Progressives at War

Progressives at War

William G. McAdoo and Newton D. Baker, 1863–1941

DOUGLAS B. CRAIG

The Johns Hopkins University Press

Baltimore

© 2013 The Johns Hopkins University Press
All rights reserved. Published 2013
Printed in the United States of America on acid-free paper
2   4   6   8   9   7   5   3   1

The Johns Hopkins University Press
2715 North Charles Street
Baltimore, Maryland 21218-4363
www.press.jhu.edu

Library of Congress Cataloging-in-Publication Data
Craig, Douglas B.
   Progressives at war : William G. McAdoo and Newton D. Baker,
1863–1941 / Douglas B. Craig.
      p. cm.
   Includes bibliographical references and index.
   ISBN 978-1-4214-0718-0 (hdbk. : alk. paper) — ISBN 1-4214-0718-3
(hdbk. : alk. paper) — ISBN 978-1-4214-0815-6 (electronic) —
ISBN 1-4214-0815-5 (electronic)
   1. McAdoo, W. G. (William Gibbs), 1863–1941.   2. Baker, Newton
Diehl, 1871–1937.   3. Cabinet officers—United States—Biography.
4. Lawyers—United States—Biography.   5. Progressivism (United
States politics)   6. United States—Politics and government—1913–1921.
7. United States—Politics and government—1865–1933.   8. World War,
1914–1918—United States.   I. Title.
   E748.M14C73 2013
   973.91'30922—dc23
   [B]

                                                                    2012018229

A catalog record for this book is available from the British Library.

Special discounts are available for bulk purchases of this book.
For more information, please contact Special Sales at 410-516-6936
or specialsales@press.jhu.edu.

The Johns Hopkins University Press uses environmentally friendly
book materials, including recycled text paper that is composed of at
least 30 percent post-consumer waste, whenever possible.

For Anne, with my love

Contents

Acknowledgments

This book has taken many years to research and write, and along the way I have accumulated a long list of debts. I owe the first of these to Robert J. Brugger, senior acquisitions editor at the Johns Hopkins University Press. Bob has supported this project from its outset, and his patience with it has been exemplary. Later Juliana McCarthy, Maria denBoer, and Kimberly Johnson formed a superb editorial team to see this project to completion. I owe them all sincere thanks.

As the bibliography indicates, I undertook most of the research for this book in the Manuscript Division of the Library of Congress. There I was blessed by the help of a team of archivists, led by Jeffrey Flannery, which included Frederick Augustyn, Fred Bauman, Jennifer Brathovde, Joseph Jackson, Patrick Kerwin, Bruce Kirby, Cathy Miller, Julia Schifini, and Lewis Wyman. I could not have done my work without them, and I could not have done it so happily without their support and friendship. Jeff and his team run one of the finest manuscript facilities in the world, and they do it with a winning combination of professionalism and warmth. My gratitude to them all runs very deep.

Other libraries and archivists across the United States have also assisted my work. The staffs of The Western Reserve Historical Association Library in Cleveland, the Bancroft Library at the University of California at Berkeley, the Davidson Library at the University of California at Santa Barbara, the Department of Special Collections at the University of California at Los Angeles, and the Huntington Library in San Marino, California, went out of their way to help me and I acknowledge them all with sincere gratitude.

I am also grateful to the institutions and copyright owners who gave their permission to reproduce the illustrations in this book. I owe a special debt to the Folger Shakespeare Library in Washington, D.C., which for many years has allowed me to stay in its scholars' residences during my research trips.

A group of scholars and friends in the United States has provided me with intellectual support and personal friendship during my frequent research trips. In Washington, D.C., and northern Virginia, Bill and Huong Bach, Fred and Jutta Bauman, Ira and Martha Berlin, Jeff and Carrie Flannery, David Kyvig, Jim

Lengle, and Beth and Stephen Van Beek have been delightful dinner companions, generous hosts, and kind friends. Jim Baughman in Madison, Susan Smulyan in Providence, Malcolm and Barbara Crystal in Boston, Caroline Ziv in Chicago, and Alletta Bredin Bell in Charlottesville have been treasured companions on my journeys. My thanks to them all are heartfelt.

Closer to home, the Australian National University has made it possible for me to conduct long-distance archival research through sabbatical leaves, research grants, and teaching assistance. I owe particular thanks to Professors David Marsh and Adam Graycar, past and present directors of the Research School of Social Sciences at ANU, for their advice and support. John Hart and Kate Lee-Koo from the School of Politics and International Relations, Caroline Bradshaw from the Colleges of Science and Medicine, Professor Peter Read of the University of Sydney, and Dr. Marivic Wyndham of the University of Technology in Sydney have been loyal friends and colleagues for many years, as has the entire staff of the School of History in the Research School of Social Sciences.

I owe my greatest debts to my family. My parents, Ronia and David, and my siblings, Andrew, Hugh, and Mary Lou, have been tireless proofreaders and devoted supporters of this and all my projects, while my own family—Anne, Lani, and Rosalie (and Mary and Duncan)—have made all things worthwhile.

Progressives at War

Introduction

Dual biographies once were unusual but now are fashionable. Nearly thirty years ago John Milton Cooper's *The Warrior and the Priest: Woodrow Wilson and Theodore Roosevelt* was lauded not only for its brilliance but also for its novelty, and in 1991 Allan Bullock's *Hitler and Stalin: Parallel Lives* was acclaimed for examining two lives that had long been connected in popular and academic thinking but were rarely analyzed together. Neither Cooper nor Bullock invented dual biography, which has a much longer pedigree, but their work reinvigorated interest in this biographical genre. Since then it has proliferated as historians explore lives in combination to bring out their individual and collective significance.

Most dual biographies focus on individuals who knew each other well; who worked either in concert or in conflict; and who individually and together encapsulate the vague but vital essence of "historical significance." Robert E. Sherwood's study of Franklin D. Roosevelt and Harry Hopkins, now more than sixty years old, is a durable example of this trope, as is Kristie Miller's recent study of Ellen and Edith Wilson. But nowadays some biographers are more adventurous: Daniel Mark Epstein's study of Walt Whitman and Abraham Lincoln deals with two subjects whose personal contact was minimal and whose knowledge of each other was almost completely one-sided.[1]

This dual biography is more conventional, in that its subjects were well acquainted with each other, worked closely together for a while, and then came into genteel but direct conflict for the rest of their lives. In examining William G. McAdoo and Newton D. Baker together, this book therefore follows esteemed footsteps. It sets out to examine the lives of two key figures in an era that encompassed reform, world war, economic depression, urban growth, corporate expansion, and changes in family structures.

I originally thought of this book as a contribution to our understanding of US wartime policy between 1914 and 1918, with an organizing theme of "citizen soldiers." As my research progressed, however, a variety of factors pushed me toward full biographies of McAdoo and Baker. These two men shared much in their southern backgrounds, legal training, Democratic Party affiliation, and contributions to public policy from Grover Cleveland's first administration until Franklin D. Roosevelt's second. Yet Baker's and McAdoo's lives are historically useful not only for what they shared but also for their differences. From similar origins they diverged in their early careers: Baker went into private legal practice and then Cleveland municipal government, and McAdoo went to New York City and pursued venture capitalism and infrastructure development. They converged again during Woodrow Wilson's presidency, serving together in the cabinet and taking leading parts in the war effort of 1917–1918.

Although Baker and McAdoo diverged again after 1918, their differences add interest, contrast, and historical significance to their stories. Woodrow Wilson was an essential triangulating influence in McAdoo's and Baker's public and private lives after 1912, inspiring both men to join the federal government and use it to further what they saw as progressive principles and policies. McAdoo's marriage to Wilson's daughter Eleanor even placed him inside the president's family circle, but this was balanced by Baker's recognized place as his true political heir. Wilson's attitude to McAdoo between 1912 and 1924 varied from amused affection to outright contempt; his attitude to Baker was consistently admiring.

After 1920 Baker and McAdoo led divergent but not disconnected lives. As lawyers, they pursued different careers; Baker founded a law firm that still enjoys a worldwide reputation for excellence, while McAdoo combined legal practice and entrepreneurial capitalism with only patchy success. The two men also diverged politically in the 1920s. McAdoo became the champion of those Democrats who sought to reinvigorate the southern and western political coalition that had won Wilson re-election to the presidency in 1916. On that basis he hankered after the 1920 Democratic presidential nomination, openly sought it in 1924, and then tried to unify the party around his version of progressivism against its more conservative urban wing. McAdoo urged aggressive federal action, and Baker more state and local autonomy, on issues such as prohibition, business regulation, and child labor. The two men also clashed over the League of Nations, with Baker supporting and McAdoo opposing this lynchpin of Wilsonian internationalism.

During the 1930s Baker and McAdoo again found themselves at loggerheads, this time over the New Deal. McAdoo was instrumental in FDR's presidential nomination in 1932 after strongly opposing Baker's half-hearted candidacy for it, and then entered the US Senate to become a loyal New Dealer. Baker, on the other hand, gave lukewarm support to FDR after his nomination in 1932 but later became a critic of the New Deal as dangerously centralist and inimical to business and personal freedom. By the end of their lives—Baker died in 1937 and McAdoo in 1941—they had traversed, both together and separately, vast swathes of American sociopolitical history, from its post–Civil War reconstruction, through its rise to urban and industrial greatness, its coming of age during World War I, and finally its emergence as a modern, more centralized state because of the Great Depression and the New Deal.

I also use these commonalities and divergences to illustrate some varieties of the progressive response to social, political, and cultural challenges from the dawn of the twentieth century until McAdoo's death in 1941. McAdoo and Baker confronted in different ways and in different spheres the inadequacies of early twentieth-century urban infrastructure; they then worked together to fund and organize the great mobilization of 1917–1918 before responding to normalcy after 1920 and then the New Deal in the 1930s. Between them they illustrate the debate and conflict between those who called themselves progressives over internationalism, the proper nature and extent of domestic reform, and the desirability of assertive government action against the Depression. These differences became sharper over time and culminated in a split within pre-1920 progressives over the New Deal after 1932. Some, like McAdoo, became disciples of the new liberalism and saw it as a natural and desirable development of the old progressivism; most, like Baker, saw the New Deal as more radical than anything that their conception of reform had ever contemplated.[2]

Other factors pushed me toward a dual biography of McAdoo and Baker. Despite their prominence within the American society and politics of their day, neither man has yet received his historical due. McAdoo published a ghost-written autobiography in 1931, and Mary Synon produced a hagiography to coincide with his run for the Democratic presidential nomination in 1924. Since then he has received only one full biography and an unpublished PhD dissertation, but otherwise patchy attention from historians who have focused on his tenure as secretary of the treasury between 1913 and 1918. This period of his life was in some ways McAdoo's finest, given his key roles in the formation of the Federal Reserve System, the Federal Farm Loan Banks, and the funding of America's and the Allies' war efforts in 1917 and 1918, but it was only a single chapter in a long life that also included an active if not always successful legal and business career, three marriages and nine children, de facto leadership of a powerful wing of the Democratic Party during the 1920s, two attempts to win the presidential nomination, and finally a term in the US Senate.

McAdoo deserves a modern, comprehensive biography to integrate these activities and do justice to his contemporary prominence and historical significance.[3]

Newton Baker has fared even worse. Only one biography, C. H. Cramer's *Newton D. Baker*, has recounted his career as one of the best-known municipal leaders in the United States, the founder of the law firm of Baker, Hostetler and Sidlo, a leader of the American war effort during World War I, a tireless advocate of the League of Nations and internationalism during the 1920s, a prominent contender for the 1932 Democratic presidential nomination, and an influential critic of the New Deal. Cramer's work is now fifty years old, and so was written without the benefit of more recent research on progressivism, World War I, and the interwar years. Only two other works, one by Frederick Palmer published in 1931 and one by Daniel Beaver in 1966, have assessed Baker's historical significance, but both were limited to his service as secretary of war.[4]

It is time to look at Baker and McAdoo again. But what is to be gained by examining them together? Separate biographies would help restore some of the historical significance that their achievements deserve, but a dual biography better allows us to see them as examples of, and actors within, important social, cultural, and political changes between Gettysburg and Pearl Harbor.

A dual biography of McAdoo and Baker also provides an opportunity to explore the contributions of two key nonpresidential actors within the statecraft of their day. The so-called presidential synthesis, in which American political history is too often reduced to a single focus on presidential personality and action, has distorted our perspective on the other political institutions that make up American government. No such institution has suffered more from this syndrome than the cabinet. Apart from their interest in the struggle between Secretary of State Thomas Jefferson and Secretary of the Treasury Alexander Hamilton in George Washington's cabinet in the 1790s, the power plays between Lincoln's cabinet secretaries during the Civil War, and the relationship between John F. Kennedy and his attorney general and younger brother Robert, historians have largely ignored the cabinet despite its popular designation as the president's "official family."[5]

Yet the cabinet does matter. Although it has always been the president's creature and servant, it has since the birth of the republic been a key institution for policy formulation and execution. During McAdoo's and Baker's time in the cabinet it loomed large in the popular and political mind; its members were acknowledged as key figures in the federal government, and their power and autonomy as political actors and decision makers were great. Woodrow Wilson was an ambitious chief executive who was determined to expand the competence of the federal government, but he could not do it by himself and found much of the day-to-day running of the executive branch boring. Once Europe descended into war in August 1914, he focused on international affairs and left his cabinet secretaries, especially those who dealt with domestic policy, largely to their own devices.

As the two most prominent members of Wilson's cabinet, McAdoo and Baker were much more than presidential mouthpieces. Wilson had little interest in financial policy or the mechanics of mobilization. After 1914 he made the lives of his secretaries of state miserable by his interference and criticism, but he left his secretaries of the treasury and war largely alone. Yet McAdoo and Baker had vital policies to devise and enact, and huge departments to administer, which directly impinged on vital interests of state and on the conduct of America's Great War. Only President Woodrow Wilson and American Expeditionary Forces (AEF) commander John J. Pershing could boast of greater contributions to America's war effort in 1917 and 1918 than Baker and McAdoo. Examining their work and ideas in the cabinet thus adds to our understanding of how the Wilson administration worked and how statecraft was done during the progressive era and World War I.

During their time in the Wilson administrations, and especially during American involvement in World War I, McAdoo and Baker redefined their portfolios so that the United States could mobilize its financial and industrial resources to fight a modern total war. The federal government spent more money between 1917 and 1919 than it had done between 1789 and 1916, and it did so without economic dislocation or logistical collapse. Within eighteen months of its declaration of war in April 1917, the United States had conscripted, mobilized, trained, and landed two million troops in France under Baker's and Pershing's leadership, and its new banking and currency system, nurtured by McAdoo, helped it emerge as the economic colossus and the pre-eminent creditor of the postwar world.

By combining Baker's and McAdoo's biographies this book also explores the significance of their differences. Both men called themselves progressives before and after World War I, although McAdoo's progressivism owed more to new views of corporate organization and social responsibility than did Baker's, which was formed by his experiences in Cleveland's municipal politics. McAdoo rose to prominence as the president of the Hudson and Manhattan Railway Company, which completed the first railroad tunnels between Manhattan and New Jersey. He founded the company and used it to further his and many other progressives' ideals of improving the productivity of labor through better working conditions. McAdoo also insisted on equal pay for equal work for women and supported female suffrage, an end to child labor, and the passage of workers' compensation laws. When he joined Woodrow Wilson's pre-nomination campaign in 1912, he was already seen as an exemplar of a new generation of socially responsible business leaders.

Newton Baker was a less flamboyant figure, but he painted an equally progressive canvas in Cleveland. His tenure as city solicitor and then mayor between 1900 and 1916 marked him as an imaginative public executive who saw cities such as his—industrial, polyglot, and burgeoning—as laboratories of social change and reform. Always a localist at heart, Baker used Cleveland's municipal government to operate the city's streetcars and generate electricity; to undertake "yardstick" competition in the provision of public recreation; and to improve the housing, health, and working conditions of the city's heavily immigrant workforce. His mayoralty was thus a model of progressive reform in action, and Baker was hailed as a leader of the movement by the time that Wilson appointed him as secretary of war in 1916. Despite his localism, Baker also found time to support progressive notions of international relations, including the submission of all international disputes to arbitration and rejection of war as a means of national policy.

Examining McAdoo's and Baker's lives together thus highlights their convergences and differences and allows the significance of each to inform that of the other. Studied together, their lives shed light on progressivism, New Deal liberalism, federal governance, and World War I. As lawyers, businessmen, and politicians, Baker and McAdoo can be seen not only as historical actors but also as indicators of the polity and society that both molded and responded to them.

I also hope that this book will contribute to our understanding of the progressive movement and its development during the first forty years of the twentieth century as well as America's World War I. Two particular areas are important to mention here. The historiography of progressivism, once a lively debate over the nature, extent, and significance of the reformist impulse that reshaped public and private institutions during and after the 1890s, has often degenerated into arguments over the coherence and usefulness of the term and the reasons for its movement's decline. This book approaches progressivism from the perspectives of my subjects, who saw themselves throughout their public careers as part of a broad progressive mindset. In this way I hope to contribute to the work of historians such as Robert Kelley, Daniel Rodgers, and Nancy Cohen, who have stressed the transatlantic connections and networks of self-conscious progressives from the 1890s until World War I.[6]

Studying McAdoo and Baker in action and in thought also shows the persistence of their progressive mindset; as far as they were concerned progressivism did not end with the United States' entry into World War I in 1917 or with Warren Harding's inauguration in 1921. Baker and McAdoo, like many of their peers, remained "progressives" for the rest of their lives. As this book's title suggests, their different definitions and experiences of progressivism before, during, and after World War I lay at the heart of their cooperation and conflict. They acted as progressives before 1917, fought World War I as progressives, and then became progressives at war as their personal and political relationship became strained.

⧓

The Great War has undergone a renaissance at the hands of political and social
historians who have sought to integrate America's wartime experience more
closely with the progressive and interwar eras that preceded and followed it. Led
by Ellis Hawley, David M. Kennedy, and William E. Leuchtenburg, they have
shown the profound legacies of the American experience of modern total war in
1917 and 1918 for ideas and practice of statecraft. Their work has challenged the old
and rigid segmentation of the early twentieth century into progressive and normalcy "eras," and has instead stressed broader trends in social, cultural, and political development under rubrics such as "corporatism," "cosmopolitanism," and a
"search for order." These approaches have most recently been combined in analyses of the origins and manifestations of modern ideas of citizen soldiers by historians such as Lisa Budreau, Jennifer Keene, Stephen Ortiz, and Richard Slotkin.[7]

By combining the biographies of two prominent progressives, Great War leaders, and interwar political figures, this book aims to further this historiographical
trend. It also hopes to provide other perspectives on Baker and McAdoo through a
discussion of their personal lives, which revealed the tensions that afflicted many
upper-middle-class families of their day. Between them Baker and McAdoo lived
compelling lives within and without their public careers, and this book aims to
show some of the ways in which their private and public lives intersected.

McAdoo's personal life is particularly suited to this approach. Following the
probable suicide of his first wife, McAdoo married Woodrow Wilson's daughter
Eleanor in 1914. As the president's son-in-law in the cabinet, he occupied a unique
position in the political and social life of his day, but that proved to be a double-
edged sword. Wilson did him few favors, and even stymied his ambitions for the
Democratic presidential nomination in 1920. After his divorce from Eleanor Wilson in the 1930s, McAdoo again attracted attention when he married a woman
more than forty years his junior. Of his nine children, seven needed their father's
financial support throughout their adult lives, four died young, two were alcoholic
depressives, and all but one went through the divorce courts at least once.

Baker's private life, a more tranquil combination of a successful legal career,
a lifelong marriage, and three independent children, provides a foil to McAdoo's
and a reminder of the unevenness with which modernity affected many American
upper-middle-class families after 1900. Baker and his wife Bess in many ways persisted with Victorian family values and structures until his death in 1937. Yet even
his privileged life was not world-proof; Baker's papers are dotted with despairing

correspondence from his brother Julian, who lost his job at the beginning of the Great Depression and was reduced to handouts from Newton as he fought a losing battle against unemployment and alcohol.

By studying these two leaders this book also aims to deepen our understanding of the political culture of their day. I focus not only on two individuals but also on the political and economic institutions they created or served, such as the Hudson and Manhattan Railway, Cleveland's municipal government, Woodrow Wilson's cabinet, the War Industries Board, and the Federal Reserve Board. Their later careers revolved around national political parties, their respective law firms, the New Deal, and the US Senate. By exploring Baker's and McAdoo's achievements and failures within those institutions we can see the ways in which two prominent figures grappled with the great challenges facing the United States in its rise to pre-eminence.

This book is divided into four parts, corresponding to the seasons in Baker's and McAdoo's lives. Each part's chapters take a combination of thematic and chronological approaches, analyzing different facets of my two subjects' lives. Whenever possible, but not to the extent of artificiality, Baker and McAdoo are treated as being both consciously and unknowingly connected. When they worked in tandem or in opposition they are dealt with together, but when they operated independently they are treated separately but always against each other's context. In so doing, this study attempts to bring substance to the idea of an integrated dual biography and to show the advantages and insights that come from looking at two actors strutting on their own stages but in a shared drama.

Spring
1863–1912

CHAPTER 1

New South Rising, 1863–1901

Living near Marietta, Georgia, in the midst of civil war, William McAdoo completed his diary entry for Saturday, October 31, 1863. He noted that he had sent four of his slaves to temporary masters in the district and that there was little news of the war that day. The big news lay much closer to home. "Today, about thirty minutes after noon, Mary gave birth to a son weighing nearly eleven pounds, with long black hair." The new baby took the name of his father, William Gibbs McAdoo, but the family soon shortened that to Willie. He was the third of Mary and William's seven children. To help make ends meet and to support the war effort, the McAdoos had taken in Confederate Colonel Albert W. Johnson's family as boarders. The Johnsons' son Tom was then 9 years old, and later recalled cradling the new McAdoo baby in his arms.[1] Nearly forty years later Tom Johnson, then the mayor of Cleveland, Ohio, would launch the political career of Newton D. Baker, the second subject of this book.

The family into which Willie McAdoo was born represented the first and the last of the Old South. McAdoo was always proud of his lineage and in 1910 paid a genealogist, Charles McGuffey, to investigate his family tree. McGuffey found that McAdoo's great-great-grandfather John McAdow, a Scot from Northern Ireland, had migrated to North America early in the eighteenth century; soon after he changed the spelling of his name to McAdoo and settled in North Carolina. By 1792 John's son had crossed the mountains into Tennessee, and his son John— Willie's grandfather—settled in Anderson County, thirty miles from Knoxville. "These early McAdoos," Willie recorded in his autobiography, "were bearded, vigorous men of Scotch descent, pioneers by instinct, rough and hearty, living close to the soil, and making their own way without seeking help or guidance. They

were all Bible-reading Presbyterians who believed in Judgement Day and the efficacy of shotguns."[2]

The McAdoos and the Gibbs were united by the marriage of John McAdoo
and Mary Ann Gibbs, Willie's paternal grandparents, in 1815. By then the McAdoos
were well established in Anderson County: upon his father's death in 1840, John
inherited two slaves and more than $6,000 in property. The Gibbs were also Scots,
but had fled to Germany during the English Civil War. From there Nicholas Gibbs
had sailed to the New World in 1725. He settled first in Pennsylvania and fought
against the British in the American Revolution; after the war he moved to North
Carolina and then to Tennessee. The Gibbs may also have had faith in the efficacy
of firearms; Willie's great-uncle George Gibbs, a lawyer, banker, and veteran of the
War of 1812, had fought a duel against a member of Congress. He survived the
encounter, but carried a bullet in his left hip for the rest of his life.[3]

Willie McAdoo could claim prominent lineage on his maternal side. His mother
Mary Faith Floyd came from an old Georgia family that had contributed prominently to the conquest of the white South. Willie's maternal great-grandfather John
Floyd had fought with Andrew Jackson in the Creek Indian War of 1813. He had led
the Georgians and Jackson the Tennesseans; after defeating the Creeks, Major General Floyd took command of the Georgia militia in Savannah in operations against
the British during the War of 1812. He served as a US representative from Georgia
between 1826 and 1828 and had been an elector on Jackson's presidential ticket
in 1832; Floyd County, Georgia, is named in his honor. John's son Charles, Willie's
grandfather, continued the family's military tradition. An officer in the Marine
Corps, he succeeded his father in command of the Georgia militia and oversaw the
removal of the Creeks and the Seminoles along the Trail of Tears to the Indian Territory in what is now Oklahoma.[4]

Born in 1820, Willie's father William Gibbs McAdoo began his working life as
a teacher, first at Union Academy in Eatonton, Georgia, between 1838 and 1840 and
then at Franklin Academy in Jacksborough, Tennessee, before returning to Union
Academy in 1841. In 1842 William enrolled at East Tennessee University and graduated in 1845. A day before his graduation he was elected, as a Whig, to the Tennessee legislature. In 1847, swept up by patriotic fervor, he resigned from the legislature and raised a company of volunteers from eastern Tennessee to fight in the war
against Mexico. Upon his return to Tennessee, William read law and was admitted
to the state bar; in the second half of the 1850s he served as district attorney general
of Tennessee for the Knoxville Circuit. By then William had been a father, wid-
ower, and new groom. In 1849 he had married Anna Horsley, who died in 1853 after
bearing him two daughters. Four years later he married Mary Faith McDonald,
née Floyd, a widow with one child. Their marriage eventually brought seven more

children, including Willie, and provided significant wealth and status in the dying days of the Old South: Mary contributed numerous slaves, and a plantation near Marietta, Georgia, to the marriage.[5]

William's second marriage brought about a reorientation of his political and social beliefs. Before 1857 he had opposed secession and was mildly opposed to slavery itself. After his second marriage, which made him a substantial slaveowner, William became a strong secessionist and committed Confederate. Knoxville, however, was unionist, and in 1859 William was defeated in his bid for re-election as district attorney general. In 1862 the family moved to their Marietta plantation, the better to protect its slave property. Upon the outbreak of war, William tried to enlist in the Confederate army, but failed on medical grounds. By 1863, the year Willie was born, the Confederacy's need for soldiers saw a relaxation of its medical standards, and William joined the colors. He fought close to home: at Kennesaw Mountain, around Atlanta, and at Macon. During the battle of Kennesaw Mountain in June 1864, the house in which Willie had been born seven months before was in the direct line of fire, which left many bullets embedded in its walls. By then the McAdoo family had fled to Milledgeville, ninety miles to the southeast.[6]

By the end of the war, William had fathered four more children. Mary's plantation was in ruins, as were two other family homes at Floyd's Neck, Georgia. "I happened to be brought up as a boy in that region where General Sherman had been a bit careless with fire," Willie recalled in 1921. The ruin of his family's property was an act of "pure vandalism" because none of it had any military significance. As a disfranchised Confederate, William could not practice law and struggled to provide for his family. Attempts to restore the Marietta plantation failed; its buildings were ruined and "the freed slaves had a notion that their new freedom, which had come to them without effort on their part, meant a perpetual license for idleness."[7]

Milledgeville offered little more promise; Sherman had ransacked it in November 1864 and in 1868 it lost its status as state capital to Atlanta. The whole area was in a "condition of poverty and depression which it is impossible to describe," Willie recalled. "The disorganization of government was complete; lawlessness was rampant, and the social order was in a deplorable state." At first the McAdoos survived on the produce from twenty acres attached to their Milledgeville house that was cultivated by some of their former slaves.[8]

The Milledgeville years were hard for the McAdoos. "I have never doubted that whatever character I have developed," Willie wrote, "has been in a large measure due to the surroundings and conditions which General Sherman forced upon the people of our section during that great war." In 1868 William regained his franchise and the right to practice law. He resumed work in Milledgeville and later became a school commissioner and county judge, but the family's finances teetered for a decade after Appomattox. Mary sold poetry and two works of romantic fiction, and William taught his children himself because there were no public schools and the family could not always afford private school fees. Willie worked as a delivery boy for a local store, a floor sweeper, and then as a soda fountain attendant in a drug store.[9]

Violence pervaded the Reconstruction South, and Milledgeville was no exception. Even Willie was not immune to the fury bubbling just below the surface of a society embittered by defeat, torn by racial conflict, and plunged into poverty. The temporary schools that Willie attended sporadically in the early 1870s were places of harsh discipline; his teachers were hardened veterans of Robert E. Lee's army who did not hesitate to beat their students into obedience. Their pupils responded in kind; Willie remembered his school days as a time "when personal courage was at a premium and no boy could refuse to fight without being regarded as a coward and suffering unendurable ostracism among his fellows." Bullying was rife, and Willie and his younger brother Malcolm learned early to defend themselves. Fights were more common than books; children in Willie's schools had to share a few copies of McGuffey's Readers and Spellers and to make do with only basic instruction in arithmetic and geography.[10]

In 1877 the family moved back to Tennessee. Knoxville had been less damaged by the war and offered better educational facilities than Milledgeville. There William secured a post at his alma mater, renamed the University of Tennessee, as an assistant professor of history and English. The McAdoos moved back into the house they had left in 1862 and Willie, now 14, returned to school.[11]

Willie thrived academically in Knoxville. He remained hot tempered and pugilistic, but his father's tuition in Milledgeville enabled him to catch up with his peers. Tenuous family finances still forced him to take jobs after school and during vacations, but in 1879 he took his place in the freshman class at the University of Tennessee. Still unsure of his future direction, and in keeping with his military heritage, Willie applied in 1880 to his Republican congressman Leonidas C. Houk for nomination to the Naval Academy at Annapolis. Willie scored well in the entrance examination, but Houk appointed a young Republican instead.[12]

Willie distinguished himself in debating at Tennessee, and joined the Kappa Sigma fraternity. By then he had decided on a legal career and even dreamed of attending the University of Virginia's law school, but his family's straitened circumstances made that impossible. At the end of 1881, halfway through his junior year, Willie took a holiday job assisting Andrew Humes, clerk of the US District Court in Knoxville. Six months later Humes offered Willie a full-time job as deputy clerk of the Chattanooga Circuit Court at $800 per year. McAdoo then gave up his dream of law school and moved to Chattanooga. Five months shy of his nine-teenth birthday, he left home for good.[13]

Life in Knoxville, though better than in Milledgeville, had not been idyllic. The McAdoos were still financially troubled, and William felt insecure in his position at the university. He worried constantly that his post would not be renewed, and fell out with his colleagues. In 1879 a rival was promoted to the full chair in history, and William moved sideways into the twin posts of librarian and composition teacher. For the next seven years, until the axe finally fell in June 1886, he feared for his job. He tried to have his *Geology of Tennessee* assigned as a school text and published some poems in the *Knoxville Sentinel*, but otherwise subsided into depression. After 1886 his income was reduced to his Mexican War pension of $8 per month, supplemented later by Willie, who gave him $10 per month as "pocket money."[14]

William passed the running of the household to Mary, who had weathered the trials of postwar life better than her husband. He died in August 1894, and Willie's matter-of-fact note of that event in his autobiography nearly forty years later contrasted with his emotional tribute to his mother, who died in 1913. "She lived a noble, unselfish life, always doing for others and never wounding," McAdoo told his lover Florence Harriman on the day his mother died. "She was resolute and gentle, with a matchless courage and a splendid mind, unostentatious, unaffected, unequalled." Willie shared his mother's indomitable temperament that thrived on activity, challenge, and adversity. William McAdoo proved to be a victim of the war; Mary was its survivor, and Willie came to see himself as its beneficiary.[15]

In Chattanooga Willie worked in the District Court and read law under Judge William DeWitt. DeWitt, McAdoo later remembered, was a fine lawyer and an honorable man whose only weakness "was that about four times a year he would get dead drunk. It was a thing he could not control and it depressed him terribly." When he was first in Chattanooga, Willie also lived in a boarding house run by an alcoholic. That experience, and Judge DeWitt's struggle with the bottle, led Willie to lifelong teetotalism and strong support of national prohibition from 1920 until 1933.[16]

Willie stayed as deputy clerk until March 1885, when Judge Humes lost his job with the advent of the first Cleveland administration. By then McAdoo was 21, had cast his first ballot (for Grover Cleveland), and was versed enough in the law to be admitted to the Tennessee bar. He rented an office in downtown Chattanooga for $5 per month, installed his one-volume legal library, "and had my shingle hanging out on an iron rod."[17]

McAdoo did not find it easy as a young lawyer. He cleared only $285 up to the end of 1885 and "picked up a few cases but not many though I somehow managed to make a living." Things got easier in 1886, when he was retained by the Richmond and Danville Railroad. Willie now had steady work, litigating rights of way, employment contracts, and disputes with suppliers. He was now part of the railroad industry which, in one way or another, would dominate his professional and political career for the next three decades. He was also a married man—on November 18, 1885, after a short courtship, he wed Sarah Houston Fleming from Savannah, Georgia. Sarah was not yet 19; her groom was 24. Their ill-starred marriage, which lasted until Sarah's death in 1912, produced seven children and provided McAdoo some property and much motivation to improve his financial standing.[18]

For the first thirty years of his career, McAdoo's chief concern was to make money. It could not have been otherwise for an ambitious lawyer with a growing family in the postwar South. Chattanooga had suffered from William Tecumseh Sherman's March to the Sea, but its rebirth offered real but risky opportunities for the entrepreneur-lawyer that McAdoo aspired to be. Unwilling to bide his time with steady but modest legal fees, McAdoo combined legal practice with real estate speculation during the second half of the 1880s and amassed $25,000 in profits. He then bought into the Chattanooga Hoe and Tool Company and rose quickly to become its president, but soon resigned to stake his fortune on street railways.[19]

Inspired by some Chattanooga associates who had bought a horse-drawn streetcar line and converted it to electric power, McAdoo decided to do the same in Knoxville. There the streetcars were still pulled by mules, but McAdoo had much grander ideas. He agreed in July 1889 to buy the Knoxville Street Railway Company for $200,000, including a $50,000 cash payment. His real estate profits provided half the deposit, but local bankers baulked at lending the remainder to a 25-year-old lawyer whose enthusiasm could not hide his inexperience. Undaunted, McAdoo sought his loan in the great financial centers of the East Coast: first in Philadelphia, then in New York, and finally in Boston, cold-calling bankers with surveys and a business plan for an electrified Knoxville streetcar line.

McAdoo received many hearings but no funds. From Boston he turned homeward, but stopped in Philadelphia for a last throw of the dice. Finally, at the Union Trust Company, he received good news: a loan of $50,000 secured by bonds to be issued on the venture's property and prospects. McAdoo then sold the bonds and made a down payment on the Knoxville Street Railway Company in August 1889. Six months later, on May 1, 1890, he inaugurated one of the first electric streetcar services in the United States.[20]

Despite its spectacular beginnings, McAdoo's first foray into venture capitalism was doomed to fail. Knoxville was too small and too poor to sustain such expensive infrastructure, and McAdoo's company was chronically undercapitalized. Electrical generation and traction was new, expensive, and unreliable; McAdoo's line ran as often on mules as it did on electricity.[21] He remained in Chattanooga at his law practice to generate funds for his ailing venture and fell $60,000 further into debt. In February 1892 the Knoxville Street Railway Company, in default of its interest payments, entered receivership. As endorser of the Union Trust loan and of his debts to the company's suppliers, McAdoo faced financial ruin. Four years of litigation, conducted by McAdoo himself to avoid paying legal fees, finally produced a settlement in 1896 that excused him from his personal liabilities.[22]

By then the McAdoos were long gone. Weighed down by debt and with a wife and two children to support, McAdoo yearned for a bigger stage and greener pastures. Mortgaging their last remaining asset—the Chattanooga house that Sarah had brought to their marriage—the McAdoos left the disappointments of Tennessee and moved to New York City in June 1892. America's largest city, the financial heart of the nation, might offer the opportunities for an ambitious lawyer-entrepreneur that the South was too poor to provide.

McAdoo landed in New York with great confidence. He rented a small office on Wall Street and moved his family into a comfortable apartment. Eager to make contacts, he joined the New York Southern Society, which fostered business networks among displaced southerners and spruiked investment opportunities in the former Confederacy. As an unknown lawyer trying to get noticed in a crowded legal and business community, McAdoo had barely made a start before disaster struck. In May 1893, less than a year after he arrived in New York, the stock market collapsed. The depression that followed lasted until 1897 and created a deflationary vortex that sucked confidence and investment from the national economy. Banks collapsed, investment dried up, and factories closed. Lawyers such as William McAdoo, so recently arrived and so little known, stood no chance of weathering the storm.[23]

The depression years were nightmarish for McAdoo and his young family. Clinging desperately to their diminishing capital, they moved to a fifth-floor walkup on the Upper West Side and then in late 1894 to cheaper real estate in Yonkers. Desperate for work, McAdoo gave up his legal practice and became a bond salesman, earning small commissions selling railroad securities in a depressed market. Picking up crumbs that fell from Wall Street investment houses was scarcely the way to wealth and prominence, but it was better than nothing. To make matters worse, Sarah, burdened by the demands of a growing family—by 1897 she had given birth to five children—fell victim to rheumatoid arthritis, which made her an invalid after the birth of her sixth child in 1904. In the face of these pressures McAdoo's optimism dimmed. "The poverty, the struggle, and the anxiety of this period are indescribable," he wrote in his autobiography. "My brain and body were put to the supreme test for several years." He suffered from a variety of anxiety-connected ailments and complained of "terrible depressions," racking headaches, and nervous disorders. McAdoo remained acutely conscious of his physical health and emotional state for the rest of his life.[24]

With time on his hands and connections to cultivate, McAdoo began to show interest in politics. As a white southerner, he considered himself to be a hereditary Democrat. Until 1896 he had supported Grover Cleveland, but William Jennings Bryan's nomination forced him to reconsider his political loyalties. McAdoo became a Gold Democrat in 1896; forswore any political activity in the campaign; and voted for John M. Palmer, the gold standard, and sound government.[25]

McAdoo's fortunes improved with the end of the depression in 1897. By then selling bonds provided a livable income, and there was more legal work as the economy shrugged off years of retrenchment. As if to draw a line under his first five years in New York, McAdoo entered into a partnership with a co-tenant in his Wall Street building with whom he had exchanged misdirected mail: William G. McAdoo. Despite their identical names, the two men could find no common ancestry, but the coincidence seemed propitious. They formed the legal firm of McAdoo and McAdoo, set up offices on 15 Wall Street, and began to build up their practice. Clients and briefs were slow to come, but at last there was progress. In 1901 McAdoo and McAdoo won a substantial fee from the new owners of the Wilkes-Barre and Hazleton Railroad. Only then, nearly ten grinding years after Willie McAdoo had arrived in New York, did he begin to feel comfortable.[26]

In Martinsburg, West Virginia—650 miles north of Marietta and perched on the fault line that separated secession from union—another established southern family grappled with the ramifications of the Civil War. Like the McAdoos far to the south, the Bakers of Martinsburg claimed a long American and southern lineage. William McAdoo learned of his family tree by paying a genealogist to investigate it; Newton Baker's genealogists worked for more sinister motives. In the early 1920s, after Baker had finished his tenure as secretary of war, Henry Ford accused him of being part of a Jewish cabal that had duped the United States into the Great War. Ford sent investigators to Martinsburg to gather evidence of Baker's Jewish antecedents. To his chagrin they discovered no Jews but many Episcopalians, Quakers, Presbyterians, and Lutherans from England, Ireland, the Netherlands, and Germany whose roots in the New World could be traced back to the eighteenth century.[27]

The Bakers originated in England, and Newton's great-great-grandfather settled in Bakersville, Maryland, in the 1750s. His grandfather Elias Baker served in the Continental army and married Mary Billmeyer from across the Potomac River in Shepherdstown, Virginia (later West Virginia). The Billmeyers, who had emigrated from Germany at about the same time as the Bakers, settled in Jefferson

County. Newton's maternal family came from Germany and Ireland; his grandfather Dukehart arrived from Württemberg early in the nineteenth century. Newton's other great-grandfather Murphy was a Scots-Irish sea captain who had died at sea; his widow took Newton's grandmother to Virginia soon after. Elias trained as a saddler before his marriage to Mary Billmeyer improved his financial standing. Elias and Mary turned to shopkeeping, owning stores in Martinsburg and then Shepherdstown.[28]

Newton Diehl Baker Sr. was born in Martinsburg in October 1841. His son recorded little of his father's early years, but they seem to have been tranquil enough until 1860. In that year Newton traveled to Springfield, Ohio, to enroll at Wittenburg College. He was sent home only a few months into his freshman year to avoid an outbreak of smallpox. By the time that the college reopened, momentous events had intervened and Newton did not return to Wittenburg.[29]

Abraham Lincoln's election opened deep divisions in the Bakers' nation, state, town, and family. Bakersville and Shepherdstown, on either side of the Potomac River, straddled the divide that threatened to split the United States in two. But in that part of the country nothing was clear cut; Virginia seceded after the outbreak of war, but Maryland remained uneasily as a "border state," sympathetic to her southern sisters but kept in the Union through force of northern arms. And then Martinsburg itself, until 1861 part of Virginia, found itself torn between the Old Dominion and the new state of West Virginia. Although West Virginia was admitted to the Union in 1863, Martinsburg and its surrounding Berkeley County did not join it until 1865. Such seismic disruption reached down beyond states and counties; many families, separated only by rivers or mountains, found themselves on either side of the great divide. In the Bakers' case secession divided even their own family.

In 1861 Newton faced a difficult choice. His father Elias was passionately unionist, while his mother Mary was equally committed to secession. Both sides of the family contributed young men to their causes. Newton was 19 and in good health; the only question was over which army he would join. He followed his mother's convictions over his father's and joined the Confederate army in 1861, serving as a trooper throughout the war under J. E. B. Stuart. Elias remained loyal to the Union despite having a son fighting for the Confederacy, and was even appointed postmaster of Shepherdstown. As postmaster, Elias delivered newspapers that brought reports of the battle at Gettysburg in July 1863, which marked the high tide of Confederate advance in the war but which also included his own son fighting on Lee's side. As the Confederacy ebbed, Newton fought for it every inch of the way. He was wounded, captured, and exchanged, and finally drifted home just before Appomattox.[30]

In 1865 Newton returned to a community straitened but not ravaged by war. The new state of West Virginia had suffered guerilla warfare but not the wholesale

destruction that had been visited upon states farther south. West Virginia's separation from Virginia placed it within the victorious northern Republican fold. The
Billmeyers' acres provided Newton with more financial security than most West
Virginians. The family did not have to start again, as had the McAdoos, and Newton's career trajectory reflected that comparative advantage. Only 24 at the end of
the war, he felt young enough to complete the education that had been so dramatically interrupted in 1860. He enrolled at the University of Maryland Medical
School in September 1865 and graduated as a physician in 1867. Dr. Baker then
returned to Martinsburg, bought a practice, and married Mary Anne Dukehart.
He would live and work in Martinsburg until his death in 1909.[31]

Domestic life for the newly married Bakers was in marked contrast to that of
the tumultuous first half of the 1860s. Even so, their transition from war to peace
was bewilderingly fast. Only four years after he laid down his arms in 1865, Newton
had become a medical practitioner, a husband, a home owner, and a father. His
and Mary's first child, a girl, died soon after her birth in July 1869. Mary then gave
birth to a son, Frank, in 1870 and to another boy on December 3, 1871. The new
baby took the name of his father, Newton Diehl Baker, but the family soon abbreviated that to "Newt." [32]

Newt grew up surrounded by a loving family and reminders of the Old South.
As a boy he played in the hills above Harpers Ferry, exploring caves in which, legend had it, John Brown had forged 30,000 pikes to use against slaveowners. Slavery
was integral to the Bakers' and Billmeyers' lives and had been the basis of their
prosperity before the Civil War. They had owned many slaves, and Newt's black
"mammy" lived with his family all her life. "I still remember her as the comforter
and protector of my youth, and certainly I learned from her humbly given, but profoundly potent lessons about humility and goodness."[33]

Memories of black retainers and stories of the Civil War from his father gave
Newt a romanticized view of the Old South and its race relations. "I think there is
no finer tribute to a race anywhere than is to be found in the records of the south
when all the white men and boys were drawn into the Confederate Army, leaving
their families and possessions to be cared for by their slaves. The history of that episode shows the most beautiful fidelity on the part of the slave men and women." All
in all, he joked in 1922, "I would like to try my second incarnation back in eighteenth
century Virginia, along the Potomac and take my turn with a coach and four."[34]

Newt was less romantic about his current incarnation. "I recall a rather moody
and difficult little boy in Martinsburg whose feelings were always being hurt."
His schools were less rambunctious than Willie McAdoo's had been, but Newt
was less able to assert himself in them. McAdoo grew tall—well over six feet—and
rangy, while Newt was short—five foot six—and slight. Quiet and bookish, he

stayed close to his family, which now included his younger brother Julian. He and his father shared a love of books and discussed history, science, and literature, and Newt read the entire *Encyclopaedia Britannica*.[35]

Most memorably of all, Newton shared with his son stories of the Civil War. "My father," Newt remembered in 1916, "accepted in word and spirit the results of the war and from my earliest childhood taught me to rejoice that our country was reunited." He spoke about the battles in which he had participated, of the valor of the southern armies, the élan of Robert E. Lee, and the perfidy of Republican carpetbaggers. He often told his son that Lee was a brilliant general because Jefferson Davis had spared him constant interference from Richmond. When, more than twenty years later, it fell to Newton's son to dispatch John J. Pershing and his men across the Atlantic, he recalled his father's lesson and did his best to live up to it.[36]

After attending Martinsburg High School for two years, Newt studied at the Episcopal High School in Alexandria, Virginia, to prepare for college. He had chosen Johns Hopkins for his undergraduate training and started there in the fall of 1889. Baker was an enthusiastic participant in university cultural and social life, sampling the musical and dramatic performances of Hopkins's staff and students, and later joining the Phi Gamma Delta fraternity, of which he became a lifelong supporter, general treasurer, and ultimately president. Not even a doctor's warning in 1889 that he should avoid any unusual stress or exertion because of a heart murmur dampened his desire to make the most of his college years. Baker eventually prospered at Hopkins but not before suffering from intellectual insecurity. Examinations brought attacks of anxiety, "with the occasional result of failing and the frequent result of not doing my best." His anxiety passed, and by the end of his undergraduate program Baker was fully immersed in his academic surroundings. He was in the audience as Visiting Professor Woodrow Wilson lectured on politics and administration, and he was at the table as Wilson lunched each day at Baker's boarding house. The two men did not formally meet at Hopkins—undergraduate students there knew their place—but their paths would cross again in 1912.[37]

Now in his element at Hopkins, Baker attended an additional year after his graduation in 1892. Although he flirted with the idea of an academic career in history, he settled on legal training. In his postgraduate year at Hopkins he read jurisprudence and Roman Law and hoped to go to Harvard Law School. Family finances could not stretch so far, so he chose instead a cheaper law school closer to home: Washington and Lee University in Lexington, Virginia. Baker was a model student, cramming the normal two-year program into a single academic year. This saved his parents money and propelled Newt much faster into the legal profession, but it came at a cost. "I have always felt," he told his daughter much later, "half educated as a consequence."[38]

Baker received a superb education, despite its intensity. Hopkins introduced him to a world of new ideas, scholarship, and even a future president of the United States. It opened intellectual doors to a bookish, shy West Virginian well versed in the classics but out of touch with Gilded Age thought. Baker then received an orthodox but complete legal education at Washington and Lee. The contrast to Willie McAdoo's legal training, which consisted of organizing court records by day and memorizing slabs of Blackstone's *Commentaries on the Laws of England* and James Kent's *Commentaries on American Law* by night, was stark. It was therefore unsurprising that they became very different types of lawyers.

McAdoo was an instrumentalist, developing his legal skills in directions determined by his own financial and business aspirations. Baker, on the other hand, was academically trained not only in the mechanics of law but also in its ideas. A year of Roman Law at Johns Hopkins was of little use in satisfying clients' needs, but it was of great importance in understanding the evolution and practice of law as a historical, social, and intellectual construction. Although the differences in Baker's and McAdoo's legal training were as much a product of their differing circumstances as they were of their opposing temperaments—completing college, let alone attending law school, was far beyond McAdoo's means in postwar Tennessee— their paths to the law were appropriate to their ambitions and interests. McAdoo, the impatient and ambitious lawyer-entrepreneur, could never have stomached Roman Law, while Baker could never imagine buying, financing, and reorganizing a struggling streetcar line.

Graduating from Washington and Lee in 1894, Baker returned to Martinsburg and set up legal practice. As McAdoo had found a decade before in Chattanooga, Baker learned that a freshly minted lawyer could expect only infrequent briefs and paltry fees. Unlike McAdoo, however, Baker lived at home and had no wife to support.

A year of waiting did little to improve Baker's practice, and in January 1896 he accepted a position as private secretary to US Postmaster General William L. Wilson. Wilson had been a Confederate cavalryman with Baker's father, had represented the Martinsburg area in Congress, and knew Baker's family well. Relieved to escape, Baker moved to Washington and stayed until June 1897.[39]

Baker's first stint in political life was stimulating. Being private secretary to the chief dispenser of patronage in the Cleveland administration was a far cry from sitting in a depressingly quiet legal office in Martinsburg. Baker quickly adapted to the work; he was diligent, well organized, and discreet. Working in such a sensitive position during an election year gave him a box seat during one of the most tumultuous presidential campaigns in history. He was impressed at the time with Cleveland's "sturdy and solid character," but later came to see that he was "all character and no brilliance."[40]

Although he was a hereditary Democrat, Baker had no time for William Jennings Bryan, the party's nominee in 1896, and his free silver ideas. He thought Bryan to be a demagogue and a "fakir," and feared for the nation when its choice was between "the dishonesty of Bryanism [and] . . . the dishonesty of McKinleyism." Like Willie McAdoo, Newt Baker supported the Gold Democrats and their platform of the gold standard, free trade, and civil service reform.[41]

Service in Washington matured Baker; in January 1897 he told his brother Frank that "I have cast off some of the 'Please—Sir' manner which use[d] to make an unfavorable impression for me everywhere, and learned to assert myself a little among men." He stayed on until June 1897, assisting Wilson's Republican successor James A. Gary to settle into his new duties. Resisting overtures to stay longer, he used his savings for a summer tour of Europe and then returned to Martinsburg.[42]

In September 1897 Baker joined two other lawyers, W. H. Flick and David Westenhaver, in a new firm. Westenhaver and Baker became lifelong friends, but after the excitements of Washington and the pleasures of Europe Baker found Martinsburg too small and too quiet. Cleveland, Ohio—a large city with close financial and legal links to West Virginia—beckoned. Despite Baker's dislike of Cleveland's "awful grime and dust," the opportunities there were irresistible. In January 1899 he joined the law firm founded by Martin Foran, a former US representative whom Baker had met in 1897. "I was a carpetbagger in reverse," Baker remembered, "although I was never made to feel so."[43]

Baker spent two productive years with Foran, McTighe and Baker. As a junior partner of a busy law firm, he inherited an extensive clientele and opportunities to become known in Cleveland's municipal, state, and federal courts. With Foran's help, Baker quickly established himself as a rising star in Cleveland's legal community. He also made a name for himself as an orator, speaking on issues concerning city government and then in support of Tom Loftin Johnson, the Democratic mayoral nominee in 1901. When Johnson won election he appointed Baker as legal advisor to the City Board of Equalization; six months later he promoted him to assistant director of law for the city of Cleveland. "He ranks with the best, highest-paid, corporation lawyers in ability and had held his public office at a constant personal sacrifice," Johnson wrote later. "This low-paid city official has seen every day . . . lawyers getting often five times the fee for bringing a suit that he got for defending it. He did for the people for love what other lawyers did for the corporations for money." In Cleveland, Johnson, and city government, Baker had found his profession, his mentor, and now his cause. After severing his connection with

Foran, McTighe and Baker in 1901, he embarked on a public career that would last twenty years.[44]

❧

By the turn of the twentieth century William McAdoo and Newton Baker had grasped the uncertain opportunities offered to them as children of the Confederacy. Of the two men, McAdoo had a harder climb out of the Old South because he had started from a much lower point. Marietta, Georgia, in 1863 was a far cry from Martinsburg, West Virginia, in 1871. McAdoo's world was literally war torn, and his family's economic foundations had been smashed. Newton Baker, also the son of a Confederate veteran, was born not into a war zone but into a community and family that had been divided but not devastated by war. That crucial difference led to dissimilarities in their childhood circumstances and educational opportunities. Yet McAdoo and Baker shared an ambition to succeed in the postwar South, and both men bumped against the upper limits of what it could offer them.

McAdoo, as the older man from the heart of the Confederacy, had bumped harder than Baker. Escaping the penury of Georgia, and then fleeing financial failure in Tennessee, McAdoo moved north to New York in search of a new start. From that time on his story became less a southern tale of regeneration and more an American saga of triumph over adversity. McAdoo remained consciously southern but proudly American, glorying in the national unity that had emerged from the Confederacy's defeat. In 1923 he denied that he had referred to Sherman's soldiers who had destroyed his home as "pillagers." Rather, he declared, "It is to the . . . glory of our country that the wounds of the Civil War have been healed and I certainly would not be a party to anything which would tend to arouse dead passions or to reflect upon the gallant men . . . who fought with a courage and heroism that is the pride and heritage of the North and the South alike."[45]

Baker also left the Old South for greater opportunity in a northern industrial city, but for less pressing reasons. A new law firm in Martinsburg, still struggling to pay its way, and then removal to Cleveland under the tutelage of a former congressman, was a more secure base than the ruins of a destroyed plantation, a collapsed streetcar line, angry bondholders, remorseless creditors, and a despairing flight to Manhattan with a young family. Yet Baker, too, had to adapt to a postwar South that was far less comfortable and much more divided than it had been before 1861. Like his father, he turned resolutely away from the defeated Confederacy and toward the victorious North and the new nation that its victory had created. Neither McAdoo nor Baker wasted time lamenting the defeat of the South, but both were forced to gamble their futures on the consequences of that defeat.[46]

By the end of 1901 both men could feel that they had won their gambles. Baker, from his more secure social, educational, and economic base, had made a smaller leap for more certain rewards. In 1901, at the age of 30, he could afford to turn his back on private practice for the lesser material gains of public service. William Mc-Adoo, who turned 38 in 1901, also made a fateful turn that put at risk his hard-won financial comfort after the struggles of 1893–1897. That turn, unlike Baker's, was to-ward the promise of greater riches as an entrepreneur-lawyer. To reach their turning points, however, both men had risen within and then away from the New South.

McAdoo and Baker had both made accommodations with their southern heri-tages and experiences. They identified as southerners throughout their careers, both remained loyal to the memory of their fathers' services to the Confederacy, and both paid obeisance to Robert E. Lee. Their nostalgia for the Old South and its legends of chivalrous men, gracious ladies, and contented slaves seemed genuine enough, but neither McAdoo nor Baker allowed this to degenerate into veneration of the Lost Cause itself. Both men were avowedly and consistently New Southerners—more nationalist than regionalist, as adoring of Lincoln as they were respectful of Lee, and convinced that the war's outcome had been beneficial to the nation as a whole.[47]

In this McAdoo and Baker were similar in background and outlook to two other southerners who would play key roles in their careers. Tom Johnson, the son of a Confederate colonel who had once held Willie McAdoo in his arms, followed a trajectory similar to McAdoo's: from childhood poverty to streetcar ventures and finally to politics. In the process Johnson also launched Newton Baker's public ca-reer. Woodrow Wilson was another child of the New South whose father had served in the Confederate army and who—like Johnson, McAdoo, and Baker—went north without rancor over the fate of his father's cause. Wilson, Johnson, McAdoo, and Baker went north not to conquer but to prosper—"carpet baggers in reverse," in Baker's phrase—and to play on the national stage that their fathers had fought so hard to destroy.[48]

CHAPTER 2

Gotham's Class A Genius and Cleveland's Little David, 1902–1911

By the end of 1901 Willie McAdoo felt justified in dropping the diminutive version of his name in favor of a more adult nickname. Having weathered the depression of 1893–1897, and his own despair, McAdoo was now an established New York lawyer. His work with the Wilkes-Barre and Hazleton Railroad had introduced him to an influential group of investors at the heart of the railroad industry, renewed his self-confidence, and revived his entrepreneurial impulse. It was little wonder that he dropped "Willie" and now preferred "Mac."

McAdoo's entrepreneurial eye saw possibilities in an inconvenience suffered by millions of New Yorkers at the turn of the century: the lack of railroad connection between Manhattan and New Jersey. Commuters who lived in New Jersey were forced to use ferries to cross the mile-wide Hudson River. Those ferries, owned by the railroads, connected passengers to rail terminals on the Jersey side and then to points west; travelers to Manhattan and then northward had to make their own way from the ferries to their workplaces in Manhattan or to railroad terminals for connections to upstate New York and New England. By the turn of the century 120 million passengers caught the ferries each year. Although free, they were slow, overcrowded, cold in winter, and sweaty in summer. As a regular user of the ferries, McAdoo wondered whether the Hudson could be crossed more efficiently.[1]

The idea of connecting Manhattan to the rest of the United States by rail tunnel was too obvious to be new. In 1873 De Witt Clinton Haskin raised $10 million to build a brick-lined tunnel between Hoboken, New Jersey, and Washington Square in Lower Manhattan. Haskin planned a single tube to allow through trains from New Jersey into the Manhattan rail network. Excavating by hand from the Jersey side below the river bed, Haskin's workers dug and lined their tunnel 1,800 feet in 6 years before its roof collapsed, the tunnel flooded, and 20 workers drowned. Ten years later a group led by the British engineering company Pearson and Son tried to complete Haskin's tunnel. Using an iron cylinder, or "shield," propelled by compressed air to excavate the tunnel, and then cast iron rings to line it, the new owners proceeded another 2,000 feet at a cost of $4 million before the tube hit a rock ledge and they abandoned the whole project. The Haskin-Pearson tunnel, now more than halfway across the river, was allowed to flood, its bondholders were left unpaid, and New Yorkers remained on the ferries for another decade.[2]

William McAdoo joined the list of tunnelers under the Hudson through coincidence. During the Wilkes-Barre and Hazleton transaction he met John R. Dos Passos, a prominent New York commercial lawyer. McAdoo mentioned his idea of a tunnel and learned that Dos Passos had invested and lost heavily in the Pearson venture and remained a member of the bondholders' association that still owned the wreckage. Dos Passos introduced McAdoo to Frederick Jennings, founding partner of the law firm of Stetson, Jennings and Russell and president of the bondholders' group. Assured by engineers that the tunnel could be completed, and calculating that the project would cost $4 million, McAdoo negotiated to buy the tunnel from the bondholders for $350,000. He now had a deal but no funds to consummate it.[3]

In floating his proposition to electrify Knoxville's streetcars in 1889 McAdoo had struggled to find a banker in Philadelphia, New York, or Boston who would lend him funds. In 1901, after a decade in New York and with letters of introduction from Dos Passos and Jennings, he found a more receptive audience. His selling skills, honed by hawking bonds during a depression, were still important—the tunnels had already cost investors dearly—but now McAdoo was armed with engineers' reports, financial plans, and well-known backers to go along with his bravado. Even half of New York's 120 million ferry passengers per year, at 3 cents a ride, would generate revenue of $2 million per year, and that would cover the tunnel's completion costs in 2 years.

Won over anew, Jennings invested $100,000, as did E. H. Gary, chairman of US Steel, and Walter Oakman, president of the Guaranty Trust Company. E. C. Converse, a prominent New York investor, contributed $200,000. McAdoo then formed the New York and Jersey Railroad Company, with Jennings, Gary, Converse, and Oakman as directors and McAdoo as president at $15,000 per year. The company then borrowed its full working capital of $6 million from the Guaranty Trust Company. Mac dissolved his partnership with William McAdoo and devoted himself to his new venture. After retaining the firm of Jacobs and Davies to repair the shield, drain the tube, and oversee construction, work to complete the Haskin-Pearson-McAdoo Tunnel began in February 1902.[4]

Pushing the tube through was slow and dangerous business, conducted at a rate of one foot per hour at depths up to one hundred feet below the river bed. Steel rings fifteen feet in diameter were placed behind the shield to form the tunnel. Air compressed to 38 pounds per square inch kept the silt and the weight of the Hudson River from collapsing the structure as the shield, pushed by hydraulic jacks, inched forward. Every thirty inches a small door was opened in the face of the shield, allowing the displaced silt to force its way into the tunnel and to be removed in trolleys. More steel rings were put in place, the shield then moved forward, the silt was removed, and the tunnel moved another yard toward Manhattan. The reef that had stymied the 1890 effort was conquered by dynamite, but not before an explosion killed an excavator.[5]

Once he was satisfied that the tunnel could be completed, McAdoo rethought the whole project. His original plan had called for a single tunnel running two-way trolley car traffic on narrow-gauge rails and terminating at both landfalls. Passengers would then have to walk to their workplaces or their train connections. As his first tube inched forward, McAdoo began to plan for an integrated railroad network that would connect to existing rail lines. This required two one-way tunnels rather than a single tube, so that tracks in each direction could be standard gauge and compatible with those in New Jersey and New York. Consequently, another tunnel was begun close to the first. This South Tube was dug by two opposing shields, one starting from New Jersey and one from Manhattan, and with more powerful jacks that enabled progress at seventy-two feet per day. The older North Tube "holed through" on March 11, 1904, while the two shields in the South Tube met on September 24, 1905.[6]

Public interest in the project grew as the tubes neared completion, and Mc-Adoo took reporters along the tunnel a day after the North Tube broke through. He met them on the New Jersey side and subjected them to procedures that were as much theatrical as practical: a doctor listened to the reporters' hearts to see if they could withstand the rigors of compressed air; they then donned oilskins and gathered for a photograph before McAdoo led them along the mile-long tunnel. "The sense that one was eighty feet below the realm of sunlight, with huge transatlantic steamers perhaps passing overhead," *The New York Times* reporter noted, "and the thought that if for a moment the compressed air machines ceased throbbing the river and its bottom might drop on all in the tunnel had something at once awing and kindling to the fancy." After decompressing in "a boilerlike contrivance" and shedding their oilskins, the reporters "celebrated their resurrection from the lower regions." The Hudson River had been conquered; Manhattan was now connected to the rest of the United States, and William McAdoo had become a hero.[7]

Four more years of construction intervened before the first passengers rode through the McAdoo tubes on February 26, 1908. By then McAdoo's original vision had blossomed into a transportation network that cost more than $70 million and linked the New Jersey railroad termini, Hoboken, Jersey City, and Manhattan. It now comprised 4 tunnels, 19 miles of track, 13 stations, its own power station, lavish terminal buildings in New Jersey, and one of Manhattan's largest office buildings at Courtlandt and Church Streets. The Hudson Terminal building—twin towers of 22 stories each—was the centerpiece of the system and provided 4,000 offices for 10,000 workers. The whole project was to *The New York Times* "one of the greatest engineering feats ever accomplished, greater perhaps than the Panama Canal will be when opened, considering the obstacles which had to be overcome."[8]

Expansion of the Hudson and Manhattan Railroad Company (H&M) took place on both landfalls of the original tunnels. In New Jersey the line continued north to Hoboken, while on the Manhattan side the tunnels continued Uptown along Sixth Avenue after Christopher Street. It reached Twenty-third Street in September 1909, and eventually terminated at Thirty-third Street. Another extension occurred downtown and involved two more tunnels under the Hudson from Exchange Place in Jersey City across to Courtlandt Street. These tunnels, completed in July 1909, could accommodate fully laden long-distance passenger trains. They were extended as far as Newark, New Jersey, and to the Midtown tunnels in August and September 1909, thus creating a network connecting seven New Jersey stations with six Manhattan stops, which linked the most populous parts of New Jersey to Manhattan workplaces. An agreement with the Pennsylvania Railroad saw its trains pass through the downtown McAdoo tunnels from Newark into Manhattan. At its peak between 1906 and 1910 the project employed 3,500 men working 24-hour days in 3 shifts, 10 shields in constant operation, and 200 executive staff.[9]

Although McAdoo was proud of his company's safety record, work behind the shields was dangerous. Labor in compressed air was risky and the perils of fire, explosion, and collapse were ever-present. On February 11, 1909, two workers were killed and another seriously injured by a blast in the spur connecting the two tunnels. The following day another employee died when a trolley carrying excavated rock crushed him. Less than two weeks later two men were electrocuted when the iron pipe they were carrying touched exposed electrical wiring.[10]

McAdoo's workforce was predominantly black, but it was supervised by Irish foremen. Although this arrangement was common at the time, it led to outbursts of tension and even violence. In May 1909 a reporter from the *New York Herald*, who had worked undercover in the downtown tubes, gave his readers some idea of these tensions. The reporter, Douglas Church, referred to one of his fellow workers as a "nigger." His workmate retaliated by throwing a metal bolt at Church's head. The bolt missed, but the black worker came after Church with a wrench. "Mike," the Irish foreman, intervened by knocking the wrench from the man's hand and ordering him out of the tunnel. "This was the first lesson I learned of the discipline maintained down there," Church told his readers. "No black man is allowed to raise his hand against a white man, no matter what the provocation is, and if he does so he is dismissed . . . Owing to the great majority of blacks over whites and the rough character of the former this rule is absolutely imperative and is never broken, no matter how good a worker the offender may be."[11]

Expansion of the original "McAdoo Tunnel" into a network required large injections of new capital. The original New York and Jersey Railroad Company was consolidated in 1906 into the H&M, with McAdoo as president and an expanded board. J. P. Morgan invested $1 million and his company underwrote H&M's bonds, which eventually totaled more than $72 million and were taken up by prominent firms and investors, including the First National Bank, the American Exchange Bank, Pliny Fisk, and Cornelius Vanderbilt.[12]

Not all of New York's financial titans were impressed by the H&M. The Delaware, Lackawanna and Western Railroad refused McAdoo use of its rights of way and yard facilities, and even bought the Hoboken ferries that conveyed its passengers across the river to Manhattan. McAdoo was dragged into lengthy litigation to secure the use of the Hoboken right of way. On the Manhattan side streetcar interests fought H&M's plans to run tubes up Sixth Avenue, and this resulted in hearings before the New York Rapid Transit Commission and more expense and delay. Using a combination of bluff and litigation, McAdoo forced a settlement by threatening to build his own line to compete with the Metropolitan Street Railway Company's franchises. After a final battle over a right of way into Jersey City in 1907, McAdoo had navigated all the political and legal obstacles to the opening of his network.[13]

At 3:30 p.m. on February 25, 1908, more than four hundred guests gathered for the inaugural passenger train service from Manhattan to New Jersey. From Washington President Theodore Roosevelt activated electric current to a train waiting in the Nineteenth Street station. After the train reached Hoboken, greeted by 20,000 spectators, McAdoo welcomed a new era in transport. "The famous Simplon, and other Alpine tunnels, do not compare with it in magnitude, and the Chinese Wall, that required centuries to build, is, by comparison, a work of insignificance." More than 50,000 passengers traveled under the Hudson River in the following twenty-four hours as they reveled in the eight-minute journey that replaced the discomforts of the ferry ride. "Hooray for McAdoo!" proclaimed the *Jersey City Journal*.[14]

Nineteen months later, on July 19, 1909, McAdoo's daughter Harriet opened the downtown tunnels. Connections between the tunnels opened over the next 3 months, and by November 1910 more than 130,000 commuters used the McAdoo tunnels every day. The excitement seemed greater in New Jersey than in New York; it mattered more to Jersey City to be only three minutes from Manhattan than for Manhattan to be three minutes from New Jersey.[15]

As McAdoo's plans matured from a single tunnel into an integrated subway system he came into conflict with the Interborough Rapid Transit Company, which enjoyed a monopoly of elevated and subway lines in Manhattan. The Interborough enjoyed strong political support from Tammany Hall, the corrupt Democratic Party machine that ran New York City. Jealous of its monopoly and protected by City Hall, the Interborough blocked the construction of competing subway lines in New York. Overcrowded and notoriously unresponsive to riders' needs, the Interborough was thoroughly unpopular. In 1910 the New York Public Service Commission called for tenders to construct an independent subway system servicing Manhattan, the Bronx, and Brooklyn. No proposals were received, and the Interborough responded by offering to operate any lines that the city built itself. Once again the forces of corrupt and cosseted monopoly seemed to have trumped public opinion and open competition.[16]

William McAdoo, operator of the only independent subway in New York, made a dramatic intervention into this impasse in November 1910. He proposed that the city build a Triborough route—servicing the Bronx, Lexington Avenue, and Broadway in Manhattan with branches into Queens, Brooklyn, and Staten Island and connections to the H&M tunnels—with public money, but that H&M would spend $50 million to equip and operate it. The arrangement would last for ten years, during which time H&M would share profits with the city, and then the city could buy the railroad out for the value of its investment plus 20 percent. The Interborough countered with an offer to split almost equally the construction costs of subway extension with the city. McAdoo and the H&M did not respond, but they won praise as a St. George to Interborough's dragon. Not for the last time, William McAdoo had challenged "the interests" and won public acclaim for it.[17]

While winning praise for his fight against the Interborough, McAdoo also won fame as an enlightened railroad operator and employer. He soon became a prominent example of a new type of progressive business owner who combined profitability with good customer service and fair treatment of his employees.

Four days before Theodore Roosevelt opened the system, McAdoo summoned all H&M employees to the new Hoboken station. He told them that the new subway would be a model of customer service and satisfaction; safety and efficiency were its primary objectives, but they would not be achieved at the expense of "civility and courtesy in dealing with the public." Implicitly contrasting his approach with that of the notoriously heavy-handed Interborough system, McAdoo declared that "the amount of courtesy you display is going to have an important bearing upon the popularity of this road. The day of 'the public be damned' is forever gone." Instead, the motto of the H&M would be "the public be pleased." McAdoo warned his staff that they would be judged on their efficiency, cleanliness, and courtesy; they should answer all questions from the public civilly and fully, be neatly dressed at all times, and never shove passengers into crowded cars. Employees could expect their jobs and promotions to depend on their efficiency and courtesy.[18]

McAdoo worked hard to present the H&M as a customer-friendly operation. Major stations were designed so that embarking and disembarking passengers entered from opposite sides of the train, and all carriages featured center doors to assist quick entry and exit. Trains and stations were cleaned daily; H&M terminals featured package pickup services, ladies' powder rooms, and movable ticket booths during peak travel times. McAdoo was an energetic enforcer of 'the public be pleased' dictum, undertaking frequent inspections and providing complaint forms in every station. Very few of those forms were used: in 1910 some 50 million H&M passengers lodged only 50 complaints.[19]

The most famous of McAdoo's measures on the H&M was also the least successful. Responding to "hundreds of letters" from female passengers complaining of smoky cars and vulgar language, McAdoo announced in March 1909 that his trains would include a "ladies only" carriage for a three-month trial period. These carriages—dubbed "hen cars" and "Jane Crow carriages"—would be voluntarily segregated; men were encouraged but not forced to vacate them, and women could ride in them if they chose. "Whether they do not care to be separated from their escorts or enjoy metropolitan crushes statistics do not show," the *New York Herald* reported in April 1909. Observation did reveal, however, that the women's carriages were largely empty, while "women clung to straps in other cars where men were seated." Three months later the *Herald* editorialized again on hen cars, but this time with a significant extrapolation: women commuters had "clamored" for carriages of their own, but had shunned them when they were provided. "Woman sometimes thinks . . . that she wants to vote. That seems abundantly sufficient ground for suspecting that she really does not want to vote at all." Hen cars did not survive their trial period.[20]

"The public be pleased" was a masterstroke in public relations, tapping into public hostility to the Interborough and riding a wave of consumer rights that propelled muckraking journalism and consumer regulation during the progressive era. Because he was the originator of the phrase and tormentor of the Interborough, McAdoo's fame spread outside New York. In July 1909 the *Boston Herald* described him as "something more than a genius," whose public service and enlightened enterprise was a "shining contrast, both on the moral and the intellectual side, to some of the other men who have figured prominently in the history of metropolitan finance during the past decade." McAdoo had shown that private profit was compatible with public benefit, and now it was up to others to follow his example. A year later the *Boston Post* described him as "Gotham's Class A genius."[21]

McAdoo addressed the Boston Chamber of Commerce on "Decent Treatment of the Public by Corporations and Regulation of Monopolies" in January 1911. He told the story of "the public be pleased," which was "another way of saying that the public shall have <u>decent treatment</u>." That this policy had won so much attention showed how far American business had drifted from its social responsibilities. Even in 1911 there survived many businessmen who "must learn that the corporations are not the masters but the servants of the people." Now "Public Opinion, Esq., must become a member, and a respected one, of every corporation Board of Directors in this country."[22]

McAdoo argued that all monopolies and trusts were restraints of trade that sprang from greed and political corruption. Regulation through the Interstate Commerce Commission (ICC) and the New York Public Service Commission was not enough to control the evils of business concentration because it did not empower consumers or encourage other enterprises into the market. There was nothing natural about the emergence of "great combinations"; they were products of "the unrestrained activities of ambitious men of highly-developed acquisitive power." The twentieth century, he predicted, would see "the renaissance of the people":

> They believe that something is wrong in our system; that in the distribution of the benefits of government, privilege has an undue advantage; that opportunity is not equal; that business is not conducted with due regard to the moralities; that political leaders betray the rights of the people. They intend to change all this. What they need is a leader . . . A man of dynamic and militant morality, who will cleave a way through greed and selfishness for the permanent benefit of the human race.[23]

The H&M workforce reached 8,500 during McAdoo's time as its president, and its working conditions compared favorably to those of other railroads. McAdoo told his staff that "there is a mutual obligation between employer and employee which should always be considered in a fair and just spirit, and it will be the purpose of the managers of this corporation . . . to see that everybody has a square deal." This rhetoric of interdependence was common during the progressive era, even among those who opposed reform, because it could be as easily used against labor organizations, higher wages, and safer work conditions as for them. At H&M workers were promised fair treatment in their job security and wages; McAdoo paid them on the basis of an eight-hour day and did not object to the organization of his workforce into unions. He also advocated, but did not enact, workers' compensation schemes and retirement plans.[24]

McAdoo's most significant advance in labor relations lay in his insistence on paying equal wages for equal work to H&M's female employees. Convinced that they were as efficient as men and better suited to the company's consumer-focused image, McAdoo hired women as ticket sellers but did not take advantage of their lower wage rates. This policy, like that concerning hen cars, received much publicity and confirmed McAdoo's reputation as a reformer. H&M did not, however, significantly extend the sphere of female employment; women workers tended to be young, unmarried, and confined to duties such as ticket selling and attending powder rooms.[25]

H&M employees were also subject to stringent codes of conduct to enforce neatness and civility. They were charged demerit points for lapses, and those who transgressed too frequently were let go. Perhaps remembering his experiences in Chattanooga, and certainly conscious of safety concerns, McAdoo insisted on employing "only men of unquestioned sobriety and character." Any employee found drinking on duty, or arriving at work under the influence of alcohol, was immediately fired. McAdoo workplace policies were sufficiently enlightened—and publicized—to win praise from progressives such as Woodrow Wilson, who were anxious to find role models for a new type of business leader.[26]

Although he told his workers that "this railroad is operated primarily for the convenience of the public," McAdoo knew that its real purpose was to make profits for its owners. Although to the commuting public the H&M was an unqualified success, it struggled to be profitable during McAdoo's tenure as president. The problem was not lack of passengers; in that regard the new tubes more than fulfilled the rosy expectations of their builders and investors. During 1910, the first full year of operation for the 2 sets of tunnels, H&M carried more than 4 million passengers a month, each paying a 5 cent fare. Monday, February 28, 1910, when 197,000 passengers rode the tunnels, was the single busiest day in H&M's history, and by then earnings had risen 61 percent since August 1909. Passenger numbers grew again in 1911, to an average of 157,530 per day in February 1911, and total annual patronage was 50,926,980 in 1911.[27] By then McAdoo's tubes were saving New Yorkers more than 4.5 million minutes per day over the old ferries across the Hudson.

H&M's financial problems lay in the cost of its debt. Completing the expanded system had cost $70 million, all of it funded from bond issues paying 4.5 percent and 5 percent interest. Servicing that debt acted as a drag on the company's profitability; bondholders had to be paid before any profits could be distributed to shareholders. Even as New Yorkers flocked through H&M's turnstiles, the company rarely made a profit during its first three years of operation. In August 1910, for example, gross monthly profit, from the difference between total revenues of

$308,480 and total expenses of $132,940, was $175,539. This was more than swallowed up by the monthly interest bill of $243,958, leaving a deficit of $16,254. There were similar results in September and November 1910, while profits of $1,945 and $11,667 were achieved in October and December 1910, respectively. In April 1911, despite announcing that nearly 51 million passengers had used its tunnels in the previous year, H&M declared a yearly deficit of $41,890.[28]

In August 1911 McAdoo told his board to expect deficits until the end of 1912 unless it was prepared to raise fares by a cent. This would require litigation in New York and submissions to the ICC in Washington. Instead, McAdoo advised patience to avoid offending either regulators or passengers. Given the fixed amount of interest payable and its relatively stable operating expenses, H&M's profitability depended on revenue and traffic growth. Passenger numbers grew slowly after 1911, so only increases in rents from the office complexes in Manhattan and New Jersey ensured that H&M was profitable after 1914. H&M, like so much of the national railroad industry, was over-indebted because of its high construction costs. McAdoo had built for the long term, and his company relied on the patience of its investors during its first decade. After 1914 H&M became more lucrative, but by then McAdoo had moved on.[29]

Although he was never as rich as his prominence suggested, McAdoo was very comfortable financially between 1902 and his departure to Washington in 1913. His salary in 1902, set by his board of directors at $15,000 per year, had risen to $25,000 by 1908, and stock bonuses nearly doubled his earnings to $50,000 per year. While this was not an astronomical income in the world of big business before World War I, it was enough to propel McAdoo and his family into the top echelon of New York comfort and society. By speculating on stock and real estate McAdoo had also accumulated significant property holdings by 1910. He owned his original house in Yonkers, a much larger one in Irvington-on-Hudson, a beach property at Bay Head, New Jersey, and a twenty-one-year lease over a house on West Forty-eighth Street in Manhattan that he used as a city residence. At Irvington-on-Hudson the family employed a domestic staff that included a butler, a nurse for his wife, a gardener, a cook, two maids, a laundress, and a nanny for his children. There was enough money left over for stock and land speculation, overseas trips, and a high-powered Mercedes car, which McAdoo loved to drive fast and not always safely.[30]

By 1909 McAdoo was also a prominent member of New York society. He was president of the Southern Society of New York; industrial and financial leaders featured in his correspondence and invitations, he supported charities and tuberculosis clinics, and he had become a favorite at parties as an accomplished dancer and lively (if teetotal) raconteur. By 1910 Mac and Sarah were parents of six living children—Harriet, born in 1886, Francis Huger in 1887, Nona in 1894, William

Gibbs in 1895, Robert in 1899, and Sara Fleming in 1904. Their father seemed to combine a strenuous business career, an active social life, overseas holidays, and a growing family with energy to spare. The *New York Herald* described him in 1906:

> A very tall, very slight, very young man sits at [his] desk. As you enter the room you decide that he looks as if he might be twenty-five; four steps further and he seems thirty . . . He told me afterward that he was forty-five. There is something suggestive of a dreamer in his deep set eyes, something of a dynamic energy in his long, slight, sinewy body, something of a fine race horse in the impression of his whole self.
>
> Despite the lines on the forehead and cheeks there is a certain unconquerable youthfulness of look which is very characteristic of him . . . He speaks lucidly and with the soft accents of the South . . .
>
> "What do you consider to be the qualities most necessary to success in life?"
>
> "Now look hyear . . . I believe in the maxim "Do or Die" . . . A man's got to be in earnest if he would succeed. He must not let one knockdown discourage him; he must get at it again."[31]

Despite the glamour and prosperity that success brought, there were more knockdowns ahead for McAdoo. His health, sorely tested during the years after 1892, continued to trouble him. As soon as he could afford it, he began to travel each year to a sanatorium at Bad Kissingen in Germany to take the "cure" under Dr. Dapper, an internist specializing in stress-related digestive problems.[32]

Before leaving on his 1910 trip to Kissingen, McAdoo thanked Sarah, who was not well herself, for being "very sweet and dear about my going. I know it is very hard to be left behind but I hope you will have Harriet & Huger & Nona & Billy with you soon & that John Barleycorn may not become a favorite." From Germany he reported that he had gained eleven pounds and that his nerves were better. "The professor gave me a very serious talk about myself today—repeating that I have no organic trouble,—but that I have irregularity of the heart & my circulation is poor . . . He says my nerves are in bad shape, and that it is imperative for me to rest them." He needed at least another three weeks to complete his treatment.[33]

McAdoo was certainly high strung and pushed himself too hard, but his health concerns were minor compared to Sarah's. During the 1890s, as her young family suffered during the depression, Sarah developed rheumatoid arthritis. Her condition became chronic and seemed to worsen with childbirth. In 1904, after the birth of her youngest child Sarah, Mrs. McAdoo became an invalid, often bedridden and generally confined to the family home in Irvington. In almost constant pain and unable to care for her large family, Sarah succumbed to depression. The contrast between her own illness and the vigor of her hyperactive husband became too great to bear. They spent more time apart as Mac worked from their Manhattan house and spent his summers in Europe. Left at home, Sarah became increasingly desperate. "You once told me that I hadn't the 'courage to face life,'" she wrote Mac early in 1909. "I, too, have known it for a long time—ever since the baby was born and I knew I couldn't get better":

> Now that Christmas is over I am only waiting my chance—Perhaps I will get it this afternoon. Billy darling I can no longer live on—the time has come when I can't be nice and patient and sweet any more . . . So if I get a chance I shall take the same old way of trying to take the long sleep this afternoon . . .
>
> Darling, what shall I say to you. Who I have loved best in all the world. There seems to be nothing except that I'm sorry and that it is all my fault. I am not brave, you see, after all—that is I can't go on. Thank you for the radiant life you gave me.[34]

This crisis passed, but Sarah still suffered at home while her husband grew famous in the world outside. "I miss you when you are away—more than you will ever know," she wrote in the summer of 1909. "Am depressed to-day and If you were here am sure would throw myself upon you with my inner thoughts to be consoled. You have never failed me yet—If I hadn't had you sometimes I don't know what I would have done." In November 1911 Mac wrote from Manhattan on their twenty-sixth wedding anniversary. "I wish I might give you a . . . new set of joints and a complete restoration to health—so that you could be in every way as young and as whole as the charming little bride of 1885! I shall see you at the matinee and we shall go home together."[35]

The McAdoos' marriage seems to have collapsed at the beginning of 1912. In January they separated after yet another crisis, and Mac wrote from a train from Irvington-on-Hudson to Manhattan:

> Dear Sarah:—
> For my own sake I was sorry not to see you this morning altho. I suppose you are glad that I did not. All that you said last night has distressed me beyond measure but in view of your frank and deliberate statements what can I do, but do as you wish? If to abandon my career would restore you to health, I would gladly do it, but as it won't, what good would it do? On the other hand, the feelings you now express would make my presence in the house anything but a pleasure—there seems nothing for me to do now but to efface myself as much as I can and this I shall try to do—having regard for your and the children's comfort and security.

McAdoo suggested that Sarah take a trip to Florida to recover her health, and he left New York for three weeks to attend Nona's wedding in Albuquerque, New

Mexico, on February 8 and to drum up western and southern support for Wood-row Wilson's campaign for the 1912 Democratic presidential nomination. Soon after his return the press announced that Sarah had died suddenly, of heart failure, on February 21, 1912. "I have just returned and have only just now heard the terri-ble news of your bereavement," Wilson cabled from Trenton. "You have my deep-est warmest and most affectionate sympathy."[36]

There is no record of Sarah suffering from heart problems, and in light of her suicidal tendencies it is likely that cardiac failure was a symptom and not a cause of her death. Suicide, like rushed marriages and divorce, was a taboo subject in polite society at the time, and McAdoo said little about Sarah after her death. In 1930 he paid a short tribute to her that ended on a note of sad liberation. "In Febru-ary of 1912, I had the great misfortune to lose my first wife." Sarah was a "noble and devoted character" who "through the long years of our struggle had stood at my side with unfaltering faith and encouragement." Soon after her death McAdoo moved with the children to New York City. "It was like beginning life over again, but a beginning that was full of long memories."[37]

※※※

As 1902 was a turning point in McAdoo's life, so too was it in Newton Baker's. On July 5 he married Elizabeth Leopold from Pottstown, Pennsylvania. The Leopolds were originally Dutch, Quaker, and "ancient Pennsylvanian." When they married Elizabeth was 29 and Newton was 31; Elizabeth, whom Newton called Bess or Betsy, was on the faculty at Wilson College in Chambersburg, but after her marriage de-voted herself to her home and family. In contrast to the McAdoos' stormy private life, the Bakers' was stable and loving; in 1911 Newton told a friend that he neither had nor wanted material wealth. "But I have a wife, Heaven bless her—and two babies: Betty (Elizabeth Baker I suppose the grand little miss will want to be called some day), and Jack Baker, whose busy baby tongue gravely announces that he is New-ton D. Baker the third . . . Betty is six and Jackie four . . . Betty is pretty, Jack win-some and both good." The Bakers' third child, Margaret (whom the family called Peggy), was born in 1912.[38]

Baker's otherwise happy family life was shadowed by anxiety over Bess's health. In 1900 she was diagnosed with Basedow's disease, a form of hyperthyroidism, and she suffered two miscarriages before 1905. She spent time at health spas, and dur-ing one of her absences in 1904 Newton wrote that "I keep saying sternly to myself 'She must be away to grow stronger and happier' and under the spell of that hope I think I am strong enough to put up with anything—even the lonliness [sic] of the clock striking twelve, Togo [the dog] snoring and—no Betsy!" [39]

Jack's birth in 1906 left Bess in poor health. "Her trouble is nervous," Newton wrote to his mother-in-law in 1910, and her doctors were concerned about her heart. Bess was badly run down, needed constant care at home, and found it difficult to look after the children. She needed Newton close by, and so he scaled down his work commitments and declined invitations outside Cleveland. In September Bess suffered "blinding and disabling, nervous headaches" that left her incoherent with pain. "As these attacks are a direct consequence of her goiter trouble and their recurrence is evidence of the fact that she is now still suffering from that disease, I find myself a good deal shaken and disturbed at this recurrence." With a sick wife, two young children, and a busy career, Newton also began to experience health problems related to stress. As Bess struggled to recover, he suffered bouts of sleeplessness and indigestion. "I have so many vices that I am at a loss to know which one to attribute this condition to," he told Bess's mother. "I think the likelihood is that I smoke too much, eat too little, work too long, vacate too little, and that the weather is bum."[40]

Baker's professional life also took unexpected turns in 1902. "I wonder, sometimes, whether I shall ever come near meeting my own ambitions and realizing any of my dreams," he wrote Bess a few months after their marriage. "My ambitions you know are to be a good lawyer and to have a large and useful practice. Sometimes it seems to me that all these political experiences are rather tending away from the law than toward it." Baker's decision to leave legal practice with Foran and McTighe for the less certain prospects of Cleveland city government had indeed led him into "political experiences." His salary of $5,000 per year as city solicitor, later raised to $6,000, was comfortable but unremarkable compared to the rewards he could expect in private practice and in comparison with McAdoo's remuneration. Even so, the Bakers lived very well in substantial houses, educated their children at private schools, and employed a domestic staff of three.[41]

Tom Johnson had initially asked Baker to stay only a year, and "at the end of his first term, and at the end of each of his other terms, I begged [him] to release me from any sense of obligation to continue in political life, as I desired to practice law and not to be in politics." If not for money, then, Baker changed direction because of the less tangible attractions of working for Tom Johnson and being part of an adventure in public policy that would captivate him for the next fourteen years until Woodrow Wilson lured him to Washington in 1916.[42]

Although Baker and Johnson were both sons of Confederate soldiers, Johnson's background was closer to McAdoo's than it was to Baker's. Like the McAdoos, the Johnsons were impoverished by the Civil War. Tom, born in 1854, received little education as his parents struggled to find a place in the New South. He went to work at 11, selling newspapers in Staunton, Virginia, and working odd jobs when his family moved to Louisville, Kentucky. In 1859 he became a cashier on Louisville's streetcar line. He rose quickly to be superintendent and invented a glass-sided fare box that he sold for $20,000 in 1876. Johnson moved to Indianapolis, bought the city's streetcar line, and for the next twenty years behaved like "a carpetbagger in reverse," as Newton Baker once described himself. Johnson proved to be a ruthless operator, buying streetcar franchises cheaply, repairing and expanding them, and then selling them at much higher prices. After Indianapolis he bought lines in St. Louis, Brooklyn, Detroit, and then Cleveland, where he settled in 1890.[43]

It was then that Johnson became a convert to Henry George's plan to redistribute income from those who lived on unearned wealth to those he called the "producing classes." Johnson was an unlikely disciple; the man dubbed the "prince of privilege" by Henry George's son had made a fortune from streetcar monopolies, watered stock, and bullying city governments in five states. Yet Johnson was an enthusiastic advocate of his new cause and won election as a Henry George Democrat to the US House of Representatives in 1890. He served two terms, preaching the single tax and free trade while managing his heavily protected steel investments and streetcar franchises. In 1894 he lost his bid for re-election and moved to Detroit, where he seemed to forget his reformist fervor and instead fought a five-year battle with Mayor Hazen Pingree over streetcar fares and franchise rights.[44]

Stymied by Pingree, Johnson sold all his streetcar interests and moved back to Cleveland in 1899. There he fought the same battles that he had lost in Detroit, but this time on the other side. He entered the mayoral race on a platform borrowed from Pingree calling for 3 cent fares and municipal ownership of streetcars. "The public utility corporations are a bunch of thieves," he told voters. "I ought to know. I was one of them." He squeaked through the 1901 Democratic mayoral primary election by five votes, but won more convincingly in the general election. He did well among Cleveland's industrial workers, but wealthier voters were wary of his wildly fluctuating convictions. Once elected, Johnson put Cleveland at the forefront of municipal good government and reform. "Tom Johnson is the best mayor of the best-governed city in the United States," Lincoln Steffens declared in 1905.[45]

The friendship between the mercurial Johnson and the cautious Newton Baker was, to say the least, incongruous. Baker never subscribed to Henry George's theories or to Johnson's rhetoric against unearned privilege and wealth. Yet Johnson never enacted single tax ideas in Cleveland, and Baker happily supported those ideas that the mayor did put into practice: lower streetcar fares, municipal ownership of utilities such as electricity generation, a new taxation regime that redistributed burdens between households and businesses, and clean government. Baker never recanted his belief that Johnson was "the greatest municipal executive I have ever known." He was a true Jeffersonian Democrat, with an abiding faith in the wisdom of the people. "As a consequence, while [Johnson] believed many things which were much in advance of possible practical adoption, he always declined to advocate anything which was not sufficiently timely to be susceptible of ready explanation and easy understanding in a public audience." After his experiences in Congress, Johnson believed that political power should devolve from Washington to the states, and then to the cities, because only when government was close could it be scrutinized and controlled by the people. Baker, himself soon to control important levers in the federal government, agreed.[46]

Reassured that Johnson was no demagogue, Baker was drawn to his warmth of character and sharpness of mind. "My association with Mr. Johnson was intensely stimulating, intellectually and morally," he wrote to Johnson's widow in 1921. "He was one of the few really great men I have ever known, and undoubtedly everything I have done or thought since I knew him, has been in some way affected by his splendid mind."[47]

Baker played a steady accompaniment to Johnson's more flamboyant political tune, and this provided stability to Cleveland voters who wanted a restraining influence on their charismatic, hyperactive mayor. The pro-business Cleveland Municipal Association, citing Baker's "blameless reputation," endorsed his election as city solicitor in 1903, 1905, and 1907, but supported Johnson for mayor only in 1905. The first decade of the twentieth century was tumultuous in Cleveland, as Johnson fought bitter campaigns against powerful streetcar interests, utility magnates, and other business groups. As Johnson's chief legal advisor, Baker was in the midst of a political maelstrom that lasted fourteen years.[48]

As part of a reorganization of Ohio municipal government, Baker's office as assistant director and then director of law was transformed into the elected office of city solicitor in 1903. He won election as city solicitor in November 1903 and remained in office for five successive two-year terms before he became mayor in January 1912. The city solicitor was responsible for prosecutions in the police court, all litigation by the city government and its officers, and advising municipal departments and officials. In 1910 the city solicitor's office included eight assistant city solicitors and five administrative staff.[49]

Despite his youth and lack of legal experience—he was 31 and had a total of six years' legal experience in Martinsburg and Cleveland—Baker quickly became Tom Johnson's most trusted advisor. Not legally trained, Johnson relied heavily on the younger man's expertise. "It is true that [Johnson] is a strong man, rather restless under restraint," Baker wrote at the beginning of 1904. "I have been frequently called upon to advise Mr. Johnson when he ardently desired that a certain line of conduct might be followed—when I have told him that the statutes made no provisions for such cases or that they provide otherwise, his universal comment has been, <u>Mr. Baker says otherwise and he is our City Solicitor, we must obey the law.</u>" "Though the youngest of us," Johnson recalled in his autobiography, Baker "was really head of the cabinet and principal adviser to us all."[50]

Threats to the independence of Baker's office came not from the headstrong Johnson but from his Republican successor Herman Baehr. In November 1909 Baker was the only member of Johnson's ticket to win re-election, leaving him as the sole Democrat in a Republican administration. For two uncomfortable years he was barred from meetings of the council that he was required to advise and forced to defend the independence of his office. The city solicitor, he reminded his erstwhile colleagues, was an independently elected official solely responsible for the city's legal business and "is not subject to question by administrative officers, nor is his conduct of matters of litigation subject to direction by them."[51]

Despite their unhappy denouement, Baker's years as city solicitor were busy and varied. Between 1900 and 1910 Cleveland's population grew by more than 40 percent, from 381,000 to 561,000. It was an important industrial city with an ethnically diverse workforce, and it had an activist mayor who courted controversy in almost everything he did. Baker had many legal opinions to give, cases to fight, and political fires to extinguish. Much of his work was routine; he was frequently asked for advice as to the proper attribution of particular costs to accounting categories, and he provided numerous interpretations of the Ohio Municipal Code. In this he usually, but not always, favored a strict construction of the city's powers.[52]

At the beginning of 1904 Baker was asked whether it was lawful for the city to maintain sidewalk water coolers originally installed by a charity. Noting that the city was "a corporation of strictly limited powers," Baker responded in the negative. The Code empowered cities to install and maintain conveniences in parks but not on public highways. He later vetoed a proposal for the City Library to charge a fee to borrowers of popular novels. The Code allowed for free libraries, Baker held, but not for institutions that charged fees of any kind. He was similarly unmoved by calls for funds raised by a city hospital tax to be used in private hospitals. "I believe, as a matter of fundamental policy, that public and private funds should not be mixed or confused in the performance of quasi-public functions, and for that reason . . . I am not in favor of the turning over of lump sums of public money to private agencies."[53]

When it came to the city saving money rather than spending it, Baker was less rigid in his reading of municipal powers. In 1904 the question arose as to whether the city might remove materials left over from construction of the Lake Erie water tunnel. City employees could do the work more cheaply than private contractors, but the Code required that public works exceeding $500 should be put out to competitive tender. It was unclear, however, what constituted public works. Having sought opinions from other Ohio city solicitors whether municipal employees could do this work without contract, Baker decided that they could. After all, he reasoned, "in Cleveland we light our own streets, clean them, lay water pipe, and do a number of such things without contract, following a long established precedent rather than any statutory designation that I have been able to find."[54]

Baker was similarly flexible in agreeing in 1903 to the city installing and operating safety devices on drawbridges over the Cuyahoga River. Streetcars belonging to the Cleveland Electric Railway Company used these bridges, as did pedestrians and other vehicles. The city used its funds and employees to protect pedestrians and ordinary vehicles, but not privately owned streetcars operating on a franchise granted by the city. Ignoring his own concern about mixing public funds and private purposes, Baker agreed to extend the city's protection to streetcars, but on the express condition that when the devices were deployed to protect streetcar traffic municipal employees were to be considered agents of the company rather than of the city. Baker would soon discover, however, that other issues concerning the Cleveland Electric Railway Company could not be so easily resolved.[55]

Baker was also called on to advise on the proper reach of Cleveland's sumptuary ordinances, which appeared to forbid playing baseball or showing movies on Sundays. Regarding baseball, Baker read the ordinance narrowly and enforced it against professional ball games but not recreational ones. "Laws are necessarily of two classes," he wrote to a clergyman concerned about such frivolity on the Sabbath, "those prohibiting things which are wrong in themselves and those regulating things innocent in themselves but which possibly by abuse become either wrongful or objectionable." Sunday baseball laws were in the latter category, and "I do not conceive that the law was ever intended . . . to prevent boys and young men from engaging in a purely athletic exercise on Sunday for their recreation, rest and pleasure." To do so would be "a tyrannous and in some cases, cruel restriction of the liberties of a portion of the people who are not so highly favored as to be able to choose the day upon which they can seek innocent diversion and recreation."[56]

Baker was not so tolerant of movies, which he described in 1910 as "better adapted to the stimulation and cultivation of impure and vicious impulses than any other form of public exhibitions we have." Although he had little time for movies on any day of the week, he saw no reason why they should be banned specifically on Sundays, and drafted an ordinance to remove that prohibition in 1908. Vaudeville theater also raised Baker's ire; he attended a show in December 1908 at the Star Theatre and found that "while the general make-up of the show was attractive and creditable, there were . . . sentences and actions of a character forbidden by law and highly objectionable." Unless the theater censored its shows, he warned the proprietor, the city would.[57]

Baker was more tolerant of political speech. Cleveland's Public Square, in the heart of the city, had several platforms from which anyone could say his or her piece. Baker defended this practice, but enforced an ordinance proscribing "huckstering in the parks" against speakers who tried to sell pamphlets. When the anarchist Emma Goldman came to Cleveland in 1908, Baker resisted calls to prevent her from speaking in the Public Square. When she did so, Baker noted that "she was not taken seriously; there was not the least disorder or trouble and it is difficult for me to see how any harm could come from allowing her to talk in public in this way."[58]

Baker brought strong views to his responsibility for criminal prosecutions. He thought that criminal justice should be as much rehabilitative as punitive, and took special interest in juvenile offenders in the belief that their offenses sprang from poor home environments rather than innate criminality. This was no idle theory. In January 1905, Baker was robbed at gunpoint of his watch and cash by two juveniles and an adult. The two younger assailants, Paul Martin and John Behan, were sent to the Ohio State Reformatory, while the older man, John Freeman, was sentenced to the State Penitentiary. Baker told the Reformatory's superintendent that he was "exceedingly solicitous that both of these boys should feel that their residence in Mansfield is disciplinary and not punitive." He hoped that they could be released quickly and undertook to find them jobs when they were.[59]

Baker later wrote to the Ohio Board of Pardons in July 1906 that John Freeman's family environment had given him little chance of an honest life. His mother was "dissolute and intemperate"; his father had died, and his sister was an inmate of a reformatory. Baker visited Freeman in jail and wrote to him regularly. "You are still young enough to lead a very useful and happy life, if you can keep away from bad associates, and remember the lesson which you are now learning." Seeking a pardon for his robber, Baker promised to find him work. Freeman was not pardoned, but he was released in 1907. Baker did find him a job, and "I am doing all I can to simulate a return of self-respect and confidence in the boy."[60]

Baker applied a humanistic approach to the law when he dealt with compensation claims by city employees. Under the laws of the day, injured workers had no recourse unless they had been injured through their employer's negligence. Even then doctrines of voluntary assumption of risk and contributory negligence often reduced an employee's payment if he or she had contributed in some way to his or her injury. This led to many injustices, and Baker acted in cases when he believed that an injured worker had sufficient "moral claim" against the city. In June 1903 he considered the case of three workmen who had suffered total paralysis from decompression sickness while working in the city's water tunnel under Lake Erie. Although Baker could not discern "any liability upon the city for this deplorable situation," he recommended *ex gratia* payments to the workers "who are now total and irre-coverable wrecks."[61]

In 1905 a police officer was shot while apprehending a burglar and needed ex-tended medical treatment. Given his "excellent record and that he is a deserving young man," Baker recommended that his medical bills be paid by the city. Rather than assume liability for injured workers, Baker urged the city to find jobs for them, but only "so far as such persons were able to perform efficient service."[62]

Baker's approach to injured workers was humane but individualized. In extend-ing generosity to those he considered to be deserving, he could salve the city's con-science while leaving its unjust liability laws in place. In the case of clean air ordi-nances he argued that suasion was better than coercion to persuade industrialists to reduce Cleveland's notorious smog. He countenanced prosecutions under the city's smoke abatement law, but only against "janitors whose employers have provided smoke consuming devices but where the janitors are too indolent or careless to work them effectively." He showed similar myopia in 1904 when he held that, although there was no legal impediment to selling rights to garbage collection from the city dump, "a large number of women, children and cripples pick an impecunious living out of this refuse and their exclusion from the dump heap would be something of a hardship more than commensurate with the advantage to the city."[63]

The most significant work of the city solicitor's office between 1903 and 1910 arose from Tom Johnson's "seven years war" against the Cleveland Electric Railway Company. The company, known as the "Con-Con," owned almost all of Cleve-land's two hundred-odd miles of streetcar lines. It was controlled by Mark Hanna, a Republican boss who sat in the US Senate. The Con-Con charged passengers a 5 cent fare, used its near-monopoly to squeeze out competitors, and paid no city taxes other than a peppercorn rent on the land beneath its lines. It had become deeply unpopular in Cleveland, and Johnson had fought hard against it in his campaign for the mayoralty in 1901. As a former streetcar franchisee himself, Johnson was no stranger to battles with city governments over fares and competition. Now the tables were turned: instead of fighting fare reductions and new operators, Johnson sought a reduction of fares to 3 cents and the granting of franchises to new operators.[64]

The battle with the Con-Con defined Johnson's mayoralty and won him a rep-utation as a fearless reformer. As his principal legal officer and closest confidant, Newton Baker was Johnson's "little David" as they battled Hanna's "Goliath." Dur-ing the Con-Con struggle Baker litigated fifty-five suits in the Ohio and federal courts and argued three cases before the Supreme Court of the United States. Ultimately, the Cleveland streetcar fight broke Tom Johnson, but it made Newton Baker.[65]

Johnson and Baker first passed an ordinance requiring streetcar fares to be re-duced to 3 cents. The Con-Con argued that this was an abrogation of existing contracts, and its contention was sustained by the Supreme Court in 1904. The city then tried to attract new 3 cent franchisees. Construction of a new line began until the Con-Con halted it by injunction. Johnson ordered this "people's line" to be completed and instructed Cleveland police to ignore the injunction. The new line did little to weaken the Con-Con's dominance of Cleveland transit lines, so Johnson and Baker turned to its franchises. The city had no power to vary these unilaterally, but it did have power either to renew them or allow them to lapse. Because of the Con-Con's assumption of its competitors' franchises, their expiration dates were in doubt. Baker maintained that all of them expired at intervals between 1904 and 1908; the Con-Con argued that they expired in 1908 and then 1914. Litigation ensued, ending twice in the Supreme Court. In 1906 the Court upheld the Con-Con's contention concerning its 1908 franchises, but in 1907 it agreed with the city that all the other franchises also expired in 1908. Baker wrote the submissions and led the argument in both Supreme Court hearings, beginning a distinguished career of nearly thirty years before that bench.[66]

The Supreme Court's 1907 decision, which effectively terminated all the Con-Con's franchises in 1908, forced the company into negotiations. Although Johnson and Baker preferred municipal ownership of streetcars, they conceded that the Municipal Code did not permit cities to own street railways and that the Con-Con could not be stripped of its property in its lines. But the expiration of its franchises meant that those lines could be operated by other concerns. Accordingly, Johnson and Baker insisted that the Con-Con's lines would be operated by a municipal corporation that would pay the company 6 percent per year on the value of its investment. Fares would be 3 cents, and any profits would return to the city. Amid much fanfare the new municipally operated system carried its first passengers on April 28, 1908.[67]

Tom Johnson soon saw defeat snatched from the jaws of victory. The municipal streetcars were hit by a strike and lost $50,000 in May and $23,000 in June 1908. Even the holy grail of the 3 cent fare proved elusive; passengers had to buy books of 3 cent tickets or pay a 5 cent cash fare. The slump of 1907–1908 reduced revenues, and there were even rumors of sabotage by the Con-Con. Influenced by a campaign funded by the Chamber of Commerce, Clevelanders voted in October 1908 to return the system to private operation.[68]

Final settlement of the streetcar wars was brokered by Judge Robert W. Tayler and drafted by Newton Baker in 1910. The new franchise, to run for twenty-five years, returned streetcar operation to the Con-Con, but under much tighter restrictions. The company was again limited to a 6 percent return on its investment, and the city took control over the routing, terminals, and schedules. A street railroad commissioner, appointed by the mayor but paid by the company, oversaw the franchise and enforced its terms. Fares were set at 3 cents, to be increased only if the 6 percent return could not be achieved. The Tayler settlement was no great triumph of principle, but it was a large step forward in the give and take of streetcar reform. Johnson's crusade for municipally owned and operated streetcars in Cleveland was finally achieved in 1942, more than thirty years after his death.[69]

During his fight against the Con-Con, Baker aligned himself more closely to what he described as the progressive wing of the Democratic Party. In 1906 he was ambivalent about legislation mandating an eight-hour working day; some occupations needed fewer working hours, and some more, "but with the general movement in favor of a reduction of the hours of labor and an increase in the wages of labor I am entirely in sympathy." On child labor, however, he had no doubts. Children were the greatest resource of the nation, and their health and education must not be stunted by premature employment. The minimum age for their labor should be raised, their hours of employment limited, and their access to urban vices curtailed. In 1911 Baker also supported a bill to restrict female working hours to eight hours a day, and successfully lobbied state legislators to pass it.[70]

During his years as city solicitor, Baker also showed interest in a cause that would later come to haunt his appointment as secretary of war. Although he was never a doctrinaire pacifist, he did oppose Theodore Roosevelt's militarism. In 1904 he congratulated his Republican congressman Theodore Burton for opposing Roosevelt's plan to increase the navy. "I cannot help believing that the accumulation of means of war and destruction is both a temptation to their use . . . and a demoralization of the peace-loving and civilized sentiment of our people." The $200 million spent on the army and navy every year was a sign that "barbarity and savagery" had not yet been conquered by "civilization and progress." In 1909 Baker anticipated a time when "international peace might come by the United States, Germany, France and England assuming to police the world." A treaty between these four powers— "and any other nations that desired to be admitted to the union"—should limit arms to levels sufficient only for nations' internal order and oblige all international disputes to be settled by arbitration.[71]

When it came to national politics Baker was a loyal but not unquestioning Democrat. "I am beginning to learn several things about politics," he wrote in June 1910. He was "in a party but not of it." The Democratic Party suited him best, "even though I do not agree with all of its doctrines or approve of all of its practical operations." Early in the century he struggled to reconcile his party loyalty with his disapproval of the populist and free-silver views of William Jennings Bryan, the Democratic presidential nominee in 1896, 1900, and 1908. In 1896 he voted for the Gold Democrats, but switched to Bryan in 1900 because of his anti-imperialism.[72]

In 1904 the Democratic Party, tiring of Bryan, nominated Alton B. Parker of New York. Parker was a very different Democrat; he was urbane, business-oriented, and conservative. Baker was thrown into a quandary; Parker seemed indistinguish-able from the Republicans—and undistinguished. He stayed loyal in 1904 because he saw Theodore Roosevelt, the incumbent president, as too egotistical, too mili-taristic, and too close to the "commercialized aristocracy" within the GOP. When Bryan again won the presidential nomination in 1908, Baker's reservations about him resurfaced. He would vote for Bryan, he told a relation, but "I am coming to the time of life when an intellectual equipment is needed to satisfy my demand." Bryan's intentions were good, "but his thinking is certainly not of a modern type."[73]

Bryan's three defeats, and an even worse performance under Parker, encour-aged Baker to advocate a new direction for the Democrats in 1912. "It does seem to me . . . that the Democratic Party is essentially a radical party," and accordingly its national electoral victories would be "occasional," he told the governor of Ohio after Bryan's third defeat in 1908. Yet because the Republicans were masters of "conservative virtues," there was no point in the Democrats attempting, as they had done in 1904, to compete on their conservative ground. Their best hope lay in "vig-orous and unwavering assertion of radical opinions rather than temporizing poli-cies" under new leadership.[74]

In 1911, however, Baker had pressing matters to attend to in Cleveland. Tom Johnson's death in April of that year robbed the city's Democrats of their standard bearer and presumptive mayoral candidate in the November elections. As the only member of Johnson's administration to survive the elections of 1909, and because of his status as Johnson's closest confidant, Baker was his obvious heir. His central campaign plank was to construct a municipal electric power plant with a bond is-sue of $2 million. With the streetcar issue now settled, he told voters, the next step to secure Johnson's legacy was to end Cleveland's electric power monopoly. "Now that he is gone and his work remains I find myself going on with it quite naturally," Baker told a Martinsburg friend in August 1911:

> Beginning October 9, our campaign will be on. You can picture us: A circus tent holding about three thousand people, three speakers, Dr. Cooley a farmer preacher and under Mr. Johnson the soul of our charities and corrections, Peter Witt an iron molder, forceful, crude, direct, incorruptible, and last me. The au-dience quiet but now and then asking questions which are always welcomed and answered so that sometimes the meetings are almost running debates. So it will run until Nov 7 when the votes will be counted and really the result seems less important to all of us than the message.[75]

Baker defeated his Republican opponent Frank Hogen by nearly 18,000 votes. He had rebuilt Johnston's coalition of immigrant and working-class voters by winning

100 percent of German, Czech, and Irish votes. The new mayor pledged to follow in Johnston's footsteps and to return his key appointees to office. "If Johnson should return," *The New York Times* noted the day after Baker's inauguration on January 1, 1912, "he would find things just as they were before his defeat and death."[76]

The first decade of the twentieth century had been good to McAdoo and Baker. Of the two men McAdoo had enjoyed the more spectacular rise from obscurity as a struggling Wall Street lawyer to national fame as a new type of business leader. Along the way he had become adept at publicizing his ventures and himself. Although he had not won the great wealth that he had dreamed of in Chattanooga, McAdoo had earned a level of comfort and security that not long before had seemed fanciful. Yet nothing in these years was easy, and much depended on his self-belief and driving ambition. Millions of dollars needed to be raised, rock ledges deep underwater needed to be blasted away, workers needed to be directed and investors appeased, and all the while his growing family had to be supported. Sarah's agonizing illness and sudden death were reminders of the cost of McAdoo's pursuit of wealth and glory. An individualist and egotist, McAdoo was convinced that those qualities had determined his success. By 1911 he had prospered as a twentieth-century Horatio Alger; his challenge after 1912 was to subordinate his sense of personal destiny to the interests of an equally strong-willed, but very differently configured, political leader.[77]

Newton Baker's rise was more measured. He was moved more by inspiration than raw ambition; he aspired to be a good and prosperous lawyer and hoped to succeed in ways that were less spectacular than McAdoo's and better suited to his personality—steady, bookish, and meditative. As city solicitor in an industrial city, Baker had a modest canvas on which to work, and that suited him perfectly. As a husband and father, he enjoyed the stability of a marriage that was more a tranquil partnership than a battle of conflicting and frustrated sensibilities. Modest and self-effacing, Baker prospered best when working with—and behind—more politically motivated mentors: William L. Wilson, then Tom Johnson, and finally Woodrow Wilson. McAdoo strove for the limelight, but Baker was content to be a supporting actor.

Baker supplied expertise and loyalty to achieve the substance of public service rather than its gaudier companions of leadership and publicity. When leadership did come in 1911, it came from loyalty and competence, not from ambition. Baker was Johnson's heir but never his rival. The years between 1911 and 1916 were therefore anomalous in his political career, as he worked on his own between the shadows of Tom Johnson and Woodrow Wilson to put his stamp on Cleveland. McAdoo, on the other hand, gravitated to Woodrow Wilson not so much as a disciple to a mentor but as an adventurer to a new opportunity for public power and prominence.

CHAPTER 3

Changing Roles

When Newton Baker became mayor of Cleveland on New Year's Day 1912, he took charge of a rapidly growing city. Cleveland's population had grown by more than 4 percent per year after 1890, and in 1910 it had 561,000 inhabitants. Ten years later its population was nearly 800,000. By 1910 it was the largest city in Ohio and had overtaken Baltimore to become the sixth largest in the nation. Cleveland, like most industrial cities, boasted an ethnically varied population; in 1910 almost 35 percent of its people were foreign born and another 40 percent had at least one parent who was foreign born. By 1912 Cleveland included large Czech, German, Irish, Italian, Polish, Russian, and Slovak communities, and the Great Migration of African Americans from the Old Confederacy had begun to make its mark. Between 1900 and 1920 the city's black population grew from 6,000 to 34,000; 9 out of every 10 black inhabitants lived in the inner east side of the city, penned in by de facto segregation, low rents, and poor housing. Cleveland was also an unhealthy place: typhoid fever caused by poor sanitation, especially in immigrant and black neighborhoods, killed two thousand Clevelanders a year.[1]

In 1910 Cleveland was one of the engine rooms of American industrial growth, positioned on the southern shore of Lake Erie with easy access to eastern markets, Appalachian coal, Great Lakes shipping, and the industrial powerhouses of Detroit and Chicago to the west and New York to the east. The Westinghouse Corporation and the Brush Electrical Company were born in Cleveland and still maintained large plants there. About half of the city's workforce was employed in manufacturing jobs concentrated in its five key industries: steelmaking and foundries, metal working, industrial and commercial machinery, electrical goods, and automobile components. Propelled by its industrial strength, and bolstered by its status as the largest city between Chicago and New York, Cleveland had a strong financial and legal community, an active Chamber of Commerce, and busy rail-road connections to Detroit, Chicago, Pittsburgh, Boston, and New York. In 1912 it was in its glory days, still two generations removed from its later sobriquet as the "mistake on the lake" and the epicenter of the rust belt that blighted the industrial Midwest at the end of the twentieth century.[2]

Between 1825 and 1930 Cleveland developed in four phases of municipal government. At first it was run by a Merchant Regime, dominated by the business organizations created by its founders. After 1878, in response to pressures generated by industrialization, immigration, and rapid growth, a Populist Regime ran the city until the end of the nineteenth century. Its failure to deliver services to Cleveland's industrial workforce led to its replacement by Tom Johnson and the Corporate Regime. City governments led by Johnson, Baehr, and Baker proved better able to deliver services to Clevelanders than their predecessors, but they largely ignored the demands of the automobile age and the need to attract new industries. After 1920 a new Realty Regime, staffed by businessmen and affiliated with the city's main industrial concerns, emphasized road building and infrastructure projects until its demise in the Great Depression.[3]

Baker's five terms as city solicitor and two as mayor between 1902 and 1916 placed him at the heart of the Corporate Regime. Although he was proud to be known as Johnson's protégé, Baker brought more than emulation to his mayoralty. He was more pragmatic than his mentor; his commitment to municipal ownership of utilities sprang from his concern about high prices and poor service rather than from adherence to Henry George's theories. As Johnson had portrayed himself as the scourge of "the interests," Baker was content to be known as the "three cent mayor," providing 3 cent streetcar fares, electricity, municipal dances, fish, and ice cream. In so doing he pushed the idea of municipal ownership much further than Johnson had dared and without his predecessor's inflamed rhetoric. Baker advocated "civitism," his own term that emphasized quality of life issues and Clevelanders' emotional attachment to their cultural environment. His style was also more inclusive than Johnson's. He was careful to work with business groups rather than against them, and he remained a member of the Chamber of Commerce until the beginning of 1914, when he resigned after it opposed him over a municipal finance bill. Even then he retained his stock in the Chamber and promised to reapply for membership upon the expiration of his term as mayor.[4]

Baker's conciliatory approach was gradual and incomplete; his municipal ownership policies often set him against Cleveland's business sector, and he remained closer to the city's intellectual and professional groups than to its entrepreneurial and corporate interests. Business groups never accepted municipal ownership, but they appreciated Baker's less confrontational style as a welcome break from the bitter controversies of the Johnson years.[5]

Baker's blunting of Johnson's sharp edges marked him as a new type of Democratic leader. Governor Judson Harmon in Ohio, Mayor John Purroy Mitchel in New York City, and Governor Woodrow Wilson in New Jersey, all elected between 1909 and 1913, promised to work with reformers, political organizations, and business groups to achieve reform. "The temper of the Democratic Party in 1910," the Cleveland *Plain Dealer* noted, "is not radical. It is sanely progressive." Baker was an example of this new Democrat who "has . . . broken away from the wild-eyed radicalism and the desire for complete upsetting and unsettling." Like Harmon, Mitchel, and Wilson, Baker worked to integrate expertise in social reform and administration—in Baker's case from Cleveland's Western Reserve University, private charities, and professional groups—with the Democratic organization to conduct city government and defuse tensions that had long plagued relations between these groups.[6]

The office to which Baker was elected in 1911 was busy and varied. At the beginning of 1914, after a reorganization of the city's government, he described his duties as a combination of the formal and the informal. As mayor, he appointed the heads of the six administrative departments of Service, Safety, Welfare, Law, Finance, and Utilities. He was also the chief executive of Cleveland, responsible for seeing that the laws of the United States, the laws of the state of Ohio, and the ordinances of the Cleveland Municipal Council were enforced. Alongside these formal duties Cleveland's mayor was the spokesman for the city and "to some extent at least a leader of public opinion in the community": "He is called upon to visit the sick, bury the dead, marry the living, welcome visiting delegations of all sorts, participate in benevolent, philanthropic, social, and political activities, and, by speeches on every conceivable subject, to encourage right thinking, right living, and higher ideals."[7]

And then there was the drudgery. Patronage was the lifeblood of politics in the first half of the twentieth century, and Cleveland was no exception. When Baker became mayor his first task was to fill the large number of jobs within his gift. Acting on recommendations from party leaders, and responding to hundreds of letters seeking employment, he devoted his first months in office to selecting heads of his executive departments, accepting resignations from Baehr's appointees, renewing those he wanted to continue, and filling hundreds of positions left vacant. The range of these positions was bewildering, from skilled and well-paid jobs such as engineering draftsman in the Parks Department paying $1,200 per year to meter readers in the Water Department, clerks in the Street Repair Department, paving foremen, and rodmen in the Engineering Department. At least five hundred jobs had to be filled, and Baker had to sign each letter of appointment. Although he believed deeply in the party system, he became a fervent proponent of civil service reform and its replacement of the spoils system by merit-based appointments. He had more important duties to perform than hiring and firing hundreds of municipal workers simply because he and the Democrats were now in charge.[8]

Baker's time as mayor saw significant additions to Cleveland's infrastructure as it struggled to accommodate rapidly growing population. The streetcar system received more cars and new lines; a new City Hall was constructed, a Union Station erected, and lakefront docks built. Baker hired more officers for the Police and Fire Departments and installed a new water main in the downtown district. A new tuberculosis sanitarium, an expanded insane asylum, and an enlarged workhouse for prisoners and the indigent updated Cleveland's ability to care for its sick, criminals, and poor. The city also began to replace its sewage system, which discharged raw effluent into Lake Erie, with one that sent it inland to the Cuyahoga valley, continued road paving programs, and instituted biweekly garbage collection from all its homes.[9]

This record of achievement was impressive, and comparable to any two terms of Johnson's more storied administration. In 1993 a survey of American mayors ranked Baker, who served only two terms, eighteenth out of all American mayors who had held office between 1820 and 1990. Tom Johnson, who served four terms, ranked second. Baker's political and personal style allowed him to justify new measures in less threatening language than Johnson had used, and he exuded a combination of intellect and warmth that many Clevelanders found attractive. His record was not perfect; his anti-vice campaign proved embarrassing when the chief of police was found in a compromising position, improvement of the sewage system proceeded too slowly, and his preference for bond issues over taxation to fund improvements left the city with debts that consumed a third of its revenues by 1915.[10]

Baker sought re-election as mayor in November 1913. By then Cleveland had a new charter and a nonpartisan preferential electoral system. This seems to have depressed Baker's vote below his 1911 majority of 18,000. With Baker's name stripped of party identification, many immigrant voters found it difficult to find him on the ballot. Although he beat his opponent Harry L. Davis by more than five thousand votes on first preferences, Baker was forced to count second-preference votes to get a majority of votes. His final majority in 1913 was 3,258, made up by large numbers of normally Republican voters who helped to offset defections from Baker's old immigrant base. "Am perfectly delighted with your reelection," McAdoo cabled from Washington. "It is a great triumph deservedly won."[11]

Baker's first major policy task was to win municipal home rule. Under the 1902 Ohio Municipal Code all cities—large and small, industrial and rural—were organized on a single template with elected office holders, municipal councils, and tight control by the state over city police powers, bond issues, and taxation. By the end of the decade many of Ohio's cities found this regime too restrictive. Small cities found the structure of elected councils, mayors, and other officers too cumbersome; larger cities such as Cleveland and Toledo chafed under state control over their bond issues and police regulations. Baker felt these constraints keenly; a "bush-beating expedition into the remote regions of southern Ohio" in 1914 showed him that "nobody who has ever seen Cleveland would believe that in the same state there could be so widely different and so completely rural a civilization."[12]

Tom Johnson and Newton Baker led the demand for an amendment to the state constitution to allow cities to opt out of the Code and formulate their own charters. Baker worked closely with his fellow mayor Brand Whitlock of Toledo to push home rule, under which the state retained its general policing and taxation powers but cities were freer to devise ordinances suited to their own conditions without fear of veto from Columbus. Baker was president of the Ohio Municipal League and then chairman of the Ohio conference of cities in 1912 that agreed on a constitutional amendment to be put to the people.[13]

Home rule was controversial. State legislators from rural areas hesitated to cede more power to cities, utilities opposed it as a license for municipal ownership, and prohibitionists worried that Cincinnati and Cleveland might undermine Ohio's dry laws. Led by Baker and Whitlock, however, home rule passed by more than 80,000 votes. Baker then created a Charter Commission to frame Cleveland's new government. The commission chose a mayor-council structure that placed executive functions under the mayor and legislative powers under the council. Other elected offices, such as city solicitor, were abolished, and municipal boards of health and public safety were replaced by departments under the mayor's control. The charter passed easily in a citywide vote in 1913.[14]

As he worked to win home rule, Baker made good his promise to build a municipally owned electric power plant. In this he both echoed and modified Johnson's legacy. Johnson had long told Clevelanders that, once the streetcars had been municipalized, electric power generation would be next. Baker endorsed this goal but was careful to modify its rationale. Whereas Johnson had argued for municipal power generation from the principle that private utility monopolies corrupted good government, Baker argued from a more pragmatic premise. The Cleveland Electric Illuminating Company (CEIC), he told Clevelanders, abused its monopoly by charging them up to 10 cents per kilowatt hour (kWh), but only 0.74 cent to large commercial customers. Because the CEIC refused to reduce prices to domestic consumers, Baker argued that a municipally owned plant, selling power at 3 cents per kWh, would reduce their electricity prices.[15]

Baker emphasized the pragmatic nature of his municipal power plans. His crusade was for cheaper electricity, not to abolish private ownership of utilities. "I believe that a private company engaged in the public service should be protected in its real investment and permitted to make a fair return thereon," he declared during the mayoral campaign of 1911. Much later, in a statement to the Republican leader Henry Stimson, Baker restated the limits of his enthusiasm for public ownership of utilities. Wherever a service was economically and fairly provided by private enterprise, municipalization was "either unnecessary or premature." Municipalities should act only when private utilities abused their market power or performed inadequately. That judgment should be left to each city rather than to state authorities; public ownership was a powerful weapon that should only be deployed at a local level to remedy bad behavior by private operators.[16]

In keeping with these ideas Baker's first move to municipal power generation was to offer to buy the CEIC's properties for their market value. Although voters had approved a bond issue to build their own municipal power station, he told the CEIC in January 1912, they wanted to avoid the acrimony, wasteful competition, and litigation that had marked the streetcar battles of 1902–1909. The CEIC declined his offer, leaving Baker with his original plan to create a separate municipal electric power plant to break the CEIC's monopoly.[17]

Cleveland had already acquired municipal power stations through its annexation of the townships of Collinwood and South Brooklyn. Both townships had operated small power plants, but their size and location made them unsuitable for generating Cleveland's power. Baker planned to use the $2 million bond issue authorized in 1911 to build a large power plant in downtown Cleveland, where it would be close to fresh water and rail lines. The Collinwood and South Brooklyn plants would act as substations, and together the three plants could generate large amounts of power. The new municipal plant, with a capacity of 20,000 kW, opened in 1914 and sold power at 3 cents per kWh.[18]

The new plant was an immediate success, covering its costs and forcing the CEIC to drop its rates. Baker claimed a triple benefit: the city saved money by powering its streetlights and streetcars from the cheaper municipal plant, consumers saved money, and the CEIC's customers benefited from the decline in its charges. Baker calculated in 1915 that the CEIC's customers had saved $800,000 since the municipal plant had opened in 1914, and in 1925 he estimated that all Cleveland consumers had saved almost $14 million over the previous eleven years. The municipal yardstick had worked exactly as he had hoped.[19]

Baker claimed other benefits from the municipal electricity plant. Under pressure from the city plant's 3 cent rate, the CEIC voluntarily submitted to price regulation by the Ohio Public Service Commission (OPSC). This was to circumvent a Cleveland ordinance limiting private utilities to a maximum price of 3 cents per kWh. Although the OPSC held that the CEIC could charge a maximum of 5 cents per kWh, Baker still claimed victory. Given that the CEIC had originally claimed to be in possession of a perpetual grant to sell electric power and that it was not subject to any regulatory authority at all, Baker argued that municipal power had not only lowered rates but also forced a powerful corporation to subject itself to regulation. Competition had transformed the CEIC into a model corporate citizen; in 1925 Baker described it as "one of the best managed public utilities with which I have any acquaintance."[20]

Cleveland's "three cent mayor" built on these initiatives to experiment with municipal intervention in other aspects of the city's life. In 1913 he announced that Cleveland would build a "model suburb" on one hundred acres of land. The suburb would have ample space for playgrounds and its five hundred houses would each be set on blocks big enough for front and back gardens. Workers from the nearby American Steel and Wire Company plant would be offered houses at rents from $4 to $12 dollars a month, and they would run the suburb through a residents' corporation. Baker hailed this project, which was inspired by Letchworth Garden City in England and Hellerau in Germany, as a way to improve Cleveland's housing stock and generate profits for other city projects. Land developers were less pleased and managed to scuttle the project. "If a municipality is to take away legitimate profit from real estate dealers," the secretary of the Cleveland Real Estate Board wondered, "what private business is there which is to be safe from ruinous municipal competition?"[21]

When Baker did extend municipal ownership and operation, it was on a smaller scale. In the summer of 1912 the price of fish caught from Lake Erie rose to exorbitant levels. The city created a Municipal Fish Company to catch and sell fish at 3 cents per pound to compete with the private market's average of 12 cents. Prices soon fell to around 3 cents, but Baker declined to continue his experiment. "The matter was done really by private enterprise rather than by the City," he wrote disingenuously at the end of 1912, "and the whole experiment was too tentative to be the basis of any philosophy on the subject." He did undertake a similar scheme in city parks, where private concession stands sold ice cream at high prices. The city set up its own stands that made profits of more than $20,000 in 1914.[22]

Attempts to improve Cleveland's dance halls combined Baker's desire to provide cheaper and better services with his goal to improve the city's moral environment. The halls, magnets for young men and women, were largely unsupervised and poorly lit. They opened early, closed late, and were, Baker thought, hotbeds of vice. They charged 5 cents for a three-minute dance, which to him seemed extortionate. At first he tried regulation, stationing a police officer in each hall to ensure that the dancers did not dance too closely or fall into the arms of pimps and other criminals.[23]

The private dance halls did improve, but they were still expensive. Baker then moved, as he had done with electricity, fish sales, and park refreshments, to provide wholesome competition through municipalization. The city erected two large pavilions in its lakeside parks and operated halls that charged 3 cents for a five-minute dance. The pavilions were well lit and supervised by city employees on the lookout for untoward behavior. That behavior included particular styles of dance (Baker objected to the tango, for example, which brought partners too close together). Girls younger than 18, unless they were accompanied by an older male relative, were forbidden entry after 9:00 p.m. The municipal dance halls were a great success; in 1914 they earned revenues of $19,000 and a profit of $5,000.[24]

Baker's dance hall reforms aimed to improve recreation for Cleveland's working class, and in 1913 he created more entertainment for it by establishing the Cleveland Municipal Orchestra (CMO) to provide "wholesome and elevating entertainment" on winter Sunday afternoons. For a modest admission fee the CMO played to audiences of two thousand "principally young men and young women engaged in industrial commerce, living in down town boarding houses." Saloons were closed on Sundays, and the dance halls were snowed in, so the CMO filled the void and tried to elevate the cultural interests of Cleveland's young people. Financial stringencies in 1915 forced the city to discontinue its subsidies to the CMO, but it was kept alive by private philanthropy.[25]

Baker's excursions into municipal ownership were eye-catching but cautious. Municipal streetcars were an inheritance from Johnson, and the power plant was justified in economic rather than ideological terms. The model suburb was cloaked in the language of sensible use of surplus public land and not in the rhetoric of socialized housing. Municipal ice cream, dance halls, and fish sales focused on the need to provide monopolies with price and service competition, and their lifespan was determined more by their success in solving these problems than by the depth of Baker's commitment to them. He defended all these initiatives but was reluctant to extend them without good cause. When a constituent suggested that the city develop its ice plant into a full-scale retail operation, Baker refused. He was not convinced that the firm that supplied ice had abused its market power, and thought it wiser to wait to see how well municipal operation of other concerns worked.[26]

Baker's reluctance to extend municipal power became most obvious during the economic slump that struck in 1914. European markets and financial networks were disrupted by the outbreak of war in August 1914, leading to unemployment and a credit squeeze in the United States. As the home of hundreds of thousands of industrial workers, Cleveland was hit hard, and by November 1914 more than

60,000 of its workers had been laid off. This raised the issue of the city government's responsibility for alleviating the economic distress of its citizens. Municipal revenues were also crimped by the slump, and Baker cut expenditures—
including funding for the CMO—wherever possible. Cleveland already maintained
a welfare system in the form of a workhouse and infirmary, but Baker resisted calls
to expand its scope to cope with the recession. He did bring forward an excavation
project budgeted for 1915 but refused to establish a municipal public works program. He chose instead to rely on a Citizens' Relief Commission that was funded
by wealthy Clevelanders. The commission raised nearly $90,000 and offered some
of the unemployed work for 25 hours a week at 17 cents an hour. This was a start,
but it was inadequate in the face of the destitution that stalked Cleveland's industrial neighborhoods.[27]

In an exchange with the chairman of the Citizens' Relief Commission Baker
accepted the proposition that destitution created "a community and social obligation" to help, but denied that it created a government obligation to do so. The
charter created municipal government for "quite definitely stated objects," including public security, sanitation, amenities, and health, "within the limits of taxation." Public works to offset unemployment might one day be seen as a proper object of city government, but they drained precious revenue from the city's coffers. "I
cannot persuade myself that with the city running far behind in its ordinary operating expenses, economizing at every point, and likely to end the year even more
deeply in debt . . . the Mayor and the Council have any right to borrow in antici-
pation of next year's revenues for the assumption of this community burden not
contemplated by law."[28]

Baker adopted similar reasoning during the much greater economic depression
twenty years later. His conflation of fiscal rectitude and strict construction of the
city charter to deny public relief for the unemployed suggested that his belief in
municipal activism depended more on its prospects of reducing prices and improving services than a commitment to relieve the economic suffering of citizens. Clevelanders found that their government could sell them electricity and ice cream, and
run their dance halls, because those activities did not drain municipal finances.
They could not, however, expect relief during a depression because that was a drain
on the city treasury. Baker's nickname as Cleveland's "three cent mayor" thus assumed a sharper edge during the slump of 1914–1915.

Baker's innovations in city amenities did not extend to less respectable recreations. Although he was no prohibitionist, he enforced closure of saloons on Sundays and banned alcohol from municipal dance halls. He was also careful to avoid
identification with saloonkeepers by emphasizing the need for saloons to operate
legally and responsibly within city and state liquor laws. It was vital for the "better

men in that business to raise the standard of the traffic and to eradicate the evils which result from the bad type of saloon, rather than by a wholesale crusade upon the entire business." Cleveland's 1,400 saloons contributed $1 million a year in city taxes. City ordinances and state laws regulating them must be observed, Baker declared, and they would be enforced. Yet their object would be to mitigate drunkenness without trying to abolish it.[29]

Brothels received harsher treatment. Johnson had tolerated Cleveland's red light district during his years as mayor; as long as prostitutes did not solicit in the streets, and brothels did not sell or provide alcohol, they and their clients were left alone. In 1912 there were perhaps three hundred "disorderly houses" in Cleveland, and Baker was determined to take a harder line. In 1914 he told police to close all the brothels they could find in the "segregated district," and afterward claimed that only thirty brothels and three hundred prostitutes remained. Baker recognized that this forced prostitution underground, but maintained that this was the lesser of two evils. Brothels were magnets for criminals, while "the clandestine prostitute is ordinarily a far more cleanly [sic] and respectable victim." All that could be done was to eliminate "prostitution in its most brutal form"—on the streets and in brothels—and wait for growing enlightenment on the dangers of syphilis and the degrading effects of commercialized sex to suppress its market. Beyond that Baker would not go; he particularly objected to "any policy of enforcement which looks to the arresting of women and the excusing of men."[30]

Baker's anti-vice campaign was controversial. His decision to close the red light district was opposed by saloonkeepers and others who feared that prostitution would diffuse through the city once it was expelled from its traditional home. Cleaning up Cleveland even cost the chief of police, Frederick Kohler, his job. Kohler had run the campaign against prostitution during the first year of Baker's mayoralty, but at the beginning of 1913 he was named as a third party in a divorce action through his adulterous affair with the wife of a Cleveland businessman. In dismissing him from office, Baker charged Kohler with "conduct unbecoming an officer and a gentleman" and "gross immorality."[31]

As the mayor of one of the largest cities in the nation and successor to the celebrated Tom Johnson, Baker enjoyed a growing reputation as a progressive Democrat after 1912. He was a strong supporter of female suffrage and direct election of US senators to bring the national government closer to the popular will and farther from "the economic inequalities of law-made favoritism." Baker was also a keen supporter of initiative and referendum, two other darlings of progressive reform. Initiative, through which the state legislature could be forced to consider measures upon petition by 10 percent of voters, and referendum—allowing voters to pass judgment on bills passed by the state legislature upon petition from 6 percent of the electorate—had been endorsed by the Ohio Democratic platforms of 1909 and 1911. Baker recognized that these measures were "merely pieces of political machinery," but believed that "a man's attitude to [them] is about the best index to his general attitude on Democratic questions that is afforded by any issue now before the people." Ohio Governor Judson Harmon, who had twice been elected on platforms promising initiative and referendum but now opposed their enactment, failed this test. Harmon was "honest, firm, but politically unintelligent . . . I should not look forward to his election as President as at all a sign of promise or progress."[32]

Baker's estimation of Harmon's presidential timber in February 1912 was indicative of his growing interest in national politics. Although he took time to choose between the contenders for the Democratic nomination, he was clear on one point: the prospect of Theodore Roosevelt running again was extremely worrying. As TR became politically active at the beginning of 1912, Baker grew more agitated. Roosevelt's support of judicial recall—which allowed state legislatures to reverse court decisions that legislation was unconstitutional—seemed to Baker grossly irresponsible. Ever the lawyer, he could not conceive of untrained voters being let loose on legal precedent and reasoning. "My opinion of Roosevelt," he wrote to his brother Frank at the beginning of March 1912, "grows gradually worse. I had not thought that possible." He also objected to TR's "utter lack of truthfulness . . . his behavior in the Panama business shows a reckless immorality . . . that makes him untrustworthy, if not dangerous." By the middle of 1912 Baker's views had hardened still more: "I think he is manifestly insane and will undoubtedly die in restraint, if not in a straight-jacket."[33]

Baker was more circumspect about other Democratic candidates. He rejected Champ Clark, Speaker of the House of Representatives and front runner for the nomination, because he drank too much and spoke too indiscreetly. William Jennings Bryan could offer the party only a repeat of his defeats in 1896, 1900, and 1908. Harmon's hopes presented more complicated issues. Baker had already dismissed Harmon as too conservative, but as governor he would probably control the Ohio delegation to the convention.[34]

Baker was initially cool to Woodrow Wilson, who had emerged as another candidate for the nomination. Baker remembered Wilson from his days at Johns Hopkins, but he was cautious about his ability to win the nomination. Although Baker declared in September 1911 that Wilson possessed the ideas and conviction that Harmon lacked, he worried about the depth of Wilson's commitment to reform. The governor of New Jersey was "a pretty recent radical," and his academic work revealed a "conservative stiffness" that marked him as more conservative than his more recent utterances suggested.[35]

Baker's doubts about Wilson persisted through the early months of 1912. He had heard Wilson criticize progressive reforms in terms that "I don't like now and didn't like then," and his writings showed signs of anti-Catholicism and a "somewhat hasty generalization about the desirability of immigrants from South European countries." If those views became widely known, they would alienate two large Democratic constituencies. Wilson's later utterances, however, and his record as governor of New Jersey, showed that he could rise above his prejudices and conservatism, and he remained the most impressive Democratic contender for the nomination. "I suppose the fact is that pretty nearly every man who is of age, has made a fool of himself a few times in his life anyhow, and if that is to be a disqualification for holding high public office we had probably better nominate the Mummy of Rameses." Now convinced that Wilson's conversion to progressivism was genuine, Baker announced his support for him in March 1912, joined him on a speaking tour in Massachusetts in April, and led the pro-Wilson and anti-Harmon movement in Ohio.[36]

In the Ohio Primary Harmon won 52 percent of the vote to Wilson's 46 percent. His supporters then tried to impose the unit rule to force all Ohio's delegates to vote for him. This affected Baker personally, for he had won election as a Wilson delegate and had no intention of voting for Harmon. He lost that fight at the state convention, but fought it again at the national convention in Baltimore. In this he sought to overturn sixty years of party practice, which had always respected decisions by state conventions on the unit rule. The Committee on Rules at Baltimore followed tradition, so Baker and his allies argued their case on the convention floor. He told the delegates that to be forced to vote for Harmon would be a betrayal of his voters. A majority of delegates agreed, the committee's decision was overturned, and Wilson counted nineteen more delegates toward his cause. Baker's success won Wilson a crucial battle and gained the Clevelander national attention.[37]

After Wilson's nomination Baker made speaking tours in Iowa and Wisconsin, raised funds, and organized Wilson's visit to Cleveland in October. He also sent information and advice to the Democratic National Committee (DNC) in Washington. William McAdoo, whom Baker had met for the first time at Baltimore, swapped suggestions over campaign appointments and worked with him to organize Wilson's visit to Cleveland.[38]

With the Republican vote split between William Howard Taft and Theodore Roosevelt's Progressive Party, Wilson enjoyed an easy victory on November 5, 1912. He won 435 electoral votes with 42 percent of the national vote, while Roosevelt and Taft won nearly 51 percent of the vote but only 96 electoral votes between them. Wilson won Ohio, and in Cleveland won 42 percent of the vote to Roosevelt's 33 percent and Taft's 14 percent. "The victory is largely an expression of confidence in you personally," Baker cabled the next day. "Surely my own satisfaction is unbounded, as I know how well justified the public confidence is." Keen to have Baker in his administration, Wilson sounded him out about a job in the cabinet. Only a year into his first term as mayor of Cleveland, Baker declined. "My place in your army is out here where I can interpret you to the virile but somewhat impatient people who are making a wonderful city of Cleveland." Three months later Wilson offered Baker the secretaryship of the Interior. Baker again declined, leaving Wilson's advisor Colonel House horrified at Baker's provincialism and his refusal "to take a broader view of the situation and do the bigger work."[39]

Although he remained in Cleveland, Baker worked with Senator Atlee Pomerone, Wilson's secretary Joe Tumulty, and William McAdoo to reward Wilson's friends and punish his enemies in Ohio. He made several trips to Washington to confer with Wilson and McAdoo on patronage matters between the election and the inauguration, and by the middle of March described McAdoo as his closest contact in Washington. "I trust you are not finding some of the burdens of public office quite so oppressive as you feared you might," he wrote in May 1913. "I know . . . how much you would prefer to be back in the Terminal Building . . . but those of us who are out on the frontier . . . realize that you are helping to do the aggregate of fine things which have already made the administration a source of joy and happiness to us all."[40]

Baker continued to advise the administration on matters of interest to Cleveland. Early in 1914 he lobbied McAdoo over the location of the Federal Reserve City in the Fourth District, which took in Ohio, eastern Kentucky, and western Pennsylvania. He traveled to Washington to put Cleveland's case directly to McAdoo, and was delighted when his city was chosen over Cincinnati. Later that year Baker was so concerned by rumors that Cleveland's Bank would be relocated to Pittsburgh that he sought reassurance from McAdoo that his city was safe. McAdoo obliged and confirmed Baker's judgment that his relations with McAdoo were "closer and more personal" than with any other member of Wilson's cabinet.[41]

Events in Europe soon put these matters into perspective. Baker was saddened but not surprised when war broke out in August 1914. All the major powers knew that war was coming, and all were party to its preparation. Although he condemned Germany for its violation of Belgian sovereignty, Baker agreed with Wilson's declaration of neutrality on August 19, 1914. He admired German culture deeply, had used German examples for his model suburb in Cleveland, and recognized "the splendid efficiency . . . with which the Germans have worked out their social and municipal relations." His dislike of militarism, he told the Austro-Hungarian consul in Cleveland in March 1915, extended equally to Germany's army and Britain's navy.[42]

Baker had other reasons to resile from the war. He had been a fervent supporter, and was later a member, of the Permanent Court of Arbitration created by the Hague Conference of 1899, was a leader of the Ohio branch of the World Peace Foundation, and had been elected vice president of the Cleveland Peace Society only a month before Europe went to war. Baker's pacifism was later much discussed and exaggerated. He was never opposed to all wars on principle, but was instead an antimilitarist who objected to wars fought without sustained attempts at diplomatic resolution. As the European war dragged on, Baker refused to join other peace organizations. By then he had decided that "the administration in Washington ought to have the united support of thoughtful people in the country and that our strength ought not to be divided up into a number of societies with special points of view." [43]

Conditions closer to home also kept Baker neutral. As mayor of Cleveland he presided over a polyglot population including 80,000 Germans and many Russians, Irish, and Britons. After hearing that war had broken out, Baker summoned his chief of police to warn him that "we are likely to have the war in miniature in our streets." The chief was less alarmed, correctly predicting that arrests stemming from christenings would outnumber those arising from ethnic conflict. At the end of 1915 Baker admitted that his fears had been unfounded and declared that he now had complete faith in the patriotism of America's foreign-born citizens in general and its Germans in particular. It was propaganda from Europe, and not tensions at home, that threatened peace on the streets of Cleveland. [44]

Baker followed Wilson's lead as the war drew closer. He praised the president's response to the sinking of the *Lusitania*, which cost 128 American lives in May 1915, because "America's policy can be made one of focusing the disapproval of the neutral world upon [Germany's] course rather than a voluntary recourse to arms by the United States." He told another correspondent that "sometimes it is necessary to tie up a bad dog and not merely frown at him, so that I am for [Wilson's] conclusion whatever it is." Soon after the *Lusitania* crisis Wilson announced a policy of "preparedness" to build up the military resources of the United States. This placed Baker, who much preferred the "high plane of idealism" than the prospect of a heavily armed America, in a quandary. He supported preparedness loyally, but with more resignation than enthusiasm. America needed arms in a world at war, he conceded, but soon humanity would return to its senses and forswear the militarism that had brought about war and that threatened to drag the United States into its vortex. [45]

By the beginning of 1916 Baker had moved significantly from his earlier view that "I am the most neutral person I know." As he had once found equal fault on both sides, he now emphasized German brutality and disregard for international law over the infractions of the British and argued that "Germany intended this war, prepared for it and began it." By its actions in Belgium and through its U-Boats on the high seas Germany had become an outlaw nation that posed a mortal threat to international decency and order. Baker was not yet ready to advocate US intervention in the war, but by January 1916—two months before he became secretary of war—he had decided the merits of the Allies' and the Central Powers' causes.[46]

In an attempt to rekindle idealism amid the orgy of profit that neutrality brought to the United States, Baker suggested a salve for the nation's conscience. Public opinion was changing, he told Wilson in the middle of December 1915, toward those who believed that America should "insist vigorously upon the maintenance of neutral rights, backing up our insistence with force, if necessary." The nation now suffered from "the moral strain of getting rich at the expense of the rest of the world," and this threatened a "depression of our national conscience" and "an enfeebling materialism." It was vital that the world should see the United States as more than a carrion bird growing fat on war profits:

> In other words America must, at the conclusion of the war, give until it hurts. Our giving ought to be directed to sustaining . . . belligerent countries until they can plant and gather their first crops and get their industries organized to the point of production and return. Much of this giving undoubtedly ought to be from those individuals who have most profited by the situation, but a great national gift distributed through some internationally recognized agency . . . would preach the sermon to our own people more impressively and also put us in a better light to the European peoples whose cooperation . . . we must win to the ideal of future peace.[47]

By this time Baker had decided not to seek a third term as mayor and to return to his legal career. Although disappointed that his political heir Peter Witt did not win the mayoralty in November 1915, Baker handed the office over to Harry Davis on January 1, 1916, with little regret and immediately formed a law firm with Joseph Hostetler and Thomas Sidlo, two former members of the Cleveland Law Department. "Personally, I am very sorry to see you retiring from public life," Wilson wrote from Washington. "I think the whole country has learned to trust you. No doubt your instinct about getting an outside view again is a correct one, but I hope that after you have got it you will come into the ranks again."[48]

The call came much sooner than even Wilson had imagined. In Washington the secretary of war, Lindley Garrison, was in deep political trouble early in 1916. Appointed in 1913, Garrison had been an outspoken secretary of war: he opposed

Philippine independence, advocated invasion of Mexico, and urged war against Germany after the sinking of the *Lusitania*. He was an earnest supporter of preparedness and believed strongly in Universal Military Training (UMT) to build up the US Army. A lawyer, but a much more conservative one than Baker, Garrison had no military experience and followed advice from the army without question. What he lacked in military knowledge he made up for in assertiveness; Garrison was imperious in his treatment of Congress, its House Military Affairs Committee, and its powerful chairman James Hay, and was argumentative in the cabinet. His nickname there, according to McAdoo, was "Secretary Garrulous." Uncompromising in his support of UMT, Garrison felt betrayed when Wilson disavowed it to placate anti-preparedness Democrats led by William Jennings Bryan. He resigned on February 10, 1916, to public congressional delight and private presidential relief.[49]

The press reported that Secretary of Interior Franklin Lane or Secretary of Agriculture David Houston would replace Garrison, and that Baker would replace whoever moved. Major General George Goethals, then governor of the Panama Canal Zone, was also mentioned as a possible replacement. This seemed plausible; with the nation perched on the edge of world war and with preparedness underway, a military man seemed necessary to oversee the army. Baker, on the other hand, was unqualified for that task; he was widely known as a pacifist and in 1914 had professed "utter non-comprehension of military matters." Yet he had other, more powerful claims to office. Wilson resisted the idea of having a soldier in the cabinet and wanted to avoid a reshuffle of Lane's or Houston's portfolio. He had already offered Baker a cabinet post—Interior, in 1913—and thought highly of the mayor from Cleveland who had fought so valiantly for him in 1912. After discussions with House and McAdoo, he decided on Baker and asked McAdoo to make the call to Cleveland.[50]

News of Baker's appointment elicited reactions ranging from measured praise to outright disdain. *The New York Times* reminded its readers that he was not the first secretary of war to be appointed without knowledge of military affairs, but elsewhere in its columns ran stories about Baker's pacifism and his recent conversion to preparedness. "Can we expect energetic action and sustained interest in this most vital problem now before the American people," asked the secretary of the National Security League, "from a person of such a decidedly pacifist tendency?" In Britain George Riddell, owner of *The News of the World*, dismissed Baker as a "nice, trim little man of the YMCA type," and in Washington Major General Leonard Wood found the thought of a pacifist leading the army during a world war "too grotesque." Wood's troubles with Baker were just beginning, and Baker was soon to test his belief that "the problems of democracy have to be worked out in experiment stations rather than by universal applications, so that I regard Cleveland and Ohio as a more hopeful place to do things than in any national station whatsoever."[51]

❖

William McAdoo's transition from president of H&M to secretary of the treasury was faster and even more unexpected than Baker's journey from Cleveland to Washington. McAdoo came to Wilson's cabinet from a very different direction, entering political life only during Wilson's campaign for the 1912 Democratic nomination and accepting appointment as secretary of the treasury upon Wilson's inauguration. His shift from business to politics, and from New York to Washington, took barely a year.

Naturally sociable and now in the public eye, Mac was led by his ambitions farther and farther from home after 1910. He was a convivial dinner companion, danced well, and liked driving cars. Automobiles were expensive playthings in the first decade of the twentieth century, but Mac was drawn to their speed and the freedom they provided from the pressures of work and home. In 1911 he owned three cars—a 1906 Mercedes, an Alco, and a Stearns—and retained a chauffeur. He also liked to drive himself, but not always to good effect. His papers are littered with letters to insurance companies explaining a succession of accidents for which he blamed everyone and everything except himself.[52]

On May 18, 1911, McAdoo's love of cars and socializing combined to injure him severely and nearly enmesh him in scandal. In 1910 he became a director of the Tuberculosis Preventorium for Children in Lakewood, New Jersey. The Preventorium had an impressive list of New Yorkers on its board, including the heiress Florence Jaffray Harriman. Harriman and Mac drove together in May 1911 to a board meeting in Lakewood, with Mac at the wheel. On the way home, near Freehold, New Jersey, their car ran off the road and rolled over. McAdoo claimed that roadwork, which left the road muddy and corrugated, was to blame. He and Harriman were thrown from the car; she was only slightly hurt, but he was thrown twenty feet, landed on his head, and was unconscious for two hours. He suffered three broken ribs, a fractured right arm, and cuts to his scalp that put him in hospital for two weeks, confined him at home for another six, and took his arm years to recover. "I consider myself," he wrote to his brother-in-law, "a lucky devil."[53]

The accident presented McAdoo with more than medical complications. It also threatened scandal, for the newspapers were unlikely to ignore the fact that a prominent New Yorker, who was also a married woman, was in the car. To head off any rumors McAdoo announced that he and Mrs. Harriman were on official business in Lakewood and that her husband J. Borden had approved of their traveling together. Mac was relieved when the press chose not to explore this aspect of the story further, for there was more to it than first appeared. More than convenience had brought Mac and Mrs. Harriman together; by then they were involved in a passionate affair. In 1911 McAdoo was 48, married to an invalid, and fêted in New York society. Florence Harriman was 41 and little constrained by her marriage to "Bordie" Harriman. She lived life to the full; even in 1927, when she was 57, a magazine called her "incorrigibly young."[54]

Although neither McAdoo nor Harriman was free to make their relationship public or permanent, they spent as much time together as they could in 1911 and 1912. In her memoir published in 1923 Harriman made no reference to their affair but described Mac as a man who "knows what he wants, goes straight after it and usually gets it. He has dash and boldness . . . none could say that Mr. McAdoo was just an ordinary man." Sometime in 1911 Mac wrote her from the parlor car of a B&O train:

> I wish you were here as I need you. I'm tired of fighting always alone and I wonder if I am ever to have a companion in <u>arms</u>. I mean this metaphorically and otherwise, especially <u>otherwise</u>—It is tough (isn't it?) when two people could do so much together and get so much out of life together, and can't. However a better day is bound to come some time . . . I send you loads of love.[55]

Harriman and McAdoo never got their "better day." Although Sarah's death in February 1912 freed McAdoo, Harriman's marriage made their relationship fraught with social danger and bereft of a future. Their relationship faded at the end of 1912, although they remained on good terms. Bordie died in October 1914, but by then McAdoo had remarried. Fortunately for his political career and his reputation as a vivacious but loyal husband to his invalid wife, Mac and Florence's affair remained secret.[56]

In 1911 McAdoo was also in the midst of a reorientation of his political loyalties. Although he later maintained that he had been a lifelong Democrat who had deserted the party only once, this was a considerable understatement. He had voted Republican in 1904 because the Democratic presidential nominee, Alton B. Parker, was "a thoroughgoing reactionary," while his Republican opponent Theodore Roosevelt was "a real progressive." But he had also voted for the Gold Democrats against William Jennings Bryan in 1896, and his allegiance to TR was deep in 1904. "I am a Southern Democrat, who was first seduced from his party allegiances by Theodore Roosevelt, the Republican candidate for Governor of the State of New York [in 1898]," McAdoo told TR in 1903. He praised Roosevelt's Panama policy and thought that he would have been justified in "forcibly bringing Panama under our sovereignty." Despite Democratic carping McAdoo felt sure that TR could rely "on the great masses of the people of this country [to] follow you wherever you carry the flag and that they will not be influenced by the over-refined hypercritics who spend their time as common-scolds in a hopeless fight against the resistless progress of manifest destiny."[57]

McAdoo and Roosevelt exchanged friendly letters over the next seven years. During the campaign of 1904 McAdoo wrote that "I am anxious that you should know personally the deep interest I feel in your election," and that "I do not believe that the Democracy should again be entrusted with power until it has . . . committed itself beyond doubt to the maintenance of the gold standard." Bryan had prevented the party from making that commitment in 1904, and he remained a threat to good government and sound currency. Roosevelt, on the other hand, was a man of "undaunted physical and moral courage, of uncompromising honesty, of high ideals and the loftiest conceptions of the duties of his exalted office." After TR's election in 1904 McAdoo hinted that he would accept appointment to the Panama Canal Commission, not only because of his deep interest in the canal's success but also because of "my loyalty to and support of your administration." Roosevelt had already promised the place, but the two men stayed friendly. TR opened the Hudson tunnels in 1908, and even in 1911, as McAdoo joined Woodrow Wilson's Democratic nomination campaign, he sent TR copies of his speeches and lunched with him at Oyster Bay.[58]

McAdoo's return to the Democratic fold was caused by several factors. His admiration for TR was motivated by his belief that the Democratic Party was unelectable so long as it nominated soft money populists like William Jennings Bryan or irredeemable conservatives such as Alton Parker. TR's forceful personality and conviction that the federal government needed to embrace the modern industrial age struck a chord in McAdoo, but when he left the White House in 1909 the chief cause of McAdoo's dalliance with the GOP disappeared.

There were ideological reasons as well. As McAdoo became more interested in politics, he grew convinced that untrammeled corporate power, called at the time the "trust problem," was the key issue of the age. Thus far he was in sympathy with TR, but McAdoo diverged from Roosevelt in his preferred solution. While Roosevelt wanted to regulate trusts instead of breaking them up, McAdoo thought that they should be split into smaller and less dominant entities. In this he parted company with TR's ideas that crystallized into his "New Nationalism" in 1912. Trusts, McAdoo argued in the middle of 1911, were organized to promote the greed of their owners and to crush their competitors. Only "the healthful stimulus of competition" would control them.[59]

As he drew closer to national politics McAdoo's ambition brought him back to the Democrats. As a self-conscious southerner, he had brighter political prospects

within the party that dominated the Old Confederacy. "The South is rapidly regaining the potential influence in the political affairs of the country which she
exercised prior to the Civil War," he told the Southern Commercial Congress in
February 1911, and he was determined to be part of that revival. As a prominent business figure born in the South but successful in New York, McAdoo was well placed
to be part of a new Democratic Party that sought to present a more business-friendly
and cross-sectional appeal to voters. His record as a socially engaged business leader
also made him attractive as a Democrat attuned to progressive reform and ready to
bring his business experience into the political arena. His confidant Byron Newton
said as much at the end of 1909. The new age of progressive politics, Newton told
Mac, "was a game of politics with the politicians left out." Instead, businessmen and
reformers could combine to reform the Democratic Party and provide new leadership to public policy and governance. "The continued glory and welfare of this headstrong country of ours depends upon strong men . . . going into the game."[60]

When McAdoo did enter the game he did so almost accidentally. As president
of the New York Southern Society, he was responsible for finding keynote speakers
for the Society's annual dinners. In February 1910 he asked his old hero Theodore
Roosevelt to speak at the dinner that December. Roosevelt declined and McAdoo
looked farther afield. He settled on Woodrow Wilson, then president of Princeton
University and soon to be the Democratic candidate for governor of New Jersey.
Wilson was a Virginian and marked as a future leader of the party. McAdoo had first
met him in 1909 at Princeton, where his son Huger was a student. By the time that
Wilson rose to speak at the Society's dinner in December 1910, he was governor-
elect of New Jersey and McAdoo introduced him as "a future president of the
United States." This was no empty courtesy; six months later McAdoo announced
his support of Wilson to be the 1912 Democratic presidential nominee.[61]

There is no evidence to suggest that McAdoo chose Wilson with any doctrinaire notions of progressivism in mind. Unlike Baker, he approached politics from
a pragmatic perspective. It was the practice, not the theory, of power and reform
that appealed to him most. As McAdoo had supported Theodore Roosevelt as a
leader who promised conviction and action, so too did he gravitate toward Wilson
as the Democrat best attuned to the necessities of the time. At the beginning of
1910, with TR out of the White House, he concluded that

> The more I reflect on existing conditions and problems, and the more speeches
> I hear of the average politician and alleged statesman, the more I am convinced
> that there are very few . . . who have correctly sensed the deep underlying feel-
> ings and aspirations of the masses of the people. We are working, undoubtedly,
> toward a broader and nobler humanitarianism, and some day a real leader, hav-

ing in his heart that breadth of human sympathy which will make him capable of truly interpreting the tendencies of the day will crystallize them and give struggling humanity a genuine up-lift.[62]

Yet Wilson was no Theodore Roosevelt in his ability to connect to the "deep underlying feelings and aspirations of the masses of the people." Wilson and TR were very different in personality and approach. Roosevelt was warm and charismatic; Wilson was distant from the human imperatives of elective politics and even his friends thought that his aloofness was his greatest electoral liability. Yet McAdoo stressed Wilson's electability as his most important attraction. His descriptions were vague on Wilson's views and focused instead on his "strength" and conviction: "I know him to be not only a great man, but a <u>clean</u> man and a <u>free</u> man, and that, if he is elected, the country will have an absolutely clean, irreproachable and able administration. I believe, furthermore, that he is the only Democrat who can be elected."[63]

McAdoo's emphasis on Wilson's electability grew stronger as it became apparent that the GOP would split in 1912. He saw Wilson as best suited to translating Republican division into Democratic victory because he was "the strongest man" in the Democratic field. Again he did not specify what strengths Wilson brought to the contest, and this suggests that McAdoo saw him more as a means than an end. McAdoo's politics were those of ambition rather than ideology; he sought political influence and office to achieve concrete policy rather than serve a cause. At first TR offered that pathway, but now it was clear to McAdoo that the Democrats promised the surer way forward. Wilson seemed to McAdoo to be the Democrat most likely to win in 1912, and so he hitched his wagon to his star.[64]

McAdoo wasted no time in making his presence felt in Wilson's nomination campaign. He joined a small group of supporters led by William F. McCombs, whom McAdoo had known in the New York Southern Society. McCombs had met Wilson while he was a student at Princeton, and from 1911 had dedicated his efforts, and sacrificed much of his mental wellbeing, to his cause. Using funds from Cleveland Dodge, Walter Hines Page, George Foster Peabody, and Dudley Field Malone, McCombs organized a speaking tour for Wilson through the West and Midwest, including Newton Baker's Cleveland, in April 1911, and in July opened a Woodrow Wilson Bureau of Information in New York City. It was there that Wilson was introduced to Edward M. House, a Texas Democratic Party powerbroker who would exercise great influence during the first six years of Wilson's presidency. McCombs also hired a publicist, Frank Parker Stockbridge, to advertise Wilson's achievements as governor of New Jersey and his program for the presidency. By tapping Princeton alumni, and his New York legal and financial contacts, McCombs raised

$193,000 before the Baltimore convention in June 1912. As McAdoo was soon to discover, however, McCombs was almost impossible to work with. Although superficially genial, he was prone to jealousy and was megalomaniac within the campaign organization.[65]

At first McAdoo assisted McCombs in spreading the Wilson gospel. He focused on the South, using his New York Southern Society mailing list to seek funds and argue that in Wilson the South had a nationally viable candidate who could lead it out of the wilderness. Below the Mason-Dixon Line Wilson's main rival was Congressman Oscar W. Underwood of Alabama. As the House majority leader and chairman of the House Ways and Means Committee, Underwood was the South's most prominent legislator. Ceding Alabama and Mississippi to the Alabamian and counting Virginia for Wilson, McAdoo concentrated on Georgia, Florida, and the Carolinas. Even in the Deep South, he thought, delegates should settle behind Wilson once they had given Underwood their votes in the first couple of ballots at the convention. "I think it is most unfortunate that the South does not unite upon her most brilliant son, Woodrow Wilson, and thus be certain that a Southern man and the ablest man in public life today . . . is made President the next time."[66]

McAdoo worked hard to shore up Wilson's position in the South, but Underwood was a strong opponent. He spent $100,000 in Georgia alone, won primaries there and in Florida, and controlled the Alabama and Mississippi delegations. Although Wilson won Texas and North Carolina, he lost the primary in Maryland, and won less than half of the Virginia delegation and only a quarter of the Tennessee delegates. Wilson had failed to parlay his southern birth and sympathies into convention votes; McAdoo and McCombs were left with only the uncertain comfort that he was likely to be the South's second choice once Underwood had had his day at Baltimore. Clark had won the largest number of delegates, mainly because of his victories in Illinois, Maryland, Massachusetts, Missouri, and California. McAdoo's efforts in the South had produced disappointing results, but Wilson's position, second behind Clark but easily ahead of Harmon and Underwood, was not hopeless.[67]

McAdoo's relationship with Wilson matured quickly. As the hero of the Hudson tunnels, McAdoo had become nationally known, and his ability to raise large sums from Wall Street provided Wilson with a high-profile business convert. McAdoo's presence in the campaign simultaneously signaled that Wilson was "safe" with business and attractive to progressives. This was important to Wilson's pitch to his party and then to the nation; he was at pains to combine the twin messages of the need for reform and the need "to remember the delicate tissue of the economic body politic." The two men also got on well; Wilson liked McAdoo's dynamism and McAdoo recognized the force of Wilson's intellect and the steel in his ambition. McAdoo soon became one of Wilson's key advisors and Wilson's main ambassador to the South. His increasing prominence within the campaign drove McCombs to fits of jealousy as he saw McAdoo as his chief rival for Wilson's attention. After seeing McAdoo mentioned in a press article in August 1911, Byron Newton reported, McComb's "face instantly took on the expression of an infuriated animal. He locked the door, seized his cane and beat it into splinters over the desk, cursing and shrieking like a maniac. When the spasm had spent itself, he fell panting and exhausted into his chair, still muttering the most hideous and blasphemous curses upon McAdoo."[68]

Wilson's pre-convention campaign nearly collapsed under the strain of McCombs's behavior. He seemed always on the verge of a nervous breakdown and spent as much energy undermining his colleagues as furthering Wilson's cause. He planted stories that McAdoo suffered from mental illness and falsely accused Stockbridge of financial impropriety before dismissing him in November 1911. He installed a new publicity manager, who created an expensive office dedicated to "selling Wilson to the country." Byron Newton complained to Wilson, who had the new advertising strategy discontinued. McCombs then turned against Newton, accusing him of soliciting funds from Wall Street sources who would embarrass Wilson's campaign against predatory wealth. This allegation was again untrue, but Newton left in disgust in February 1912. Increasingly erratic, McCombs spent long periods away from the office and obsessed about rivals plotting to poison his relationship with Wilson.[69]

Despite his reputation for ruthlessness in his personal relationships, Wilson was outwardly tolerant of McCombs's behavior. Although aware of the troubles within his campaign, he refused repeated requests to dismiss his manager. McCombs was a mental and physical wreck, but Wilson insisted that his weaknesses be overlooked because of his loyalty to the cause. In other moods he was less generous, comparing McCombs to a vampire sucking his blood.[70]

McAdoo spent as little time as possible at the Bureau and focused on winning southerners to Wilson's standard. As it became clear that Roosevelt would run for the presidency again, either with or without the GOP, McAdoo emphasized that only Wilson could defeat TR in a national contest. Underwood was unelectable outside the South; Clark was vapid and Harmon too conservative. Wilson, on the other hand, was strong in the East, where the Democrats had to win if they were to defeat TR and the Republicans. Given Clark's and Underwood's strong showings in the primaries, it was now essential for Wilson to win as many second-choice instructions as possible so that he would be in a strong position once the convention's early ballots, and the delegates' promises to their favorite sons, had played themselves out.[71]

This strategy relied on the Democrats' rule that candidates needed two-thirds of the delegates to win the nomination. McAdoo's first task was to persuade Underwood's forces to remain firm and to make no deals with Clark; he then committed Wilson to a similar pledge in the hope that Clark would fail to win a two-thirds majority. McAdoo then made plans for Wilson to break the deadlock. Once Clark had been blocked, Underwood's delegates were to be persuaded to throw their weight behind Wilson as a fellow southerner with national appeal. Wilson had run second to Underwood in the states that the Alabamian had won, and so McAdoo hoped that Wilson would be the ultimate beneficiary of his votes.[72]

McCombs and McAdoo's convention strategy also required the support of William Jennings Bryan, who still wielded great influence over western and southern Democrats. McAdoo worked hard to warm the frosty relations between Bryan and Wilson by stressing the need to nominate a truly progressive candidate like Wilson rather than a machine politician like Clark or a provincial southerner like Underwood. This was a delicate assignment; Bryan had vague designs upon the nomination himself, and Wilson had not endeared himself by disparaging Bryan and his populist backers. McAdoo's task was to disabuse Bryan of his hopes for a fourth nomination and to persuade him that he could still strike a blow against reaction by swinging his support to Wilson. In this way the Great Commoner could broker the nomination of the next Democratic president.[73]

When the Democratic convention opened on June 25, 1912, McAdoo worked as Wilson's floor manager. McCombs was still technically in charge, but because of their poor relationship the two men worked separately. McAdoo had won election as a New York delegate, but this placed him in an anomalous position. New York had adopted the same unit rule that Baker had succeeded in overturning for Ohio, forcing McAdoo to vote for Harmon and then Clark while working for Wilson. He was allowed to vote for Wilson only once, in the final ballot of the convention. The unit rule, he later concluded, was "one of the most stupid devices ever conceived by the human intellect."[74]

McCombs almost ruined the plan. When New York switched on the tenth ballot from Harmon to Clark, the Missourian reached a bare majority of the convention's 1,088 votes. Although he needed nearly two hundred more delegates to reach a two-thirds majority, no contender since 1844 who had reached the 50 percent mark had failed to win the nomination. Without consulting McAdoo, McCombs advised Wilson that the fight was lost and to draft a telegram releasing his delegates. McAdoo strenuously disagreed and argued that Clark's wave had peaked; Wilson would soon reap the benefits of the "second choice" strategy. "You astound me," McAdoo yelled at McCombs. "You have sold him out." In desperation McAdoo telephoned Wilson and persuaded him to countermand his telegram. As

McAdoo predicted, Clark's majority melted away during subsequent ballots. On the fourteenth ballot Bryan announced his support for Wilson, and then Indiana and Iowa switched to him from Clark. On the twenty-eighth ballot Wilson's delegate tally passed Clark's, and Illinois, Virginia, and West Virginia changed sides on the forty-third ballot. After the forty-fifth ballot and four days of voting, Underwood's votes went to Wilson and Clark withdrew from the race. Years later McAdoo thought that the two-thirds rule "usually results in the elimination of all the powerful candidates." He had forgotten that this "mischievous and asinine" rule was the basis of his strategy to nominate Wilson at Baltimore, and was the reason for its success.[75]

The triumph at Baltimore did nothing to improve relations within the Wilson campaign. Despite his manifest unsuitability for the job, McCombs pushed hard to be appointed chairman of the DNC and head of Wilson's election campaign. He even engineered a torrent of telegrams, allegedly from Democrats across the nation but actually from McComb's friends, that urged his appointment. Already sensitive about his reputation for ingratitude, and anxious to avoid dissention in his camp, Wilson agreed. He then tested his new friendship with McAdoo by asking him to become McComb's deputy. "You are the only man living for whom I would accept this post," McAdoo replied. "If I do less well than you expect, only remember that I am not in command and that that necessarily restricts opportunity." Rarely was a more volatile combination created; McCombs was sick, unstable, and hypersensitive, while his deputy was dynamic and tactless. Not surprisingly, their duet functioned only when they worked apart.[76]

Fortunately for Wilson, McCombs's poor health kept him away from Wilson's headquarters for much of the campaign. His rages at McAdoo worsened as his mental equilibrium deteriorated, and McAdoo found himself in a deputy's nightmare as his decisions during McCombs's absences were revoked as soon as the chairman returned to the office. In the middle of August, as the campaign entered its critical phase, McCombs's mental and physical health collapsed and he was sent home for two months' rest. After recalling Byron Newton, McAdoo concentrated on bringing order to the campaign's financial affairs by instituting clear accounting methods and demanding costings for all expenditures. He called this the application of business principles to politics, but it was also a desperate effort to bring order to a campaign that had drifted dangerously because of McCombs's eccentricities.[77]

McCombs returned from his sickbed in the middle of October to accuse McAdoo of risking Wilson's reformist reputation by soliciting funds from Wall Street. Telling the press that he had been forced to foil the plot and avoid "a great scandal," McCombs stamped his authority on the last days of Wilson's campaign. McAdoo's preparations for a Wilson and Marshall Day celebration on November 2 were upended; his name was excised from publicity materials and substituted with McCombs's, and 100,000 copies of a letter to voters signed by McAdoo were destroyed. McAdoo left headquarters and returned to H&M, but not before writing to McCombs that he had tolerated enough of his insults and megalomania. "I will pull as hard with you as any man can for success," he declared, "but there is a certain respect and consideration which is not only indispensable, but which must not be ignored." From then on he only appeared when McCombs was out of the office.[78]

Wilson's victory on November 5, 1912, turned attention to the composition of his cabinet. The press was sure that McAdoo would become secretary of the treasury; his status as Wilson's best known supporter from New York and his prominent role in the campaign made him the obvious choice. Well before the election Wilson had discussed with Colonel House the advisability of appointing McAdoo to Treasury, and his admiration for his de facto campaign manager only increased as McCombs grew more erratic. Wilson acknowledged to McAdoo "the generous and efficient part, the self-sacrificing and sometimes painful part, you have played in pushing forward the common cause," and told him that he would not forget his role in the victory. As for McCombs, Wilson had heard and seen enough to convince him that he should not be appointed to the cabinet. An ambassadorship would be gratitude enough, with the added advantage that it would send McCombs abroad and prevent further embarrassment. McCombs was duly offered the ambassadorship to France, which he refused as an expensive exile. With his political debt to McCombs paid, Wilson's tone toward him changed from gratitude to imperiousness. "Whether you did little or much, remember that God ordained that I should be the next President of the United States. Neither you nor any other mortal or mortals could have prevented it."[79]

McCombs had other ideas. On the basis of his experience as a New York lawyer, his success at fundraising, and his titular leadership of the election campaign, he considered himself eminently suitable for Treasury. Rightly judging McAdoo to be his chief rival for that post, he enlisted his friends to persuade Wilson that McAdoo could not be trusted to be a force for progressive reform and would instead be a tool of Wall Street. This was ironic, for although McAdoo had raised millions of dollars from Wall Street to finance the H&M, he was neither its darling nor its champion and distrusted it all his adult life. Oswald Garrison Villard, editorial writer of *The Nation* and a leader of progressive opinion, threw his weight behind McCombs's claim to be secretary of treasury by damning McAdoo as "one of the least valuable of Wilson's advisers on questions of policy for his advice was rarely actuated by principle, usually by political intuition." McCombs, in contrast, was a sincere and determined progressive, loyal to Wilson through conviction rather than ambition.[80]

Although McAdoo had originally told Wilson that "I would not accept any office from [you] if [you] should be nominated and elected President of the United States," no one believed him. Villard found the idea "profoundly amusing" and noted that McAdoo had asked him to lobby Wilson on his behalf. McAdoo also sought House's aid to persuade Wilson to appoint him to Treasury, and even William Jennings Bryan put in a good word. Bryan did, however, note that he had heard that McAdoo was too friendly to Wall Street, and suggested that Wilson might consider other cabinet positions to which these reservations would not apply. Wilson paid no heed and asked McAdoo to be secretary of the treasury. Despite the fact that a cabinet secretary's salary of $12,000 was less than a quarter of his income from H&M, McAdoo accepted with alacrity and his nomination was confirmed by the Senate on March 5, 1913. "I'm awfully glad that you got into the cabinet," his 12-year-old son Robert wrote. "I knew you would all the time."[81]

CHAPTER 4

Newton Baker, William McAdoo, and Progressivism

Four decades of demolition have left little standing from the old idea of a coherent progressive *movement*. Each case study of progressive reform has added to the rubble; some progressives in the North worked for enforcement of African Americans' rights, while at the same time in the South many whites who supported racial segregation and disfranchisement also called themselves progressives. Progressives even divided over a single issue such as female suffrage. What was once thought to be a coherent movement is now seen as little more than a vague and partially shared mindset that sporadically coalesced to achieve often contradictory reforms.[1]

Yet the idea of a progressive *era* has been a hardy survivor. Most historians now agree that progressivism was incoherent, but many have clung to it to both separate and link the Gilded Age of the 1880s and the Jazz Age of the 1920s. No matter how many stakes are driven through the heart of progressivism as a coherent movement it has survived as a historical category and identifier. Now hedged with qualifications and reservations, it has proved much easier to deconstruct than to replace. Instead of being cohesive, it is now seen as a set of shared concerns and methods which, although not universal or consistent, demarcated those who wished to change their society and its institutions from those who saw no need for reform.[2]

Central to that demarcation was a belief that classical liberalism—laissez faire economics, negative statism, and decentralization of public authority—had become inappropriate to urban and industrial societies. The verities of old liberalism may have suited the chaos of early industrial society, but by the 1890s they had proved inadequate as mass immigration, urbanization, and industrialization revolutionized America. Progressives espoused new institutions, laws, and attitudes to modernize, but not abolish, notions of individual liberty, responsibility, competition, and property rights. Central to their dismissal of the old individualism was their rejection of the idea that misfortunes such as unemployment and poverty were simply products of personal failings. Progressives subscribed instead to new ideas of social welfare that acknowledged social and structural causes of private economic distress and which looked to institutional reform, not just individual redemption, for their solutions.[3]

Many progressives therefore used government power and institutions to blunt the sharp edges of nineteenth-century politics, economic development, and individualism without excavating the foundations of their society or their own assumptions about class and racial power within it. The progressive mindset was often engaged by issues arising from urbanization, immigration, and industrialization, but it was usually blind to America's racial divide. When Jane Edna Hunter, an African American nurse, came to Cleveland in 1905, she found that Tom Johnson's and Newton Baker's city, already famous for its progressive reform, offered her very little. Hunter was refused employment as a nurse and forced to work as a cleaner, and she found it impossible to find accommodation anywhere outside the grimy inner city. After years of struggle she created her own version of progressive reform by opening a shelter for African American women, but her achievement was exceptional. Few progressives tried to improve the position of African Americans or to include them in their vision of a transformed nation and public.[4]

In keeping with their middle-class orientation, progressives did not seek to destroy the social structures that had made them comfortable, but instead tried to make them fairer and more transparent. Yet progressivism was not altruism; it sought to remake America in ways that cemented its proponents' position and influence within it. Progressives were certainly motivated by moral outrage, but their ferocity did not spring from the rage of the dispossessed. Although many progressives thought that maldistribution of wealth was the key problem facing the United States—Amos Pinchot declared that "the whole political question in America seems one of making the poor man richer and the rich man poorer. That is all there is to it"—few supported the idea of drastic income redistribution. Income taxes that took disproportionately from the rich were as far as they would go; outright confiscation was not only unconstitutional and un-American; it was also unprogressive.[5]

The other common thread in progressivism was statism. Progressives of all stripes turned to public authority for solutions to the social ills they saw around them. The site of that public authority varied over time according to the problem and to the social location of its combatants; municipal and labor reformers looked to city government and the states, while those concerned with national problems turned to the federal government. To the progressive mindset, however, local problems soon became national concerns; its stress on the interrelation of social development fostered broader perspectives and encouraged national action. This centripetal tendency was accelerated by the influence of the two great progressive presidents, Theodore Roosevelt and Woodrow Wilson, who publicized their versions of progressivism by mobilizing public opinion and imposing their agendas on Congress. Faith in government, and desire to build or rebuild its structures to cope with new problems, was as close to a universal characteristic that progressivism possessed.[6]

Progressives also thought hard about power, and how to both limit and use it. While they railed against the corporations that controlled their markets, crushed competitors, and corrupted legislatures, and against the power of urban political bosses who grew rich from their poor constituents, progressives were adept at augmenting those institutions that they could create and control. Heavily influenced by late nineteenth-century ideas of social engineering and efficiency, and motivated by their dislike of unrestrained individualism, progressives set about reinvigorating public sources of authority as counterweights to private corporations, corrupt political organizations, and cabals of self-seeking officeholders. Keen to redefine and expand the public sphere, progressives were anxious to define who should and should not be part of the public. Those who had earned their disapproval, such as urban bosses, illiterate immigrants, and unschooled African Americans, were shoved aside in favor of native stock American men and women and the well-educated.[7]

Progressive municipal reform consequently aimed to reduce the power of political machines and patronage through at-large representation, city manager government, fiscal rectitude, and merit-based bureaucratic employment. At the state level progressives targeted corruption and patronage, and advocated reforms such as direct primaries, initiative and referendum, equitable taxation regimes, and efficient and honest provision of infrastructure. As they looked increasingly to Washington, progressive reformers emphasized executive regulation over legislative enactment and structural reforms such as a federal income tax, female suffrage, and direct election of US senators to open the federal administrative structure not only to the light of day but also to their own expertise. "Social justice" in many progressives' eyes encompassed measures as diverse as factory labor laws, prohibition, anti-vice laws, and public hygiene regulation; "civic engagement" included female suffrage, initiative and referendum on the one hand and racial segregation and immigration restriction on the other. The very plasticity of these terms gave progressivism its breadth, but also its contradictions and incoherence.[8]

At all levels of government, however, most progressives united around a distrust of institutions that owed too much to pliant voters or public apathy. They also shared an admiration for power that was less dependent on local democracy and more reliant on expertise and public spiritedness. Democracy could not be left to evolve in undirected ways, for that was part of the drift that had afflicted America through laissez-faire thinking. Like all social institutions, democracy had to be directed through the expertise of social scientists possessed of vision and skills to steer society away from demagoguery, bossism, corruption, and greed. Citizens should be free to fulfill their talents, but the complexity and interdependence of modern society meant that the duties that citizens owed to each other were now as important as their liberties. The progressives' collective insight was to see that those liberties and duties were so interrelated that each depended on the other for their protection and advancement.[9]

Less universally, but still commonly, progressives respected those they recognized as experts and sought to integrate them into the governmental and reform process. They also tended to be environmentalist in their conception of human nature and capability, stressing the need to improve education, housing, working conditions, health, and recreation to make citizens more capable and fulfilled. Much of progressivism was also underpinned by a sense of the innate potential of human beings once they had been liberated from the constraints of poor environments, outdated social institutions, unenlightened laws, and corrupt rulers.[10]

The most telling manifestation of a progressive mindset lay in the reformers themselves. Many of them believed that they were part of an inchoate but still very real movement. While their historians have carefully distinguished waves of social and intellectual development that separated classical liberalism from progressivism and then New Deal liberalism, their subjects were not so discriminating. Some called themselves "progressives," others used "liberal" or "insurgent," and some like Newton Baker even occasionally described themselves as "radicals." Baker most frequently described himself as a "liberal," which he defined in terms that could apply equally to nineteenth-century mugwumps, turn-of-the-century progressives, and twentieth-century New Dealers:

> Liberalism is a state of mind which causes one who has it to approach all public questions with a desire to solve them in the general public good rather than for the interest of any class, group, or individual. It is also a sure feeling that things get better in this world rather than worse and have their best chance of improvement when they rest for approval upon the informed conscience of the common man.[11]

Some progressives rejected their entire inheritance from classical liberal values, while others retained elements of it in their economic thinking or in their desire to protect individuals from ever more active and intrusive governments. Confused by the variety of "progressive" causes, and by their conflicting means and objectives, progressives often blurred their commonalities and their differences. They were sure that they belonged to a broad movement, but they struggled to define exactly with what and with whom they identified. Most gave up even trying.[12]

Ideological consistency came in a poor second to political necessity and expedience, but reformers as diverse as Jane Addams, Theodore Roosevelt, Woodrow Wilson, Louis Brandeis, Walter Lippmann, Tom Johnson, Newton Baker, and William McAdoo all felt that they were part of an amorphous movement to modernize the United States. They recognized each other as fellow soldiers in an army with many theaters of battle, many enemies to fight, many generals to follow, and many strategies and tactics to execute. They recognized the breadth, the contradictions, and even the incoherence of their progressive army, but none seemed to question its existence. Historians who seek to carve progressivism's epitaph too deeply must first come to terms with their historical actors who found much more life, and much more meaning, in a movement that has been so often dismissed as unworthy of the name. William McAdoo and Newton Baker provide clear examples of this sentiment at work.

❖❖

Although their trajectories into, through, and out of the progressive era differed, Baker and McAdoo shared a sense of belonging to a broad movement. They identified themselves as progressives and saw progressivism as a way of thinking instead of a single political and philosophical entity. "Political philosophies are nearly always questions of speed and rarely questions of principle," Baker declared in 1927. Most people agreed on the key goals of human development—"how much well-being and education and opportunity there ought to be in the life of everybody in the world"—but they disagreed on how soon these objectives should be gained: "Some people would want them immediately. They are radicals. Some people would want them the day after tomorrow. They are progressives. Some people would want to be continuously making headway toward them without a fixed date. They would be liberals. And some people would want them postponed until it becomes entirely convenient to do them. They would be conservatives." By that reckoning Baker and McAdoo were either "progressives" or "liberals," depending on the issues involved, rarely "radicals," and never "conservatives."[13]

Baker and McAdoo observed progressivism and saw their own reflections in it. Those reflections revealed different motivations and interests, but they were progressive reflections nevertheless. Baker's and McAdoo's experiences in progressivism remind us not only of the vibrancy of progressivism but also of its diversity. Most of all, they remind us that participants in the progressive movement were less concerned with coherence and ideological consistency than their critics and historians have been.

Recent studies of progressivism have stressed the importance of organizations and networks in engendering common purpose within groups of reformers. Progressives were inveterate joiners, forming a galaxy of organizations that spanned the nation and the Atlantic to discuss social problems, share ideas, mourn failures, and trumpet successes. These organizations also provided sites of belonging that created communities of reform from geographically scattered and politically isolated individuals and groups. From these grew mailing lists that could address and publicize issues across the nation, from municipal governments to state capitols, from the states to Washington, and even to transatlantic bodies such as the Hague Tribunal.[14]

Newton Baker typified this impulse. As city solicitor and then mayor of Cleveland he worked hard to develop a network of municipal reformers, first in Ohio and then farther afield. As he and Tom Johnson fought for municipal control of streetcars, others interested in the same cause around the country wrote in search of advice and support. Johnson's tent meetings, which aimed to educate citizens about issues facing the city, were inspired by Charles Sprague Smith's People's Forums in New York City. Baker also sought out a network of Ohio municipal leaders, attending conferences and maintaining correspondence with mayors such as Brand Whitlock in Toledo and Henry Hunt in Cincinnati on issues of common concern.[15]

Although he was focused on Cleveland, Baker knew that his city was not unique in its problems. When it came to improving Cleveland's dance halls, Baker borrowed from similar campaigns by Belle Moskowitz's Committee on Amusements and Vacation Resources for Working Girls in New York City and Chicago's Dance Hall and Ballroom Managers' Association. In his concerns about the effect of movies on young people Baker looked to Jane Addams, who recognized them to be "the only possible road to the realms of mystery and romance" for urban young people, but also worried about their exaggerated emotions and alluring sensuality.[16]

Baker won national prominence during Cleveland's streetcar wars between 1902 and 1909. Urban transit had become a pressing issue in cities all over America, and Baker's advice was widely sought. His later forays into municipal ownership of electric power, and his pronouncements on public control of other utilities such as gas and steam heating, cemented his reputation as a leader of urban reform. His prominence arose from the influence that large cities exercised in the political life of the nation; in the years before the expansion of the federal government's capabilities during World War I it was in the cities and not Washington that early progressives cut their teeth. Reform of municipal government, Woodrow Wilson argued in 1885, was a national priority because it was there that new ideas of social efficiency and financial accountability could be most effectively instituted. Far from being written off as social and economic failures, as they would be in the 1970s, America's industrial cities were seen during the progressive era as vital social laboratories in which great problems of the age could be solved. As chief legal officer and then mayor of one of America's largest industrial cities, Baker was therefore prominent in the progressive community long before he joined Woodrow Wilson's cabinet.[17]

Baker supported a wide variety of reform organizations. These included groups dedicated to law reform, abolition of capital punishment, adult education, world peace, religious tolerance, abolition of child labor, urban design, consumer rights, and public health. His papers contain minutes of meetings, appeals for donations, invitations to speak, and requests to join boards from more than one hundred organizations from all over the Northeast of the United States and Western Europe. The idea of a community of reformers, banded together in a web of organizations with interlinked memberships but diverse interests, was reflected in Baker's mail, diaries, and checkbooks through the first quarter of the twentieth century.[18]

Baker's third major connection to the progressive movement was through the world of ideas. Always bookish, he was a voracious reader and the collector of a library so extensive that its annotated catalogue would eventually be published. While at Johns Hopkins in the early 1890s, Baker read the new social, economic, and legal thought that assailed the determinism and romantic individualism of social Darwinism, laissez-faire economic theory, and legal formalism. After college and law school he kept up with the work of American progressive intellectuals, including Jane Addams, Herbert Croly, Richard Ely, Thorstein Veblen, Louis Brandeis, Oliver Wendell Holmes, and, of course, Woodrow Wilson. As a reader of Greek, Latin, and German, he also became familiar with classical and modern European thought.[19]

McAdoo came to progressivism through different avenues. Historians have discerned three main streams in progressive language: antimonopolism, social justice, and social efficiency. Baker belonged to the second of these streams, while McAdoo arose from and then transcended the first. Those in business who considered themselves to be progressives formed a new class of corporate leadership, trained in management and a generation younger than the founders of the great business organizations that they now controlled. This new managerial class systematized the financial and production processes of their corporations, imposed more thorough supervision of their employees, and engaged more closely with the emerging regulatory and police powers of the state. These business progressives did not share the enthusiastic statism of other progressives, but they were a far cry from their corporations' aggressively individualistic founding fathers. For this new breed, the emerging state could serve business interests and profits more than the needs of workers and consumers.[20]

Business progressives were corporatists rather than social reformers; they saw society as made up of competing groups and were determined that business should be at the top of the new social hierarchy. Concerned predominantly with restructuring their operations along efficient and "progressive" lines, the new managerial class was aloof from social justice reformers and engaged in reform mainly to protect business from venal politicians, assertive employees, and active consumer groups. Their interactions with the broader progressive impulse tended to be sporadic, tightly focused, and contentious. Their modernity owed more to necessity than to ideology as their corporations grew more powerful and complex, and their engagement with progressivism owed more to self-interest than to civic-mindedness as they jostled with competing interest groups.[21]

McAdoo emerged as a different type of business progressive. He shared little with the new managerial class; he was never a manager, was certainly not an inheritor and then reformer of business structures, and was closer to the entrepreneurial and promoting spirit of the pre-managerial age. McAdoo's talent lay in creating but not managing enterprises; it was no accident that his move to politics coincided with the maturation of H&M beyond its building phase, which fascinated him, into a period of consolidation, which interested him much less. Early in 1912 McAdoo focused on Wilson's nomination campaign rather than on his railroad, and when he resigned from H&M in March 1913 his separation from it was permanent. He mentioned it seldom in his correspondence and soon sold all of his stock in it. He was a dynamic promoter, happy to hire the managerial class but uninterested in joining it.

Yet McAdoo was no robber baron reincarnate. Although he played up the rugged individualism of his early career, often retelling his humble beginnings as a penniless southerner pitching for funds on Wall Street, he never doubted that he and his business were parts of an interdependent economy and society. He did not need to be persuaded that corporations owed obligations to their consumers and workers as well as to their shareholders, and that those obligations underpinned the privileges that gave American corporate life its freedoms and profits. When he announced H&M's "public be pleased" policy in 1909, he acknowledged that "recognition by the corporation of the just rights of the people results in recognition by the people of the just rights of the corporation. A square deal for the people and a square deal for the corporation. The latter is as essential as the former and they are not incompatible."[22]

Baker became a reformer through education, reading, networks, and conviction; McAdoo did so through different means. His education had been crimped by poverty and by its intellectual ambience; the University of Tennessee in the late 1870s offered nothing like the breadth of Johns Hopkins ten years later. McAdoo learned his law not in a university but at nights under a local judge. He was never bookish, and learned what he needed about law, business, and politics through doing and listening rather than reading. "I have long since come to the conclusion that the vast majority of books are of no value," he wrote in his autobiography. "Nine out of ten of them are written by those who lack the experience, the capacity, and the ideas which are necessary for the creation of a significant literary work." He was bored by ideas without practical application. "I do not like ideas that are suspended in air," he confessed. "There is not much metaphysics in my temperament." Admirers lauded this trait as flexible and open-minded; his critics saw it as expedient and shallow.[23]

As he preferred to play a lone hand in his business career, McAdoo also avoided the organizations that nurtured other progressives. His associationalism was more business networking than participation in a reform community. The New York Southern Society and Kappa Sigma were scarcely hotbeds of reform, progressive or otherwise, and McAdoo's papers reveal far fewer affiliations and civic activities than do Baker's. His work for tubercular children, which so nearly cost him his life and reputation in 1911, was the sort of philanthropy that had long been expected from business leaders and did not represent a new spirit of reform. With a railroad to run, six children to support, and an invalid wife to nurse, McAdoo had little time for the networks and correspondence that Newton Baker maintained throughout his career.

McAdoo's reputation as a reformer before 1912 therefore rested on his actions rather than his ideas and through his self-identification rather than his associations. In New York he portrayed himself as an outsider who had succeeded through the force of his initiative and personality and through his defiance of monopoly and corruption. As president of H&M, he presented himself as a new type of businessman who combined an eye for profit with a sense of social responsibility. To be a progressive in business, McAdoo maintained, was "practical and wise altruism" that promised both social benefit and private profit. While this propelled him to the forefront of progressive business reform and caught the eye of Theodore Roosevelt and Woodrow Wilson, it is also hard to discern the line between good public relations and genuine reformist conviction, and, in Walter Lippmann's phrase, to distinguish McAdoo the statesman from McAdoo the promoter.[24]

This ambivalence lay at the heart of McAdoo's conduct of the H&M. His initiatives on equal pay for female ticket sellers, hen cars, and complaint books, all publicized under "the public be pleased" motto, were innovative but not unique. They attracted publicity and goodwill, but they were not a progressive manifesto. Even on their own terms, H&M's innovations were limited and sometimes tokenistic. There were relatively few ticket sellers, and their equal pay did not extend to other female employees. Hen cars received more publicity than passengers and were soon discontinued. The complaint books were prominently displayed but little used. The suspicion remains that these measures were more devices for publicity than indications of a deep commitment to reform. McAdoo's emphasis on customer service may have been symbolic of a desire to create a socially responsible corporation, but it was also a magnet for publicity.

Urban transit played a pivotal role in McAdoo's and Baker's careers before 1912 and in the creation of their progressive reputations. Cleveland's municipal streetcars and the H&M were notable for combating rapacious monopoly and their reliance upon the goodwill of their customers. In Cleveland the Con-Con had become unpopular because of its disregard for passengers' comfort and pocketbooks, and in New York McAdoo played on Manhattanites' rage at the Interborough's monopoly. In both cities urban transit was of great importance to the middle class, who were increasingly resident in suburbs distant from their workplaces but not yet beneficiaries of the automobile age. Crammed into overcrowded streetcars and subway carriages and overcharged for poor service, the urban middle class—a key constituency of progressive reform—felt itself at the mercy of monopolies. Baker and McAdoo responded by creating new entities to break their respective transit monopolies and to provide better service to longsuffering commuters in Cleveland and New York. In this broader context, and independent of McAdoo's gaudy public relations efforts, both men's efforts were eminently progressive.[25]

The key difference between McAdoo's project and Baker's crusade lay in the statism that underpinned the campaign to municipalize Cleveland's streetcars. McAdoo's railroad was a privately funded corporation established to make private profit. In Cleveland, Johnson and Baker employed public resources to operate streetcars for public benefit. Cleveland's municipal streetcars were an experiment in governmental power to usurp private capital and enterprise and to provide cheaper and better service to passengers. Inspired by similar undertakings in Europe and propelled by voters disgusted by the Con-Con, municipalization was on the cutting edge of Cleveland politics in particular and progressive reform in general. McAdoo's railroad, in contrast, provided a much more orthodox solution to the transport and political challenges facing New York's commuters at the turn of the twentieth century. The Interborough's monopoly was challenged by competition, not municipalization, and the H&M was run on commercial, not civic, principles.[26]

This is not to say that McAdoo was a fake progressive or that his innovations were shams. Equal pay for female ticket sellers was consistent with his advanced views on the role and rights of women in American society. Like Baker, McAdoo was a strong supporter of female suffrage. "Democracy does not mean rule of men, it means rule of the people," he declared in 1920. "There can be no genuine democracy until this truth is recognized." Although less interested than Baker in foreign affairs, McAdoo played a prominent role in the National Citizens' Committee established in 1911 to protest against Russian anti-Semitism, and he joined the American Peace and Arbitration League. He was also vocal in his opposition to Tammany Hall and prominent in his support of honest government and clean administration.[27]

McAdoo also shared progressive concerns about the social costs of untrammeled corporate power; his opposition to overweening corporations, monopolies, and their financial handmaidens on Wall Street was also genuine. Concern that TR was too complacent about large corporations contributed to McAdoo's defection to Wilson, and his resolve that business should take its social obligations seriously extended beyond the slogan of "the public be pleased." By 1910 he had emerged as a hybrid entrepreneur-reformer who had supped at Wall Street's table but kept his independence from it, and who had demonstrated that pursuit of profit was compatible with civic improvement and corporate responsibility. In so doing he demonstrated progressivism's ability to function alongside private enterprise and to improve it. If that achievement came at the cost of reformism that conflated progressivism with innovation and civic-mindedness with self-promotion, McAdoo at least had shown that progressivism, as he defined it, could still be good business.[28]

Once established in Wilson's cabinet, McAdoo became more closely aligned with the statist element of the progressive mindset. He proved to be a committed centralist in the fight for the Federal Reserve Act, insisting that the federal government should replace Wall Street "in the saddle" of the nation's banking system. At the end of 1914, concerned that the United States was unable to trade with whomever it chose, McAdoo argued for the creation of a government-owned merchant marine. By then he was a convinced statist:

> What is Government for? Is it something in a straitjacket? Is it sitting in a corner like a thing with palsied hands afraid to act, or is it something vital? Is it a flexible instrument in the hands of the people of this country to be used within constitutional limitations for their relief and for their benefit? Is it . . . something to come to the front and do things for the American people when private capital can not be commanded or commandeered or persuaded to that purpose? It does not seem to me that there is room for argument.[29]

Once the United States entered World War I, McAdoo extended his new faith in government action. In 1918 he even controlled the US Railroad Administration (USRRA), which operated the nation's railroads. This was progressivism writ large, and municipalization on a grand scale, but it did not add to McAdoo's reputation for ideological consistency.

Newton Baker undertook his own journey from progressivism in Cleveland to reform in Washington and from peace to war. Unlike McAdoo, he found no inspiration in Theodore Roosevelt, whom he described as totally lacking in humility. His first hero was Tom Johnson, with his affinity with the common man and hatred of unearned economic privilege. Baker's own policy of civitism promised, in a typically progressive mix of the practical and the spiritual, a new age of civic pride bolstered by "more beautiful parks, cleaner streets, upright government and widespread adherence to justice as the ideal of social and economic relations." Baker was also typically progressive in his support of initiative, referendum, and civil service reform.[30]

As his reputation and experience developed, Baker spoke out on issues that extended well beyond Cleveland. Now confident in the success of his city's municipal streetcars, he urged municipalization of other utilities, including gas, electric light, water, "and perhaps telephones and telegraphs." In 1912, soon after his election as mayor and Wilson's to the presidency, Baker had become even more adventurous. "I think I am the original railroad nationalizer in the country," he declared in December 1912, and predicted that "the great trans-continental lines will be owned by the government with perhaps state lines and city owned terminals completing the picture." There were vested interests to overcome and constitutions to amend, but "whatever the philosophers may be willing to do, the people are not willing to wait and the demand for state control I think is going to be irresistible."[31]

Whether from courtesy to his correspondents or from enthusiasm at the progress of reform, Baker even had kind words to say about socialism. In 1912 he wrote that socialists were right to say that too many individuals had enriched themselves at the expense of their fellow citizens, but the "ingrown habit of selfish acquisition as the dominant characteristic in business and industry" made their theories impossible to implement fully in the United States. Yet failure to deal with unequal distribution of wealth would surely lead to experiments with aspects of socialism. Progressive reform, Baker believed, was therefore essential to save capitalism from itself. He would never be so tolerant of socialism again, although his concern that free enterprise might self-destruct resurfaced during the Great Depression.[32]

While McAdoo said little about labor relations before 1914, Baker could not afford to be so reticent. McAdoo did recognize the presence of organized labor at H&M but made no statements in its support or about its role in industrial life. He maintained that paying good wages created happier employees and therefore better customer service, and he was proud that his subway suffered no significant industrial unrest during his time as its president. Yet he did not venture beyond tolerance for unions, payment of fair wages, and institution of an eight-hour working day. He paid lip-service to workers' compensation and pension plans, but did nothing to implement them. McAdoo was a fair employer, but certainly not a practitioner of the welfare capitalism that began to emerge within some large corporations after 1914. Baker, on the other hand, was forced to express clearer views on the role of organized labor and prospects for industrial peace. As Cleveland's city solicitor and then mayor, he had to confront industrial relations in ways that McAdoo, insulated from elective politics and content to implement his own "square deal" for employees, was not.[33]

Although it did not suffer the same traumas as Detroit, Chicago, and Pittsburgh during the 1890s, Cleveland was not left unscathed by the depression of 1893–1897. More than eighty strikes closed the city's industries, including two violent streetcar strikes in 1892 and 1899 and a riot by unemployed workers in 1894. The 1899 streetcar strike, which lasted four months and involved strikebreakers and the National Guard, was particularly divisive. It provided the backdrop for Johnson's campaign in 1901 for the mayoralty and for his promises to municipalize streetcars and encourage industrial harmony in the city. Cleveland's Democrats were particularly divided by the 1899 strike, and almost lost the support of industrial workers and immigrants. Under Johnson the party managed to mend its political fences and create a coalition of reformers and organized labor that added a working-class base to the progressives' middle-class constituency. As Johnson's chief legal officer and confidant, Baker developed his progressivism with the electoral power of labor firmly in mind and became a beneficiary of Cleveland's version of a working class-progressive alliance.[34]

Although he relied on workers' votes, Baker kept his distance from their organizations. His background and temperament did not lend themselves to the rough and tumble of working-class political culture, and he relied on Peter Witt, a former iron molder who had joined City Hall during Tom Johnson's mayoralty, to build his bridges to labor. As mayor, Baker contented himself with statements of support for labor that did not alarm Cleveland's business interests and conservative voters. He declared his sympathy with the objectives of trade unions, but noted that often their noble aims had been betrayed by leaders who preached class conflict to the detriment of the rank and file. In July 1915 he sharpened his attack upon "the professional labor organizer" who "seems to have gotten a mistaken notion that his duty is to be a business disorganizer." Instead of working to ameliorate workers' alienation from their work—"pretty nearly every industrial worker I have talked with has about the same attitude towards his factory that prisoners have toward their place of confinement"—union leaders only worsened relations between employers and employees by accentuating conflict over cooperation and self-interest over "the sense of contribution to the general economic output."[35]

Baker's views on labor issues were always judicious and they hardened over time. His stress on workplace cooperation was well intentioned but unrealistic, and carried seeds of a less sympathetic attitude once industrial conditions degenerated into violence or prolonged strikes. Shocked by the radical syndicalism of the International Workers of the World (IWW) and by their violent strikes in 1919, Baker became a prominent advocate of the open shop and ruptured the vicarious links he had formed with organized labor in Cleveland. McAdoo, on the other hand, moved in the opposite direction. Despite his reticence on labor issues before World War I, McAdoo courted labor assiduously as director general of the USRRA, and the railroad brotherhoods repaid the favor by strongly supporting his presidential ambitions in the 1920s.

❧⊰✦⊱❧

Progressivism haunted Baker and McAdoo long after its era had closed. As the demands of elective politics had kept Baker within the reformist camp before World War I, he seemed to drift away from it after 1917. Conversely, the allure of political office after the war encouraged McAdoo to assume a progressive mantle more assertively during the 1920s and 1930s. This prompted their critics to assert that Baker's reformist arteries had hardened after 1921 and that McAdoo's pragmatism had soured into opportunism. Neither criticism was entirely fair, but they pointed to the importance of the progressive legacy to Baker's and McAdoo's postwar careers.[36]

McAdoo, typically enough, spent little time musing on the fate of progressivism. He remained convinced of the electoral viability of his own brand of reform and later threw in his lot with the New Deal. McAdoo did not provide a detailed analysis of his thought other than to insist that ideas had to change with the times and that "I like movement and change." His contemporaries, who had already decided that McAdoo was either an effective and pragmatic progressive or an inveterate opportunist, devoted little attention to his ideas and concentrated instead on his deeds.[37]

Newton Baker was a different matter. Because he was a more cerebral politician than McAdoo, his relationship with progressivism after 1920 was more closely observed and more harshly criticized. He noted in 1935 that he had been described as a reactionary ex-liberal and a dangerous radical. "Somewhere between these extremes I think I see my unchanged self, but perhaps I am wrong about that."[38]

It was the nature of this "unchanged self" that troubled Baker's friends as they tried to make sense of his alleged defection from progressivism after 1920. Baker insisted that the times, and not he, had changed. What had seemed radical in 1912 had become staid in 1932, but he declined to update his thinking. Apart from a half-heated tilt at the 1932 Democratic presidential nomination, he forswore elected office from 1916 until his death in 1937. Freed from the need to win votes and to stay abreast of public opinion, he could now afford the luxury of taking stock, reasserting his beliefs, and being left behind by relative motion. He could also afford the luxury of honesty; an elected politician needs to give at least the impression of having solutions to crises, but Baker often had none to offer and was frank enough to say so.[39]

In 1926 Baker thought that most of his reform agenda had been achieved. Municipal governments were now more honest, more efficient, and freer to govern through home rule, and they now had better parks, schools, and sanitation, and more control over their utilities. In addition, reforms such as initiative and referendum and at-large representation had proven to be less useful than he had once hoped. The optimism of prewar reform had also been dissipated by dissension among its practitioners and disillusion after the war. Liberalism and reform would rise again, Baker thought, but just now the "stricken and terrified world demanded a respite."[40]

Respite did not mean reaction, and Baker resented charges that he had surrendered to it. As a lawyer familiar with the evolution of the common law, he was aware that social institutions needed to adapt to changed circumstances. "The trunk of a tree must grow larger every year to sustain the new branches and the more numerous leaves," and government was no different. "I think from my earliest youth my mind has been hospitable to liberal ideas," he mused in 1932, "but I had, even as a young man, a feeling that changes had to come gradually and by growth in order to be beneficial and enduring." During the 1930s the New Deal brought not evolution but revolution, and that offended his natural caution.[41]

Baker was not the only progressive who found the New Deal objectionable. An examination of the attitudes of more than one hundred former progressives to the New Deal found that a majority of them opposed it. Josephus Daniels, who had served as secretary of the navy between 1913 and 1921, remarked in 1936 that of Wilson's cabinet only he, Postmaster General Alfred Burleson, and McAdoo supported the New Deal and that "I fear Newton Baker is in the cave." Baker was indeed typical of those progressives who later opposed the New Deal; he had been born in a small town, was well educated, was unmoved by the radicalism of the populists in the 1880s and 1890s, entered public life before and during World War I, and then had taken lucrative private employment during the 1920s and the Great Depression.[42]

Lawyers among the old progressives opposed the New Deal by a margin of two to one, and most of them rejected, as did Baker, the coercive powers assumed by the federal executive after 1932. To many of the old progressives Franklin Roosevelt seemed too eager to please, too flexible in his views, and too bereft of convictions. His progressive critics tended to be localists who were, like Baker, more accepting of activist government close to home rather than in Washington. Most of all, they objected to the new corporatist idea that society was made up of competing interest groups and classes that fought for influence within government and swapped their votes and donations for favors from it. "As a consequence our

Government for the last three years," Baker thought in 1936, "has been the mere tossing of tubs to each whale as it grows bold enough to stick its head out of the water."[43]

McAdoo responded differently to the challenges of the 1920s and to the innovations of the New Deal. His campaigns for the presidential nomination in 1920 and 1924 kept him engaged with postwar political culture and public opinion. When FDR won the White House in 1932, McAdoo won a seat in the US Senate. There his own convictions and his hopes for a second term kept him loyal to the New Deal. McAdoo, like FDR, had long been dismissed as facile and opportunistic, and often attacked for his centralist instincts. Both men saw flexibility and pragmatism as virtues, and expanding the role of the federal government during the Great Depression seemed to them to be common sense rather than a betrayal of progressivism.

In 1913 this lay in the future, for in that year all seemed well among progressives. At the end of 1912 Woodrow Wilson won the presidency, in January 1913 Baker took office as mayor of Cleveland, and in March McAdoo took his place in Wilson's cabinet. When Baker came to Washington in March 1916 as secretary of war, he sat alongside Wilson and McAdoo as the administration's leading progressives. In peace and then war, the three men struggled to impose their versions of progressivism on the problems that confronted them, their nation, and each other.

Summer

1913–1920

✦❋✦

CHAPTER 5

In Woodrow Wilson's Cabinet, 1913–1921

Like many other visitors to Washington, D.C. in March 1913, Franklin Lane wanted very much to meet Woodrow Wilson. One of the crowd who surrounded Wilson before his inauguration, Lane managed to introduce himself to the president-elect. Wilson greeted him cordially but briefly. There were so many people to meet, and so many decisions to make. Yet Lane had pressing reasons to make Wilson's acquaintance. He had been designated as secretary of the interior, a post originally offered to Newton Baker, but had never even met Wilson. After their brief meeting on Inauguration Day and then a perfunctory confirmation by the Senate on March 6, 1913, Lane joined Wilson's cabinet and remained there until 1920.[1]

Although it is often described as the president's "official family," the cabinet has rarely lived up to the influence and intimacy that this term suggests. Instead, its role has been subject to each president's executive style, political imperatives, and personal prejudices. Washington allowed his cabinet to be dominated by feuds between his Secretary of State Thomas Jefferson and Secretary of the Treasury Alexander Hamilton, Lincoln used it to keep his political enemies close to hand, and Franklin Roosevelt used it to gauge opinion on policies that his White House staff had already devised.[2]

As the scope of the federal government has expanded, and as the powers of the president have grown, so too has the size of the cabinet. John Adams had five departmental secretaries in 1800, Woodrow Wilson had ten in 1913, and George W. Bush had fifteen in 2008. Mere growth, however, has not made the cabinet more powerful. Cabinet secretaries have become less influential as the sizes of the president's White House staff, the National Security Council, and the Office of Management and Budget have grown. The "official family" has an all-powerful parent who demands obedience and loyalty, and who treats its members as subordinates to implement presidential policies rather than as autonomous policy makers.[3]

Woodrow Wilson's two presidential terms, dominated by an active domestic policy agenda before 1917 and then the demands of fighting a world war, ushered in a new era of federal activism. Wilson's departmental heads were swept up in the increasing demands on the federal government, but they did so without the assistance of more recently created executive agencies such as a large White House staff or presidential advisory bodies. Wilson's own staff was small and chiefly clerical. Before the creation of extra-congressional and extra-cabinet organizations such as the War Industries Board, he relied on his personal advisor Colonel Edward House, his political secretary Joseph Tumulty, prominent Democrats in the legislature, and his cabinet secretaries for advice and policy ideas. In this Wilson was in the same position as his predecessors, but he did have one key advantage: as a political scientist he could draw on his own ideas as they had evolved during his pre-presidential career about the proper role of the cabinet within the federal government.

Wilson's earliest thoughts on the role of cabinet were radical and impractical. In "Cabinet Government in the United States," which he wrote as a senior at Princeton in 1879, he suggested that the new demands of governing the nation required a British-style cabinet drawn from, and responsible to, Congress. By expanding the executive to include the president and the cabinet as equal actors, he thought, the federal government could draw on a wider pool of expertise while retaining its accountability to the people. Convinced of the need to reinvigorate Gilded-Age governance from its torpor and corruption, Wilson brushed aside the obvious constitutional impediments to his suggestions.[4]

Increasingly influenced by progressivism and by Theodore Roosevelt's assertive presidency, Wilson changed his views on the cabinet during the early twentieth century. His earlier advocacy of the British system was now tempered by constitutional reality and by a new appreciation of the benefits of centralized executive power. In *Constitutional Government in the United States*, first published in 1908, Wilson emphasized the cabinet as an integral part of the president's executive functions. He now conceded that the status quo, in which the president appointed department heads from outside Congress, was desirable. The business of government was now so complicated that the president needed to delegate his powers to the best cabinet officers he could find. Presidents had to limit themselves to setting broad policy directions, addressing specific issues, and overseeing their chief delegates. Cabinet secretaries were therefore vital to the smooth running of the national government, and so had to be chosen for their particular skills and experience.[5]

In positioning the cabinet so firmly within the executive branch Wilson had moved from his earlier idea of connecting them to the legislature. Although he recognized that "the Secretaries are in the leading-strings of statutes, and all their duties look towards a strict obedience to Congress," he argued in 1908 that the legislature could not impose close oversight over executive departments. Endless congressional inquiry could "violently disturb, but it cannot often fathom, the waters of the sea in which the bigger fish of the civil service swim and feed." All Congress could do was to ensure that the president's cabinet was composed of competent and honorable men who sought public benefit over political preferment.[6]

With Congress largely out of the picture, Wilson concluded that each president was free to use his cabinet as he saw fit. He could take it fully into his confidence, or not at all; he could allow his secretaries to run their departments with only minimal oversight, or he could control them as delegates operating with clear instructions. "The character of the cabinet may be made a nice index of the theory of the presidential office, as well as of the President's theory of party government; but the one view is, so far as I can see, as constitutional as the other." Each cabinet was as good, as effective, and as useful as each president allowed it to be.[7]

Wilson adopted some, but not all, of these ideas after his election to the presidency. His earlier strictures against cabinet appointments to repay political debts or appease electoral constituencies were early casualties. Even before his election Wilson had agreed that William Jennings Bryan should join the cabinet; his support at Baltimore had been very important and he had won many votes for Wilson during the election campaign. Bryan's inclusion in the cabinet would also assist liaison with congressional Democrats and help keep an old hero of Democratic agrarian radicalism on Wilson's side. Despite his inexperience in foreign affairs, Bryan was offered State because it was the most senior position in the cabinet and the Great Commoner would have accepted nothing less. His selection was a perfect example of the politics of cabinet appointment, but it was a far cry from Wilson's earlier belief that only the best and the brightest should be in charge of departments that reflected their expertise.

Rather than selecting the rest of his cabinet himself, Wilson entrusted the job to his new friend and advisor Edward House. Wilson had already offered House any cabinet post except State, but the Texan declined in favor of an informal advisory role. He proposed a cabinet that reflected a broad range of Democratic Party opinion that was loyal to Wilson and friendly to House; five of the ten secretaries were southerners and two more came from west of the Mississippi. Wilson accepted most of House's recommendations, including McAdoo for Treasury,

William Redfield for Commerce, Albert Burleson for Postmaster General, Josephus Daniels for Navy, David F. Houston for Agriculture, and William B. Wilson for Labor.[8]

Wilson did add his preferences for specific cabinet posts, but they were not always practicable. For Interior he wanted Newton Baker, but after Baker decided to stay in Cleveland he accepted House's recommendation of Franklin Lane. For attorney general Wilson preferred Louis Brandeis, but was persuaded by House to appoint James C. McReynolds, a much less controversial figure who had been Theodore Roosevelt's assistant attorney general. A. Mitchell Palmer, who later served as attorney general, was offered the Department of War but declined because he was a Quaker; three days before his inauguration Wilson asked Joe Tumulty to find a replacement. Tumulty suggested Lindley Garrison, whom he had known in New Jersey. Garrison was summoned to Washington, introduced to Wilson, and, according to McAdoo, "a place in the Cabinet descended upon him like manna from heaven."[9]

Once in place, Wilson's cabinet learned quickly about his way of conducting its meetings. As he had earlier predicted, Wilson saw that "the character of the cabinet may be made a nice index of the theory of the presidential office." In his case the cabinet was not an executive body but rather a loose collection of his delegates. He did not hold regularly scheduled cabinet meetings and held fewer than most of his predecessors and all of his successors. This was especially so during Wilson's second term, when the pressures of war, his trips to Europe, and then his illness made full cabinet meetings rare. Throughout his presidency Wilson preferred to deal with his cabinet secretaries individually rather than collectively, and over specific issues without formal agendas for general discussion.[10]

Wilson's departmental heads responded in kind. Because they each owed their jobs to Wilson, and because Wilson preferred to discuss important matters in private conferences rather than in open debate, his cabinet shared little esprit de corps. "[They] do not seem to have the habit of frankness with one another," Walter Hines Page noted in September 1916. "Each lives and works in a water-tight compartment." When Josephus Daniels suggested to Secretary of War Garrison that they should work together to improve coordination between the army and the navy, Garrison would have none of it. "I don't care a damn about the Navy and you don't care a damn about the Army. You run your machine and I'll run mine." Wilson seemed to encourage such attitudes. Commerce Secretary Redfield remembered being upbraided for continuing a discussion with McAdoo after a cabinet meeting had finished. "President Wilson came and asked if we were talking business and said the business meeting had adjourned and it was no longer in order to discuss business."[11]

As a result Wilson's cabinet meetings were seldom forums for serious debate. Secretary Bryan spoke frequently, but rarely on point. Wilson, mindful of Bryan's political value to his administration, treated his secretary of state with great courtesy and put up with his ineptitude in foreign policy until the stakes grew too high after the sinking of the *Lusitania* in May 1915. Although he was able and hardworking, Secretary of War Garrison spoke so much that he won the nickname of "Secretary Garrulous" from McAdoo and increasing irritation from Wilson. Garrison also delighted in goading Bryan, whom he detested. Newton Baker recalled that Bryan and Garrison shared a "capacity for continued discussion after the question was settled" that irritated the president in cabinet meetings.[12]

Wilson found Postmaster General Albert Burleson to be so pompous that he privately called him "the Cardinal," and he found Redfield's frequent contributions to cabinet discussions tiresome. Attorney General McReynolds remained aloof from his colleagues and Wilson. Nor did Wilson warm to Franklin Lane, but he did overlook his failure to keep the cabinet's secrets. Secretary of Commerce Redfield and Secretary of Labor William B. Wilson dwelt on the periphery of Wilson's attention and affection, and both felt slighted by his inattention.[13]

In the cabinet McAdoo was Wilson's most useful secretary but not the most loved. Josephus Daniels seemed to be the president's favorite and was one of four secretaries from Wilson's original cabinet who stayed for the whole of his tenure. Burleson, "Billy" Wilson, and Houston were the other survivors, in Burleson's and Wilson's cases as much because they did no harm and remained steadfastly loyal than because of their closeness to the president. David Houston, the fourth of the survivors, was another of the president's favorites; Wilson respected his secretary of agriculture's intellect and appreciated his sense of humor. When Newton Baker replaced Garrison in March 1916, he too earned the president's affection and respect.[14]

The president often opened cabinet meetings by reciting limericks and snippets of Washington gossip, and then turned discussion to whatever issue was on his mind and which he felt inclined to share. He sought his secretaries' advice on the congressional situation and the state of public opinion, but rarely sought their counsel on tactics and never called for a vote on courses of action. This was in keeping with his habit of weighing advice from many quarters before deciding important matters on his own. The cabinet could be useful in the preliminary stages of this process, but it was neither his only nor his most important source of advice.[15]

Although Wilson now saw his cabinet as mere delegates of his executive powers, the scope of that delegation depended on the department, the times, and the secretary. In departments and issues in which he was not particularly interested, such as Lane's Interior, Wilson's Labor, and Redfield's Commerce, Wilson gave his secretaries wide freedom of action. Wilson expected them to make him aware of any significant issues and policies that they confronted or initiated, but otherwise he was content to leave them to it. In areas in which he was interested, however, Wilson kept a close eye on his secretaries. Early in his presidency he worked with McAdoo to shepherd major banking legislation through Congress, and in 1915 he became increasingly involved in foreign policy and issues arising from the European war. He lost interest in domestic policy, and thus in the work of those secretaries whose departments were not directly affected by the war. Instead, Wilson effectively became his own secretary of state, accepting Bryan's resignation in June 1915 and then closely supervising Robert Lansing.[16]

Wilson's treatment of his cabinet changed during the course of his administrations. Increasingly dependent on House for political advice and grief-stricken by his first wife's death in August 1914, Wilson withdrew from the empty camaraderie of his cabinet meetings. His reserve was deepened by Secretary Lane's tendency to leak its deliberations. Wilson was well aware of Lane's tendency to tell tales outside the cabinet room, but shrank from dismissing him. Instead, he ceased to raise sensitive issues before the full cabinet and increasingly relied on private conferences with his secretaries. The result, according to Lindley Garrison, was that cabinet meetings became "an interesting waste of time," and Wilson confessed to Edward House that he now understood how little interest the people had in the cabinet and that he sympathized with their indifference.[17]

The outbreak of war in August 1914 added to Wilson's increasingly taciturn demeanor toward his cabinet. This became more obvious as the war dragged on. From March 1916, after the sinking of the *Sussex* by a German submarine, senior cabinet members, including McAdoo, Redfield, Burleson, and Houston, argued that war with Germany was not only inevitable but desirable and that it should not be postponed. Wilson refused to be pushed into belligerency and thereafter avoided discussion of foreign policy with his cabinet.[18]

When Wilson did ask his cabinet for its views on February 23 and March 20, 1917, as to how the United States should deal with Germany, he seemed irritated that all but two of its members urged him to declare war. "McAdoo wants war—war to the hilt," House later noted. "He said his appetite for it was so strong that he would like to quit the cabinet, raise a regiment, and go to the front." Wilson replied that he wanted sensible suggestions, not bravado and the "code duello." He did not consult the cabinet again about the international situation, did not inform it of the Zimmerman Telegram and its attempt to excite Mexico into joining the war against the United States, and did not show it an advance copy of his speech to Congress calling for a declaration of war.[19]

Once at war, Wilson further reduced the cabinet's collective role and its meetings became largely inconsequential. Secretary of the Interior Lane complained in March 1918 that the cabinet discussed nothing that "would interest a nation, a family or a child." It spent its meetings "largely in telling stories." The real work was done privately between the president and his senior secretaries, and in the weekly meetings of the war cabinet, made up of the president, the secretaries of treasury, war, and navy and the heads of the War Industries Board, the US Food Administration, and other war agencies.[20]

By excluding those cabinet secretaries whose work was least affected by the war, and by including extra-cabinet agencies, the war cabinet became Wilson's key executive body during the war. Although its discussions were marred by turf disputes between the new agencies and the old departments, and by clashes between McAdoo and Food Administrator Herbert Hoover over railroad and shipping priorities, the war cabinet worked much more effectively than the full cabinet.[21]

After the armistice, between Wilson's two long trips to the Versailles peace conference, and before his stroke in September 1919, the cabinet briefly regained its position as the nation's most important executive council. After Wilson's collapse, however, it met rarely and its members grew more autonomous. Wilson withdrew into the care of his wife, doctor, and secretary, and during the last eighteen months of his presidency he had neither the energy nor the inclination for even the formalities of the "cabinet government" he had once so strongly advocated.

***

When William McAdoo received Wilson's invitation to become secretary of the treasury, his first concern was about money. A cabinet secretary's salary in 1913 was $12,000 a year, less than half McAdoo's average salary at H&M. A 50 percent pay cut was bad enough, but the expenses of life in Washington made it worse. Cabinet members ranked high in Washington's social hierarchy and were expected to live accordingly. McAdoo would have to rent or purchase a large house, employ a retinue of servants, and entertain frequently. He would even have to maintain a carriage, a pair of horses, and a driver dressed in livery. When the costs of his six children were added, McAdoo could expect to spend all his salary, and more, while he served the federal government. Yet the allure of high office was irresistible; he accepted the president's offer, moved his family into a four-storey house in Washington, installed his 18-year-old daughter Nona as the social head of his household, and was confirmed by the Senate on March 5, 1913.[22]

Only twice in the history of the republic has the metaphor of the cabinet as the president's "official family" taken on literal meaning. In 1961 John F. Kennedy

appointed his brother Robert as attorney general, and their partnership in government has been much analyzed. Much less discussed is the earlier instance of family ties in the cabinet between Woodrow Wilson and William McAdoo. In contrast to the Kennedys in 1961, Wilson and McAdoo had no family connection when
McAdoo joined the cabinet. Only in May 1914, when McAdoo married Wilson's
youngest daughter Eleanor, did the two men enter a more personal relationship.
Despite reservations about the couple's difference in age—Mac was 51 and Eleanor
was 25—and his affection for Eleanor's former beau Ben King, Wilson gave his
blessing to their marriage. "The dear little girl is the apple of my eye," he wrote
when the engagement was announced. "No man is good enough for her. But
McAdoo comes as near being so as any man could." From then on he had not only
had a star in cabinet but also a son-in-law.[23]

McAdoo offered to resign from the cabinet, but Wilson would not hear of it.
This was puzzling because of the conflict of interest that they now faced. Their
subordinate-superior relationship would be blurred, in the public's perception at
least, by their new connection, and relations within the cabinet were sure to be
affected by it. In January 1915 the Philadelphia *North American*, no friend to either
McAdoo or Wilson, reported that "McAdoo is feared and deferred to by every other
member of the cabinet, not because he has shown himself to be the strongest man
in cabinet, but because he is the president's son-in-law." His colleagues might best
McAdoo in debate around the cabinet table, but how could they win their arguments with a secretary who could chat with the president over lunch as a member
of his family?[24]

Nine months later the Charleston *News and Courier* provided another example
of the blurring between the political and the personal in an editorial criticizing
McAdoo's proposal for a publicly funded merchant marine. "It is difficult to believe that Mr. McAdoo's father-in-law approves of this plan, and it will be interesting to see whether he possesses a quasi-parental authority sufficient to pry Mr.
McAdoo loose from his obsession." McAdoo complained that "it grieves me that a
problem of such great importance . . . should be approached from the standpoint of
the family relations existing between the President and myself," but both he and
Wilson must have known that such perceptions were neither unforeseeable nor
rare.[25]

Wilson's decision to keep McAdoo in the cabinet also sat uneasily with his professed dislike of nepotism. He refused to appoint his brother Joseph to any paid
position and later criticized House and Lansing for appointing their relatives to
the Peace Commission in 1919. "The truth is that the President feels very strongly
about the appointment of relatives to office," McAdoo told an office-seeking
cousin only two months before he married Eleanor, "and I am sure, from what he

has said to me, that he thinks it unwise that Cabinet officers should appoint theirs."[26]

McAdoo stayed in Wilson's cabinet for five and a half years, but not without flirting with the idea of more lucrative employment. In October 1914 he was offered the presidency of the Metropolitan Life Insurance Company at a salary of $85,000 per year, and rumors that he would return to private life swirled around Washington in 1916. McAdoo declined the Met's offer, but privately declared that he could not afford to stay in the cabinet indefinitely.[27]

Money worries aside, McAdoo quickly asserted himself in Wilson's cabinet as an energetic executive. "McAdoo was a dynamo of energy: no member of Wilson's cabinet was more avaricious of labour than he," Ray Stannard Baker wrote in his biography of Wilson. "If a difficult task appeared anywhere upon the horizon, McAdoo saw it first and . . . demanded eagerly 'Let me do it.'"[28]

As the spearhead of Wilson's administration, McAdoo won praise for his energy and vision. "I rate him very highly," Louis Brandeis declared in 1916. "He is farseeing, courageous, inventive, effective . . . and I do not know of any department of his work in which he has failed to exhibit the qualities of a master." Elihu Root, although a Republican, thought McAdoo the most impressive of Wilson's cabinet secretaries and as uniquely free from "the general paralysis of Wilsonism." Later analysts have agreed, ranking McAdoo as one of the best cabinet secretaries of the first half of the twentieth century.[29]

To colleagues who did not suffer from his insatiable desire for wider fields of action McAdoo was the leading light in the cabinet. Navy Secretary Daniels admired his energy and decisiveness so much that he later became an ardent supporter of his presidential ambitions. In the cabinet the two men exchanged bonhomie and political favors; in 1916 Daniels asked McAdoo to expedite funding for a project in Chapel Hill and in the following year reciprocated by arranging a naval commission for McAdoo's son Huger. Secretary of the Interior Lane felt that McAdoo's vigor needed to be husbanded for the good of the nation. "Please for the sake of all of us take a good rest," he wrote to him in October 1914. "I'm a conservationist & my first concern is to conserve the best Sec'y of the Treasury this country has had since Hamilton."[30]

Others were less impressed. "The truth is," Secretary of Agriculture Houston thought, "McAdoo is a solitaire player . . . He is self-reliant and has dash, boldness, and courage, but he does not cultivate Cabinet team work and does not invite discussion or suggestion from the Cabinet as a whole." While reluctant to seek his colleagues' advice, though, McAdoo frequently tried to invade their turfs. Even his friends despaired of the transparency of his ambition and the ruthlessness of his empire-building. "As a man . . . in spite of his brilliance," Charles Hamlin of

the Federal Reserve Board confided in his diary at the end of 1917, "he was vindictive, rather treacherous, vain conceited & wildly jealous of anyone with him
receiving credit."[31]

Attorney General McReynolds was the first to feel the secretary of the treasury
breathing down his neck. In 1913 he consulted the president about the construction of a new building for the Department of Justice and won approval to draft a
bill for its construction. That bill was introduced into Congress early in 1914, but a
substitute, prepared without McReynolds's knowledge, gave Treasury control over
the project. This, McAdoo told McReynolds, would ensure that it would proceed
with "economy, efficiency and speed." McReynolds was furious. "To say the least,"
he told McAdoo, "the method of your action was objectionable to me." The president had decided that Justice should have carriage of the project, and McAdoo
should butt out. Postmaster General Burleson was asked to mediate between
them, and McReynolds emerged the victor. "I trust both of us can regard the mis-
understanding as at an end," he wrote to McAdoo, "and without power to interfere
with our future cordial relations."[32]

Even Daniels had to beat McAdoo off. In July 1916 McAdoo wrote to Wilson to
seek an Executive Order to assign enforcement of neutrality laws to Treasury rather
than to the Navy. "It is, of course, unnecessary for me to say that the Treasury Department is not looking for new responsibilities, but so far as merchant vessels are
concerned it is clear to my mind that the enforcement of the neutrality laws falls
more naturally and fits more readily into the duties and functions of the Treasury
than any other Department of the Government." Enforcement should be a matter
for the Coast Guard, under McAdoo's control, rather than for Daniels's Navy. The
North Carolinian begged to differ, forcing Wilson to mediate a compromise.[33]

McAdoo's most bruising battles were with Secretary of Commerce William
Redfield. Their departments shared authority over a number of "twilight zones,"
as Newton Baker called them, including navigation regulations and customs clearances. McAdoo wanted to consolidate these in his department, but Redfield was
strongly opposed. In March 1914 McAdoo fired the first shot in a long battle when
he demanded control over anchorages used by interstate and international shipping. These were under Commerce's control, but McAdoo argued that they belonged in Treasury because they were enforced by its revenue cutters. Redfield
acceded, but not without protest.[34]

More serious disputes broke out between the two men after the declaration of
war against Germany. Redfield was mortified by McAdoo's usurpation of a life insurance scheme for US military personnel; he insisted that Commerce had originated the idea, but that McAdoo had persuaded Wilson to approve Treasury's rival
plan. McAdoo pleaded ignorance of Commerce's scheme and claimed paternity

of the whole idea, but Redfield was unconvinced. Their dispute was complicated by the fact that Newton Baker's Department of War, in concert with American Federation of Labor (AFL) President Samuel Gompers, had devised its own war risk insurance scheme and had drafted legislation to enact it.[35]

McAdoo argued that war risk insurance was "a matter of finance" and so belonged in his department; Redfield contended that it lay in Commerce's domain, and Baker pointed to the benefits of attaching soldiers' insurance policies to their records held by the War Department. "I cannot go forward with satisfaction or success," McAdoo told Wilson, "unless I am permitted to have direction of the matter." The president sided with McAdoo, leaving Redfield and Baker fuming on the sidelines. "Oh Mr. Secretary!" Gompers complained to Baker. "McAdoo is stealing my baby."[36]

In April 1917 McAdoo moved in another direction against Redfield by suggesting to Wilson that the new Shipping Board be placed in Treasury. Wilson declined, and considered putting it under Commerce instead. McAdoo shot back a letter suggesting that the postmaster general or the secretary of labor would be better guardians of the Shipping Board. "Either of these men would be very helpful—more so than the Secretary of Commerce under existing conditions."[37]

McAdoo and Redfield clashed again over customs clearances for international shipping. Under prewar legislation these were the responsibility of the Department of Commerce, but an Executive Order in August 1914 transferred them to the Coast Guard, under Treasury's control. US entry into the war, however, automatically transferred the Coast Guard from Treasury to Navy and the Trading with the Enemy Act returned customs clearances to Commerce. McAdoo lobbied Congress behind Redfield's back to return them to Treasury and told him in a testy exchange of letters that he needed to maintain control over all international trade for the duration of the war to avoid "confusion, harm and friction." By then relations between the two men had become poisonous; Redfield considered resigning and McAdoo described Redfield as "a slow-witted person with very little initiative or energy."[38]

Reports of tensions between Redfield and McAdoo appeared in the press and became the subject of Washington gossip. Years later "Uncle Henry" in *Collier's* recalled that McAdoo had the rest of Wilson's cabinet on constant alert "an' nobody dared to put anything outside the window to cool." Lansing took all his possessions home at night for fear of McAdoo stealing them; Redfield refused to leave his office to prevent him from moving in, "Lane never went to bed without takin' in the national parks an' Daniels kept the navy under lock an' key . . . and even Woodrow had to set spring guns around the executive offices, an' put up 'No Trespass' signs."[39]

Inside the administration there was less levity about McAdoo's covetousness. Some suspected that his attempt to control customs clearances was part of a plan to control gold exports and thus exercise influence over the banking system. Even in 1917 rumors were rife that McAdoo wanted the presidential nomination in 1920, and that his control of war risk insurance aimed to curry favor with the new legions of American soldiers. At the height of the McAdoo-Redfield dispute Edward House confided in his diary that McAdoo was beginning to irritate Wilson by his empire-building. McAdoo wanted customs clearances, war risk insurance, control over the Embargo Board, the Shipping Board, the Purchasing Board, and even to see all the foreign dispatches of the State Department. "When you sum up, it means he would be in complete control of the Government." [40]

With a war to fight, Wilson had little patience for interdepartmental squabbles. He backed Redfield over customs clearances and gold export licenses and ordered McAdoo to cooperate with Commerce's jurisdiction over them. McAdoo acceded gracelessly, complaining that Redfield was "standing so much on his technical rights" that he was impeding the war effort. He also complained to House that Wilson was making his job impossible by not telling him "what is in his mind," and by appeasing those cabinet members who felt threatened by McAdoo's executive abilities and ambitions. This was because of his status as Wilson's son-in-law; "he thinks it is embarrassing to the President to decide in his favor, because there is always a latent suspicion that family relationship has something to do with it." [41]

Wilson had indeed grown weary of McAdoo's grandstanding. In May 1918 he complained that McAdoo "had gotten so arbitrary that he presumed that, sooner or later, it would have to come to a crisis between them." McAdoo had drawn up important income tax legislation without consulting him, and now had objected to a coal price agreement that would add significantly to the railroads' operating costs. "Son-in-law or no son-in-law, if he wants to resign he can do so." [42]

Wilson may have sometimes wished to be rid of McAdoo, but he was not yet ready to demand his resignation. Certainly McAdoo was abrasive, but his appetite for work and executive ability made him a vital member of the administration. Yet with each accretion to his power McAdoo grew more eager to expand his domain. At the end of 1916 he privately criticized Wilson for becoming so engrossed in foreign policy that he had lost track of the work in many of his departments. He needed to revamp his cabinet by firing its weaker members; he had lost his "punch" and had allowed his administration to drift. Tired of being overruled through Wilson's aversion to conflict within the cabinet, McAdoo felt frustrated by his distant and distracted executive style. [43]

Wilson's exasperation with McAdoo burned on a slow fuse, but it increased steadily between 1915 and 1918. He grew tired of his son-in-law's tendency not only to intrude into other cabinet members' portfolios but also to give him gratuitous advice. Problems caused by McAdoo within the cabinet over jurisdictional boundaries were bad enough, but the president found his son-in-law's incursions into foreign policy even more galling. "Yesterday," he wrote to his bride-to-be Edith in June 1915, "a talk with Mac in which he benevolently and with the best intentions sought to render assistance in Mexican and other foreign matters which are none of his business." The secretary of the treasury had assumed unofficial leadership of the cabinet's belligerent group after the sinking of the *Lusitania* in May 1915, and had spoken frequently of the need to declare war against Germany sooner rather than later. Wilson, desperate to keep his options open, resented McAdoo's advice. "That was a terribly confident opinion you fired at me the other day," Wilson told him during the *Lusitania* crisis. "I wish the matter looked as simple as that to me."[44]

McAdoo continued to argue the case against Germany throughout 1916 and with great fervor during the final crisis at the beginning of 1917. His insistence in the cabinet that Wilson should arm US merchant vessels without waiting for congressional approval earned him a rebuke. Appearing "somewhat nettled" by McAdoo's insistence, Wilson reminded him that they both worked within a government of laws. Congress had the power to declare war and Wilson would "do nothing which savored of dictatorship."[45] By then he knew that McAdoo would have to be watched carefully, but in April 1917 there was a war to win and McAdoo's virtues still outweighed his faults.

❖❖❖

When Newton Baker joined the cabinet in March 1916 he learned quickly about his colleagues' strengths and weaknesses. Apart from the president, he thought, David Houston had the best intellect in the cabinet. William Wilson was "kindly, canny and sagacious," and Attorney General Gregory "made upon me the most favorable impression from the fineness of his character and the loyalty and devotion of his public service. I made no friend in Washington whom I value more highly." Albert Burleson, the postmaster general, was "a good, frank and grim old war horse who spoke his mind for what it was worth." Burleson had no great intellect, but his devotion to Wilson was boundless and he took his ribbing as "the Cardinal" in good spirit. Secretary Redfield was a "fine fellow," but was "too much of a fuss-budget."[46]

Soon after he arrived in Washington, Baker worried that he would be blamed for a leak concerning the Department of War. Burleson reassured him that there was no need for concern because the president knew all about Secretary Lane's propensity to "sit and 'gas' at lunch." Baker later observed that "the truth about Lane is that he was moody, ambitious and very cock-sure part of the time and very

cock-unsure part of the time!" No such criticism could be leveled at William
McAdoo, who had "the greatest lust for power I ever saw." Baker soon divined that
"there was some jealousy of him in the Cabinet because of his tendency to exercise wide power and encroach in domains not his own." Some of those domains
were Baker's, and the two men spent their time in the cabinet as uneasy colleagues,
with Baker trying, not always successfully, to resist McAdoo's incursions into his
territory.[47]

The war spawned a multitude of government powers and agencies, and McAdoo
seemed to lay claim to them all. First it was the war risk insurance scheme, and
then Baker and McAdoo clashed over the best way to coordinate the purchase of
military and civilian materiels. McAdoo argued that it should be under the control
of one person—he had his friend Bernard Baruch in mind—who was independent
of the military bureaucracy. Baker demurred, arguing that the Council of National
Defense (CND), which he chaired, already coordinated military purchases. He
won that round when Wilson appointed a War Industries Board (WIB) under the
Department of War rather than a single and independent purchasing czar. The
same issue flared up in January 1918, when McAdoo persuaded the president,
against Baker's protests, to appoint Baruch as chairman of the WIB with independent powers.[48]

McAdoo and Baker continued to bicker over wartime agencies and departmental
jurisdiction. McAdoo complained that draft boards in New York had been hijacked
by Republicans who exempted their sons and drafted their Democratic opponents.
Baker promised to watch for any signs of such behavior, but declined to appoint
McAdoo's friends to draft boards in the Empire State. In November 1917 McAdoo
responded to press reports that the CND was considering regulating the flow of capital to wartime industries. This issue was "peculiarly financial," he told Baker, and "if
such a policy should be adopted, the Treasury would be compelled to shoulder the
load." The CND and the Department of War should therefore back off. Baker replied coolly, denying that neither the CND nor the WIB had any such plans.[49]

By then Baker had seen enough of McAdoo's power grabs to discern their motivations. He thought that McAdoo genuinely believed that Wilson wanted him to
range widely across the war effort, exercising his executive ability on tasks regardless of their departmental boundaries. Convinced that he was the most effective
member of the cabinet, McAdoo felt justified in riding roughshod over his colleagues' realms and sensitivities. "He lived throughout his Washington experience
under the strange illusion that he was personally doing everything significant done
there." Baker's own relations with McAdoo were cordial, "but some of my Cabinet
associates literally wept on my shoulder at his encroachments on their authority
and responsibilities."[50]

Baker also noted McAdoo's "queer penchant for having his name on everything." During the war "everyone was expected to be self-effacing, and the spreading of 'William Gibbs McAdoo' on . . . all sorts of printed matter seemed to offend the public sense." In 1918 Arthur Guiterman parodied McAdoo's propensity for self-promotion:

> The Who, preeminently Who,
> Is William Gibbs McAdoo.
> (Whom I should like to hail but daren't
> As Royal Prince and Heir apparent.)
> A Man of high intrinsic Worth,
> The Greatest Son-in-Law on Earth—
> With all the burdens thence accruing,
> He's always up and McAdooing.
> From Sun to Star and Star to Sun,
> His work is never McAdone.
> He regulates our Circumstances,
> Our Buildings, Industries, Finances,
> And Railways, while the wires buzz
> To tell us what he McAdoes . . .
> I don't believe he ever hid
> A single thing he McAdid!

For his part McAdoo told Edward House in May 1918 that Baker had too much influence over Wilson and that "Baker [was] antagonistic to him." Four months later he thought that Baker was "of the Wilson type, neither of them, in his opinion, having much executive ability."[51]

Baker's closest relationship in the cabinet was with Secretary of the Navy Daniels. They had first met at the Baltimore convention in 1912, and had exchanged friendly correspondence while Daniels was secretary of the navy and Baker was mayor of Cleveland. Only minutes after McAdoo called to relay the president's invitation to join the cabinet, Baker wrote to Daniels that "I shall have to rely on your experience and wisdom for help at every point, but I know already how generous you are."[52]

In the cabinet the two men did indeed work closely together. Baker had none of Garrison's hostility to interservice cooperation, and the coming of war in April 1917 made harmonious relations and close coordination with the navy essential. Baker ensured that the Marines were an integral part of the American Expeditionary Forces (AEF) in Europe, and the two secretaries worked to ensure that their departments did not bid against each other for scarce materiel such as steel plate, gunpowder, and cotton. They exchanged a steady stream of correspondence and met frequently to resolve issues arising from their conduct of the war effort. In keeping with the personalized politics of the day, much of that correspondence revolved around favors given and received. Daniels seemed to do more asking than Baker, but the secretary of war complied even beyond the limits of propriety. In February 1917, for example, he extended a furlough granted to a soldier who was an employee at the Raleigh *News and Observer*, which Daniels owned. The man had a sick father at home, and was a valued employee who brought much revenue to Daniels's newspaper.[53]

"[Baker] and I were yoke fellows in everything and stimulated the perfect working together of the Army and Navy," Daniels recalled, "which made them invincible in the World War." Despite a divergence in their views after the war—Daniels was a strong supporter of McAdoo's presidential aspirations in the 1920s and of Franklin Roosevelt's New Deal in the 1930s—the two men exchanged frequent and affectionate correspondence for the rest of Baker's life. "Read and return," Daniels annotated a letter in December 1934. "Baker's friendship is very dear to me."[54]

Baker's most important political relationship during his years in the cabinet, naturally enough, was with Woodrow Wilson. Baker believed that Daniels and House enjoyed closer personal relations with the president, but there is no doubting the bond that he and Wilson developed. They shared much in their southern origins, scholarly interests, and political views. "[Secretary Baker] is one of the most genuine and gifted men that I know," Wilson told a correspondent in May 1916, and at about the same time he told his future biographer Ray Stannard Baker that "I am delighted with your namesake in the cabinet. It is a comfort to have him with me." The new secretary of war "had a trained mind: an administrative mind & his experience as Mayor of Cleveland . . . made him especially useful." Wilson believed then that Baker had already proved himself superior to Lindley Garrison. "Garrison was intensely argumentative. He wore me out with argument. When he met a fact, instead of accepting it . . . he wanted to argue about it indefinitely. Baker accepts it, makes room for it & goes ahead."[55]

As a professor Wilson had argued that cabinet members should be chosen on the basis of expertise rather than political expediency, but as president he applied this precept only selectively. It was clear that McAdoo was suited to Treasury because of his experience as a financier, but Baker had no obvious qualifications to be secretary of war and in fact had great liabilities because of his pacifist associations. Undeterred, Wilson offered Baker the job in March 1916 because he wanted him in the cabinet, Baker was available, and War was the only vacancy.[56]

With his re-election won and war imminent, Wilson reconsidered his cabinet. Baker, following custom, offered his resignation after the 1916 election, but Wilson brushed it aside. "Suffice it to say," he wrote in November 1916, "that I should deem myself an unfaithful servant of the nation if I permitted you to leave an office in which you have rendered such admirable service." Edward House, who never thought as highly of Baker, suggested to Wilson in March 1917 that "he had taken a gamble that there would be no war and had lost," and that he now needed to find "better timber than was generally thought to be in the War and Navy Departments." House suggested that Baker become ambassador to Britain, but Wilson seemed more taken with the idea that he should replace Robert Lansing as secretary of state. He decided to leave Baker, Daniels, and Lansing in their places, postponing rather than rejecting the idea that Baker was qualified for State. So highly did Wilson rate Baker's diplomatic skills that at the end of the war he planned to include him in the delegation to the Versailles peace conference, but McAdoo's resignation forced him to keep Baker at home.[57]

Baker reciprocated Wilson's admiration in spades. He identified so closely with the president that William McCombs dubbed him the "lickspittle of the White House," and reported that "Baker never made a move without Wilson's direction." In fact Baker told General James Harbord in 1929 that "I think the world and you would be very much surprised if you could realize how completely President Wilson let me run the War Department without ever an order, and with only the rarest suggestions, from him." He had consulted Wilson on only three major issues—his refusal to send Theodore Roosevelt to war, his decision to deny General Leonard Wood a battlefield command, and his selection of John J. Pershing as commander of the AEF—and in all three instances Wilson had happily concurred.[58]

Despite enormous political pressure to do so, Wilson never interfered with Baker's decisions on promotion of officers or enforcement of military discipline. They shared a distaste for capital punishment and agreed that it should be imposed only when soldiers had been convicted of offenses carrying the death penalty under civilian law. The two men, in Baker's memory, disagreed only once over a major issue when Wilson decided in 1918 to send a military expedition to Russia.[59]

In the cabinet Baker was discreet and intensely loyal to Wilson. "I think I knew his mind completely and entirely," he remembered in 1937, "not only from what he said to me but because I had come to have a very sensitive appreciation of the way his mind worked." Where McAdoo was shameless in pushing himself forward in the cabinet, Baker won Wilson's gratitude for his graceful acquiescence over the war risk insurance scheme and then over federal control of the railroads. Baker sensed Wilson's dislike of conflict and acted as his spear carrier when there were disagreements between cabinet members to resolve. In 1917, for example, Franklin Lane took it upon himself to set a price for coal. Lane's price was too high, and Wilson decided to repudiate his decision. Fearing that a presidential rebuke would result in Lane's resignation, Baker offered to renounce the deal himself as chairman of the CND, of which Lane was a member. Wilson agreed and Baker cancelled Lane's deal. The secretary of the interior felt deeply aggrieved but remained in the cabinet.[60]

As relations with Germany worsened, Baker remained supportive of the president's policy of exploring all avenues of peaceful settlement. He did not join the cabinet belligerents, led by McAdoo, until the very last. Had Germany not resumed unrestricted submarine warfare in January 1917, Baker thought, Wilson would not have declared war. Regardless of the "code duello" of his hot-blooded son-in-law, Wilson remained committed until the middle of March 1917 to neutrality and to brokering peace between the combatants. Baker agreed with this and worked to calm more excitable voices both within and outside the cabinet room. When Baker did decide that war was inevitable, and told the cabinet on March 23, his colleagues correctly assumed that Wilson had come to the same conclusion.[61]

Unlike McAdoo, Baker stayed in the cabinet until the end of Wilson's second term. The two years and four months that separated the Armistice from Inauguration Day in 1921 were grim times for the Wilson administration. The president's long periods at Versailles, the Senate's refusal to ratify the resulting treaty, and Wilson's illness reduced his administration to a shambles. Secretary Houston bumped into Baker a week after the president's collapse in September 1919. "I am scared literally to death," Baker told him, and "he looked it." Reliant only on press reports and occasional statements from the president's doctor, Baker recalled in 1926 that "the cabinet was in a helpless position . . . It was thoroughly bad that [it] was kept so much in the dark."[62]

At first Baker underestimated the gravity of Wilson's illness. "He will need rest to get back to his old self," he wrote to the president's wife Edith at the end of September 1919. Wilson needed much more than rest, but Baker parroted the official line that the president was mentally alert and steadily regaining his strength. In October 1919, a month after Wilson's catastrophic stroke, Baker assured former Army Chief of Staff Tasker Bliss that the president was "quite his old self as far as clearness of mind and decision of will are concerned." He was unable to see Wilson until the end of November, and then only briefly, and was not permitted to see him again for another two months. "I hear that his progress is steady but slow," he told House in January 1920, "so it will be a long time before we can feel his full hand at the helm."[63]

A government without its head cannot operate coherently, but its limbs can continue to thrash around. There were so many pressing issues bearing down on the cabinet—demobilization of the armed forces, winding down production programs, returning the railroads to their owners, making a postwar economic settlement with the Allies, quelling industrial unrest, and dealing with rampant Republican majorities in both houses of Congress—that the pressures on it were overwhelming. At first no cabinet member was permitted to see the president, or even to send messages to him. Once Wilson's condition had stabilized Baker and his colleagues sent documents to his sickbed for his signature, but they received no directions from him. Baker's experiences were typical; he sent the president occasional memoranda that were returned with terse indications of agreement or disapproval, but otherwise he operated without guidance from the White House.[64]

The president's bedside administration—Edith Wilson, Cary Grayson, and Joseph Tumulty—was now in charge, and would remain so for the remainder of his presidency. When Wilson did meet his official cabinet, he was uninterested in conducting prolonged or substantive meetings.[65]

Members of the cabinet therefore had to fend for themselves, making such decisions as they could, conferring with each other on matters requiring joint action, and trying to get time with Wilson to discuss issues that needed his consideration and approval. Baker and Daniels continued to work closely together, coordinating the repatriation and demobilization of soldiers, sailors, and marines, unwinding procurement contracts, dismantling training camps, and mothballing warships. Some secretaries took advantage of their autonomy. Attorney General Palmer authorized on his own initiative a campaign against communist sympathizers and labor activists. His "Red Scare," featuring mass deportations, arrests without warrant, and police brutality, further unsettled the nation and divided the cabinet.

Robert Lansing, the cabinet's most senior secretary, grew impatient with the silence from the White House. On October 6, 1919, with Baker's support, he called a cabinet meeting to discuss the situation. Summoned to describe the state of the president's health, Grayson described Wilson's condition as "encouraging," but added that he needed rest and should be disturbed only for matters of the greatest urgency. Wilson's body was weak, Grayson warned, but his mind was "clear and very active"—and he was livid at Lansing for calling the meeting without his permission. "From time to time thereafter," Baker recalled, "we assembled in the cabinet room, discussed matters which we thought ought to be brought to the President's attention, transmitted them to him through Dr. Grayson and received messages back from the President." Despite rumors to the contrary, Baker denied that the cabinet ever discussed whether Vice President Thomas Marshall should be asked to assume the presidency.[66]

Calling that meeting cost Lansing his job, and it was rumored that Baker also offered to resign when he realized how angry Wilson was about it. Baker neither confirmed nor denied those rumors, but maintained that the meeting was held only to facilitate the business of government while the president was incapacitated.

The president had other reasons to dismiss Lansing, who had made no secret of his dismay at Wilson's monomania on the League of Nations, and to spare Baker, whose work as secretary of war had met with consistent presidential approval. Despite his earlier belief that Baker would make an excellent secretary of state, however, Wilson appointed the undistinguished Bainbridge Colby to replace Lansing. Edward House, by then exiled from the White House, thought that Baker had been "shelved" by the bedroom government because of his role in the Lansing cabinet meeting.[67]

"The final moments of the Cabinet on Tuesday," Wilson's secretaries wrote in a letter to him on March 3, 1921, "found us quite unable to express the poignant feelings with which we realized that the hour of leave-taking and official dispersal had arrived." The poignancy of the moment was real, and much deeper than would ordinarily be expected at the end of a presidential term. In 1921 Wilson was an invalid, unwilling or unable to communicate effectively with his cabinet, his party, or his nation. Wilsonianism had been repudiated, first by the voters in the 1918 congressional elections, then by the Senate in its rejection of the League of Nations, and finally by the nation in Warren Harding's landslide election to the presidency in November 1920. Wilson's administration had publicly and painfully imploded since September 1919, and all of his cabinet greeted their return to private life with relief.[68]

McAdoo and Baker viewed Inauguration Day in 1921 from different vantage points. By then McAdoo was long gone from cabinet, having resigned at the end of 1918, and was establishing himself as a lawyer and aspirant for the 1924 presidential nomination. Despite his position as the president's son-in-law, McAdoo would never again be close to Wilson. Ill and bitter, Wilson valued loyalty above all other qualities, and by then he thought that McAdoo had failed that test.

In spite of rumors that Baker and Wilson had fallen out over Lansing's cabinet meeting, relations between them remained warm. Certainly Baker remained loyal, and he dedicated his political energies after March 1921 to the realization of Wilson's dream of US membership in the League of Nations. "You will understand," he wrote to Wilson as he left office, "the happiness with which I record the exaltation with which I have seen you remake the moral relations of nations and lead America, like a little child, to the altar of right." McAdoo had begun the Wilson years as the star of the cabinet, but Baker ended them as Wilson's political and spiritual heir.[69]

Holing through the first Hudson River Tunnel. William McAdoo (*center*),
Chief Engineer Charles Jacobs (*to McAdoo's right*) and gentlemen
of the press, March 12, 1904.
McAdoo MSS, Container 322, File: "Jan. 2, 1926."

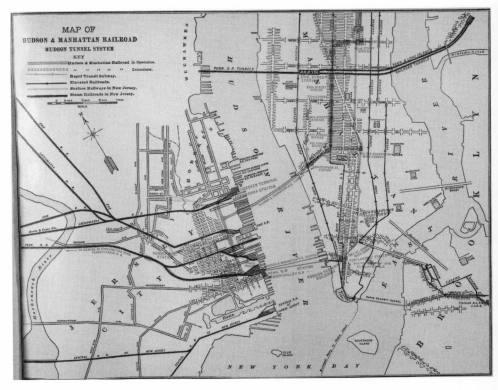

Map of the Hudson and Manhattan Railroad system, December 31, 1912.
From the Fourth Annual Report of the Hudson and Manhattan Railroad Company,
Year ended December 31, 1912.

Annual report of Hudson & Manhattan Railroad Company New York, N.Y.: Hudson and Manhattan
Railroad Company Electronic reproduction. 1910–1950. New York, N.Y.: Columbia University Libraries,
2008. JPEG use copy available via the World Wide Web. Master service copy stored locally on [9]
DVDs#: Hudson and Manhattan Railroad Company 01-09. Archival raw master images stored
locally on DVDs named: Hudson and Manhattan Railroad Company. Columbia
University Libraries Electronic Books. 2006. Thomas J. Watson Library
of Business and Economics, Columbia University in the City of New York.

Newton D. Baker, secretary of war.
Undated and uncaptioned photograph, LC USZ62-26506, Library of Congress
Prints and Photographs Division, Biographical File: "Baker, Newton Diehl."

Jay N. "Ding" Darling Cartoon, "Picture of William G. McAdoo
Going to Work in the Morning," March 13, 1918
Courtesy of the Jay N. "Ding" Darling Wildlife Society.

From left to right, front row: Addie Daniels, Secretary of Navy Josephus Daniels, Secretary of War Newton Baker, Eleanor Wilson McAdoo, and Secretary of Treasury William McAdoo, Liberty Loan meeting on the Ellipse, c. 1917.
Papers of the Wilson-McAdoo Family, Library of Congress Manuscript Division, Box 16, File: "Wilson Family Clippings—William G. McAdoo, Biographical Articles, 16-5."

Inscribed photograph: "To Hon. W.G. McAdoo, "With Happy Recollections
of Great Years Together, Newton D. Baker, February 3, 1921."
McAdoo MSS, Container 645.

From left to right: Betty Baker (*seated*); in the painting, *clockwise from bottom left*, Bess, Betty, Jack, and Peggy Baker; artist Seymour Stone (*right of painting*); May 17, 1920.
Library of Congress Prints and Photographs Collection, Biographical File:
"Baker, Newton Diehl Family."

Mac, Eleanor, Ellen, and Faith, c. 1924.
Papers of the Wilson-McAdoo Family, Library of Congress Manuscript Division, Container 8,
File: "Photographs, 1924 and undated." Provenance unknown.

Clifford Berryman cartoon, "Oh, How I wish Woodrow had never given him that thing!" *Washington Star*, January 19, 1932.
Baker MSS, Hayes-Baker Correspondence, Container 264, File: "Jan–Feb, 1932."

King maker at last: William Gibbs McAdoo after announcing California's shift to FDR at the 1932 Democratic National Convention. Jim Farley is to McAdoo's immediate left.

Undated and uncaptioned photograph, provenance unknown: McAdoo MSS, Container 646.

CHAPTER 6

Secretaries at Peace

When William McAdoo became secretary of the treasury in March 1913 he knew little about his new department. "I resolved that . . . my hand would be on the steering-wheel—that is, as soon as I could find out where the steering-wheel was." At first he lived alone in a Washington hotel while his younger children stayed at home in Irvington-on-Hudson. In October 1913 Nona, Sally, and their father set up house at 1709 Massachusetts Avenue, only a short walk from the Treasury Building.[1]

McAdoo's first task was to select his executive assistants. He appointed Byron Newton, a journalist who had served as publicity chief during Wilson's presidential campaign, as his private secretary. When Newton was promoted to assistant secretary of the treasury in August 1913, his place was taken by George Cooksey, another former newspaperman. McAdoo chose John Skelton Williams as assistant secretary in charge of the fiscal bureaus and Charles S. Hamlin as assistant secretary in charge of customs. Williams and Hamlin became McAdoo's closest advisors, and were rewarded with major promotions in 1914: Williams to comptroller of the currency and Hamlin to governor of the new Federal Reserve Board (FRB).[2]

Byron Newton kept a diary during his first months as McAdoo's private secretary, and recorded the deluge of patronage requests that threatened to overwhelm him. From the moment they took office McAdoo and Newton were besieged by job applicants. McAdoo announced that he would receive no job seekers personally and that all applications should be made in writing, but still they came. "The hungry throng continued to march into my room," Newton recalled, "beginning at nine in the morning and remaining there until I left, oftentimes in a state of utter exhaustion at nine or later at night. It was a constant strain of resistance,

holding back, combating, explaining, directing, appealing, refusing, all day long."
"By Jove, the demands for positions in the Treasury Department will yet put me in
the lunatic asylum," McAdoo told Josephus Daniels in November 1913. "If a man
could only devote his time to the big questions of vital moment to the country,
instead of spending at least two-thirds of it as I do on patronage matters . . . it
would not be so difficult."[3]

Patronage might have been onerous, but it was also vital to early twentieth-
century politics. Although civil service reform had reduced the number of political appointments in the federal bureaucracy, growth in governmental agencies
after 1900 meant that there were still thousands of jobs to be filled when a new
administration took office. This was particularly so when there was a change in
party control of the executive. When Wilson won the White House in 1912, the
Democrats had been out of power for sixteen years, and there were thousands of
GOP appointees to replace with those whom William Jennings Bryan called "deserving Democrats." Albert Burleson's Postmaster General's Department was the
engine room of federal patronage, but McAdoo's Treasury, with its customs collec-
tors, tax assessors, clerks, laborers, and messengers, also had thousands of jobs to
dispense. There were also promotions and demotions to make to reward Democrats, punish Republicans, repay political debts, and satisfy political grudges.[4]

Patronage politics were personal and intricate. Departments' salary budgets
had to be carefully balanced, and so for every beneficiary a victim had to be found.
When McAdoo gave John McTeer, a bookkeeping clerk, a pay raise of $200 per
year another employee had to suffer an equal reduction. Charles Miller, a 70-year-old
clerk, was selected to bear the loss because he was "among the least efficient of the
aged employees in his office." No reason was given for McTeer's good fortune
other than that McAdoo wished it to be so. Despite his exasperation with the minute details and oppressive volume of patronage, he played the game with vigor and
assured party leaders that "so far as my Department is concerned, we are supplant-
ing Republicans with Democrats as rapidly as we can."[5]

As a dispenser of federal patronage and transplanted southerner, McAdoo came
under pressure from southern Democrats eager to reclaim the spoils of office
and to reassert white supremacy. "The solidarity of the Democracy of Georgia
and the entire South," the Brunswick, Georgia Board of Trade declared, "results
from a determined opposition of our people to any semblance of negro domination.
We feel that our support of Democracy entitles us to protection from such wanton
disregard for our wishes." McAdoo usually acceded to such demands and placed
African Americans only in posts that "the negroes had come to regard . . . as being
a distinct recognition of their race." Even in the North, far from segregation and
disfranchisement laws, he appointed African Americans only to positions that had

traditionally been filled by them or to areas with a black constituency that could reward patronage favors.[6]

Patronage also enabled McAdoo to build his own power base. This was particularly so in New York, his adopted home and springboard for his future political ambitions. New York was also home to Treasury's richest patronage plums; the collector of the Port of New York, the nation's best paid political position, was responsible for four thousand jobs. From the outset McAdoo used patronage to punish his enemies and reward his friends. At first he focused on his enemies, and especially Tammany Hall, which had opposed Wilson's nomination in 1912 and threatened to block McAdoo's own political plans. Determined to create a Democratic organization in New York that was independent of Tammany, loyal to Wilson, and beholden to himself, McAdoo tried to persuade Wilson to appoint his friend Frank Polk to the collectorship. McAdoo's scheme was stymied by James O'Gorman, the Democratic senator from New York, who was close to Tammany. Wilson eventually appointed Frank Purroy Mitchel, an independent anti-Tammany candidate. McAdoo's machinations seemed to Wilson to be self-serving and were an early sign that his secretary of the treasury needed to be watched as well as admired.[7]

Wilson's wariness was echoed in January 1916 by *The New York Times*, which alleged that McAdoo had installed a niece, a cousin, a nephew, and the husband of his housekeeper to jobs in New York. His defense rested more on technicality than principle; his alleged cousin was merely a family friend, his "nephew" was no relation at all, and the husband of his "housekeeper" was actually the husband of his cook. McAdoo did admit to appointing his niece because "she is one of the brightest and most capable women I know . . . Why shouldn't I approve the appointment of people whom I personally know to be fit for the position? Isn't that one of my duties?"[8]

⤞⧓⤝

McAdoo also courted controversy through his attitude to racial segregation. Wilson's election brought the first southerner into the White House since Andrew Johnson in 1865, and came soon after the legitimation in 1896 of segregation by the Supreme Court in *Plessy v. Ferguson*. Although in 1912 Wilson had promised African Americans "absolute fair dealing and for everything by which I could assist in advancing the interests of their race," his record was not promising. He had attacked Reconstruction in the South, had supported black disfranchisement during the 1890s, was an advocate of segregation, and had barred African American students from Princeton. Even so, his vague promises were better than Theodore Roosevelt's hostility and William Howard Taft's disdain. W. E. B. Du Bois,

William Monroe Trotter, and Oswald Garrison Villard, chairman of the National Association for the Advancement of Colored People (NAACP), endorsed Wilson, and 100,000 African Americans voted for him. They would soon be bitterly disappointed.[9]

The federal bureaucracy was, officially at least, racially integrated while it was in Republican hands. Black and white employees worked in shared facilities, although their respective numbers, incomes, and promotion prospects were grossly unequal. Upon his election Wilson appointed five southerners—William McAdoo, Albert Burleson, Josephus Daniels, James McReynolds, and David Houston—to his cabinet, and all except Houston were committed segregationalists. Postmaster General Burleson took the lead, telling the cabinet in April 1913 that he would segregate the Railway Mail Service—"it is very unpleasant for [whites] to work in a car with negroes where it is almost impossible to have different drinking vessels and different towels"—and urging his colleagues to follow his example. Wilson noted that he had promised African Americans justice, but not integration, and that his primary goal was to avoid "friction" between the races. His secretaries left the meeting with the president's implicit approval to segregate their departments if they so desired.[10]

McAdoo's attitude to African Americans veered between sentimentality born of childhood memories of loyal ex-slaves and his adult belief in the innate differences between African Americans and whites. Paramount was the need to avoid racial tension by limiting black and white interaction and by privileging white prejudice over African American rights. McAdoo remembered well the violence whipped up by whites' resentment of racial equality, and he supported segregation to maintain harmony when blacks and whites shared physical and social spaces.

McAdoo defended provision of separate restrooms for black employees by noting that this appeased whites who resented close contact with African Americans, "especially when such consideration does not involve the deprivation of the negro of an essential and inherent right—any more, for instance than the provision of separate toilets for the higher officials of [the] department would be a denial of the rights of the ordinary employees." McAdoo remained a segregationalist all his life, remarking in 1929 that "I think it is a dream of the negroes that all barriers to social intercourse and to the intermarriage of the races will disappear in time. I am, of course, strong for the integrity of the white race and I could not be a party to any view, even by implication, that this sort of thing could be justified in any circumstances."[11]

McAdoo's first plan was to make Treasury's Registry Division an all-black bureau, headed by an African American. Under this scheme African Americans would not be hired elsewhere in the department while the Registry Division could be held up as evidence of the administration's willingness to employ black employ-ees. "I know Mr. McAdoo's motive and respect it," Oswald Garrison Villard pro-tested to Woodrow Wilson, "but he does not see that in his well-meant desire to give the colored clerks an opportunity to contrast, as a group, more clearly with the white clerks . . . this division will immediately be called the 'nigger division' and that the precedent thus established will be of the utmost danger to the colored people long after the motive had been forgotten." Villard was too kind; McAdoo's plan was indeed segregation writ large and a ploy to appease whites while seeking political benefit from African Americans. It failed when it became clear that a black registrar could not win confirmation in the Senate.[12]

Foiled in this strategy, McAdoo then quietly allowed his subordinates to segre-gate their bureaus. His chief accomplice was Assistant Secretary John Skelton Wil-liams, a Virginian who, according to his fellow Assistant Secretary Charles Ham-lin, refused to sign letters to African Americans addressed "Dear Sir" or "Dear Madam," and did not allow black employees or visitors to sit down in his presence. Acting as secretary while McAdoo was on vacation in the summer of 1913, Williams ordered the segregation of all work areas, toilets, and dining rooms in the depart-ment. When the director of the Bureau of Printing and Engraving posted "Whites Only" signs on some bathrooms, however, McAdoo insisted that they be removed. Throughout the Treasury African American employees found their workspaces screened off from those of whites, their previously shared restrooms segregated, and their dining facilities divided. When Rosebud Murray, an African American clerk at Printing and Engraving, complained about the segregated dining room, she was dismissed. Segregation was to be imposed with the minimum of fuss—or evidence.[13]

At the end of October 1913 Villard organized a public meeting to express "our unqualified abhorrence and condemnation of such reactionary and un-Democratic practices" in the Treasury. "I am . . . so clear in my own mind as to the terrible dan-gers from the segregation policy and the gross injustice of it all," he told McAdoo, "that I must speak out."McAdoo's reply was revealing, not only of the embarrass-ment underlying his denial that there was a formal policy of segregation in the Treasury Department—Williams's segregation order had by then been quietly countermanded—but also of the segregationalist spirit that animated his own views.[14]

McAdoo denied that there was "a segregation issue" in his department. "It has always been a mischievous exaggeration . . . [If] the colored girls" in Printing and Engraving ate their lunch in the toilets, then that was their choice. He did concede that black and white workspaces had been segregated "to remove causes of com-plaint and irritation where white women have been forced unnecessarily to sit at desks with colored men." Such segregation imparted no stigma on African Americans, but recognized the desires of workers, both white and black, to associate with their own racial groups. "I shall not be a party to the enforced and unwelcome juxtaposition of white and negro employes [sic] when it is unnecessary and avoidable without prejudice to anybody, and when such enforcement would serve only to engender race animosities detrimental to the welfare of both races and injurious to the public service."[15]

The torrent of protest from black leaders and their white supporters embarrassed and irritated Wilson and McAdoo, but it did not change their convictions. When appeals to morality failed, however, political considerations had more impact. Wilson and McAdoo were taken aback by the assertiveness with which African American leaders reminded them of the promises made to them in 1912, and of the electoral support they had received in return. Wilson was so affronted by Trotter's protests—"We are not here as wards. We are not here as dependents . . . We are here as full-fledged American citizens, vouchsafed equality of citizenship by the federal Constitution"—that he banned him from the White House. Undeterred, Trotter and Villard mobilized African American newspapers and church groups to show the administration that it would pay a price for its adoption of segregation.[16]

Chastened by this reaction, Wilson and his cabinet retreated in 1913 and 1914. McAdoo rescinded Williams's order and released figures showing that more than twice as many African Americans had been promoted in his department in 1913 and 1914 than during the last two years of Taft's administration. John Skelton Williams, Treasury's arch-segregator, was promoted to comptroller of the currency, and his place was temporarily taken by Charles Hamlin, an outspoken opponent of segregation. Hamlin and McAdoo issued instructions in March 1914 forbidding formal segregation in Treasury offices and promulgated four "general rules: (1) justice to all; (2) no notices to be posted in toilet rooms; (3) no discrimination in promotions; and (4) no partitions in dressing rooms." These were well publicized and carefully noted; Villard sent his congratulations, the Boston Advertiser declared that "Segregation is Being Undone," and the NAACP expressed its delight.[17]

Forcing an administration led by southerners and in thrall to southern congressional leaders to abandon formal segregation in its departments was an important but incomplete achievement. Even Hamlin recognized that official orders in Treasury had been replaced by informal arrangements that enforced segregation through quiet understandings instead of formal directives. In November 1914, long after Hamlin's four rules had been promulgated and the NAACP had claimed its victory, Trotter complained to Wilson that in Printing and Engraving "there is segregation not only in dressing rooms, but in working positions; Afro-American employees being herded at separate tables, in eating and in toilets." Segregation by "custom" had replaced segregation by direction, but it remained nonetheless.[18]

McAdoo's decisive responses to policy challenges in 1913 and 1914 contrasted to his wallowing in the politics of patronage and his obfuscation on segregation. Each summer farmers in the South and West rushed their banks for loans to pay for the shipping of their crops. Previous administrations had responded by placing federal funds in major New York banks, which then lent the money to banks in the hinterland. This caused delay and increased interest rates paid by farmers. McAdoo complained that New York banks in general, and the National City Bank in particular, exploited the harvest credit squeeze by charging local banks 7 percent interest on these funds, which translated into rates of up to 10 percent for farmers.[19]

With large southern and western constituencies to satisfy, McAdoo bypassed the New York banks and sent federal money—$46 million in 1913 and $34 million in 1914—directly to banks in the cotton and grain states. Federal funds now attracted interest of 2 percent, were quarantined from speculative use, and were returnable within nine months. Southern and western farmers and their banks were pleased by the speed with which credit now reached their communities, but the New York banks, accustomed each summer to large injections of interest-free federal funds, were not. McAdoo had won many friends in the hinterland, but his relationship with the major New York banks, used to deference and favors from Washington, had begun badly.[20]

McAdoo grew more adventurous in his use of federal funds to calm troubled financial waters. In 1913, responding to fears of a credit squeeze, he announced that he would place up to $60 million in banks across the country. This would flood them with capital charged at 2 percent. As it turned out no funds at all were needed; mere knowledge of them was enough to quell panic in financial markets. But McAdoo's point had been made: from now on the federal government, and not the New York banks, would take responsibility for the health of the nation's credit system. He "had electrified the country by the epoch making announcement that the bankers of the United States no longer had to appeal to Wall Street for aid or advice," the New York Sun noted. No longer would the "money hoarders" profit from periodic credit squeezes. In 1907 Theodore Roosevelt's secretary of the treasury had begged Wall Street to bail the economy out, but "when Secretary McAdoo walks in Wall Street," one newspaper noted, "he carries his hat on his head—not in his hand."[21]

Two of McAdoo's early decisions, one symbolic and the other substantive, deepened the big banks' concern that he was hostile to their privileges. The nation's largest bank, the National City of New York, had long stationed one of its employees in the Treasury Department. McAdoo saw this as "entirely wrong and indefensible" and ordered it to stop. Although it was scarcely an expulsion of the money changers from the temple, his action was a declaration that changes in policy would no longer be telegraphed in advance to those specially favored within the banking community.[22]

McAdoo's second action cost the banks money as well as influence. Treasury had long parked its surplus funds in banks scattered around the country. Recipient banks were known as government depositaries, a title that they advertised as a sign of their financial solidity. They were selected by the secretary of the treasury, a power that had long been used to reward political allies and campaign contributors. Depositaries fell into two classes: inactive depositaries, in which the federal government held largely static funds; and active depositaries, which held much larger Treasury accounts and acted as financial agents of the government. At the beginning of 1913 there were 900 inactive depositaries in the United States, each holding only $1,000 of government funds. In return for the benefits conferred by their designation, inactive depositaries paid 2 percent interest on their Treasury funds. The 559 active depositary banks, which included the largest and most powerful banks in the country, held nearly $47 million of Treasury funds in April 1913 but paid no interest on them. This was allegedly to compensate them for frequent transactions on their government money, but in fact the banks made large profits from their free deposits.

On April 30, 1913, McAdoo announced that active depositaries would be charged 2 percent interest on their Treasury deposits. Because its funds would now earn interest, McAdoo also announced that Treasury would deposit $10 million more of its surplus in its active depositaries. Levying interest on these funds would contribute more than $1.5 million a year to revenue, and depositaries would be able to extend more loans on the basis of their increased Treasury deposits. Had 2 percent interest been charged on Treasury funds from 1896 until 1913, McAdoo calculated, the federal government would have been $30 million richer. The banks were furious, but only nine—including National City, already smarting over the removal of its Treasury spy—gave up their depositary status.[23]

The major banks' reservations about McAdoo deepened as they witnessed the unfolding of a bitter dispute between the secretary and the Riggs National Bank of Washington. The so-called Riggs War heightened fears that behind McAdoo's dynamism lay a vindictive spirit that was quick to anger and slow to forgive. In 1917 Wilson had accused McAdoo of subscribing to a "code duello" in his attitude to Germany. America's leading bankers had come to a similar conclusion two years earlier as they witnessed McAdoo's campaign against the Riggs Bank.

The origins of the Riggs War are obscure. John Skelton Williams had crossed swords with Milton Ailes, vice president of Riggs, when Ailes had testified against Williams's nomination as comptroller of the currency in January 1914. McAdoo had his own reasons for suspecting Ailes of hostility when he objected vociferously to McAdoo's decision to charge interest on government funds in active depositaries. McAdoo suspected Ailes of feeding stories to the press that Williams and McAdoo were using their offices for personal aggrandizement. He confronted Ailes in December 1913 over these rumors and then ordered him out of his office. Both proud southerners, Williams and McAdoo set out to avenge their honor.[24]

McAdoo fired the first shot in May 1914. The Treasury had long deposited additional funds each summer in all eleven of the District of Columbia's depositary banks to allow for withdrawals to pay District taxes. In 1914 McAdoo authorized these extra funds for all the banks except Riggs. When asked by Riggs President Charles Glover for his reasons, the secretary replied that "I do not consider it in the public interest to keep Government funds on deposit in your bank," and intimated that he would withdraw all Treasury funds from it. At the beginning of July he made good on his threat and also stripped Riggs of its status as a government depositary.[25]

Knowing that Glover and Ailes would fight back, McAdoo and Williams sought evidence of the bank's wrongdoing. They discovered that Ailes, who had been Theodore Roosevelt's assistant secretary of the treasury, had transferred $3 million of government funds to the Riggs Bank four days before he resigned to take up his position there. Riggs had then extended loans of $25,000 to Secretary of the Treasury Leslie M. Shaw. McAdoo and Williams also investigated allegations that several of Riggs's directors had illegally approved loans to themselves via dummy borrowers. Riggs refused to cooperate with the investigation, and Williams levied a $5,000 fine against it. The bank then initiated litigation alleging that McAdoo and Williams had conspired to ruin it. That litigation dragged on until May 1916, when the bank lost on all counts except on a technicality concerning the $5,000 fine.[26]

Although McAdoo and Williams claimed that they had been vindicated, some of their colleagues were less sure. Lindley Garrison and Thomas Gregory thought that McAdoo had acted more from spite than principle, and Brandeis advised early settlement of the case to avoid further embarrassment. Treasury Assistant Secretary Hamlin feared that McAdoo and Williams had abused their powers to conduct a private vendetta against Ailes. Hamlin had already fallen out with Williams over segregation, and the Riggs War further convinced him that Williams was an "evil genius" who exercised unhealthy influence over McAdoo.[27]

McAdoo's motives in the Riggs War were political as well as personal. Riggs was a convenient target; it had been a "pet bank" of previous Republican administrations and it epitomized the eastern banking establishment that McAdoo had resolved to vanquish. Riggs's transgressions were egregious, but hardly unique within the murky network of mutual favors and shady bargains between the nation's big banks and Washington's politicians. By confronting the Riggs Bank so publicly McAdoo did more than assuage his personal resentments: eastern banks and Wall Street were unpopular institutions, and for millions of voters they were good enemies for an ambitious Democrat to have. McAdoo's crusade against Riggs was also an advertisement of his credentials as a reformer unafraid to confront powerful and corrupt bankers who had grown rich on Republican favors. He would apply the same logic to the debate and implementation of the Federal Reserve Act of 1913.

❧⊰⊱❧

Enmeshed in patronage, preoccupied with the disposition of Treasury funds, and embroiled in disputes with the National City and Riggs Banks, McAdoo exercised little influence over the Democratic legislative agenda in the first months of 1913. Tariff reform was the first item on the congressional calendar. Although his department was responsible for administering tariffs, McAdoo deferred to Oscar Underwood in the House and Furnifold Simmons in the Senate to take charge of tariff reform and the negotiations needed for its passage.[28]

McAdoo was also detached from the new federal income tax, authorized by a constitutional amendment in 1913 and enacted as part of the Underwood-Simmons tariff. Although he championed federal income tax as an advance in social and economic justice, McAdoo was cautious using it to soak the rich. The 1913 legislation taxed corporations 1 percent of their net profits, individuals at 1 percent of their incomes above $4,000 per year, and levied surtaxes of up to 3 percent on incomes over $20,000. When new revenue had to be found in 1916 McAdoo suggested that the tax threshold should fall to $3,000 rather than having its rate increased. He was no friend to the rich, but was concerned that higher rates would increase tax evasion. Simmons and Congress demurred, and raised the basic income tax rate to 2 percent, sharply increased surtaxes on high incomes, and left the thresholds unchanged.[29]

McAdoo was more active in influencing the Federal Reserve Act, which became the Democrats' greatest legislative achievement during Wilson's presidency. Reform of the nation's banking system—if "system" is the right description of an unregulated mishmash of state and federally chartered banks—had become a pressing issue after a bank panic in 1907 reduced Treasury's reserves to $21 million and forced Theodore Roosevelt and his secretary of the treasury to beg the New York banks to come to their rescue. Those with longer memories recalled four other credit crises, two of which, in 1873 and 1893, had triggered nationwide economic distress, and twenty-four smaller panics between 1873 and 1909. Contemporaries decried the American banking system of the late nineteenth century as one of the worst in the Western world, but agreeing on ways to improve it was much harder than diagnosing its ills.[30]

Stung into action in 1908, Congress passed the Aldrich-Vreeland Act to authorize emergency currency to relieve credit shortages. Congress also established a Monetary Commission to recommend a new structure for American banking. In 1912 the commission suggested the creation of a single national bank based in Washington with fifteen branches across the country. Control of the National Reserve Association would reside in a board of forty-two bankers and ten delegates of the federal government. This scheme, named after Republican Senator Nelson Aldrich, polarized political opinion. Eastern Republicans supported it as their creation and reflective of their concerns, but Democrats and former populists attacked it as a recipe for Wall Street and Republican control of the nation's banking.[31]

Wilson's victory in the presidential election of 1912 ensured that the Aldrich Plan would be reworked by Democratic majorities in both houses of Congress. In the House, banking legislation came under the control of Carter Glass of Virginia, who chaired the relevant subcommittee of the Banking Committee. In the Senate Robert L. Owen of Oklahoma took the chair of the Senate Committee on Banking and Currency. These men had very different ideas about banking reform. Glass had little patience with ex-populist and new ideas about the need for government oversight of banking. Owen, on the other hand, had more radical views. Before he entered the Senate, he had run a bank in Oklahoma that had almost collapsed during the depression of 1893, and that experience convinced him of the "complete instability" of the US banking system. Owen had objected to the Aldrich-Vreeland Act and the Aldrich Plan as creatures of predatory Wall Street interests.[32]

Owen was also influenced by the House of Representatives' Pujo Committee, which investigated Wall Street's "money trust" in 1912. Led by its counsel Samuel Untermeyer, the committee recommended sweeping reforms to eradicate interlocking directorates, stock-watering, and secret commissions. Closely aligned with William Jennings Bryan, now Wilson's secretary of state, Owen was determined that the new banking system should be protected from the money trust through strong federal regulation. His main concerns were that the currency should be an obligation of the government rather than of its chartered banks, and that the government should control all appointments to any board established to oversee the banking system.[33]

Glass made the early running, seeking Wilson's approval to draft an alternative to the Aldrich Plan. Wilson agreed, and used McAdoo as his liaison with Glass and Owen. In place of Aldrich's single bank with fifteen branches, Glass favored a decentralized model of up to twenty regional Federal Reserve Banks. Beneath each Reserve Bank would be an unlimited number of member banks—there were about nine thousand in 1930—which could join the Federal Reserve System by buying stock in their Reserve Bank and subjecting themselves to its rules. Once part of the system, banks could exchange commercial paper taken as collateral for currency issued by their Reserve Bank, which charged rediscount fees depending on the quality of the paper presented to them. When member banks wished to reduce their currency holdings, they could redeem their Federal Reserve banknotes for the commercial paper they had lodged with their Reserve Bank.[34]

The Aldrich Plan had envisaged a single rediscount rate, but Glass's model allowed each Federal Reserve Bank to set its own. Rediscounts operated as interest rates because they were the price of currency to member banks, and so under Glass's plan they could vary according to the conditions prevailing in each Reserve District. Glass required each Federal Reserve Bank to accept the discounted paper of other Reserve Banks, thus providing the system with some, but not much, coordination. Federally chartered banks would be obliged to join the Federal Reserve System, but state-chartered banks could retain their independence. If they wished to use the new rediscount and currency facilities, however, they had to join the new banking system.

Most significantly from Owen's, Bryan's, McAdoo's, and ultimately Wilson's points of view, Glass's plan was based on private control of Federal Reserve Banks. Of the forty-three members of Glass's FRB, Owen noted with disgust, forty were to be chosen by the banks, with only the secretary of the treasury, the comptroller of the currency, and the attorney general given seats from which to fly the public's flag. Owen refused to accept Glass's plan, and they asked Wilson to resolve their differences.[35]

Glass and Owen disagreed over the role of the federal government in the new banking system, over its degree of centralization, and over the status of its currency. These were difficult issues to resolve, partly because bankers were divided over them. The big banks of the Northeast had united behind the Aldrich Plan; their smaller competitors were much less enthusiastic, and southern and western bankers were hostile. When Glass put forward his alternative to the Aldrich Plan he consulted with prominent New York bankers and then received their support. The more numerous western and southern bankers personified by Robert Owen, however, wanted reform that limited the New Yorkers' influence. Because these hinterland bankers dealt with customers who retained some loyalty to the populists and their anti-bank rhetoric, and who had recently voted Wilson into the White House, their influence in 1913 was significant. It was therefore unsurprising that Wilson's first intervention in the Glass-Owen dispute was to agree with Owen that all members of the FRB should be nominated by the president and confirmed by the Senate.[36]

As to centralization, Glass sensed that his structure was too loose for the reformers to accept. At Wilson's suggestion he modified his plan to include an FRB charged with supervising the whole system. Even so, the eventual Federal Reserve Act lacked strong central control over the credit policies of its component Federal Reserve Banks; rediscount rates were still locally determined, banks could evade the system and its liquidity requirements by continuing as state-chartered banks, and a member bank could drop out at any time and seek a charter from its home state.[37]

The status of the new Federal Reserve currency was again resolved in Owen's favor, albeit ambiguously. Owen and his Bryanite supporters wanted a single currency bearing the imprimatur of the federal government. Glass strenuously objected, arguing that each Federal Reserve Bank should issue notes backed by its own assets. Paul Warburg, a prominent New York banker who later sat on the FRB, argued that Owen's plan would dangerously stretch the credit of the United States, while Owen argued that public confidence in the new banking system depended on the federal government standing behind its currency. Wilson compromised by giving Owen his symbolism and Glass his substance; Federal Reserve bank notes were declared to be obligations of the US government but were issued by each Federal Reserve Bank on the basis of its holdings of commercial paper.[38]

McAdoo's role in the formulation of the Federal Reserve Act was significant but complex. Although they later squabbled over their respective contributions to it, McAdoo and Glass worked closely over the formulation of the new legislation. As negotiations dragged on, however, McAdoo moved closer to Owen's views. As was so often the case, his fluid allegiances and changing convictions arose from the interaction of his ideological, political, and personal interests.

Although they agreed on a regional reserve bank system made up of autonomous banks, McAdoo had moved away from Glass's view that control of it should be in bankers' hands. "The more I have studied this question," he wrote to House in June 1913, "the more I have become convinced that the right measure is the one which puts the Government in the saddle." Mindful of his recent disputes with the National City Bank and the active depository banks, McAdoo now declared that "I am not the least afraid of a Government bank whose functions are limited to dealings with the banks throughout the country, exercising, at the same time an altruistic control which will prevent the selfish and arbitrary exercise of power now too frequently exerted by certain powerful interests in this country." This position allied him more closely with Owen, Bryan, and their congressional allies than

had previously been the case. The more statist McAdoo became on banking reform, the more he worried Glass and the bankers, and the more opposition he
sensed from the banks, the more determined he was to put the government "in the
saddle."[39]

McAdoo even proposed a revision of Glass's plan to create a central bank wholly
controlled by the government through the Treasury Department and operated
through twenty subtreasuries across the nation. In a nod to Owen's crusade for
a government-backed currency, McAdoo's plan also envisaged replacement of
all existing bank notes with a single US currency only partially backed by gold.
Although he later claimed that this scheme was a ruse to frighten the banks into
supporting Glass's more moderate proposals, others were not so sure. Assistant
Secretary of the Treasury Williams prepared a memorandum on how this scheme
would work without any hint that it was anything other than a serious proposal;
Glass was horrified at McAdoo's "bastard greenback scheme," House opposed it as
an unnecessary provocation of the major banks, and Wilson disowned it.[40]

McAdoo's espousal of federal control over banking was part of a broader trend
in his thinking. He now saw the federal government as the most effective guardian
of the public interest in American society and as the best regulator of capitalism's
excesses and weaknesses. Much to the consternation of the bankers, Glass, and
perhaps even the president, but to the delight of Owen and Bryan's supporters, this
change in McAdoo's thinking became apparent during the struggle to enact banking reform.[41]

Political as well as philosophical considerations also moved McAdoo closer to
the Owen-Bryanites. One of the rationales for his currency plan was that the Glass
bill would not win a majority of congressional Democrats unless it was radically
changed; Bryan and his southern and western allies would oppose any bill that
gave eastern bankers control of the new system. After abandoning his currency
scheme, McAdoo worked closely with Glass, and then Owen, to win congressional
support for a modified version of Glass's bill that bore clear signs of compromise
toward the more statist concerns of the Owen-Bryan group.[42]

This was necessary to get the bill through Congress, but opposition from the
major banks grew with each of Owen's victories.[43] Glass's original bill had been
too decentralized for the New York banks, but after the Democratic victory in 1912
it seemed to them to be the best outcome in bad political weather. The more that
McAdoo helped to amend the Glass plan to meet congressional approval, the
more he confirmed major bankers' fears that he was ruining Glass's bill to curry
favor with southern and western ex-populists. This was exaggerated; McAdoo
worked closely with Glass throughout 1913, kept in close contact with Wilson,
and was motivated more by Democratic congressional opinion than by desire for

personal political gain. Nevertheless, the bankers were correct to see that one consequence of McAdoo's shift toward Owen's position was that his powers as secretary of the treasury would be much greater than Glass had originally envisaged.

Owen insisted that Glass drop his demand that all Treasury revenues be placed
in the Federal Reserve Banks in favor of a provision empowering the secretary of
the treasury to deposit funds as he saw fit. Owen saw this as protecting the independence of the Treasury, but it also enabled McAdoo to discipline member banks
without constraint from the FRB. His powers were further protected by Section 10
of the Federal Reserve Act, which declared that wherever powers created by the
new act conflicted with the secretary of the treasury's existing authority "such
powers shall be exercised subject to the supervision and control of the Secretary."
McAdoo was to chair the Federal Reserve Organization Committee to determine
the boundaries and Federal Reserve Cities of the Federal Reserve Districts, and
then chair the FRB itself.[44]

With its compromises made, the Glass-Owen bill made its way through Congress in the second half of 1913. Legislators came under pressure from all sides;
farmers' groups urged support of the bill against the northeastern banks, while
banking groups conducted surveys showing that large majorities of banks opposed
the Glass-Owen bill. Encouraged by leading questions such as "Do you believe
that it is wise and safe to place such vast powers in the hands of the appointed
FRB, the personnel of which need not necessarily be composed of either bankers
or business men?" one survey conducted in October 1913 reported 2,247 banks in
favor of further amendment to the bill and only 132 content with it; 631 federally
chartered banks threatened to refuse to join the new system and to seek state
charters instead.[45]

McAdoo's staff noted his mail's diversity. New Yorkers were critical, westerners
were supportive, and many from outside New York made suggestions that sought
to improve, but not demolish, the banking bill. Lacking coherence and regionally
divided, the banks' efforts cancelled each other out and left lawmakers to their
own devices. The big banks won only one major concession when they had Glass
veto Owen's suggestion that the government insure all bank deposits. Owen and
McAdoo eventually won this battle in 1933, but not before hundreds of thousands
of Americans had lost their savings in the first years of the Great Depression.[46]

The House moved quickly once Glass's bill was reported out of the Committee
on Banking on September 9, 1913. The bill passed the House on September 19 by
287 votes to 85, with nearly 80 percent of Republicans voting in the negative and
13 progressives and progressive Republicans voting with the Democratic majority.
The bill's progress in the Senate was more tortuous. After long debate Owen introduced a substitute bill that increased the permissible number of Federal Reserve

Districts from 10 to 12 and required all national banks to join the system. The substitute bill passed the Senate on December 20 by 54 to 34, with Republicans making up the entire minority and only 6 voting in the affirmative. The two bills were quickly reconciled, and the Federal Reserve Act received Wilson's approval on December 23, 1913. "The impossible has happened," Secretary of Agriculture Houston recorded in his diary. "[The banking bill] was passed by a Congress dominated by the Democrats, two thirds of whom had been unsound on currency questions and a majority of whom can scarcely be said to have understood what the measure meant and would accomplish."[47]

＊＊＊

With the Federal Reserve Act in place, McAdoo's first task was to chair the committee to determine the boundaries of no less than eight and no more than twelve Federal Reserve Districts and to designate a Federal Reserve City for each one. The biggest problem facing the Organization Committee concerned the maldistribution of the nation's banking resources. Paul Warburg, who would soon sit on the FRB, pointed out that banks based in the state of New York alone represented one-quarter of the nation's banking capital and surplus. "The little corner on the map" encompassing New York, New England, and Pennsylvania held nearly half of the national total, and the great quadrant stretching south from the Canadian border with Minnesota to Kansas City and then east to Delaware—one-sixth of the nation's territory—contained 74 percent of the nation's banking resources. Warburg suggested the creation of eight districts, which agglomerated the South into a single district focused on Washington, D.C., divided the Northeast into three districts led by New York, Boston, and Philadelphia, covered the Midwest, Great Plains, and Mountain states with three districts based in Chicago, Cincinnati, and St. Louis, and created an eighth district out of the three Pacific Coast states. Dividing the nation into more than eight districts, Warburg warned, would only magnify New York's preponderance.[48]

Although it was very important that the new system not be organized in ways that increased New York's banking dominance—populists and progressives had fought the "money trust" too hard to tolerate that—other factors influenced the demarcation of Federal Reserve Districts. Congress had required them to be drawn with regard to "convenience and customary course of business," and this required consideration of their physical size. Warburg's scheme involved gigantic districts covering the entire South and trans-Mississippi West, which would have made it difficult for member banks to have their commercial paper discounted in a Federal Reserve City far from their communities. Such large districts would also have made it almost impossible for Federal Reserve Banks to set discount rates in sympathy with economic and trade conditions, which could vary greatly across their huge domains.

After conducting public hearings across the country in January and February 1914, McAdoo's Organization Committee decided on twelve districts, the act's maximum number, rather than Warburg's eight. This was to reduce the physical size of the western and southern districts and to lend to them more regional and economic coherence. The committee also took advantage of Congress's direction that it could disregard state boundaries if it saw fit.[49]

Some decisions were easy. In keeping with Warburg's original plan, New York was given its own district. It was also logical to agglomerate New England and to create a third district from the eastern two-thirds of Pennsylvania, Delaware, and the Maryland counties of the Delmarva Peninsula. Beyond that the committee's decisions became more complex. Communities across the nation, and especially those near the proposed boundaries of the twelve Federal Reserve Districts, argued that they should join their neighboring district because the flow of their business was in that direction. As a result of these representations the committee's districts often bisected states with jagged lines; southern parts of Arizona, Illinois, Indiana, New Mexico, and Wisconsin were separated from their northern counties; Kentucky, Louisiana, Mississippi, and Tennessee were cut in half; and Oklahoma's southeastern counties, which did more business and banking with Texans than with their fellow Sooners, were separated from the rest of the state. McAdoo's committee even dared to add a postscript to a bitter chapter in Civil War history when it reunited the Virginias within the Fifth Federal Reserve District.[50]

Although McAdoo's committee drew boundaries that reflected business and banking flows, it could do little to mitigate the centripetal nature of American banking through which commercial paper from across the nation was sucked into New York. As Warburg had predicted, the twelve-district formula created one dominant district in New York, a second smaller hub in Chicago, three yet smaller but still significant centers in New England, the upper Midwest, and the middle Atlantic, and seven minnows in the South, the Great Plains, and the West. When the Federal Reserve System came into operation at the end of 1914 the Second District, based in New York, boasted more than $1 billion worth of bank assets; the Fifth District, based in Richmond, held a little more than $7 million. The McAdoo Committee had done its work carefully, but it could not change the facts of American life.[51]

The Organizational Committee's second task, to select a Federal Reserve City for each district, proved even more contentious. Although McAdoo maintained that selection of the reserve cities was "subsidiary and relatively simple, waiving considerations of local pride and prestige," those considerations prompted a blizzard of lobbying to descend on McAdoo and Houston.[52] Thirty-seven cities vied for the twelve prizes, but half of the decisions were straightforward. In 1914 the nation's six largest cities were New York, Chicago, Philadelphia, St. Louis, Boston, and Newton Baker's Cleveland, and they were all chosen as the seats of their respective districts.

Battles over the remaining six cities were intense. Denver and Omaha fought against Kansas City, New Orleans against Dallas and Atlanta, Houston against Dallas, and Baltimore and Washington, D.C. against Richmond. Dallas proclaimed itself to be Texas's banking center and most important city, ideally placed to serve not only the Lone Star State but also Oklahoman counties and Louisianan parishes; Houston objected that "we do not want to be the tail to anybody's kite," and that "SOME OF OUR LOCAL BANKERS DO NOT THINK WE SHOULD HAVE A RESERVE BANK, BUT SUCH MEN WOULD NOT HAVE BUILT THE MCADOO TUNNELS OR THE PANAMA CANAL." Atlanta described itself as the railroad, insurance, and banking capital of the Southeast, dwarfing Savannah, Jacksonville, Mobile, Chattanooga, and New Orleans in its importance. William Jennings Bryan pleaded in vain for Lincoln, Nebraska, but no one was surprised when Richmond, in Carter Glass's Virginia, was selected ahead of Baltimore and Washington, D.C.[53]

Designation as a Federal Reserve City marked its recipient as the leading commercial center of its district, and provided real benefits in the speed and convenience with which commercial collateral could be discounted. The presence of a Federal Reserve Bank encouraged retail banks to concentrate around it, providing the nucleus of vibrant banking sectors in Richmond, Kansas City, and Minneapolis that might otherwise have struggled to compete against nearby and larger banking sectors in Washington, D.C., Denver, and Chicago. Federal Reserve Cities have not changed since 1914, allowing the benefits of their status to accrue over time. San Francisco was the pre-eminent city in California in 1914, but Los Angeles is today. San Francisco, however, retains its status as the center of western banking thanks to McAdoo and Houston's decisions nearly a century ago.

McAdoo was less successful in controlling the makeup of the FRB. The act established the board with seven members, made up of the secretary of the treasury and the comptroller of the currency *ex officio* and five members appointed by the president with the advice and consent of the Senate. McAdoo was determined to have appointees who were "sympathetic"—his critics thought he really meant subservient—to his vision of the new structure. Edward House was equally determined to use board appointments to mend fences with the banking community. The two men fought hard for Wilson's ear; even before the president signed the Federal Reserve Act McAdoo put his case emphatically and personally:

The immediate success of the new system . . . depends almost wholly upon this Board. It must be composed not only of able men, but men who are in sympathy with the purposes of the bill and the aims of the administration, and it is <u>essential</u> that they shall be acceptable to your Secretary of the Treasury. My difficulties and responsibilities are great, and if I should be associated with uncongenial men, who would not work loyally and unselfishly, my usefulness would be greatly impaired if not destroyed.[54]

Wilson was unmoved, telling House that he did not want a board that was "in any way personal," and that it should be at arm's length from McAdoo, who seemed to want to form a "social club." McAdoo tried again in May 1914. "Please don't think me unduly fearful of the 'Money Trust.' I am not. I simply know, after a year's experience in the Treasury, that it is not a fiction, but a real thing and I want to keep the upper hand for the people while we have it."[55]

Always wary of ambitious subordinates, Wilson ignored McAdoo's entreaties. He was persuaded that the big banks needed reassurance that the Federal Reserve System would be independent and conservative, and he nominated five members who were eminently acceptable to them: Paul Warburg of Kuhn, Loeb & Company; Thomas D. Jones from Chicago; William P. G. Harding, a banker from Birmingham, Alabama; Adolph C. Miller from the University of California; and Charles Hamlin. Jones ran into senatorial opposition and was replaced by Franklin A. Delano, a former president of the Wabash Railroad. Apart from his former Assistant Secretaries Williams and Hamlin, McAdoo saw few allies on the board. Wall Street was delighted, and progressives were horrified. The big banks, defeated in Congress, seemed to have been handed victory by the White House.[56]

McAdoo's relationship with the FRB never recovered. Paul Warburg, in particular, remained a thorn in his side. In 1915 he objected to McAdoo's shifting of Treasury funds around member banks to relieve agricultural credit shortages. Pointing out the incongruity through which McAdoo as secretary of the treasury could move funds without the knowledge or consent of the FRB, which he chaired, Warburg tried unsuccessfully to have the act amended to clip McAdoo's wings. He also led the board in its refusal after August 1914 to allow banks to rediscount bills of exchange from munitions purchases. Warburg claimed that this contravened US neutrality; McAdoo argued that it damaged the national interest. McAdoo complained to the president that Warburg—who had been born in Germany and had taken US citizenship in 1911—was doing Germany's bidding. His insinuations enraged Warburg and permanently estranged the two men. Warburg served out his term on the FRB but declined to be considered for a second term.

So many people, he told Wilson, had impugned his loyalty that his reappointment would expose the board to yet more attack by "unscrupulous and unreasoning people."[57]

⬥⬥⬥

Even before he declared that the Federal Reserve Banks would begin operations on November 16, 1914, McAdoo's attention had turned to international issues, and especially to the dislocation in international finance, trade, and shipping caused by the outbreak of war in Europe in August 1914.

The most pressing problem lay on Wall Street. In the last days of peace all the major European stock markets, except the French, had closed. This left the New York Stock Exchange (NYSE) vulnerable to panic selling as European investors rushed to liquidate their holdings. At the end of June 1914 Europeans held $4 billion of stock on the NYSE, while the national banks held only slightly more than $1 billion in gold. Liquidation of only a quarter of Europeans' holdings would therefore have exhausted the banks' bullion, and any greater sell-down would have forced the United States off the gold standard. In the last week of July 1914 more than $45 million in gold left the United States, and much more was likely to follow.[58]

With a new banking system to launch and the nation's currency to protect, McAdoo needed to act promptly. Abandonment of the gold standard would destabilize the dollar and severely damage the financial reputation of the United States. McAdoo moved instead to limit Europeans' opportunities to drain American gold supplies by pressuring the NYSE to close on July 31, 1914. It remained closed until December 15, although an unofficial curb exchange saw some trading continue. McAdoo addressed the currency crisis brought about by the flight of gold to Europe by authorizing $370 million of emergency currency under the Aldrich-Vreeland Act. Although gold exports remained very high—$15 million in August and $19 million in September—they stayed within the banks' bullion reserves.[59]

Confident that their banks would not run out of currency, American depositors left their funds untouched and the financial crisis dissipated. When the Federal Reserve Banks opened for business the value of the dollar had stabilized, the "dollar discount" to the pound had disappeared, and the gold standard had been maintained. Soon European gold came flooding back and the gold crisis of 1914 was forgotten.[60]

Although World War I ultimately proved to be an economic bonanza for the United States, and the catalyst for its pre-eminence in international trade and finance, at first it caused more problems than it solved. When war broke out the United States was in the grip of economic recession. The year 1914 saw the largest number of business failures of any single year up to that time and more than a million workers were unemployed. War struck hard at the nation's accounts; customs revenue fell by $10 million in August 1914, and McAdoo wrongly predicted that Treasury would suffer losses of $60 million in customs revenue between August 1914 and June 1915.[61]

Worried about federal revenue and anxious to maximize the opportunities created by the war, McAdoo soon chafed against the constraints of neutrality. The administration upheld the right of Americans to sell supplies to both sides, although the effectiveness of the Royal Navy's blockade of Germany made that trade increasingly one-sided. Even so the influence of war-related commerce was profound. By the middle of 1915, as the Allies placed huge orders for food, clothing, and munitions with American producers, the recession of 1914 was swept away by unprecedented economic growth and prosperity. Britain, France, Russia, and Germany paid for their orders by selling their American assets, quickly transforming the United States' balance of payments from chronic deficit to overwhelming surplus. Farmers received high prices for their produce, manufacturers struggled to expand production to meet demand, and financiers grew rich on their commissions. "Our prosperity is dependent on our continued and enlarged foreign trade," McAdoo told Wilson in August 1915. "To preserve that we must do everything we can to assist our customers to buy."[62]

McAdoo urged Wilson to relax restrictions on the belligerent nations' ability to raise funds in the United States. France and Germany had early in the war sold bonds to Americans, but Wilson had prohibited that activity as unneutral. McAdoo had no such qualms; trade with the Allies was now too important to the American economy. Sooner rather than later the Europeans would exhaust their gold and American securities, and then their orders would dry up. The proprieties of neutrality would be satisfied by refusing to extend government loans to either side, but they should not prevent arrangements with American bankers to raise funds. It was illogical, McAdoo maintained, for the United States to declare that the purchase of materiel was lawful but that the establishment of credit facilities for those purchases was unneutral. Secretary of State Robert Lansing and Edward House agreed, and with McAdoo persuaded Wilson to allow private loans to all the belligerents.[63]

As he worked to free US trade from the constraints of neutrality McAdoo also moved to improve American access to markets in South America that were suddenly evacuated by Britain and Germany. Rhetorically at least, the United States had long considered Central and South America to be within its sphere of influence, but the reality before 1914 was much more complex. It was true that a quarter of the United States' foreign trade was with nations to its south, but nearly half of that amount was with Mexico and the nations and colonies within the Caribbean basin. Britain and Germany, not the United States, controlled trade with South

American nations, and British banks dominated the financial networks necessary for it. Bills of exchange were denominated in pounds sterling, drawn on banks in London, and funded by loans from British and German banks. The result was that Britain, and to a lesser extent Germany, ruled the finance and trade of those that President James Monroe had called "our southern brethren."

All this changed soon after the outbreak of war on August 4, 1914. Suddenly British and German capital flows to South America dried up and their shipping was redirected. South American nations found their bonds unsubscribed, their imports restricted, and their produce unshipped. Although US trade with Britain, France, and Russia boomed between 1915 and 1918, the South American trade languished.[64]

There had always been something of the imperialist in McAdoo. His first political hero had been Theodore Roosevelt, his first political cause had been to support TR's grab of the Panama Canal Zone, and even his friends recognized a strong strain of opportunism in his character. These characteristics came together in his campaign for more assertive US trade and diplomatic policies in Central and South America. He had been a strong supporter of the purchase of the Danish West Indian (Virgin) Islands in 1916 for $25 million, and he even tried to talk Wilson into offering to buy the Baja Peninsula from Mexico in 1915. With Britain and Germany now at each other's throats, he argued, the time had come for the United States to make good on the previously unexplored implications of the Monroe Doctrine.[65]

With Wilson's backing McAdoo won congressional authority to call a conference of all Central and South American governments to forge "closer and more satisfactory financial relations." Eighteen nations sent forty-four representatives to the First Pan American Financial Conference in Washington on May 24, 1915, to be joined by a US delegation of forty-four bankers and business leaders selected by McAdoo. Secretary of State Bryan, Secretary of Commerce Redfield, and Secretary of the Navy Daniels were also invited to the conference, but it was made clear that it was to be McAdoo's show. By seniority Bryan should have run the meeting, and by jurisdiction Redfield had a strong claim to take the lead. McAdoo demanded pre-eminence by claiming a congressional mandate and because the Federal Reserve Act allowed member banks to establish foreign branches. McAdoo had sidelined Redfield before, and would do so again, but the Pan American Conference was a particularly brazen example of his bureaucratic imperialism.[66]

The conference was declared by its chairman to be a great success. The delegates agreed that US banks should provide prompt and ample credits to Latin America. They unanimously approved two more of McAdoo's priorities by agreeing to improve facilities in major South American ports and to an International High Commission to formulate uniform commercial laws for the Western Hemisphere. McAdoo appointed himself as the High Commission's chair and named to it eight US representatives, including E. H. Gary, chairman of the board of US Steel; Henry Davidson of J. P. Morgan and Company; and the banker Samuel Untermeyer. The commission, it was agreed, would meet in Buenos Aires.[67]

On March 8, 1916, McAdoo and his delegation sailed south on the USS *Tennessee*, stopping in the Caribbean, Brazil, Uruguay, and Argentina. "Everywhere we went," he reported, "there was a genuinely friendly attitude and a complete absence of that suspicion and distrust of the United States which has, until recently, existed . . . in some, at least, of the Central American countries." The conference lasted ten days. Participants discussed the uniform treatment of bills of exchange, visas for commercial travelers, and protection of copyright and trade marks. Discussions also began on two more of McAdoo's pet projects: to complete a railroad from New York to Buenos Aires and to support a much enlarged merchant marine.[68]

The Pan American financial movement soon petered out as its governments, not least that of the United States, became enmeshed in World War I. Pancho Villa's raid on Columbus, New Mexico, in March 1916, which coincided with both McAdoo's departure for Buenos Aires and Newton Baker's arrival at the Department of War, distracted Wilson and his administration from the visionary plans emanating from Buenos Aires to the less elevated business of policing Mexico. McAdoo often reminded Wilson of the important work in South America that still remained to be done, but after May 1916 the moment had passed.[69]

⊰⊱

The Pan American conferences had focused attention on shipping shortages brought about by the war. "We have been a department store without a delivery system," Secretary of Commerce Redfield observed, "depending on our rivals for the use of their wagons." The coming of war starkly revealed this anomaly: the Royal Navy swept the oceans clear of German merchant ships or bottled them up in ports; German U-Boats sank British tonnage faster than it could be replaced; and the United States had very little shipping of its own to transport its burgeoning exports. In 1914 British-flagged ships carried 70 percent of the United States' trade, but much of that shipping was soon requisitioned for military purposes. The resulting shortage caused ocean freight rates to skyrocket; by January 1915 average rates from Savannah to Liverpool and to Bremen had risen 250 percent and 900 percent over their August 1914 levels. America needed its own wagons, and it needed them quickly. This seemed to be more Secretary of Commerce Redfield's problem than the secretary of the treasury's, but again McAdoo muscled him out of the way.[70]

Displaying a still more statist impulse than he had demonstrated over the Federal Reserve Act, McAdoo proposed in August 1914 the creation of a shipping corporation to purchase and construct a large merchant fleet as quickly as possible. The federal government would own 51 percent of the stock in the new corporation, and would sell the remainder to private investors. McAdoo estimated that the corporation, using shipyards in Britain and the United States, could build 700,000 tons of merchant shipping in 18 months.[71]

In reply to charges that he was entering a socialist wedge into the American economy, McAdoo argued that the emergency was too great to allow for niceties. "Whatever may be said about the principle of government ownership, it ought not to apply to a great national emergency where the vital interests of the nation are at stake and where private capital is not only unwilling to come forward, but refuses to come forward and meet the problem." He then undertook a speaking tour to put his case for the shipping bill, stressing the need for decisive action to capitalize on the wartime boom that was transforming the United States into the most powerful economy on earth.[72]

McAdoo's arguments cut no ice with Republicans, who delayed the shipping bill in the House and then filibustered it to death in the Senate in March 1915. Led by Elihu Root and Henry Cabot Lodge, Senate Republicans charged that McAdoo's shipping corporation was dangerously socialist and a threat to American neutrality. It would compulsorily purchase German ships interned in American harbors, Root claimed, and this would alienate Germany. "It is buying a quarrel, not a ship." Undeterred, McAdoo next considered building large numbers of ships for the navy "as fleet scouts" and then using them as cargo ships.[73]

Secretary of Commerce Redfield, who by now had become very wary of McAdoo's empire-building, dismissed that shipping plan as fanciful. Redfield questioned whether the problem might solve itself—by August 1915 the US shipping register had swelled by more than half a million tons as owners fled to the neutral American flag as protection against German submarines—and doubted whether there was sufficient capacity in British or American yards to undertake McAdoo's ambitious plans. If the shipping shortage was so severe, Redfield wondered, how was it that US exports were growing at unprecedented rates as the embattled Allies bought as much American food, munitions, steel, and other materiel as could be produced?[74]

McAdoo tried again in February 1916 with a new version of the shipping bill. This time it included provisions that the board would operate ships only as a last resort and would cease operations five years after the end of the war. McAdoo described the new bill as "tremendously emasculated," but Congress passed it on August 30, 1916.[75]

"Mr. McAdoo is certainly a busy body, and as busy about calling attention to his attempts to be of assistance to everybody as about anything else," *The New York*

Times noted in February 1915, "but the list of finished accomplishments to his credit is not embarrassingly long." By the middle of 1916, however, his list had lengthened significantly; the Federal Reserve Banks were open, the Pan American conferences were making progress, and the shipping bill was through Congress. McAdoo was the most prominent member of the cabinet and had even become Wilson's son-in-law. His drive and flair for publicity had made him the president's most dynamic lieutenant and the crown prince of the cabinet.[76]

❖✴❖

Newton Baker traveled alone to Washington in March 1916 to join the cabinet as secretary of war. Bess remained in Cleveland so that Elizabeth and Jack could complete the school year, and so Newton took up residence at the University Club. The family was reunited in the summer and moved to Georgetown, which in 1916 offered lower rents than more fashionable neighborhoods in the capital. Baker did not suffer the same precipitous drop in income as McAdoo had in 1913, but he had not been able to accumulate much wealth while he was in Cleveland. He was determined to live within his means and refused attempts by wealthy friends to assist him. Bess was happy to live simply in Washington; she was intimidated by the social demands of her position and uncomfortable with the complexities of etiquette surrounding diplomats, heads of state, and military officers.[77]

Baker's first day in office, March 7, 1916, began normally enough but ended in high drama. His first interview was with the president, and then he met the press. "I looked wise, pleasant, smiling, grave and all my other looks for them in series . . . and finally escaped from them to Mr. Daniels office where I found a very genuine welcome and in a few minutes was in the War Department." There he met his advisors, led by Army Chief of Staff Hugh Scott. "I am an innocent," Baker told Scott. "I don't know anything about this job. You must treat me as a father would his son. I am going to do what you advise me." He had good reason to feel intimidated. If they had heard of him at all, his subordinates knew their new secretary to be a pacifist who had been a spokesman for the League to Enforce Peace and a founding member of the League to Limit Armaments. Utterly inexperienced in military affairs, Baker had much to learn and many skeptics to convince.[78]

The office that Baker assumed in March 1916 incorporated a bewildering variety of duties. The secretary of war, through the US Army Corps of Engineers, conducted flood prevention work; the Department's Insular Bureau controlled the Panama Canal, the Philippines, and Puerto Rico; the secretary was chairman of the National Forest Restoration Commission, supervisor of public buildings and grounds in the District of Columbia, and even superintendent of the cleaning and care of the Statue of Liberty. "You would be interested in the sort of things I have to do here," Baker wrote to a friend in Cleveland after three months in the job. "To most people the War Department means war business and is entirely unattractive, but when I took hold I was astonished to find that . . . only a small part of my time is taken up with military things." Even so, there was the US Army, with nearly 5,000 officers and more than 100,000 enlisted men, to run.[79]

Third in the cabinet pecking order behind State and Treasury, the Department of War had long been divided between its civilian and military leadership. Before 1900 the secretary of war directed the administrative staff of the department while the commanding general of the army controlled military facilities and personnel. This division of responsibilities entrenched conflict between secretaries of war and their commanding generals, leaving the department's technical bureaus— including Artillery, Engineering, and Ordnance—as largely autonomous. In 1903, after his department's bumbling conduct of the Spanish-American War, Secretary of War Elihu Root had Congress abolish the position of commanding general and replace it with a general staff. The general staff was expressly subordinate to the secretary of war, who was now responsible for the administrative and technical bureaus as well as for all military facilities and operations. Not surprisingly, Root's successors, including Newton Baker, venerated him as the savior of their office.[80]

Root's reforms only partially tilted the balance of power within the Department of War toward its civilian leadership. Secretaries of war were political appointees, usually with short tenures and little experience in military affairs. They tended to focus on the political, legal, and administrative aspects of their work and deferred to the general staff and the bureaus on military matters. Baker's immediate predecessor, Lindley Garrison, had become so identified with the general staff's plans for universal military training (UMT) and an expanded army that his relations with Wilson and key congressional Democrats suffered irreparable damage. Baker would eventually prove more independent of his military advisors, but at first he was as prone to capture by his uniformed subordinates as his predecessors had been.[81]

Any hope that Baker held for a leisurely introduction to his duties was dashed before lunch on his first day. No sooner had he made his introductions than reports came that Columbus, New Mexico, had been attacked by a guerilla force led by Pancho Villa. Within ninety minutes Villa's men had killed eighteen Americans and looted Columbus. "Instantly there were conferences and pow-wows enough to make me realize just what sort of rumpusey [sic] business life is after all," Baker reported to his wife. Initial fears that Mexico had invaded the United States proved groundless; it was soon clear that Villa was a renegade at war with Venustiano Carranza's regime and intent on pillage rather than conquest. "I am assured that nobody intended this Mexican situation to develop on the first day of my being here," Baker wrote home on March 10, "but here it is and about the only comfort I can find is that the work may get easier for it cannot get much harder."[82]

As each dispatch from the border was decoded, "I call for the General Staff and preside over a council of grizzled veteran soldiers in determining what to do next. The decision is up to me, but these fine soldiers help enormously through their long experience and frank helpfulness." Wilson had left Washington, but former Secretary Garrison returned to give advice, and Baker put the best face on his lack of experience for the task at hand. "Of course we are not at war with anybody," he told Bess five days after Villa's raid, "and the problem of dispersing Villa's marauding bands is a police problem of the kind I used to have with Chief Kohler [in Cleveland] except it is on a larger scale."[83]

Baker and the general staff recommended that Wilson authorize a Punitive Expedition, led by Brigadier General John J. Pershing, to pursue Villa into Mexico. "I am afraid this is the forerunner of intervention on a comprehensive scale," McAdoo wrote from the USS *Tennessee* on his way to Buenos Aires, "but to tell the truth I am not at all averse to it, because I think we have reached the point where it is necessary for the Government to take vigorous and decisive action." Aware that Villa was a creature of civil war rather than an agent of the Carranza regime, Wilson insisted that Mexican government troops encountered by the expedition be "treated with courtesy and their cooperation welcomed," and "upon no account or pretext . . . shall this expedition become or be given the appearance of being hostile to the integrity or dignity of the Republic of Mexico." Pershing was authorized to engage Mexican government troops only if his expedition was attacked by them.[84]

Pershing and five thousand men crossed the border on March 16, 1916. They soon found themselves ever deeper into Mexico and ever closer to confrontation with Carranza's forces. Increasingly worried by this prospect, the Department of War doubled the number of Pershing's troops and prepared plans to mobilize 150,000 army and militia troops and undertake a full-scale invasion of Mexico.[85]

War with Mexico was averted through mutual restraint. Although Pershing's expedition was an affront to Mexican sovereignty, its full implications were ignored by both governments. In Mexico Carranza's regime was too weak to respond as Pershing's forces ventured farther south; in Washington Wilson and Baker stressed Pershing's limited objectives and their desire to withdraw his forces as soon as Villa and his men had been captured or killed. Both sides had public opinion to placate; Mexicans were inflamed by the presence of US troops on their soil, while Americans demanded revenge for the outrage at Columbus. "So far as I have any feeling about this situation at all," Baker told a correspondent in June 1916, "it is that our paramount duty as a nation is to protect the lives of men, women and children who live in American towns on the Mexican border, that we have no sort of right to interfere with Mexico's national and political concerns, and that we have no right to invade Mexico . . . except to the extent that it is plainly necessary to protect life on our own side."[86]

Baker reminded his correspondents that Villa was a bloodthirsty brigand whose offenses against the United States demanded justice be done, but also that Villa represented neither Mexico's government nor its people. Mexico was incapable of bringing Villa to justice, but the United States could vindicate the rule of law on behalf of both nations. In October 1916 Baker noted that the American Revolution had created conditions similar to those afflicting Mexico. George Washington's men, he told an audience in Jersey City, were hungry and ill-clad at Valley Forge, the former colonies were bankrupt, and the Loyalists were dispossessed. His foray into historical relativism earned him hundreds of denunciatory letters and demands for his resignation from the Daughters of the American Revolution.[87]

Whatever their stated mission, ten thousand uninvited US troops looked like an invasion, and the very name of the Punitive Expedition was more in the spirit of Theodore Roosevelt than Woodrow Wilson. The expedition's failure to capture Villa was embarrassing, and each day took Pershing deeper into Mexico. Baker realized that the expedition could not leave "without being followed by an excited and lawless band . . . inflamed with the feeling that they were chasing American soldiers out of Mexico." Negotiations with Mexico to withdraw the expedition began in October 1916, but progress was slow. The Americans could not leave Mexico empty-handed, but the Mexicans could not neutralize Villa on their own.[88]

Baker's instructions to the commission entrusted with negotiating an end to the impasse emphasized two themes: the United States must protect its citizens and property along the border, and it much preferred Mexico to solve its own problems. "If the Mexican Commissioners want to avoid intervention, they ought to understand that there is no other way than by the suppression of aggression, and that we intend to suppress it if they don't." As negotiations dragged on his position weakened; Pershing could not stay in Mexico forever, and his presence threatened to curdle relations with Mexico for a generation. At the end of 1916 the commissioners agreed to secure the border jointly; Mexico promised to pacify its northern states, and the United States stationed 40,000 troops on the border.[89]

The Punitive Expedition was ordered home in January 1917. Although they had not captured Villa, Pershing's men had dispersed his forces and avoided escalation of the conflict. Pershing was promoted to major general as much for his restraint as his valor, and further honors soon came. "The tact, dignity and loyalty with which Pershing carried out this difficult measure," Baker remembered, "had . . . a great deal to do with his ultimate selection to command our forces in France."[90]

While Pershing's men pursued Pancho Villa, Baker's attention was drawn to the implementation of the preparedness policy announced by Wilson in December 1915. In April 1916, a month after he had taken office, Baker submitted a memorandum, drafted by General Enoch Crowder, outlining what was needed for prosecution of a modern total war. Experience in Europe showed that "mobilization of the industrial, commercial, financial and social resources of the country is as important as the mobilization of either the Army or the Navy." To that end Howard Coffin, president of the Society of Automotive Engineers, had begun an inventory of the nation's industrial assets and their ability to switch to war production. What was needed now, Baker told Wilson, was "a certain amount of new national machinery"—a "council of national strength"—to coordinate this process. This would provide the "third element of preparedness" to work "through sympathetic cooperation between the Government and business interests of the country" rather than "coercive action."[91]

Coffin's inventory of industrial resources was never completed, but the idea of a "council of national strength" quickly assumed tangible form. This owed much to the Naval Consulting Board, set up by Secretary of the Navy Daniels in 1915 and chaired by Thomas Edison, to assess developments in naval technology. Unlike Daniels's board, however, Baker's council focused on interdepartmental coordination rather than adoption of military technology. Baker's council was made up of the secretaries of agriculture, commerce, interior, labor, navy, and war, with the secretary of war as the chair. Congress established the renamed Council for National Defense (CND) in August 1916. Congress also established a National Defense Advisory Commission (NDAC) to provide the CND with plans for mobilizing and expanding war-related industries. The NDAC was made up of business, professional, and labor leaders such as Daniel Willard, president of the Baltimore and Ohio Railroad; Franklin Martin, the secretary general of the American College of Surgeons; Bernard Baruch, a prominent Wall Street financier; and Samuel Gompers, president of the American Federation of Labor (AFL).[92]

"Should the United States be called suddenly into war," Baker and Crowder warned in April 1916, "the disorganization which would result in our industry by a calling out of the State Militia and the acceptance of volunteers . . . would be profound." Within a month Baker had endorsed military training through "some sort of selection." Coming so soon after Garrison's battle over UMT, Baker's policy needed careful nuance. He told the press that he did not suggest that every citizen be transformed into a soldier-in-waiting, but that a system of "selection" would ensure that vital industrial workers were not lost to the army in a rush of volunteering. It was a small step from "selection" to conscription, and Baker was already a long way down that path before the United States entered World War I.[93]

The NDAC was a manifestation of Baker's desire to develop policy through associations of individuals and interest groups rather than through expansion of the federal government's capacities. In 1916 the federal government had yet to develop the ability to implement ambitious schemes such as Coffin's industrial inventory or national industrial mobilization. The need for preparedness was urgent, but expansion of the federal bureaucracy would take time. Baker was also anxious not to create permanent and powerful federal structures in the name of preparedness. Always the localist, he was convinced that the demands of war could be met without permanent change to federal capacities or diminution of state and local authority.[94]

The NDAC and the CND began work at the end of 1916. The CND met regularly—two or three times a week after April 1917—to coordinate federal departments to avoid duplication of effort and resources in the event of war. The NDAC began meetings in December 1916, with each commissioner agreeing to lead the organization of their particular industries and to forward reports to the CND. Until the United States declared war in April 1917, however, the CND and the NDAC struggled to make headway. Wilson was preoccupied with ending the war rather than planning for it; the Department of War's bureaus resented civilian interference in their fiefdoms; and industries were slow to respond to the NDAC's calls for detailed information about their actual and potential capacities. Although these difficulties lessened after the United States entered the war, the CND and the NDAC were partially replaced by newer and more effective organizations such as the War Industries Board.[95]

⋙⊁⋘

Baker and McAdoo moved at different speeds to the conclusion that the United States should declare war against Germany. McAdoo, characteristically enough, moved faster than Baker. Although he had publicly supported neutrality he was privately sympathetic to the Allies. He thought that Germany was responsible for the outbreak of war and condemned its U-Boats as barbaric threats to neutral nations' right to freedom of the seas. The cultural and economic ties between Britain and America were also too strong to countenance siding with Germany. The combination of the British blockade and the flood of Allied orders that bankrolled American prosperity ensured that her neutrality was grossly one-sided, and this accorded with McAdoo's personal sympathies and his assessment of American national interests.[96]

Although he was prepared to go to war over the sinking of the *Lusitania* in May 1915, McAdoo kept that view private. He did, however, find ways to assist the Allied cause. Despite being aware of rumors that the *Lusitania* had carried munitions, he denied that it was anything other than a passenger liner. In July 1915 he inflamed public opinion by leaking German plans to incite industrial unrest in American munitions plants and to spread propaganda through writers and speakers.[97]

McAdoo's commitment to neutrality and peace was increasingly qualified after May 1915. "I believe that the people of this country want peace," he wrote during the height of the *Lusitania* crisis, "but they are unwilling to have it, except with honor." A year later he declared that "the President and every member of cabinet are bending their energies to preserve peace but, of course, it must be peace with honor. The President has been very patient in trying circumstances, and I assure you that our peace will not be broken if it can be preserved without the sacrifice of honor and self-respect." By this he meant that the United States could not tolerate limits to its ability to trade and to protect its citizens as they traveled on neutral ships. In light of the *Lusitania*'s fate, and Germany's declaration in 1916 of unrestricted submarine warfare, he was convinced that German diplomacy toward the United States was more expedient than genuine. He argued strenuously for naval and army expansion, and only the thought that peace would be a potent electoral weapon in 1916 restrained his conviction that war with Germany was inevitable, imminent, and desirable.[98]

With the 1916 elections safely won, McAdoo reacted to the final breach in US-German relations with relief. Wilson had struggled to uphold American rights and honor, but the new German declaration of unrestricted submarine warfare had left the United States with no choice but to enter the war. "I am myself," he wrote to his daughter Harriet in February 1917, "full of fight and energy and am glad to have the definite issue drawn at last."[99]

Newton Baker had good reason to be a wholehearted supporter of neutrality. As mayor of Cleveland, he had a polyglot population to govern and a large German American constituency to placate. Strict neutrality was the best way to maintain municipal peace, and Baker adhered to it closely. He also had personal reasons to be a fervent supporter of neutrality: he was identified with the antiwar movement and with Woodrow Wilson. Apart from heartfelt appeals to Clevelanders to keep the peace, he was happy to leave public discussion of international affairs well alone.

After he ceased to be mayor Baker became more forthcoming about the war's significance. He told his brother Frank in January 1916 that he now subscribed to four key propositions. First and foremost, "Germany intended this war, prepared for it and began it." He was also clear that German "brutalities" in Belgium and on the high seas had shown that the Allies "were dealing with an adversary who had abandoned all the conventions and restraints of civilization." Baker also rejected the German argument that U-Boat warfare was morally equivalent to the Royal Navy's blockade. The blockade prevented trade, he argued, while the U-Boats killed innocent civilians. Compensation and arbitration could rectify property losses, but nothing could make up for the loss of human life. Germany had also "debased the coinage of the common thought of the world" by breaking treaties and trampling the rule of law.[100]

In the cabinet after March 1916, Baker inherited preparedness policies without objection. Although his energies were at first focused on the Mexican crisis, he observed the war in Europe with horror. He remained committed to American neutrality, arguing in April 1916 that "the disaster in Europe is already large enough to satisfy the worst fears of the world, and any addition to it would be an insupportable burden, to be avoided at almost any cost." Trench warfare in France struck him "as very terrible, very pathetically, hopelessly cruel, but very magnificent." After seeing a British film on female industrial workers, he remarked that they "looked so strong and happy," and so "evidently equal to their share of the task of saving England that I want to meet the next man or woman who says that women are not entitled to vote."[101]

Baker did not translate his sympathy with the Allies into a decision for US military intervention until the beginning of 1917. In the cabinet he joined Burleson, Daniels, and Gregory against the belligerents led by Lansing and McAdoo. In April 1916, after Wilson demanded that Germany cease attacks on unarmed ships, Baker still held "a deep conviction that we shall not be drawn into the war and surely that is my hope as it is of the President."[102]

Although not yet ready to go to war, Baker grew impatient with German complaints about the unequal impact of American neutrality. He was aware that America was growing rich by supplying the Allies' war needs but maintained that "I think something can be said for a nation endeavoring to ameliorate, so far as it can, the economic disaster thrust upon it by the war activities of others." In May 1916 he replied to criticism that American-made munitions were critical to the Allied war effort by claiming that they "now comprise only something less than five percent of the total which the Allies are now using," and that he had been told that more German soldiers had been killed by German-made munitions sold to the Allies before the war than by ammunition made in America. In any case "the legal case for any country to sell munitions is clear; and I think it is equally clear that if we were to change the rule in the middle of the war, it would be an unneutral act." This awkward mixture of legalism and anecdote stretched German credulity and Baker's reputation for clear thinking. When the Allies launched their offensive at the Somme in July 1916, three-quarters of their light artillery shells had been manufactured in the United States.[103]

Baker finally decided for war sometime in February 1917. He agreed with Wilson that Germany had left the United States with no choice; nearly two years of negotiations had so wedded Wilson's policies to the protection of neutral shipping and citizens that a back-down now was unthinkable. Baker also subscribed to Wilson's portrayal of the moral issues now at stake. "America is in arms now to vindicate upon the battlefield the right of democracy to exist against the denials of autocracy," he declared in August 1917. "We entered this war to remove from ourselves, our children and our children's children the menace which threatened to deny us that right."[104]

Baker had begun to implement mobilization plans even before Wilson called for a declaration of war. On February 7, 1917, he reported that, "upon a given signal," telegraph and telephone systems would be given over to government use, railroads had been alerted to the imminence of mobilization, the Department of War had placed secret orders for food, clothing, and tents, and that its arsenals had doubled their production. On March 21, 1917, Baker joined McAdoo and the other belligerents in the cabinet in favor of a declaration of war. When Congress obliged on April 6, 1917, Newton Baker began to learn the wisdom of Mr. Dooley's advice to "Be sicrety of war, if ye will; but niver be sicrety of A war!"[105]

CHAPTER 7

Wartime Service, 1917

William McAdoo had been the best known member of the cabinet during Woodrow Wilson's first term. As soon as Congress declared war against Germany on April 6, 1917, however, Newton Baker usurped his place as Wilson's most visible lieutenant. The onset of war brought an abrupt end to the president's domestic agenda, which McAdoo had dominated, and shifted the political and policy focus onto Baker's department. Although McAdoo was deeply involved in the war effort—managing the budget, overseeing tax policies, arranging financial support for the Allies, leading four Liberty Loan campaigns, and controlling the nation's railroads—Baker's duties as secretary of war were even more important and publicly apparent.

In contrast to McAdoo, Baker found public attention uncomfortable. In Wilson's cabinet for barely a year before the declaration of war, he had yet to win over critics who thought him too bookish, too reformist, and even too short to be capable of managing the greatest military undertaking since the Civil War. "These people," he remarked, "wouldn't believe I was Secretary of War unless I was six feet tall and had guns strapped around my waist." Nor could they forgive Baker's connections to the antiwar movement. "I do not see how we can hope to win the war with a pacifist, a professed pacifist, an out-and-out pacifist at the head of the War Department," wrote the editor of the *Providence Journal*.[1]

Baker began his wartime service with a mixture of optimism and apprehension. "But Lord what a job we are up against!" he told a friend at the end of April 1917. "Oh there is a catalogue quite full of troubles if one wants them—but our country is compensatingly magnificent isn't it?"[2]

At the head of a large bureaucracy about to undergo rapid growth, Baker needed competent and loyal staff. His private secretary was of particular importance, and he asked Ralph Hayes, who was then 22 years old, to take the job. Hayes left to join the American Expeditionary Forces (AEF) in July 1918, but returned to Washington immediately after his discharge in May 1919. Six months later he was promoted to assistant to the secretary of war. In 1921 he began a business career that led to the presidency of the Coca Cola Company. He remained devoted to Baker, writing to him in the mid-1930s that "I shall never cease to be grateful that you took me in and so far adopted me that you have been more of parent and priest to me than anyone else I've known." Hayes's mentor and friend returned his affection in spades. "Merry Christmas, my dear Ralph," Baker wrote in 1933, "and grateful hosannas to that kind Providence which brought you into my life. You know how I both admire and love you!"[3]

With his personal office in safe hands, Baker drew reformers and old Cleveland associates into his department. Frank Scott came from the Cleveland Chamber of Commerce to join the General Munitions Board in April 1917 and then the War Industries Board (WIB) in July; Baker also found jobs for Walter Lippmann, the young editor of the New Republic; the future Supreme Court Associate Justice Felix Frankfurter; Eugene Meyer, later the publisher of the Washington Post; Frederick Keppell, who would become head of the Carnegie Corporation; and Stanley King, a future president of Amherst College. Baker also encouraged other progressives, including Grace Abbott, Josephine Goldmark, and Florence Kelley, to contribute to the work of his department. In this he was at the forefront of the administration's efforts to give reformers and business leaders prominent roles in the war effort.[4]

Augmenting the civilian personnel of the War Department was much easier than controlling its military administration. In 1916 Baker inherited a department only partially reformed by Elihu Root in 1903 and still riven between its uniformed and civilian leadership. The military bureaus, in charge of materiel, logistics, and purchasing, retained their budgetary autonomy and undermined the general staff's planning and coordination. As a result, the general staff was completely inadequate to its tasks; in April 1917 it included only 19 officers. When they went to war in August 1914, the German general staff had 650 officers, and the British 232.[5]

Baker was slow to assert his authority over his department's fiefdoms. Aware of his lack of military experience, he at first relied heavily on General Hugh L. Scott, his first chief of staff, for advice. Scott had much experience dealing with the bureaus and their chiefs but little stomach for clipping their wings. He advised Baker to keep the peace by leaving the bureaus alone. Short of friends in a department about which he knew little, Baker was at first happy to follow this advice.[6]

General Scott retired in September 1917 and was replaced by Tasker H. Bliss. By then mobilization was under way and severe shortages of supplies had become apparent. Still reluctant to undertake wholesale reform of the bureaus, Baker and Bliss merely tinkered with their administrative machinery. In November 1917 Baker appointed Benedict Crowell, chairman of a large Cleveland construction company, to be assistant secretary in charge of military supply. Crowell soon resolved to wrest control over purchasing from the bureaus into a centralized system controlled by the secretary of war. Trenchant opposition from the bureaus made Baker realize that change was now not only desirable but essential.[7]

Alarmed by moves led by George E. Chamberlain, chairman of the Senate Committee on Military Affairs, to create a separate Munitions Department, Baker stripped the bureaus of much of their autonomy at the beginning of 1918. Instead of augmenting Crowell's responsibilities, however, he allowed his new chief of staff Peyton C. March to control supply coordination from his office. More dynamic and ruthless than Scott or Bliss, March chose General George W. Goethals as his chief coordinator of the bureaus, took control over major procurement and transport programs, and bypassed the Quartermaster Corps and Ordnance Bureau. Baker, March, and Goethals had struck a significant blow against the bureaus, but they did not surrender all their autonomy until well after the war.[8]

Baker's changing relationship with his three chiefs of staff was indicative of his growing confidence. He had relied on Scott to guide him through the labyrinthine bureaucracy of his new department and had treated him with the same mixture of affection and gratitude that he had bestowed on William Wilson and Tom Johnson. Tasker Bliss and Baker's relationship was more equal. Now more comfortable in his role, Baker worked with Bliss instead of simply following his lead. They began the delicate work of streamlining the War Department's administrative machinery, and their relationship reflected that collaborative spirit; Baker came to think of Bliss as his partner rather than as his mentor. "Taking him all in all," Baker wrote in 1930, "I think [Bliss] was the finest and largest of my wartime army friends."[9]

Baker's relationship with Peyton C. March transcended those he had established with Scott and Bliss. From the outset he was more assertive with Marsh than he had been with Scott and Bliss; he had inherited Scott and Bliss through seniority rather than selecting them himself. In March 1918, however, Baker personally chose March to be chief of staff and recalled him from France over Pershing's objections. March thus owed his job to Baker, and later came to depend on him for political support. Baker appointed March to undertake reforms that he had determined to be vital to the war effort and to safeguard his department against congressional meddling. There was never any doubt that March was Baker's man, and his appointment was a turning point in the secretary's authority within the department.[10]

March was an energetic administrator whose drive was unleavened by either tact or political sensitivity. Even Baker described him as "arrogant, harsh, dictatorial and opinionated." Congressional leaders thought him insufferably rude, Hayes found him overbearing, and Pershing disliked him. "It may be that somebody like me was necessary to act as a yoke to hold them together for [March and Pershing's] combined work," Baker recalled. That he could now "yoke" two powerful generals spoke volumes about his increased authority and confidence. Baker never regretted his promotion and protection of March. "The war was won by days," he told him after the Armistice. "Your energy and drive supplied the days necessary for our side to win."[11]

Baker needed less time to learn the political aspects of military leadership. This was clear in his response to Theodore Roosevelt's bid to re-enact on the Western Front his earlier glories in Cuba. Soon after Wilson broke relations with Germany, TR sought permission to raise and lead a division of volunteers in Europe. This was not the first time that he had offered to ride out of retirement at the head of a new generation of Rough Riders; in July 1916 he had tried to raise a division of volunteers in the event of war with Mexico. That request was easily pigeonholed, but in 1917 TR ran a much louder campaign to return to the colors. He offered to raise a division made up of three brigades of infantry, a brigade each of cavalry and artillery and an "aero squadron," and had even decided that his chief of staff and brigade commanders should include Generals Leonard Wood and John J. Pershing. TR's plan was leaked to the press and won much support; even Baker's brother Julian offered to serve.[12]

Baker thanked Roosevelt for his offer but noted that plans were afoot to form a much larger army whenever Congress so decided and that its commanders would be drawn from the regular army and not from volunteers. Three days later TR reminded Baker that he was a retired commander in chief who had led troops in the field. Irritated by TR's failure to take a hint, Baker replied that "the military record to which you call my attention is, of course, a part of the permanent records of this Department and is available, in detail, for consideration."[13]

The American declaration of war made Roosevelt redouble his efforts. He promised to persuade Congress to pass a conscription law and again offered to raise a division in advance of a new conscripted army. Concerns about his age were groundless, the 59-year-old claimed, because General Paul von Hindenburg had emerged from retirement at 67 to lead the German army on the Eastern Front. TR did concede that "I am not a Hindenburg!" but insisted that he could "raise and handle this division in a way that will do credit to the American people, and to you, and to the President."[14]

Baker was scathing of Roosevelt's request and its motives. TR's release of their correspondence showed that he hoped to embarrass Baker into approving his scheme, and his protestations of support rang hollow because of his antipathy toward Wilson and contempt for Baker. "Nice Mr. Baker," he had declared during the 1916 presidential campaign, "he knits." TR worked closely with Republican Senate leader Henry Cabot Lodge, coordinating his request to raise a division with Lodge's effort to discredit the Democrats' war policy as too little, too late.[15]

Roosevelt combined these approaches in an eighteen-page letter to Baker. He argued that his division would help rectify the "very grave blunder" of not instituting conscription in August 1914. Had Wilson and the Democrats done so then America would now have a million trained soldiers to turn the war's tide. A single division now could be trained more quickly than a whole army, and TR's men could soon support the Allies in advance of the American regular army. "If the people of a town do not prepare a fire company until the fire breaks out, they are foolish. But they are more foolish still if when the fire breaks out, they then decline to try to put it out with any means at hand, on the ground that they prefer to wait and drill a fire company."[16]

Baker drew his correspondence with TR to a close in the middle of May 1917. "I do not like Mr. Roosevelt," he confessed to Wilson. He had long considered him to be self-obsessed, and saw this episode as further proof of that judgment. Roosevelt was "a useful man" who had served the nation admirably, Baker told a friend after the war, "except for the last two years of his life, when he was mad." TR was restless in retirement, still politically ambitious, and in declining health. His bravado in Cuba twenty years before had been at the expense of a ragtag Spanish army and one-fifth of his men's lives. The consequences of letting him loose on the Western Front were too horrendous to contemplate.[17]

As politics infused Roosevelt's offer, so too did they influence Baker's refusal. It was no secret that TR wanted the 1920 Republican presidential nomination, and Baker was in no mood to give him a springboard to it. "It would have been quite impossible for Colonel Roosevelt to forget that he had been President of the United States . . . If [he] had been in France, politicians and military men alike would have regarded him as qualified to speak on both national and on military policy and the confusion would have been very great." This would be embarrassing to the actual American commander in the field, who would feel constrained by having a former commander in chief under his authority.[18]

Selection of the commander of the AEF presented other difficulties. Of the army's senior generals most were disqualified by their age or poor health. Baker's shortlist was soon reduced to two men: TR's friend Leonard Wood, who had served in Cuba, in the Philippines, and on the general staff, and John J. Pershing, who had led the Punitive Expedition into Mexico. Both were Republicans, but Wood had been more outspoken. He had called for war with Germany after the sinking of the *Lusitania*, criticized the administration for its slow progress on preparedness, and backed TR's quest for his own division. He had also described Baker as deplorably weak. Wilson was aware of Wood's antipathy and told Baker in January 1917 that "personally I have no confidence either in General Wood's discretion or in his loyalty to his superiors." Baker had observed him while he was on the general staff, and called him his most "insubordinate subordinate." Wood's great weakness, Baker thought, was his desire to be a great soldier and a great politician at the same time. "This combination I do not believe to be possible in the United States and I am glad it is not."[19]

Pershing, on the other hand, had shown during his foray into Mexico his ability to lead a large military formation in the field. He knew his place as a military commander under civilian superiors, while Wood clearly did not. In May 1917 Baker formally recommended to Wilson that he appoint Pershing to lead the AEF. [20]

Subsequent events confirmed Baker in the wisdom of his choice. Wood was assigned to the army's Southeastern Department to oversee construction of the camps there. He remained close to TR and Lodge, feeding them information to embarrass Baker. Wood was later appointed to lead a combat division, and again irritated Baker by criticizing Pershing during a trip to Europe. He also tried to organize a trip to the Italian front, but by then Baker was anxious to have his troublesome general back home. He resolved that Pershing would never again be undermined by Wood's unrestrained egotism.[21]

Baker acted at the end of May 1918. By then Wood's division had completed its training and was about to embark for Europe. En route to the coast Wood received orders to leave his division and take charge of the army's Western Department in San Francisco. He rushed to Washington to object, only to be told by Baker that his relief had been requested by Pershing, who "most decidedly does not want you in Europe." Wood protested that Baker had rendered every army officer's career hostage to Pershing's whims, and that this was "very unjust and very dangerous."[22]

Wood beat a sullen retreat to San Francisco. His actions there warranted his dismissal from the army altogether, but Baker was content to sideline him far from the war. To Wood's biographer Hermann Hagerdorn, Baker and the general presented a contrast that reflected no credit on the former. Wood was "rugged, powerful, self possessed," while Baker was "slender, boyish, with all his brilliancy, unimpressive . . . It seemed the maddest irony that, in the midst of the greatest of wars, this groping sentimentalist should be this realist's master."[23]

Baker was as indulgent of Pershing as he was uncompromising with Wood. Like almost everyone else, he found Pershing prickly and aloof, "an interesting and somewhat baffling personality," who combined military daring with an obsessive concern for detail. "He is the only combination of telescope and microscope I know."

Remembering his discussions with his father in Martinsburg, Baker resolved not to repeat Secretary of War Edwin M. Stanton's interference in the Union's military planning during the Civil War. Jefferson Davis, by contrast, had allowed Robert E. Lee to fight the war his way, and Baker was determined to follow his example. The result was that Pershing enjoyed, with only a few exceptions, a free hand. Baker supported Pershing's incessant demands for more troops and his frequent changes to specifications for AEF aircraft, artillery, and other materiel. He took responsibility for Wood's exile to San Francisco and supported Pershing against the bureaus' attempts to control the contracts between the AEF and its European suppliers. "No American general in the field," Pershing later declared, "ever received the perfect support accorded to me by Mr. Baker. His attitude . . . is a model for the guidance of future secretaries in such an emergency." For his part, Baker ranked Pershing, with March and Bliss, as the three most important contributors to the American war effort.[24]

Baker's support of Pershing wore thin only near the end of the war. His self-proclaimed role as a "yoke" between March and Pershing became increasingly difficult as the two clashed over the extent of their authority. Encouraged by Baker to exercise independent control over the AEF, Pershing resented March's assertion of the general staff's overarching responsibility for the war effort. This struggle involved Baker, for March and the general staff were instruments through which the president, through his secretary of war, operated as commander in chief. Although loyal to Pershing, Baker increasingly saw March's point that the secretary of war needed to maintain the principle that the military was under civilian authority. The war ended before this conflict could be resolved, but Baker certainly sided more frequently with the general staff against Pershing in the latter half of 1918 than during the first twelve months of Pershing's tenure.[25]

Pershing tested the limits of his independence toward the end of October 1918. Amid rumors that the Germans would sue for peace on the basis of Wilson's Fourteen Points, Pershing told his British and French counterparts that only unconditional surrender was acceptable. Continuing the war until Germany's complete collapse would give the United States a more prominent role in the victory and strengthen its hand in the peace settlement that would follow. This contradicted Wilson's policy, and Baker objected to Pershing's "usurpation" of it. He wrote a letter of reprimand that reminded Pershing that he was subordinate to civilian authority. That letter was never sent, but Pershing was brought to heel by Edward House. By so upbraiding Pershing at the end of the war, Baker had returned to the same concerns that had led him at its beginning to scuttle Wood's ambition to lead the AEF.[26]

Entry into the war required a massive expansion of the US Army and brought into sharp relief the problem of recruiting millions of new soldiers. It is clear that Wilson and Baker preferred voluntary service over conscription until February 1917. Wilson's refusal to countenance compulsory military service in 1916 had precipitated Garrison's resignation as secretary of war, and his successor entered the cabinet believing that soldiering should be a voluntary privilege rather than a legal obligation. Conscription also revived unpleasant memories of the Civil War, with its draft riots and iniquitous substitution system.[27]

Baker and then Wilson reconsidered their positions in the weeks immediately before the Declaration of War. The imminent prospect of war concentrated Baker's mind on the requirements of mass mobilization. Relying on patriotic fervor to create a huge army risked chaos or failure, as millions of young men either flocked to, or ran from, recruiting stations. Conscription's ability to ensure orderly mobilization needed to be weighed against its unsavory ideological and historical baggage.

A central concern of progressivism since 1900 was to rethink old convictions that individualism and limited government were the foundations of social progress. The modern age required coordination of individual initiative toward community goals by more active governments and more engaged citizens. Modern war seemed to many progressives to require reconsideration of the role of the federal government in setting and enforcing national priorities and policies. Under conscription, Wilson's secretary Joseph Tumulty explained, the government and not the individual would decide whether a man could best serve his country at work or at the front. Baker had been persuaded by this argument by the beginning of March 1917.[28]

Although some historians have seen Wilson and Baker's conversion to conscription as a panicked response to TR's attempt to raise a volunteer division, this is unlikely. Roosevelt's offer had captured the public's imagination, but he was also an advocate of compulsory military service and never suggested that volunteer divisions could be a substitute for it. His grandstanding was embarrassing to Wilson and Baker, but it was not sufficient to force such an abrupt change in policy. The imminence of war, and the logic of progressivism, were much more influential than the irritation of what David Kennedy has called TR's "martial buffoonery."[29]

Now converted to conscription, Baker had to persuade the president. He did so during a discussion in March 1917, telling Wilson that conscription was the only way to ensure that the costs of war could be equitably shared and economic production maximized. Wilson agreed, and authorized General Enoch Crowder, the judge advocate general, to formulate a conscription bill for presentation to Congress in the event that it decided to declare war.[30]

The army bill caused a sensation. It called for the immediate expansion of the regular army to 500,000 men, with provision for another 500,000 if needed, to be recruited wholly by a selective national draft of men between 19 and 25. No substitution was allowed, although the bill did allow exemptions for workers in essential industries, for those who were physically, mentally, or morally unfit, and for conscientious objectors. Men with economically dependent wives and children could also receive a deferment of their military service.[31]

The bill was well received in the Senate, but it faced an uncertain future in the House. Speaker Champ Clark declared that there was "precious little difference between a conscript and a convict," and others accused Wilson of trying to Prussianize America. James Reed, a Democratic senator from Missouri, warned Baker that "you will have the streets of our American cities running red with blood on Registration Day." Many western congressmen feared the wholesale loss of farm labor, and their southern colleagues worried about the prospect of uniformed and armed African Americans in their midst. During his appearance before the House Military Affairs Committee in support of the bill, Baker was asked why the administration was not prepared to trial a volunteer system. Samuel Nicholls, a Democrat from South Carolina, declared that a volunteer army would be more effective because "[men] who wanted to go would make the best soldiers." "I am not so sure," Baker replied, "that lust for battle is necessarily a valuable asset for a soldier. Willingness to do his duty is enough."[32]

Those who extolled the inherent superiority of volunteer soldiers had to face the fact that only 4,355 men had come forward in the first 10 days after the declaration of war. Even if volunteers now flooded in, Baker warned, the nation would suffer "because you would have combed the country of all those brave spirited men, and killed them off." Only a draft would ensure that slackers would play their part and key industries could retain their workforces. Ex-President William Howard Taft congratulated Baker and offered his assistance to win over Congress. "It is hard to tear away from the traditions of volunteering handed down to us from the various wars regarded only in the light of ultimate success, and without the slightest analysis of the enormous waste and useless slaughter due to such an illogical and really absurd system." Amendments raised the minimum draft age to 21, paid draftees generously, and permitted—but did not require—the president to authorize volunteer regiments such as TR's. Wilson signed conscription into law on May 18, 1917.[33]

Baker now had his draft, but he did not yet have his army. Crowder had devised a registration system designed to avoid the chief failings of the Union's draft during the Civil War. Conscription then was conducted by uniformed army personnel, which in Crowder's view "bared the teeth of the Federal Government in every home within the loyal states." In 1917 he decided that conscription would be administered by civilian draft boards staffed by "friends and neighbors of the men to be affected." The nation would have 4,500 draft boards which, in Crowder's memorable image, "became the buffers between the individual citizen and the Federal Government, and thus they attracted and diverted, like grounding wires in an electric coil, such resentment . . . as might have proved a serious obstacle to war measures, had it been focused on the central authorities." Baker also ensured that Registration Day, June 5, 1917, was preceded by intense publicity to "relieve as far as possible the prejudice which remains . . . in the popular mind against the draft by reason of Civil War memories."[34]

The result was that conscription in World War I was an unwieldy combination of policy imposed by the federal government but implemented by local administrative structures. Although its initial implementation was successful, closer examination of conscription in 1917 and 1918 reveals its flaws. Baker was so focused on the need to avoid repeating the mistakes of 1863–1865, and so enamored of community-based mobilization, that he allowed less admirable features of local politics and social hierarchies to mold, and often pervert, the creation of a national army.[35]

Despite Reed's predictions Registration Day was not accompanied by blood in the streets. There were no major disturbances reported from anywhere in the country as nearly ten million men registered for the draft. Registrars filled out a card for each man, recording his name, date and place of birth, marital status, race, and occupation. Each registrant was assigned a number between 1 and 10,500, and on July 20, 1917, Baker, blindfolded, reached into a bowl of 10,500 capsules and drew out number 258. Over the next sixteen hours a procession of dignitaries and clerks drew out the remainder of the capsules.[36]

Registrants were then called before their draft boards in the order that their numbers had been picked. Those who failed medical tests were exempted, and those with economic dependents were granted deferments. Much to the chagrin of McAdoo and others in the cabinet, Baker issued blanket exemptions only to shipbuilding employees and forced railroad employees, farm workers, and coal miners to argue for exemption on the basis of their essential employment. McAdoo tried and failed twice to persuade Baker to classify all railroad employees as essential workers.[37]

Baker and Crowder's policy of entrusting "friends and neighbors" to determine eligibility for military service led to inconsistent results. Some Democrats complained that Republican governors had appointed cronies to draft boards, who then applied exemption and deferment criteria more strictly to Democrats than to their friends' sons. In Democratic areas troubles also arose; McAdoo complained that too few of his allies sat on New York draft boards, and across the nation Americans of both parties objected to the different definitions of economic dependence applied by local boards. Some assumed that all wives were economically dependent on their husbands, while others examined each case carefully and sometimes intrusively. The result was that married men were inducted into the AEF at rates that varied from 6 to 38 percent across the nation's draft districts.[38]

All southern men were subject to conscription, but African Americans found their inclusion to be grudging and certainly not a validation of their full citizenship. A study of four southern draft boards has shown that they were made up of propertied white men who actively discriminated against out-groups. The Coweta County, Georgia, board routinely exempted African Americans; the manly, active, and patriotic duty of the soldier was reserved for white men while African Americans remained subservient at home in the cotton fields. The Fulton County, Georgia, draft board discriminated against African Americans in the opposite way, this time exempting 65 percent of white registrants but only 3 percent of African Americans.[39]

By the end of the war African Americans, who represented 10 percent of the national population, made up 13 percent of draftees. Despite numerous complaints Baker disbanded only three draft boards for systematic racial discrimination. The result was that African Americans were drafted or exempted on the basis of white prejudices and economic interests. Life picking cotton was less dangerous than in the AEF, even in its labor battalions, but it also denied African Americans the citizenship and financial benefits of serving their nation in its time of need.[40]

By November 1918, 14 million men had registered for the draft and 2,800,000 of them had joined the army and navy. In August 1918 the minimum draft age was dropped to 18 and the maximum rose to 45, and by the end of the war the United States had mobilized 20 percent of its males in this cohort compared to the British figure of 60 percent. Despite intensive publicity campaigns and government pressure nearly 340,000 men failed to report for induction. In Georgia and New Jersey about 5 percent of registrants failed to attend their eligibility interviews, and many more declined to register at all. Of those who did enter the AEF, the typical draftee was between 21 and 23 years old and single. Nearly 30 percent of the initial registrants were rejected on medical grounds, 5 percent could not understand English, 31 percent were functionally illiterate, and during the course of the war nearly 260,000 men with venereal disease enlisted.[41]

Despite these unedifying statistics Baker remained intensely proud of the men who joined the AEF. He refused to call them "conscripts," preferring "selectees" and "servicemen" to distinguish them from their Civil War forebears. "You are the army of a free people, yourselves free men;" he told the 86th Division before it embarked for France in July 1918. "You are fighting for a cause which is almost a romance in its purity and freedom from selfishness or taint of any kind." [42]

At the end of the war Baker told Wilson that the AEF was "the sanest, most sober, and least criminalistic body engaged in the great war, under any flag, or that could be found in any group the same size in civil life." The men of the AEF, despite the horrors they had witnessed in France, suffered lower insanity and suicide rates than had the regular army before the war, and less than 100 of them had been repatriated for alcoholism. In New York City, which had about the same number of adult males as there were in the AEF, by contrast, 10,000 men passed through hospital alcoholic wards every year. Only 2,000 of the 2 million-strong AEF were convicted of crimes, compared to 210,000 arrests per year among New York's male population and a 12 percent discharge rate from the regular army for criminal wrongdoing in 1915. Baker attributed these differences to psychiatric testing, control over soldiers' access to alcohol, and the AEF's patriotism. [43]

Transforming millions of "selectees" and the greatly expanded National Guard into battle-ready soldiers presented enormous challenges. Between April 1917 and November 1918 soldiers made more than 8,700,000 train journeys between collection centers, training camps, and embarkation ports. Transportation of a single combat division required 60 trains of 14 cars each, and by the end of the war there were more than 40 AEF divisions in France. Each one included about 28,000 officers and men organized in infantry brigades, artillery regiments, machine gun companies, medical detachments, supply companies, and headquarters staff, and mounted on trucks, motorcycles, bicycles, horses, and mules. Nearly four million new soldiers, sailors, and National Guardsmen also required huge quantities of food, water, arms, ammunition, clothing, and footwear. [44]

To house its new troops the War Department built 9 mobilization centers, 16 army cantonments, 16 National Guard camps, 3 Engineers' and 5 medical camps, 9 reserve officers' camps, 8 airfields, and 3 embarkation ports. Each cantonment was like a small city with its own electricity, water, and sewerage systems and up to 1,200 wooden barracks for between 25,000 and 40,000 men. All this construction consumed entire forests, employed thousands of soldiers and private contractors, and cost three-quarters of the sum spent building the Panama Canal—but this time it was spent in 3 months rather than the Canal's 10 years. [45]

The commercial and patriotic possibilities of lucrative construction contracts, and then the stationing of tens of thousands of trainees paid $1 a day, created fierce competition among communities for camps to be built in their midst. Beyond specifying that facilities should be near rail lines, and stating a preference for milder climates, the War Department left camp locations up to the commanders of its six military districts. As McAdoo discovered when he selected Federal

Reserve Cities in 1914, the politics of distributing federal largesse were never easy. Army and National Guard camps were prime political pork, and politicians fought hard for their share.

Nineteen of the thirty-two facilities were built in the states of the Old Confederacy and Kentucky, ostensibly because of their warmer weather. The entire West Coast won only three camps, and the upper Midwest, Great Plains, and Rocky Mountain states received none at all. Not surprisingly, their communities and representatives felt aggrieved; Senator Warren G. Harding of Ohio, a state that received only one camp, wondered how training in the steamy South could prepare troops to fight in northern France. Indiana, denied even a single camp, complained that its barracks near Indianapolis had been ignored in favor of building a brand-new facility in nearby northern Kentucky. Others noted that every Democratic member of the House Military Affairs Committee had been favored with a camp in their district.[46]

Even in the South there were powerful losers. Senator Kenneth McKellar complained that no less than ten camps and cantonments had been approved in seven of the eight states that bordered his own state of Tennessee, but still it had received nothing. Senator Duncan Fletcher of Florida was incensed by the rejection of Leonard Wood's recommendation to build a camp in Florida, writing to Baker that this put him "in a most embarrassing and humiliating position . . . I might as well resign my seat here if that is the treatment we are to have."[47]

The politics of camp location were obscure and, to Baker, exasperating. Congressmen and senators were parochial enough, but life was made even more difficult by Leonard Wood, then in command of the southeastern military district. Despite the War Department's policy to place camps near rail junctions, Wood held that they should be located near ports. To this end he drummed up support by leaking his views to the press. Wood promised Tennesseans that Memphis would get a camp, and Floridians that Jacksonville would be selected, despite decisions to the contrary in Washington. His indiscretions reinforced Baker's doubts about his trustworthiness and contributed to his decision not to reward him with a division in France.[48]

Baker's troubles did not end there; toward the end of 1917 southern camps were hit by unseasonably cold weather. Heavy snow and subzero temperatures made a mockery of the mild climate that had justified the location of so many camps in the South, and wreaked havoc on the newly constructed installations and their inhabitants. Men shivered without blankets or coats, water pipes froze, sewerage systems broke down, and pneumonia, meningitis, and dysentery broke out. Press reports and letters from suffering draftees embarrassed Baker and his department as they struggled to keep camp hospitals operating and essential supplies flowing. A congressional committee accused the War Department of underestimating their residents' need for warm clothing. These criticisms presaged the much greater difficulties that Baker would encounter from Congress in 1918, and added to controversies over camp location, construction, and administration that had dogged the program from its inception.[49]

Within the camps draftees were subjected to intensive physical fitness programs, endless parade drills, and basic military training. As they awaited the manufacture of rifles, bayonets, and machine guns, many of them practiced with broomsticks to the derision of critics who feared for the War Department under the leadership of a pacifist. Baker's other ideas for military training gave his critics more ammunition. He was determined that camp life would not only make men into soldiers, but also into better citizens. To that end he established the Commission on Training Camp Activities (CTCA) under the direction of Raymond Fosdick to devise a program of moral education for the AEF.[50]

Fosdick had studied army camps along the Mexican border, and was horrified to learn that they were encircled by saloons, casinos, and brothels catering to soldiers with money to spend and time on their hands. He resolved to do better with the AEF by providing what Baker described as "wholesome recreation so as pleasantly and, if possible, profitably to occupy the leisure hours of the soldier." Millions of American men had been taken from their families in the name of a great national crusade, he declared, and in return the government was under an obligation to return them sound in morals, if not in body. Draftees were to be provided with "invisible armor" to protect them from vice. Baker also knew that venereal disease and alcohol poisoning severely depleted an army's fighting strength. In 1917 the British Expeditionary Force had the equivalent of two divisions under treatment for syphilis and gonorrhea, and the French army had recorded a million cases since the beginning of the war.[51]

The CTCA focused on prostitution and saloons as the greatest threats to the soldiers' moral and physical welfare. Sale of alcohol was prohibited within a five-mile radius of army camps, as were "houses of ill fame, brothels, or bawdy houses." Committing the CTCA to a "fit to fight" campaign, Fosdick shut down every red light district in the country that was in reach of the AEF. Prostitutes and "promiscuous women" were arrested and imprisoned, while their uniformed customers were fined and sent to clinics for painful treatment. Fosdick and the CTCA succeeded in driving prostitution off city streets, but not in eradicating sin. The mayor of New Orleans complained to Baker that suppression of his city's brothels denied "the God-given right of men to be men," and one AEF officer wrote that "You ask us to give our lives for our beloved country, which we are only too willing to do—but you deprive us of the privilege of a glass of wine or beer even at our meals—and—most of all you deny us the freedom of our God-given rights of manhood!"[52]

The CTCA proffered carrots as well as sticks. It coordinated organizations such as universities, the YMCA, the Jewish Welfare Board, and the Playground and Recreation Association to provide athletic equipment, reading classes, lectures on science and literature, concerts, motion picture showings, and dramatic performances. The American Library Association donated works of approved literature and banned books that smacked of pacifism, anarchism, or German propaganda.[53]

Baker's commitment to the CTCA echoed his work in Cleveland's dance halls and red light district. The CTCA combined three elements of his progressivism: efficiency, morality, and social justice. Men free of venereal disease and alcoholism were better soldiers; if they could be steered toward wholesome physical activity, they would learn the value of self-improvement that would serve them well after the war. There was also a strong theme of personal and social uplift in the CTCA's work, in which working-class recreations like drinking and gambling were discouraged in favor of middle-class virtues of education, middlebrow culture, personal cleanliness, and temperance. "The work which Mr. Fosdick and his Committee have undertaken at my request," Baker told Pershing's aide in France, "has been so important for the building up of the morale of the soldiers that I would not be far wrong if I were to characterize it as one of the most important activities of the War Department."[54]

❧⧉☙

William McAdoo greeted the declaration of war by offering to resign from cabinet to raise a volunteer regiment to fight in France. His offer was symbolic; he was 54 years old, unqualified to lead troops into battle, and TR's demand for his own division had produced embarrassment enough for the administration. His martial dreams shelved, McAdoo found plenty to do at home. Although Baker was now the lynchpin of the war effort, there was still wide scope for an empire builder like McAdoo. "I am doing all I can with the Treasury," he told Colonel House in June 1917, "which, of course, must bear the brunt of everything that is done . . . so far as the conduct of the war is concerned."[55]

McAdoo's primary responsibility during the war was to ensure that there were enough funds to finance not only America's war effort but also to help those of Britain, France, Italy, and Russia. He therefore insisted on the centralization of all fiscal and monetary policy into his department. As chairman of the Federal Reserve Board (FRB), he subordinated its policies to Treasury, even to the extent of making it the government's bond-seller during the four Liberty Loan campaigns of 1917–1918. Although much vaunted in 1913, the independence of the FRB had been compromised by the role of the secretary of the treasury as its chairman. The subjugation of its independence to the federal government in 1917–1918 was the consequence of McAdoo's resolve that federal government, through him, should be "in the saddle."[56]

Modern war proved to be ruinously expensive, not only in soldiers' lives but also in resources. In 1916, the last full year of peace, the federal government spent $740 million. Expenditures more than doubled to $2 billion during 1917, multiplied 6 times in 1918, and then peaked at $19 billion in 1919. The federal government spent almost double its total 1916 annual expenditures every month during the 1918 fiscal year. By 1920 the war had cost $35 billion, 10 times the cost of the Civil War and about the same as all the federal government's expenditures during its first century of existence. The full cost of the war, including forgiven loans and soldiers' pensions, amounted to $54 billion by 1950.[57]

War financing had traditionally come from three sources: taxation, bonds, and creation of new currency. During the Civil War the Union had raised 20 percent of its costs from taxation and had used bonds and greenbacks to fund the remainder. Although he was publicly deferential to congressional prerogatives over revenue measures, McAdoo insisted that taxation should play a much larger part in war finance than it had in the past. In negotiations with congressional leaders in the first few months after the declaration of war he urged that half the projected cost of the war be raised through taxation, with the rest coming from bonds.[58]

McAdoo argued for a balance between taxation and bonds for a number of reasons. Relying too heavily on bonds would strain the nation's credit and drain stock markets while raising interest rates and creating inflationary pressure. The social consequences of war taxation also appealed to him. Bonds were government obligations, repayable thirty years after their issue. Their cost was mostly borne by the next generation, who would repay the principal, while the generation who prosecuted the war was responsible only for the interest. Taxation forced the present generation to shoulder more of the financial burden of war instead of deferring the bulk of it to its children. Bond financing also had significant implications for social equity within the wartime generation. Instead of paying high taxes, better-off Americans could buy bonds and earn interest exempt from federal taxation. Bonds offered investors, especially those who could buy many of them, an opportunity to make money out of the war rather than involuntarily donate to it. "Good fortune has for many years favored us, and we have grown healthy, wealthy and fat," McAdoo told *The New York Times* in May 1917. "Wholesome taxation for a noble purpose is the best antidote for the fatty degeneration with which we have been long threatened as a nation."[59]

At first McAdoo's arguments held sway in Congress. He consulted with Claude Kitchin, chairman of the House Ways and Means Committee, to formulate the first wartime revenue bill. It called for $3.5 billion of extra funding, half of which was to come from taxation. Kitchin's committee proposed a raft of tax increases, including a halving of the threshold for the 2 percent federal income tax to $1,500 per year for single and $3,000 for married taxpayers, surtaxes from 1 percent to 33 percent on incomes between $5,000 and $2 million per year, a doubling of the excess profits tax, increases in the inheritance tax, new stamp duties, increases in liquor and tobacco taxes, and new taxes on jewelry, cosmetics, movie tickets, railroad tickets, and telephone calls.[60]

Despite opposition from Republicans the bill passed the House in three weeks. In the Senate it met more effective resistance that held the bill up until October 1917. In the meantime McAdoo quintupled his original estimate of the cost of the war during the 1917–1918 fiscal year to $15 billion, but did not ask for further revenue measures. Correctly assuming that senators and representatives were happier to approve bond issues that paid their constituents interest rather than cost them in higher taxes, he dropped his earlier insistence that taxation provide half of the war's cost. That concession left many progressives skeptical about his commitment to their principles.[61]

McAdoo rediscovered some of his earlier zeal for using taxation to achieve social equity during negotiations over revenue legislation for the 1918–1919 fiscal year. By then the federal government had floated three bond issues totaling $8.5 billion and had raised $4.5 billion in taxes. This represented a one-third:two-thirds ratio between taxation and loans, but projected expenditure for 1918–1919 of $24 billion threatened to tilt the balance further toward loans unless higher taxes were enacted. Although reluctant to raise taxes in an election year, McAdoo worried that greater reliance on bonds might run investment funds dry and escalate inflation. He therefore suggested that taxes be raised to $8 billion per year— almost double the figure for 1917–1918—to keep the one-third:two-thirds ratio for 1918–1919.[62]

Rather than increase the excess profits tax, McAdoo pushed Kitchin to agree to a flat 80 percent war profits tax on profits above 8 percent on capital. This would not only close the revenue gap but recapture inflated profits from generous "cost-plus" contracts designed to stimulate production through high prices. "The laboring men of the country," McAdoo told Kitchin, ". . . will not rest content while corporations engaged in war industries pay huge dividends from Government war contracts or Government price fixing." He also suggested that income tax rise to 6 percent on incomes less than $4,000 per year, 12 percent on incomes above that figure, and surtaxes up to 65 percent on very high incomes. Unearned income from dividends, rent, and interest should also be taxed at double the rate as income derived from wages and salaries. Because Liberty Loans, floated to pay for the war, were exempt from such taxation their attractiveness would be heightened without the need to lift their interest rates.[63]

Kitchin was doubtful of congressional support for such a radical plan but agreed to back it. Congress did refuse to enact a war profits tax, and the rest of the war revenue bill of 1918 was still in committee when the war ended. After the Armistice McAdoo dropped his demands for more revenue and his calls for a more equitable distribution of the war's costs. Ultimately, taxation provided 35 percent of the cost of the war, nearly double the share achieved by the North during the Civil War but a far cry from the vision of inter- and intragenerational equity that had underpinned McAdoo's original demand for a 50–50 share between loans and taxation.[64]

War bonds excited far less opposition than high war taxation. In April 1917 Congress authorized McAdoo to issue up to $5 billion in bonds and $2 billion in certificates of indebtedness. Treasury officials, FRB members, and prominent investment bankers engaged in spirited debate over the maximum amount of bonds that could be absorbed by investors, their interest rate, and their relationship to the nation's currency supply. Given that no one could predict the duration or ultimate cost of the war, McAdoo and his advisors also had to factor in the likelihood of several more bond issues.[65]

It was widely agreed that the first bond issue should be offered at a low interest rate to prevent funds from being drained from savings accounts and to leave room to lift interest rates on subsequent issues. McAdoo's advisors suggested an initial rate of 3.5 percent, but with a right to convert into subsequent issues if they were offered at higher rates. A low interest rate, however, might limit the amount of bonds that would be taken up. J. P. Morgan, America's most prominent banker, thought that only $1 billion worth could be sold at 3.5 percent, while Comptroller of the Currency John Skelton Williams and Paul Warburg of the FRB argued that patriotism and publicity could sell $2 billion at 3.5 percent, as long as there was a right of conversion and exemption from federal taxes.[66]

McAdoo was also advised to calibrate taxation to foster a market for war bonds. Although he was determined to make those bonds widely available, it was clear that most of them would be bought by financial institutions and wealthy investors. It was therefore essential, the mining magnate Cleveland H. Dodge advised, to thwart calls for high levels of taxation. "If the newspaper rumors are correct that large incomes are to be taxed up to 60%, and there is to be an enormous increase in the excess profits tax," Dodge warned, "it is doubtful whether you could place any bonds at all."[67]

McAdoo took these arguments seriously, but was aware of the self-interest that ran through them. "No matter what tax is evolved there are very few people who think it equitable," he replied to Dodge, "except those who have not to bear the tax!" Heavy taxation of wealthy Americans and luxury goods was essential because the former ensured that the costs of war would be equitably distributed and the latter depressed nonessential spending. "Wars cannot be fought without sacrifices, sacrifices not alone of life but sacrifices of property."[68]

Quite prepared to use intensive advertising and patriotic pressure to make up for low interest rates on war bonds, McAdoo also enlisted the Federal Reserve Banks to reduce the risk of currency contraction that was inherent in deficit financing. Banks were allowed to lend money to buy war bonds by accepting the bonds themselves as collateral, which then enabled them to receive currency from their Federal Reserve Bank on the basis of those bonds. The national money supply would increase with the amount of war bonds sold and thus limit inflationary pressure. This policy was only partially successful; between 1916 and 1920 the nation's money supply grew by 75 percent, but the consumer price index doubled.[69]

On May 2, 1917, McAdoo announced that $2 billion of war bonds, called Liberty Loans, would be offered for sale. They would mature in 30 years, pay 3.5 percent interest, be sold in denominations from $50 to $100,000, and be exempt from federal, state, and municipal taxes. Purchasers of the first Liberty Loans could convert their holdings into future issues and they could pay for their bonds in five installments over three months. McAdoo also announced a publicity campaign "to acquaint the people with the nature of the loan and the advisability of subscribing both from the standpoint of the investor and the patriot." The first Liberty Loan would be devoted to extending credit to Britain, France, Italy, and Russia, and would be spent entirely in the United States. Liberty Loans would therefore provide not only gilt-edged security for investors but also jobs and profits for all Americans. Subscriptions flooded into the Federal Reserve Banks at the rate of $500,000 per day immediately after McAdoo's announcement, calming earlier fears that the loans would fail.[70]

Analysts of American economic policy during World War I have been critical of McAdoo's key decisions on the Liberty Loans. Floating them below prevailing market rates distorted credit markets by flooding them with huge volumes of low-yield bonds. When combined with their long maturity periods, and many subscribers' tendency to sell their bonds soon after each Liberty Loan campaign, war bonds lost value very quickly. Bonds from the second campaign were already selling at a 4 percent discount when the Third Liberty Loan opened, and by 1920 all the loans sold at 20 percent below their face value. By then the great majority of them were held by banks as the basis of their currency holdings. The consequent increase in the money supply, based on a mass of low-yield government securities, created inflationary pressure that was contained only by a recession between 1920 and 1922.[71]

McAdoo justified keeping Liberty Loan interest rates low on grounds of inter-generational equity. By keeping the war's cost to a minimum the burden on the present and future generations to repay the loans was less than it might otherwise have been. On its face this was a plausible argument, but it was undermined by the exemption of Liberty Loans from income taxes. Always defensive about the low interest on Liberty Loans, McAdoo overcompensated by granting this concession to increase their attractiveness. That meant that the bonds' real return rose with their purchasers' incomes, and so created a situation in which a married man earning $1,500 per year paid federal income tax while much wealthier citizens who could direct their wealth into Liberty Loans paid no tax at all on them. If tax exemption was the price paid for a low-interest rate, it came at significant cost to McAdoo's aim to distribute the costs and benefits of war fairly.[72]

"Thank you heartily for your characteristically generous and thoughtful note," McAdoo wrote to Baker after the first Liberty Loan had closed. "I am watching for the final returns—not yet received—before I permit myself to accept congratulations on the result . . . I want to be certain as to the size of the 'chicken' we have hatched!" Although response to the first Liberty Loan exceeded all expectations, McAdoo left nothing to chance in selling its successors. The second and third issues each bore a higher interest rate than its predecessor, rising to 4.5 percent for the third and fourth Liberty Loans, although each issue offered lower than its current market rates. The second, third, and fourth Liberty Loans also incorporated shorter maturity periods. On the other hand, and to contrary effect, the second and subsequent Liberty Loans were subject to federal income surtaxes, and the third and fourth Liberty Loans were stripped of conversion rights. By the end of 1918 there had been four Liberty Loans, all of them over-subscribed, which raised a total of $17 billion.[73]

Although concerned about the failure of war bonds to maintain their face value, McAdoo refused to change their terms to discourage holders from selling their bonds early. He preferred to aim patriotic ire rather than policy at those who did. "I cannot think of any man as less than a traitor," he said in July 1917, "who would deliberately sell such a bond below par." It is little wonder that many of his contemporaries and historians have criticized McAdoo's handling of wartime financial policy as expedient, contradictory, and consistent only in its preference for the path of least political resistance.[74]

Advertising for the Liberty Loans became better organized, more pervasive, and increasingly strident in each of the four campaigns. Led by Robert W. Woolley and then Oscar A. Price, and publicized by an army of "salesmen" including 60,000 women led by McAdoo's friend Antoinette Funk, Americans were deluged by a marketing strategy that was unprecedented in its scope. Funded by donations from advertising agencies, banks, and large corporations, the Liberty Loan campaigns were the culmination of the administration's desire to encourage and enforce patriotism by a combination of modern advertising methods and state surveillance.[75]

McAdoo was at the forefront of all the Liberty Loan campaigns, publicizing himself as a leading light of the administration and the financial mastermind of the war. His penchant for self-promotion placed him happily in the role described by the *Buffalo Times* as "Commander-in-Chief of the Liberty Loan drive." He undertook speaking tours for three of the campaigns, his speeches were printed by the millions and distributed across the nation, and he ensured that Liberty Loans were floated with a close eye to their political advantage and electoral palatability. While Baker often squirmed in the spotlight of national attention, McAdoo actively courted it. The results simultaneously confirmed the opinion of his champions that he was indeed the dynamo of the Wilson administration but also his critics' charge that his many virtues were undermined by political ambition and personal vanity.[76]

Within his own department McAdoo oversaw a campaign to have every employee who earned more than $840 per year invest 10 percent of his or her salary in Liberty Loans. McAdoo led by example, buying up to $1,750 worth of bonds from his salary of $12,000 during each campaign, but this represented little real sacrifice to a man with other sources of wealth. Public lists of individual subscriptions placed enormous pressure on less well-paid Treasury employees to contribute beyond their means. The whole department was expected to subscribe $1 million during the fourth campaign, and even the poorest employees, earning less than $16 per week, were "encouraged" to buy a $50 war bond on installment. As director general of the nation's railroads in 1918, McAdoo also pressured his employees, who had recently received generous pay rises, to buy war bonds. He published the names of those lines that reported 100 percent subscription rates, and castigated the selfishness of railroad workers, whatever their salaries, who declined to buy a bond. [77]

McAdoo's "volunteerism" extended beyond his own department. When Senator Warren G. Harding complained that the first Liberty Loan campaign was "hysterical and unseemly," McAdoo replied that "it is nothing short of dastardly for any one to attempt to discredit the patriotic effort being made by bankers, business men, and people of all classes and noble women of America to make the Liberty Loan a success." Later he condemned the head of the Farmers' National Conference for his "utterly unpatriotic and indefensible attitude" in not contributing to the second loan campaign, and in 1918 he criticized businesses in St. Louis for "actually helping the Kaiser" through their slow take-up of the fourth loan. Heartfelt letters from drought-stricken farmers in South Dakota received little sympathy from McAdoo, who saw subversion behind every unfilled quota.[78]

McAdoo featured prominently in advertising for all four of the Liberty Loans. His speaking tours combined salesmanship with self-promotion because they enabled him to meet political leaders from all over the nation and to present himself to tens of thousands of voters as a leader of the great national crusade. In a letter written to his wife during his tour for the First Liberty Loan he reported warm receptions in every town and city along his journey. In one Colorado town he was greeted by a "fine reception," with each member of the crowd wearing a badge emblazoned with the American flag and a flattering greeting:

> How'de do! McAdoo!
> We're proud of you!
> We're just "folks":
> Citizens of Limon, Colorado.

"I enclose one of these badges—wasn't that bully?" At Denver a large crowd lined the streets to greet him, and he spoke to an audience of six thousand. At Des Moines his speech was interrupted by three standing ovations, and at the civic reception there a guest passed him a note saying "I want to vote for you for President some day. I, of course, told him 'nothing doing!'"[79]

Treasury printed 377,000 copies of McAdoo's speech at Des Moines, and some Iowa Democrats noted that it had convinced them that he was Wilson's true successor. In Milwaukee the *Journal* reported that his speech was "clear, strong and telling," and that his audience "discerned in him a man with a keen, fine mind; a man of high education, of unusual poise and far-seeing judgment." The *Wall Street Journal* noted that the first Liberty Loan "is now spoken of as an achievement which will be sure to be ranked with the historical achievements of the Treasury Department."[80]

McAdoo's speeches for the Liberty Loans focused on the reasons for going to war, the necessity of adequate war funding, and the advantages of buying war bonds. In Boston in June 1917 he told the City Club that America faced a crisis even greater than that of 1861. During the Civil War the worst that could have happened was that the nation would have divided in two, but in 1917 it faced a foreign enemy "which threatens civilization and the integrity of America itself." "I am a Southerner," he told an audience in Sioux City, "my people fought on the other side, but I thank God they did not succeed, because we would not have had a united America to-day to resist this alien despot." Now the Kaiser's submarines had reduced the Atlantic to "no more than a stream," and if the United States did not win the war in Europe it would soon have to fight a rampant Germany at home.[81]

Purchase of Liberty Loans was not just a patriotic act; it was "the best investment, the finest security, upon the face of God's earth." It was even better than the currency in audiences' pockets: a war bond paid interest while currency did not, yet it was "as good as cash in your hand if you want to sell it, and it is the best security you can have if you offer it to your bank." Cash raised by the bonds did not leave the country but would equip American soldiers and enable the Allies to buy more American goods. If Americans economized in their own consumption, not to the extreme of "unnecessary self-denial" but "to the extent of preventing waste, preventing extravagance," and bought Liberty Loans, they "will keep Uncle Sam lusty and sturdy and vigorous and able to fight and able to win this victory which is essential for us as well as for civilization."[82]

McAdoo's rhetoric of German perfidy, financial patriotism, and self-interest sharpened during the third Liberty Loan campaign. "Some day we will be annealed into a real nation," he promised in April 1918, "and there will be no room on our soil for those who have not the National spirit and the National ideal." The Kaiser could not be allowed to "impale civilization upon the bayonet," and there cannot be "any talk of peace except a peace rammed down the throats of the military autocrats of Europe . . . with the steel of American bayonets." Buying Liberty Loans transformed those unable to fight into "true soldiers of liberty," but only if they held them at least until the end of the war. Buying and then selling bonds depressed the market and forced interest rates on subsequent issues to rise. Even a rise of one-quarter of 1 percent on $10 billion of bonds would cost the nation an extra $250 million per year.[83]

Raising money was a major element of McAdoo's wartime duties, but it was a means rather than an end. The primary purposes of Liberty Loans and taxation were to fund the war effort and to assist the Allies. For McAdoo the first task was straightforward, requiring him to ensure that there were sufficient funds to meet the appropriations passed by Congress at the behest of Secretary of War Baker and Secretary of Navy Daniels. The second task, to ensure that the Allies received enough credit to sustain their own war efforts, plunged him into much murkier waters.[84]

Intimations of the Allied financial crisis reached Washington even before Congress declared war. On March 6, 1917, US Ambassador to Great Britain Walter Hines Page reported that Britain had almost exhausted its capacity to pay for its purchases in America. By then responsible for French and Russian credit needs as well as her own, Britain had so far been able to pay her debts, but not for much longer. Continued purchases required shipment of large amounts of gold to the United States, but this was not possible because it was required at home to buttress the pound. Soon the Allies would be unable to pay their debts, and the result would be the collapse of their trade, German victory in the war, profound economic dislocation in the United States, and "a world-wide panic for an indefinite period." America needed to make credit available to Britain, France, and Russia, but this would be un-neutral. "Perhaps our going to war is the only way in which our present preeminent trade position can be maintained," Page concluded, "and a panic averted."[85]

Alerted to the depth of the crisis facing the Allies, McAdoo ordered his officials to make plans for immediate financial assistance to them in the event that the United States entered the war. When Wilson did call for war on April 2, 1917, McAdoo notified American ambassadors in London, Paris, and Petrograd that the Allies should send requests for funds as soon as Congress passed the Declaration of War. With Allied bankruptcy and defeat in the offing time was of the essence. "It is fortunate for the United States that in this critical time," the *Washington Post* editorialized on April 11, "there is at the head of the Treasury Department a man of remarkable breadth of vision, moral courage, and sound judgment."[86]

The Allies rushed to respond to McAdoo's invitation. On April 6, 1917, the same day that Congress declared war, the new government of Russia asked for a loan of $500 million, and over the next four months McAdoo authorized credits to it of $325 million. "It is of course understood," he reminded the secretary of state in August 1917, "that these credits are available only during the time Russia is engaged in war against Germany." After the Bolsheviks assumed power in the October 1917 and sued for peace, American credit was frozen and McAdoo arranged for hundreds of locomotives under construction for Russia to be diverted to other purposes.[87]

Negotiations with the other Allies had a happier outcome, but they were complicated by issues of national prestige and jostling for postwar primacy. When Wilson called for a declaration of war Britain and France were almost bankrupt. On April 2, 1917, the British chancellor of the exchequer Andrew Bonar Law told his cabinet that Britain had only $577 million in American-based assets and bullion with which to pay its "overdraft" of $358 million held by J. P. Morgan and Company. At current rates of expenditure of $75 million per week, Britain could cover its American debts for only three more weeks. Britain's financial position, Bonar Law concluded, was "a very black one indeed." Only America could save the Allies now.[88]

Four days later America came to the rescue. McAdoo immediately authorized loans of $200 million to Britain and France, and billions more soon followed. By

November 1918 the United States had lent $7.3 billion to the Allies, and another $3 billion in the following months. Of that sum a little more than $2 billion went to Italy, more than $3.8 billion to France, and more than $4.4 billion to Britain, all in the form of interest-bearing loans. Although these loans would later create enormous tension between the United States and its debtors, in April and May 1917 they were welcomed as the difference between solvency and collapse, and victory and defeat.[89]

McAdoo tried to use this flood of credit to wring concessions from the Allies and to indulge in personal empire-building. Soon after the Declaration of War he insisted that Britain remove restrictions on maritime insurance for US vessels trading with South America. He then tried to create an Allied Purchasing Commission, chosen by him and chaired by Bernard Baruch, to determine priorities for the Allies' purchases. McAdoo was worried that Britain, France, Italy, Russia, and now the United States were buying huge amounts of supplies without any coordination. As a result, they were competing against themselves, driving up prices, and creating production bottlenecks. His commission would also forestall congressional criticism that credit was being diverted to British rather than American needs.[90]

McAdoo insisted that creation of a Purchasing Commission under American control should be a condition of loans to the Allies. Britain agreed, but the others did not. They preferred to use their American loans to buy priority in the market rather than let an American commission impose it. Although McAdoo forced agreement from all the Allies to the creation of his commission in July 1917, it never achieved all that he hoped. Denied clear and exclusive powers, it functioned largely as an advisory body and its decisions were frequently ignored or circumvented.[91]

None of the Allies liked McAdoo's next idea of an Inter-Ally Council, made up of representatives of the major Allies' governments to make recommendations to McAdoo "as to the amount of loans that shall be made from time to time to them by the United States." Wilson approved this idea, but the Allies were extremely reluctant. A Purchasing Commission in Washington was one thing, but a council made up of Allied representatives making submissions to an American secretary of the treasury was quite another. Britain, France, and Italy were adept at making representations directly to Wilson, and the prospect of working through McAdoo was unpalatable. McAdoo eventually got his Inter-Ally Council, but the Allies insisted on their right to make direct and private representations to the president whenever they saw fit.[92]

Apart from their concerns about dilution of their diplomatic influence through the Inter-Ally Council, the British soon grew tired of McAdoo's handling of their loans. At first he seemed generous and decisive; Allied requests during the first months of American belligerency were promptly met on generous terms. The United States charged the Allies the same interest rate that it paid its own creditors and accepted their securities as collateral without discount. This led the British to hope that the flow of American credit would be unstinting and unquestioned.

Trouble emerged in July 1917 over the "Morgan overdraft." That facility was a revolving short-term credit, and when the United States entered the war it stood at more than $400 million. At the end of June the British government and J. P. Morgan and Co. applied for a loan to pay off the overdraft. Publicly concerned that the Liberty Loan legislation did not allow for liquidation of British debts contracted before April 6, 1917, and privately alive to the political consequences of using American taxpayers' funds to pay off debts owed by Britain to the hated House of Morgan, McAdoo refused the request and froze all credit transfers to Britain.[93]

British officials believed that McAdoo had signaled a worrying change in American policy. They now feared that he and Wilson would impose onerous conditions on further credits, and that those conditions would look as much to the postwar world as they did to war finance. Fears that McAdoo wanted to tie war loans with geopolitical strings were correct, but the Allies' assumption that Wilson agreed with his son-in-law's timing were not. Colonel House warned Wilson of the dangers of pushing American long-term interests too soon. "The English, of course, want to maintain the pound sterling," he wrote in August 1917, "and I see a disposition on the part of McAdoo . . . to substitute the dollar as the standard of value throughout the world. This, I am afraid, will finally come to be the crux of the difference between the two nations, and if we are not careful, it will make for trouble." Wilson agreed, and concluded that "when the war is over we can force them to our way of thinking, because by that time they will . . . be financially in our hands." But now the priority was to win the war and to preserve unity against the Germans.[94]

Relations between McAdoo and the British had soured badly. The head of the British mission, Sir Hardman Lever, reported that "the Secretary of the Treasury is chiefly concerned with providing himself with a political defence against attacks which he expects when it becomes known he is providing funds to repay Wall St." Lever's deputy Andrew McFadyean described McAdoo as "a Wall Street failure" who was driven by political ambition. Both McAdoo and his assistant secretary Oscar T. Crosby in "their inexperience and their fearfulness . . . are incapable of any wide outlook or real grasp, and take refuge in red tape and petty detail." Sensing Lever's disdain, McAdoo insisted on his recall.[95]

Lord Northcliffe and then Lord Reading took Lever's place, and relations between the two sides improved. The issue, however, remained as to what British quid McAdoo had in mind for America's quo. A promise not to use American credit to pay off the Morgan overdraft was forthcoming, but McAdoo soon sought other concessions. On June 30, 1917, he prepared a note to the British chancellor of the exchequer seeking assurances that Britain would not use American loans to expand its postwar navy or to effect "preferential trade relations effective either during the war or after." Wilson put a stop to that time bomb after Lansing called it "a grave mistake" that would damage Anglo-American relations at exactly the wrong time.[96]

Although prevented from forcing geopolitical concessions from Britain, McAdoo did succeed in adding tighter conditions on subsequent loans, including promises not to use them to buttress the value of the pound against currencies other than the American dollar, and to direct all British war purchases through the Allied Purchasing Commission. McAdoo was a hard bargainer who was unafraid to ruffle British feathers in his determination that the United States should take Britain's place at the apex of the world's financial structure at the end of the war.[97]

British officials, resentful at McAdoo's high-handedness but also desperate for funds, bombarded him with detailed accounts of their parlous position. "It is after having supported an expenditure of this magnitude for three years that Great Britain ventures to appeal to the United States for sympathetic consideration in financial discussions where the excessive urgency of her need and the precarious position in which she is may somewhat lend a tone of insistence to her requests for assistance which under ordinary circumstances would be out of place." By the end of August 1917 the crisis had passed; American credit again flowed easily and the British had learned that on Wilson's leash McAdoo's bark was worse than his bite. "Situation here is better than when I left," Sir William Wiseman of the British Secret Intelligence Service in New York cabled Sir Eric Drummond in Whitehall on September 20, 1917. "McAdoo is more inclined to be helpful because he now realizes the very serious responsibility which he would assume if Allied finance collapsed through any petty action of his."[98]

Closer to home McAdoo took every chance to augment his department's influence and his own public profile. His empire building most often irritated only his cabinet colleagues, but occasionally it even raised the president's ire. This was especially true when McAdoo strayed too far into foreign policy, as he did in attempting to expand the role of the Inter-Ally Council.

Soon after the council was established in London and Paris, McAdoo asked Baker to attach a representative to it from the War Department. Baker agreed, and assigned General Bliss. When Wilson was informed, he sent a shot across

McAdoo's bows. "I hope, my dear Mac, that hereafter you will let me see these messages before they are sent and not after, because they touch matters of vital policy upon which it is imperative that I should retain control." McAdoo apologized, not so much for usurping Wilson's prerogatives but for his trust in Baker's judgment. "I perhaps jumped to the conclusion that you and [Baker] had conferred about the matter and that he was advising me not only as to his own views, but as to yours as well."[99]

McAdoo also tried to use the wartime crisis to broaden the powers of the Shipping Board for which he had fought so hard in 1915 and 1916. He suggested that the board commandeer all American-flagged ships, totaling 1,500 vessels and 2.5 million tons, and more than 700,000 tons of German ships impounded in American harbors. By the beginning of 1918, because of the huge stockpile of unshipped goods and losses to U-Boats, the shipping shortage had become so severe that he persuaded Wilson to allow the Shipping Board to requisition 163 vessels currently under construction for the British. "Shipping . . . is so intimately related to the application of the credits we are giving to the foreign governments that unless it can be completely coordinated with the work of the Treasury, I am frank to say that I think advances to the Allies are scarcely worth considering." Just why coordination of shipping should be the task of Treasury, and not of the War Department or even the Department of Commerce, was never as clear to others as it was to McAdoo. Wilson killed the other part of his scheme by telling his cabinet that proposals to appropriate German shipping "offended him . . . America must set an example of splendid conduct of war."[100]

Undismayed by presidential rebuke or cabinet resentment, McAdoo continued to claim responsibilities that lay outside Treasury's normal scope but that propelled him further into the spotlight. After shoving Baker and Redfield aside from the war risk insurance scheme, he held a conference of life insurance companies in July 1917 and announced that they had agreed that the task was too great for them. Only the government could ensure that "every American soldier shall go to the front with the comforting and supreme satisfaction of knowing that his loved ones are not dependent upon charity" should the worst happen.[101]

Under the scheme servicemen could buy insurance policies from $1,000 to $10,000 at premiums from $3 to $33 a month. Four million soldiers and sailors eventually took out policies at an average value of $8,700; 128,300 policyholders died in service, and 3,200 were totally disabled, triggering payments of $1.17 billion. War risk insurance, McAdoo argued, was an eminently progressive way to fight a war because it created a "scientific, well-balanced, equitable and comprehensive" program in place of the capricious and corrupt system of congressionally awarded payments. He hailed the scheme as "one of the greatest humanitarian measures ever enacted by any government," and took credit for it for the rest of his career.[102]

⧓⧓⧓

Characteristically enough, it was McAdoo and not Baker who released a press statement recounting his department's achievements during the first year of the war. McAdoo listed many achievements, including two Liberty Loan campaigns, the enactment of a multitude of wartime taxes, insurance of more than 12,000 cargoes of American goods and 1,500,000 American servicemen, the provision of $75 million in loans through the Farm Loan Board, and an expansion of the Customs Service. The statement concluded that the president on December 28, 1917, had appointed McAdoo to be director-general of the US Railroad Administration (USRRA) to take control of the nation's 250,000 miles of track and all its rolling stock in the New Year. "I very much fear that you do not know the way opinion is changing about you in the marts of trade," J. H. O'Neill wrote from Boston at the end of November 1917. "Wall Street is beginning to swear by you, and State Street pretty much the same way. Of course, in their very smug hypocrisy they say that you have grown, but I do not let it go at that. I tell them that they have grown wiser, that is all."[103]

CHAPTER 8

Wartime Service, 1918

Newton Baker had spent 1917 organizing the American Expeditionary Forces (AEF); he spent 1918 overseeing its deployment. The numbers involved were mind-numbing and the human cost was heartbreaking. Although his commitment to the war did not waver, Baker's horror at it steeled his determination that it would be mankind's last war. "When this war is over and it is definitely decided among the children of men that autocracy is bidden to veil its face forever," he declared in August 1917, "it will then be said . . . that the dawn of liberty for all men all over the world dates from that day when our soldiers landed in France and began the final conquest for freedom."[1]

But first there was the war to be won. At the end of 1917 there were only 157,000 US servicemen in France, but the tempo of arrivals increased as they completed their basic training. In January 1918, 47,000 troops disembarked in France, 162,000 more in May, and 300,000 in July. By the war's end nearly 2 million US soldiers, Marines, and National Guardsmen were on the Western Front, and 2 million more were at home in various stages of training.[2]

The AEF fired its first angry shot on October 23, 1917, and fought in thirteen major battles during the rest of the war. Detached units and then divisional formations fought with the French at Cambrai in November 1917, with the British on the Somme and at Lys in March and April 1918, on the Aisne and at Noyon-Montdidier in May and June, with Australian troops at Hamel on July 4, 1918, and then at Champagne-Marne. These battles engaged a total of 145,000 American troops, while the rest of the AEF was deployed on its own section of the front in Lorraine. There it continued to train, but that released more French and British troops for combat. In this way the AEF contributed significantly to the war, but it did not play a major part in blunting the German offensives of March and April 1918. By the end of March 1918 there were only three complete AEF divisions on the line and none were in combat.[3]

In May 1918 the AEF held 55 kilometers of front and was ready to take a more active role in the fighting. It participated in the Allied counterattacks in the summer and fall of 1918, providing a quarter of the men deployed at Aisne-Marne in July and August, and then contributing to offensives on the Somme, at Oisne-Aisne, and at Ypres. The AEF fought its own battles at Cantigny in May, Belleau Wood in June, Château-Thierry in July and August, and St-Mihiel in September, and then undertook its own campaign at Meuse-Argonne in October.[4]

The AEF's allies and enemies had high praise for the individual doughboy but not for the quality of his leadership. Pershing and his commanders were dismissive of the "bite and hold" tactics featuring close coordination of artillery, tank, infantry, and air power that the Allies had developed after 1916. He was convinced that American valor would triumph through heavy artillery barrages, massed infantry attacks, and good marksmanship. At St-Mihiel he felt vindicated when the AEF captured more than 400 guns and 13,000 prisoners in a single day. The first day of the Meuse-Argonne offensive was equally encouraging, but the AEF soon bogged down as poor planning, inexperienced troops, and difficult terrain took their toll. The AEF then suffered high casualty rates as Pershing wasted his men's lives trying to fight the war his way. "It was magnificent fighting," General Joseph Dickman wrote later, "but it was not modern war." The doughboys eventually broke through, but at terrible cost.[5]

The AEF's chief contribution to victory was through its present and future weight of numbers, which sapped German morale, and through its occupation of quiet sectors of the front to allow the Allies to halt and then reverse the German offensives of 1918. Baker never claimed that the United States and the AEF won the war. He was sure, however, that its presence and growing numbers did prevent the Allies from losing it.[6]

As secretary of war Baker took no role in devising military tactics. His job was to oversee the formation, training, and transportation of the AEF and to ensure its supply. "War is no longer Samson with his shield and spear and sword, and David with his sling," he told the press in May 1917. "It is the conflict of smokestacks now, it is the combat of the driving wheel and of the engine."[7]

Baker's main concern early in 1918 was to regain control over purchasing priorities and coordination. By the middle of 1917 production shortfalls, competition between American and Allied purchasers, and escalating prices had revealed deep flaws in his mobilization plans. The War Department's bureaus, its general staff, the Council of National Defense (CND), the National Defense Advisory Commission (NDAC), and the Allied Purchasing Commission were better at competition than coordination, forcing prices up while production and shipping shortages reduced supplies to critical levels. Led by McAdoo, many called for a new regime of economic coordination, but Baker was proud of his advisory committees. He was also committed to War Department control over industrial mobilization. The resulting struggle lasted for the rest of the war and showed Baker to be a stubborn infighter whose motives combined high principle and jurisdictional jealousy.[8]

In May 1917 McAdoo called for the creation of a single agency to control military purchasing and priorities. Executive power in the War Industries Board (WIB) would be vested in a chairman, whose authority would come directly from the president rather than through the Department of War. McAdoo suggested that Bernard Baruch, then a member of the CND, should be chair of the WIB. McAdoo and Baruch were already friendly, and Baruch would later become a generous supporter of his presidential ambitions. Baker dissented, arguing that the CND, established under his authority and composed of representatives from industry and the Departments of War and the Navy, was sufficient. Americans would not stand for great power in the hands of a single unelected official, and the demands of a modern war required a broad range of expertise best gained from an advisory body.[9]

Baker and McAdoo could not resolve their differences, forcing Wilson to impose a compromise. On July 28, 1917, he announced the disbanding of the NDAC and the creation of the WIB, but as a subordinate agency of the CND under the secretary of war. The WIB had three members, including Baruch, but it was chaired by the Cleveland industrialist Frank Scott. The WIB was advisory to the secretary of war and lacked legal authority to decide priorities. "I am genuinely discouraged that such a complicated piece of machinery has been set up," McAdoo declared, and predicted that it could not provide coherent and authoritative economic direction. Baker, on the other hand, congratulated Wilson on this new arrangement.[10]

Wilson's compromise unraveled during the second half of 1917. The WIB struggled within its limited mandate and Scott's authority was undermined by his disappointed colleague Baruch. Scott resigned at the end of October 1917 and was replaced by Daniel Willard, who left in January 1918. Without coercive powers and beholden to the CND, the WIB became an orphan agency largely ignored by Baker and his department's still-powerful bureaus.[11]

Problems with procurement had become dire at the end of 1917. A Senate inquiry in January 1918 led by George Chamberlain heard from witnesses, including Baruch, Willard, and Waddill Catchings of the US Chamber of Commerce, who criticized the War Department and its advisory bodies. Willard and Baruch pushed again for authority over purchasing and priorities to be vested in a single person, and Catchings described current arrangements as "pernicious" and "woe-fully chaotic."[12]

The travails of the WIB and Chamberlain's inquiry emboldened McAdoo and Baruch to revive their proposals to give the WIB legal teeth and a powerful chair-man. Since July McAdoo had seethed over Baker's emasculation of the WIB and his refusal to support Baruch's appointment as its chairman, and this time he would not be denied. Arguing that both the facts and the politics of mobilization demanded the revamping of the WIB and the whole process of war purchasing, he persuaded Wilson to direct Baker to begin consultations with Baruch.[13]

In their discussions Baker and Baruch agreed to greater control by the WIB over military and civilian production, purchasing, and priorities. Although Baker insisted that the army and the navy retain control over their own purchases, he agreed that the WIB should act independently of his department, that the WIB should be vested with coercive powers to commandeer plants, set prices, and de-termine production priorities, and that all major military and civilian purchasing programs should be submitted to the chairman of the WIB for his "final alloca-tion, distribution and judgment."[14]

Baker's concessions to Baruch were grudging. He was determined to ensure that his department's committees would play a key role in the war effort, subject only to the WIB's final approval. Baker also continued to oppose Baruch's assump-tion of the chairmanship of the WIB, explaining that it should be led by "a great industrial captain," and that "I doubted whether the country would accept as an ideal appointment a man whose success in life had been largely that of a Wall Street financier."[15]

When he heard from Baruch about Baker's refusal to support his appointment, McAdoo "split the air with expletives" and insisted to Wilson that Baruch was the best person to fix the mess that Baker had created. Wilson, impressed with Baruch's work on the WIB and delighted to find a Democrat on Wall Street, needed no more convincing. On March 4, 1918, he announced Baruch's appointment as chair-man of the WIB and pointedly annotated Baker's copy of Baruch's letter of appoint-ment that "[I] afford myself the opportunity of asking if you will not be kind enough, whenever the occasion arises, to afford the War Industries Board the full-est possible cooperation of your department."[16]

The reasons behind Baker's opposition to Baruch's appointment are unclear. Baruch suspected that anti-Semitism lay at its heart, but Baker's papers reveal no such sentiment. He maintained that his opposition to Baruch arose from a belief that his business experience was inappropriate to control economic mobilization. Behind this lay a disdain, shared by many in the business community, for stock speculation. Samuel Untermeyer, a fellow Jew, was outspoken in his contempt for

Baruch. In a "strictly private" letter to Baker, Untermeyer noted that Baruch "has never been engaged in or even remotely connected to any legitimate business unless you regard the occupation of a professional speculator who gambles on the short side of the stock market as a legitimate business."[17]

Whatever the reason, there was bad blood between Baker and Baruch that predated the WIB and lingered for the rest of their lives. There was even gossip that Baker was jealous of Baruch's gregariousness, his influence over Wilson, and even his tall stature. Although their relationship improved after March 1918, it remained formal and was often strained.[18]

McAdoo, on the other hand, remained close to Baruch during and after the war. "If McAdoo believed in you," Baruch wrote in his autobiography, "nothing could ever make him waver in his determination to carry through for you to the end." When Claude Swanson, chairman of the Senate Naval Affairs Committee, asked if the navy should defer to the WIB, McAdoo replied that "if any damn fool interferes with Baruch he will get his block knocked off." The only exception was for McAdoo himself, as he insisted that transportation priorities were his prerogative as director general of the US Railroad Administration (USRRA).[19]

Baker's relationship with the WIB was as conflicted as his attitude to its chairman. This arose from more than mere bureaucratic jealousy, although he was anxious to protect his department's place at the center of the war effort. More important was his opposition to the creation of a powerful agency dedicated to direction of the economy. The WIB and its ambitious chairman, he feared, would introduce controls that would long outlive the war. Although he conceded that his mobilization machinery was cumbersome, he maintained that it had the great advantages of impermanence and clear lines of responsibility to him. This upheld the authority of public officers while using, but not surrendering to, the expertise of unelected businessmen.[20]

Hemmed in by the compromises forced on it by Baker's intransigence and Wilson's caution, the WIB fulfilled neither Baruch's hopes nor Baker's fears. Peyton C. March, appointed as chief of the general staff on the same day that Baruch became chairman of the WIB, gave the board only minimal cooperation and the WIB rarely quibbled with his decisions. As Baker and Wilson had feared, Baruch was generous to large corporations, granting them high prices to generate maximum production in minimum time. This assisted larger firms, which usually owned the most efficient plants, to consolidate their market power while growing rich on WIB-approved prices. Baruch picked his targets carefully and used bluster more than his contested powers to get his way. The WIB did bring more cohesion to mobilization than the CND or the NDAC, but it was never the all-powerful force that Baker had feared.[21]

Baker's role in and against the federal government's movement toward wartime production control was hesitant and often inglorious. He was slow to grasp the full implications of total war; only at the end of 1917, when accumulated production, supply, and transport problems brought mobilization almost to a halt, did he accept the necessity of significant government intervention, even "regimentation," in the economic life of the nation at war.[22]

Once converted to the doctrine of total war, Baker supported a significant expansion of federal government activity during 1918. Shipping and railroads came under federal control, prices of key commodities were fixed by wartime agencies, and Baker grew less jealous of his own turf and more aware of the necessity to mobilize the whole economy. The result was that 1918 witnessed turning points not only in the war itself, but also in Baker's conception of his role within it.[23]

Supply problems pushed him into unfamiliar territory. The AEF required huge amounts of explosives for its artillery, but nitrocellulose, used as propellant, was more difficult to manufacture than the nitroglycerine used in high explosives. Two American manufacturers, DuPont and Hercules, had supplied the British and French with nitrocellulose since 1915 but neither had enough capacity to supply the AEF as well. Soon after the Declaration of War the War Department called for the building of two new explosives plants at a cost of $90 million each. It negotiated with DuPont to construct and operate one of the plants, "Old Hickory" near Nashville, but the company drove a hard bargain. Unwilling to saddle itself with a huge plant destined to become a white elephant as soon as the war was over, DuPont demanded terms that guaranteed it profits of between $60 and $70 million. Citing the extreme urgency of the situation, Baker approved the contract without consulting the WIB.[24]

The WIB objected strongly and argued that if DuPont insisted on making huge profits from the war then the government should own and operate its own explosives plants. Baker then cancelled the Old Hickory contract and authorized construction of a government-owned facility at Nitro, West Virginia. This opened in September 1918 and by November had produced forty-five million pounds of explosives. DuPont, embarrassed by its portrayal as unpatriotic and greedy, agreed to build and operate Old Hickory and to sell nitrocellulose at cost. The AEF remained dependent on French explosives while Baker, DuPont, and the WIB argued over the terms of their contracts and the desirability of government-operated military infrastructure.[25]

Baker's experiences with aviation during the war were even more hesitant and unproductive. In April 1917 the army had only thirty-five trained pilots and a handful of aircraft. Determined to catch up, Congress appropriated $700 million in July 1917 to produce more than 22,000 airframes and 45,500 aircraft engines and to send 4,500 planes to Europe. Before the war was over it had voted another $1 billion in pursuit of an air force worthy of a major military power. By November 1918 the United States had produced more than 11,000 planes and 13,000 Liberty aircraft engines, which went into army, navy, French, and British airframes.[26]

Behind these impressive numbers lay inglorious realities. American taxpayers spent mightily to create an air force out of nothing, but the AEF remained dependent on French planes, pilots, and engines. On November 11, 1918, it had only 196 American-built aircraft deployed in combat. Baker had entrusted airplane production to Howard E. Coffin, previously a vice president of the Hudson Motor Company, who had grossly exaggerated American capacity to produce thousands of aircraft and engines of the latest type in the space of a year. Baker acknowledged the danger of "the importation of the advertising methods of American private business into a Government department," but thought that "progress made in aircraft development has been remarkable and will . . . produce a real result."[27]

Baker's critics were less forgiving. Congressional Republicans sifted through Coffin's records hoping to discover incompetence and dishonesty, but they found extravagance and inefficiency instead. In April 1918 aircraft production was put under the control of John D. Ryan, and finally some planes were shipped to Europe. Even then the promised air armada never eventuated. Baker insisted that Germany would have been overwhelmed by tens of thousands of American pilots and planes in 1919 and 1920, but even his kindest biographer described the aircraft program as a "fiasco."[28]

Baker was more confident dealing with the sociological aspects of running an army. Always proud of the AEF, he worked hard to engender its spirit. Military life required obedience to superiors, but the army needed to remember that its officers and men were republican citizens united in a crusade for democracy. Baker's faith in the AEF's virtues extended beyond its democratic tendencies; he indignantly refused a French offer to provide brothels for American troops and cited statistics showing a reduction in venereal disease between newly inducted conscripts and men who had served at the front. The army thought that its medical examinations were responsible for this, but Baker had other ideas. "[I] attribute the major part of it to the substitution of attractive recreation opportunities, which did for our Army just what it does for college boys."[29]

Sometimes the AEF failed to live up to Baker's high ideals. Four million men under arms generated a steady stream of offenses against civilian and military law. Pershing sought power to carry out all court-martial sentences in France, but Baker demurred. He persuaded Wilson that Pershing should determine appeals only for offenses against civilian law. Serious breaches of military law were to be referred to Washington before sentences could be carried out. The result was that soldiers convicted of offenses attracting the death penalty in civilian life were dealt with by courts martial and Pershing, while those condemned under military law could appeal to Baker and Wilson. The results were stark: between April 1917 and November 1918 twenty-five soldiers were executed in the United States, and ten more in France, after Pershing had reviewed their cases. No soldier condemned under military regulations, on the other hand, was executed during Baker's tenure as secretary of war.[30]

In April 1918, for example, Baker reviewed the cases of four soldiers tried by courts martial and sentenced to death. Jeff Cook and Forrest Sebastian were convicted of sleeping at their posts after doing sentry duty for twenty-six hours without rest. Both men were conscripts and the oldest had just turned 20. "I can not believe that youths of so little military experience, placed for the first time under circumstances so exhausting," Baker told Wilson, "can be held to deserve the death penalty." Two other soldiers, Stanley Fishback and Olon Ledoyen, were convicted of willful disobedience after they refused orders to attend drill. They were sentenced to death, but Baker again recommended clemency. "It is perfectly obvious that this order ought to have been obeyed," he told Wilson, and the men's insubordination "ought to be punished with a suitable punishment." This, he thought, would be a jail term at Fort Leavenworth. Wilson agreed, as he did with all Baker's recommendations for mercy.[31]

Baker's solicitude for men who chose not to fight was patchier. He promised that "in the midst of our military enterprises we must be equally loyal to our own political theories," but often ignored curtailment of freedoms and rights that in other moods he held dear. As a result he sent mixed messages about combining martial fervor against Germans abroad and moderation toward dissenters at home.

"You and I know many Germans," he told an audience in May 1917. "Many of them have been our . . . friends, and a more gentle and more neighborly and more kindly set of acquaintances none of us ever had. It is not in their nature to spread poisoned candy and to poison wells . . . it is no more part of their nature than of anybody else's to resort to barbarity." Six months later he repeated that sentiment to a group of police chiefs, declaring that "You and I are both too wise . . . to imagine that a broken accent means a broken mind, or that a non-American name . . . means any lack of loyalty in the man." This time, however, he added a warning: "But never let us hesitate for a second when we find a man living here, eating of our bread and drinking of the milk of plenty, when we find that man disloyal! The man who strikes us in the back, who undertakes to sap our strength through fire or otherwise, let us see that he is rendered harmless to accomplish any such purpose against the Government and our people."[32]

Conscientious objectors were the first to feel Baker's inconsistency. The draft law exempted those who had a religious objection to war, and in March 1918 Baker persuaded Wilson to extend exemption to nonreligious objectors. Those who declared themselves to be conscientious objectors were inducted into AEF training camps and their claims assessed there. Baker thus left them to the tender mercies of army discipline and peer group pressure rather than in the hands of the civilian courts. About 25,000 inductees initially claimed to be nonreligious objectors, but only 5,000 persisted after being exposed to the AEF's powers of persuasion, and of these 504 were court-martialed for false claims to exemption.[33]

Baker initially declared that genuine conscientious objectors should be treated with civility. In September 1917 he reported that only 27 of the 18,000 men inducted into Camp Meade had declared themselves objectors. Eleven were Amish, three were Quakers, and one "was a Russian-born Jew who claimed to be an international socialist and who, I think, is simply lazy and obstinate." Most of them were "simple-minded young people who . . . really have no comprehension of the world outside of their own rural and peculiar community. Only two of those with whom I talked seemed quite normal mentally." They were separated from the other inductees, but kept close enough to see the camaraderie between the new soldiers. "As a consequence the young fellows every now and then . . . 'withdraw the objection' and put on a uniform and are soon drilling or playing football like other youngsters."[34]

Behind Baker's schoolyard imagery lay tougher realities. Far from yearning to play football, many objectors were bullied into enlistment. In March 1918 Baker ordered that they be subjected to psychological testing and that those who were "sullen and defiant" should be tried by court martial; issued honorable discharges to officers who had severely beaten objectors at Camp Funston; and never conceded that objectors had been treated badly by the AEF.[35]

Baker was similarly ambivalent about the rights of organized labor during the war as he oscillated between his dislike of closed-shop unionism and his concern to avoid production delays through strikes. Although he warned employers not to erode working conditions, Baker also declined to allow unions to win permanent gains during the wartime emergency. This seemingly even-handed approach worked to limit employees' rights to organize their workplaces by subordinating their interests to the imperative of maximum production in minimum time.[36]

Labor groups that transgressed Baker's conceptions of patriotism and cooperation received little sympathy. This was particularly true of the International Workers of the World (IWW), which was singled out for close surveillance and persecution. Baker was convinced that the IWW was a traitorous group and showed no mercy to its leaders, who received heavy sentences for sedition after hasty and biased trials. "The fact is that these men were themselves actually engaged in making war upon the people of the United States," he told the American Civil Liberties Union (ACLU) in 1929, "and instead of being objectors to violence, they . . . resorted to violence with which to wage war upon innocent and defenseless non-combatants."[37]

Baker's attitude to African Americans was more complex. Although not as outspoken as McAdoo, he was uninterested in improving African Americans' place in society or the army. In keeping with most progressives, Baker agreed with segregation in military and civilian life and rejected the idea of racial equality. As secretary of war he dealt gingerly with racial issues, responding out of necessity rather than principle and from expediency rather than conviction. "There is no intention on the part of the War Department at this time," he declared in November 1917, "to settle the so-called race question." The paramount task was to win the war, and African Americans, like all others, needed to subordinate their individual aspirations to that goal.[38]

The scale of the war effort soon undid Baker's desire to wish racial disadvantage and tension away. Of the 400,000 African American men conscripted into the AEF about half served in France and 42,000 were in combat. Although the army had included some black troops since the Civil War, their large numbers in 1917 and 1918 presented new challenges to it. There were many African American non-commissioned officers, but very few black lieutenants and captains, and promotion beyond those ranks was very rare. That African Americans would train in segregated camps and serve in segregated units was unquestioned, but whether or not to train black officers caused much debate. Baker's advisors conceded that black officers could assist in training and campaigning their troops, but insisted that they should not be assigned to white units. Southern congressmen would not hear of biracial officer training, and Baker was noncommittal on this issue while the bill made its way through Congress.[39]

Black leaders were also divided, with some hesitating to endorse a black officers' camp for fear of being seen to acquiesce to segregation in general. In 1917, however, the choice was between a segregated camp and none at all, and in May a "Committee of 100 Colored Citizens" petitioned Wilson to create one. "Our young men are so anxious to serve their country in this crisis that they are willing to accept a separate camp. This opportunity for our representative young men to receive training as officers is not only necessary for the proper efficiency of the army but it is also essential to the active and hearty patriotism of ten million Colored citizens." By then Baker was on their side, and Wilson agreed to create a black officers' camp at Fort Des Moines, Iowa. The camp graduated 639 officers before it was shut down in October 1917. During the war a total of 1,353 black officers graduated from other camps in Puerto Rico, Hawaii, and Panama.[40]

Baker oscillated between condescension and detachment in his attitude to black soldiers. Observing them sailing to Europe through heavy weather at the end of August 1918, he told his wife that "the negroes . . . are a perpetual joy. They are grouped just outside my windows watching the waves with childish exclamations and delight and behave much as children do on a roller-coaster at Luna Park, yelling with joy at the big ones." Five years later he told a journalist that African Americans had benefited enormously from war service; their health, nutrition, and education had improved and their contribution to a great patriotic undertaking had given them a sense of worth and belonging. He did not acknowledge any contributions that they had made in return.[41]

Baker also responded ambivalently to outbreaks of racial violence during the war. On August 23, 1917, one hundred black soldiers in Houston, enraged by harassment from local police, went on a rampage that left fifteen whites dead. Fifty-four of the soldiers were court-martialed in November 1917; thirteen were sentenced to death, and the rest were imprisoned for life. The condemned men were hanged on December 22, 1917, without petitioning the president for clemency. African American leaders argued that the Houston rioters had been denied basic legal rights because of their color and the army's desire to make an example of them.[42]

A second and a third round of courts martial of the Houston rioters in December 1917 and March 1918 brought another sixteen death sentences. By then Baker, responding to criticism of the speed with which the first thirteen rioters had been executed, had decided that all death sentences imposed on soldiers within the United States should be reviewed by the judge advocate general (JAG). The JAG found no errors in the second and third trials and confirmed their verdicts. Through a petition organized by the National Association for the Advancement of Colored People (NAACP) and signed by 12,000 citizens, Wilson then came under pressure to commute those death sentences to life imprisonment.[43]

In response to Wilson's request for advice, Baker stressed political concerns above legality or morality. He thought that the thirteen had suffered no miscarriage of justice, and that they had committed offenses of the "greatest gravity." Yet African American support of the war effort made it prudent "to recognize their loyalty by a concession against the extreme penalty executed upon so many members of the race." Baker suggested that Wilson distinguish between those convicted of nonspecific acts of violence and those who had been personally involved in acts of murder. The former should be spared, but the latter should not. Wilson accordingly extended clemency to seven of the thirteen rioters and allowed the execution of the other six.[44]

Baker's reaction was typical of his general attitude toward racial discrimination. Determined not to allow the war to become a crusade for racial justice, he assisted African Americans only when he was forced to. Even then he opted for symbolism over substance. In October 1917 he appointed Emmett Scott, from the Tuskegee Institute, as special assistant on issues of concern to African American soldiers. Scott soon found that his role was only advisory and usually ineffective. Policies discouraging promotion of black officers, and imposing segregation of military units, remained in place, and Scott spent most of his time trying to ameliorate the War Department's ferocious response to the Houston riot.[45]

Although Baker's vacillating pragmatism on African American rights and grievances earned him criticism from black organizations, his most pressing concerns, and his most influential critics, sprang from white America. Sometimes the barbs were personal. In 1917 the First Lady of South Carolina worried that none of her guests "would be gracious or polite enough to the Secretary of War" at her Thanksgiving dinner, and in 1922 a former AEF officer wrote to remind Baker of his "characteristic imbecility" and his status as "PARAGON OF BONEHEADS." "Verily you deserve the booby prize that everybody has awarded to you, Newt."[46]

Baker's fiercest critic was Theodore Roosevelt, still furious about Baker's rejection of his military services, who declared at every opportunity that he was unfit to be secretary of war. Appointing him in 1916 was "evil enough," but "keeping him on during a great war was a criminal thing." In Congress Baker's critics were equally rabid. "From the time we entered the war until January 1918," Baker recalled, "Senators, Republican and Democratic alike, hunted me with dogs."[47]

Republican attacks were predictable, but Baker also made powerful Democratic enemies. Chief of these was Senator George E. Chamberlain of Oregon, chairman of the Senate Committee on Military Affairs. Chamberlain had hoped to become secretary of war and repaid Wilson for his decision to appoint Baker instead with bitterness and obstruction. Spurred by the mobilization crisis and bolstered by TR's support, Chamberlain launched an investigation into the War Department's leadership, procedures, and efficiency. He found that the army lacked machine guns and artillery; its aviation program was far behind schedule, draftees were forced to train in substandard clothing and with broomsticks instead of rifles, a shortage of wool had led to a dearth of blankets in the training camps, poor housing conditions had caused high mortality rates among the AEF trainees, and as yet few American troops had landed in France. "The military establishment of the United States of America," Chamberlain declared in December 1917, "has fallen down . . . It has almost stopped functioning, my friends . . . I speak not as a Democrat, but as an American citizen."[48]

Baker at first ignored Chamberlain's attacks, but the Oregonian would not be brushed aside. During his testimony to Chamberlain's committee on January 10, 1918, Baker conceded that there had been delays and wastage but maintained that these were inevitable. Never before had the country equipped, trained, and shipped two million soldiers. Ten years' warning would have helped enormously, but neither the Germans nor Congress had obliged. "His complacency and smartness of rejoinder when asked legitimate questions," *The New York Times* thought, "did not become an official with his powers and responsibilities."[49]

Pressure from congressional Democrats led by Chamberlain, from Republicans encouraged by Theodore Roosevelt, and from the press placed Baker under great pressure in January 1918. "At the base of the criticism against you," one of McAdoo's friends wrote to Baker, "is a misconception of your personality, a belief that you have been debonair when you should have been serious." Influential editors such as Adolph Ochs of *The New York Times* and Oswald Villard Garrison of the *New York Evening Post* debated whether Baker should remain in office, and he considered resigning to spare Wilson further embarrassment.[50]

Baker returned to give a more robust defense of his management and to rebut each of Chamberlain's charges. He detailed the supply of rifles, blankets, and overcoats and denied that the camps were overcrowded or unhealthy; the draftees' health was in fact better than that of the general population. "Has any army in history ever, since the beginning of time, been so raised and cared for as this army has?"[51]

Baker's testimony won widespread praise. "Don't let the wolves worry you!" McAdoo wrote. "I know you won't anyway but I want you to know as well how sincerely I sympathize with you in the utterly unfair attacks that are being made upon you and how confident I am that everything will come right." One Democratic senator rushed to the White House during a break in Baker's testimony. "Jesus," Oliver James told Wilson, "you ought to see that little Baker. He's eating them up!" Baker's testimony was a turning point in his reputation on Capitol Hill; no longer did he seem a soft target but now was doughty and well informed. He even made peace with some of his critics, but not with Chamberlain, Roosevelt, or Wood. Baker later told McAdoo that the Senate had assisted the efficiency and honesty of mobilization by warning his subordinates that "anything they did on Tuesday was likely to be investigated on Wednesday." The Chamberlain hearings also spurred reorganization of the War Department and the revamp of the WIB. These changes lessened Baker's responsibilities for domestic mobilization—perhaps no bad thing—and let him focus on the military and diplomatic demands of coalition warfare.[52]

The most persistent of these arose from the transportation and deployment of the AEF. In May 1917 Wilson had agreed to send soldiers to France, and the size of that force grew as the Allies made clear their desperate need for American manpower. At first Baker suggested that 12,000 soldiers and Marines be dispatched to France as soon as possible to bolster French morale. To save shipping these American soldiers were equipped with French rifles, artillery, and ammunition and operated within the French army. This first contingent arrived in France on June 28, 1917, to a rapturous welcome. Pershing, alive to the effect of even a few American troops in France, made the most of the opportunity. In Paris at the head of his troops on July 4, 1917, he kissed Napoleon's sword and told an aide to declare that "Lafayette, nous voilà!"[53]

Pershing's orders were to form an independent American army. Although Wilson and Baker knew that delays in shipping and training would cause some postponement of that goal, they insisted that US troops retain their separate identity and fight under American commanders. At first this caused little difficulty; the time required to train the AEF meant that it embarked in numbers that could be easily shipped across the Atlantic and then housed in training camps behind the front.[54]

Events at the end of 1917 disrupted this schedule. Russia's withdrawal from the war raised the prospect of one million German soldiers moving from the east to the Western Front, and British and French troop strength and morale had declined in 1917. By the end of that year, on the other hand, AEF training camps were in full swing, graduating legions of soldiers ready for final training. Questions arising from the shipping and deployment of the AEF, however, brought two interwoven issues into sharp relief. The first involved shipping. As McAdoo had predicted in 1914, the United States did not possess enough ships to transport its army across the Atlantic; American vessels could carry only half the monthly output of the AEF training camps to France. Only the British had sufficient capacity to transport the remainder.[55]

The British drove a hard bargain for their ships. They were keen to maintain as much of their international commerce as possible, and with their own supplies to ship, the French to supply, their empire to protect, and the depredations of German submarines to replace, they placed the AEF's needs low on their list of priorities. At the end of December 1917 Tasker Bliss warned Baker that it would take an additional two million tons of shipping to transport the men that Pershing had promised the Allies.

Given that this amount of shipping was not immediately available, and that American troops would require some months of training in France before they went into combat, the AEF was faced with the possibility that it would not play a major part in the war until 1919. That timetable made the Allies vulnerable to German offensives in 1918, and so Britain needed to decide whether or not it wanted the AEF in France in large numbers in that year. If it did, then much of its shipping would have to be diverted to transport and supply it. Otherwise the war might be lost while one million American soldiers languished on the wrong side of the Atlantic.[56]

The British countered with a proposal of their own. They could not spare the shipping to transport entire American divisions at Pershing's rate of two per month, but they could provide enough for 150,000 American infantrymen and machine gunners who would be integrated into the British army to replace its losses. Pershing and Bliss inquired how it was possible for shipping to be available for 150,000 infantrymen but not for the same number of soldiers in entire divisions, to be told that the infantry would be shipped with only their uniforms and rifles, and so would require much less shipping than full divisions with their artillery, transport, and engineers. The pressing need was for infantrymen to repel German offensives in the spring of 1918. "They all seemed to be badly rattled," Bliss reported to Baker.[57]

Wilson and Baker kept in close touch with these negotiations and were aware of the parlous state of Allied forces. "If we do not make the greatest sacrifices now and, as a result, great disaster should come," Bliss wrote in February 1918, "we will never forgive ourselves nor will the world forgive us." Although he was prepared to see AEF infantry train with the British, Baker insisted that this should only be temporary. "This for two reasons," he cabled Wilson at the end of March 1918, "first—we do not want either [Britain and France] to rely upon us for replacements, and, second—we want the Germans to know that we are augmenting the present allied forces and not merely making good its losses." Bliss brokered a compromise in which the British agreed to ship six entire American divisions, with their infantry to be sent to train with the British army. Then the doughboys would return to their divisions.[58]

Shipping remained a sore point in Anglo-American relations for the rest of the war. "There is just a little disposition on the part of both British and French to feel that they are in a position to demand, or at least to insist, upon the fulfillment of expectations on their part," Baker told Bliss in April 1918, "as against a right on the part of the United States to pursue its own policy." Still suspicious that commercial concerns lay behind British protestations about its shipping shortage, Baker told the Inter-Allied Maritime Council in September 1918 that current vessel assignments meant that the AEF could not assemble enough troops in France to ensure the successful outcome of the war until the end of 1919. The war ended before either Baker's fears or the Allies' promises could be further tested.[59]

Negotiations over shipping created another controversy that threatened to disrupt cooperation between the United States and the Allies. Britain's offer to ship only American infantrymen to France, ostensibly because of a shortage of shipping, also served another objective: to persuade Wilson to abandon the idea of an autonomous AEF in favor of "brigading" American troops with the British army. This meant that doughboys would fight in units embedded in British divisions and under British command. The Allies were persistent in their pressure for brigading, while Wilson, Baker, and Pershing stuck to their principle of an autonomous AEF while compromising over its implementation. The result was a battle of wills that periodically erupted into acrimony and threatened to derail the war effort at its most critical juncture.[60]

Several considerations lay behind both sides' attitude to brigading. The British and French stressed the urgency of training AEF troops as quickly as possible. Three years of attrition had thinned their armies' ranks, and Germany seemed ready to strike. British Prime Minister David Lloyd George wrote an impassioned note to his ambassador in Washington, Lord Reading, to outline the Allies' plight. Germany now had 196 divisions on the Western Front, with another 5 on their way from Russia, compared to the combined British and French total of 166 undermanned divisions. "The position of the Allies as a whole," Lloyd George concluded, "will ere long be in dire peril . . . There can be little doubt that victory or defeat for the Allies depends upon the arrival of the American infantry."[61]

This was powerful reasoning, and Wilson and Baker were impressed by it. Their sympathy, however, was tempered by suspicion that other factors were also at work. French claims that brigading would protect US troops while they learned the brutal ways of the Western Front struck Baker as disingenuous. The real reason, he thought, was that the Allies wanted to use the doughboys to make good their own losses and to avoid amalgamating divisions that were no longer viable. Pershing, who objected strongly to brigading, was even blunter. He thought that the "French have not been entirely frank, as unofficial information indicates they really want to incorporate our regiments into their divisions for such services in the trenches as they desire," and the British saw brigading as an excuse to relax their increasingly unpopular draft laws.[62]

Brigading suited not only Allied needs but also the poor opinion in Paris and London of the quality of the AEF's leadership. Georges Clemenceau, Joseph Joffre, and Douglas Haig thought little of Pershing's tactical or strategic skills, and argued privately that doughboys did much better when brigaded with their troops. Even in October 1918, according to British sources, "the American Army is disorganized, ill-equipped and ill-trained, with very few non-commissioned officers and officers of experience. It has suffered severely through ignorance of modern war and it must take at least a year before it becomes a serious fighting force." Aware of these criticisms, Bliss and Pershing argued that the British underestimated the AEF and its commanders to justify prolonged brigading.[63]

Wilson and Baker had their own reasons for opposing brigading. They thought it unseemly to place American troops under direct foreign command, for how could America make the world safe for democracy when its troops were dispersed throughout the British army? American families and voters, particularly those of Irish descent, would not tolerate their boys being subsumed into the British army; even the Canadians and Australians, despite the bonds of empire, had their own army corps and it was unthinkable that the United States accept anything less.[64]

Prolonged brigading would also bring out other tensions between American soldiers and their hosts. At the end of the war Baker told Wilson that "American soldiers get along well with the Canadians, fairly well with the Australians, but not at all with the British." Americans had different eating habits and higher expectations for their amenities than the French and British, and they would not accept lower standards. There were other implications to consider. "The French view of the sex privilege of soldiers, in sharp contrast to our own attitude on the sex question, would prevail, to the horror of our people," and white doughboys would be "demoralized" by contact with dark-skinned troops in the French and British armies. This logic applied in reverse when four of the US Army's black regiments were assigned to fight in the French army. This was the only instance in which the United States encouraged brigading; its commitment to segregation easily outweighed Baker's arguments against long-term brigading of white American soldiers.[65]

Tensions over brigading ran deep. During a visit to London in September 1918 Baker joined Lloyd George and Lloyd Griscom, Pershing's representative at the War Office, for dinner. After dessert Lloyd George, according to Baker, "half turned his chair . . . so that he faced me and then with vehement emphasis complained that the American Army in France was of no service to the British at all." Pershing had scuttled the compromise over brigading by recalling American infantrymen so quickly that they had been useless to the British. "Mr. Baker interrupted him," according to Griscom, "jumped to his feet, banged on the table, and said that under the circumstances, he was sure the President would agree that we send no more troops to France." Lloyd George abruptly changed the subject, and the following morning sent word that Baker "should think no more about the matter which [I] raised for discussion last night at dinner."[66]

Staring down the British prime minister showed Baker's diplomatic mettle, but his trips to the Western Front in 1918 left more profound impressions on him. "When you receive this," he wrote to his daughter Betty on March 9, 1918, "you will know that I am in France, not to see the gay things which usually take people to Paris, but to see our soldiers and talk to our generals and observe with my own eyes all the war things which have taken up my time for so long." He spent nearly a month in France and Italy, visiting AEF port facilities and then inspecting its troops and commanders. He met Generals Haig and Philippe Pétain, and King Albert of Belgium, to discuss strategy and consulted at length with Pershing. Even so, he found time to see some of France's wonders. "I would soon get the cathedral habit if I traveled much with Secretary Baker," General James Harbord noted in his diary. "It is only when I travel with him that I seem to have time to visit them."[67]

Baker returned to France in September 1918. His visit coincided with the Battle of St-Mihiel, in which 550,000 AEF and 50,000 French troops recaptured a salient that had jutted twenty miles west of the main front since 1914. Baker saw the attack unfold and described it to his wife:

> The cannonading began at about midnight and the infantry advanced at dawn, so that when I arrived at a high hill which overlooked the mountains and valleys which comprise the battlefield it required a field glass to follow the "rolling barrage" and to see our soldiers advancing behind it. But I saw the long lines of prisoners being sent to the rear, talked with many of them, saw our wounded men in ambulances and hospital and so practically witnessed the whole battle. And really the feeling one has in the American camps about the wonderful boys who comprise our army magnifies as you follow them through such an experience. They literally romp into battle and are just indescribably splendid, and the best part of it all is that they are not spoiled. A Frenchman said to me "their modesty is as great as their courage."[68]

Baker also saw the personal cost of war. Just before he left France he found the grave of Lieutenant Thomas Kern, whose father was an old friend. Thomas had died at Château Thierry, and Baker took pictures of his grave to send to his father. Dr. Kern replied with grief and gratitude. "There is in me that which longs for and wants to touch everything and anything in any way associated with my boy."[69]

William McAdoo did not visit Europe during the war. His work was at home, and there was plenty of it: by November 1918 the war cost the United States $60 million per day; there were taxation policies to implement, Liberty Loan campaigns to conduct, soldiers' and sailors' lives to insure, the Federal Farm Loan Board to run, the War Finance Corporation to chair, the Federal Reserve Board to supervise, and the Allies to fund. These tasks became more pressing during 1917 and through 1918, and McAdoo was responsible for them all.[70] And then, on December 27, 1917, Wilson announced that McAdoo would also become director general of the USRRA.

Federal control of the railroads, the nation's largest industry and biggest employer, had long been a goal of the Grange and populist movements of the nineteenth century. Some progressives had adopted the cause, this time in the name of national efficiency. Successful public operation of railroads might also spur nationalization of other key industries such as the telegraph and telephone networks.[71]

Wartime demands fed into this reformist agenda. The Army Appropriations Act of 1916 authorized the president, through the secretary of war, to take over transportation systems to facilitate the war effort. Wilson at first encouraged but did not force railroad coordination through agencies created by the Department of War. Daniel Willard, president of the Baltimore and Ohio Railroad and now a member of the Appropriations Committee, worked through its Transportation Committee to coordinate the roads to speed desperately needed materiel across the continent.[72]

Willard's efforts were hampered by logistical pressure, railroads' reluctance to cede autonomy, and bad weather. Determined to make the most of the enormous increase in freight brought about by the Allies' military needs, the roads applied to the Interstate Commerce Commission (ICC) in March 1917 for a rate increase of 15 percent. Shippers petitioned the ICC to restrain the increases, while investors demanded a higher return on assets that had languished under tight regulation. Pressure from wartime administrators, hopeful reformers, and resentful shippers pushed the administration to revisit its emergency powers. In December the ICC came out in favor of unified operation of railroads through either voluntary integration or the president's powers under the Army Appropriations Act.[73]

McAdoo pushed hard for the latter option. Immediately after the ICC's declaration he told Wilson that "I came to the conclusion some weeks ago that the only solution compatible with the genuine interests of the great masses of the American people was the prompt assumption by you of the control and operation of the railroads during the period of the war." The railroads were incapable of voluntary integration, Baker's rickety administrative structure was inadequate, and now the ICC had failed to reconcile the interests of the railroads and their shippers. Rate increases alone would not create the efficiencies and integration necessary to transport huge amounts of supplies generated by mobilization. "By a stroke of the pen" Wilson could eliminate wasteful competition between railroads and their "jealously guarded rights and prerogatives." Only then could they contribute fully to the war effort.[74]

By then Wilson was persuaded, but he hesitated over the terms by which the federal government would take over the railroads. McAdoo first thought that owners should be paid a "rental" based on their earnings in 1916. The government would also maintain the lines' rolling stock and infrastructure, with the value of improvements to be charged to each line at the end of its federal control. This arrangement was generous because 1916 had been a prosperous year for the railroads. Wilson and

McAdoo were persuaded to amend their plan so that net earnings were calculated on an average of a railroad's profits in 1915, 1916, and 1917.[75]

Wilson's other problem was whom to appoint to run the railroads. McAdoo had made it clear that he wanted the job but Wilson was dubious, not through lack of faith in his son-in-law but because he thought that he already had too much to do. Joseph Tumulty reassured him that "if you want to get a thing done, the best man to apply to is to a busy man, and this maxim applies to Mr. McAdoo most conspicuously."[76]

One more complexity embarrassed the president. The Army Appropriations Act empowered him, through the secretary of war, to operate the railroads. Well aware that his two secretaries were more often opposed than allied, Wilson feared that Baker would be hurt by yet another usurpation by his pushy colleague. "It was the only time that Mr. Wilson ever appeared . . . hesitant and a bit 'sheepish,'" Baker recalled. Ever loyal, he signed the proclamation and then appointed McAdoo as director general of the railroads. McAdoo, after all, had actually run a railroad, and Baker had not.[77]

Congress also needed to legislate the details of the federal takeover. The Federal Control Act of March 1918 limited federal control to a maximum of twenty-one months after the declaration of peace and mandated a "standard return" to the railroads based on their earnings over the previous three years. Congress also suspended the ICC's powers to set freight rates and authorized the USRRA to fix them as it saw fit. In response to pressure from shippers, the ICC did retain power to investigate rates, but its findings were subordinated to the judgment of the director general. When McAdoo raised rates by 25 percent in May 1918, he created appeal procedures that sidelined the ICC and muzzled shippers' complaints. The act also made clear that the USRRA was not subject to the Appropriations Committee or the WIB over purchasing and transportation priorities.[78]

Wilson's proclamation and McAdoo's appointment met with widespread but not universal praise. Prominent bankers welcomed them as the best solutions to the railroad industry's problems, shipping interests were delighted to be spared immediate freight rate increases, railroad brotherhoods hailed them in hopes that their wages and conditions would finally improve, and shareholders were pleased at the prospect of a guaranteed return on their investment. Even the railroads expressed approval of the scheme, and especially of its retention of their executives and its temporal limitation.[79]

In Congress some Republicans expressed reservations. "As a temporary expedient and war measure it may be necessary," Senator Harry New of Indiana conceded. "If it shall lead, however, to the development of sentiment for Government ownership, it would be calamitous." Frederick Gillett of Massachusetts noted Mc-

Adoo's multiple roles as secretary of the treasury, chairman of the Federal Reserve Board, "great dispenser of patronage and the political advisor to the President," and now director general of the USRRA. "He is already the Pooh-Bah of this administration, and there are other members of the cabinet who would have excited less distrust." Medill McCormick, then a Republican candidate for US senator from Illinois, told the press that "it is not good practical business . . . to charge one man, however, fertile, active, agile and energetic, with such a conglomeration of duties as [McAdoo's]."[80]

Others were more generous. "No Secretary of the Treasury has ever accomplished so much," a St. Louis banker wrote, "and I believe great wreaths and laurels will be heaped on your record as a Railroad Dictator." Earlier comparisons of McAdoo's achievements as secretary of the treasury with Alexander Hamilton's were repeated, and one periodical even elevated him to stand "among the great war financiers of history, like Saul among the sons of Israel of old." Bruce Barton, who after the war became America's most famous advertising guru, wrote that "a man in my office said to me today, 'did it ever occur to you that Mr. McAdoo now has concentrated in his hands more power than any man in the world?'" Early in 1918 *The Outlook* printed this poem by Alvah Bushnell:

> POOR MISTER MCADOO!
> Poor Mr. McAdoo!
> Think of the jobs he's hitched up to do!—
> The Treasury, the Railroad crew,
> The Income Tax and then a few.
> Each week they hand him something new
> To tax his time and temper too.
> He has to know when loans are due,
> What source to get his billions through,
> What funds to pass each dollar to,
> Which tax is what, and who is who;
> What bonds to sell and what renew,
> Which "trust" to coax and which to sue.
> He stretches out each day to two
> To do the things he has to do.
> The job would flounder me or you—
> But it's a cinch for Mr. McAdoo![81]

McAdoo assumed his new powers with vigor. He was now master of 300,000 miles of track, 57 canals and thousands of miles of inland waterways, 2,000 railroad corporations, and 1.5 million employees. His two aims, he declared, were to win the war and leave the railroads in better condition than he had inherited them. "The thing that lay under my hand and control was a run-down, confused, chaotic mess; an entire industry that was sliding rapidly downhill. It was anemic, undernourished, and subject to alarming attacks of heart failure."[82]

McAdoo first worked through the railroads' corporate structures. His Order No. 1 declared all railroad employees to be agents of the USRRA and that the roads would be administered "as a national system of transportation, the common and national needs being in all instances held paramount to any actual or supposed corporate advantage." Led by McAdoo, his deputy Walker D. Hines from the Atchison, Topeka and Santa Fe Railroad, and John Skelton Williams from the Treasury, the USRRA set about forcing the railroads to work cooperatively. They were told to ignore shippers' route preferences if they conflicted with efficiency, to share rolling stock, and to maintain ICC-approved freight rates and passenger fares.[83]

Old habits died hard. In May 1918 McAdoo announced that the railroads would no longer be run through their corporations but through seven regional districts, each with a federal manager appointed by the USRRA. The previous system had failed, he told Wilson, because railroad executives had favored the interests of their shareholders over those of the USRRA. Railroads would continue to operate with their own executives, but now under their federal managers' orders.[84]

McAdoo worked hard to integrate the railroads. He banned their solicitation of traffic and consolidated their ticket offices and freight depots. Passenger services were rationalized to eliminate duplicate services and tickets were sold without reference to particular railroads so that passengers could ride whichever service suited them best. Civilians were told, however, that the USRRA's first priority was to move troops, so they would have to make do with fewer trains and more crowded compartments.[85]

The USRRA also paid close attention to freight transport. Early in 1918 Europe faced a severe shortage of cereals, but American wheat sat in silos because of railroad congestion, car shortages, and severe weather. Within a month the USRRA had shipped enough grain to eastern ports to satisfy the Allies' needs, but it was stymied by lack of shipping to take it across the Atlantic. Again the freight cars, this time laden with grain, accumulated in their thousands. McAdoo threatened Food Administrator Herbert Hoover with an embargo on further deliveries unless he could provide sufficient shipping for it. Hoover obliged, but McAdoo took the credit. The USRRA had "saved the day for America and the Allies, because a failure to meet the food crisis at that time would have been an irretrievable disaster."[86]

Chastened by the food crisis, McAdoo ordered the construction of 2,500 locomotives and 100,000 freight cars and commandeered others from western and
southern lines for work in the East. He also directed that rolling stock be standard-
ized, freight yards shared, less-than-carload shipments held up, and trains routed
only on the basis of shortest travel time. The USRRA imposed penalties for shipment delays and idle trains and cancelled all transportation priority orders established by other government agencies in favor of its own. Through its Division of
Inland Waterways it also deepened the Cape Cod Canal to expedite coal shipments to New England, expanded the nation's fleet of river barges, and intensified
operations on the Erie Canal and the Mississippi River.[87]

The result, McAdoo reported to the president, was that eastward freight movements rose markedly during the first six months of federal operation. Coal shipments to New England rose by more than 50 percent and new freight records were
set along rail lines through Pennsylvania. On January 1, 1918, there were 41,000
freight cars holding nearly 2 million tons of freight bottled up in eastern yards; 5
months later there were only 28,000 and further reductions came during the summer. At the same time the railroads transported 4.3 million soldiers and sailors and
millions more civilians to their destinations. "I really think the improvement in
the railroad situation little short of miraculous," Newton Baker wrote in June
1918.[88]

McAdoo was in his element in the USRRA, for here was a task that appealed to
his love of action and penchant for self-promotion in ways that financial management did not. The USRRA also returned him to the industry in which he had first
become famous, but this time on a national scale with direct impact on the war
effort. McAdoo's new role also offered more personal benefits because by then his
presidential ambitions had been fully awakened. Controlling the nation's largest
industry that employed nearly two million Americans promised great political rewards. McAdoo worked best when he combined public service with personal ambition, and the USRRA offered wide scope for both.

Nowhere was this confluence of interest more evident than in his USRRA wage
policies. Because of the railroads' financial frailty after 1910, and the ICC's reluctance to grant large rate increases, their wages had not kept pace with the cost of
living. This became more pressing after the outbreak of war in August 1914, when
worsening inflation left railroad wages even farther behind. By the end of 1917
railroad employees, led by their well-organized Brotherhoods, were restless.[89]

McAdoo moved quickly to calm the situation. In January 1918 he created a
Railroad Wage Commission that recommended wage increases of up to 50 percent
for all but the best paid railroad employees. McAdoo enacted all these increases

through General Order No. 27 at the end of May and backdated them to January 1, 1918. The raises were generous and gave the lowest-paid workers the highest percentage gains. Flagmen's wages jumped 50 percent to nearly $60 per month; engineers won raises of 42 percent, firemen received 35 percent, and freight conductors' wages rose 20 percent. Only those who earned more than $250 per month missed out altogether. General Order No. 27 also mandated equal pay for equal work for female and African American employees and paid overtime after eight hours per day or for work on Sundays and public holidays. The total cost of these measures ran to more than $784 million in 1918.[90]

Labor leaders were delighted. Hugh Frayne, an American Federation of Labor (AFL) organizer and member of the WIB, hailed General Order No. 27 as "a marked progressive step" that delivered wage justice to millions of workers and entrenched equal pay for equal work, an eight-hour workday, and overtime for Sundays. Even railroad owners, secure in their rental payments and comforted by McAdoo's promise to offset higher wages by increases in rates and fares, reacted with equanimity.[91]

As Baruch had done within the WIB, McAdoo used high prices, this time for labor, to elicit maximum production. Purchasing industrial peace on the railroads was not only an exercise in social justice but also a calculated concession to a key element of the workforce to encourage its wholehearted participation in the war effort. Now that their grievances had been addressed it was as much the duty of railroad employees to stay at their posts as it was for AEF soldiers to stay in their trenches. McAdoo made clear the terms of this bargain in his reply to railroad machinists who had protested about the size of their wage rise:

> The time has come when we must give our undivided thought and attention to our work in order that we may turn out the amount of transportation absolutely required to make our Armies victorious on the fields of France and our Navy triumphant on the high seas . . . We cannot justify to the American people the great increase in wages and the immense improvement in working conditions already granted unless every employee proves . . . that he is worthy of it.[92]

There was also another deal in the making. Two million employees were a tempting constituency for someone with presidential ambitions, and McAdoo worked hard to cultivate it. As director general, in confirmation of Baker's observation that McAdoo had "a queer penchant for having his name on everything," McAdoo insisted that every railroad employee's paycheck bear his signature. "The political implications involved in that act," Ivy Lee noted after the war, "were such as to make unnecessary any comment." The employees were also aware of the favors they could bestow in return for generous treatment. Just before the promulgation of General Order No. 27 some clerks from the Northern Pacific Railroad sent McAdoo this piece of doggerel:

> McAdoo, McAdoo why don't you speak,
> Don't you hear all the Railroad Men squeak?
> Why don't you give us the promised raise
> If you do it quick, then you we will praise . . .
> Now have a heart, make your decision quick,
> Don't lose any time but turn the trick,
> We will take off our hats to you and send,
> You to the Whitehouse as our next PRESIDENT.[93]

African American and female leaders also applauded McAdoo's reforms, but in a time of southern black disfranchisement and before the passage of the Nineteenth Amendment they had fewer votes to offer. One black employee, William McKinney, wrote that "the Negroes of the country bless the Powers for taking over the railroads, and above all they bless the selection of a man . . . who has the courage to see that each human being is justly treated, no matter what may be his station in life or the color of his skin." Nearly twenty years later Thomas Webb thanked McAdoo for his stand on equal pay. Webb had taken a job with the Pullman Company in 1917 at $85 a month while his white colleagues earned $125. After General Order No. 27 Webb's pay rose to $125, and he received $200 in back pay. Webb, a Californian, could vote and years later he was proud to say that he had done so for McAdoo in the 1932 Senate election.[94]

McAdoo's belief in racial hierarchy and segregation, nurtured in his youth and shown by his desire to segregate the Treasury Department, did not change when he was appointed to the USRRA or when he granted equal pay to its black employees. Equal pay suited white workers as much as it pleased African Americans because white males had long resented substitution of their labor for that of lower-waged African Americans and women. McAdoo was sympathetic to these concerns; when the USRRA regional director in Chicago reported agitation by whites against hiring African Americans, he promised to honor existing agreements between railroad Brotherhoods and their employers to limit black employment.[95]

As he had done in the Treasury Department, McAdoo upheld segregation while taking steps to improve the quantity and quality of its separate facilities. He began by declaring that the USRRA would abide by state railroad segregation laws where they did not compromise efficiency or the war effort. To that end he accepted separate train compartments and station facilities in compliance with local customs and laws. "As a Southern man, I know, however," McAdoo wrote to his regional director in Atlanta, "that the facilities provided for the colored people on trains and in stations are frequently not only inadequate, but are of a very inferior and unsatisfactory quality." He ordered African American facilities to be kept as clean and comfortable as white accommodations, but little was actually done to bring substance to "separate but equal" on southern railroads.[96]

McAdoo also applied some of the measures that he had instituted at H&M to the USRRA. He banned consumption of alcohol by staff during working hours, created a Bureau of Suggestions and Complaints, and ordered employees to deal with the public with courtesy, helpfulness, and respect. He even revived the H&M's slogan as the catch-cry of the USRRA. "The 'public-be-damned' policy will in no circumstances be tolerated on the railroads under Government control," he announced, because now all railroad employees were "direct servants of the public."[97]

Although he announced his resignation as director general of the USRRA on November 22, 1918, McAdoo remained in office until January 11, 1919. By then debate over the railroads had focused on the future of the USRRA, because once the Treaty of Versailles was signed in June 1919 the time limit of twenty-one months established by the Federal Control Act began to tick away. Unless new legislation came into force the railroads would return to their owners no later than March 1921.

McAdoo was always alive to the political ramifications of federal railroad control, and at the end of November 1918 he warned Wilson that the situation was worrying. The Republicans, who had just won majorities in both houses of Congress, would hound the president over railroad policy. Determined to return them to their owners, the GOP had a vested interest in undermining the USRRA. The administration would be politically harmed and the railroads made inefficient at great cost to the postwar economy. Twenty-one months was too short a time to invest the sums needed to improve the roads, but too long to suffer Republican politicking on them.[98]

Instead, McAdoo argued, Wilson should propose a five-year extension of the USRRA. This would buy time for Congress to decide on a permanent railroad policy and take the issue out the 1920 election campaign. If Congress did not oblige, then Wilson should return the railroads to their owners on March 4, 1919. This would force Congress to decide railroad policy without embroiling the administration in partisan point-scoring at the expense of the railroads and Democratic electoral prospects.[99]

McAdoo denied that his proposal was a Trojan horse for nationalization. The point of his plan, he told the Senate Interstate Commerce Committee in January 1919, was to allow the USRRA to make the railroads more efficient while Congress made permanent arrangements for them. His own preference was for "unified control of some character," but not for outright public ownership.[100]

McAdoo's views sparked much debate. Labor groups, led by the Brotherhoods that had done so well from the USRRA, backed the Plumb Plan, under which the roads would be nationalized and then run through a board composed of government representatives, management, and employees. McAdoo opposed the Plumb Plan as ruinously expensive—the total capitalization of the railroads was almost $20 billion in 1918—and impractical. It was better to save the expense of buying them and instead to submit their owners to robust federal regulation. It was also inconceivable that Congress, so recently turned Republican, would countenance nationalization of any industry, let alone one as large and important as the railroads.[101]

Others were unconvinced. *The New York Times* noted that McAdoo's proposal, had it come from a socialist committed to public ownership of key industries, "would everywhere been recognized as well contrived, adroit, and, if accepted, sufficient to accomplish its purpose." Five more years of government control of the railroads, and continuation of its generous wage policies, would create a powerful constituency that would force Congress to make it permanent. "Mr. McAdoo's plan puts the country on the straight road to Government ownership."[102]

McAdoo dismissed this as an attempt to discredit the whole notion of federal control. "As in the case of the Federal Reserve Act and the Ship Bill in 1914," he told the editor of *Review of Reviews* at the end of 1918, "I find arrayed against [me] all of the conservative and reactionary forces in the country." By then it was clear that the Republicans in Congress would not act on his proposal; they even legislated to prevent early relinquishment of the railroads and to empower the ICC to overturn any rate and fare increases by the USRRA. Wilson vetoed that bill, but also abandoned hope that Congress would extend federal control beyond the original deadline of March 1921. Acting on Hines and McAdoo's advice, and with the agreement of Newton Baker as his co-signatory of the original proclamation in 1917, he announced in May 1919 that the railroads would return to their owners on January 1, 1920, fourteen months ahead of schedule and ten months before the next election. Railroad policy was now the Republicans' problem.[103]

Forced into action, congressional Republicans struggled to reach a consensus, and this delayed Wilson's handover for two months until March 1, 1920. In its final form the Transportation Act of 1920, also known as the Esch-Cummins Act, covered the railroad owners' operating losses for the next six months, provided for an extra "rental" payment of $453 million from the federal government, and directed the ICC to ensure a return of 5.5 percent on the railroads' capital for two years. Railroad owners and shippers were pleased by the Esch-Cummins Act; their employees, on the other hand, who had done so well out of the USRRA and then supported the Plumb Plan, looked with apprehension on the new order.[104]

Now back in private life but still deeply interested in politics, McAdoo decried the Esch-Cummins Act as a gift to the same interests that had undermined the USRRA. Making good the railroads' losses for six months after the handover was legitimate enough, but nothing could justify the $450 million "rental" for tracks and rolling stock that the government no longer operated. According to McAdoo the owners soon undid much of the USRRA's good work; the car shortage re-emerged, freight rates increased, and the railroads degenerated into their old destructive competition.[105]

McAdoo continued to attack the Esch-Cummins Act, defend the USRRA, remind railroaders of their wage increases for the rest of his career, and to argue that the best way to run the roads was to place them under strong national regulation. Although he remained fiercely critical of the "railroad interests," he opposed nationalization or permanent government operation and saw the USRRA only as a regulatory model and not as a blueprint for future government ownership. It was true that the USRRA had run the roads at a deficit, but that was because it had spent millions of dollars on improvements and delivered wage justice to its employees. This had cost $200 million in 1918 and $500 million in 1919, but that was a small price to pay for a more efficient rail system that had played a critical role in the war and that had provided a lasting example of the benefits of centralized administration and coordination.[106]

Like so much else in the Wilson administration, the USRRA went out with a whimper. The president, preoccupied with the peace treaty and then incapacitated by ill health, paid little attention to the railroads. McAdoo and Hines received no support from Wilson or his cabinet as they sang the USRRA's praises and defended their management of it, and many reformers who had welcomed the USRRA in 1918 now turned against it. Dismayed by McAdoo's conduct of the USRRA, Senator Hiram Johnson of California renounced his earlier enthusiasm for federal railroad control. McAdoo had effectively bribed railroad employees with General Order No. 27, but he had not raised freight rates sufficiently to relieve taxpayers of the need to fund the USRRA's operating deficits. "God pity the forgotten middle class who foot the bill!" Thanks to McAdoo the cause of government ownership had been set back fifty years.[107]

McAdoo linked his defense of the USRRA to his own political fortunes in the first half of the 1920s, and criticism of it also became part of political attacks on him and his presidential ambitions. Only months after the passage of the Esch-Cummins Act the Macon, the Georgia *Daily Telegraph* objected to McAdoo's "bragging" about railroad wage rises that had cost the rest of the population billions of dollars in increased fares, freight rates, and huge USRRA deficits. "McAdoo's idealism as regards the railroads and his management were predicated upon Uncle

Sam's pocketbook. What fool couldn't take over the railroads or any other enterprise and work wonders with it in bringing about reforms . . . for one class of people, if the undertaking were backed by the taxing power of the United States government?"[108]

The New York Times was also skeptical about McAdoo's claim that the USRRA had operated the railroads more cheaply than their private operators. According to the *Times*, the USRRA had under-maintained the railroads, and left them with an unsustainable wage bill and an inadequate revenue base. Even on McAdoo's figures the USRRA had run at a loss of more than $2 million per day. The *New-York Tribune* noted in September 1923 that McAdoo's "reckless" wage raises and parsimonious rate increases not only pillaged the Treasury but also left the railroads vulnerable to postwar recession.[109]

The USRRA deserves more historical attention than it has so far received, for it was one of the most significant of the mobilization measures of 1917–1918 and represented a major expansion of governmental competence to run the nation's largest industry. McAdoo's generosity in General Order No. 27 was more than a downpayment on his later political career; by lifting wages faster than freight rates and passenger fares he shifted some of the costs of wage increases and railroad integration into USRRA operating deficits and then onto taxpayers. His reliance on taxation to achieve industrial reorganization was not unprecedented, but the scale and the cost of the USRRA were. Acting under the pressure of war, McAdoo used the USRRA to undertake wealth redistributive policies on a scale that would not be exceeded until the New Deal in the 1930s. The New Deal, borrowing what William E. Leuchtenburg has called the "analogue of war," undertook a massive expansion of federal competence and authority that owed much more to the USRRA than it did to the Transportation Act of 1920. As William McAdoo had been at the forefront of the USRRA in 1918, so too was he a prominent cheerleader for the much greater revival of its spirit fifteen years later.[110]

❖❖❖

Baker and McAdoo followed accounts of Germany's military reverses in the second half of 1918 with rising excitement. When Germany did sue for peace both of them urged a quick armistice. "It will be such a boon to humanity to secure peace on our terms," McAdoo wrote to his wife at the end of October, "and to stop further horrible slaughter & human misery." Despite advice to the contrary from Bliss, March, and Pershing, Baker saw no point in wringing unconditional surrender from Germany and he worried about the AEF's growing supply problems. President Wilson agreed with his two secretaries and told the Allies that the war should end forthwith.[111]

Baker and McAdoo led the outpouring of congratulation and relief that greeted the Armistice on November 11, 1918. They sat together as Wilson read its terms to Congress and joined the rapturous applause when the president ended his recitation with "the war thus comes to an end." Baker congratulated the AEF for contributing to "the great victory for the forces of civilization and humanity," and McAdoo told an AEF representative in Switzerland that "I am a very happy man that all this bloodshed and slaughter has been stopped, not only for the sake of my own sons but for the sake of everybody else's sons, husbands, fathers, brothers, wives and children."[112]

McAdoo soon had another announcement to make. On November 14, 1918, only three days after the Armistice, he submitted his resignation from the cabinet and the USRRA to the president. Nearly six years of public service, he told Wilson, had so damaged his health and fortune that it was now time to recoup both. Wilson's reply was gracious. "I shall not allow our intimate personal relation to deprive me of the pleasure of saying that in my judgment the country has never had an abler, a more resourceful and yet prudent . . . Secretary of the Treasury." He agreed that McAdoo should leave the Treasury upon the appointment of his successor, and the railroads in the New Year. Carter Glass, who had done so much to formulate the Federal Reserve Act of 1913, became secretary of the treasury on December 16, 1918, and McAdoo's deputy Walker D. Hines became director general of the USRRA on January 30, 1919.[113]

McAdoo's resignation took the press by surprise. *The New York Times* noted that the nation had lost a brilliant public servant, and that it should combine deep gratitude to McAdoo with "some sense of shame . . . [at] the niggardliness of our democracy toward its servants." The *Los Angeles Times* mourned the departure of "the brains of the Wilson cabinet," the *Los Angeles Express* admired McAdoo's "Herculean job," and the *New York Tribune* paid tribute to "the most powerful man in America next to the President." More than 350 people wrote to thank him for his service, and a group of railroad workers in St. Louis even promised to send him $2,000 a month to augment his salary so that he might remain in public life.[114]

McAdoo always insisted that his stated reasons for resigning were genuine. He had been concerned about his health since his hungry years in New York during the 1890s; his Liberty Loan tours had been abbreviated by laryngitis and tonsillitis, and he complained often of "nervous exhaustion." He had been frequently confined to home, and twice sent on long holidays, to recover his health, and shortly before his resignation he had contracted influenza. His physician Frank E. Miller prescribed him medications for a wide range of complaints. In June 1918 Miller inquired whether the Glycero-phosphate of Lime and Soda to combat McAdoo's lethargy, the Argyrol to assist his earache, the Euliol to alleviate his sinus pain, the Diastos to relieve "intestinal complications," and the Respalis to reduce "congestion about the base of the brain where the Will centers are," had had their desired effects.[115]

It was also true that McAdoo was worried about money. Living and entertaining in Washington cost him $35,000 per year, which was nearly 3 times his salary. At the end of 1914 he sold $14,000 of bonds at a discount because "it is impossible for a man in my position and with as large a family as I have, to live on the salary that the Government pays." In 1916 he sold a property on Vinalhaven Island, Maine, and then two blocks of land at Bayhead, New Jersey, for $30,000, and a year later offered some bonds to Cleveland H. Dodge at 90 percent of their face value. "I am selling the bonds merely because I must do so in order to replenish my income which . . . is not sufficient to enable me to stay in office. Confidentially, I shall probably go back to private life within the next twelve months simply because I am unable to stand the expense here any longer." A week before his resignation he acknowledged a loan of $9,500 from W. H. Osborn, another wealthy Democrat.[116]

And yet many still wondered. In his letter of resignation McAdoo himself noted that "I do not wish to convey the impression that there is any actual impairment of my health because such is not the fact." He was more tired than ill, and needed only "a reasonable period of genuine rest to replenish my energy." Nor did money problems entirely explain the timing of his resignation. *The New York Times* conceded that McAdoo could not live in Washington on his salary, but noted that he had never been able to do so and that there were many who would lend him money on generous terms. McAdoo brushed aside alluring offers of employment immediately after his resignation, preferring instead to take a long holiday in California. Not surprisingly other reasons for his departure began to emerge from the Washington rumor mill.[117]

These rumors focused on the timing of McAdoo's resignation. It seemed odd that Wilson's best known cabinet member, and his son-in-law to boot, should desert him at such a critical time. Certainly the war had been won, but peace had still to be negotiated and Wilson had announced that he would travel to Paris to oversee it. With the president and secretary of state overseas for an extended period the administration needed leadership at home, and yet McAdoo had chosen that very time to depart. Surely his money problems and fatigue could have waited a few months more. Why had he deserted Washington and his father-in-law at such a difficult time?

All of the answers focused on the deterioration of Wilson and McAdoo's relationship. There were stories that Wilson had tired of McAdoo's appetite for bureaucratic turf and personal publicity, and that he had distributed patronage with more concern for his own political future than for that of the administration. Other stories circulated that McAdoo had objected so vociferously to Wilson's call to voters to return a Democratic Congress in the 1918 elections that the president had decided to release him. The Providence, Rhode Island, *Daily Journal* reported that McAdoo and Wilson had fallen out over railroad policy, while Cory Grayson, the president's doctor, told Colonel House that McAdoo had been incensed that Wilson planned to take Baker and not him to the Versailles peace conference. Others saw in McAdoo's resignation ambition rather than jealousy; hungry for the 1920 nomination, he wanted to distance himself from Wilson to run his own presidential campaign.[118]

There was some fire behind this smoke. Despite their denials, Wilson and McAdoo had indeed moved apart, and their relationship had become distant and sometimes hostile. They had differed frequently over postwar policies, and McAdoo had certainly angled for an invitation to Versailles. Rumor had it that he had asked Wilson three times to take him to France, but each time the president had refused on the grounds that McAdoo did not "belong" on the peace delegation "and he couldn't be put on it on account of family relationship." Wilson did not explain how that "family relationship" prevented McAdoo from going to Versailles but had not stopped him from serving in the cabinet for more than four years after his marriage to Eleanor.[119]

Embarrassed by his declining influence in the White House, McAdoo also justified the timing of his resignation by referring to his status as presidential son-in-law. Wilson and Secretary of State Robert Lansing's being in France, he told Baker, meant that he, as the second-ranking cabinet member, would be in charge of domestic policy. "The 'dynasty' and 'family affair' business would have been played up by the hostile press, and my usefulness would have been seriously impaired."[120]

Wilson's public graciousness about McAdoo's resignation also hid a more private but deep sense of betrayal and a conviction that his ambitious son-in-law was not presidential timber. McAdoo was aware of most if not all of these factors, but had pressing personal and political reasons to attribute his resignation to reasons other than the breakdown in his relationship with his father-in-law.[121]

Newton Baker joined the surprised chorus that greeted McAdoo's resignation. "Really I can hardly think of going on with your strong hand and splendid instincts withdrawn both from the councils of the administration and from the Treasury upon which we all rely for the support of all we do. For all your personal support and kindness to me I am deeply grateful and I can wish you nothing better than that your future happiness may be somewhat in proportion to your past great services." McAdoo's reply hinted at more private disagreements and disappointments as reasons for his departure. "My retirement was inevitable, forced by circumstances beyond my control, and that at least gives me comfort. If it had been optional, I might have doubted my judgment, but in the circumstances, the path of duty and honor was perfectly clear and I had to follow it regardless of personal consequences."[122]

There were personal consequences for Baker as well. Mac's departure from cabinet, he told Wilson, made it impossible for him to go to Versailles. Now that McAdoo had jumped ship Baker would have to stay in Washington. "I am persuaded that the country would feel more concerned about your own absence if two members of the Cabinet were with you now that the Secretary of the Treasury's post will have to be filled by a man new to those responsibilities."[123]

This was not the first or the last time that McAdoo had disrupted Baker's plans. This time, however, Baker found it difficult to forgive him for deserting Wilson. He, too, felt worn out and poor by the end of the war, he later told McAdoo, but "I did not feel free to [resign] and, of course, your presence in the Cabinet was vastly more important than mine." Wilson clearly felt the contrast keenly, and did not forget it. By one account he told Baker that he was "utterly disgusted" at McAdoo's timing. It fell now to Baker to be cabinet's leading light amid the diplomatic disappointments, political catastrophe, and ill health that blighted Wilson's final two years in office. McAdoo's resignation brought his relationship with Wilson to a crisis from which it would never recover, but it also cemented the president's conviction that Baker was a more deserving political heir than his errant son-in-law.[124]

CHAPTER 9

The Heir Apparent, the Crown Prince, and Woodrow Wilson, 1918–1924

The Wilson administration failed to respond to the challenges of demobilization and peacemaking between the Armistice of November 11, 1918, and Warren Harding's inauguration on March 4, 1921. Wilson himself, hailed at the end of 1918 as mankind's best hope for a more enlightened future, was by the end of 1919 so diminished by illness, diplomatic failure, and political miscalculation that he was reduced to a querulous invalid. Baker and McAdoo suffered less dramatically from the unraveling of Wilson's presidency, but it still had profound consequences for their public and private careers. Although no longer in the cabinet, McAdoo was still Wilson's son-in-law, but that affiliation proved double-edged as he publicly reveled in his role as Wilson's "crown prince," but privately struggled to reconcile his political ambition with his deteriorating relationship with his father-in-law.

Baker's experiences were less complicated but also disappointing. McAdoo's sudden resignation not only derailed his hope to accompany Wilson to Versailles but also convinced him to stay in office during the president's lengthy trips to France and then his illness. McAdoo may have been the president's son-in-law but, according to one writer at least, Baker "was the son Wilson never had."[1]

Baker's reputation became hostage to the precipitous decline in Wilson's popularity and authority. As McAdoo suffered the personal and political costs of his disloyalty to Wilson, Baker also paid a price for his deep and public loyalty to him. The result was that Wilson's shadow followed both men for the rest of their lives.

As McAdoo packed his bags, Baker's work still lay in Washington—not only to dismantle the war effort but also to provide leadership in the absence of the president, the secretary of state, and now the secretary of the treasury. Baker's conception of postwar adjustment was very limited. His job in April 1917 had been to build the nation's military capabilities as quickly as possible; now that the war was over it was to unwind wartime institutions equally fast. Conscription was shut down on Armistice Day, trains full of inductees were turned around, and within two months the American Expeditionary Forces (AEF) had discharged more than 800,000 soldiers. The War Industries Board (WIB) shut down on January 1, 1919, only six weeks after the Armistice, and Baker rapidly disbanded the myriad of other wartime agencies and committees. Army contracts were cancelled, supply ships in the mid-Atlantic were ordered back to port, and the AEF ceased construction and procurement. The Armistice was only a truce, but as far as Baker was concerned the war was over.[2]

Ending conscription and cancelling contracts was easy enough, but extricating the AEF from Europe involved more complicated planning, politics, and diplomacy. The Armistice transformed two million American soldiers into spectators, and the French were keen to set them to work. Marshall Ferdinand Foch asked to use the AEF in reconstruction work under French authority, but that cut across two of Pershing's key post-Armistice objectives: to improve the AEF's military capabilities and to bring it home as soon as possible. Alert to its political and diplomatic implications, Pershing forwarded Foch's request to Baker and recommended that it be denied. The AEF had come to Europe as warriors to save civilization, not as laborers to rebuild it.[3]

Baker agreed with the substance of Pershing's reaction but worked to soften its tone. He reiterated US policy to repatriate the AEF as soon as possible and confirmed that American soldiers would not be used as laborers. Individual members of the AEF could, however, provide a "gift of service" and voluntarily assist in reconstruction. Baker did not explain how these volunteers might donate their labor in the midst of their military training and despite their commanding general's opposition to the whole idea. He may have taken his compromise seriously, but no one else did.[4]

As a result the AEF spent the rest of its time in France on parade grounds, on firing ranges, and in camps. Baker was also determined that no member of the AEF should return to America without first improving his education. Those who were poor in literacy and numeracy attended remedial classes; those who wished to pursue trades received training, and in the bigger camps there were "soldier universities" in which thousands of doughboys took classes in liberal arts, science, agriculture, divinity, medicine, and law. Their lecturers were fellow soldiers who had been conscripted into the AEF from the academy or the professions, and Baker was delighted to learn that privates lectured majors on calculus and that "the military hierarchy is completely upset by the intellectual hierarchy." More than three thousand American soldiers attended British and French universities, including Oxford, Cambridge, and the Sorbonne, while they awaited repatriation.[5]

Wilson and Baker wanted to recall the troops as soon as possible, but several factors conspired against them. Although no one seriously considered that the war might resume after the Armistice, it did remain a possibility until a permanent peace had been signed. A sizeable American army therefore needed to remain in Europe until that time. Lack of shipping to transport two million soldiers and their equipment also restricted repatriation efforts. As Baker had struggled to persuade the British to provide shipping for the rapid deployment to France of the AEF during the war, he found it even harder to secure ships to take them home. This time the British argued that their Empire troops, who had been fighting since 1915, should be repatriated first and that the AEF would have to wait its turn.

Baker conceded this "equitable right to an earlier return," but his troops did not. Captain Walter Lippmann, then stationed with the Peace Commission, noted in January 1919 that doughboys exhibited acute homesickness and "an inescapable sense of disillusionment." If the AEF could be transported to Europe at the rate of 300,000 men a month when the Allies needed them, they wondered, "why can't they get us home just as fast when they are through with us?" Anxious at the prospect of millions of impatient families at home, and about the possibility of unrest among the soldiers in France, Baker ordered their repatriation on American naval vessels and cargo ships. Twenty-six thousand soldiers returned in November 1918, and nearly 100,000 more in December, but at that rate the whole process would have taken nearly 3 years. It was not until April 1919 that enough British ships were available to make large inroads into the task. In May 1919, 300,000 US troops left France, and by the end of August only 300,000 remained as an occupation force in Germany. Most of those troops returned in September and October 1919.[6]

Repatriation of the AEF's living soldiers was a question of shipping and time, but the disposition of its dead was a more delicate matter. Baker had originally promised that all American war dead would be buried either in Arlington National Cemetery or at home, but once the enormity of the task of recovering and transporting tens of thousands of bodies became clear he suggested that fallen AEF soldiers should remain in "fields of honor" in France. Many of their families, however, insisted that their sons be brought home, and so Baker allowed each family to decide for itself. Nearly 60 percent opted for repatriation, and eventually 45,500 bodies were brought home while 32,000 remained in France in 6 American war cemeteries.[7]

Baker visited France in March and April 1919. "Every place I went, wherever I spoke to the boys, they chanted in a very respectful but audible chorus, 'We want to go home.'" In Germany with American troops stationed in the Army of Occupation, he found "the most entrancing situation that one can imagine. It is Spring and the birds are out and the trees are in bloom." Although they were under orders not to fraternize with German adults, the men of the AEF "have been just as unable to resist the German children as they were to resist the French children, and you see American soldiers everywhere with little Hans and Fritz and Gretchen."[8]

Enmeshed in peace negotiations, Wilson showed little interest in military policy or demobilization. When he did intervene, however, the results were catastrophic. The president committed US troops to two separate military operations in Russia, both times against Baker and March's advice. In July 1918, after Russia had withdrawn from the war and descended into civil war, Wilson agreed to send six thousand American troops to Archangel, six hundred miles north of Moscow. The British were concerned that military supplies there might fall into German hands, and hoped that Allied troops would encourage "loyal" Russians to re-enter the war. Baker believed that any diversion of American soldiers from the Western Front would delay victory. Intervention also ran contrary to Wilson's recently promulgated Fourteen Points, which promised that Russians would be left to work out their own destiny. The president, however, was swayed by other considerations. He had been forced to deny so many British and French requests, particularly those concerning brigading of U.S. troops in Allied armies, that he wanted to agree to this one.[9]

Baker thought the Archangel expedition was "nonsense from the beginning," and later described it as "the only real disagreement I ever had with President Wilson." He took no satisfaction from failure at Archangel; the Germans secured the military stockpiles there before the Allies even reached Russia and the expedition was dragged into the Russian civil war by assisting the White Russians in their losing struggle against the Bolsheviks.[10]

Wilson committed troops to another Russian expedition, this time to Vladivostok at the eastern terminus of the Trans-Siberian Railway. Japan had offered to secure the terminus to prevent shipment of supplies to German forces in Europe, but Wilson suspected that its real motive was to control as much of eastern Russia as it could. "Looking from Tokio [sic], one might regard Russia as a huge cake," Pershing was advised, "—a bonbon big enough for two." Determined not to allow Japan a free hand, and again contrary to Baker's advice, Wilson sent eight thousand troops to Vladivostok in August 1918.[11]

Baker pushed Wilson to withdraw both expeditions as soon after the Armistice as possible. The Archangel force served no military purpose, and in Vladivostok the Americans did little more than provide the Japanese with diplomatic cover as they pillaged eastern Siberia. "My own judgment," Baker wrote to Wilson at the end of November 1918, "is that we ought simply to order our forces home by the first boat." Wilson thought otherwise, and American troops stayed at Archangel until June 1919 and at Vladivostok until March 1920. By then nearly four hundred of them had died in Russia for no appreciable gain, and Russo-American relations had been poisoned for a decade. Always loyal to Wilson and mindful of the service of American troops in Russia, Baker never publicly criticized the Russian expeditions. Privately, however, he conceded that both had been disastrous.[12]

Their differences over the Russian expeditions aside, Baker and Wilson worked together as harmoniously as circumstances allowed. At first their interaction was limited by the president's absences; trips to Europe took him away for six weeks after December 1918 and then for four months between March and July 1919. He then spent only a month in the White House before beginning a tour that ended with his collapse in Colorado at the end of September. Four days after his return to Washington on September 28, 1919, Wilson suffered a massive stroke that severely limited his capacity to undertake the physical and mental demands of the presidency for the rest of his term. During this time he displayed only sporadic interest in domestic policy and politics, leaving Baker and the rest of the cabinet to manage demobilization without presidential direction or support.[13]

Wilson's absences and illness affected Baker greatly. They had grown close after March 1916, but after the Armistice they saw little of each other. After his stroke Wilson remained in the White House, isolated by a protective troika of his wife Edith, his doctor Cary Grayson, and his secretary Joseph Tumulty. He did not meet his cabinet for eight months after his stroke, but its members communicated with the White House through notes. To mask the extent of Wilson's incapacity his inner circle orchestrated a conspiracy of false optimism about his health and acuity through press releases and stage-managed meetings.[14]

Baker and the rest of the cabinet were willing participants in this conspiracy. "I have seen Grayson several times and of course see Tumulty often," Baker told Bliss in October 1919, "and I gather from their manner and their talk that they are beginning to be more cheerful and hopeful than they were two weeks ago." Baker had not seen the president since his collapse, but he had received memoranda "which show that he is quite his old self so far as clearness of mind and decision of will are concerned." Wilson's powers of concentration fluctuated wildly for the rest of his term, yet neither Baker nor his colleagues ever revealed the extent of his incapacity to the public.[15]

Accounts of the true state of Wilson's health were consigned to diaries and private correspondence. Breckinridge Long, third assistant secretary of state, saw Wilson in May 1920 and was shocked. "His face has lost many of its heavy lines and all of its ruddy color. The flesh is no longer of the firm appearance it was . . . His mouth has a tendency to stay open." Long introduced the Uruguayan ambassador, but Wilson seemed distracted and forgetful. Afterward the ambassador, at Long's request, told the press that he found Wilson to be "doing well, bright of mind and very gracious." For his part Baker announced that Wilson was recovering slowly but steadily and had retained all his mental faculties. In 1928 he maintained that there had been no need for the president to resign after his stroke because "Wilson had a better mind at his sickest moment . . . than anyone else at his best." Even so "it was thoroughly bad that the Cabinet was kept so much in the dark" about his health.[16]

Reluctant to formulate his own vision for demobilization, and without any clear direction from the president, Baker focused on specific issues rather than policy formulation. With an invalid in the White House, a resurgent Republican Party, and increasingly hostile public opinion, he and his colleagues could do little more than watch as all that they had made together slipped away.

Baker's loyalty to Wilson was most obvious in his views on the Treaty of Versailles and the League of Nations. Once the treaty was made public he told its critics that it was indeed flawed, but Wilson had done his best. Rather than entrust hopes for an enlightened peace to the tender mercies of the British and French, Wilson had "stuck it out on the theory that with all his disappointments he would get a better thing for the world than would happen if he were to leave." Later Baker told a friend that, but for Wilson, "the peace finally patched up in Paris would have made the looting of Peking look like a Sabbath School scolding." Wilson had been beaten by the vindictiveness and "parochial zeal" of the Allies, "but [he] did coerce on his cynical associates the idea of the League and, unless I am more wrong than I have ever been in my life, that is at once the most handsome and enduring idea born."[17]

Baker's conviction that the sins of the treaty were redeemed by the League corresponded exactly to Wilson's own view. The president had staked his political authority and personal prestige on the treaty, with the League embedded in its terms, and upon its ratification by the US Senate. Hardliners within the GOP Senate majority, led by Henry Cabot Lodge of Massachusetts, were equally determined to vote the treaty down. This left Wilson and the Democrats little option but to compromise with moderate Republicans to pass the treaty with amendments. In December 1919, following rejection of the treaty by the Senate, the president refused any compromise and instructed Democrats in the Senate to follow suit.[18]

Wilson's intransigence divided Senate Democrats and his own administration. In the Senate his loyalists under Gilbert Hitchcock of Nebraska fought Democratic compromisers led by Oscar Underwood. In the cabinet Lansing and Lane argued for an amended treaty as better than no treaty at all, but Secretary of the

Treasury Carter Glass, Secretary of the Navy Daniels, Postmaster General Burleson, and Newton Baker opposed them. Lansing singled Baker and Daniels out for special criticism:

> After the President has taken action, these two always endorse it. They seem to have no minds when the President has made up his. They act as if he could not possibly make a mistake. This form of flattery . . . gives them much more popularity with their chief and results in an intimacy which those who show independence of judgment do not enjoy . . . To me this course is inconsistent with manliness, with self-respect and with a true sense of public duty. However, it cannot be denied that these two gentlemen are in high favor with the President, who is very responsive to praise of his conduct and politics.

By his own measure Lansing was not short of "a true sense of public duty," and his views soon cost him his place in Wilson's cabinet.[19]

Baker argued Wilson's case for the treaty without amendment. "I should much prefer to see the whole treaty beaten," he declared in November 1919, "than to have the stingy, go-lightly performance which Lodge has made of it with his reservations." Even if Wilson accepted the reservations, the Republicans would find other reasons to reject the treaty; the reservations were also impractical because the victorious powers would need to reconvene the peace conference to agree to them and then put the amended treaty to the Germans. America would one day join the League, Baker told Walter Lippmann in January 1920, but "we will come into it like a timid miser, late because we delayed outside to hide our valuables for fear that our associates might pick our pockets." On March 19, 1920, the treaty was again rejected by the Senate, this time through a strange alliance of Democrats loyal to Wilson and Republicans loyal to Lodge.[20]

Limitations in Baker's post-Armistice vision were made clear by his treatment of two issues left unresolved from the war. The first concerned African Americans in the army. Although all black conscripts soon returned to civilian life, those who had enlisted before 1917 remained in uniform. The war had provided black soldiers with new, albeit limited, opportunities, and now Baker came under pressure from both sides of the army's racial divide as they argued over recognition of African American wartime achievements and postwar aspirations.

In May 1919 Baker heard that General Charles C. Ballou, a white officer who had commanded the African American officers' training camp at Des Moines and then the 92nd Division in France, now found himself "ground between the upper and nether mill stone of feeling over the colored man as an officer in the army." On the one hand General Leonard Wood declared that black soldiers had performed poorly in combat and had shown that "the negro would not make an officer," while on the other W. E. B. DuBois criticized Ballou for being insufficiently assertive of the rights of his black subordinates. Wood wanted to force black officers out of the army, "while the colored men will want to demand a much fuller recognition of race equality."

Baker responded with the same hesitance that had marked his treatment of racial issues during the war. He agreed that the army should provide African Americans with "every opportunity . . . to develop individually and as a people," but he also stressed that those opportunities did not include desegregation or social equality. "Our government has never undertaken to regulate people's social relations; they flow naturally from the admiration and respect of people for one another, and their sure basis is their spontaneity." Baker promised that African American officers and men would receive "fair play" for their wartime service, but he made no promises about their postwar futures.[21]

Although he was ambivalent about black soldiers after the war, Baker made some effort to correct the record of their achievements during it. Press stories and army gossip claimed that the 368th Infantry Regiment of the 92nd Division, made up of African American troops and white officers, had broken and run during the Battle of Argonne in September 1918. Baker investigated these rumors and found that no blame could be attributed to the officers or men in the field. The regiment had advanced without artillery support or enough wire-cutting equipment, and it had withdrawn under orders and not through panic or cowardice.[22]

Correcting the record was one thing, but changing attitudes was another. In October 1920 McAdoo passed on a complaint from L. L. Burkhead, a newspaper editor in Columbus, New Mexico, about the conduct of African American troops there. Nearly three thousand black troops, along with their "camp followers," were running liquor and drugs across the Mexican border and threatening the town's white inhabitants. Burkhead also warned that the troops, all of whom voted Republican, might tilt New Mexico against the Democrats in the 1920 elections. "I think these people ought to have relief," McAdoo wrote. Baker again focused on the particular problem but not the broader issue. The inspector general investigated allegations of drug-running and found them to be baseless, and Baker ascertained that state law prohibited soldiers from other states from casting votes in New Mexico elections. Moving black troops from Columbus, he concluded, would only heighten racial tension because they were "not desired anywhere." Hiding them away in the desert seemed the best option.[23]

Baker dealt with conscientious objectors with similar obfuscation. Once the war was over, Wilson came under pressure to release all wartime dissenters. With presidential dreams of his own, McAdoo told Wilson that "the great mass of men and women in the country of liberal thought and tendencies" supported an amnesty. "These are your friends, and it is to them . . . we must look for support in the coming campaign." This time Wilson sought the views of Postmaster General Burleson, Attorney General Palmer, and Baker. Burleson agreed to an amnesty but Palmer, engaged in his own campaign against radicals, did not. "The country is not yet entirely free from enemies within," he warned, and an amnesty would send troublemakers the wrong message.[24]

Baker also demurred. More than 2,700 dissenters remained in jail because of their wartime utterances and actions. They were "anarchists and agitators whose conduct in prison has been such as to make it clear that they would either be a menace, or by agitation arouse serious resentment and perhaps local disorders, if released." Those who had been sincere in their objections had already been freed, but the rest still required "the curative and helpful discipline of prison."[25]

Insistence on the moral turpitude of conscientious objectors sat uncomfortably with Baker's other conviction that, as he told Walter Lippmann in 1920, the "right of free speech can not be limited to the right to speak freely unimportant opinions on immaterial subjects." Aware of this contradiction, Baker tried to reconcile it by making judgments about the genuineness and social costs of the dissenters' objections. He thought, for example, that Eugene Debs, who had been sentenced to ten years in jail for opposing conscription, had done much more than simply express an opinion. He had instead made a "deliberate and determined effort . . . to defeat the execution of the draft law and recruiting for the Army." That made him a willful obstructer of the war and deserving of severe punishment. Wilson agreed, and Debs languished in prison until President Warren Harding released him in December 1921.[26]

Baker failed in his one attempt to achieve postwar structural change. In August 1919 he and Peyton March sent Congress a bill that created an army of 500,000 men, three months' universal military training (UMT), and permanent federalization of the National Guard. Hearings on the bill focused on its cost, and ultimately the Army Act of 1920 established an army of fewer than 300,000, no UMT, and the retention of state control of the National Guard. Remembering its earlier battles with Baker over the role of the general staff, Congress also authorized it to advise Congress independently of the Department of War. This was an attack on the authority of the secretary of war, on the principle of civilian control over military administration, and on Baker's ability to control his fractious, and frequently Republican, senior generals.[27]

Criticism of Baker's plan was not limited to congressional penny-pinching and politicking. Many of those who had led the peace movement before 1917, and who now championed Wilson's vision of a world free of militarism, wondered how their former ally could advocate a large standing army and UMT. Always sensitive to charges of apostasy, Baker justified his plan through a combination of realism and idealism. When he had joined the cabinet, he told a friend, he was convinced that war was irrational and wasteful, and "my three years as Secretary of War have not changed these beliefs." His plans were not "consciously at least, at variance with the President's appeal to America that she lead the world into an era of justice accomplished by peaceful negotiation." He calculated that an army of 500,000, backed by millions more through UMT, was needed so that it "can be expanded by mere multiplication and will not have to be entirely recast should an emergency require its use."

Baker then injected a note of idealism into his pragmatic acceptance of a large army and UMT. Until the Armistice the army had been assembled and trained solely to fight the war, but now it could also be an educational institution. Recent experience in the AEF camps had shown that soldiers could use their time in uniform to gain educational qualifications that would make them better citizens. Far from making militarists out of all young men, three months of UMT would improve their health, fitness, and hygiene. These arguments did not convince Congress or Baker's critics, who feared that he had grown too close to his military advisors. Baker's reputation as a lapsed progressive, seduced from reform by too close an association with his military subordinates and later his business and legal colleagues, took root at the end of the war and remained for the rest of his life.[28]

❧✦❦

Unlike Baker, McAdoo had time to plan his future after the Armistice. "It is rather a tough job to start life again at the age of 55," he told Cleveland Dodge soon after his resignation, "but with unimpaired health and my increased enthusiasms . . . I shall begin all over again certainly with resolution and, I hope, success."[29]

Having long since severed his connection to H&M, McAdoo returned to his original training as a lawyer. He invited George Franklin, whom he had appointed to the War Finance Commission in 1917, to join him in legal practice in New York City. Franklin agreed and brought Joseph P. Cotton, who been counsel to the Federal Reserve Board (FRB), with him. "There should be a moderate fortune in it for you," Cotton predicted to McAdoo, "and very substantial incomes for the rest of us." McAdoo also asked Francis Huger, his eldest son, to join the new firm of McAdoo, Cotton and Franklin. They opened an office in May 1919 and McAdoo set to work. "If you ever have need for a 'one-hoss' lawyer (I know that you have plenty of talent of the better order)," McAdoo reminded Dodge, "please do not forget me!"[30]

McAdoo's resignation from the cabinet also necessitated a reconfiguring of his relationship with Woodrow Wilson. The consequences of their separation were profound for them, their wives, and even the body politic. Their contemporaries and historians assumed that the two men had grown close during their years in power, and McAdoo always maintained that this was the case. He even made a virtue of the lack of evidence on this point. "So much of my discussion with the president of public questions was personal, because of my peculiar intimacy with him," he told Wilson's official biographer in 1929, "that I have, perhaps, fewer notes from him than any other member of the Cabinet." Lack of evidence may have reflected lack of substance; after McAdoo's engagement to Eleanor, Wilson had distanced himself from his secretary of the treasury. Behind closed doors he made it clear that it would be inappropriate for them to live in the White House, and in May 1916 Edward House confided in his diary that "the President evidently does not tell McAdoo much of what is in his mind. I was surprised to find that he knows so little excepting of matters current in his own department."[31]

Wilson's brother-in-law Stockton Axson attributed tensions between Wilson and McAdoo to their conflicting personalities. Wilson was artistic, full of intro- spection, "harassed nerves," and "resentment at being torn away . . . from a line of intense, all-absorbing thought." McAdoo, on the other hand, was a businessman, "full of schemes . . . a man of action," who pestered Wilson by "talking business" with him whenever he could. Wilson responded by shrinking from his pushy son- in-law and by seeking out more meditative companions:

> There have been ridiculous stories about the animosity between this father-in- law and son-in-law . . . which friends have denied stridently. And yet it is curious how the newspapermen sometimes get a germ of the truth . . . There has never been the suggestion of a rift in the Wilson household, but that Mr. Wilson rather avoids serious discussion with Mr. McAdoo is true . . . Nobody in the Wilson family talks of these things; nobody in the McAdoo family. Neither Mr. Wilson nor Mr. McAdoo would admit to themselves or to each other that there was any division, and yet . . . Without being conscious of it, Mr. Wilson has caused pain to one of his own blood whom he loves with a peculiar devo- tion. Nell, so she is known, has always been . . . his closest companion of the three [daughters] . . . And yet he has hurt her—she is too loyal to admit it—but one does not have to be a clairvoyant to know it.[32]

Even the White House barber knew that relations between Wilson and McAdoo were tense. The president "certainly does love his son-in-law, Mr. Sayre [who had married Wilson's middle daughter Jessie]," John Mays gossiped in March 1917:

But I think he's getting tired of Mr. McAdoo. Why a few weeks ago Mr. McAdoo bounded up to the President's room and walked right in—My, but the President was mad. He didn't say anything cross to Mr. McAdoo, but he wasn't very cordial . . . When he left the President said "Damn it, he makes me tired. He's got too much nerve and presumes on the fact that he's my son-in-law to take up with me in my private apartment matters that a Cabinet Officer ought to take up in my office. I'm getting damn sick of it."[33]

Relations were further strained by McAdoo's frosty relationship with Edith Bolling Wilson. Wilson's first wife Ellen died in August 1914, and the president married Edith in December 1915. Eleanor found it hard to accept Wilson's infatuation, which she thought had come too soon after Ellen's death, and House, Tumulty, and McAdoo were concerned about the political implications of Wilson's remarriage before the elections in 1916. Only McAdoo had the courage, or the effrontery, to confront Wilson with his colleagues' advice that his marriage might best be postponed until after his re-election. McAdoo concocted a story that Wilson was in danger of blackmail over letters he had written to Mary Hulbert some years previously. Wilson's letters certainly existed, but the blackmail did not. Edith resented McAdoo's attempt to derail her engagement, and from then on thought him duplicitous and opportunistic. They clashed repeatedly during the next twenty-five years: first over McAdoo's position on the League of Nations in 1920 and 1924, then over Edith's right to dispose of parts of Wilson's estate, then over McAdoo's use of Wilson's letters to encourage opposition to Al Smith's presidential nomination in 1928, and finally over Edith's memoirs, in which she made plain her distaste for McAdoo's machinations against her in 1915.[34]

McAdoo and Eleanor were in New Mexico when Wilson collapsed in September 1919. They rushed to Washington and immediately fell in with the conspiracy of optimism about the president's health. Wilson suffered only from "nervous prostration," McAdoo told the press, and "we all feel confident . . . that he will be fully restored to health in the near future. You can disregard all the base and ridiculous rumors that are being circulated about the [his] condition." More than a year later he told Frank Cobb, editor of the New York World, that Wilson "is looking better and seemed better than he has been at any time since his illness," and that Dr. Grayson had noted "a decided improvement recently in his physical condition."[35]

The truth, of course, was much less rosy, as was the reality of McAdoo's relationship with Wilson. Their contact was in fact very limited after Wilson's stroke, with only occasional and often unacknowledged letters from McAdoo and rare personal meetings. At the end of 1920 McAdoo told the Philadelphia Record that he saw the president only rarely and never about matters of substance, and in December 1921 he confessed to Baker that he had not heard from Wilson for more than six weeks, although "we hear of his condition frequently from members of the family."[36]

Political differences increased the personal distance between McAdoo and Wilson. This first became apparent over the Treaty of Versailles and the League of Nations. Although McAdoo seemed to support Wilson's position that the treaty should be ratified without amendment, a note of compromise pervaded his statements on the issue. In November 1919 he pointed out to his former companion Florence Harriman that any American amendments to the treaty would necessitate reformation of the peace conference. Reservations, on the other hand, were "merely explanatory statements of our views . . . which will govern us in their interpretation." As such they did not require the peace conference to reconvene, but the "reservations" proposed by the Republican senators were actually amendments in disguise. "This is a palpable deception and should meet with prompt condemnation and defeat." Immediate ratification of the treaty would reduce the possibility of war, assist in the eradication of poverty, and reduce taxes.[37]

By distinguishing amendments from reservations McAdoo had suggested that some could be countenanced because they were "merely explanatory statements." Wilson had declared that no reservations would be acceptable, and so McAdoo's position contradicted his father-in-law's. Reports in February 1920 that McAdoo had broken ranks on this totemic issue forced him to reassure Wilson that he remained loyal. The press had "garbled" his argument, he wrote, because he had suggested only that "there would be no difficulty about adopting reservations which would not emasculate or destroy the value of the treaty."[38]

Wilson was furious, believing that McAdoo had betrayed him for his own political gain. Unabashed, McAdoo sent word that he had stood by the president in all of his speeches on the League. "I wish you would mention this to him," McAdoo appealed to Grayson, "when you see him." He then tried a more direct approach, writing to Wilson in May 1920 that the Republicans had convinced Americans that it was his "obstinacy," and not GOP obstruction, that had defeated the treaty. "It is all so grossly unfair that I never think of it without indignation, but we must face the facts." Wilson should now resubmit the treaty to the Senate, this time with a list of reservations that were "unobjectionable." This would create an alliance between Democrats and Republican "mild reservationists" sufficient to ratify the treaty.[39]

The president was in no mood to see any reservations as "unobjectionable," and saw only betrayal in McAdoo's suggestions. He did not even reply to McAdoo's letter, and soon after publicly scuttled his son-in-law's hopes to win the 1920 presidential nomination. For his part McAdoo maintained that Wilson's failure to accept any amendments had played into the hands of Republican irreconcilables and had denied the world its best chance to begin anew.[40]

Complexities in the McAdoo-Wilson relationship reached a crescendo over the 1920 Democratic presidential nomination. McAdoo should have been the front-runner for that prize: he had been the most prominent member of Wilson's cabinet, he now had time to campaign for the nomination, and—publicly at least—he was close to the president. Jouett Shouse, a Democratic congressman from Kansas and one of McAdoo's most active supporters, wrote in January 1918 that "I am looking to you as the logical and the probable candidate of our party for the presidency in 1920." Others declared that McAdoo was the most electable candidate on the Democratic horizon. "Keep cool, say little," one wrote in 1918, "and work like the Devil."[41]

McAdoo was receptive to these early soundings. Although he declared that it was too early to canvass possible successors to Wilson, McAdoo encouraged his supporters, led by Shouse, John Elliot, Antoinette Funk, Daniel Roper, and Robert Woolley, to form unofficial organizations to boost his candidacy. Bernard Baruch provided most of the funding that this low-profile effort required.[42]

McAdoo gave an interview to *The Independent* and its survey of "Some Likely Candidates for 1920," outlining his achievements as secretary of the treasury and reminding readers what he had done for the railroads. He repeated that he was "unequivocally" for the League of Nations, albeit with "reservations that are clarifying or interpretative," and promised to reduce taxes and to support female suffrage. He later added more planks to his platform by calling for justice to workers who had lost earning power through wartime inflation and promising a rapid return to freedoms of speech and assembly. As director general of the US Railroad Administration (USRRA), McAdoo had wooed labor through generous wage increases, and in March 1920 he committed himself to a "square deal" for every American worker "to maintain himself and his family in comfort, and give them the advantages which every decent American wants in the way of education, moral training and equal opportunity."[43]

From the outset, however, McAdoo's presidential boom faced political and personal obstacles. Democratic reverses in the congressional elections of 1918, and Wilson's rapidly declining popularity, suggested that 1920 would not be a good year to win the Democratic nomination. These problems were difficult enough, but they were nothing compared to those presented by Woodrow Wilson. The president watched McAdoo's rise with increasing distaste, perhaps even jealousy, and decided that he was not fit for the presidency. He said this only in the strictest confidence but with increasing vigor. According to Stockton Axson, Wilson declared in August 1919 that McAdoo, unlike Newton Baker, lacked the intellectual depth to lead a "successful and wise administration." No one could devise plans with more flair, or enact them with more vigor, "but I never caught Mac reflecting." Instead of airing his family's dirty laundry in public, Wilson explained his silence over McAdoo's presidential ambitions as a determination to avoid any hint of nepotism. Joseph Tumulty later noted that McAdoo lost both ways from his relationship with Wilson. "While every effort was being made by Mr. McAdoo's enemies to give the impression that the Federal machine was being used to advance his candidacy, the President was engaged wholly in ignoring [it]." [44]

Wilson had another reason for undermining McAdoo's quest for the 1920 nomination. Against all political and personal logic, the president had his own ambitions for a third term. This was despite his unpopularity, the potency of the two-term tradition, and the appalling state of his health. Mortified by the Senate's rejection of the treaty, Wilson had visions of presiding over "a great and solemn referendum on the League" in 1920, and then its ratification during his third term. He declared that the convention should be left free to select the best candidate for the nomination. That probably meant Wilson, and certainly did not mean McAdoo. "I think he would have accepted the nomination if it had been tendered to him," Baker wrote later, "and that he expected it." Wilson wrote drafts of his platform and even jotted down a list of cabinet members for his third administration. Nothing illustrated the poignancy of his delusions better than his choice of William McAdoo for secretary of the treasury. [45]

Aware of Wilson's dreams but convinced they were impossible, McAdoo was impaled on the horns of a political and personal dilemma. As the president's son-in-law, he could not actively seek the nomination without Wilson's acquiescence, but the president had said nothing. The consequences of running for the nomination against Wilson's wishes were unthinkable on both a political level, because McAdoo's campaign would be based on his assumed role as Wilson's political heir, and also personally, for it would put his wife in an impossible situation.

The result was that McAdoo floundered in indecision over the 1920 nomination. He refused to enter primary elections but declared that "my friends are free to discuss my availability as much as they like," and that "I have been persuaded . . . that if the convention should finally decide that I am the most available man to make the fight, I ought to do it." He therefore asked for a convention free of binding commitments to announced candidates. This was the same as Wilson's position because in both cases an open convention suited their private, and conflicting, ambitions. [46]

Reduced to sniping from the sidelines, McAdoo denigrated his rivals. Herbert Hoover had done well during the war, but had not yet declared his party loyalty.

McAdoo rightly suspected him of Republicanism and was incensed. "What have we come to? Are we to be nothing more than a party of the Republicans' cast offs?" Newton Baker was Wilson's favorite, but was widely derided by voters. Mitchell Palmer had won prominence as the scourge of Bolshevism, but his home state of Pennsylvania was too Republican. "Of one thing I am certain," McAdoo wrote in June 1920, "that if Palmer should be nominated it would be an invitation to certain defeat." Governor James M. Cox of Ohio was too "wet" on prohibition, too far from Wilson, and too close to the party bosses to be worthy of the nomination.[47]

Behind these criticisms lay McAdoo's conviction that he was the obvious candidate, a belief buttressed by press comment and public opinion. In June 1920, on the eve of the convention, a *Literary Digest* poll found McAdoo to be the favorite for the nomination, winning more than 100,000 votes to Wilson's 87,000 and Cox's 32,000. Although he did not enter the primaries, McAdoo won write-in votes and many delegates were instructed to support his nomination. He could count on every delegate from Florida, Idaho, Kansas, Mississippi, Missouri, Montana, North and South Carolina, Oregon, and Vermont, and significant support from Alabama and Virginia.[48]

McAdoo's friends begged him to commit to the race. "I realize that for many reasons . . . you are unwilling to antagonize the President and hence his failure to declare himself out of the race is a great draw back to you," Bruce Barton wrote in January 1920, but "if your friends do not soon get organized and actively at work the convention will be packed against you or rather made up in the interest of some other candidate." If McAdoo could not "take the bull by the horns," Antoinette Funk wrote early in April, then "I think it must be done by some one very, very soon."[49]

Barton and Funk were right to be worried because by then other Democrats, including Newton Baker, had been sounded out. Unbeknownst to McAdoo, Baker had swatted these approaches away. "I have held public office too long to have any illusions about it, and I hope it is not all indolence, but I frankly have no taste or inclination for further public service." The presidency, he told a friend in 1918, "does not interest me in the slightest . . . my present mood is one of waiting release, and home and friends and in no sense being willing to return to the scramble."[50]

Baker was circumspect about his colleagues' claims to the nomination. "McAdoo is a genius . . . with a fierce energy, a fiercer temper and generally a capacity for keeping every accessible hornets nest violently agitated which would make the four years of his administration a fiery furnace." His nomination was therefore "unwise." This echoed Walter Lippmann's description of McAdoo in June 1920 as "a statesman grafted upon a promoter," who "does not hesitate or brood or procrastinate or reflect at length . . . McAdoo is distinctly not a safe person in the ordinary sense of the word . . . He has length and breadth if not depth."[51]

Baker was also aware of Wilson's ambitions for the nomination and of his antipathy to McAdoo. Convinced that Wilson's hopes were as wrongheaded as McAdoo's were dangerous, Baker quietly supported his fellow Ohioan James Cox. Torn between his loyalty to Wilson, his support of Cox, and his discomfort with McAdoo, Baker opted out of the intense politicking that gripped the party in 1919 and 1920. He did not even go to the convention at San Francisco because the "embarrassments" of the Wilson-McAdoo-Cox struggle had shown him "just how complex some questions of loyalty can become."[52]

A coalition of city bosses, led by Charles Murphy of Tammany Hall and Tom Taggart from Indiana, also coalesced against McAdoo. Some old scores were settled and new feuds begun when William McCombs, who had fallen out with McAdoo so bitterly in 1912, came out for Cox, and Tammany Hall backed the new governor of New York Alfred E. Smith as a dark horse. Coal-mining interests who had been offended by McAdoo's support of their miners during a bitter strike in 1919 worked against him, as did bankers who had chafed under his management of the Federal Reserve System. McAdoo was proud of his enemies. "I would not have their imprimatur on me for any consideration on earth," he told Mary Synon. "Oblivion is preferable." He could not, however, ignore his father-in-law's silent opposition.[53]

And so the hidden drama unfolded. McAdoo tried and failed five times to see Wilson in April and May 1920, and told Cary Grayson that he hoped the president would soon make a definite statement on the nomination:

> Things are taking a turn which is exceedingly embarrassing to me. My hand is being forced, against my wish, and at a time when I am frank to say that my indecision is very great . . . I do not remain in a state of indecision long as a rule but the factors in this situation are difficult to appraise and reckon with.
>
> Of course, the President's silence makes it very awkward for me, even if I had an inclination to stand for the presidency—which, as you know, I have not, — but it is not possible to resist the demands of one's friends to state either that they may proceed or that they may not. In the latter case I should have to say flatfootedly that in no circumstances would I permit my name to be considered at the Convention. It seems hardly fair to do this now with so many uncertain elements in the situation . . .
>
> Any suggestions you may have to offer I shall appreciate. I am really very much perplexed.[54]

Wilson again refused to take the bait. In May McAdoo sent another plea to Eleanor:

Every one I meet is most friendly & either urge me to run for President or tell me they are for me—It makes me rather sad because I feel that I really cannot undertake it . . . I shall have to try very soon to head this thing off. If you have an opportunity to discuss this situation with the Boss, I wish you would get his ideas about the whole thing. Tell him, if you discuss it, that I have practically determined to keep out in any circumstances.

You would be surprised if you could hear what people say to me everywhere I go—that I am the only hope for the party & that I can be elected if I will run—It is fine to have so many friends. Railroad people everywhere are simply bully to me.[55]

A week later he wrote directly to Wilson:

Doubtless you know that I have consistently refused to seek, and that I am not seeking, the nomination. I have declined to permit my name to be entered in primaries in every State where I had the right to withdraw it. I have stated re-peatedly . . . that I do not want the nomination and that I hope my name will not be considered at the Convention . . .

Even if I desired to be President, I would, in no circumstances, permit my name to be considered if I thought that you desired to have your name placed before the Convention.[56]

Wilson did not reply, but on June 18, 1920, condemned the "vanity" and "un-charitable or selfish impulses" of unnamed pretenders to the nomination that he coveted. Later that day McAdoo announced his "irrevocable" decision not to seek the nomination. "One thing about my action of yesterday that distresses me very much," he told a supporter, "is the disappointment I know I have given to my many splendid friends," but his family's need for financial security came first. Aware that he seemed to put money before duty, McAdoo hinted that other factors lay behind his decision. These were "conscientious reasons which I need not detail," he told a friend, and to another he attributed his withdrawal to "inexorable circumstances."[57]

Even this did not mollify Wilson, who noted that McAdoo had not said that he would refuse the nomination if he were offered it. "Methinks thou dost protest too much," a Missouri delegate wrote, "and therefore I am asking that you modify your pronouncements, so far as to admit that you are quite willing for our friends to go out and get the nomination for you." McAdoo agreed, and his organizers an-nounced that he would accept but not seek the nomination. "I am still hoping that the convention will settle on some one else," he told his daughter Harriet, "but there appears to be little encouragement for that hope." He was not formally nomi-nated, but his name was placed before the delegates. Wilson's was not; by then, but not before he had scuttled McAdoo's chances, his wife and friends had persuaded him not to seek another term.[58]

Newton Baker made the best of the San Francisco convention by describing it as "the least bossed of any similar gathering we have had in this country for a long time." "The scramble for your delegates when your announcement came out reminded me a little of the hungry heirs when they receive the news that a rich relative has passed on," Antoinette Funk told McAdoo. Some of his delegates went to Palmer, some to Cox, a few went to John W. Davis, but most of them stayed loyal.[59]

McAdoo's lieutenants planned to park his delegates behind Carter Glass during the early ballots, but the crusty Virginian was no crowd-pleaser and failed to win support from delegations outside his home state. In the end McAdoo's name stayed before the convention, albeit with declining support, for forty-three ballots before the delegates chose Cox on the forty-fourth. In the White House, according to Wilson's stenographer, "the President was a bitter man over the nomination of Cox—not that he disliked Cox but because he didn't get it himself. As between Cox and McAdoo he preferred Cox I believe—solely out of jealousy toward McAdoo."[60]

"Don't be disappointed," McAdoo told Antoinette Funk after Cox won the nomination on July 6, 1920. "I am neither disappointed nor disgruntled." To another friend he confessed that "no one is to blame for defeat except myself, because I am sure that if I had gone into the fight . . . we might have had a different story to tell." That immodest conclusion has been endorsed by historians, who have pointed to Wilson's obstructionism and McAdoo's consequent vacillation as key factors in his failure to win the nomination. He congratulated Cox, offered to support his campaign, and told his supporters that "we are all young yet, and the world is before us!" Mary Synon was more direct: "Congratulations on deferred candidacy which will make success even more certain yours for Nineteen Twenty Four."[61]

True to his word, McAdoo delivered speeches for Cox in the last three weeks of October. He did mention Cox's qualifications for the presidency, but stressed the achievements of the Wilson administration, the qualities of the party's platform, and the dangers presented by the "forces of reaction" arrayed behind Republican candidate Senator Warren Harding. By his own estimation he spoke to more than 200,000 people, but found them unmoved by his calls for a new mandate for liberal reform and internationalism. When Cox lost the election in a landslide, McAdoo was unsurprised. Harding's campaign had been well funded and well targeted, and "this, in addition to the blunders of our own side, made the result inevitable. I am sorry, but a sober time is ahead of us." Others took more comfort from Harding's victory. "Republicanism and Americanism have triumphed over Wilsonism and socialism," three voters cabled McAdoo on Election Day. "You almost ruined the railroads but we will trust to President Harding to bring us back to normal. Best wishes on your journey to the sea of oblivion."[62]

⥈⥇⥈

Oblivion was too strong a word for it, but a chapter in Baker's and McAdoo's lives had closed. "So far as the election is concerned," Baker wrote after Harding's victory, "I find myself wholly philosophical and untroubled." Wilson had tried to elevate America's domestic life and international relations, and if he had exceeded his people's capacity for virtue then at least he had provided an example that would not be forgotten. "It never does to forget, though, that this is at best a naughty world, which washes its face and brushes its hair occasionally." In the meantime, as Baker saw out the last three months of Wilson's presidency, his thoughts turned from Washington to Cleveland, and from politics to the law. On March 7, 1921, he and his family were welcomed home by the mayor of Cleveland and the Cleveland Bar Association. He would never hold public office again.[63]

"In the matter of ingenuity and knowledge, my military I.Q. was subnormal," Baker wrote about his time as secretary of war, "but in my capacity to realize that people were carrying heavy burdens bravely and needed the encouragement of a hand on their shoulder, I think I made a fair success." He was proud of the rapidity and honesty of mobilization, of the activities of the Commission on Training Camp Activities (CTCA), and of his role as the political lightning rod for the military, bearing the brunt of congressional hostility and public criticism while Pershing and his men did their jobs in France. Secretary of the Navy Daniels recalled an occasion when Tasker Bliss hesitated over an unpopular decision. "I will give the order and let any criticism come to me," Baker told him, "That is what a civilian secretary is for, to take the blame."[64]

Throughout the 1920s Baker defended his department's treatment of conscientious objectors. Appointed to a committee established in 1923 to make recommendations on the fate of those still imprisoned for their wartime activities, he did recommend their release but declared that their crimes had been real and their trials had been fair. Later he opposed the restoration of citizenship rights to those convicted of wartime sedition because they had worked against their country and had forfeited their right to vote.[65]

Those who had been closest to the War Department rated Baker's performance higher than those who had observed him from a distance. His subordinates spoke of his loyalty, wisdom, and modesty; Brigadier General Douglas MacArthur, then superintendent of West Point, told Baker in 1921 that his departure was a matter of "sincere regret" and lauded his "fearless justice, your human moderation, your gentle courtesy, and your inflexible determination and fortitude under shameless calumny." Another member of the AEF, this time a private rather than a general, wrote that "my conscience hurts for criticizing adversely your conduct of the war in war days . . . I can see now that you were a godsend, because you were willing to be the antithesis of everything showy and especially because you were the first civilian in power who let the professional soldiers alone during a war." Even *The New York Times*, which had led criticism of Baker during the war, forgave him after it. Baker had made mistakes, it conceded in 1929, but "citizens somewhat on the inside of the war machine know that he supplied the absolute prerequisite of brilliant, toiling leadership."[66]

Not everyone was as quick to forgive and forget. Leonard Wood led the Republican attack, citing Baker's reluctance to take hard decisions about army procurement processes. Hampered by his lack of military experience, Baker traded on his closeness to Wilson to obscure his administrative failings and his ignorance of how a modern war should be organized. Oswald Garrison Villard, editor of *The Nation* and spokesman for those progressives who saw Baker as a traitor to their cause, condemned his surrender to militarism after 1916. In 1919, Villard noted, when liberals everywhere demanded permanent reductions of armaments and armies, Baker had instead advocated UMT and 500,000 men in uniform. "That once great liberal and democrat then and there began his rapid descent into the camp of the enemy."[67]

Those farther to the left were even more damning. Norman Thomas, later a six-time presidential candidate for the Socialist Party of America, accused Baker of eroding civilian control of the military through his deference to his uniformed subordinates. "It is an old story," Thomas wrote in 1924. "The system—the Army—proved bigger than the man. It did not break him; it bent and molded him. At the end of Mr. Baker's career it was often said the voice was the voice of Newton D. Baker, but the will was the will of the chief of staff." In 1917 Baker had urged respect for those who objected to the war, but by the end of his term he refused to consider a general amnesty to objectors and had even advocated peacetime UMT. In between, Thomas charged, Baker had abdicated his authority to Pershing, failed to detect massive frauds in army procurement, and had done nothing to reform the army's disciplinary processes.[68]

Criticism from a socialist and champion of wartime political prisoners was expected, but Baker's friends were shocked by his treatment at the hands of the *Encyclopedia Britannica*. Its 1922 edition contained a two-hundred-word entry on Baker, describing him as "an American politician" (McAdoo received the loftier title of "public official") and stating that "his career generally as Secretary was widely condemned throughout the United States as lacking in energy, foresight, and ability and especially for his failure to prepare adequately in the months immediately preceding the American declaration of war." This was true as far as it went, but it also ignored the encomiums that Baker had won for his efforts. His colleagues rushed to his support; Woodrow Wilson wrote from his sickbed that the entry had made him "indignant," Douglas MacArthur wrote that the piece "fills me with that feeling of nausea which always comes to fair minded men when confronted with the exhibition of a great injustice," and William McAdoo wrote that "I was disgusted by the dastardly attack on you in the *Encyclopedia Britannica*."[69]

Ralph Hayes led the counterattack, organizing a letter-writing campaign to demand revision of Baker's entry. Hayes forwarded more than five hundred letters from prominent Democrats, including all of Baker's cabinet colleagues, leading military figures such as Pershing, Bliss, and Harbord, and even Republicans such as Senator James Wadsworth of New York. The *Britannica* initially held firm, refusing to name the author of its entry and asserting its right to publish what it chose. Its next edition, however, included a revised entry that recognized Baker's achievements as well as his critics, and in 1926 an entirely new entry acknowledged the partisan attacks to which he had been subjected throughout the war. Hayes was delighted, but Baker remained equable; even at the height of the controversy he admitted that "I have never been able to stir myself up much about the article in the Encyclopedia."[70]

Baker did deserve better than the *Britannica*'s disdain. As Mr. Dooley had warned, it was indeed difficult to be "be sicrety of A war!" Few have had to deal with major conflicts, and Baker's war was the largest military undertaking since the Civil War and the second largest of the twentieth century. He had to oversee hothouse mobilization and deployment of more than four million soldiers in nineteen months, and that he did so without catastrophe or widespread corruption, and with no military experience of his own to draw on, was an enormous achievement. As secretary of war Baker was responsible for one of the four greatest military undertakings in the history of the United States, and for that he deserves more accolades than brickbats.

And yet some of the criticisms were justified. Baker was too deferential toward his uniformed subordinates and too easily convinced that his lack of military experience disqualified him from asserting civilian authority over the army. His obstruction of the WIB, whether through personal animus against Baruch or a conviction against excessive regulation of private business, did hinder the war effort and revealed his slowness to realize that modern war required radical changes to the ways in which America had traditionally operated. As a late and reluctant convert to the doctrine of total war, Baker upheld his own values and those of his upbringing, but he also made the task of rapid and massive mobilization more difficult. His mobilization was much better than the muddle his critics accused it of being, but its inefficiencies and deliberate transience made it less effective than it could have been.[71]

Other criticisms carry less weight. Baker was certainly naïve about conscientious objectors and conscription, but he was not as hypocritical as their champions made out. His refusal to countenance brigading may have resulted in some delay, but it was also necessary to maintain support for the war and to fulfill Wilson's determination that America should act in association with, but not subordinate to, Britain and France. Baker certainly stayed very close to Wilson, but that represented not weakness but realism. He enjoyed more political power than military authority, and his close relationship with the president was a reflection and a consequence of that fact. As his critics never tired of pointing out, Baker was a most unlikely secretary of war, and so his effectiveness was heavily dependent on support from the White House. That, Baker thought, was as it should be. He might be secretary of war, and secretary of a war, but most of all he was Woodrow Wilson's secretary of war. Neither he nor Wilson forgot that fundamental truth, and Baker never shrank from the personal and political costs that came with it.

❧

Both Baker and McAdoo moved away from Wilson after 1921, but McAdoo moved much farther. From Cleveland Baker kept in touch through frequent letters and occasional visits. His letters combined news, political gossip, and references to classical literature. "Do not feel called upon to answer or acknowledge this note," he wrote in May 1921, "it is just an <u>ad interim</u> report to the chief and I shall feel freer to send them if I know that they impose no burden beyond the reading." Consequently he wrote often and Wilson replied sometimes but always affectionately. Personal visits were a different matter; Baker was upset by Wilson's infirmity and in January 1924 told his wife that "unless it is thought that I can be useful I think I will not often call when I come down. It is quite too depressing."[72]

McAdoo's move from Wilson was more literal. On March 1, 1922, he announced that he and Eleanor would move to California. Huger stayed in New York to form a new firm with Cotton and Franklin, while his father set out for Los Angeles. "I am quite sure that one can get a larger satisfaction out of life in this part of the country than he can in the over-crowded East," McAdoo told Baker. "If you ever come to California, you may be assured of a warm welcome at the McAdoo house."[73]

McAdoo also left New York for political reasons. His experience in 1920 showed that his political future in New York was limited, and in California he hoped to establish a power base far from the party bosses who had worked against him in 1920 and who would surely do so again in 1924. Wilson, too, had revealed his hostility to McAdoo's presidential ambitions, and putting three thousand miles between them might help McAdoo distance himself from his father-in-law's personal bitterness and unhelpful political legacies.[74]

Eleanor McAdoo's place in this personal-political decision was uncomfortable, to say the least. As she set out for California, she revealed the price she had paid because of the breach between her husband and her father:

> I couldn't go down to Washington to tell you good-bye—not because there wasn't time but because I couldn't bear to say good-bye to you. This is the only way I can stand it at all—going so far away from you . . . I feel as if I were chopping a great big piece off my heart when I put four days, instead of five hours between you and us. I don't see how I'm going to stand it, Father darling. I wish I knew how to tell you what you and your love mean to me.[75]

McAdoo maintained a veneer of friendliness with his father-in-law. He sent numerous letters, chiefly about the children, and even sent him a movie of their new home and garden. Wilson replied briefly but without much warmth. His reservations about his son-in-law's political and personal loyalty ran very deep. For his part McAdoo was deeply hurt by Wilson's opposition to his presidential ambitions in 1920. In 1928 he wrote to Edith Wilson in a tone that was more self-pitying than bewildered, and which ignored his own attempts to trade on Wilson's name and legacy:

> Since 1911 . . . I have been his constant defender against calumny, misrepresentation and unscrupulous charlatans . . . But I have been meticulously careful never to claim anything for myself because of my association with him. From 1920 to 1924 when I was the most discussed man for the Democratic Presidential Nomination, I never spoke once to him on the subject, never sought his aid and never used his name to advance my interests, although my political enemies constantly circulated stories that he was opposed to me and used his name to my disadvantage.[76]

Woodrow Wilson died on February 3, 1924. McAdoo and Baker both eulogized the man who had dominated their public and private lives for so long, but the difference in their emotional intensity was telling. McAdoo told the press that "Woodrow Wilson, the man, is dead; but Woodrow Wilson, the apostle of peace, the lover of mankind, will live forever." Three months later, at the Democratic National Convention in New York, Baker delivered an impassioned speech that spoke to Wilson as if he were still alive: "I did my best, I am doing it now. You are still the captain of my soul."[77]

Autumn

1921–1932

⋯⋇⋯

CHAPTER 10

Lawyers and Businessmen

"My dear Baker," McAdoo wrote in March 1921, "my warmest congratulations on the resumption of your professional work and my best wishes for a prosperous and even more distinguished career than you have already had." Harding's inauguration propelled Baker and McAdoo back to legal practice, but they returned from different directions and in different states of mind. Although he had established the firm of McAdoo, Cotton and Franklin in New York after leaving the cabinet, McAdoo's main concern was to maneuver for the 1920 presidential nomination. Stymied in that ambition, he practiced law more as a default than as a return to his true calling.[1]

Baker, on the other hand, returned to legal practice with genuine relief. In the two months between finishing as mayor of Cleveland and becoming secretary of war in 1916 he had established a firm in Cleveland and had long looked forward to returning to it. The allure of home grew during the last dispiriting days of Wilson's presidency. At the end of June 1920 he told Joseph Hostetler that he wished only "for a roof to keep out the rain, a few more windows to lock at night, and an additional dozen frail porcelain gods and goddesses which my romping babies may break."[2]

"When I left Washington in 1921," Baker recalled, "I was tired and needed both rest and change of occupation," but as "I had no accumulations and did have a family, I plunged head long into professional work." He had shared in his firm's profits while he was in Washington, but insisted that it accept no work connected to his department. "I am afraid that you will think I am unnecessarily 'thin skinned' about this matter," he told Sidlo, "but I do so deeply object to the thought of profit being made out of official position that I would far rather see even my friends lose than have an unjust appearance of impropriety." In 1919 he had Congress ban former employees of his department from presenting any claim arising from war-time contracts, and for the rest of his career refused to accept any cases pertaining to his time as secretary of war.[3]

Baker's return to Cleveland rapidly elevated his firm's profitability and prestige. Baker, Hostetler, and Sidlo moved to larger offices in 1924, included twenty-two partners by 1935, and soon developed a national reputation. Baker was central to his firm's rise, attracting prominent clients, earning hefty fees, and winning recognition as one of the finest lawyers of his generation. The firm that he founded in 1916 still retains his name and now includes more than six hundred lawyers in ten offices.[4]

⬥❈⬥

Success at first also came quickly to McAdoo in his reincarnation as a lawyer. Not having practiced law for twenty years, he conceded that "my greatest value to [McAdoo, Cotton, and Franklin] will be in commanding business." He did this by approaching prominent Democrats, and those who wished to do business with the Wilson administration, to retain his new firm. Bernard Baruch came up with $15,000 a year and Owen D. Young, vice president of the General Electric Company (GEC), paid $12,000. McAdoo also received $50,000 from the Virginia Shipbuilding Company (VSC) and $10,000 from the oil speculator Edward L. Doheny. The largest fee came from Douglas Fairbanks, Mary Pickford, and Charlie Chaplin, who paid him $50,000 to be general counsel to their United Artists Corporation (UA). Altogether McAdoo, Cotton and Franklin received $68,000 in 1919 and more than $270,000 in 1920. McAdoo's share of its profits in 1920 was more than $100,000—nearly 7 times his old cabinet salary.[5]

Some of these retainers were little more than donations. Baruch saw his as assistance to McAdoo in his transition from public office to private life, made few claims on his legal expertise, and had his brother Herman lend McAdoo $50,000 to pursue investment opportunities. McAdoo did so little work for GEC in 1919 that he returned his 1920 retainer of $7,500, but billed it $8,000 for professional services in 1922.[6]

McAdoo worked harder for some of his other clients, but later wished that he had not. Within a year he had fallen out with Fairbanks and his retainer from UA soon ceased. Two other clients came back to haunt McAdoo's campaign for the 1924 Democratic presidential nomination. In 1919 he appeared before the Shipping Board in a dispute between VSC and the Emergency Fleet Corporation. Charles Morse, who controlled VSC, had been imprisoned for misappropriating corporate funds and was indicted soon after McAdoo appeared for him on a conspiracy charge. Morse was acquitted, but not before McAdoo had been cited as an unwitting source of false information to the board. He was exonerated, and told the press that his employment "was a perfectly proper thing for any law firm to do," but many doubted the propriety of his appearance before the Shipping Board that he once controlled.[7]

Doheny's retainer, though welcome in 1919, caused even more damage to McAdoo's political career. To avoid nationalization of his Mexican oil leases, Doheny employed McAdoo to lobby his former cabinet colleagues and to put his case directly to Mexican President Álvaro Obregon in 1921. "Do you not think you are taking a risk in representing the Mexican Petroleum Company?" Tumulty wrote from the White House in November 1919. "I have the highest opinion of Mr. Doheny but if you intend to be a candidate for the Presidency, the Mexican question is bound to be acute at the time of the campaign and your acceptance of a retainer from Mexican interests is sure to come up and embarrass you."[8]

McAdoo showed little compunction in undertaking briefs that related to his work in the Wilson administration. In 1919 he accepted $10,000 from the Republic Iron and Steel Company to represent it before a Treasury Department Board of Appeal over the taxation of its invested capital. McAdoo won the argument, saved Republic Iron and Steel $2 million, and received $140,000 in fees. He also kept active the contacts he had made while he was director general of the US Railroad Administration (USRRA) and sought their assistance to buy equipment for two of his clients. Away from the Treasury and the USRRA, but still within the administration, he pursued claims against the War and Navy Departments over compensation for assets requisitioned during the war. When these cases came to light in 1924 McAdoo rejected any hint of impropriety and argued that every lawyer had the right to support his family. Charles Evans Hughes had practiced law after leaving public office, so why shouldn't he?[9]

His rivals held that McAdoo's retainers tainted his electoral viability, and his critics saw his activities as unethical. "Some men leave public office to practice law," The Nation noted in February 1924. "Mr. McAdoo left to practice son-in-law." Legally he may have been entitled to accept retainers from Morse, Doheny, and Republic Iron and Steel, but ethically he was not. "His inability to understand the fitness of things and his readiness to sell his personal and political influence in the guise of legal service combine to stamp him as an unfit candidate" for the presidency.[10]

Felix Frankfurter, then a Harvard Law professor and later to become an associate justice of the Supreme Court, sought Newton Baker's opinion on the ethical issues raised by McAdoo's conduct. Baker replied carefully, but concluded that McAdoo had acted unwisely and possibly unethically during the remainder of

Wilson's term. He was franker to another correspondent, confessing a "very uneasy feeling" about McAdoo's actions, which he thought were "essentially improper."[11]

McAdoo, Cotton and Franklin also undertook work that was unequivocally legal and apolitical. In 1919 the firm wrote and registered documents for the Columbia Graphophone Manufacturing Company of New York, drafted deeds for Dunlop America Limited, registered trademarks for another Manhattan manufacturer, drafted certificates of incorporation for the Hughes Petroleum Company, and undertook litigation for the American Can Company, the American Silk Spinning Company, and the California Wine Association. Given McAdoo's focus on winning retainers and lobbying the administration, it is likely that his colleagues handled these more mundane matters. The minutiae of legal drafting and forms of pleading interested him little and required specialized expertise that he had long ago forsworn in favor of business and politics.[12]

There were exceptions, but they proved the rule. "I am 56!" he reminded Eleanor on October 31, 1919. "I was glad I was able to celebrate the day with a victory in the court in the first case I have argued in more than 20 years." The hearing was in Kansas City and concerned the constitutionality of the Federal Farm Loan Banks. McAdoo appeared alongside Charles Evans Hughes and George Wickersham, two of the best-known trial lawyers of the day. The public gallery was full, he noted, because "Hughes & Wickersham and myself appearing all at once was considered something of an event." He addressed the court for ninety minutes, focusing on the intent of the Farm Loan legislation. "I seemed to get more applause than any of the others, although Hughes was a close second." Justice Arba Van Valkenburg decided in favor of the Farm Loan Banks, "showing a very clear grip of the principles involved and a very comprehensive understanding of the whole situation." The disappointed plaintiff vowed to appeal to the Supreme Court, "so I suppose I shall have to argue the case in Washington this winter."[13]

McAdoo never got to the Supreme Court, and appeared rarely in other federal courts. Perhaps because of his unfamiliarity with the rules of evidence he avoided jury trials and limited himself to appellate hearings in which he could speak to briefs prepared by junior colleagues. When he ran a trial in Augusta, Georgia, in May 1923, he instructed a local lawyer to argue an important pre-trial evidentiary motion. "I decided that it was too long a trip for me to make merely to debate a point of law," he told Edward House. "If the hearing goes up on the merits, I shall attend."[14]

Few committed litigators would avoid arguing a point of law if their trial depended on it. Baker, by contrast, reveled in courtroom argument; in 1929 he told his wife that the demands of trying cases left him feeling either ecstatic or wishing he had chosen another profession. Yet the highs outnumbered the lows, and he was sure that cross-examination of witnesses was the "most powerful weapon civilized man has yet invented for discovering the truth and if we are to have any kind of social order the truth must be found and brought to light."[15]

As McAdoo had done before him, Baker set out to translate his public prominence into professional success, but he did so in very different circumstances. McAdoo's early departure from Wilson's cabinet allowed him to offer clients access to the administration. Baker, on the other hand, resumed his practice at the same time as Harding's Republicans replaced Wilson's Democrats in Washington. This meant that Baker's cachet, even if he had desired to use it, had largely evaporated. As McAdoo found that his list of retained clients contracted after March 1921, Baker would have struggled to establish himself as a prominent Democratic lawyer in a suddenly Republican town.

Yet Baker never wanted that kind of career. His future lay in Cleveland, where his legal reputation was already established. Although he had left private practice in 1902 he had remained visible in Cleveland's legal community as city solicitor and then mayor, and during his time in Washington he oversaw huge army supply contracts with some of the largest corporations in the country. More so than McAdoo, whose career between 1902 and 1918 led him from legal practice to entrepreneurial capitalism and then financial policy, Baker's public career had burnished his legal skills and reputation.[16]

Baker's return to Cleveland coincided with reorientations in his city's economic activities from the Corporate Regime's reliance on heavy manufacturing toward a Realty Regime that emphasized real estate and infrastructure development, and it was to these activities that Baker directed his firm. Chief among this new economic order were the Van Sweringen brothers, who by the end of the 1920s controlled nearly 30,000 miles of railroad track, significant coal resources, numerous streetcar operations, and electricity generators across the nation. In Cleveland they owned the Union Station office complex and suburban housing developments. Baker and his firm became the Van Sweringens' preferred counsel for their property transactions and for Vaness, their personal holding company. Both sides prospered from their relationship; in 1927 Baker, Hostetler and Sidlo billed Vaness $75,000, and Baker counted both Van Sweringen brothers as his friends and neighbors.[17]

The Van Sweringens were Baker's star clients, but his firm soon had many other corporations and individuals on its books. Although Baker's fame as a courtroom lawyer grew during the 1920s and 1930s, he was not a full-time litigator. One of his partners recalled that he spent three or four weeks a year in court; most of his time was spent resolving matters through negotiation and pre-trial settlement, drafting advice to clients, and reviewing precedents. He was helped in these tasks by the firm's junior lawyers and younger partners, who did much of the research and drafting that large commercial transactions and complicated trials required.[18]

Baker was more than the Van Sweringens' pet lawyer and more than a corporate property specialist. Long after his death his former colleagues compiled a list of his most significant trials, most of them in the superior federal courts and some in the Supreme Court, that concerned constitutional, copyright, and patent law, zoning matters, employment and labor disputes, banking and Federal Reserve issues, international law, appearances for state and municipal governments, corporate law, antitrust law, administration of estates and wardship, and the freedom of the press. He even ran a case against the extradition of a suspected Chicago fraudster (John "Jake the Barber" Factor) from the United States to Great Britain.[19]

In the 1920s Baker twice represented the state of Wisconsin in the Supreme Court in its fight against the diversion of water from Lake Michigan to the Mississippi River via the Chicago River. Later he led litigation over federal powers in the Supreme Court, first in 1931 over the application of the Federal Water Power Act to the New River in Virginia, then in 1933 over the Agricultural Adjustment Act's processing tax, and again in 1936 over the legality of the Tennessee Valley Authority's sale of electric power. "During the era of Mr. Baker's active practice," one of his partners noted, "in the opinion of many, and probably of most, informed lawyers, Baker, John W. Davis and Charles Evans Hughes were the most distinguished and outstanding members of the American bar."[20]

Baker attracted large corporations and wealthy individuals with complex legal needs. In 1920 he represented the Youngstown Steel and Tube Company in litigation arising from its proposed merger with the Bethlehem Steel Corporation. Baker lost at trial but won on appeal, and his firm was rumored to have earned $1 million. In another well-publicized case ten years later concerning Cyrus McCormick's estate, Baker sought a fee of $500,000 after successfully arguing that McCormick's mentally incompetent son Stanley should receive a much larger income from the estate.[21]

It was easy for Baker's critics to assume that these fees were typical of his practice, but those that attracted public attention arose from long-running cases that consumed many lawyers' time and drew heavily on the expensive infrastructure of a large law firm. The McCormick litigation, for example, occupied Baker, two other partners, and numerous junior lawyers for three years, required numerous trips to California, painstaking research through decades of financial and medical records, and lengthy litigation in two states. Given that overheads typically consumed half of Baker, Hostetler and Sidlo's fees, and that all its profits were shared between its partners, Baker's fees were not quite the rivers of gold that his critics imagined.[22]

Even so, Baker acquired "a few more windows to lock at night." Despite his protest in 1935 that "I make a good income but my accumulations are negligible," he was by then a very wealthy man. In 1936 he paid $43,000 in taxes and gave away another $58,000, and upon his death his net estate was valued at $236,301. He had already given more than $380,000 and the family home to his wife, and an additional $115,000 to his children, so that his real net worth was nearly $750,000. This sum was equivalent to more than $12 million in 2011 values.[23]

Baker's wealth, earned from some of the largest and least popular corporations in America, attracted a growing chorus of criticism. Tom Johnson's "little David" now seemed too close to the forces of economic privilege that he had fought as city solicitor and then mayor of Cleveland. Even in 1922 *The Cleveland Press* noted that "the old easy Baker manner of pre-war days has been buried under a heavy coating of great dignity and heavy solemnity." In 1914 he had resigned from the Cleveland Chamber of Commerce, but in 1922 he was its president, and now it seemed that "the manner of the money-making attorney is naturally different from that of the affable City Hall politician." Eleven years later a candidate for mayor of Cleveland described him as "Jekyll and Hyde," one moment speaking out against the utilities and the next appearing for a power company. Perhaps, some Clevelanders and many of Baker's old progressive colleagues thought, Baker had turned his back on reform and had adopted the views of his plutocratic clients.[24]

Baker was shy about his wealth but resented criticism that he had sold his soul to earn it. His former partner William Bemis argued that Baker undertook much *pro bono* work and that "to characterize [him] as seeking only clients who could pay large . . . fees and ignoring other matters is wholly fallacious . . . Mr. Baker was never one to turn down a client because of the modest fee . . . that [was] involved in the question." Another partner denied that Baker was avaricious. He was, in fact, "the least acquisitive lawyer with whom I have ever been associated . . . If Mr. Baker had had the sole say in fixing the amount of charges made for his time and efforts, the fees would indeed have been modest."[25]

Baker was unrepentant when George Foster Peabody, a past progressive and present New Dealer, wrote in 1934 in "grief and distress of heart and mind" about Baker's rapacious clients. To be a lawyer was to "belong to a priestly caste," obliged to defend every client's legal rights. Baker was as happy to defend an unpopular corporation as he was to represent "a negro prisoner accused of a grave crime" because "I have no more respect for the lynching of a corporation by an excited and popular prejudice against it . . . than I have for the lynching of an individual by a mob inflamed to passion." His critics lauded the principle but mourned the fact that he seemed always to act for large corporations and never for persecuted African

Americans, and that his "priestly caste" earned him handsome rewards in the midst of the Great Depression.[26]

※※※

A combination of factors drove McAdoo from New York at beginning of 1922. His retainers had evaporated with the Wilson administration, his hopes for the 1920 nomination had been dashed by Woodrow Wilson in Washington and Tammany Hall in New York, and two new friends promised him lucrative fees and business opportunities in California. Los Angeles was particularly attractive: in 1920 its population was more than half a million, which was nearly double its size in 1910, and its transformation from a regional city reliant on agricultural processing to a thriving industrial center sparked by World War I spending, sustained by the Panama Canal, and made glamorous by the movie industry, was well under way in the early 1920s.[27]

McAdoo's first Californian suitor was Thomas Storke, a prominent Democrat, businessman, and owner-editor of the *Santa Barbara News-Press*. His other western siren was A. P. Giannini, president of the Bank of Italy (later to become the Bank of America). In 1922 Giannini's bank was already one of the largest west of the Mississippi with 66 branches in California and deposits of $225 million. Attracted by McAdoo's connection with the Federal Reserve System and his contacts with its regulators, Giannini offered him an annual retainer of $50,000.[28]

"Everything has started off most interestingly and encouragingly for us out here," McAdoo told Baruch in early April 1922. "I find that no army of new clients is knocking at the door, but there are a good many encouraging symptoms." His first task was to assist the Bank of Italy. He urged friends and associates, including Edward Doheny, to deposit funds in it and lobbied the Federal Reserve Board (FRB) to allow it to open more branches. At the end of 1924 he set up a firm with William H. Neblett, a well-known Californian lawyer, and they occupied offices in the Bank of Italy Building until 1937. Despite McAdoo's early hopes, however, his retainer from the Bank of Italy lasted only two years and his relationship with Giannini was never as close or profitable as that between Newton Baker and the Van Sweringens.[29]

McAdoo, Neblett and their new partner J. F. T. O'Connor established a viable firm in Los Angeles, but its success and reputation ultimately disappointed them. "I am not in touch with the big business interests in this City," McAdoo confessed in 1926, "my practice does not lead in that direction." Although involved in politics and distracted by other business ventures, he touted for work at every opportunity. Besides registering mortgages, drafting documents, and establishing corporations for his own ventures, McAdoo's firm worked for the Georgia and Florida Railroad, the Piggly Wiggly retail chain, real estate developers and speculators, commercial leasing companies, oil explorers, deceased estates, individual taxpayers, the Julian Petroleum Company, and the Venice Consumers Water Company.[30]

McAdoo's firm also did work for Storke's business empire, and through his influence received briefs from several Los Angeles newspapers. Generally, however, McAdoo, Neblett and O'Connor's clients tended to be McAdoo's Democratic Party friends and supporters, emerging entrepreneurs, and small corporations who generated relatively straightforward transactions and small fees. "Winners are popular," the Los Angeles Examiner reported in March 1925. "Report has it that William G. McAdoo's legal services are in less demand by plutocratic clients than they were before he lost the Democratic nomination. The Doheny incident also did not help McAdoo's standing with the kind of clients that formerly flocked to him."[31]

Drawing on his experience with the Pan American Financial Conference and the Liberty Loans, McAdoo offered his services in 1924 to South American nations hoping to raise loans in the United States. That idea came to nothing, but in 1925 he tried again to combine his experience in international finance with his lobbying and legal contacts, this time in relation to a hydroelectric project in France. McAdoo and two French associates offered to assist the French government in placing bonds for this project through Dillon, Read & Company, a New York broker with close connections to Bernard Baruch, for a commission of 1.5 percent of the bonds up to $54 million. That project also collapsed when Dillon, Read objected to the size of McAdoo's fee, questions were raised about the credibility of his French partners, and the French government lost interest in the scheme.[32]

Another alluring proposal drew McAdoo to Washington in 1927. H. P. Wilson, who had helped fund McAdoo's bid for the nomination in 1924, asked him to act in a set of consolidation and de-merger transactions involving two Washington streetcar companies and an electric utility. The consolidated streetcar company was then to be separated from the utility to satisfy regulatory rules. These transactions required intricate documentation and detailed negotiations and would take at least a year to complete. Wilson promised McAdoo and his firm half his profits.[33]

McAdoo jumped at the chance. Wilson's transactions involved complexities of corporate law that lay beyond McAdoo's legal experience and ability, but its mixture of streetcars, corporate reorganization, negotiation with regulators, and large profits was irresistible. McAdoo, Neblett and O'Connor opened a Washington office in the summer of 1927 under the control of Brice Clagett, McAdoo's former secretary and now son-in-law. McAdoo also spent a great deal of time on the case, shuttling back and forth from Los Angeles to oversee the drafting of documents and to shepherd the transactions through the District of Columbia courts and ultimately Congress.[34]

At first the Washington streetcar merger seemed to be the answer to McAdoo's prayers. "Now, my darling," he wrote to Eleanor during one of his many trips to Washington, "it <u>looks certain</u> that I shall get that <u>large</u> remuneration we have talked about—It will simply transform our situation into one of comfort and with no future anxieties." Yet the merger went much slower than Wilson had predicted and McAdoo had hoped. Both streetcar companies had lodged applications for a fare increase to increase their individual values before the merger, and they disagreed on the value of their corporations. Fare increases required court approval, and dissension between the parties stalled that process; the court also proved to be less amenable to the prospect of a consolidated streetcar operation than Wilson and McAdoo had been led to believe. The entire transaction also required congressional approval, but McAdoo had difficulty even getting it included in successive legislative calendars.[35]

The slow progress of the streetcar merger hurt McAdoo, Neblett and O'Connor's financial position. In 1928, the last full year before the Wall Street Crash, the firm made a profit of $28,000, and it generated $29,000 in fees in the first quarter of 1929. This return would have been higher had it not been for the Washington office, which incurred losses in each year of its existence. Profits of this size, split between three partners, were insufficient to support McAdoo and his family in their accustomed style and forced him to devote time to other ventures. The Depression then pinched the firm's earnings, a slump in the oil price diminished McAdoo's investment income, and running offices on both sides of the nation made his overheads burdensome. And still the streetcar merger dragged on.[36]

In 1931 McAdoo, who had yet to receive any payment for his work on the merger, closed the Washington office. "I am carrying a terrible load at the moment," he told Clagett, "but I hope to heavens there will be some sunlight a little later on. As you say, this depression is certainly hell for everybody." At the beginning of 1932 he unsuccessfully sought a progress payment on the merger case, and in February 1933 requested $165,000 for his services over the past 5 years. Wilson paid $65,000, which was almost entirely consumed by the firm's accumulated debts. By then O'Connor had left the firm and McAdoo had entered the Senate and could take no further role in the merger negotiations. Even so, 1932 was a better year for McAdoo and Neblett; they made a net profit of $55,000 on fees of nearly $87,000 drawn from 82 clients. That was enough to keep them busy, but not enough to make them rich.[37]

McAdoo's election to the Senate promised better prospects for his firm. In 1933 he sought an opinion from Attorney General Homer Cummings on whether incumbent senators could try cases in US courts. Cummings thought they could, but told McAdoo that he should not appear before executive departments or agencies. McAdoo then represented clients in federal courts and sought briefs from the federal government in actions over Californian oil properties. "I don't see why a Democratic law firm of such prominence as mine should be passed over," he grumbled in August 1933. "I am serving the American people for almost nothing."[38]

In 1933 McAdoo and Neblett made a profit of $46,758, of which McAdoo received $10,200—$1,700 more than his senatorial salary that year. The firm made $48,000 in 1934, but both partners were frustrated at the business they were forced to decline because it involved federal bureaus and programs. In 1936 their firm returned a profit of only $8,700.[39]

McAdoo's status as a senator, which once seemed so promising for the firm, had now become its chief liability. Neblett, without a Senate salary behind him, had the most to lose. He and McAdoo dissolved their firm in September 1937 because "we want to keep politics out of the office," but they bickered over their final payments from it. McAdoo continued to represent clients for the rest of his Senate term; in 1938 he asked a district court judge in Louisiana to reschedule hearings for a matter so that he could fit it into his "official business in Washington," and later apologized to a constituent for neglecting his correspondence while he had been trying a case in Los Angeles. Combining public office and private practice, he confessed, "has created the most difficult two-ring circus for me in many years."[40]

❧❦❧

Outside their practices McAdoo and Baker cut very different figures within the legal profession. This was the result of differences in their legal training, their approaches to the law, and their professional reputations. Having learned his law from a judge in the county court at Chattanooga, McAdoo had a limited legal education in comparison to Baker's. He understood law more as an instrument of commerce than as an intellectual discipline. Although he was a member of the American Bar Association (ABA) all his career, McAdoo was not prominent within it. When he was invited to join the ABA's Public Utility Section in 1929, he accepted with alacrity but arranged for his paper on public utility law to be written by John Dickinson, a Princeton law professor who had served under him in the Treasury Department.[41]

Baker occupied a more esteemed place within the profession and its organizations. Steeped in legal history at Johns Hopkins and Washington and Lee, he maintained a deep interest in the development of the common law and of legal institutions. He received many of the profession's highest honors and contributed frequently to debates about law and society. In an address to the Cleveland Bar Association in 1932 entitled "The Lawyer's Place in Society," Baker argued that lawyers should see their profession as "a great consistent science covering the whole subject of human relations." The law and its practitioners should be more than handmaidens of commerce; lawyers were part of a "learned and honorable calling" that owed great obligations to the society that rewarded them so well.[42]

Baker tried to practice what he preached. He was active in the Cleveland Bar Association and served as its president in 1925. On the national stage he was a colonel in the Judge Advocate General's Reserve Officer Corps, was the honorary president of the American Arbitration Association in 1927, was appointed in 1928 to the Permanent Court of Arbitration at The Hague, and in 1936 was elected president of the American Judicature Society. He served on the ABA's Board of Governors in the 1930s but declined its presidency in 1937 because of his failing health.[43]

Although his practice focused on commercial and constitutional law, Baker wrote on labor law in the *American Bar Association Journal* and was very interested in criminal law. In 1925 he joined Franklin Roosevelt's National Crime Commission and contributed to its work on the causes and psychology of crime, the parole system, and criminal procedure. He also joined the General Committee of the National Society of Penal Information in 1929, served seven terms as president of the Cleveland Association for Criminal Justice, and was appointed to the National Committee on Law Observance and Enforcement (NCLOE) in 1929.[44]

Baker also spoke and published on the social implications of criminal law. In 1915, while mayor of Cleveland, he argued that his city's experience with labor disputes, saloons, street crime, and brothels showed that police departments and criminal codes were effective only when they operated in communities that valued knowledge above force. Age-old institutions such as jury trials and the presumption of innocence relied on a social consensus as to what behavior deserved criminal sanction, and no amount of policing could alter that. It was therefore vital to recruit police officers who reflected community values rather than imposed their own.[45]

Baker returned to these themes in "Crimes and the Criminal," published in *The Clevelander* in 1930. Cleveland was then in the grip of a crime wave with more citizens coming before the courts and serving longer jail terms. Citing William Blackstone in the eighteenth century and American prison reformers in the twentieth, Baker called for the simplification of criminal codes and the shortening of sentences for lesser offenses. Only then could communities focus on the causes of crime instead of punishing criminal behavior with little thought to the rehabilitation of transgressors.[46]

This is not to say that Baker was soft on criminals or criminality. Although "the reason we have so much crime in America is because public opinion is tolerant of it and tolerant of its causes," and that "many criminals are products of the environment which society allows to surround them," he did not think that they should escape severe consequences for their actions. Although he opposed capital punishment, Baker advocated life imprisonment without parole for premeditated murder as a more effective deterrent. For other offenses he thought that prisons should be rehabilitative and not punitive institutions. After their detention convicts should be released to make financial restitution to their victims, but Baker reminded parole boards to ensure that prisoners' repentance and rehabilitation were genuine before they acted.[47]

Baker also worked to elevate the moral standards of the Cleveland bar, but he did so in condescending and exclusionary ways. In 1930 he wrote to a Cleveland judge that Martin Miller, an African American lawyer, was rumored to have lodged a false affidavit. Mr. Miller should be counseled on his obligations as an officer of the court because "the whole racial problem in Cleveland is delicate, if not dangerous," and black leaders such as Miller needed to "retain the confidence of thoughtful and earnest white people." Three years later he wrote to the federal attorney general about the nomination of Justice Florence Allen of the Ohio Supreme Court to the US Circuit Court of Appeals. Judge Allen was "the most highly qualified lawyer or judge in Ohio," and if the president wanted to nominate a woman she would be a superb candidate. "I think it only fair to say," Baker went on, "that I do not urge the appointment of a woman to this vacancy." Whether or not to "stimulate the ambition of girls to become lawyers may be an open question of social policy," but he felt uncomfortable at the thought of women infiltrating his "priestly caste."[48]

Baker's concern about the intellectual and ethical qualities of many lawyers led him to conclude that "the great body of the profession has been diluted by the reckless admission of recently naturalized foreigners of very limited education and almost complete lack of sympathy with the American tradition." Naturalized citizens should be barred from legal practice and "Washington's order, 'None but Americans on guard tonight,' might be good marching orders for the Bar as a profession."[49]

McAdoo's reputation as a lawyer, on the other hand, was publicly dissected during investigations in 1924 of his dealings with Morse and Doheny, and it never recovered. These investigations coincided with his campaign for the presidential nomination that year and were colored by partisan attacks. In Congress Israel Foster, a Republican from Ohio, took the floor to discuss "McAdoo the Lawyer." Foster reviewed McAdoo's large retainers from UA, Morse, and Doheny and noted the common belief that he had earned his fees through influence rather than talent. "I do not recall having read of Mr. McAdoo having been violently legal either before or during his time in Cabinet. My information is that he was a broker, then a contractor for the Hudson tunnel, and then entered national politics." And yet he commanded huge fees from clients who wanted something from the administration that McAdoo had so recently served. These retainers were not illegal but they were unethical, Foster concluded, and "[a] President should be something more than a non-criminal."[50]

Newton Baker's legal reputation, by contrast, rose even as his political stock fell. Alongside his professional honors he received honorary doctorates in law from universities and colleges across the nation, including Brown, Bucknell, Johns Hopkins, Princeton, Michigan, North Carolina, Ohio State, Virginia, Western Reserve, Yale, Amherst, Dartmouth, Oberlin, and Williams. In 1937, at the height of the court-packing controversy, the American Institute of Public Opinion polled 175,000 lawyers as to who should be appointed to an expanded Supreme Court. Baker was one of the seven leading choices along with Felix Frankfurter, John W. Davis, Robert Wagner, William E. Borah, Roscoe Pound, and Learned Hand. This honor was significant but ironic because Baker was critical of the court-packing proposal.[51]

Baker's appointment in 1928 to the Permanent Court of Arbitration particularly pleased him; Charles Evans Hughes, already a member, wrote to say that it was "a position which has greater dignity and less work than any other I know of in this democratic community." Baker, indeed, did little work for the court but reveled in the honor it bestowed. "Curiously enough this appointment is addressed to the only ambition I have ever had of a personal sort . . . I have sometimes thought that about the best that could come to me would be to be considered a good lawyer. In a way to be named with Root, Hughes and [John Bassett] Moore does satisfy that wish."[52]

⋙✕⋘

In business, unlike the law, McAdoo surpassed Baker in interest if not achievement. This was in keeping with his lifelong attraction to commerce, the entrepreneurial bent of his legal practice, and the financial demands of his family and lifestyle. By the mid-1930s McAdoo had a large family to support: his third wife Doris, his ex-wife Eleanor, eight children, and several grandchildren. Of his children only one, Huger, was self-sufficient; the others relied on their father's resources to maintain a lifestyle that they and their parents assumed was their due.

McAdoo also had expensive tastes. He maintained houses on both coasts, an airplane and pilot, and numerous automobiles and a chauffeur, and paid dues to expensive city and country clubs. His house at Irvington-on-the-Hudson, which he had bought while president of the H&M, sat on four and a half acres and included nine bedrooms, six bathrooms, and six servants' rooms. In 1913 it was worth $75,000—nearly $1.8 million in 2011 values—and by 1925 McAdoo also owned properties at Santa Barbara, Bayhead, New Jersey, and Huntington, Long Island, a ranch near Phoenix, Arizona, and the family's California residence at 5 Berkeley Square in Los Angeles. His total income in 1919 was large—more than $218,000 then or $2.8 million in 2011—but nearly half of it went in interest payments to service his mortgages and other debts. In 1924 his total expenses were more than $67,000, and they rose steadily until their peak of $155,000 in 1929. Even in the depths of the Great Depression it cost McAdoo nearly $110,000 per year—$1.9 million in 2011 values—to maintain his assets and support his family. Although he lived a millionaire's lifestyle in the 1920s and 1930s, he always felt poor and turned to a variety of business ventures to support a way of life he considered appropriate to a prominent man and his large family.[53]

"There are some real and wonderful opportunities out here in the oil fields close to Los Angeles," McAdoo told Tom Chadbourne, a wealthy Democrat and supporter, in 1922. "I have some clients in the business who are straight shooters, and I am turning up some very good things every now and then." He joined numerous syndicates through the Jameson Petroleum Company and asked friends to invest with him. In November 1922 he told Bernard Baruch about 2 wells that produced 2,500 barrels per day of high-quality oil worth $1.55 per barrel. More wells would increase returns, and so McAdoo invited Baruch to join the syndicate. "In no case would I want you to put more than $25,000 into it. That is what I expect to do myself."[54]

Baruch declined, but lent McAdoo $30,000 to expand his own oil interests. Between October 1923 and September 1925 McAdoo received nearly $44,000 in dividends from Jameson Petroleum. By then he had become so enthusiastic about oil that he encouraged Huger to invest $10,000 in 6 leases and funded his second son Billy to enter the oil business. "I made up my mind when I came here that I would get even with oil!" he told Huger in November 1922. "I am sure now that I have done so, and will have some velvet beside." By May 1926 he had stakes in 18 wells in California, Oklahoma, and Texas which returned nearly $12,000, and in 1928 he and Eleanor earned $24,000 from Jameson Petroleum. Ten years later he invested another $50,000 in 3 wells, which returned $130 per day, and 2 undeveloped leases.[55]

Oil exploration was always risky, and McAdoo soon learned that its "velvet" came with hard edges. When a lease in Texas proved dry in 1921 he was philosophical. "No one can expect an oil investment like this to prove a sure thing," he consoled one of his partners, "and, notwithstanding our hope of large profits, we have met the fate which befalls so many of the inexperienced and have lost our money." In 1924 he bought a half share in a well near Long Beach that cost $189,000 to drill. No oil emerged, and McAdoo was left with a loss of $95,000. In 1927 he complained that the promises that had induced him to invest in an Oklahoma lease had proved to be false. Two wells yielded 395 barrels instead of 20,000; three others were much farther from production than he had been led to believe, and another produced less than 10 percent of its stated capacity. McAdoo conceded that there was always "uncertainty in the oil game," but these discrepancies were suspicious. "The thing that disturbs me most about it is that I allowed one of my daughters, Sally, who can't afford to lose the money, to take an interest. Of course, I shall have to make this good for her."[56]

The disappointments of the "oil game" encouraged McAdoo to pursue other business opportunities in the 1920s. "You know I have always had a great weakness for railroads," he told Baruch at the end of 1924. "It is a pity that we cannot get into that game in a big way and do some real constructive work for the industry." McAdoo identified a struggling road, the Denver and Salt Lake, as a promising prospect. Like so many of his schemes, this one involved a combination of Baruch's money and McAdoo's management. "Like myself," he told Baruch, "you need an outlet for your abundant energy. Neither of us can afford to dry up." Although he often helped McAdoo with his projects, Baruch drew the line at buying him a railroad.[57]

Newspapers and radio next caught McAdoo's eye. In 1925 the Los Angeles *Evening Express*, which also owned radio station KNX, came onto the market. As McAdoo was attracted to railroads as a combination of his business and personal enthusiasms, newspaper ownership was an alluring combination of business and politics. "If we could take this paper," he told J. F. T. O'Connor in April 1925, "my idea is that it should be run as a strictly independent newspaper along progressively Democratic as well as Progressively Republican lines . . . A great service can be rendered to the people of this State by keeping control of this great news agency out of the hands of the reactionaries, who will certainly buy it if the opportunity slips us." A controlling interest could be had for $800,000, and with good management the *Evening Express* could make net profits of half a million dollars a year.[58]

"I do not want, and therefore it is not my idea," McAdoo assured his prospective investors, "to make this a personal organ." He would instead lead a syndicate of investors who wished to combine civic duty with personal profit. "My children and your children," he warned Baruch in yet another appeal for funds, "may have to face the day when a few great independent newspapers may speak with a clarion voice to the people and successfully parry the deadly thrust of privilege and reaction." "Bernie not interested," O'Connor reported back, and McAdoo dropped the whole idea.[59]

As a transplanted westerner with business and political interests on the East Coast, McAdoo saw great possibilities in commercial aviation. There was also something very personal in his attraction to airplanes; he had long driven cars too fast and flying promised even greater excitement. "The road cops are really quite a pest," he told Nell in 1929. "One reason why I like flying is the freedom from pests, grade crossings, other traffic and general obstructions . . . You take an airline through God's majestic highway and find yourself <u>free</u>. I have never before felt the glow of real freedom and it is worth a chance even of death, to find it."[60]

"You cannot try an aeroplane and go scooting around the country," McAdoo's daughter Nona chided him in January 1928. "I would be worried to death every minute about you & you are much too valuable & your life entwined by too many children to be so reckless." Undeterred, he did buy a plane, a Buhl five-seater, but did not try to fly it himself. In July 1929 he bought a more powerful Lockheed Vega, which he named *Blue Streak*. As the Depression dragged on, *Blue Streak* became an expensive luxury; his pilot's salary was $200 per month and the plane needed costly repairs and hangar facilities. In 1932, after spending $30,000 on *Blue Streak,* he put it on the market and eventually sold it for less than a third of its purchase price.[61]

McAdoo was convinced that there was money as well as adventure in aviation. In October 1928 he bought an airport near Culver City, a few miles east of Santa Monica. McAdoo installed his son Billy as operator of the airport and as the local dealer for Buhl planes. The airport also maintained a flying school and hangar facilities. Like most aviation concerns, however, Culver City Airport struggled to cover its costs during the Depression and added even more red ink to McAdoo's ledger.[62]

Early in 1929 McAdoo announced the formation of Southern Sky-Lines to run mail and passenger services between Los Angeles, Atlanta, Washington, D.C., New York, Florida, and New Orleans. He also envisaged an airmail route to Havana, and flew in the Vega from Washington to Miami, and then to Cuba, to publicize his plans. He distributed prospectuses to the postmaster general, the Cuban government, and investors, including Bernard Baruch, H. P. Wilson, Edward Hurley, John F. Sinclair, Daniel Willard, Daniel Roper, William H. Woodin, and William Neblett. "This will give me an interesting thing to play with," he told one prospective investor. "My mind has always turned to concrete acts. Building something always appeals to my interest and imagination enormously. This new field has a great future."[63]

Like so many of McAdoo's schemes, Southern Sky-Lines did not get off the ground. His timing was exquisitely bad as he hawked his prospectus while Wall Street collapsed in October 1929, and his attempts to win mail contracts for an operation that had only one plane, his Vega, and only one employee, his pilot, were doomed to fail. Not surprisingly McAdoo found it difficult to raise capital; an advisor to Bernard Baruch described the proposal as full of "magnificent conclusions" based on overestimated revenue and underestimated costs. Baruch and his colleagues begged off McAdoo's proposition, established companies won the mail contracts, the Cubans refused his offer, and by April 1930 he had dropped the scheme. "There is no use in putting money into a rat-hole," he concluded, and there was no money to put into it anyway.[64]

McAdoo also turned to more conventional ways of making money during the Jazz Age. Chief of these was land speculation in California and Florida. Real estate was attractive to McAdoo because it required little capital of his own. His interest in Californian land began even before he moved there in 1922. Along with his retainer from UA, McAdoo and Douglas Fairbanks bought 170 acres of land at Santa Barbara and planned to subdivide it. This transaction was bankrolled by Fairbanks, while McAdoo paid for his half share of $15,000 through a personal note on a two-year term, in which time the blocks would be resold and the original owner paid from their profits. Relations between McAdoo and Fairbanks cooled in 1920 over subdivision and development costs, and at the end of the year Fairbanks sold his share to Tom Storke. By then McAdoo had grown nervous at the scale of the development and the size of his debt, and he and Storke sold the land in 1921 at a much smaller profit than they had once hoped for. They continued to buy and sell Californian land, but Fairbanks and McAdoo did not do business together again.[65]

McAdoo also joined in the Florida land bubble, which began to inflate at the same time as California's burst in 1924. "I honestly believe that if we were to spend the winter in Florida," he told Eleanor in September 1925, "I could make a million dollars." Four blocks he had bought in Sarasota in February had already doubled in value, and he expected large gains from his other properties there. McAdoo invested in real estate as he did in oil: through syndicates and borrowed money. In March 1925 he borrowed $80,000 from Baruch to buy a 5 percent share in 180,000 acres in Okeechobee for $8 an acre. Six months later the syndicate sold the land for $15 per acre, which delivered McAdoo a net profit of $70,000. "Isn't this fine," he gloated to Eleanor, "especially since I didn't put up <u>any money</u>—simply used my credit?"[66]

McAdoo did most of his Florida speculation late in the boom. He was a short-term speculator, making quick profits in an overheated market. He rarely took more than half shares in property purchases, and mostly took small stakes in syndicates arranged by John F. Sinclair, a Floridian land broker. The bubble, McAdoo told Sinclair in October 1925, would not last forever "so I think the prudent thing to do is to get rid of these investments as quickly as we can." The market did break in 1926, leaving him with large losses on properties bought at boom prices. But those losses were generally shared, his holdings were limited by his focus on quick turnarounds, and he had happy memories of riding the Florida boom while it lasted.[67]

McAdoo also rode the stock market boom of the 1920s. As he had done in land, he bought stocks for quick profit rather than long-term gain. As the market grew after 1924 so did McAdoo's share trading; he bought and sold stock in nearly 200 companies between 1926 and 1936, ran margin accounts with 3 New York brokers, and made about 20 percent profit per year before the crash in October 1929. In the first half of 1924 he received $22,000 in dividends, which comfortably exceeded the $13,500 and $13,000 he received from his law firm and land speculation, respectively. That combined income of $48,000 was reduced by interest payments on the debts that funded McAdoo's investments and assets; in 1927 his debts included $67,000 to Baruch, $45,000 to mortgagees in New York, $25,000 to his stockbrokers, and $30,000 on his house in Los Angeles. In the first 6 months of 1927 he paid $28,000—more than half his gross income—in interest payments.[68]

As he had done in Florida, McAdoo counseled caution but practiced risk on Wall Street. "I am so disgusted at myself not to have acted long ago on my judgment about General Motors," he told Huger in August 1926. "I have concluded that I am a very poor specimen of businessman and a worse one as a speculator! I hope you got in on the present rise. I have been out of it altogether." Despite this uncharacteristic self-deprecation, McAdoo was far from risk-averse in the 1920s. He continued to borrow money to buy stocks, made profits on all three of his margin accounts, and in July 1927 calculated his and Eleanor's total net worth to be nearly $461,000—the equivalent of nearly $6 million in 2011 values.[69]

At the beginning of 1929, having made significant profits for eight years, McAdoo sensed that the market had reached its peak. When stock prices did break in February he read this temporary fall as the major correction he had predicted, and so re-entered the market. Armed with inside information from Tom Storke and others, McAdoo began to buy stocks and make moderate profits on high trading turnover. He was also a beneficiary of J. P. Morgan's "preferred list" that allowed prominent politicians to buy into the Alleghany Corporation in 1929 at half its market price. McAdoo subscribed to five hundred Alleghany shares, while Newton Baker took two thousand. When the preferred list became public knowledge in 1933, McAdoo explained that his participation came through his friendship with a J. P. Morgan partner and decried attempts "to impart some sinister feature into perfectly proper business transactions" that had delivered him a net profit of nearly $5,000. Baker received his shares through the Van Sweringens but held on to them too long and lost money on the deal.[70]

When the music stopped in October 1929, McAdoo was left holding a large portfolio. "It has been a terrible market but I hope the worst is over," he wrote Huger on October 30, 1929. "One never can realize until too late what an utter damn fool one has been! But I didn't get seriously hurt." As the market declined further, however, so did McAdoo's equanimity. In the middle of 1930 he sold stocks at a loss to cover his margin accounts, called in some debts, and postponed his own. In 1931 he resigned from most of his clubs, and in 1932 sold his beloved *Blue Streak*. Early in 1934 he asked a friend to make good his guarantee that stock McAdoo had bought in 1930 would not fall in value. "I have suffered so many losses the past four years," McAdoo confessed, "that I am under great pressure at this time." By the middle of the 1930s he felt poor again, and when he died in 1941 there was almost nothing left.[71]

❖

The best example of the differences between Baker's and McAdoo's business instincts lay in their patents. McAdoo held two: one for an insulated flask with storable handles that he registered in 1927, and one that he lodged in 1934 for a better packaging of razor blades. In 1935 he and his son Robert sought a manufacturer for his razor package, but two years later the Gillette Company released a similar product. McAdoo threatened to sue but did not proceed to litigation. Baker also held a patent, for a vacuum cleaner for shelved books. He was lawyer enough to register it but not businessman enough to commercialize it. McAdoo rued another lost opportunity; Baker gave copies of his invention to his friends.[72]

Baker always presented himself as an ingénue in business matters, preferring instead to emphasize his legal and intellectual concerns. While McAdoo created and pursued many business opportunities while he practiced law, Baker showed little interest or ability in the ways of a lawyer-entrepreneur. Yet he too was in charge of a business—Baker, Hostetler and Sidlo—and he skillfully nurtured it into a rapidly expanding and profitable concern. Having started life with modest resources, Baker had by the mid-1920s become a very wealthy man at the head of a booming law firm. On that measure he had succeeded in business well beyond his own expectations and far ahead of McAdoo, who won and lost several fortunes but at the end of his life was almost bankrupt.

Although his family was neither as complex nor as large as McAdoo's, the need to support it during and after his lifetime loomed large in Baker's thinking. Unable to take out life insurance because of his weak heart, he worried about his family's financial future in the event that he died young. "I not only have not millions," he told a correspondent in 1934, "but I am very doubtful whether my family will be able to live on my savings without changing the very modest mode of life to which they are accustomed." These fears were either neurotic or disingenuous, for by then Baker and his firm had done so well for so long that there were "accumulations" enough for not only the present generation of Bakers but those in the future as well.[73]

Baker professed ignorance of financial matters, but fortunately for him his friends did not. Soon after he went to Washington in 1916 four Cleveland associates, R. L. Fuller, R. H. Bishop, Carl Osborne, and S. L. Mather, formed an investment syndicate called FBOMB. Baker was invited to become the final "B" on generous terms. The others contributed $5,000 each to the syndicate, but Baker's share was paid by a loan from them payable from future profits. FBOMB invested in war-related stocks such as American Shipbuilding and Lackawanna Steel, and within a year had returned dividends of $3,000 to each member. By January 1917 it had doubled its assets, and by July Baker had paid back his loan. After that FBOMB delivered handsomely; between July and October 1918 Baker received $10,671, which equaled his annual cabinet salary. "Never having made any money in my life that I did not work for with both hands and both feet," he wrote Osborne, "the idea that I am making money by reading these occasional statements seems quite incredible, although I confess highly agreeable." Sustained by his friends during the war and confident of his future after it, Baker negotiated a large mortgage on a block in Cleveland's wealthiest neighborhood, close by his prize clients the Van Sweringens and adjacent to the Shaker Heights Country Club.[74]

Prestigious appointments in the business community soon followed. In 1922 Baker served as president of the Cleveland Chamber of Commerce, and he became a director of the Cleveland Trust Company, the city's largest bank, in 1923. In that year he also joined the board of the Baltimore and Ohio Railroad at the behest of its president Daniel Willard, who had worked with Baker during the war. Other directorships followed: the Mutual Life Insurance Company in 1931, the Radio Corporation of America and the National Broadcasting Company in 1933, and the Goodyear Tire and Rubber Company in 1934. These jobs were not lucrative in themselves—Baker received $50 per meeting from Goodyear—but they came with benefits such as discounted stock prices, free travel on the B&O, and tires from Goodyear. Baker, Hostetler and Sidlo also received briefs from these companies.[75]

Baker enjoyed his association with these corporations and the men who ran them. He retained his air of financial innocence even as he sat on the boards of some of the most powerful corporations in the nation, but provided them with legal advice, supported them against insurgent shareholder groups and the anti-business tide of public opinion during the Depression, and batted away critics who accused him of betraying his reformist zeal. "I have just been elected a director of the Cleveland Trust Company," he wrote to his daughter Betty in 1923:

> No doubt you will wonder why—so do I! Banks are usually supposed to have to do with money and anybody can testify that I am not an expert on that subject. But you see I am getting more and more tied to business interests in Cleveland, so I suppose I can count upon finishing my days here without further excursions into public life. You will have to be content to have Daddy directing railroads and banks instead of armies and nations. Don't grieve over it, I like it.[76]

CHAPTER 11

Lost Causes, 1921–1929

McAdoo's and Baker's return to private life during the 1920s did not mean their retreat from politics. In McAdoo's case his legal practice and business schemes were poor substitutes but necessary interstices between attempts to return to public life and prominence. Baker's retirement was more genuine because its motivating ambitions were professional rather than political, but he also had unfinished political business to complete. McAdoo's causes were more selfish than Baker's and their failures more dramatic, but for both of them the 1920s proved to be a decade of lost causes.

No one doubted that McAdoo would seek the 1924 presidential nomination, but declaring his hand too early would reinforce his reputation for overweening ambition and give his enemies more time to organize against him. "There should be active, systematic work," Robert Woolley wrote in November 1921, "but it should be so quietly done that the right hand would not know what the left hand was up to." McAdoo had much to gain from a restoration of Democratic fortunes after the catastrophic losses of 1918 and 1920; he insisted that the party, now evicted from the White House and reduced to minorities in Congress, should combine criticism of the Republicans with a plan to help farmers, return German American property confiscated during the war, and reduce taxes on moderate incomes.[1]

McAdoo soon added the soldiers' bonus to his list. Pressure from veterans' groups saw a scheme of "adjusted compensation" for members of the American Expeditionary Forces (AEF) and the navy introduced into Congress. Conscripted soldiers and sailors were promised an extra $1 a day for service at home and $1.25

per day for overseas service. This effectively doubled their pay to compensate them for their loss of earnings during the war. Veterans could receive their bonuses in cash or in certificates bearing interest over twenty years. An amended version of the bonus, providing only for a deferred payment in 1945, eventually became law over a presidential veto in 1924.[2]

McAdoo strongly supported the bonus and suggested that its cost be met from British and French loan repayments. American servicemen had been underpaid while others enjoyed the wartime boom, and now it was time to make amends. Four million veterans formed a solid base for McAdoo's presidential ambitions, but other factors were also at work. He had used the US Rail Road Administration (USRRA) to redistribute wealth and saw the bonus as another opportunity to do so. "Of course, my enemies are trying to make it appear . . . that I was too kind to labor when I was Director General of the Railroads," he wrote in July 1922. "I was not of course . . . The trouble is that in our democratic form of Government, the greatest difficulty we have always encountered is to get justice to the common man and woman, and to see that they get their just share of the benefit of Government."[3]

McAdoo's redistributive agenda and its electoral possibilities were not lost on his critics. "It cost the country many millions of tax money paid for unearned railway wages to enroll the railway vote under the McAdoo banner," *The New York Times* grumbled, "and it would only cost $1,600,000,000 to make the soldier vote solid for him." The *Times* also criticized McAdoo's proposal for a "living wage" sufficient for every worker to "maintain himself and family in reasonable comfort, educate his children and save something against emergency and old age." This plan, the *Times* noted, coincided with reports that McAdoo would seek the nomination and aimed to broaden his appeal beyond railroad workers and veterans.[4]

McAdoo was used to criticism from the *Times*, but some of his friends echoed its complaint. Bernard Baruch wrote that business groups saw the bonus as a bribe to veterans, and that "no election can be won with the business interests solidly against you." Daniel Roper thought that McAdoo's support of the bonus reinforced the suspicion that he was too ready to use the public purse to buy votes, and George Foster Peabody withdrew altogether in protest at what he saw as McAdoo's pandering to the American Legion. In Cleveland Newton Baker confessed that the economic arguments for and against the bonus left him cold; what concerned him was the demeaning of the idea that fighting for one's country was a patriotic duty. It was wrong to compensate individuals regardless of their actual sacrifices; many doughboys had entered the army illiterate and unhealthy and left it "better in body and mind, better fed, clothed and housed and with better prospects of useful and happy lives than they could ever have had but for their military service. To give them a bonus in addition is absurd."[5]

McAdoo hoped to align the South and the West behind his candidacy because those sections of the country had delivered Wilson victory in 1916 and would do so again for the right candidate in 1924. "The East is more stand-pat than the West," he told Senator Thomas Walsh of Montana, "and is more dominated by those interests against which democracy must continually fight." Westerners and southerners could unite around prohibition, agricultural and railroad reform, and a moderate tariff, but northeasterners were too close to anti-prohibition sentiment, in thrall to the urban bosses who had obstructed Wilson and then nominated Cox, and too partial to business interests. [6]

By then Newton Baker was drifting into that camp on domestic policy, but his main concern during the 1920s was to advocate American entry into the League of Nations. In this he not only continued Wilson's campaign but also made it his own through his public statements and prominence in organizations such as the League of Nations Non-Partisan Association, the Council on Foreign Relations, the Woodrow Wilson and Carnegie Foundations, the Cleveland and American World Court Committees, and the Foreign Policy Association. No audience was safe from Baker's obsession over the League and America's place in it. "I have been talking League of Nations ever since I got on the boat," he wrote to his daughter Betty on his way to Europe in September 1923. "As you can imagine I have been having a good time—and I hope I have done some good."[7]

As Wilson's influence waned Baker asserted his own rationale for entry into the League and even began to work with sympathetic Republicans to urge a rethink of Harding's foreign policy. He knew that Wilson was opposed to such cooperation as a betrayal of his great cause, but he saw no other way forward. "W.W. is not going to live long enough to get even with all his enemies . . . Frankly I want to get into the League now and if not today, then tomorrow and I would not consent to a day's delay for a chance to punish every enemy I have or ever had."[8]

Baker's support of the League was predictable, but some of his other contributions to political debate were surprising. In 1922 he was elected president of the Cleveland Chamber of Commerce. "It is a hopeful sign that a man of your high character and idealism should be willing to accept the presidency of your chamber of commerce," McAdoo wrote, "and it is highly creditable to its members that they should turn to you." Baker used his position to denounce compulsory union membership. "Enlightened and determined public opinion" demanded instead "the principle of the Open Shop: the shop in which every worker's chance is as good as every other worker's chance and from which no worker is shut out because he holds a union card and from which no worker is shut out because he has no union card."[9]

American Federation of Labor (AFL) president Samuel Gompers responded that "this alleged conversion of yours to all that is detrimental to the interests of the wage earners proved a very great shock." Why was Baker now blind to fact that "the so-called 'open shop' is indeed a closed shop, as any hint that a worker is a member of a union immediately erects a bar to his employment"? "I learned to respect you very highly for what I believed to be your high principles where Labor is concerned, but now I mourn the terrible step you have taken—one that I cannot understand and can hardly believe."[10]

Gompers and Baker continued their discussion in published letters. Baker declared that "if I were a worker I would join a union and be very active in it." The AFL had struggled against low wages and exploitative working conditions and had made vital contributions to society. Yet he believed that a closed shop was an affront to liberty because an individual's choice whether or not to join a union should not determine his or her ability to work. Accordingly, Baker found Gompers's demand for a closed union shop and employers' calls for a closed non-union shop equally wrong. In Cleveland the Chamber of Commerce had endorsed a truly open shop in which individual workers could join or not join unions, and industrial relations had proceeded in a cooperative atmosphere rather than "class war."[11]

"I do not for a moment doubt your intentions, nor do I doubt your belief that there can be such a thing . . . as a true open shop," Gompers replied. "The point is that you are deluding yourself." Anti-union employers had used sentiments such as Baker's as a "pious cloak for their iniquity" to deny recognition to labor organizations and to persecute their members. "I maintain that you cannot hold this position . . . and remain friendly to the organizations of workers." Employer groups wanted the open shop because it kept workers unorganized and vulnerable. To argue otherwise was to ignore the realities of power in the workplace that left individual workers helpless to assert their rights without the collective power of unions behind them.[12]

Those who thought of Baker as a friend to reform shared Gompers's bewilderment. "Because you use the war-cry of one of the combatants—'the open shop'— your influence is thrown, willy-nilly, on the side of that combatant," Felix Frankfurter wrote, "and the education of the general interest, which I know is anxiously close to you, is correspondingly weakened and confused." It was too late to define the open shop as a genuinely free workplace because it had long since been appropriated by anti-union forces. Frankfurter urged Baker to endorse the "preferential union shop" in which workers were free to join unions and employers were encouraged to bargain through them. Individual liberties and collective protections could then be reconciled and Baker's reputation saved from the charge that he had turned his back on industrial justice and the rights of working people. Baker later declared that "I have no special objection to the preferential union shop," and reiterated that "I believe not only in the right, but in the wisdom of Labor to organize itself in to Unions," but lasting damage had been done to his standing among progressive and labor leaders.[13]

The consequences of this controversy soon became apparent. Baker had long served as president of the National Consumers' League (NCL), which mobilized consumers against sweatshops and child labor. Under its general secretary Florence Kelley the NCL had developed close ties with the AFL. Baker supported the NCL from its inception in 1898 and described Kelley as "one of the most brilliant women I have ever known," but his breach with the AFL embarrassed it. He offered to resign in August 1922, but with Kelley's support was re-elected for another term. A year later pressure to align NCL leadership with AFL policy had become too great and he resigned the presidency. He remained a vice president until 1937, when NCL's strong support of the New Deal led him to sever all ties with it.[14]

Despite their disagreement over the open shop, Baker remained close to Kelley and to elements of the progressive movement during the 1920s. After the Supreme Court overturned a federal ban on the interstate commerce of goods made by juvenile workers, the NCL lobbied for a constitutional amendment against child labor. Although "by every instinct and tradition I am in favor of limiting the concentration of power in Washington because I believe things are more democratically done when they are locally done," Baker agreed that children's health was so important that it was worthy of federal regulation.[15]

Baker also supported the campaign to keep the enormous hydroelectric dam at Muscle Shoals, Alabama, under federal control. Construction of the dam had begun during Baker's time as secretary of war to provide power for the nitrate plant at Old Hickory. The Armistice reduced military demand for nitrate, and Henry Ford offered to lease the dam to produce fertilizer and electric power.[16]

Ford's offer was anathema to those who wanted Muscle Shoals to provide cheap electricity to develop its impoverished region. These ideas later crystallized in the Tennessee Valley Authority (TVA), but in the 1920s they focused on keeping Muscle Shoals in public hands. Baker actively supported this campaign, lobbying Congress to decline Ford's offer and suggesting that the dam be operated by the US Army Corps of Engineers or by a public corporation. "I have no desire to see the government of the United States enter the field of industry in competition with private initiative and am still old fashioned enough to believe that the government ought not to undertake . . . anything that can be better or even as well done privately." But Muscle Shoals was a special case: America needed to use hydro-electricity as its coal reserves dwindled, and Baker's experiences with Cleveland's streetcars had convinced him that monopoly infrastructure was best kept under public control.[17]

Baker was also more supportive of government ownership of railroads than was the former director general of the USRRA. While McAdoo now sought only to regulate railroads, Baker argued in 1922 that they should be nationalized because they "have never been as well managed in this country as they were during Mc-Adoo's control." Two years later he conceded that the prospect of miring railroads in bureaucracy and centralization now made nationalization an unpalatable last resort, and his critics pointed to this newfound caution as evidence of his drift from reform. Even so, his position was more adventurous than McAdoo's.[18]

⋙※⋘

After the 1922 congressional elections McAdoo told his friends that "it is my duty as a good citizen to stand for the nomination if a sufficient sentiment for me becomes apparent." He still cloaked his ambition and compared his reluctance to re-enter public life with George Washington's. "But what's the use of such reflections?" he asked Tom Chadbourne. "If a man must . . . sacrifice even his life for his country, to say nothing of his happiness, it must be done if the Republic is to endure." Chadbourne was irritated by McAdoo's false humility. "I could stand it no longer. I told him frankly that if he ever made the remark again he must make up his mind to do without my support as I had no use for men who tried to fool either themselves or their friends. 'I know that you are crazy for the nomination and so does everybody else,' I said. 'What is there to be ashamed of?'"[19]

McAdoo corresponded with Democrats across the country, seeking news of their local situations and implicitly encouraging them to support him for the next presidential nomination. In Ohio he tried hard to enlist Baker to his cause. "I think it was fine of Baker also to take the chairmanship of his Country Committee," McAdoo told Byron Newton in April 1922. "I appreciate his friendship very much." In May 1922 Baker noted that the Republicans were misrepresenting McAdoo's conduct of the USRRA and that "I am arming myself as fast as I can find the time to be prepared to defend your administration on the stump if anybody raises a question about it here in Ohio." Although his letters were cordial, Baker did not commit himself to McAdoo, but in 1922 he was more supportive than he would be later. According to Byron Newton, Baker thought then that "Mac is a genius and ought to have a practically clear road to the nomination in 1924, despite the fact that Brother Jimmie Cox is traveling the same road, or thinks he is. As we all know, Baker is a wise little man but I think he is a good friend of yours. He surely says so with emphasis."[20]

McAdoo chose David Ladd Rockwell, who had led Cox's fight at the 1920 convention, as his campaign manager. Rockwell was a volatile character and his failings soon became apparent. He clashed repeatedly with others in McAdoo's inner circle, including Bernard Baruch, Thomas Chadbourne, and Daniel Roper, and he was often deaf to the subtleties of political campaigning. At first, though, he was effective in assembling mailing lists and raising funds. Bernard Baruch and Dixon Williams, a Chicago industrialist, provided $10,000 each, and Chadbourne and John Skelton Williams donated smaller amounts. McAdoo's initial war chest amounted to $50,000, and there were plans to raise another $50,000 later. By the standards of the day this was a generous fund for a nomination campaign.[21]

Rockwell and Chadbourne created McAdoo clubs in states that seemed most promising. The Texas McAdoo Campaign Committee, for example, included members from twenty of the state's thirty-one senatorial districts. "Texas is yours," the editor of the Fort Worth *Record* reported at the end of 1923, "without a question." McAdoo hoped to be treated as a favorite son in three states: Georgia, where he was born; Tennessee, where he had studied and worked; and California, where he now lived. In Alabama, Indiana, Nebraska, Ohio, Virginia, and West Virginia, on the other hand, his supporters did little because those states had favorite-son candidates in Oscar Underwood, Senator Samuel Ralston, Governor Charles W. Bryan, James Cox, Carter Glass, and John W. Davis, respectively, and their support might be needed later.[22]

This was important because it was unlikely that McAdoo would go to the convention with the two-thirds of delegates that he needed to win the nomination; negotiation would be needed to win the votes of favorite sons after they had had their moments of glory. States with complicated political situations required more nuanced strategies. In Missouri McAdoo's friends devised a three-part plan that aimed first for an instructed delegation or, in the event that ex-Governor Frederick Gardner entered the contest, a delegation friendly to McAdoo as its second choice. If Gardner withdrew in favor of Senator James Reed, then McAdoo would go to war for Missouri's delegates.[23]

The New York Times noted in November 1923 that McAdoo's strongest rival for the nomination was Senator Oscar Underwood of Alabama, who combined southern support with respect from northeasterners over his pro-business views and opposition to prohibition and the Ku Klux Klan (KKK). McAdoo thought that Underwood was unelectable, and announced his own candidacy in December 1923.[24]

McAdoo outlined the themes of his campaign in a radio address in January 1924. He promised to reduce federal income taxes, but not surtaxes on incomes over $50,000 per year, and to tax investment income more heavily than wages. Farmers needed relief from freight rates and consumers deserved a "reformed tariff" to lower the cost of living. He combined his personal past and political future by reminding his audience of his support of women's rights at H&M and then the USRRA. He had been a teetotaler since his days in Chattanooga and now urged strict enforcement of prohibition. "The clarion call of a new crusade of moral and political righteousness rings out in the land," he concluded, and he would heed its call.[25]

Some planks in his platform created problems with business. Wall Street originally disliked McAdoo, the *New York World* reported in March 1924, because of H&M's "the public be pleased" motto. It liked him less when he financed the war at low interest rates and "it positively abhorred him" after General Order No. 27. From St. Louis Breckinridge Long reported that he knew only one businessman who supported McAdoo; the rest saw him as "unsafe, Socialistic, radical." He needed urgently to reassure business because "if it is postponed too long, the sentiment against him, already very solid in industrial and financial circles, will have congealed to such an extent that it will be very difficult, if not impossible, to get any support for him in the campaign from these elements."[26]

McAdoo was surprised at criticism of his record in Treasury, which he saw as "absolutely helpful and constructive in every direction" to business. Of course, corporate America had objected to General Order No. 27 and now to tighter railroad regulation and the soldiers' bonus, but that was because they disliked paying for them. He would not alter his policies because "whether popular or unpopular, these are my views and I am not willing to dodge." There were also many votes to be won from the bonus and Wall Street's hostility, but he did restate his objection to public ownership of the railroads and told Roper to tell business groups that he opposed an excess-profits tax. Beyond that he maintained his views on the desirability of surtaxes and inheritance taxes despite business opposition to both measures.[27]

Business hostility was never fully offset by support from those who McAdoo hoped would love him for the enemies he had made. Railroad reformers found his ideas inadequate compared to Robert M. La Follette's gradual nationalization plan that featured in his own presidential campaign in 1924. "The time has COME," one correspondent told McAdoo, "when we MUST, regardless of party, stand for a REAL PROGRESSIVE, whether it be McAdoo . . . La Follette or some other . . . Shall you sit on the fence in [sic] public ownership? There is no middle ground. Either we MUST own the railroads or they OWN US." Nor did McAdoo's backing of the soldiers' bonus win the support of all veterans. A North Carolinian reported that "the ex-soldiers are divided in sentiment" and that "I am of the opinion that if the people believed that there could be no tax reduction, if the Bonus is granted, that they would overwhelmingly oppose the Bonus."[28]

McAdoo was also disappointed that railroad workers did not flock to him in memory of his generosity to them in 1918. Committed to nationalization of railroads, the Brotherhoods refused even to endorse McAdoo for the Democratic nomination and backed La Follette for the presidency. This, he told the editor of *Labor* in 1931, "deprived me immediately of the <u>organized support of the railroad workers</u>, and consequently, left me to battle, single-handed and alone, with the powerful interests which had been antagonized by my support of the railroad workers."[29]

"Despite the extraordinary efforts that the big and sinister interests in Wall Street, including the railroad executives and every crooked influence in the country, are making against me in every state," McAdoo complained, "what astonishes me is the fact that those who believe, as I believe, in progressive democracy and in fighting the battle of the people against these great interests are doing so little to help me." In June 1924 *The Nation*, the most influential progressive publication of all, lauded McAdoo's record in Washington but concluded that his nomination would be "a moral disaster for the whole country." He had sold his influence to Doheny and Morse; "he is an imperialist abroad and at home; his race prejudices are deep and insurmountable . . . We join the New York *World* in saying that this man's candidacy will not do."[30]

Foreign policy also created dilemmas as some Democrats demanded that the party promise to join the League while others hoped to put its electoral poison behind them. "Among the great body of the American electorate there is a strong revulsion of Europe at this time," McAdoo told Chadbourne in December 1923. "I think it is going too far but it nevertheless warns us that to deal with this great question wisely and effectively we must not shut our eyes to facts nor butt our heads against stone walls, just for the fun of having our brains ooze out." Hollins Randolph urged him to disavow the League despite his connection to Wilson. It would be at least a generation before a majority of Americans would accept the League, and in the meantime no candidate who espoused it could hope to win a presidential election.[31]

Yet large numbers of Democrats remained loyal to Wilson's crusade, and they would fight hard against McAdoo's nomination if he turned his back on it. In 1924 he tried again to navigate between Wilson's unconditional approval of the League and the more measured views of the reservationists, but because he saw the League as a political problem instead of a moral crusade he alienated Democrats like his father-in-law and Newton Baker. "These people, like my friend McAdoo, who are soft-peddling the League of Nations," Baker thought, "are like the false prophets of Baal, [and] not one of them should escape."[32]

McAdoo broke cover in February 1924. Declaring that divisions over the League were too deep to be resolved amid a presidential election, he proposed a national plebiscite on it in 1925. To Breckinridge Long this was "a stroke of genius" because "it puts the League discussion in the discard" until after the election. "Mr. Wilson wanted a 'solemn referendum' on this issue and never got it," McAdoo told the press. "I want to see that 'solemn referendum' because I know that as a result the American people will endorse by a decisive majority cooperation by the United States."[33]

McAdoo's support of the bonus and his League policy reawakened gossip about his relationship with Woodrow Wilson. As he had done in 1920, Wilson refused to support any candidate for the 1924 nomination, spurring speculation as to why he again refused to help his son-in-law. That speculation focused on their differences over the bonus and the League. "I know that the Governor does not agree with me about increased compensation to our soldiers," McAdoo told Edith Wilson in December 1923, but "if it is commercializing patriotism to increase the pay of these men from one dollar a day to two dollars per day . . . it was equally commercializing patriotism to pay them even one dollar per day."[34]

Wilson also believed that the 1924 election should focus on the League and was disgusted by McAdoo's proposed plebiscite on it. McAdoo assured him that he still believed in the League but doubted its electoral viability, but his father-in-law would have none of it. "Democratic chieftains make all sorts of guesses why Wilson is not for McAdoo," Edmund Lowry wrote in *Collier's* in November 1923. "Everybody is agreed on one point: That something happened between [them] that caused the latter's sudden resignation from the Cabinet, but that that something, for family reasons, has been kept secret." Newton Baker's friend Raymond Fosdick shared the feeling. "From the way [Wilson] talked to me I am sure he was thinking of you and Huston [sic] [for the 1924 nomination]—and somewhat reluctantly of McAdoo. He certainly never spoke enthusiastically of McAdoo to me." During the last months of his life, as McAdoo's campaign for the nomination grew heated, Wilson avoided even being in the same room as his son-in-law.[35]

Wilson also had himself in mind as he obstructed McAdoo. Byron Newton reported at the end of 1922 that Wilson's "flabby-brained friends" had encouraged him to reassert his leadership, and perhaps even seek the presidential nomination, of the Democratic Party. That notion was even more fanciful in 1924 than it had been in 1920, but Wilson did draft ideas for his acceptance speech and Inaugural Address. McAdoo's supporters did not take Wilson's delusions seriously, but they did worry that he might scuttle McAdoo's campaign by making his opposition to him public.[36]

As he did the League of Nations, McAdoo treated the KKK as a strategic rather than a moral problem. Reborn in Georgia in 1915, the second Klan quickly out-grew the South and by 1923 claimed four million members across the nation. Al-though less focused on African Americans than its predecessor in the 1860s and 1870s had been, the Klan remained fiercely supportive of segregation and disfran-chisement in the South and virulently against Catholics, Jews, and immigrants in the North. During the first half of the 1920s it was powerful across many southern, midwestern, and western states, and politicians trod warily around it. "Of course the thing will not last much longer and is very foolish and wicked and ignorant," Newton Baker told his wife at the end of 1923, ". . . but people are always more or less crazy after a war and we just have to live through these things."[37]

Aiming to assemble a southern and western electoral coalition during the Klan's heyday, McAdoo had no choice but to deal with it. As was the case with the League of Nations, he faced deep division within his party and a perilous combi-nation of political calculation and moral choice over the Klan. He tried first to skirt it and then to compromise on it, and this delivered short-term gains but caused profound damage to his self-proclaimed role as a progressive force in American po-litical life.

McAdoo was warned early about the KKK. At the end of 1922 Thomas Walsh reported that it was strong across the South and had spread even to Montana. Yet the Klan remained southern in the national imagination, and unless that percep-tion changed "this country will never again place its destinies in the hands of a party drawing its chief strength from that section." McAdoo replied that "I had not supposed that it was so serious as you think it is." Walsh need not worry about 1924, however, because groups like the KKK regularly appeared and then disappeared from American life. McAdoo then reassured Walsh, himself a Catholic, that "I have no patience whatever with intolerance or bigotry in any form."[38]

Walsh sharpened his warning three months later by passing on rumors that Tom Love, one of McAdoo's closest advisors, had assisted the Klansman Earle Mayfield in his Texas senatorial contest in 1922. McAdoo declined to disassociate himself from Love and Mayfield, but soon after complained of "cheap skunks throughout the country" who spread stories that "the Ku Klux Klan are supporting me and inferentially, therefore, that I am in sympathy with them, this for the pur-pose of estranging the Catholics, the Jews and the foreign populations generally." It was true that he had congratulated Mayfield on his election, but that was noth-ing more than common courtesy to a leader in a state that would be vital to his nomination.[39]

McAdoo continued to treat the KKK with public reserve and private accommodation. Because Underwood had condemned the Klan, McAdoo hoped that he could win its votes by default. The KKK was "troublesome," Milton told McAdoo, but "I think you are doing right to ignore it. Not a national question. We must carry Tenn, Ga, and enough other southern states to break Underwood." In Texas a McAdoo supporter reported that "Underwood, in my judgment, couldn't carry a single District in the State." He had denounced the KKK, "and the Klan in this State is in the majority." McAdoo agreed that "it would of course be foolish of me to involve myself in a lot of collateral issues and notice the attacks my enemies are constantly making."[40]

The Klan responded positively to McAdoo's silence. In Oregon it endorsed him "without qualification or equivocation," and in Washington State James Bell promised that 86,000 Klansmen "are for you to the finish, [and] will endeavor to send a delegation that will stay by you during the whole fight." In Kansas Sam Abidon reported that the KKK had endorsed Governor Jonathan M. Davis but would ultimately back McAdoo. "I do not want to antagonize them because they are powerful here and I want their support for you." In Texas Cato Sells reported that "Underwood's positive declaration against the klan [sic] has antagonized their membership so positively that I have not found it necessary to do otherwise than remain in a passive and receptive attitude . . . Their attitude so far as we are concerned seems to be friendly without any effort to embarrass."[41]

The other half of McAdoo's strategy, which assumed that anti-Klan Democrats would forgive his dalliance with it, was more problematic. Many northeastern and urban midwestern Democrats insisted that he condemn the Klan as a poisonous influence in American life. Herbert Bayard Swope, editor of the New York World, passed on rumors in October 1923 that McAdoo was a member of the Klan. "I agree that you can not stop any group of men from supporting you; I think, however, that it may become your duty to disassociate your name from alleged adhesion to the K.K.K." From Nebraska Arthur Mullen reported that "some frank statement should be made on the general question of intolerance. It is of the utmost important [sic] that you do not be put forward as the preferential candidate of the Klan."[42]

Similar views flooded in early in 1924. In Colorado Morris Shapforth thought that the KKK was in decline and would be a liability to any candidate thought to be close to it. Antoinette Funk advised that McAdoo should condemn the Klan "when you grow a little further in delegate strength," and Mullen reported that McAdoo's silence on it had cost him dearly in Wisconsin and Ohio. Samuel Untermeyer, a New Yorker who had donated to McAdoo's campaign, wrote that "the time has about come" to condemn the KKK because otherwise McAdoo would lose the Northeast.[43]

McAdoo's reluctance to denounce the Klan was politically rather than person- ally motivated. Although he was committed to segregation he had never been a member of the KKK or sympathetic to its goals. He had shown little evidence of nativism or anti-Catholicism, and counted Jews such as Bernard Baruch and Sam- uel Untermeyer among his closest allies. He had long been a Mason, but never a diligent one, and had shown no interest in any other secret organizations. His im- age as the Klan's candidate in 1924 was therefore personally unfair but politically deserved. Determined to go to the convention with as many delegates as possible, and reliant on southern and western votes, McAdoo kept quiet about the KKK to reap the benefits of its approval while avoiding the obloquy of endorsing it.[44]

By early 1924 the costs of McAdoo's accommodation began to outweigh its ben- efits. The primary elections that he needed to win had not yet begun, but pressure on him to denounce the KKK had become intense. On March 15, 1924, he finally broke his silence, but in a way that neither disturbed the Klan nor placated its en- emies. In Macon, Georgia he was asked "How do you stand on the Ku Klux Klan?" He replied that "I stand four square with respect to this and . . . to every other or- ganization on the immutable question of liberty contained in the first amendment of the Constitution of the United States, namely, freedom of religious worship, freedom of speech, freedom of the press and the right of peaceful assembly." As denunciations went, this one was particularly weak; the KKK endorsed its senti- ments and its opponents reported that it "didn't get very far with the Catholics." John O'Neill cabled from Boston that "Newspapers worse than ever. Something must be done. Smith people using Kluklux against you with effect." By then, how- ever, the die was cast. McAdoo had supped with the devil, but with too short a spoon.[45]

<hr>

"Unless there is some radical change," McAdoo told a friend in January 1924, "I think that the outcome of the Convention is not at all in doubt." That "radical change" came two weeks later when Edward Doheny testified to Irvine Lenroot's Senate Public Lands Committee about his dealings with Secretary of the Interior Albert Fall over the naval oil reserve at Teapot Dome, Wyoming. Doheny admit- ted to "lending" Fall $100,000 in return for the right to drill the reserve, and then returned on February 1 to reveal McAdoo's retainer. That related to Mexican oil and not Teapot Dome, but its disclosure was very damaging because it linked McAdoo to Doheny. Now confronted by a new president and a national economy in strong recovery, the Democrats' main hope in 1924 was to campaign against Republican corruption. Doheny's evidence threatened the salience of that issue if the Democrats nominated McAdoo.[46]

Doheny's testimony coincided with a sharp deterioration in Woodrow Wilson's health. Urgently summoned from California, McAdoo and Eleanor arrived too late to see Wilson, who died on February 3. McAdoo was left to combine mourning his father-in-law with his own political damage control. He released a statement on Doheny's testimony and appeared before Lenroot's committee on February 11 to confirm the retainer, outline the work he did for it, and repeat that he had had nothing to do with Teapot Dome. He also revealed that Doheny had promised him a success fee of up to $900,000 if he saved his Mexican holdings from confiscation. That fee was never paid, and in any case McAdoo denied that it was corrupt. "What I have done is within my rights as a lawyer . . . If my conduct . . . is open to criticisms, then no lawyer can take a cabinet office unless he be rich enough to give up all professional employment . . . when he comes out of office."[47]

McAdoo's supporters discussed Doheny's testimony as they gathered for Wilson's funeral. "Tragedies have become common in the lives of men and nations," Norman Hapgood told McAdoo after talking with Baruch, House, and Love. "We are confronted with one of these in our political plans." Hapgood and his friends agreed that McAdoo was entitled to take Doheny's retainer, but they thought that feeling against Doheny was so strong that McAdoo was no longer electable. They advised him to withdraw from the race and to aim instead for 1928. Baruch and House agreed that McAdoo should withdraw, but hoped that the 1924 convention might draft him if it deadlocked. Breckinridge Long first thought that Doheny had damaged McAdoo's candidacy beyond repair, but later reconsidered because the delegates had not yet had their say. Of McAdoo's other friends only Carter Glass, Antoinette Funk, and David Ladd Rockwell urged him to fight on.[48]

McAdoo was in no mood to surrender and was heartened by letters and telegrams from supporters across the country and by sympathetic coverage from mainly southern newspapers. More skeptical opinions came from the Northeast. The New York World editorialized that "Mr. McAdoo, with all his strong qualities, simply cannot qualify as the leader of a party which will promise the country a return to purer and sterner standards of public conduct." The publisher of the Newark, New Jersey, Ledger told McAdoo that "there has never been much hope for you in this particular section," and now there was even less. In West Virginia a Morgantown lawyer told John W. Davis, who had emerged as that state's favorite-son candidate, that "McAdoo is very definitely out of the picture. He has been both erased and effaced."[49]

Hoping to reinvigorate his campaign before the primaries, McAdoo called his friends to Chicago to decide if his candidacy was still viable. "If they think I am unavailable I shall gladly withdraw and fight as a private in the ranks; if they think

I should lead, I will do so with all the power that is in me." Nearly three hundred people came to the meeting on February 18. "He looks badly," Breckinridge Long observed. "He is thin, and nervous as a cat . . . [but] from the beginning there was no doubt of the ultimate decision. Everyone was for McAdoo continuing the fight. There was no other answer possible. There is no other man."[50]

McAdoo preached to the converted in Chicago, but others were unconvinced. Newton Baker thought that "oil is in so much disfavor that a man who burns kerosene in his lamp could not be elected constable." John W. Davis observed that "today Brother McAdoo assembles his division commanders in Chicago. No doubt they will give him a hearty cheer. It seems to me, however, that when the captain of the boat, after denying that she has been torpedoed, calls the crew together to consider how many hours she will float, it is not calculated to improve the morale of the passengers." Thomas Walsh supported McAdoo until the cumulative weight of his dealings with Doheny and his appearances in tax cases before the Treasury Department made "the load . . . too heavy for you or your friends to carry . . . I give you my candid judgment that you are no longer available as a candidate; at least that the oil scandal issue would be lost to us if you should be nominated."[51]

Doheny's bombshell also affected McAdoo's headquarters. Unhappy that McAdoo had disregarded his advice to withdraw, Baruch ended his financial support after a final donation of $7,500. Rockwell raised only $27,000 of his $50,000 target, and the campaign remained poor until the convention. Even worse, Frank Frazier, the Chicago office manager, resigned and announced that McAdoo was unelectable. The only way to beat President Calvin Coolidge, Frazier told the press, was to find another "upstanding, vigorous, somewhat radical progressive" like Thomas Walsh. Rockwell and Roper fell out over the Frazier affair and ignored each other until the convention. Early in June Antoinette Funk cabled McAdoo that "Your manager drinking heavily and running amok . . . there is no limit to damage that may be done to your cause." McAdoo stood by Rockwell and placated Roper, but the atmosphere in his headquarters remained poisonous.[52]

Beset by these difficulties, McAdoo limped to the 1924 nomination season. In 1924 only fifteen states held primaries, while the others chose delegations through conventions. McAdoo did well in the early contests; in March he defeated Underwood in Georgia after speaking throughout the state and visiting his birthplace at Marietta to reinforce his credentials as a native son. Georgia was an important test after Doheny's testimony and McAdoo's comment on the KKK, and he was relieved to find that neither had done him much damage.[53]

In Missouri McAdoo's supporters waged a bitter battle against Senator James A. Reed, who had entered the contest as an avowedly anti-McAdoo candidate. Both sides exchanged allegations of personal misconduct and political corruption. Even though McAdoo stayed aloof from this campaign, Reed won only 7 of the state's 118 counties. In April the state convention elected an uninstructed delegation that included a large majority of McAdoo supporters. By the beginning of April he had won instructed delegations from Nebraska and the Dakotas, uninstructed but friendly delegations from Iowa and Kansas, and a majority of delegates from Arizona. Even the *New York World* conceded that McAdoo's nickname of "McAdieu," earned after Doheny's testimony, may have been premature.[54]

Elsewhere, though, it was clear that McAdoo had been damaged by the bad publicity and unsavory associations that his campaign had attracted. In Seattle his organizer wrote that "there has been a little hesitancy on the part of some of the Democrats here that they didn't seem to have before to work vigorously for an instructed delegation for you." Daniel Kelleher thought that a majority of the delegation from Washington would be in McAdoo's favor but that it could not be instructed for him. Nevada's Democrats also refused to bind themselves to McAdoo, and even in his home state an anti-McAdoo ticket emerged because of fears that the oil scandal had made his candidacy unwise. In Wisconsin his chief organizer reported that the "booze crowd" in Milwaukee was working against him and that his success in Georgia had convinced many Catholics that he was indeed the Klan's candidate. McAdoo could now count on only fourteen of Wisconsin's twenty-six delegates but had no chance of having the remainder instructed for him.[55]

To the south and east the news only got worse. Illinois, controlled by Chicago boss George Brennan, was a lost cause and increasingly identified with Al Smith. In Ohio the party coalesced behind its favorite son and 1920 nominee James Cox. In keeping with his policy on favorite sons, McAdoo tried to stay friendly with Cox, but Edward House told him at the end of January that he "was not for you, [and] that he did not like what you stood for" on labor, the soldiers' bonus, and the League of Nations.[56]

In Cleveland Newton Baker was torn as he surveyed the candidates for the nomination. He was aware that McAdoo was the front runner, and always admired his vitality and ability. "He is a bit given to apple sauce, chiefly about himself," he told his wife, "but he is a very brilliant man." Yet his reservations about McAdoo's suitability for the presidency had only strengthened since 1920. "My chief criticism of him and his candidacy," Baker wrote in February 1924, "is that it seems to be wholly without leadership on the question of our foreign affairs, and to me that is so much the dominant issue that I am unable to take seriously a program of domestic reform which is not based upon first getting our foreign relations straightened out and put upon a general co-operative plan." McAdoo had gone cold on the League and was obdurate on war debts, and was instead content with "tinkering with the tariff and other old pots and pans" such as the soldiers' bonus and prohibition.[57]

Baker also saw no reason to rethink the reservations about McAdoo's temperament that he had first expressed during their time together in Wilson's cabinet. He told Walter Lippmann in October 1923 that "from all I have ever seen, I believe his tendencies are really democratic, but he has an unconscious love of power and a fondness for seeing the machine go in response to his urging which makes him restless and unhappy, unless he is doing something that either makes a flash or a loud noise." He was even franker to Betsy. "I should be I suppose for Mr. McAdoo when he gets the nomination, but why is it that I feel repelled by the very ardor of his pursuit of the prize? It is entirely proper for him to want to be President, most men do, but somehow his attitude and behavior displeases me."[58]

Baker was more impressed by James Cox and John W. Davis. He had known Cox for years and had worked for his election in 1920, but he had lost too badly then to be a viable candidate in 1924. Baker rated Cox's chances of renomination and then election as infinitesimal. "But he has been faithful to my beliefs on international questions and I owe him a lot for that."[59]

Baker's other loyalty was to John W. Davis. Born two years and thirty miles apart, the two West Virginians had met as students at Washington and Lee. They had worked together in the Wilson administration, which Davis served as solicitor general and then ambassador to the Court of St. James. In 1921 he established a law firm in New York with Frank Polk and Allen Wardwell, and became president of the American Bar Association. "Every time I hear you," Baker told Davis after seeing him in court in 1935, "I make up my mind to come as near imitating you as I can." Davis was also a strong supporter of the League of Nations. In October 1923 Baker noted that "Mr. McAdoo is making the most fuss just now about being President but whether he is making the most progress I do not know. My own hope is that the Democrats will get tied up in a deadlock and . . . will choose Mr. John W. Davis . . . I could vote and work for Mr. McAdoo but with more enthusiasm for Mr. Davis."[60]

Baker grew more enthusiastic about Cox because of his outspoken support of the League of Nations, which contrasted with McAdoo's silence on it. His respect for Davis was undiminished, and so he went to New York with two candidates in mind, both of whom he thought superior to McAdoo.[61]

Having defeated Underwood so decisively in Georgia, McAdoo now focused on Al Smith. Right across the East and especially in New England, Homer

Cummings reported to Rockwell; Smith had gained strength at McAdoo's expense because of Doheny and the KKK. McAdoo knew little about Smith but treated him with the same courtesy that he accorded all favorite sons who were not overtly hostile to him. Although he dismissed the possibility that the Catholic, wet, and Tammanyite Smith might win the nomination, McAdoo was alive to the possibility that he might deadlock the convention. It was therefore important to remain on good terms with him so that he might later withdraw in McAdoo's favor. He therefore told Smith that "I thought he was entitled to the State and I naturally would not contest it with him."[62]

This strategy was undone in the heat of the 1924 primaries. In the South McAdoo's friends lambasted Underwood as a tool of Wall Street and compared his outspoken opposition to the KKK to McAdoo's reticence. They also pointed to Underwood's and Smith's opposition to prohibition and suggested that they would cooperate to nominate a conservative, wet, and perhaps even Catholic candidate. Smith noted the tone of McAdoo's fight against Underwood and took it personally. "The religious issue is in this campaign and can not be eliminated," he told Tom Chadbourne. "The only way it could have been eliminated would have been by my not being a candidate, and that I never would have consented to [because] I do not propose that my religion shall disenfranchise me from aspiring to the greatest office in the country." To win his battles in the South, McAdoo allowed his tactics to negate his strategy and alienated the only favorite son who could win enough votes to deny him the nomination.[63]

As he grappled with Smith in the east McAdoo consolidated his western and southern flanks. In the middle of April he claimed two hundred delegates and seventy-six more from Washington and North Carolina in early May. Twenty-four more votes came from Tennessee and forty from Texas. His victory there was marred by rumors of connivance with the KKK. McAdoo had won another tactical victory at great strategic cost, for he had further enraged those who opposed him as the KKK's favorite son.[64]

By the end of May McAdoo claimed every delegate west of the Mississippi River and south of the Ohio River, either through instruction or second preference, and outside that arc he had some votes in Illinois, Michigan, Pennsylvania, and Wisconsin. By his own reckoning he held more than 400 of the Convention's 1,094 delegates, which was enough to block a nomination but well short of the 730 he needed to win it. Smith had 300 votes, which left him only 65 short of his own veto. Early in his campaign McAdoo had boasted that he would win enough delegates to have the two-thirds rule abrogated, but now he depended on it to keep his candidacy alive. First he would see Smith off, and then "I will stake my life on the prophesy [sic] that if we get, as I am sure that we shall, a majority of the

Convention at any time, we shall get the necessary two-thirds. I know what I am talking about."[65]

⊰⊱

"I am sorry, for your own sake," McAdoo told his son Robert, "that you are not going to attend the Democratic National Convention, because there is no more thrilling and interesting experience than a National Convention with a hard contest on." In New York Breckinridge Long and twelve assistants organized delegates on the floor, while McAdoo chaired a "Board of Strategy" with Rockwell and Roper at the Vanderbilt Hotel. Baker arrived with the Ohio delegation, which instructed him to support denunciation of the KKK by name and immediate entry into the League of Nations. "There is no forecast of when we shall get through," he told Betsy as the convention began on Thursday, June 26, "but I still believe the delegates will find New York expensive and begin to get impatient as they get poor, so that Monday or Tuesday should see the finish."[66]

After selecting its officers the convention turned to the nomination speeches. There were nineteen candidates in all, and nominating them took three days. Following the alphabetical order of their home states, Underwood from Alabama came first and McAdoo from California came next. James Phelan's nomination speech met with a long demonstration by McAdoo's delegates accompanied by taunts from the galleries. "We don't care what Easterners do," chanted the delegates, "the South and West are for McAdoo!" New York's turn came the following day when Franklin Roosevelt nominated Al Smith in a speech now famous for its description of him as the "Happy Warrior." The parade that followed lasted ninety minutes as Smith's delegates and the public galleries combined to reduce the convention to bedlam.[67]

Cox had to wait until the third day before his nomination. Newton Baker used his nominating speech as much to rehearse his coming battles over the platform as to sing his fellow Ohioan's praises. He began by alluding to the election of 1920. "There is nobility in a defeat when it is but a temporary set-back in the assertion of principles eternally true." Americans then were not ready for the responsibilities of peace, and "our leaders having led us, morally, back to the age of the mound builders, the largest mound built in America, in a period of four years, is a nation-wide secret society which parades in the darkening moon, wrapped in sheets [and] arouses prejudice against that tolerance in matters of race and religion which has ever been the choice tradition of the American spirit."

But now the League "has gathered to it the great liberals of the old world. It has yielded nothing to force, it has defied skepticism and dared to believe, as liberals always believe, in the power of good will." Americans were now ready to join the

League that Cox had argued for so valiantly in 1920, and "Ohio feels that her son, once only her favorite, has become the nation's favorite . . . I present to you the name of James M. Cox!" Afterward Baker told Betsy that "I seemed to have complete attention and a kindly reception. The particular thing I watched was the attitude of the audience to the League of Nations and with that I am entirely satisfied."[68]

After all the candidates were nominated the convention turned to the platform. A drafting committee had deadlocked over the KKK and the League of Nations, with McAdoo's delegates supporting a general condemnation of intolerance without specific mention of the KKK, while delegates from Smith's Northeast, the urban Midwest, and Underwood's Alabama demanded that it denounce it by name. Baker voted on the platform committee for an express denunciation, but McAdoo's wording prevailed by a majority of 40:14. Baker confessed that "I cannot worry much about anything so intrinsically absurd being very permanent or very powerful." He was much more concerned about the party's position on the League. McAdoo's supporters backed an advisory plebiscite, but Baker insisted that the platform commit to membership without delay. He won scattered support from thirty-one state delegations, but none from those in McAdoo's hands. After losing in the Platform Committee, Baker vowed to take his case to the full convention.[69]

The assembled delegates decided on the League and KKK planks when they met to endorse the platform on June 28. Exhausted by his struggles in the Platform Committee, Baker led debate over his League plank with a speech that many considered to be the greatest they had ever heard. "There is no subject on this earth, apart from my relations to my God and my duty to my family," he began, "which compares even remotely in importance with me [as] the League of Nations." With all that was "left of me at the end of five days, with about two hours sleep in each night of the five," he appealed "to every emotion you have in your heart, and to every thought that your intellects can generate." The majority's plank was so prevaricating that "when my son is dead on a battle field that I have been trying to keep him from going to, they will have reached fullest consideration. And somebody, somebody will put a tombstone over that boy's grave and over the graves of other boys, your boys, and on them will be written: 'Died in battle after fullest consideration.'"

McAdoo's League plank was legally unsound and morally suspect. There was no constitutional power to conduct a plebiscite, so how might it be conducted? Nothing would come of it other than to bury the League of Nations and all that it promised. Baker ended on a familiar note. "On battlefields in Europe I closed the eyes of soldiers in American uniform who were dying and who whispered to me messages to bring to their mothers." He had welcomed the AEF home with joy and relief, but to the dead he had promised that their sacrifice had not been in vain. Baker then addressed Woodrow Wilson, who "is standing at the throne of a God whose approval he won and has received. As he looks down from there I say to him, 'I did my best. I am doing it now. You are still the captain of my soul.' "[70]

Although it was much lauded, Baker's speech won few converts. Leading the case for the majority, Alfred Lucking of Michigan ignored Baker's arguments against the constitutionality of the plebiscite. Instead, he reminded the delegates of Cox's catastrophic loss in 1920 and warned that another flatfooted endorsement of the League would cause the same result in 1924. Senator Key Pittman, a delegate from Nevada and a McAdoo supporter, was less polite. Baker, "with his wild burst of oratory, with his tears in his eyes and his broken-down, tottering body across this table here, is trying to appeal to your sympathies, not your judgment."[71]

Large sections of the audience hissed their disapproval of Pittman's rudeness but then voted by a large majority against Baker's plank. All of McAdoo's delegations voted nay while Smith's delegates and the favorite sons divided. James Cox's Ohio, Carter Glass's Virginia, and John Davis's West Virginia voted with Baker while Indiana and Montana opposed him. The final vote was 742½ votes to 355½, but Baker was neither surprised nor dismayed. He confessed only to "a regret that I was not able a little more to restrain the emotional side . . . but the audience quite carried me away by its enthusiasm for the Wilson tradition and, perhaps because I was weary, I started with a deep distaste for those counsels of expediency which were leading my associates into timid and impermanent policies."[72]

While the fight over the League was Baker's personal crusade, the struggle to name the Klan engaged all the party's factions in passionate debate. The majority plank had come from the McAdoo camp, which remained wedded to its pre-convention strategy of publicly ignoring the Klan. By then McAdoo was trapped by his own strategy; his failure to condemn the KKK had so galvanized his opposition that it was now too late to change course. "The more the Smith forces were built up the more solid our forces became," Breckinridge Long noted in his diary immediately after the convention. "So there was no sense in [condemning] the Klan and entering upon the impossible task of competing with Smith for the Catholic vote, for that is just what it amounted to."[73]

Debate over the minority plank that condemned the KKK by name sparked fistfights on the floor and jeering from the galleries. McAdoo's delegates argued that naming the Klan would only publicize it further and alienate the party's most loyal voters. Robert L. Owen, who had worked closely with McAdoo on the Federal Reserve Act in 1913, argued that the convention should not condemn the whole barrel because of a few bad apples, and William Jennings Bryan castigated those who were prepared to ruin the party's chances for the sake of "three little words." Those in favor of the minority plank argued with equal passion that the Klan was an affront to American principles of tolerance and to millions of Catholic and immigrant voters.[74]

The majority plank squeaked through by a single vote. Apart from Underwood's Alabamians, southern delegates voted uniformly for it as did those from Idaho, Nevada, Oklahoma, and Washington. McAdoo's California divided, with nineteen delegates supporting the majority and seven opposing it. New York, New Jersey, Delaware, and Rhode Island voted unanimously to condemn the Klan, while the other delegations split unevenly. The closeness of the result made the majority plank's victory pyrrhic, and its implications were dire for McAdoo. If his KKK plank could win only the barest majority of delegates, then his chances of winning two-thirds of them for his nomination were slim indeed.[75]

Voting on the nomination began on June 30. McAdoo led Smith by 431½ votes to 241 on the first ballot, followed by the gaggle of favorite sons. McAdoo received almost all his votes from the South and West, while Smith won none from the South and only a few outside the Northeast. Most of McAdoo's supporters had voted against naming the Klan, and all but one of Smith's had voted to denounce it. McAdoo's 39.4 percent of the vote was well below the majority that he hoped would cow his rivals, and Smith's 22 percent was more than one hundred votes short of the one-third he needed to block McAdoo. By the end of the day four favorite sons had dropped out, but this had not changed the main candidates' relative standing; McAdoo won forty-eight new votes but Smith countered with sixty-five of his own. Newton Baker received a single vote on the fifteenth ballot, but he was already tiring of the show. "We seem to have settled down to endless roll calls and purposeless repetitions," he wrote home the next day. "Nobody is gaining, nobody losing. For all I can see there is no reason why this should be over until after the November election!"[76]

McAdoo's first pre-convention strategy aimed to win a simple majority of delegates before the convention and then to have the two-thirds rule overturned before balloting began. After that plan became impracticable, he cultivated the favorite sons so they would throw their support to him once they had strutted on the national stage. After he had won half of the delegates, McAdoo would ask the other candidates to concede and drive him through the two-thirds barrier. This strategy, ironically enough, was similar to Champ Clark's at Baltimore in 1912 before it was derailed by McAdoo and Baker on behalf of Woodrow Wilson.[77]

Unlike Clark at Baltimore, however, McAdoo went to New York in 1924 well short of a majority of delegates. The convention fight over the Klan then so polarized the party, and so identified McAdoo with the KKK, that the favorite sons hesitated to hitch their stars to his wagon. McAdoo's failure to win a majority of delegates in ballot after ballot also encouraged them to stay in the contest in hopes that they would ultimately benefit from the deadlock. Virginia's Carter Glass earned particular censure from McAdoo for his "duplicity and treachery" in staying in the race rather than ceding his delegates to McAdoo. "You are dead right about the two-thirds' rule," McAdoo told Tom Love in 1925. "I am sorry now that we didn't make the fight for its abandonment in the pre-convention campaign . . . but I never supposed that the 'favorite sons' would make common cause (for as many as thirty ballots even) with the bosses to deadlock the convention."[78]

Flaws in McAdoo's strategy became obvious as the balloting entered its fifth day. Samuel Ralston of Indiana withdrew after the sixty-third ballot, but his votes divided to keep the balance between McAdoo and Smith. Cox pulled out at the same time, but Ohio's delegates went neither to McAdoo nor to Smith but to Newton Baker. Ohio had swapped one favorite son for another, but the new one had no illusions. "Ohio's '48 votes for Baker' were a very pleasant compliment, but there never was any chance for it to prove serious and since last Saturday when I made a League of Nations speech I have simply been a brave but indiscreet man whom the Convention admires for courage but could on no account follow."[79]

"Hold fast till hell freezes over," a McAdoo supporter cabled on July 3. On July 4 McAdoo declared that "the fight is proceeding along certain inevitable lines which will lead . . . to an inevitable victory." On the 69th ballot he won 530 votes and 48.3 percent of the delegates. This was to be his zenith, but he was still 20 votes short of a majority. Smith had also inched towards one-third of the delegates, and 234 votes remained with favorite sons. By the 77th ballot McAdoo had slipped to 513 votes while Smith had gained Ohio's votes to reach 367 delegates, or a third of the convention. "Poor McAdoo does not deserve to win, indeed he richly deserves to lose and I think must lose if there is to be anything left of the Democratic Party," Baker told Betsy, "but it is a tragic hour for him and I am sorry to realize how much he is suffering. But for him, or when he is eliminated, we can close up our task quickly."[80]

McAdoo and Smith met after the 93rd ballot on July 8. By McAdoo's account Smith "was, at the time, in the state that constant drinkers frequently find themselves—not intoxicated but well tanked." Smith admitted that he could not win and that he stayed in the race only to block McAdoo. They then discussed compromise candidates but could not agree on any of them. To McAdoo, Smith was "an obstructionist and a wrecker." There would be no peace between the two men, but no victory either.[81]

McAdoo regained some of his vote, but any hope of a breakthrough was gone. At the end of the 99th ballot he and Smith polled 353 votes each, but attention had turned to John W. Davis's growing support, which stood at 210 votes. Before the convention began its 100th ballot at 2:00 a.m. on July 9, McAdoo announced that he was "unwilling to contribute to a continuation of a hopeless deadlock. Therefore, I have determined to leave my friends and supporters free to take such action as . . . may best serve the interests of the party." This was not a withdrawal, but it was treated that way by the exhausted delegates. In the next ballot McAdoo's total dropped to 190 while Smith and Davis showed no change. McAdoo was down to 52 votes after the 101st ballot, while Smith had declined to 121. Davis now stood at 316 votes; Texas and Georgia shifted to him on the 102nd ballot, and during the 103rd he won a majority and then two-thirds of the votes. After ten days the convention had finally stumbled on a nominee. "We died game," a Texan cabled McAdoo after the news of Davis's nomination reached Amarillo. "We still love you [and] we are for you in 1928."[82]

McAdoo and his family left for Europe on July 12. Doubtless thinking of his own problems with Doheny's retainer, he defended Davis's record as a prominent Wall Street attorney "because a lawyer's views on economic, political and social questions are no more to be judged by his professional associations than is a physician to be judged by the character of his patients." Privately he was not so sure; Davis seemed resistant to farm relief and railroad reform, and "I am not at all sure that he can convince the country as to his progressivism." These reservations were mutual; Davis disliked the platform, which reflected McAdoo's ideas rather than his own, and decided to disregard its "unsound" features. The League plebiscite was especially difficult because Davis agreed with Baker that it was unconstitutional.[83]

McAdoo was bitter about the outcome of the convention and blamed everyone but himself for it. "The corrupt bosses . . . in combination with the liquor interests and other sinister influences," he wrote from Europe, had subverted "the will of a great majority of the rank and file of the Democratic Party." McAdoo's enemies, and their "hoodlums and hirelings" in Tammany Hall, had stolen victory from him. "I have never seen such foul methods employed in a Convention or in the press as were employed against me." His delegates had been plied with whiskey, he had been falsely accused of belonging to the KKK, and his reputation had been traduced by "a fake religious issue" that solidified Catholic opposition against him.[84]

"Welcome home," Davis cabled McAdoo on September 21. "I hope to have the pleasure of seeing you soon." By then his campaign was in deep trouble, but McAdoo was unsympathetic. "I am not responsible for the present situation, and there is really no reason why I should respond to the Macedonian cries for help from those who created this situation and destroyed all prospects of a Democratic victory." Davis's strategy was all wrong; instead of campaigning against the Republicans he had attacked La Follette, and in wooing the economically conservative and wet Northeast he had endangered the Democrats' solid South.[85]

Instead of campaigning for Davis's lost cause McAdoo entered the hospital to undergo prostate surgery. Skeptics dismissed this as an excuse to sit out the campaign, but McAdoo's condition was real and its treatment painful. He stayed in the hospital for two weeks, and emerged even more reluctant to help Davis. "I don't give a damn what my enemies say. I owe them nothing . . . I think those eminent gentlemen who helped to create this mess . . . might do the work." By then the election was ten days away, and McAdoo's contribution to it amounted to three speeches from the back of the train as he traveled to California, and then an address in Los Angeles on October 30.[86]

In Ohio Baker was more supportive. Having opposed McAdoo's nomination, he was happy with the convention's outcome. Somehow the delegates had chosen "the ablest man now living in the Democratic Party." Baker could overlook the League plank that McAdoo had bequeathed because Davis was a true internationalist. He made several speeches for Davis and tried to persuade progressives to support him over La Follette. "You may be interested to have me confess," he told Jonathan Daniels many years later, "that the low point in my own hope for the ultimate success of our experiment in democracy was reached when John W. Davis was defeated for the presidency." Davis had his limitations as a campaigner, and his plutocratic clients made him an unlikely progressive, but he deserved better than his crushing defeat. His 28.8 percent of the vote was much closer to La Follette's 16.6 percent than to Coolidge's 54 percent. "Esquimaux, I am told, reject candy for blubber," Baker told him after the election. "Apparently our fellow citizens just now are in an arctic mood."[87]

The events of 1924 propelled McAdoo's political career for the rest of the decade. The lesson of Davis's defeat, he wrote after the election, was that "[it] is hopeless for the Democratic Party to expect to carry the East any time, no matter who it may nominate . . . [it] must look to the liberal elements in the West and the South for success, and until this lesson is learned there is no hope." Convinced that his defeat in New York had shown that the party had lost its way, McAdoo was determined that he, and not the men who had blocked him, should guide it out of the wilderness.[88]

As he tried to reassert his position in the party after the bloodbath of 1924 McAdoo became more explicit about his philosophy of government. In May 1926 he delivered a speech, entitled "States Rights and the Jeffersonian Idea," which challenged the views of conservatives who had opposed him in 1924 and who threatened to do so again. He began by noting the growing interdependence of American society because "[to] rest upon a solid basis the prosperity of every class in the community must go hand in hand with the prosperity of every other class. They must all co-operate." Business groups had long understood this imperative "but they have frequently been tempted to use the power produced by their internal cooperation to the disadvantage of other elements in society." Government action was essential to prevent exploitation of less well organized groups because "democratic government is, after all, nothing but nation-wide co-operation. Its highest duty is to protect all the individuals and classes of a community . . . against the invasion of those interests by any other individual or class; in short, to preserve social, political and economic equality."

McAdoo argued that Americans had long divided over the proper role of government. Some relied on it to solve all social ills without understanding its limitations, while others preferred that it do as little as possible. "Both views are fallacious because they conceive of government as something external . . . instead of looking on it as merely the servant of the people for their common purpose." Thomas Jefferson understood this, and so should Democrats in the 1920s. Jefferson had been misrepresented as a friend of small government by conservatives uneasy with state activism. In political matters he did insist on noninterference by the state, but he also agreed that protection of the economic rights of all sometimes required curtailment of the liberties of some. Modern Democrats must never be beguiled by conservatives' co-option of Jefferson's ideas because their patron saint had bequeathed them a rationale for government action, not inactivity, to combat the same "sinister forces" that McAdoo had battled in New York.

Jefferson and the Democrats' catch-cry of states' rights had also been perverted to suit conservative ends. Jefferson had championed local government against the federal Alien and Sedition Acts, but "he would have been the last man to invoke it, as do the champions of the new states' rights doctrine, as a protection for great interstate monopolies or for great systems of national traffic of an anti-social character with which the individual states are impotent to cope." Interdependence had created a single economic entity in the United States, and only the federal government had the resources and authority to regulate it in the public interest.[89]

McAdoo's defense of federal activism in the name of economic justice justified his initiatives as secretary of the treasury and director general of the USRRA, and it underpinned his proposals during the early 1920s for the soldiers' bonus, railroad reform, and farm relief. After 1924 he sharpened his arguments over the relationship between private rights and public authority as he positioned himself as a defender of national prohibition. In 1924 he had courted dry votes and blamed the wets for orchestrating his defeat in New York; as he contemplated his prospects for

1928 he calculated that a full-blooded defense of prohibition might mobilize the South and West against the East and its proliferating speakeasies. Already New York and Rhode Island had repealed their prohibition laws, and opposition to the Eighteenth Amendment was rife in Al Smith's wing of the party. Dry Democrats needed a champion after William Jennings Bryan's death in July 1925, and McAdoo considered himself to be the rightful heir of the Great Commoner's dry constituency.

McAdoo applied his analysis of individual rights, community interest, and state action to national prohibition in a series of speeches that he published in 1928. He denied the wets' claim that regulation of personal behavior had no place in the Constitution by evoking his version of Jeffersonian republicanism. "If the community as a whole, acting through constitutional channels, solemnly concludes that a particular kind of private conduct is hurtful to the interests of other individuals to the point of impairing the general welfare, then the community is entitled to interdict such conduct." He denied that Jefferson believed that individual rights were immune to government action; inherent or natural rights belonged instead to communities and "he insisted that the rights of individuals within a society are and must be determined by the laws of that society, and are subject to whatever changes and modifications are effected by the will of a constitutional majority." Individual rights "must be more or less flexible" depending on their social context and regulated according to the competing demands of the community's welfare and individuals' liberties.[90]

McAdoo therefore argued for rigorous enforcement of prohibition. The Eighteenth Amendment had been ratified because the majority of the community had decided that the social good of outlawing the liquor trade outweighed individuals' right to engage in it. Now that the amendment had passed, "every unlawful effort on the part of any individual or group to thwart it or defeat it is in direct contravention of the supreme law of the land." The amendment specified that the federal government and the states had concurrent jurisdiction to enforce it, and so efforts by states like Al Smith's New York to repeal their prohibition laws were contrary to their constitutional obligations.

As a teetotaler and vocal supporter of prohibition, McAdoo was well suited to mobilize dry Democrats for another tilt for the nomination. At first he began locally, working in California for the nomination of a dry senatorial candidate in 1926 and pushing a strict enforcement plank through the state Democratic convention. This was seen as the first shot in his battle to prevent California from becoming a Smith state in 1928. Neither man had yet made any announcements about 1928, but both seemed determined to repeat their fight at Madison Square Garden. McAdoo wooed prohibitionists by portraying himself as an implacable defender of their cause. Those who sought modification or nullification of prohibition, he told the Women's Christian Temperance Union (WCTU) in October 1926, were staging a "rebellion against the United States . . . Anarchy and license or regulated liberty? There is but one choice and we unhesitatingly make it—liberty under law and supremacy of the Constitution now and forever!"[91]

Pressure on McAdoo to announce his position on the 1928 nomination began to build toward the end of 1926. His old supporters divided over his prospects; George Fort Milton editorialized in the Chattanooga News that although "not all progressives are dry, and not all dries are progressive," only McAdoo could unite both groups. Other former supporters took the opposite view. "Why don't you do what I have done," Jouett Shouse wrote "[and] simply put politics behind you and enjoy life?" Smith would run again, and this time "a vast number of very thoughtful people in this country [including Shouse himself], who were originally in favor of national Prohibition, have come to the conclusion that the present situation is intolerable and want to see some change in it." If not for the two-thirds rule Smith would win the nomination on the first ballot in 1928, and nothing that McAdoo might do or say could stop him.[92]

Nevertheless, McAdoo tested the waters for yet another nomination campaign. He followed his WCTU speech with one to the Ohio State Bar Association that stressed the evils of Tammany Hall and by implication its acolyte Al Smith. "Behind the propaganda against the Eighteenth Amendment, corrupt municipal politics is making a concerted and nation-wide drive to encompass with its fatal embrace the national politics of this country." To The New York Times McAdoo's speech showed that "he is again a Presidential candidate. And he is coming out in a way not to bring peace but a sword."[93]

The more that McAdoo appealed to the drys, however, the more he marginalized his candidacy. Strict enforcement of prohibition, The New York Times noted after his Ohio speech, was a "blind alley" because it provided no alternative to the Republicans' position. "The country does not show the least sign of rallying to phrases and shibboleths which everybody now feels to have become frayed and worn out." Disregard of prohibition was on the rise everywhere, and calls for its enforcement were doomed to fail. By championing strict enforcement McAdoo appealed to a declining constituency and cheapened his cause by using it as a club to beat his nemesis Al Smith. He thus could offer Democrats only a rerun of the destructive battle of 1924 instead of a new progressive platform. "If the McAdoo cause was to be taken up by his party, the result would be very little rule and a great deal of ruin."[94]

The Times exaggerated the strength of anti-prohibition sentiment in 1927, but even McAdoo worried that his candidacy would be seen as an anti-Smith crusade instead of a campaign for progressive reform. "The difference between Smith and me," he told Mark Sullivan, "is a difference of principles, policies and attitudes to public questions generally." He did not hate Smith personally, but he objected to his Tammany affiliations and his policies. Becoming the darling of the dries mobilized a vocal section of the party, but it also cast him as the hero of an embattled constituency opposed to all that Smith represented. There was indeed a fundamental division in the party, he told Bernard Baruch, but it was not between Smith and McAdoo, or even the wets and the dries, but between Tammany Hall and "progressive elements" of the party whose reformism included, but was not limited to, prohibition.[95]

The response to McAdoo's call was dispiriting. In an inversion of the situation in 1924, now McAdoo and not Smith played the role of blocker, and it was he who bore the brunt of his party's determination not to repeat the debacle of Madison Square Garden. The bitterness of that contest even become a rationale for Smith's nomination in 1928. Arthur Brisbane, editor of the New York *Evening Journal*, told McAdoo in March 1927 that "if Governor Smith is defeated for the nomination, his friends will feel that he was defeated because he was a Catholic. And I believe that under those conditions so many Democrats would refuse to vote the Democratic ticket as to make Democratic victory impossible."[96]

At the beginning of 1926 *The New York Times* noted that attempts to revive McAdoo's candidacy had proven "somewhat disappointing." A year later he detected "a rather hopeless feeling . . . about the possibility of effecting my nomination if I should be a candidate." Edwin Meredith, Wilson's secretary of agriculture and a passionate dry, noted in April 1927 that Smith was gaining strength all over the country, and unless progressive and dry Democrats organized soon the fight would be lost. Yet "they are up in the air without any central figure around whom they are organizing." That central figure was McAdoo, but Meredith feared that his supporters had lost confidence in his prospects.[97]

Rumors of McAdoo's withdrawal from the race for the 1928 Democratic presidential nomination circulated in the press during the first half of 1927. In April he traveled to Washington to consult with his supporters, but was depressed by their response. Even George Fort Milton, his strongest advocate, thought that Democrats who would have jumped on McAdoo's bandwagon three months before now supported Smith. McAdoo decided that his cause was hopeless, but delayed announcing his decision in case the situation changed during the summer. When President Coolidge unexpectedly announced in August 1927 that he would not seek re-election, Milton thought that McAdoo's luck had changed. Democrats might now rethink their flirtation with Smith, with all his electoral liabilities, in favor of McAdoo's safer candidacy in an election they might now win.[98]

McAdoo felt differently. Regardless of Coolidge's decision, "it seems to me that there is an extraordinary apathy and indifference in the ranks of the progressive Democrats which it is difficult, if not impossible, to overcome." His supporters had dispersed and there was no money to mount a campaign. He therefore announced on September 15, 1927, that to defend national prohibition, assist farmers, and ensure "social and economic justice for all classes . . . I prefer to stand aside in order that the field may be left clear, so far as I can clear it, for the development of a leadership that can more effectively gain these ends."[99]

"Well," *The Nation* editorialized, "nothing in his political career has pleased us more than the manner of his leaving it." McAdoo's candidacy had been dead in the water for some time, and now his party could move beyond "the moral wreck of the Wilson administration" and anoint a new leader. McAdoo agreed that his decision "will lead to the party being gobbled up in the maw of the Tammany Tiger," and accepted that his presidential dreams were over. He had tried to defend the interests of "the plain people," he told his wife Eleanor, "but the forces arrayed against me are too strong to ever admit of my nomination . . . I don't care a bit for myself but I sometimes feel that when a man has had all the wonderful experience that I have had, it is a pity that it can't be used for the good of the country."[100]

McAdoo's influence declined rapidly after his withdrawal. His criticisms of Smith became sharper, but neither his target nor his audience seemed to care. In February 1928 he told the Anti-Saloon League that Smith was unworthy of the nomination because he was beholden to liquor interests and Tammany Hall. By signing the repeal of New York's prohibition enforcement law in 1923 Smith had nullified the Eighteenth Amendment's requirement of concurrent state and federal enforcement, and the idea that he would enforce prohibition from the White House was "upon its face an absurdity." This was a familiar argument, and Smith brushed it away by pointing to Article VI of the Constitution that required state judges to enforce federal laws. "The gentleman simply does not know his Constitution," the unschooled Smith said of the lawyer McAdoo. "Further than that, deponent sayeth nothing."[101]

Edwin Meredith was McAdoo's initial choice for the 1928 nomination, but Meredith soon withdrew from consideration and endorsed Newton Baker and Thomas Walsh. To McAdoo Baker was out of the question. "Nothing would be less to Mr. McAdoo's taste than that there should be any serious talk about me as a candidate," Baker told Ralph Hayes. "My beliefs are not adequately zealous in the dry direction, and his doubts about my being 100% pure on that subject would be strongly seconded by his belief that other people have been very much more helpful to him in the New York Convention than I and therefore much better fitted to be his heirs."[102]

For McAdoo Walsh was a more viable candidate; he was well known from his Teapot Dome investigation and as chairman of the New York convention. He was also progressive, dry, and Catholic. This last attribute allowed McAdoo to oppose Smith without suspicion of bigotry. Walsh's progressive credentials were also unimpeachable and his support of prohibition was genuine. With him, unlike Smith, Democrats could fight for agricultural reform, enforcement of prohibition, and clean government. Walsh was receptive to the idea but worried that McAdoo's support might damage his cause. "Don't you see it is hatred for Smith that makes McAdoo put you—another strong Democrat—against Smith?" a supporter warned. "You two will 'kill' each other politically." Walsh entered some early primaries, lost them all, and retired from the race. This left McAdoo with no one to stop Smith. "It is the same old proposition," Meredith told him, "of not being able to beat someone with no one."[103]

In a stunning reversal of 1924 Smith won the 1928 nomination on the first ballot. "The Smith nomination would never have been made if I had stayed in the fight," McAdoo told his daughter Sally, but now he was in an awkward position. He hinted that he might endorse Smith in return for a pledge to enforce prohibition, but Smith was not interested. "All I can say," Franklin Roosevelt told McAdoo after the election, "is to repeat that it was a stupid piece of bungling."[104]

McAdoo waited until three days before the election to announce that "I am absolutely opposed to Governor Smith's position on prohibition and the Eighteenth Amendment, but I shall preserve my party allegiance." This endorsement was so late and so backhanded as to be useless, and McAdoo made it only "for strategic reasons, namely, to be able to fight within the party . . . against the very things that Smith represented." Smith lost in a landslide, and McAdoo felt vindicated. "I had hoped that you would feel that you could do something of this kind and I was gratified that you found it possible," Homer Cummings wrote. "I think it leaves the record in better position that it would have been had you remained silent."[105]

⋙✦⋘

Newton Baker also struggled with the legacies of 1924, but without McAdoo's burden of political ambition. He supported Franklin Roosevelt's call in 1925 for Democrats to formulate "a liberal program of principles" instead of fighting over candidacies, and he worked to enshrine internationalism at the heart of that program. That did not mean flogging the dead horse of immediate entry into the League, but it did involve "every sort of official sympathy from the United States to the League without reopening the question at present of American membership."[106]

Baker now argued for internationalism over discrete issues instead of the one great cause of joining the League. In 1926 he criticized insistence on full payment of wartime loans because America did best with a prosperous Europe rather than a resentful continent struggling to pay its debts. If Americans were obdurate about their loans the Allies would require full payment of reparations from Germany, and then everyone would lose.[107]

Correspondents with letterheads and typewriters, and newspapers close to centers of international trade, were supportive of Baker's views. *The New York Times* doubted that Congress would cancel any loans but saw the wisdom of his case, and Raymond Fosdick wrote from Geneva that his article was "a fresh breeze in a parched land . . . Woodrow Wilson told me of his prophetic belief that you would one day succeed him. He was as sure of it as he was of the future of the League of Nations." Others were less complimentary. "You damn fool," a "True American" wrote. England, France, and Italy had each won territory out of the war, but "what did we get out of this deal [?] Nothing . . . all we done was to leave our brave boys there."[108]

Baker hoped that cancellation of war debts would promote multilateral solutions to common problems. American trade would find wealthier European consumers, the German economy would benefit from reduced reparations, and the United States would win moral authority in its campaign for gradual disarmament. His arguments fell on deaf ears, and linkage of reparations with war debts continued to poison European relations and cripple world trade. Baker opposed the settlement negotiated by Owen D. Young in 1929 that required Germany to pay half a billion dollars per year, two-thirds of which would flow across the Atlantic to repay the Allies' debts for the next two generations. "This seems to me the most unimaginative disaster I can think of," Baker told Ralph Hayes. By making the Allies conduits for war loan repayments and by giving Americans a vested interest in reparations, Young had tied Americans to a system that would bankrupt Europe before plunging it into another war.[109]

As he surveyed the candidates for the 1928 presidential nomination Baker at first saw little hope. In 1925 he feared that McAdoo and Smith would repeat their suicidal contest and ruin the party's prospects for another twenty years. A year later he was more optimistic because his opinion of Smith had improved. The New Yorker had won many friends as a strong campaigner against prohibition and as an effective governor of New York. Baker still doubted that Smith was electable because dislike of Tammany and support for prohibition remained strong in the West and South, but he now considered him to be the outstanding candidate for the nomination.[110]

Another possibility beckoned. Ralph Hayes and others urged Baker to run for the nomination himself on a platform of internationalism abroad and reform at home, but he was unresponsive. His wife was strongly opposed, and "I have lived close to the presidency twice and each time have gone away with the settled conviction that no man who knew anything about [its] responsibilities and burdens . . . would be willing to take it if he could honorably escape." Yet "somebody has to be President and I would not shirk if a situation arose where other people, <u>without stimulation</u>, decided that it was my job . . . Frankly I dread the havoc of prejudice which Smith's nomination would bring and scarcely less the passionate fury which McAdoo would arouse. But there must be somebody, at least as qualified as I, who wants it—would we not all be doing our wisest if we looked for him?"[111]

Much to his relief Baker's presidential boom came to nothing and he attended the Houston convention as an ordinary member of the Ohio delegation. He voted happily for Smith, but was less pleased by other developments. Walter Lippmann lobbied for him to become Smith's running mate to fortify the Happy Warrior's foreign policy credentials. Smith was interested, but ultimately chose Senator Joseph T. Robinson of Arkansas. Baker would have accepted the call but was relieved that it did not come. "If he came home a candidate," Hayes thought, "Mrs. Baker wouldn't let him in the house."[112]

Baker was much less happy with Smith's platform, which said nothing about Muscle Shoals and subordinated tariff reform to the "maintenance of legitimate business and a high standard of wages for American labor." This echoed Republican protectionism and was a major shift from the Democrats' traditional position. The Houston platform was also silent on the League of Nations and condemned "entangling political alliances with foreign nations." Baker was horrified by the platform. "McKinley could have run on the tariff plank," he complained to Franklin Roosevelt, "and Lodge on the one on international relations." Smith was "trying to be more Republican than the Republicans," and voters might well prefer the real thing.[113]

Despite his reservations Baker donated to Smith's campaign and made speeches for him. "My wife and I sit at the radio listening to the speeches of the candidates and every now and then I notice that her face becomes quite radiant. When I ask her if she is particularly pleased at what the candidates are saying, she says, 'No, but I am thanking God I am not listening to you.'" Baker's role in the 1928 campaign came to an abrupt halt in October, when he suffered a heart attack on the way to give a speech for Smith in St. Louis. He was ordered to bed for three weeks and spent the rest of the campaign there. Smith's landslide defeat did not surprise him; he thought that the power of prosperity was too great for any Democrat to overcome and this, rather than religious prejudice, had beaten the Happy Warrior. Hoover had won a great victory, but "he comes into power when prosperity is at the high tide, at which it is impossible to maintain it." The tide did indeed turn, and more quickly than either Baker or McAdoo could have imagined. How they and their party reacted to the ebb of Republican prosperity would widen their political and personal divergence in the troubled decade ahead.[114]

CHAPTER 12

The Great Depression

The Great Depression brought out the best and the worst in Baker and McAdoo. Neither was surprised by the end of prosperity in 1929 because they were convinced that Republican policies had set the economy on a course to catastrophe. Yet the severity and duration of the crisis challenged them both. McAdoo reacted with a rush of ideas, but few of them were well thought out. Baker was bewildered by the crisis and produced few new ideas to combat it. This eroded his reformist reputation even while many Democrats saw him as a presidential possibility in 1932.

Although their personal resources enabled them to avoid the poverty that afflicted millions of their fellow citizens, Baker and McAdoo were alive to the ramifications of the economic collapse. Divergences in their responses to the Depression became increasingly pronounced until their spectacular climax at the 1932 Democratic convention, where they clashed with lasting consequences for their careers and reputations. Baker became a presidential possibility despite himself, and McAdoo played the role of king maker that he had coveted since 1924. That his king-making came at direct and calculated cost to Baker's tentative ambitions made clear in 1932 what had been latent since McAdoo's resignation from the cabinet in 1918. Then they had worked together during the national emergency of World War I; now they divided as their party grappled with the new emergency of the Great Depression.

Despite his disappointment at the outcome of the 1928 election Baker soon answered President Herbert Hoover's call to duty. In his Inaugural Address Hoover announced the creation of a National Commission on Law Enforcement and Observance (NCLEO) "to make such recommendations for the reorganization of

the administration of federal laws and court procedure as may be found desirable."
He appointed George W. Wickersham, who had been President William Howard
Taft's attorney general, as chairman with ten commissioners, including the legal
scholar Roscoe Pound, the sociologist Ada Comstock, five judges, and Newton
Baker.[1]

Unlike McAdoo, Baker had avoided public comment on prohibition and his
private opinions on it were erratic. He had opposed the Eighteenth Amendment in
1920, but in 1923 recognized that "the country is becoming drier and drier." He
still believed that national prohibition was unfortunate because it denied communities the right to regulate liquor in ways that suited their own conditions, but it
was the law of the land and so he obeyed it. He remained respectful of prohibition
but supported Al Smith's wet campaign in 1928. "I am not wet enough for the wets
nor dry enough for the drys and my views on this subject as yet have no approval
from either camp."[2]

Baker's legal skills, Democratic identification, and reticence on prohibition
made him an attractive appointment to the Wickersham Commission, but he did
not seek the honor. He was busy with his law firm, and only reluctantly agreed to
Hoover's request. McAdoo also felt the "obligations of good citizenship," and had
a friend suggest his name to Hoover. "Frankly, I think that it would redound
greatly to the advantage of the President and his administration if I could be induced to serve." Far from being induced, McAdoo was not even asked.[3]

The Wickersham Commission was asked to investigate a range of issues, but it
quickly focused on prohibition. Assisted by a staff of researchers, and bombarded
by ideas from the public, Baker and his colleagues struggled to agree on the future
of the Eighteenth Amendment. "The subject never interested me very much," he
confessed to his brother. "I never think about it except when I am sitting as a member of the Wickersham Commission and if I had my way I would report to the
President that the 18th Amendment should be repealed as a nuisance." Federal
control over something as local and personal as drinking could not work, and
nothing that he learned on the commission convinced him otherwise. Prohibition
also raised issues about the future of American federalism, which had echoes of
the past and warnings for the future:

> I do not like to see the ice broken by the creation of a centralized national police
> power in Washington. Our country is too large and the difficulties of honest and
> efficient administration are too great. If the ice be broken in the interest of Pro-
> hibition, I can imagine many other subjects which will soon have bands of
> propagandists wanting the Federal Government to take over their regulation
> from the States . . . and we shall have all over again the agitation and unhappi-

ness which we had before the Civil War, when Massachusetts was quite sure it knew exactly how Virginia ought to deal with a problem domestic to Virginia.[4]

The Wickersham Commission released its report on prohibition in January 1931. All the commissioners signed twelve recommendations that began by endorsing the Eighteenth Amendment, but that finding was undermined by its successors. These ranged from declarations against any change to the Volstead Act, which enforced prohibition, to a suggestion that the Eighteenth Amendment be amended to allow regulation as well as prohibition of liquor. Some commissioners thought that prohibition was enforceable with more effort; others believed it should be amended, and the rest thought it should be repealed. Each commissioner also appended a personal statement. Baker began his by saying that "in my opinion the 18th Amendment should be repealed and the whole question of policy and enforcement with regard to intoxicating liquors remitted to the States." If immediate repeal was impracticable, then the commission's amendment should be presented to the people. [5]

Response to the report was incredulous. It was a waste of $500,000, a "Wicked-Sham commission," and *The New Yorker* summarized its findings as follows:

> Prohibition is an awful flop.
> We like it.
> It can't stop what it's meant to stop.
> We like it.
> It's left a trail of graft and slime
> It don't prohibit worth a dime
> It's filled our land with vice and crime,
> Nevertheless, we're for it.[6]

McAdoo was scathing of the commission he had once tried to join. He had long criticized those who "[ran] with the hare and hunted with the hounds" on prohibition, and Baker and his colleagues had done just that. Baker preferred another explanation. The Wickersham Committee was expected by the dries to uphold prohibition and by the wets to condemn it. It did neither and so invoked the "fury of the zealous" on both sides. The zealous were indeed furious, but those without axes to grind were also puzzled by the report's contradictions. "It was neither wet nor dry," Congressman Loring Black of New York declared, "—just foggy."[7]

Service on the Wickersham Commission added little to Baker's reputation as a policy maker, but it confirmed his view that "the Constitution of the United States was being endangered by the educated and propertied classes . . . who were gayly defying it because the Eighteenth Amendment interfered with their habits." One day wealthy Americans might need to rely on the Constitution's protection of private property, but they would be reminded by the less well-off that they had disobeyed it when it suited them. Prohibition was indeed swept away in 1933, and by then Baker could see the beginnings of the wider struggle that he had predicted from its decline and fall.[8]

❧❦❧

"Market uncertain," Thomas Gaunt cabled McAdoo on October 17, 1929. "Advise keeping out for the present." Wall Street crashed a week later, ruining the investments of the well-off and beginning a decade of privation for the less fortunate. "I did manage to escape the Wall Street cataclysm," McAdoo told Byron Newton a week after the Crash, "but my investments, like everybody else's, are much reduced in value and one feels a good deal poorer than he was before." He still had stock bought with loans from his brokers, and these had to be covered with cash, and in early November he sold his speculative stock at a loss for fear that the market would fall farther. "This about wipes out the profits I made in stocks for the past six months," he told Eleanor, "but it leaves intact the stocks we already had. I felt that I could not imperil them—so we are out of the market and what we own is paid for."[9]

Baker had invested more conservatively than McAdoo, preferring municipal bonds to stocks and blue-chip companies to speculative concerns, and so he suffered less on Black Thursday. Free of debt and sustained by regular dividends from his law firm, Baker could afford to ride the Depression out. He and his family lived well in their large Cleveland house and continued to take holidays overseas. In 1930 they enjoyed chauffeured tours of Europe and England, and in 1931 paid $3,300 for berths on the SS *Britannic* to the Azores, Gibraltar, Greece, Constantinople, and Egypt. This was a handsome sum in the depths of the Depression, but Baker could easily afford it. McAdoo, on the other hand, with a large and improvident family, shakier professional income, and volatile business ventures, was forced to economize as the 1930s dragged on and worried about money for the rest of his life.[10]

Reminders of the human cost of the Depression soon arrived. A mutual friend told McAdoo in July 1931 that "your friend and admirer Bryon [sic] Newton . . . is despondent. Inactivity and the loss of all his securities upset his constitution. He has reached a stage wherein he is planning to harm himself . . . An invitation for a rest on an estate or a voyage . . . would probably yield the best results." Frank Eichler wrote from the Santa Barbara YMCA with a simpler request. "I need a pair of shoes—size 10 or 10½E if you have a pair not in use please let me have them." Another Californian asked McAdoo to help pay her mortgage. "I'm ashamed to ask—<u>beg</u>—burn this don't let anyone see it. You can come <u>investigate</u> me. I am truthful. But I hate to beg—or loose [sic] my home."[11]

McAdoo was quick to see the political implications of the crisis. Soon after the Crash he told Eleanor that the same interests that had fought him so bitterly in 1913 and 1924 now begged him to "undertake some leadership," but that task belonged to those who had led the nation to ruin. "If, as is sure to happen, business suffers from this panic, the Republicans will lose in 1932 if the Democrats show any intelligence at all—it takes years to get over a financial cataclysm like this one." At the end of 1931 he saw "evidence of an amazing amount of unrest and discontent under the crust . . . here is a deep feeling . . . that it is time [to put] somebody in the White House who will see that they get justice and a fair deal."[12]

McAdoo saw the political implications of the Depression clearly but was hazy on its causes. He blamed Republican taxation and tariff and farm policies for distorting world trade and maldistributing wealth at home. Sensitive to criticism of the Federal Reserve System that he had done so much to create, he thought that the Federal Reserve Board (FRB), but not the whole system, was partly to blame for the Great Crash. In June 1929 he criticized its belated attempts to cool the rampant speculation that had inflated the stock market. Once the Depression had taken hold, however, he attacked the FRB for being too timid. In 1914 he had published the names of banks that had restricted their lending after the outbreak of war, and he suggested that the same tactic might shame banks into loosening credit during the Depression.[13]

McAdoo floated other solutions to the economic crisis. In August 1930 he suggested that all corporations be required to devote some of their earnings to a "reserve for unemployment" to assist employees who lost their jobs during economic downturns. Beyond noting that this would require legislation by all state and federal governments, however, he did not explain how this idea would work. A year later he advocated the creation of a "Peace Industries Board," modeled on the old War Industries Board (WIB), to balance industrial and agricultural production with consumption, and he even suggested a way out of the war debts problem. Cancellation was not politically possible, but Britain and France could surrender some of their colonies to the United States in partial repayment of their loans. Bermuda, Jamaica, Guadeloupe, and Martinique were worth about half of the Allies' war debts, he thought, and the other half could come from bonds issued over British and French assets. "I have observed that neither France nor Great Britain has any sentiment about taking over the possessions of other peoples, including the inhabitants, and I cannot see, therefore, any reason for super-sensitiveness or sentimentality about transferring these island possessions to us."[14]

Closer to home McAdoo proposed in 1930 that the Federal Farm Board provide 60,000 bushels of wheat to help feed the unemployed during the coming winter. After the war Congress had appropriated large sums to feed Belgium and France, and now it was time to help the needy at home. The wheat could be converted into flour and bread to revive employment in the transport, milling, and retail industries and ward off the destitution that threatened millions of Americans.[15]

McAdoo also suggested a plan to combine farm relief with wider economic reform. He thought that raising agricultural incomes, which were 50 percent lower than the urban average, would improve national purchasing power and help end the Depression. He therefore proposed a scheme of compulsory crop management to limit production, reduce stockpiles, and lift prices for major products such as cotton, wheat, and oil. Tariffs on these commodities would also rise to give farmers and oilmen, including McAdoo, "a reasonable return on domestic consumption." He gave no details about how his scheme would operate, but made speeches on its virtues in 1932, and in 1933 endorsed the Agricultural Adjustment Act, which bore a faint resemblance to it.[16]

Baker had more metaphysical explanations for the causes of the Depression but fewer ideas for its alleviation. "The whole story begins with the wastefulness and folly of the World War. We cannot indulge in four years of savagery and destruction without paying the price both materially and spiritually." Wilsonian idealism had been perverted by Republican materialism and now the harvest had come. "Perhaps the one good thing to come out of it all," Baker thought at the beginning of 1933, "is that it is making us all more sympathetic and human. As I look back on the bogus splendor of 1929 . . . I feel quite satisfied that the best prayer for the new year will be the return of a little of our old prosperity and the retention of all our new humanity."[17]

"I do not want to pronounce a credo at this moment," Baker told Ralph Hayes in 1930, "but I will admit to you that I am heartily ashamed of the ineptitudes of our present industrial arrangement." It was unacceptable to make workers bear all the burdens of the trade cycle. He even confessed to his brother Frank that "I am far from sure that the Russians, out of their welter of suffering and wrong headedness are not going to make some contribution to Social theory which will help us all." Baker had not become a Communist, but "of this I am quite sure: that capitalism as we have it cannot and ought not to satisfy a thoughtful person. Involuntary poverty is explosive and it grows daily more so."[18]

But what *was* to be done? Baker found it hard to translate his bewilderment into a coherent plan. "In a general way I am dissatisfied with the almost universal loss of security which the modern man faces. Just how we are to readjust our institutions, I confess I do not know . . . Often it is better to stand still and think than to keep on going if one is merely going in circles, and so for the moment I am standing still and thinking." Beyond suggesting that all banks should be brought into the Federal Reserve System, Baker hesitated to expand federal powers to combat the Depression. Instead of trying to create jobs it was better to limit the working day to six hours to share those that were left.[19]

Otherwise he hesitated to endorse innovative remedies. "We must not let ourselves be satisfied with slogans like 'unemployment insurance,' 'stabilization of industry,' 'immediate relief to all unemployed,' for each of these phrases denotes a principle difficult to apply, with limitations which must be studied and about which honest differences of opinion arise." The government's highest duty was to balance its budget to reduce taxes on private enterprise. Although he criticized Hoover for not doing enough to fight the Depression, Baker also found fault in what he did try to do. In 1932 he declined the president's invitation to lead the Reconstruction Finance Commission (RFC), which sought to revive employment by lending funds to banks and large corporations, because he had no expertise in finance and believed that "the lending of large sums of money, Government money, at low rates of interest to industries to enable them to make goods which nobody can afford to buy . . . does not seem to me to contain the seeds of prosperity."[20]

Old verities promised safer ways out of the crisis. Baker opposed government economic planning because it inevitably led to tyranny. Instead, the United States should create "conditions of freedom under which progress is possible." Of these, two were of paramount importance: world peace and tariff reduction. America had shunned the League of Nations, but it could still support disarmament and mediation of international disputes. Protectionism had eroded global trade, trust, and prosperity; now the time had come to reduce it by coordinated international action that would simultaneously improve the world economy and further the cause of peace.[21]

"In the meantime," Baker declared in August 1932, "we are all entitled to our theories but all theories must give way in the presence of a hungry child." It was vital to give charity to the unemployed, "and those who devote themselves to it must not be regarded as being 'complacent' about the more fundamental remedies which in time must be applied." He donated generously to Cleveland's Community Chest and served as its chairman in 1934. In 1931 he joined the President's Organization on Unemployment Relief to oversee federal, state, and private relief for the winter ahead, and he became chairman of the National Citizens' Committee for Welfare and Relief Mobilization of 1932. This was the kind of activity that Baker liked; wary of economic theorizing, yet desperate to alleviate the suffering he saw around him, relief work confirmed his view that government worked best when it coordinated and augmented, but did not usurp, private philanthropy.[22]

Baker worked hard for the National Citizens' Committee and led it for four years. Although Congress had appropriated $300 million for relief in 1932, this was nowhere near enough to sustain the nation's unemployed, and Baker's committee mobilized local communities to make up the shortfall. "America will be on trial this winter," he warned in September 1932. "The peacetime battle which is being waged against unemployment may not be as spectacular as were some of our World War battles, but the consequences in terms of human values may be even more devastating." He ran similar campaigns in 1933 and 1934, and in 1935 successfully lobbied for tax exemption of corporate gifts to Community Chests.[23]

Baker's belief that private charity and local action were preferable to government welfare hardened as the New Dealers extended the federal government's reach after 1932. Federal funds and programs were important to ameliorate the effects of the Depression, but they should operate only as last resorts after private and local agencies had exhausted their resources. "The deterioration in the manhood and self-reliance of our people attendant upon the necessity of accepting material relief is in itself disastrous," Baker told a correspondent," but if there be withdrawn at the same time the sympathy, social service and understanding which modern character building agencies have learned how to supply, the picture becomes many shades darker."[24]

Baker's retreat into traditionalism hastened as the Depression dragged on. In October 1934 he published "Can Uncle Sam Do Our Good Neighboring?" in the *Saturday Evening Post*. The Depression was now five years old and there was no end in sight. Private charity, with its focus on the health, education, and character of the poor, had been replaced by government relief that addressed only the material needs of its recipients. Old virtues of independence and personal responsibility had been sapped by public welfare, and "it is an insidious development that honest folk do not at first recognize because their need for assistance is so great and a bit of dole so welcome." Federal relief treated recipients as if their problems were all the same; private and local charity focused on individual needs, and propinquity of giver and recipient ensured that help was neither wasted nor taken for granted. Uncle Sam would need to keep paying relief for some time yet, but his money should be dispensed by local charities and communities instead of Washington bureaucrats.[25]

Two months later Baker turned from localism to individualism. In "The Decay of Self-Reliance," published in the *Atlantic Monthly*, he mourned the loss of America's "pioneer spirit." Two years of war, the "moral disaster" of prohibition, and now the Depression had eroded the dignity and autonomy of the individual. Government now bore many of the responsibilities once left to individuals, to the detriment of their industry and thrift. "Only yesterday, a woman who had long served as a domestic in the family of one of my friends presented her resignation and explained it by saying that she and her husband had decided to visit the

World's Fair in Chicago and on their return to go on relief!" Baker did not doubt the need for federal supplementation of local and private charity but feared that "we are coming more and more to regard the State as a legitimate and responsible carrier of all individual, group, and class burdens."[26]

Philosophy was one thing but practice was another. "Human nature is such," he remarked in 1932, "that almost any one will give a handout once with some little grace, but continuous handouts day after day are often not so generously bestowed." In March 1934 a Cleveland socialite offered to sell him her string of pearls. "<u>Only this crisis</u> forces me to dispose of my necklace, for which my husband paid seven thousand dollars . . . I would 'sacrifice' it for . . . $2500 (a real bargain)." Baker brusquely declined, but was gentler three months later with another Clevelander who sought a job for her husband. "You will realize Mr. Baker what this all means to us when I tell you there is seven in the family and we are trying so hard to keep our spirits up but this terrible deadly fear is getting into our hearts." Baker replied with sympathy but little assistance; "the tragedy of this depression reaches everybody in one way or another and nobody's personal means or capacity for helpful advice is equal to dealing with even a fraction of the pathetic and undeserved distresses which come to his attention."[27]

Letters from strangers could be brushed off, but when the Depression affected Baker's own family it was harder to philosophize away. Before the Great War his younger brother Julian had drifted into alcoholism and stumbled from job to job. Julian had served in the American Expeditionary Forces (AEF) but could not settle back into civilian life. In 1922 he was unemployed, drinking heavily, and reliant on his brothers for financial support. "It isn't pleasant to be without an overcoat and shoes," he wrote from New York City in December. By 1930 Julian had moved to Cleveland. "He has also lost all his teeth," Newton told his other brother Frank, "and generally does not look well, though well dressed and sober this last visit." Between them he and Frank supported Julian and paid for his children's education and upkeep.[28]

Through Julian Newton learned about the underside of Cleveland's Depression. "I have been out every day from six in the morning making the rounds of shops, employment agencies and every place where I thought there might be a chance," Julian reported in April 1930, "but industrially, the town is dead. Unemployment is worse now than at any time since last Oct. And steadily growing worse." Newton replied with good cheer and small checks. "By the way," Julian wrote in September 1930, "will you tell me how old I am? I have lied so much about it trying to get a job that I have myself puzzled." He was 53, and his prospects of finding work were bleak indeed.[29]

In 1932 Newton lent Julian money to buy a grocery in Cleveland. Within a year, and without repaying the loan, Julian had sold the store. "After reading your article in the Sat. Eve. Post I wondered if I dared write you again for help," he wrote in 1934. "It kind of made me feel a good deal like a laboratory guinea pig on which you had been trying out your theories and had found them unsuccessful." Newton's checks resumed and whatever was left of Julian's pioneer spirit was not tested again. Those checks to Julian made the difference between his want and destitution, but they were also regular reminders that "all theories must give way in the presence of a hungry child."[30]

Baker was drawn into the 1932 presidential race almost—but not quite—despite himself. Democratic prospects rose as the Depression deepened; the party did very well in the 1930 congressional elections and it had high hopes for the presidential election in 1932. As interest in the Democratic nomination became more intense, Baker was drawn into a vortex of speculation from which he only half-heartedly tried to escape. By the end of 1931 he had become an unofficial but reluctant candidate who felt uneasy about running but unwilling to disappoint his friends by withdrawing.

At first Baker preferred to discuss policies instead of candidacies. At the end of 1930, with his experiences with the Wickersham Commission in mind, he argued against focusing on prohibition in 1932. Democrats should instead restate their opposition to high tariffs and their Wilsonian internationalist convictions. This did not mean immediate entry into the League of Nations, but it did involve working with it to revive trade and untangle war debts and reparations. "I have a feeling that we are now in a time when idealism is again possible. The present economic depression has made us all poor together and . . . only the poor can have enough sympathy to generate an idealistic philosophy." Besides repeating his desire to extend the Federal Reserve System, however, he offered few suggestions on domestic policies.[31]

In July 1931 Baker spoke at Williams College on "World Economic Planning." The global economy was now so interdependent that an international conference needed to enact simultaneous tariff reductions. Above all, nations must cooperate to forge a lasting peace because "modern war is a loaded pistol, aimed at the heart of civilization itself with its hair-trigger held by an unsteady hand." Prosperity was impossible without peace, and peace was impossible without prosperity. Americans had refused the internationalist call in 1919, but Baker was sure that they would now answer it.[32]

Baker's speech excited speculation over whether it signaled his intention to seek the 1932 nomination. His answer seemed clear at the beginning of 1931 but grew vague as the year wore on. In April he told George Foster Peabody that he did not want to be president because he had already contributed enough to public life and his candidacy "would simply reopen a lot of old war time controversies." He remembered hearing a preacher once say that a man needed to be sure of two calls before he took the pulpit: "he had to be quite sure that he was called to preach the Gospel and, second, he had to be equally sure that other people were called to hear him preach it . . . and I am quite determined that I am not going to fool myself into supposing that I have either of these calls if I can help it."[33]

His friends were not so sure. Ralph Hayes, his former secretary and now a senior executive in the Coca-Cola Company, distributed copies of Baker's Williams College speech and created detailed lists of their recipients. Baker reacted with affection and embarrassment. "That you are to me a child of my spirit, you know," he told Hayes in August 1931, "but I tremble when I see how ruthlessly you apply the principle of 'loyalty first' to yourself and for my benefit!" "I suppose I could end it all by imitating General Sherman," Baker wrote in September 1931, "but somehow I hardly feel I have the right to do that although I have the deepest wish to have this Presidential talk end."[34]

Hayes's determination to impose presidential burdens on Baker was encouraged by a poll of Democratic newspaper editors in September 1931, which showed that most of them expected FDR to win the nomination but that a majority thought Baker the better choice. "Here is a man without press agents, propagandists, or organization, who is not even an avowed candidate," the *Richmond News Leader* noted, "and yet . . . he was the first choice of the editors interviewed in thirty-four states." The convention was still nine months away, but the poll suggested that influential Democrats were worried that FDR—described by Baker's supporter Walter Lippmann as "an amiable boy scout" and "a pleasant man who, without any important qualifications for the office, would very much like to be president"—had more charm than substance.[35]

Encouraged by the editors' poll but still without formal approval from Baker, Hayes sounded out anti-Roosevelt Democrats. He found that many Pennsylvanians wanted to have Baker on their primary ballot and that he could expect to win sixty of the Keystone State's seventy-two delegates. Hayes also made contact with Jouett Shouse, head of the Democratic National Committee's (DNC) permanent organization, and Belle Moskowitz, Al Smith's closest political advisor, to discuss tactics. Smith and FDR had fallen out, and the Happy Warrior was determined to block Roosevelt's nomination. Hayes reported to Baker that "X [Shouse] tells me today that if you will consent to be supported, Z [Smith] will not only eliminate himself, but will throw to you every particle of strength he can muster." After talking with Moskowitz, Hayes reported that "[Smith's] immediate group are loyal to him and their ambition is not dead but they think he will not, and probably should not, be nominated and their sincere alternative choice is B." Even FDR knew about these talks. "Confidentially," he told Josephus Daniels, "I understand that the Smith-Shouse-Raskob crowd really want Young, but that the latter declines to run and that they will turn with a deep sigh to Newton Baker":

> I don't need to tell you how much I admire Newton and what a wonderful asset he can be to the Party during the next four years if we win. The trouble is that he labors under very definite political handicaps. Because of, or rather in spite of, his perfectly legitimate law practice he is labeled by many progressives as the attorney for J. P. Morgan and the Van Schweringens; he is opposed by Labor; he would be opposed by the German Americans; and also by the bulk of the Irish because of his consistent League of Nations attitude up to this year. As they say, "them are the sad facts"![36]

Baker's ambivalence did not make Hayes's job easy. He declined to enter the Pennsylvania primary or to have Ohio's delegation pledged to him, and told Hayes that "It is . . . clear to me that X and Y [Shouse and Moskowitz] are looking wildly about for a charger to ride in their battle, and that I ought not to bare my back for their saddle . . . I hope you will not think me difficult or unbending about this but I am not as enthusiastic as you are to accomplish the particular end you have in view."[37]

Yet his friends sensed that Baker's resistance was weakening. Instead of saying that he did not want the nomination, he now told them that he did not think that it would come to him. Two factions supported his nomination: those who "wanted any stick that could beat Roosevelt," and those who saw him as the "legatee of the Wilson tradition," but they were so antagonistic that they would not cooperate to nominate him. Baker explained in December 1931 that he had no desire to be president, but

> I am obliged to say, however, that I do regard the present situation in this country and in the world as of such tragic importance that there are conceivable circumstances in which I would not feel that I had a right to consult my own preferences or my own judgment. So you see my hope is that the Party will adopt a candid and constructive platform and will be able to select a standard bearer whom I can follow, but I cannot exclude myself from the possibility, however remote it may be, that for reasons which I cannot control this thing may present an obligation which I have no right to decline.[38]

Others now looked harder at Baker's prospects. In April 1931 Desha Breckinridge, editor of the *Lexington* (Kentucky) *Herald*, thought that "if he can reconcile the Wickersham report which he has signed, with his personal opinion which he wrote, I think he would be just the man to reconcile the factional differences in the Democratic Party." Claude Bowers told FDR in June that Baker was now his main rival. He "would like the nomination, provided it fell into his lap," but his liabilities were heavy. Ordinary voters found him "up-stage and intellectually high hat," and he was closely identified with the unpopular League of Nations. Six months later Bowers still believed that "it will either be Roosevelt or Baker," but noted that "there has been a tremendous ground swell Baker-ward recently."[39]

Baker had become a key player in the struggle for the nomination whether he liked it or not. By the end of 1931 Hayes had become excited by his prospects but exasperated by his reticence. "Your refusal to run is being capitalized as a final refusal in propaganda from quarters where your elimination would be regarded as the Summum Bonum," he wrote at the end of November. Couldn't Baker say something publicly "with possibly—or God's sake—1/2 of 1% more receptivity injected into it? . . . if you hand over this nomination and election by default to the boy scouts or stuffed shirts, I intend to bellow like a bull for the rest of my life." [40]

At the beginning of 1932 Baker relented, but only slightly. He allowed Hayes to release a medical opinion on his ability to withstand the rigors of campaigning. Professor R. W. Scott of Western Reserve University concluded that Baker had sufficiently recovered from his heart attack in 1928 to run a campaign in 1932 "provided that it be not too strenuous." This was scarcely a ringing endorsement, but to Hayes it showed that Baker's health was at least as good as Roosevelt's.[41]

Baker also agreed to clarify his position on the League of Nations, which was his biggest electoral liability. Baker's stance on the League had changed during the 1920s from passionate support of immediate entry to a more measured view that the United States should assist but not join it, and yet voters retained "an idée fixe that hell and hot water may not thaw out of them—namely that your chief political concern and title is that of a kleagle in an evil international hierarchy engaged in preying on honest Americans." Why not try again to reassure them? "I don't want to see you put in the position, within the national party, of a kind of curio to be regarded with unbounded admiration but not to be taken off the shelf and used."[42]

Hayes's fears deepened after Baker's speech to the League of Nations Association in January 1932. Baker had sung the League's praises and bemoaned America's failure to join it in 1920, and the press read this as proof that he was still committed to that policy. In fact, he had thought since 1926 that immediate entry was not politically possible. He therefore believed that Democrats should promise in 1932 to work with the League "in every way we can without incurring the domestic discord which would be involved in premature membership." At Hayes's urging he repeated this point before he left on a cruise to Mexico, this time stating that

"I would not take the United States into the League if I had the power to do so until there is an informed and convinced majority sentiment in favor of that action in the United States."[43]

By removing this major obstacle to his nomination, Baker's statement was seen as a declaration of his eagerness to accept it. Yet he denied that it had a "political purpose." He had merely restated a view that he had held for some years, and had no desire to use his statement as a springboard to the nomination.[44]

This was disingenuous. Baker's statement was designed to make Hayes's job easier, because otherwise he would not have made it. This is not to say that he had decided to seek the nomination in the conventional way, but he had now allowed Hayes to promote him as a compromise candidate should the party need him. Clarifying his position on the League and releasing his medical details were part of that limited brief; Hayes and Lippmann implored Baker to follow his League statement with a manifesto on domestic issues, but he refused because that "would tend to cast him in the role of a candidate." He had already stated that war debts should be cancelled, tariffs reduced, Muscle Shoals kept in public ownership, the Federal Reserve System expanded, and federal expenditures retrenched, and that would have to do.[45]

Publicly aloof from the fray, Baker was polite about its protagonists. He contributed ideas on foreign policy to FDR's campaign and assured him that he had no intention of creating a deadlock at the convention. Off the record he was more critical. FDR had renounced the League, opposed cancellation of war loans, and criticized efforts to join the World Court. Baker thought this "a very thoughtless utterance on a very grave problem," and it further convinced him that FDR was too "politically minded" to deserve the presidency. He praised John Garner, the Texan favorite son, as "a wise, honest man [who] would make an informed and firm President," save only for his lack of interest in foreign affairs. He repeated his opinion that Al Smith had been the best governor of New York since the Civil War and was "so real and genuine a man and so valiant a leader," but also that he had no chance of winning the nomination.[46]

Hayes was frustrated by Baker's reticence but never doubted that it was genuine. Outsiders, though, saw it as evidence of weakness. The longer that Baker stayed out of the race while hinting that he would accept its prize the more he appeared too weak or too proud to fight for it. "I should like to have Baker on the [Supreme] Court, and I think he would make a good Secretary of State under the directing authority of another man," Felix Frankfurter noted in February 1932. "Not the least amazing thing to me is that the same people, e.g. Walter Lippmann, who get apoplectic about Frank Roosevelt's lack of courage should be passionate about Baker. If ever there was a fellow who lacked leadership, his name is Newton

Deal [sic] Baker." Oswald Garrison Villard, editor of *The Nation*, was even more damning. Baker had long since betrayed the liberal ideals of his youth and now hid his conservatism behind eloquence and sentimentality. "Newton Baker has in him the makings of a splendid fascist President." He was as likely as Hoover to fall in with Wall Street financiers, and "should it be necessary to shoot down hungry Americans [he] would do it without turning a hair, and then do a beautiful speech about it with sobs in his voice and a clear message from God in it." [47]

Others saw arrogance behind Baker's refusal to be measured by the primaries or even to declare that he would accept the nomination. Jouett Shouse told Hayes in March 1932 that Smith had no chance for the nomination and would ultimately throw his support to Baker if only he and his supporters "were less chilled by what they regard as your aloofness from any indication of willingness to submit to a call." Baker's quasi-candidacy gained momentum because of Hayes's efforts, some Democrats' concerns about FDR, and Roosevelt's failure to win two-thirds of the delegates before the convention met, but Baker did little to help his cause. "[Leonard] Ayers [sic] and I dined in a speakeasy last night and cried in our beer for an hour over your execrable habits and conduct in this respect," Hayes wrote. "It isn't right." [48]

<hr/>

William McAdoo approached the 1932 election from a different perspective. His failure to win the nomination in 1924 and then to influence it four years later left him searching for a new role within the party. "Except for occasional lapses, I am as full of energy, determination and spirit as I ever was, and whether I last long or not, I intend to continue to 'dare dangerously' until I go," he told his daughter Nona a few months before his sixty-sixth birthday and the Wall Street Crash. "A flat life makes no appeal to me. There are some things that I wanted to do for the people of the United States before I go, but that chance is gone and I am reconciled to it. There are many interesting things left for a private citizen to do if he knows how to do them." [49]

Private life had its attractions, but its allure for McAdoo was never as strong as it was for Baker. His legal practice was much worse affected by the Depression than was Baker's, and his real estate and oil speculations fared badly after 1929. This left him with time to re-engage in public life, and he was alive to the political opportunities that the Depression had created.

At first he focused on internal party politics. He saw Smith's defeat in 1928 as proof of the dangers of flirting with anti-prohibition and pro-business policies, and he was determined that Democrats should not make the same mistake again. When Smith's chairman of the DNC John J. Raskob tried to push the party toward anti-prohibition and a conservative economic platform in 1932, McAdoo swung into action. "When the party made the frightful blunder of surrendering to Smith and the wet elements in the east in 1928," he told Josephus Daniels, "it was a decree of death so far as party success in that campaign was concerned. Why should the party be compelled to follow that leadership any longer, and why should the wet millstone be continued around its neck?"[50]

The 1928 campaign had left the party heavily in debt, and Raskob's creation in 1929 of a permanent publicity organization within the DNC meant that it remained heavily dependent on his money. Raskob lent the DNC $10,000 each month between January 1928 and June 1932 to cover its costs, but his largesse came with strings. It was in the form of loans and not gifts, leaving the party deeply in debt to its national chairman, and his strong identification with anti-prohibition, eastern business, and Al Smith made other Democrats nervous that he would use his hold over the party to commit it to the repeal of prohibition. These concerns were well founded; Raskob called a meeting of the DNC in March 1931 to discuss a plan to institute "home rule" by which individual states could opt out of the Eighteenth Amendment and control liquor consumption according to their own conditions and preferences. This change was seen as part of Raskob's wider agenda to support Smith in 1932 and to deflect the party from adopting adventurous economic policies to combat the Depression.[51]

Democrats like McAdoo, who supported prohibition and objected to Smith and his business allies, reacted strongly against Raskob's attempts to use the DNC to change party policy. McAdoo declined to attend Raskob's DNC meeting, preferring instead to release a statement that "to impinge the next national campaign, as [Raskob] proposes, upon restoration of the liquor traffic, to the subordination of the grave economic and social problems now tearing at the vitals of democracy . . . would be fatuous in the extreme."[52]

The DNC deferred a decision on Raskob's prohibition plan until an unspecified later date. It did, however, make clear that the party was divided not only over prohibition but also over the economic and political implications of Raskob's proposals. Franklin Roosevelt, recently elected to a second term as governor of New York, organized opposition to Raskob to win favor with southern and western Democrats in advance of his own campaign for the 1932 presidential nomination. By linking anti-prohibition to economic conservatism and Al Smith, FDR hoped not only to block Raskob's attempts to have the DNC assume a policy-making role but also to direct the party away from the "Eastern Group" that had nominated Smith and now pushed for an electoral strategy to emphasize repeal of prohibition over a reformist economic platform.[53]

McAdoo sympathized with advocates of bread before booze, not only because he was committed to the Eighteenth Amendment but also because "relegalizing liquor will not put food into a single hungry mouth, nor provide employment for the great army of jobless men and women in the United States." Yet he was slow to see the implications of FDR's opposition to Raskob. He could not forget that Roosevelt had led opposition to him at the New York convention in 1924 and that in 1928 had again supported Smith. Since then FDR had joined Smith and Raskob in supporting repeal of prohibition and had failed to curb Tammany Hall. "I don't want you to assume," McAdoo told a friend after the DNC meeting, "that I base my opinions about Roosevelt on his personal course toward me. I disregard that. It is what he has descended to and now stands for that renders him, in my judgment, one of the weakest men we could nominate for the Presidency." FDR was "not a man of great ability," his health was poor, and the country had had enough of presidential candidates from New York.[54]

By opposing Raskob and courting southerners and westerners, FDR had built a coalition very similar to McAdoo's in 1924, but McAdoo was slow to realize this. "Without meaning to be vain," he told Edward House in January 1931, "I think I had a very strong hold on the masses. I don't know how strong it is now . . . but it might be vitalized if I were willing to make the effort." He was still undecided, but "if the Democrats could put forward some militant and progressive man who has some hold on the popular imagination, who is free from boss and machine taint or control, and who is, at the same time, sound on prohibition . . . and who has some really definite and constructive ideas about the economic and sociological problems of the day," they would win easily in 1932. It was not hard to guess who he had in mind.[55]

McAdoo's presidential ambitions, never far from the surface, were aroused as he surveyed the Democratic field for the 1932 nomination. Having written FDR off, he found significant faults in all his other rivals. Owen Young, he told Baruch in May 1931, was certainly the ablest of the possible nominees, but through his presidency of General Electric was identified with that company's open shop policy and with corporate interests more generally. Voters would see little difference between Young and Hoover, and so would have no reason to change.[56]

By then McAdoo had also decided that Newton Baker was an unacceptable candidate. The Ohioan was "an able fellow but nothing like so able as Young," and his health was poor. He had also supported the wets on the Wickersham Commission, had alienated labor by his support of the open shop, and was too close to big business through his legal practice. "His repeal statement was a surprise," George Fort Milton wrote in February 1932, "and of course eliminates him from any consideration by our group." McAdoo agreed that Baker had cast aside his old reformist ideas and now thought him disloyal. "As you know," he told Byron Newton in September 1931, "I have always thought well of Baker, but I could never understand why, in view of our past association and the very definite and valuable marks of friendship I have given him, he allied himself with my enemies in the 1924 convention." Baker, he thought, was "thoroughly cold blooded and selfish."[57]

McAdoo then tested his own support. "I am foolish enough to think," he told the publisher William Kiplinger in June 1930, "that I could come nearer [to] winning a victory for the Democrats than any other man now in sight. I say this without egotism." His nomination was unlikely because those who had blocked him in 1924 would surely try to do so again, and so he would not actively seek the honor. "Of course, to be perfectly frank, conditions might develop where I might change my mind." The response in 1930 was underwhelming, but he tried again a year later and toyed with the idea of a national speaking tour. "I am getting a good many letters from friends throughout the country urging me to sanction movements in my behalf," he told a supporter in Missouri. He was not ready to do so yet, but saw no reason why others should not work for his nomination.[58]

Everywhere that McAdoo looked for support in 1931, however, he found that FDR had been there before him. Roosevelt had by then won prominent single-issue Progressives, including George W. Norris on water power, Cordell Hull on tariff reduction, Key Pittman and Burton K. Wheeler on remonetarization of silver, and Thomas Walsh on the St. Lawrence Seaway, to his cause. With the exception of Wheeler, who had run on La Follette's ticket, these men had all supported McAdoo in 1924 but were now in FDR's camp. Even the South now waved Roosevelt's banner and had forgotten its native son in California.[59]

Of the single-issue reformers only prohibitionists remained enthusiastic for McAdoo, but public opinion had so turned against them that they could not deliver enough votes to win his nomination. To the contrary, one supporter told him, "there has been recently a very systematic effort made to convince [us] . . . that we shall have to consent . . . to the nomination of an opponent of prohibition, and along that line much missionary work is being done for Roosevelt and Baker." When some prohibitionists came out for McAdoo in October 1931, *The Outlook and Independent* was scornful. "Alas for these good people! In the realm of practical politics their hero is now as dead as so much burned-over timber. Mr. McAdoo was not strong enough to win the Democratic nomination in 1924 when the drys had the party in a stranglehold. What chance has he of winning it now that the drys have lost their grip? . . . By 1928 McAdoo was as outmoded as Bryanism; today he is but a walking monument to a hopelessly lost cause."[60]

More dispiriting news came in 1931. By June McAdoo knew about the split between Smith and Roosevelt and that FDR's support was wide but not deep because of concerns over his character and policies, but it seemed that Baker, or perhaps Young, would be the beneficiaries of these developments. Baker and Young had weaknesses as nominees, James H. Moyle told McAdoo in November 1931, because of doubts that "their hearts beat in sympathy with that of the average man." There was no doubt about McAdoo's popular appeal, "except for the fact that you seem to have dropped out of the picture, and your followers are wandering in the wilderness for the lack of a real leader with not only the right ideals and record, but activity."[61]

Friends closer to home were even more discouraging. Bernard Baruch declined to fund McAdoo's campaign because he wanted to remain publicly neutral in 1932. George Fort Milton, who had fought so hard for McAdoo in 1924, reported that "I do not see how a successful fight can be conducted to take the Democratic Party out of its present hands . . . , and I would hate very much to see you sacrificed in a hopeless and a futile combat." Brice Clagett wrote in September 1931 that "I believe it extremely doubtful, to put it mildly, whether there is any chance for your nomination." The wets were on the ascendant and no one wanted to revisit the acrimony that had almost destroyed the party in 1924. "I hope much that Roper and House and you," FDR told Homer Cummings, "can pour oil on the somewhat troubled waters of [McAdoo's] mind. Mac is a fine fellow, but I don't think that he has any perspective about the present situation and that it is only his real friends who can persuade him that a last minute insurgency will get him nowhere and will do harm to the progressive ideals with which all of us were associated in the old days."[62]

Discouraged on all sides, McAdoo renounced his presidential dreams at the end of September 1931. "Under the present plutocratic control of the Democratic party," he told Senator Furnifold Simmons, "I would have no show whatever in a Democratic national convention. Moreover, even if I were willing to seek the nomination, I haven't the money to make the fight, and I don't know where I could get it."[63]

McAdoo soon bounced back. Distrustful of FDR, opposed to Baker, skeptical of Young, and hostile to Smith, he looked elsewhere to find a candidate and settled on Speaker of the House of Representatives John Garner of Texas. Garner supported prohibition, had long opposed Wall Street interests, demanded full repayment of war loans, and rejected internationalist remedies for the economic crisis. "Really, of all the men mentioned, I think best of him," McAdoo told friends in February 1932. "He is not a scholar or a statesman like Woodrow Wilson, but he has the cardinal virtues, is a loyal and dependable man, and I believe that he would be a better President than any of those who are prominently mentioned for the office." Ralph Hayes reported to Newton Baker that McAdoo had endorsed Garner for intensely personal reasons. "I think that what is most in [his] mind is to prevent the nomination from going to New York. He has a 'hate' against all of New York because of his experience in 1924."[64]

Garner's chief backer was the newspaper magnate William Randolph Hearst, who supported him to block Smith, Baker, and Roosevelt. Hearst despised Smith and Baker with equal ferocity; he and the Happy Warrior had been sworn enemies since 1919, and Baker's identification with Wilson and internationalism disqualified him as a weak echo of a president and worldview that Hearst detested. "There are in the United States of America approximately 125,000,000 persons," he told delegates to the Chicago convention, "and among the least desirable of these as a candidate for President is Newton D. Baker of Ohio." Hearst's objections to FDR were less visceral, but he dismissed him as intellectually shallow, too partial to internationalism, and—even worse—insufficiently deferential to Hearst.[65]

According to McAdoo's confidant Tom Storke, Hearst asked McAdoo to lead the campaign for Garner in the California primary in return for his support if McAdoo later ran for the US Senate. California's forty-four delegates, with Garner's forty-six Texans, would make the Speaker a significant player at the convention. McAdoo jumped at the chance; winning California for Garner would propel him back onto the national political stage, and the prospect of running for the Senate backed by Hearst's deep pockets and influential newspapers was appealing.[66]

McAdoo's announcement for Garner attracted much attention, but its impact was unclear. It coincided with Smith's own declaration that he would seek the nomination and seemed to place McAdoo in the anti-Roosevelt camp. Yet FDR's supporters were undismayed. "The statement of Mr. McAdoo is wholesome," Daniel Roper told him, "in that it releases those McAdoo men who, like myself, are already committed to you, but who were under a cloud of suspicion as belonging to a McAdoo movement under cover." By withdrawing from the race McAdoo had ensured that the Democrats would not suffer a repeat of his battle with Smith in 1924, but their antagonism made it unlikely that he would help Smith win the nomination. McAdoo's differences with Baker were also well enough known to discredit the notion that he supported Garner as a stalking horse for Baker.[67]

McAdoo's differences with FDR were nothing like as bitter as his conflict with Smith or as deep as his differences with Baker, so FDR's group felt that they could bargain with him at the convention if they needed to. Garner's friends thought that McAdoo's endorsement had significantly boosted his campaign, but it had also put Garner in a double bind: he was now seen as an anti-Roosevelt candidate, which hurt his chances of inheriting FDR's support should he fail to win the nomination himself, but it also damaged his standing with Smith and Baker's supporters. "Of course New York has never liked McAdoo," Peyton March told Baker, "and McAdoo's support of Garner is the finishing blow to any consideration of his name by the eastern group."[68]

But first there was the California primary to win. McAdoo led the Garner ticket and stumped the state, urging voters to reject Roosevelt and Smith because they had had enough of New Yorkers, Tammany Hall, and Wall Street. Garner, by contrast, was a son of Texan soil, experienced in national politics, and unafraid of the financial titans who had led the nation to ruin. "We must put the mace of power into the hands of a man like GARNER, who has the Jacksonian courage to drive the crooks and money changers from the temple of government and demonstrate that a strong, clean, and economical administration of national affairs can be secured for the people." McAdoo said nothing about prohibition because Californians were decidedly wet, and the less that they knew about Garner's dry views the better.[69]

The California primary on May 4, 1932, was a triumph for Garner, Hearst, and McAdoo. Roosevelt and Smith split the wet vote, while McAdoo's campaigning and Hearst's publicity delivered the Texan a clear victory. "Well, Mac, you've swung California all right," a friend wrote, "and it was a damned good job, and one that has put confusion in the Philistines." McAdoo had rejoined the great game of national politics and went to Chicago determined to make the most of the hand that he had been dealt. "Bill McAdoo has staged the biggest comeback in a generation," his old colleague Josephus Daniels announced. "He is here with the goods, and you had better keep your eyes on him during this convention."[70]

⋨⋇⋩

The Democratic convention of 1932 has become one of the best known in American history, partly because of its own drama but mostly because of its importance as the dawn of the Age of Roosevelt. It was clear by the summer of 1932 that the Democrats would win the presidency, and so the stakes at the convention were very high. Had the party chosen differently, Elliot Rosen has concluded, "the course of our nation's history would have been radically different. There would have been no New Deal."[71]

Baker and McAdoo played key roles in this critical moment, and they played them in conscious opposition to each other. Their roles reflected their temperaments: McAdoo was deeply involved in the intrigue at Chicago, while Baker remained in Cleveland as the *deus ex machina*, ready to break a deadlock created by professional politicians whom he understood but could not fully join. In the end the professionals won, but Baker came closer to the nomination and the presidency than he had ever imagined or Hayes had ever hoped.

Hayes arrived in Chicago some days before the convention began and lobbied delegates to support Baker as their second choice. His argument was straightforward: FDR had come to Chicago with a majority, but not two-thirds, of the delegates and his chances of winning any more were slim. Smith's delegates were rock solid because of their bitterness at Roosevelt's treatment of him; Garner's patron Hearst was hostile to FDR, and none of the other favorite sons had enough votes to swing the nomination. If the party was to avoid an impasse like the one that had ruined it in 1924, it had to find a compromise candidate quickly. That person should be Baker, who offered a record of strong leadership during the national emergency of 1917–1918. Because he had stayed out of the nomination fight, Baker owed no favors to the party's factions and could unite them against the GOP in the election.[72]

Hayes was delighted to find that Baker was indeed the second choice of many delegations, particularly in the South but also in the Midwest and on the East Coast. He was repeatedly told that FDR would hold his strength for three ballots, but then his delegates would melt into Baker's column. It was therefore vital to block Roosevelt's attempt to abolish the two-thirds rule before voting began. To that end Baker announced that delegates had been elected on the basis that the two-thirds rule would apply, and "sensitive men would find it difficult to defend a candidate who started out with a moral flaw in his title."[73]

McAdoo also arrived early for the convention and set to work for Garner. He found that the Texan had very little support outside his own state and California, leaving him no hope of winning the nomination himself but with ninety votes with which to bargain. McAdoo met Jim Farley and Breckinridge Long from FDR's campaign, but told them that he would not help them "unless Baker became a real threat." He also made a well-publicized call on Al Smith. The two men, with Baruch in the middle, talked for some time but emerged tight lipped as to what they had discussed. Smith later claimed that McAdoo had agreed to hold California firm for Garner until FDR had been knocked out of the contest, but McAdoo always denied that he had given any such undertaking. He had agreed only to give Smith notice of any change in California's vote if that was "feasible," and to use his influence to prevent a repetition of the disaster at Madison Square Garden. Baruch opted out of this dispute, but most historians have concluded that Smith had the better of the argument and that McAdoo later reneged on his promises.[74]

As California's representative on the resolutions committee, McAdoo argued for full repayment of war debts, a referendum on prohibition, and a federal guarantee of bank deposits. "The provision about cancellation of debts is stupid," Baker told a friend, "and was put in to enable Mr. McAdoo to make a campaign in California on the theory that having contracted the debts he wants to be sent to Washington to collect them." McAdoo won that plank, but could not head off a commitment to repeal the Eighteenth Amendment, and his deposit guarantee lost to a combination of Roosevelt and conservative forces. Ultimately the platform was much wetter and more conservative than McAdoo thought wise; its emphasis on balanced budgets and government economy seemed too solicitous of the Wall Street interests that had spawned Raskob, sustained Smith, and stymied him. Having suffered from the two-thirds rule in 1924, McAdoo was more sympathetic than Baker to its abolition, but as the head of a delegation pledged to Garner he supported it in 1932. The proposal was dropped, handing FDR a defeat even before balloting for the nomination began.[75]

Once the convention got under way its initial votes confirmed Roosevelt's fears. On the first ballot he won 666½ votes, 104 votes short of a two-thirds majority. Smith won 201 votes and Garner 90¼. FDR's managers planned to start a bandwagon on the second ballot by deploying votes held back from the first, but that scheme backfired when his tally increased by only 10 votes. Smith's vote subsided slightly to 194, and Garner's remained steady. A third ballot saw Roosevelt's total increase by only 5 to 682, still 88 votes short of two-thirds, Smith's decline to 190, and Garner's increase to 101. The other delegates divided between 5 favorite sons, leaving Garner in a powerful position. Acting in concert, the other favorite sons might have swung the nomination to Roosevelt, but Garner's 101 votes were enough either to block or to nominate FDR.[76]

Because he was an unannounced candidate without delegates of his own, Baker's name was not put to the convention. Yet Hayes was at work behind the scenes. Arguing that Roosevelt's support had peaked and that the contest would soon be deadlocked, he urged wavering delegations to move to Baker sooner rather than later. He had arranged for thousands of telegrams to be sent to delegates urging them to support Baker, and he activated his plan during an adjournment after the third ballot. Hayes thought this was effective in reaching delegates he might not have otherwise contacted, but in other ways it was unwise; FDR's organizers accused the utilities of organizing the telegrams, and they reminded delegates of criticism that Baker was too close to corporate interests.[77]

The telegrams were a misstep, but Hayes did manage to mobilize support for Baker in nearly every delegation that he approached. Mississippi agreed to move from FDR to Baker on the fourth ballot; Iowa and Kansas also sent word that they would switch on the fourth or fifth vote. Alabama, the Dakotas, Indiana, Minnesota, North Carolina, Ohio, Oklahoma, and Pennsylvania all seemed ready to join a Baker bandwagon, and Smith's delegates from Massachusetts and New Jersey also seemed willing to move. Hayes was now confident that FDR's house of cards would collapse during the fourth ballot. This was more than bravado; FDR himself almost believed it. "It now looks as though the Chicago Convention is in a jam and that they will turn to you," he told Baker on the telephone a few hours before the delegates voted for the fourth time. "I will do anything I can to bring that about it you want it." Baker was not so sure, and advised FDR to wait to see what the delegates would do.[78]

McAdoo was also busy during the adjournment, but he had very different objectives. Increasingly desperate for a breakthrough before it was too late, FDR's managers focused on Garner's two delegations. That meant winning over Hearst who, despite McAdoo's pretensions, ultimately called the shots in California. Joseph Kennedy undertook to persuade Hearst to support Roosevelt. Garner could not win, but Baker probably would if FDR did not. "Do you want that man Baker running our country? That great defender of the League of Nations, that ardent internationalist whose policies you despise? No, of course you don't. But that's just who you're going to get if you keep holding out your delegates from Roosevelt." Hearst was skeptical of Roosevelt but swallowed his reservations for fear of someone much worse. He sent word to Garner that he should support FDR to save the nation from Newton Baker.[79]

Neither Garner nor McAdoo wished to be seen as Hearst's puppets and never acknowledged his influence on their fates. "At the Chicago convention I supported this man," Garner pointed to FDR, "instead of Baker because I thought he was not linked up with big business or the Wall Street crowd as Baker was." Hearst may have been all-powerful in California, but at Chicago Garner's delegates were pledged to him and would do nothing without his approval. After talking things over with his colleague Sam Rayburn, Garner agreed to release his Texan delegates to FDR and to accept the vice presidential nomination.[80]

McAdoo always insisted that he and not Hearst had been the king maker at Chicago. There was some truth behind his vanity because only McAdoo could effect Hearst's change of heart on the convention floor. Roosevelt's friends knew this and saw him as the chief executor of Hearst's switch. They did so with some distaste because they knew of McAdoo's criticisms of FDR and had some of their own in return. "I have always thought that he is one of the most arrogant men I have ever met," Farley noted in his diary. "He always thinks he is right. He is rather a difficult fellow to get along with . . . I have always thought he was selfish and thinks [only] of McAdoo."[81]

Gritting his teeth, Farley went cap in hand to McAdoo's camp. Unless California switched on the next ballot, he told Tom Storke and Hamilton Cotton, "Roosevelt is lost and Baker wins." If McAdoo delivered California he could have

any job, including the vice presidency, secretary of state, or secretary of the treasury, that he wanted. McAdoo sent word that he sought no office for himself, but
that Garner should be FDR's running mate and that McAdoo should have a veto
over Roosevelt's choices for State and Treasury, control over federal patronage in
California, and a clear run at the nomination for the Senate. By then FDR was in
the mood to accept almost anything, and he agreed to McAdoo's terms on the
phone. After a desultory meeting with Smith's group, McAdoo set about persuading the Californian delegation that it was now time to switch horses.[82]

McAdoo had more trouble with the Californians than he expected. They were
so divided over dropping Garner for FDR that their meeting descended into a shout-
ing match. McAdoo dared not risk a vote on the switch but persuaded the delegation
to allow a subcommittee to make the decision. It hastily agreed to vote for FDR on
the next ballot and McAdoo rushed to the convention to announce the news.
Amid boos from Smith's supporters in the galleries, he became a king maker at
last:

California came here to nominate a President of the United States. She did not
come here to deadlock this convention or to engage in another disastrous contest like that of 1924 . . .

Sometimes, in major operations, where skillful surgery is required, the life of
the patient may be destroyed if there is unnecessary delay. We believe . . . that
California should take a stand tonight that will bring this contest to a swift and,
we hope, satisfactory conclusion . . .

The two-thirds rule . . . makes it difficult to nominate any man. I say therefore that when a candidate has not only a majority but is within reach of the
two-thirds . . . he is entitled to the nomination . . .

California casts forty-four votes for Franklin D. Roosevelt.

"Bernie," Al Smith remarked to Baruch, "your long-legged friend has run out
on us, just as I thought he would." California's switch nipped Baker's charge in the
bud. States that had wavered now stayed loyal to FDR, and those of the other favorite sons fell in behind him. McAdoo had stolen the limelight from Garner and
Texas, but the Lone Star State's votes finally pushed FDR through the two-thirds
barrier.[83]

Most of his contemporaries attributed McAdoo's dramatic intervention at Chicago to his desire to even the score with Smith. FDR was nominated "by the flop
of the slippery McAdoo," H. L. Mencken noted, "who hated Smith even more than
the frank Ku Kluxers, and was full of a yen to ruin him." Why else had McAdoo

taken the stage and personally delivered the coup de grace to the man who had denied him the prize in 1924?[84]

McAdoo was certainly a good hater, but revenge against Smith was of only minor importance to him during the climactic events before and during the fourth ballot at Chicago. Overemphasis on the McAdoo-Smith feud obscures more significant factors in the decision to back Roosevelt on the fourth ballot. William Randolph Hearst was crucial to that decision, and McAdoo's role was to bring it about. By the time of the fourth ballot it was obvious to every politician in Chicago, and to Smith himself, that the Happy Warrior had no chance of winning the 1932 nomination; he stayed in the race only to block Roosevelt. McAdoo knew this, and he and Hearst focused on Baker, and not Smith, as their most dangerous opponent. Hearst objected to Baker's internationalism while McAdoo thought him too conservative, but both agreed that he was unacceptable. Now that the nomination contest had boiled down to Roosevelt versus Baker, Hearst and McAdoo chose FDR as the more palatable choice.[85]

Convinced that the move to Baker would occur in the fourth ballot, McAdoo needed to act urgently. Voting California once more for Garner and waiting for Texas to announce the switch might have let Baker's charge gather irresistible momentum. California came fourth in the roll call; Texas was thirty-seventh, and in between were states that Hayes had readied to turn to Baker. Announcing California's shift before Garner's home state was bad manners, but time was too short for niceties. There was also a strong element of self-promotion in McAdoo's decision. California could have yielded to Texas and allowed it to announce the change, but eager for the limelight and now anxious to win favor with Roosevelt, McAdoo took the stage alone. He had come very late to FDR's party, but he arrived in the most spectacular way possible.

Newton Baker's lieutenants were in no doubt that it was fear of their man, and not hatred of Al Smith, that had changed Hearst's and McAdoo's thinking. "Even as it was," Roy Howard told Baker after it was all over, "I think you came a damn sight nearer being nominated than you suspect. Had McAdoo not turned the trick at the very time he did, there is not the slightest doubt in my mind but that the Roosevelt tide would have started to ebb on the fourth ballot." Another correspondent was even blunter. "I firmly believe," Edward Wade told Baker, "that had California come further down the alphabetical line you would have been the nominee."[86]

Baker was philosophical about the fate of his crypto-candidacy. "Dear Boy," he cabled Hayes, "I wish you could be as contented as I am." He was touched by the faith that so many had shown in him, but was never fully convinced that he wanted or deserved the presidency. "Cheer Ralph all you can," he told a mutual friend.

"The fact is that I made his task impossible from the beginning." Public office was an important duty but it was no longer, if it ever had been, his burning ambition. If the call had come he would have answered it, but when it did not he was relieved. "The fact is," he told an old supporter in 1936, "that I never wanted to be president . . . [and] as I look back over the past four years, I realize what a tremendous responsibility it would have meant and I have never had a moment's regret that I was not chosen."[87]

Although untroubled by his defeat, Baker disliked the manner of FDR's victory. "At the moment," he wrote soon after the convention, "I am bowed down with the thought of his obligations to Hearst who has for years seemed to me the worst influence in the public and private life of the country . . . Hearst is a ruthless user of the power he acquires and Frank will have to show sterner virtues than I know him to have to escape from that alliance with his soul." McAdoo's gleeful announcement, Baker told a friend, was in "execrable taste." A month later he confessed that "I have used every brand of toothpaste and tooth powder I know without being able to get the bad taste out of my mouth which arose from the McAdoo-Hearst-Garner episode . . . whenever I sleep uneasily I have visions of McAdoo announcing the decision, and I do not like my nightmares to take personal form like this."[88]

"So far as Governor Roosevelt is concerned, I must say that I am holding my breath. I have, of course, known him for many years and know the charm of his personality. There is, however, a certain immaturity and impulsiveness about him which Walter Lippmann once summed up in the statement that there was about him 'a fatal touch of the boy scout.'" Baker would help FDR's campaign "in exact proportion as I satisfy myself that I am not helping Hearst," but there were good omens as well as bad. The platform, except for the "lurking embarrassment in the debt cancellation question," was a great improvement over 1928; its call for repeal of prohibition was timely and its silence on radical remedies for the Depression was wise. FDR also extended an olive branch by asking Baker to join a group led by Raymond Moley to devise policies during the campaign. Baker was pleased to be asked, and thought that "our candidate" should avoid discussion of the League of Nations but back the World Court, support multilateral tariff reductions, and ignore McAdoo's debt cancellation plank.[89]

By October Baker was excited by the thought of evicting Hoover from the White House. The GOP had foisted isolationism on the nation to the detriment of its place in the world and its prosperity at home. The Democrats, on the other hand, would revive Wilson's internationalism and regain America's moral and diplomatic leadership of the world. When Baker took to the stump in Boston, Cleveland, and New York, his speeches focused more on attacking Hoover than on praising Roosevelt, but his conclusion was clear: the Republicans had led the nation to ruin, and so "I venture to advise you to vote for Roosevelt and Garner."[90]

⊰⊱•⊰⊱

McAdoo had one more part to play in the drama of 1932. Between his tilts at the presidential nomination during the 1920s he had considered running for the US Senate but had resisted the temptation. California was firmly Republican, its Democrats were divided over prohibition and between their northern and southern wings, and he still hoped to make his fortune from oil and legal practice. And besides, he told a friend in 1925, "my tendencies are too strongly executive, and I am sure that I should be impatient under the restraints imposed by Senatorial courtesy, etc."[91]

All these reservations had receded by 1932. It was now clear that California would vote Democratic in the coming elections; the Depression had so reduced McAdoo's income that a senatorial salary was now attractive, and a Senate seat promised influence within the new political order. McAdoo told Baruch in February 1932 that "I may be forced to run for the United States Senate as the pressure is very strong, and I may be persuaded that it is a public duty to do it." He was more frank to another friend. "I would like to have the opportunity of telling the country, from the floor of the Senate, what I think about a good many things. I might be able to render some service of value, even in that capacity." At the end of June, just before his *bravura* performance in Chicago, McAdoo declared his candidacy for the Senate.[92]

Events in Chicago both helped and hindered McAdoo's Senate campaign. His prominence there confirmed his reputation as California's best known Democrat who had played a leading role in nominating Franklin Roosevelt, but he had leapfrogged others who had strong claims to Roosevelt's loyalty. Justus Wardell, who had run FDR's primary campaign in Northern California, also had senatorial ambitions and expected Roosevelt's support in the primary; Isidore Dockweiler had led FDR's campaign in Southern California and wanted to control patronage there after the election. During his negotiations with Farley at Chicago McAdoo had demanded a clear run at the Senate nomination and control of Californian patronage, but this conflicted with FDR's understandings to Wardell and Dockweiler. FDR had dumped them for McAdoo at Chicago, and this left a legacy of bad feeling.[93]

Angry at his treatment in Chicago, Wardell entered the Senate primary as a wet and Bob Shuler entered as a dry. This left McAdoo, a committed prohibitionist now promising to abide by the wet national platform, languishing between his opponents' more consistent positions. Dockweiler strongly supported Wardell and warned Farley that McAdoo had upset Democrats by not supporting Smith in 1928 and by his "intellectual dishonesty" over prohibition. "I don't know of any outstanding citizen in the banking, manufacturing, commercial or business activities of our state that regards McAdoo with other than political abhorrence."[94]

McAdoo funded his campaign with donations from friends in Los Angeles. Although he spoke in San Francisco and kept an office there, he focused on Southern California. The primary campaign was hard fought; Wardell was strong in the north and Shuler was popular among drys in the south who had once looked on McAdoo as their hero. Despite his earlier promises Hearst now hedged between McAdoo and Wardell, and the railroad Brotherhoods remained neutral because they also counted Wardell as a friend.[95]

Despite these setbacks McAdoo won an easy victory in the primary on August 30, winning 52 percent of the vote to Wardell's 23 percent and Shuler's 17 percent. He did much better in the south than in the north, where Wardell's campaign left deep wounds. "There is a terrible bitter feeling throughout Northern California against Mr. McAdoo," a friend in San Mateo reported. "I have been visiting counties and it is anything but pleasant to hear the name of Mr. McAdoo mentioned."[96]

Still nervous about Californians' loyalty to the GOP, McAdoo and FDR worked to create a semblance of Democratic unity in the Golden State. That required improving McAdoo's standing among wet voters in the north, winning over Smith's supporters alienated by events in Chicago, and persuading Wardell and Dockweiler to support his campaign. Whatever support McAdoo had expected from drys evaporated when Shuler contested the general election on the Prohibition Party ticket, leaving McAdoo to persuade wets that he was a reformed character by promising to vote for repeal if he was elected. Smith's voters needed more attention. McAdoo reacted to reports that FDR and the Happy Warrior had reconciled by asking Smith to endorse him in California. Smith declined, but his declaration in favor of Roosevelt's election defused the danger of wholesale defections by his partisans in November.[97]

Dockweiler and Wardell also presented difficulties. When FDR visited California in September both men demanded prominent roles in the welcoming ceremonies and in the management of the local campaign. McAdoo refused to have Wardell on the train carrying FDR south from San Francisco and insisted that he alone would control patronage in California. He was convinced that Wardell and Dockweiler were undermining him to ensure that they would represent the new administration in California, and he saw Northern California as hostile territory throughout the campaign. Breckinridge Long worried that division within the state party was so deep that McAdoo had become a liability to the whole ticket;

instead of carrying California for Roosevelt, FDR would now have to carry California for McAdoo. Many Northern Californian voters did not believe that McAdoo genuinely supported the repeal plank, while Shuler did well with voters disgusted by McAdoo's change of heart on prohibition. Tallant Tubbs, the Republican candidate, was an outspoken wet and threatened to win disaffected Democratic wets from McAdoo.[98]

Tensions between McAdoo and Wardell simmered during the campaign. Wardell did only the minimum in San Francisco, but McAdoo ran an active campaign in Southern California. After the primary Hearst delivered editorial and financial support, and McAdoo used it to campaign strenuously. He promised to protect California's oil and agricultural industries, to give immediate payment of the soldiers' bonus his "most friendly and fair consideration," and to be "the President's strong right arm and an effective representative of California and its interests."[99]

McAdoo ran hard against Republican attempts to combat the Depression. This was no time, he declared, for "pussy cat words and poodle dog phrases." There was only one issue in the campaign, and that was "how can prosperity be returned to the land?" Eleven million unemployed workers and their families demanded immediate relief and long-term reform. The GOP had done much to bring about the Depression and little to alleviate it. It had allowed the speculative bubble of the 1920s to inflate and had sat by while worthless foreign bonds were sold to American investors. Now that the crash had come the "Hoover theory" of simply waiting for recovery was unacceptable; the Democrats would provide extensive public works to employ that in need. "In ordinary times I would be opposed to any direct federal relief, but when people are starving, I care nothing for theories of government."[100]

Preferring not to dwell on the platform's repeal plank, McAdoo emphasized its promises to reduce government expenditure and balance the budget but ignored the contradiction between cutting the budget with one hand and creating unemployment relief and public works with the other. He also ran on his own record, reminding voters that his Hudson River tunnels had "amazed the country" and marked him as "a Progressive of Progressives" who combined entrepreneurial flair with enlightened policies on equal pay and "the customer be pleased." He had also established the Federal Reserve System, controlled Wall Street interests, funded the war effort, and administered the nation's railroads. "Builder, executive, financier and statesman," McAdoo's campaign flyer declared, "his record entitles him to be regarded as the great administrative genius of his day . . . No apprenticeship will be required of him . . . for he will take a leader's place at once."[101]

By October McAdoo felt confident. Tubbs had run a listless campaign and Shuler's dry constituency had dwindled. Yet Northern California was still problematic and FDR seemed hesitant to lend McAdoo his full-blooded support. McAdoo asked him to send "as strong a telegram as you [can] expressing your hope that the people of California would send me to the Senate because of assistance I could give," but no cable came from Hyde Park. Garner sent one from Texas instead.[102]

McAdoo won easily on Election Day, with 43 percent of the vote to Tubbs's 31 percent and Shuler's 26 percent. He won 13 of the 16 counties below Monterey and a majority in Los Angeles of nearly 100,000 votes. He did less well in Northern California, winning only 33 of the 42 counties there and losing badly in San Francisco. "The gang there certainly knifed me to the limit," he told George Creel. "I got less than half as many votes as Roosevelt received, which shows the character of the organization." Even so, he was going back to Washington and had just celebrated his sixty-ninth birthday.[103]

CHAPTER 13

Husbands and Fathers

At the end of 1915 Newton Baker declined the Cleveland Chamber of Commerce's request for a family photograph. "I do not think it good for the children to have their pictures taken in any official association and generally I disapprove of the way people's private lives get mixed up with their public activities." He therefore led his public career largely without his family and kept his household sheltered from the public's gaze. William McAdoo also felt protective of his family's privacy but found it much harder to achieve. That was because of circumstance—marrying the president's daughter was not a recipe for domestic privacy—but also because of his own inconsistency. McAdoo accepted publicity of his family that he could control but resented scrutiny that he could not. While Baker and McAdoo shared traditional views about their wives' and children's roles, only Baker's family cooperated to realize them. McAdoo's family, on the other hand, lived much more chaotic and public lives that made a mockery of his ideas of propriety and privacy. Together the Bakers and McAdoos embodied a transition from stable Victorian family values and structures to the more varied and turbulent lives that characterized many American families during and after the twentieth century.[1]

Upon hearing of a friend's divorce in 1903, Baker told his wife Bess that "tragedies like this always make me melancholy, and it does seem unutterably pathetic that after twelve or fourteen years together they cannot finish it out." He and Bess certainly "finished it out." Their marriage lasted thirty-four years, and their children Elizabeth (Betty), Newton Diehl III (Jack), and Margaret (Peggy) formed families of their own and remained close to their parents. The Bakers had their problems, but they were never as damaging or as public as the McAdoos'.[2]

Bess and Newton created a tightly knit household between 1902 and 1916. Their marriage obeyed Victorian dictates of propriety and separate spheres; in 1933 Baker reflected that "I have been married now thirty-one years and one of the most deeply impressed lessons of my life is that I must not interfere with my domestic establishment . . . If I were to undertake to discuss the relative merits of milk dealers, I should immediately have Mrs. Baker moving my law office from the Union Trust Building." His sense of propriety changed little over time; in 1929 he was shocked to find a woman in the chair next to his in a barber shop. "I did not like it," he told Bess. "Usually I take my coat off, but of course I did not undress before a woman, and somehow I resented having either to have her present at my toilet as having to be present at hers."[3]

The Bakers' spheres were separate but not antagonistic. Newton was more gregarious than Bess, but his favorite pastime was reading, best done in his living room with his pipe and family close by. He also enjoyed travel, particularly to Europe, but usually went with male friends while Bess summered in Ohio or West Virginia. Their separations were entirely amicable; Bess preferred to leave Newton to his cathedrals and to have time with the children instead. August, however, was reserved for family holidays, and Newton refused all engagements for that month.[4]

The Bakers also took holidays from Cleveland's winters in the Mediterranean, Hawaii, Mexico, and Central America. They were quiet tourists, keeping to themselves and soaking in the sun and sights of their journeys. "Mrs. Baker, Peggy, and I had a restful and enjoyable cruise in the Mediterranean," Newton reported in 1934, "and by avoiding the general run of our fellow passengers, succeeded in not becoming involved in bridge tournaments, fancy dress parties, and horse racing on the decks. This gave us all an opportunity to read and drowse and rest."[5]

Immediately after her husband's appointment to Wilson's cabinet in March 1916 Bess stayed with the children in Cleveland but was distressed by their separation. "The babies complicate things a good deal," she told Secretary of the Navy Josephus Daniels's wife Addie, "for I don't want to take them from school, they need me and I am miserable without Mr. Baker." Alone in Washington and swamped by his new duties, Newton could do little to help. "You poor dear child," he wrote in April. "How can you get low spirited when you know how I love you and want you here?"[6]

Bess dreaded the life that awaited her in Washington. "I know nothing of the city and less of what my duties will be," she told Addie Daniels. The "nerves" that had afflicted her since Elizabeth's birth, compounded by her retiring nature, made her hesitant to move. "I have but one fear in the world in which you figure," Newton wrote in April 1916, "and that is that the excitement of this life is going to be bad for you and that out of a sense of duty . . . you will sacrifice strength and break yourself down. But both of us have pretty good sense after all and we can determine to do just as much as we can afford, financially and nervously and let it go at that."[7]

Bess and the children moved to Washington in the summer of 1916. With Addie Daniels's help she learned the intricacies of Washington etiquette but was never comfortable with them. By March 1921 she and her husband were keen to go home. Newton had his law firm to build and Bess longed for her new home and garden. Back in Cleveland and mindful of the sacrifices that Bess had made, Newton was careful to preserve his family's newfound stability. He declined attractive jobs, including the presidencies of Washington and Lee and the University of Virginia, because Bess was unwilling to move again. "She is a good soldier and I am sure would go uncomplainingly," he told the president of Washington and Lee in 1928, "but it would mean separation from our children . . . which would be hard for me but even more difficult for her."[8]

Solicitude for Bess suited Newton's own desire to remain in private life, but it was still genuine. Aware of her own limitations and worried about Newton's health after his heart attack in 1928, Bess discouraged suggestions that he return to public life and dampened his presidential ambitions in 1932. Newton's "good soldier" would have supported him had the Chicago convention decided differently, but she was relieved that both of them escaped that fate.[9]

Bess's medical troubles were not simply "nervous." In the 1930s she suffered severe sinusitis and rheumatoid arthritis that forced her to move to a warmer climate in the winter. In 1937 she stayed in Arizona under an osteopath's care until May. "Mother is more and more incapacitated," Newton told Peggy, but "fortunately her spirit is brave and she is infinitely better off in her attitude and feelings than she was before she went to Arizona." A month later, with Bess back in Cleveland, he was still worried that she showed no sign of recovery. He remained anxious about her health for the rest of his life, but she outlived him by fourteen years.[10]

Baker was an attentive husband and a solicitous father. He remained close to all his children and watched carefully over their progress. Modern consumer culture often raised his paternal ire. In July 1918 he complained about movies with "suggestive squirmings and too passionate grimaces which unsettle young people in the audience," and criticized a Charlie Chaplin film as "sordid, overwrought and muscular without being interesting." As the father of two daughters he was sensitive to what to him were unacceptable female fashions. Crossing the Atlantic in 1923 he noticed a fellow passenger who "paints her lips with carmine colored paint until it is literally repulsive. How can they do it?" he asked Betty. "And what do they do it for? I would frankly rather kiss the cork of a red ink bottle!"[11]

Baker's oldest child Betty was 11 when her father became secretary of war. She completed her schooling in Washington and in 1923 attended the Institut de Mont Choisi, a finishing school in Switzerland. There she improved her French, studied art history, and toured Florence and Rome. Evidently she did not find the Institut confining; she had not been there long before her father admonished her about too many champagne suppers. "You naughty child. Cut it out! A very good rule by the way, as to champagne, is to drink it and other intoxicants only socially and in the company of older people."[12]

After her year at Lausanne Betty enrolled at Wellesley. "Our bargain is that you are to go one year for me and as many more as you like for yourself," Baker reminded her. "I think you will go all four years if some boy or boys do not interfere." One boy was particularly distracting: Betty had known Jack McGean for some time and by the time she went to Wellesley their relationship had become serious. "I have always delighted in your regard for one another," Baker told her, "and I have only two wishes: 1. that you shall not hurt each other, and 2. that you don't sacrifice the enduring satisfactions of mature life by mere impatience while you are young." Jack wanted to get married as soon as possible, and Betty asked her father if she could leave Wellesley after her first semester. "I can't help you about loving Jack," Baker replied, "but the more you do love him the less you want to spoil him by getting him married before he is finished or getting him married to an unfinished wife."[13]

Betty did poorly in her first semester at Wellesley but returned to complete the year that she had promised her father. She scraped through her first year and returned in September 1925, but it was clear that she would not complete her degree. Jack had left college and moved to Los Angeles to work in his uncle's insurance company, but their separation was traumatic. He left California in May, begged Betty to elope, and returned to his job only after she agreed to marry him sooner rather than later. She left Wellesley at the end of her sophomore year, married Jack in December 1926, and returned with him to Los Angeles.[14]

Betty and Jack's early married life was a struggle. Betty was soon pregnant, and Jack was overwhelmed by his new responsibilities. "I have done more than I have ever done for anyone else, with no sign in any respect of appreciation," his uncle complained in September 1927. "When one continuously does these things, only to hear that the beneficiary is dissatisfied and that enough has not been done, and that Los Angeles is a rotten place to live, and that Cleveland is a wonderful city— you cannot continue indefinitely." Anxious to start afresh, but without a job and expecting a child, Betty and Jack moved back to Cleveland and into her parents' house.[15]

Jack's false start in California showed his emotional fragility and impetuosity. Baker was very differently configured, but he and Bess were pleased to have company again in their large house and delighted to get to know their grandsons Michael and Lee. They still worried, however, that Jack was slow to heed Baker's advice that "being in a position to be married means being in a position to do so without a disabling and embarrassing sense of dependence."[16]

Jack eventually found his feet. Through his father-in-law's influence he joined the Cleveland Trust Company and rose to become its assistant vice president in 1937. By then, however, the McGeans' marriage was in trouble. Jack and the boys moved back into Newton and Bess's home while Betty stayed in the house that her parents had bought them. Baker reported to Bess, in Florida seeking relief for her arthritis, that Jack was dogmatic and self-centered with "certain patches of immaturity," but that he loved Betty, Michael, and Lee. Betty was disappointed in her husband, but her father counseled caution. All men had weaknesses, some of them much worse than Jack's. "But she knows all that and what she does not know she will learn only out of her own head and heart. How little we can really help our children!"[17]

Newton and Bess also worked hard to help their middle child Jack, who had just turned 10 when his father went to Washington. "When you come down you will be interested, at my office, to see the beautiful models of the battleships of the Navy. They are in glass cases so that you can see them clearly and there are a great many of them." In the meantime he urged Jack to work hard at lessons that he already found difficult. "Next year I want you to be able to read as well as any of these Washington boys of your age and to do as well in arithmetic so that you can get your school work done easily and leave lots of time to see the wonderful things here."[18]

In Washington Jack attended a succession of schools and performed poorly in all of them. When the family returned home in 1921 he was 15 and his patchy school career had taken its toll. In 1923 he was at the bottom of his class at the University School in Cleveland and had collected demerits for "lack of responsibility, some disorder, some cutting." His French teacher noted that "he's much more sure of his ignorance than his knowledge. If he will get interested in asserting the positive instead of the negative, we'll gradually see gratifying progress."[19]

Jack failed to make progress at University School and in September 1924 moved to northern Virginia to the Episcopal School in Alexandria. "Jack is having the dickens of a time," his father told Betty. "Has written three letters to say that he can't stay and called me on the long distance telephone to tell me that after having been at school 24 hours he has come to the conclusion that he is not learning anything and that I ought not to waste my money keeping him there." Within a month he had returned to Cleveland to enroll in a public high school. "Jack really is a very special problem," Baker ruefully explained to the principal of Episcopal, "due in large part, no doubt, to the fact that throughout all of the younger years of his life I was so much occupied with public burdens that I had to neglect my family, so that he now suffers for the attention he ought then to have had."[20]

Jack finished high school in Cleveland in 1925 but needed further tuition to qualify for college. He went to a preparatory school in Cheshire, Connecticut, but his father doubted whether he would stay. The Roxbury School was expensive, but it offered students tuition in classes limited to four students. "The boy and I are good friends," Baker told the principal. "He is honest, clean-minded, too sophisticated and quite unable to see why the difficulties of life ought not automatically to disappear as he approaches them." At Roxbury he did better in his scientific courses than in English, French, and history, but nothing academic came easily to him.[21]

Jack finished his year at Roxbury, but chose not to go to college. He worked in a Cleveland factory and then with an aviation firm. He was happy there, but his prospects without qualifications were limited. He was now 22, and "if a father's judgment is to be trusted in such matters the following would be my summary: Good personality; good character; industrious; fair, but not expert, knowledge; a happy disposition which makes it easy for him to get along with others."[22]

Jack eventually found congenial work at Standard Oil and in the summer of 1931 married Kezia Strong, the daughter of a prominent Pennsylvanian industrialist. His father was delighted, but soon after Jack suffered a collapsed lung brought about by a tubercular infection. At Baker's expense Jack and Kezia, now pregnant, moved to a sanatorium in Tucson, Arizona. Baker told its director that "such anxiety as I have about the boy at the moment is largely on the psychological side" and "the problem which it seems to me he faces is to accept his year of inaction without having it create an emotional invalidism on his part." Jack's spirits and health did improve, and he stayed only five months in Tucson before returning to Cleveland. He and Kezia had two children, Charles Henry and Newton Diehl Baker IV, and they remained close to Newton for the rest of his life.[23]

Newton and Bess's youngest child Peggy was 4 when the Bakers moved to Washington. When the family returned to Cleveland she attended a local school and stayed close to home. "Bess feels that she cannot go [to Europe] for a prolonged stay," Newton told a friend in 1924, "largely because Peggy, in the absence of companionship of children of her own age in our suburban neighborhood, has come to depend upon her mother for companionship in a way that quite upsets her high-strung nervous organization if Bess is away over night." Baker was vigilant for signs that the children had inherited Bess's "nerves," and worried that Peggy "filled her usually philosophical mind with misgivings on slight occasions."[24]

Peggy was certainly sensitive. In 1925, when she was 12, she went to summer camp in Vermont but left after a month. "She has had the admiration and affection of all of us here," the matron reported, "and I think it is her youth and her temperament that makes her wish to be with you rather than finish out the summer." Baker agreed, but noted that Peggy and her mother had spent so much time together that "Peggy is undoubtedly much more grown up in many ways than little girls of her age often are." In 1930 she went to Sarah Lawrence College, and within an hour of her departure Baker wrote with some last-minute advice:

> P.S. No. 1
> Do not wear high-heeled shoes on hilly ground, they make one walk lop-sided and distort your form.
> P.S. No. 2
> Use lip-stick very sparingly, if at all. As a matter of fact Providence did a pretty good job with your lips and you have little or nothing to disguise or cover up about them.[25]

Peggy enjoyed college and her father encouraged her to make the most of her opportunities. "In all matters affecting Peggy's disposition and wishes," he told the registrar of absences in 1931, "the College has my consent to . . . trust to her discretion." His only stipulation to the college was that "I prefer not to have Peggy travel by airplane unless the proposed trip is one involving a critical emergency," and his only warning to Peggy was that "Yes, my sex is worth studying to some extent—but preferably with a telescope at present, young miss!"[26]

During her freshman year Baker urged Peggy to create a trust for the stocks that he and Bess had given her. "Some of these days you may marry and it is a very good thing for a girl to have her money in a trust so that she will not be so likely to turn it over to her wonderful husband to speculate with. Even if you do not marry a trust is a good thing for a lady schoolteacher to have!" In fact, Peggy did both; after college she taught at a school in Cleveland, but not for long. "He seems a very attractive, though somewhat serious, young man," Baker wrote of her beau Fulton Wright. "I am perfectly prepared either to accept this young man, if that is Peggy's wish, or to endorse any change she may make in the candidate she tenders." Fulton stayed, and in May 1934 he and Peggy married and moved to St. Louis. As they had done for Peggy's siblings, the Bakers gave the young couple $21,500 to buy a house, paid medical bills arising from the birth of their son Fulton in 1937, and each year gave Peggy a parcel of stock for the trust that she had created on her father's advice.[27]

On May 7, 1914, two months before the Bakers celebrated their twelfth wedding anniversary, William McAdoo married for the second time. By then he was 50 years old and had been widowed for more than two years. After Sarah's death in 1912 he had become a star of Washington society; although a teetotaler, he was gregarious and an excellent dancer. Unaware of his affair with Florence Harriman, gossips hinted that McAdoo had several admirers, one of whom often sent roses to his office.[28]

At the end of 1913 McAdoo was indeed courting. Eleanor Wilson, the president's youngest daughter, was three years younger than McAdoo's eldest daughter Harriet. Less serious-minded than her siblings Margaret and Jessie, Eleanor (Nell) was her father's favorite because she had "the virtue of not being too good." After completing high school in Princeton, she spent two years at St. Mary's College in North Carolina and then studied at the Academy of Fine Arts in Philadelphia. In December 1911 she went on holiday to Mexico, where she met Ben King. The couple were caught up in the Mexican Civil War and escaped to Texas after four months of adventure, danger, and romance. By then they had decided to marry, but their engagement was kept secret during Wilson's presidential campaign. That secrecy continued through 1913, but their betrothal was welcomed by both families.[29]

Eleanor and McAdoo met in 1911 when he visited the Wilsons at Sea Girt, New Jersey. "We agreed that he was most attractive," Nell recalled, "and Margaret asked, 'Is he married?' I answered with dignity, 'He has a wife, and a houseful of children.'" In 1913 Nell and McAdoo, whom she called Mac, saw more of each other. "The President's youngest daughter admired him too, but shyly, with a touch of awe," Nell remembered. "Mr. McAdoo, born and raised in the old South, where pursuit was left to the men, found this attractive."[30]

McAdoo was an ardent suitor. When the Wilsons spent Christmas 1913 on the Gulf Coast, he wrote every day. "Adorable person, I like to think that you are basking in sunshine at Pass Christian today and that it is the sunshine you took with you from Washington." He proposed when Eleanor returned to Washington. Still engaged to Ben King, she now had a choice to make. She agreed with her mother to break her engagement to King and to have no contact with Mac while she thought things through. The Wilsons were troubled by Eleanor's news; they were fond of King, McAdoo was more than twice Nell's age with six children, and they disapproved of "what looked like double dealing on my part."[31]

"I think the course you have adopted is an eminently wise one," McAdoo wrote from Denver, "and I begin at once to co-operate by writing this little note to tell you so and I make it platonic for that reason only." Even so, he arranged for Cary Grayson, his friend and Wilson's physician, to send Nell flowers on his behalf and coded telegrams to McAdoo on her state of mind. "Roneal has appeared much concerned about something of which she does not speak," Grayson cabled ten days later, "but she is happier now apparently and is delighted at the mention of your name and interested about everything concerning you." A few days later she accepted McAdoo's proposal over the phone. "Sweetest Darling," he wrote, "you do make me so infinitely happy." Ben King was left bewildered and hurt, but remained on good terms with Wilson and later reconciled with his former fiancée and his rival.[32]

The engagement became public in March 1914. "We were holding it back for the very purpose of enabling us to write to our intimate friends and to members of our respective families," McAdoo complained after the news had broken. "Even [my children] Harriet and Robert got their first news from the papers." The significant difference between Eleanor's and Mac's ages attracted attention. "The bride-elect is only 24 years old, while the sturdy secretary has turned the fateful corner of 50," the Quincy (Illinois) *Journal* noted. "According to the traditions, this constitutes an element of unsuitability." Yet Eleanor had chosen a healthy, active man who carried his years lightly, and "better ten years with such a man as McAdoo, than thirty years with some helpless weakling, some colorless mollycoddle."[33]

Nell and Mac married in the Blue Room of the White House on May 7, 1914. It was a simple ceremony because Ellen Wilson was already ill with the nephritis that took her life three months later. Even so the wedding was covered on the front page of every newspaper in the nation in accounts that described the twenty-five-piece Marine Band, the groom's military aides in dress uniform, the bridesmaids' Egyptian crepe dresses, Eleanor's ivory satin gown, and presents from members of the cabinet, Congress, the Supreme Court, and the diplomatic corps. The Reverend Sylvanus Beach, the Wilsons' minister from Princeton, led one hundred guests in a brief service. After supper the Eleanor and Mac left for their honeymoon at Cornish, New Hampshire. There, the *Milwaukee Journal* reported, "from the minute of their arrival the couple has been in strictest seclusion" in "a world of just two people."[34]

❧

All eyes were on the family that McAdoo had married into, but Nell had the more complex situation to deal with. Marriage to McAdoo, twenty-six years her senior, meant that Eleanor became a stepmother as well as a wife. Sarah McAdoo's death had left Mac as the sole parent of six children. Harriet was 26 and had just married when Sarah died, and their oldest son Huger was 24 and establishing a legal career in New York. Nona and Billy were 19 and 16, and only Robert and Sarah (Sally), ages 13 and 5, were still children.

By the standards of the day and within the constraints of his career McAdoo was an engaged and loving father. As Sarah's health deteriorated, he had become increasingly involved in his children's lives and remained close to them through-out his life. By 1941 he had married three times, fathered nine children, adopted a grandson, and accumulated a volatile collection of sons- and daughters-in-law. They kept him young, poorer, and exasperated. Only three of his ten children managed to make independent lives after their privileged but disrupted child-hoods, and because of their parents' prominence their difficulties were subject to attention in the press. McAdoo's fame as a cabinet member, presidential son-in-law, presidential aspirant, and finally senator ensured that his personal and politi-cal careers were played out in public view over three decades, and his wives and children paid a heavy price for the privileges that his prominence gave them.[35]

Tragedy pursued the McAdoos relentlessly. Harriet married Taber Martin just before her mother's death, and in 1914 she presented McAdoo with his first grand-child. By then Taber was ill with tuberculosis, which worsened despite spells in sanitariums in Arizona and then California. He died in November 1915, and McAdoo rushed to send money and reassurance. "If you were a woman of means to bear these expenses yourself, it would be a different matter, but never, so long as I have breath in my body and am able to do such things for my children, will I fail to do them." He paid Harriet's expenses until 1918, when she married Clayton Platt, an insurance executive from Philadelphia. The Platts had children of their own, but their marriage grew troubled and finally dissolved. "I have gone through ten years of misery & humiliation on account of Clayton's drinking," Harriet told McAdoo in 1935. "It has not only ruined my life but the children's."[36]

Of all his children McAdoo worried least about Francis Huger and Sally. Huger was 25 when his mother died and had already graduated from Princeton Law School. He joined a New York firm but enlisted in the navy a month before the Declaration of War. Huger served first in Chesapeake Bay, but at the end of 1917 sought to have his boat transferred to Annapolis. "If the thing could be initiated by your commanding officers in some way," McAdoo advised him, "and I could be apprised of it, I could help it along." The boat stayed in Chesapeake Bay, but Huger was transferred to the Naval Academy to be commissioned as an ensign. In June 1918 he again sought his father's help to be transferred to Europe, and was soon serving as an assistant navigator on a destroyer in French waters.[37]

After the war Huger resumed his legal career, this time with his father's new firm in New York. He stayed there when McAdoo moved to California in 1922, but they continued to work together in legal and business ventures. By the mid-1920s Huger was an established lawyer with a comfortable income and had begun to contribute to the financial support of his less fortunate siblings. When he divorced his first wife Ethel, his father brokered a separation agreement that ensured that he kept in contact with their children. "You have always been so sweet to me and you know how much I care for you," Ethel wrote later to her former father-in-law. She and Huger found new spouses, and McAdoo kept on good terms with them all.[38]

Sally, born in March 1904, was 8 when her mother died and 10 when her father remarried. She and Eleanor got on well, and Sally stayed at home and attended the Holton-Arms School in Bethesda. From there she went to Bryn Mawr, where she was diligent but undistinguished. "I hope that you are not worrying about your college exams," her father wrote in 1922. "Just have confidence in yourself and don't conjure up unnecessary specters, and you will do much better." Sally was determined to earn her own living after college, but first had to convince her father. "I am very averse to having her take a job," he told Huger in 1926. "I suppose that is a survival of my old training about women. Nevertheless, I am reconciled to anything which she thinks essential to her happiness, and I must say that I admire her for her desire to do something useful in the world."[39]

Sally did take a job as a proof-reader at a news agency, but she soon had another surprise for her family. Early in 1928 Brice Clagett, who had been McAdoo's secretary during the war and was now his law partner in Washington, asked for Sally's hand in marriage. Mac and Eleanor were surprised; they had no idea that Sally and Brice were romantically involved, but they did know that he was married and had only recently separated from his wife. "He was very pale and agitated, poor chap," Mac told Nell, "but tremendously happy when I told him that you and I both had a genuine affection for him and that we would be glad to have him in the family after the period of 'probation' was over." Clagett soon won his divorce, and he and Sally married in November 1928. Their union proved durable, and McAdoo remained close to both of them for the rest of his life.[40]

Nona, McAdoo and Sarah's third child, caused more anxiety. When the McAdoos moved to Washington in 1913 she was 19 and the social head of the household. The *Houston Chronicle* noted that her "dazzling facial charms attracted general attention and Mr. McAdoo was kept busy introducing her to admirers." In 1914, however, rumors of Nona's jealousy of Nell reached the gossip columns. "Poor Nona," one reported in April 1914. "She has left no doubt in anybody's mind as to her attitude toward this marriage which will dispossess her of her official empire in Washington in favor of one as much of a girl as herself." The sight of Nell on her father's arm at a ball caused her "to have a fit of hysterics from which she recovered in such a limp and dejected condition that she was obliged to go home."[41]

A year later Nona was in the news again. After McAdoo's wedding she and a friend volunteered to nurse soldiers in France. Press reports in February 1915 suggested that they were unhappy and would return home. McAdoo explained that he had ordered Nona home because the strain was too much for her, demanded that the reporter be dismissed, and asked Newton Baker whether he could sue to restore her reputation. "I object to no criticism of myself personally and officially, but when it comes to such detestable methods as lying about the ladies of my household . . . I feel that indignation which any man with decent blood in his veins must feel in such circumstances." Baker replied with personal sympathy but legal caution; the report was "blackguardism," but Nona was powerless to prevent it.[42]

McAdoo browbeat the newspapers into retracting the story, but there was truth to the rumors that all was not well between Nona and Eleanor. They found it difficult to live in the same house and tension between them contributed to Nona's departure for France. "I don't know that Nona will be much less of a problem in a larger house than she has been in the small one," Woodrow Wilson confided to Edith Bolling Galt after Nona returned. "But fortunately she is a great deal away . . . and it may be that some adventurous youngster, deluded by beauty, may marry her soon! That's a hateful remark, I admit . . . [but] it must be said that Nona is not an admirable person." Even after Nona established her own home her relations with Eleanor remained poisonous. In 1918 she accused Nell of using her furniture without permission. "Of course I would not think of using anything of yours again," Eleanor replied, "and I shall put them all away immediately and try to forget that you have hurt me very much."[43]

Nona married Ferdinand de Mohrenschildt, a Russian diplomat, in May 1917. She reveled in Washington's diplomatic community, but calamity struck two years later when Ferdinand died days after the birth of their daughter Fernanda (Fedya). "It is a tragedy of the first order and nothing now can mitigate its severity," McAdoo told Bernard Baruch. "I was devoted to de Mohrenschildt. He was an exceptional man and I feel as if some real light had gone out of the life of our family."[44]

"Papa darling," Nona wrote in November 1922:

I have been thinking how I married full of ambition for a brilliant future for Fedya and therefore myself, with a life ahead full of opportunity to meet interesting people . . . and here I am leading an aimless existence . . . I feel I am somebody, you have made me so, I resent not being known . . . [I] don't want to be a non entity—I long to have power for in having such it is not only for oneself but places you in a position to help friends, family and other miserable creatures . . . Any woman can be a good mother but I want more—I want to go forward and I am not—the only solution as I see it is marriage naturally but that is so easy to say . . . I wish I were like Harriet, could marry one of these rich dull men and be happy with my children—but I can't. I am made differently & and I am vain restless and ambitious . . . what shall I do? [45]

With McAdoo's help Nona established a dress shop in New York City. Chez Ninon became one of Manhattan's most exclusive salons and provided Nona with the glamour that she had not known since the days in Washington before Eleanor usurped her. Her father was proud of Nona's success, but admitted that "I have always hated to have you and Sally take a job. You will have to be patient with my old-fashioned notions. I am sure they are silly in the light of the modern development of women . . . so I am reconciled so long as it makes you happy." [46]

Nona's search for personal happiness was more complicated. In 1927 she married Edward Cowles, a prominent Manhattan physician. In May 1935, however, the New York American noted that "in soft whispers along Fifth and Park avs, the news is filtering out to the effect [that] Dr. and Mrs. . . . . Cowles are not as congenial as they once were . . . Everyone is distressed over the news—for the Cowleses have been one of our most interesting couples—she so chic and he so intelligent." Nona was divorced later that year. She married Francis Taylor a month later but divorced him in 1938 and married Darragh Park in 1943. [47]

The most troubled of McAdoo's brood was his second son William Gibbs III. Billy, as the family called him, was born in May 1895 and attended St. Paul's School in Concord, New Hampshire. From there he went to Princeton, but only because of his father's contacts and an extra year of preparation. At Princeton he struggled academically and behaved erratically. In 1914 he was jailed overnight in Portsmouth, New Hampshire, after a drunken altercation with a police officer. The story was covered in the press and left his father embarrassed and concerned. "Let me have an exact and truthful statement of the whole affair. You may be sure that I am not going to scold or be harsh about it; I only want to help you." [48]

Billy left Princeton in 1917 without graduating and joined the Naval Reserve. He trained in naval aviation and joined the American Expeditionary Forces (AEF) in September 1918. When the war ended two months later he was a lieutenant, but influenza had kept him from active service. He did not return to Princeton after the war but went to Kansas to work on one of his father's oil leases. He found the work discouraging and drank heavily. "You are going through . . . a very trying time in a young man's life," McAdoo wrote in May 1921, "but you can be certain of one thing: that with fidelity to your standards and with continued fighting the skies will clear and you will get into the sun-light of the open without the shadow of a doubt." Billy's skies, however, did not clear and his 1920s were marked by a steady decline into alcoholism, depression, and financial dependence on his father. [49]

Time and again McAdoo arranged for Billy to join his business associates in oil ventures, but each time the experience ended badly. As Billy's health and behavior worsened, his father was reduced to reimbursing his employers for his wages. Drinking ever more heavily, Billy continually broke the gentleman's code: he borrowed money from his employers and did not repay his loans and club fees; he fell in with "bad company," and mixed lassitude with a jarring sense of entitlement. All the while he accumulated unpaid creditors, angry employers, and a lengthening charge sheet in police departments from New York to Arizona. McAdoo's letters were always supportive, but increasingly admonitory. "Really, my dear boy," he wrote like a latter-day Polonius to his 26-year-old son in 1921:

> You have got to realize that appearances in this world mean little or nothing. It is what men do that counts. Do not, above all things, live beyond your means or merely for the sake of keeping up appearances. Live within your earnings, and save money beside. In that way you will . . . lay the firm ground of self-respect which is absolutely essential to a successful career . . .
>
> I want to repeat, in all kindness, dear boy, but with none the less firmness, that I will not stand for a repetition of any such conduct as that which John and yourself were guilty of in New York.[50]

Billy drifted from "opportunity" to "opportunity" and slipped further into alcoholism. He married Molly Ferguson in 1922 and soon added two grandchildren to his father's long list of dependents. Their marriage was blighted by his drinking and punctuated by frequent separations. "He sees nothing whatever of Huger, Nona, or Ribs," Molly told Nell in March 1933. "Billy just called and said he was considering killing himself—such a mess but he got calmed down and said he felt better after talking to me. Sorry to bother you darling & please don't tell his father or anyone. He said he'd be alright if he didn't feel so alone."[51]

In 1932, while he campaigned for election to the US Senate, McAdoo sent Billy to New York under the care of Nona's then-husband Edward Cowles. Dr. Cowles reported that Billy had arrived drunk and often left his clinic without permission. Once he was away for four days, returning in the company of two policemen. Cowles diagnosed Billy as a chronic alcoholic and psychopathic personality. He recommended intensive psychiatric treatment and advised that for too long McAdoo had picked up after Billy, shielded him from reality, and allowed him to escape the consequences of his actions. "Billy is one of the most stubborn, the most egotistical and the most selfish men I have seen in a long time." McAdoo wrote back to request that Billy be given "as much latitude as possible."[52]

Billy continued to deteriorate. He and Molly separated for the last time in 1934 and divorced in 1936. In 1934 Billy, now 38, was arrested in New York City with a

22-year-old model after a fight in a restaurant. Following his father's intervention, Billy was released after a night in the cells, but not before the newspapers had featured the story. "I am sorry to say," McAdoo wrote to William Randolph Hearst to complain about the story being published, "that this youngster once in a while gets on the rampage—he can't take a little liquor without taking too much." McAdoo sent a clipping about this incident to Nell in California. "It makes me very unhappy but what can I do? <u>Nothing</u>. What a pity he has thrown his life away. I fear he is beyond reclaim."[53]

In 1935 McAdoo found Billy yet another job, this time with the National Aeronautical Association. McAdoo had recently been elected to its presidency, and he and Huger reimbursed it for Billy's salary. Billy was soon unemployed again, and a year later wrote from Florida to say that he had married Sarah Lummus, who had been arrested with him at the restaurant in New York, and to ask for a $100 wedding present. Billy also warned—or threatened—that he would take a New Deal relief job unless Mac increased his allowance. McAdoo sent the check and wrote to welcome Sarah into the family.[54]

Later that year McAdoo found another job for Billy, this time with Pan American Airways, courtesy of its founder Juan Trippe. "I assured him that you would stick to it and that he would never have occasion to be ashamed of you." Six months later Billy had received a promotion and a raise. "All this is hopeful. The boy may yet be rescued and be able to do something for his family." In fact, there was little improvement, and Billy never managed to stop drinking or to make his own way in life. He outlived his father by nearly twenty years but died by his own hand at Bellevue Hospital in 1960.[55]

Mac and Sarah's youngest son Robert was 11 when his mother died. The family called him Ribbs, and his personality was very different from that of his siblings. His father described him as "a very sensitive and shy boy, with an extremely humble opinion of himself . . . because he has gotten into the habit of thinking himself a 'bonehead,' as he puts it, and I think he is a bit discouraged." Eager to join Huger and Billy in the war, Ribbs joined the Naval Reserve after finishing high school in 1917. McAdoo arranged with Secretary of the Navy Daniels for Ribbs to be transferred to the Hampton Roads School for Ensigns and then to the Massachusetts Institute of Technology to train as a naval aviator. "You have never failed heretofore where you have tried, and you won't fail in the future," Mac reassured him. "I am telling you this merely because you depreciate yourself and your own capacity too much. It is a wrong attitude."[56]

The war ended before Ribbs could finish his training, and he enrolled at Princeton in February 1919. In July 1920 he was suspended on academic grounds, having failed three courses. He was readmitted in the fall, but in December was suspended again, this time after a drunken prank at a dance. Ribbs admitted to drinking that night, but denied that he was drunk. His father believed him but, doubtless thinking of Billy's problems, reminded him that "I think that it is much better never to take even one cocktail or one drink except in case of illness." Ribbs left Princeton soon after and completed his studies at the Babson Business Institute in Wellesley, Massachusetts.[57]

"Some way or other I hate to think of your becoming a <u>Wall Street</u> stock broker or banker," McAdoo wrote after Ribbs graduated from Babson. Remembering his own struggles in New York during the 1890s, and currently engaged in a campaign against Wall Street, McAdoo encouraged Ribbs to move to Los Angeles. His friends in the Bank of Italy had agreed to hire him in their bond department, and "you would not have to 'beat the sidewalks' here because they would take you into the office end of the work . . . I need not tell you how happy Nell and I would be to have you come and live with us . . . but you must make up your own mind about it."[58]

Ribbs stayed in New York. "Would it be too much trouble if I sent you a 'Directory of Directors' of N.Y. City to look it over? There are probably a great many people in it who could be of great help to me that you know." His bond business did not improve, and he moved to Los Angeles in 1923 to join his father in real estate speculation. He continued to drink heavily, married Lorraine Rowan, and returned to New York. Lorraine and Ribbs did not have children and they divorced in 1936.[59]

Ribbs died of double pneumonia in January 1937. He was ill for only three days and was unconscious by the time that McAdoo reached his sick bed. To his father Ribbs's death was "a blow that I have found it difficult to sustain, notwithstanding the philosophy I have always tried to cultivate about the hard knocks one must take in life." Ribbs was interred in the Arlington National Cemetery in a site that his father and Billy would eventually share. "It comforts me to feel that we shall at least be near each other in this way," McAdoo wrote in 1937, "if in no other."[60]

❧❦❧

These tribulations all lay in the future when McAdoo married Eleanor Wilson in May 1914. For some years their marriage sustained the intensity that had carried them through their tumultuous courtship. "I seem to have been in a strange daze in '14 and '15," Nell later recalled. "The war and mother & childbirth and the strain of the McAdoo family all apparently made a sort of automaton out of me." McAdoo resented any separation from his new wife and then from Ellen and Faith, who were born in May 1915 and April 1920. "Darling entrancing and enchanting being, your adorable blue eyes haunt me every minute in the most beautiful way and make me yearn for you more and more as the leaden weighted minutes go by," he wrote in September 1915. Eleanor felt their separation with equal intensity. "You're such a dear companion, as well as the most wonderful and fascinating lover that ever lived, that I couldn't live a day without you," she wrote in October 1919. "I love you, I love you beloved, darling, wonderful Man—and I shall love you forever and ever."[61]

McAdoo tried hard to protect his new family's privacy. In July 1914 he threatened a *Washington Times* photographer who had taken an unauthorized picture of Eleanor that "if he did not destroy the negative I would smash the camera or thrash him." His wife was not a "public character," and should be left alone. As the daughter of a president and wife of a prominent man, however, Eleanor *was* a public figure. Even in 1932, after McAdoo had won election to the Senate, a reporter noted that she still turned more heads than many Hollywood movie stars. Her hair was "iron-gray," but the 43-year-old was "younger and better looking than she ever was before in her life." Ellen and Faith, now 17 and 13, would adorn Washington society and their mother "will play the game gallantly as 'Mac's wife.' "[62]

By the late 1920s, however, the game was not so gallant in the McAdoos' marriage. McAdoo shuttled between Los Angeles and Washington and a new tone crept into their correspondence. "There is no reason to worry in any direction," he wrote from a train at the end of 1927. "Oh, if I can only help you by making you see this, my darling, I am sure that your overtired nerves will respond so quickly that you will believe in miracles!" McAdoo stayed in Washington for more than a month, and his letters home became fraught. "I had hoped that my absence would really help your nerves," he wrote in January 1928, "and I shall be grievously disappointed if you fail to get a benefit." Eleanor's replies revealed the depth of her emotional crisis:

> I want to try to explain—I had thought that you understood what I tried to say to you in that other letter—that, in this struggle I am making to become a normal person again and the right kind of wife to you, my dearest, it seemed better for me to be away from you for a few months . . . when I am with you I am in a constant nervous turmoil and so full of misery and despair that there is no hope of getting myself back into shape again . . . There is something awfully wrong with me, but I can conquer it, if I have more time and a chance to get some health again.[63]

McAdoo hurried home, but stayed only a week. "Darling, darling Mac," Eleanor wrote after he returned to Washington. "It seems to me that I am living in some sort of a dream—a very dreary dream about being lost in the dark—and I don't seem to think of little happy surprises and things . . . when this is all over, we will travel about and be gay and happy again and not worry about anything." Eleanor's wan optimism lifted McAdoo's spirits. "Isn't it strange?" he wrote back. "It is the very way I seem to have been groping for a year—my darling it is clear we have felt that way because we have been worrying about each other. I am sure it is only that!"[64]

This time McAdoo stayed in Washington until the summer. "You poor darling," he wrote in March, "I suppose the whole burden is thrown on you and that you will be worn out—losing perhaps whatever you have gained in the last month that I have been away." His demands that Nell provide daily reports on her activities and state of mind left her feeling pressured and peeved. "It is so upsetting, darling, that I never really please you or make you really happy no matter what I do."[65]

Eleanor visited Washington briefly, and McAdoo returned to California in June 1928 and stayed until the fall, but she was still in emotional turmoil. "As long as we really love each other there is nothing to worry about except health, and I am sure we can get yours back as soon as we quit needless worrying," Mac wrote in December. He came home for Christmas, but left soon after. By then his long absences and short returns reflected a marriage that had become spatially and emotionally distant. Nell went to Europe with her sister Margaret in 1929, and Mac offered to join her once his work in Washington was done. She declined because "If you had come out so soon, I could not have had the benefit of being away from you all to be calm and get my nerves in shape." He returned to California and the children instead. "Please believe me when I say that I am not hurt and that you need not think I am nor worry about it. But I do think it better for you if I don't write any more."[66]

"How is Mrs. McAdoo?" Byron Newton inquired in October 1929. "I thought I saw indications a year ago that she was drifting toward the borderland of that hell in which I have been living for the past three years . . . try to assure her that . . . it WILL SURELY PASS . . . Stand guard at the portals of thought . . . Hurl back every gloomy thought and image of disaster and despair." Physicians found little wrong with her, but Eleanor became increasingly depressed. "Every letter tells of a fight for health and happiness," her sister Jessie wrote in August 1931, and Mac put the best face on her anxiety and depression. "Nell does not sleep as well as she should and does not seem to regain her nervous vitality," he wrote in April 1930. "She isn't ill but she is just below par and we don't seem to be able to pull her back, but she has a lot of courage about it and is determined to get better and I expect that she will in time."[67]

The normally voluminous family correspondence in the McAdoo collections is thin for 1932 and 1933. Elected to the Senate in November 1932, McAdoo spent much of 1933 in Washington while Eleanor stayed in California. By May 1934, when their preserved correspondence resumes, dramatic changes were afoot. McAdoo had spent four weeks in the Bethesda Naval Hospital in April and early May suffering from a staphylococcus infection manifested by numerous painful carbuncles. "I had supposed that you would, at least, have sent me a few letters of encouragement and cheer," he wrote. "I had never imagined that you could be so heartless, so callous, so indifferent." Eleanor and McAdoo had separated at the end of 1933, and the seriousness of their breach was made clear in an appeal to Eleanor in May 1934 by her brother-in-law Francis Sayre:

> Poor Mac has gone through profound deeps of suffering through the past weeks . . . I am distressed and grieved by what he tells me—that you want a divorce. Oh dear Nell, I wonder, I wonder. Is it really <u>necessary</u>? Of course, I don't know your mind and heart; but I do know you don't want to hurt your children, or wrong Mac, or cloud the memory of your father and mother . . . As to Mac, of course it will break his life, and I fear it will break his spirit . . . and I can't help wondering if it's fair to him.[68]

Sayre's plea went unheeded. "I am so at sea, so confused about your attitude," Mac wrote two weeks later. "I have done everything I could think of to gratify every wish or whim of yours—but nothing seems to satisfy—nothing I suppose except the divorce you seek. It is incomprehensible to me—what it may do to me and to the children, [whom] you do not seem to have considered." Molly was currently divorcing Billy, and now it seemed that both father and son "would be dragged into court at the same time. It is a lovely picture to contemplate."[69]

Eleanor and Mac executed a property settlement that included a vacant lot in Beverly Hills, a cash payment of $5,000, an annuity of $6,000, and 10 percent of McAdoo's estate upon his death. "I do not hesitate to say," Nell's lawyer advised, "that it is the most unfair agreement I have ever seen a man submit to his wife." But haste was more important to Nell than haggling, and on July 17, 1934, she won a divorce in the Los Angeles Superior Court. She based her case on mental cruelty and neglect, deposing that she was interested in the arts while her husband "devotes his time to public affairs," and that his frequent absences in Washington deprived her of companionship for prolonged periods. McAdoo did not attend the hearing or contest the action, and their divorce was granted forty minutes after Eleanor filed her claim.[70]

Eleanor and Mac hoped to minimize publicity through a speedy hearing, but their plan backfired. News of their divorce received prominent coverage in the newspapers and questions were raised about its unusual speed. Allegations of sharp lawyering and political favoritism caused the presiding judge of the superior court to castigate Eleanor's lawyer for "contemptible if not contumacious" conduct in causing "a group of people to believe there is one procedure, slow and tedious, for the poor, and another, quick and active for the rich and prominent."[71]

"How are you, darling Father?" Sally McAdoo inquired. "The news in the morning's paper was no great surprise, but sad nonetheless . . . Maybe it feels pretty good to be a free lover after so many years of restraint—for one of your charms and proclivities!" Although his divorce had attracted much publicity, McAdoo hoped that it would be forgotten by the time that he sought re-election to the Senate in 1938. He had some grounds for this optimism. In 1870 the national divorce rate stood at 1.5 per 1,000 marriages, but by 1920 it had risen to 7.7 and was 7.4 in 1934.[72]

Although by the 1930s divorce was no more prevalent among the wealthy than the poor, its social stigma was stronger among the better off than the less wealthy. Newton Baker always held the views he had expressed in 1903, and in 1937 rebuked Walter Lippmann for leaving his wife. "I have been in the habit, for many years," he told Ralph Hayes, "of regarding as fatal controversies between well-bred people leading to divorce and the action of Walter in this regard seems to me to be beyond redemption." He also wondered whether Mrs. Simpson was "worth the gesture" of King Edward VIII's abdication and noted that "if we happened to have a bachelor president who fell in love with an experienced divorcee in the course of her second venture . . . I think sober American opinion would be greatly shocked." He was probably right; even in 1964 Nelson Rockefeller's divorce hurt his campaign for the Republican presidential nomination, and it was not until Ronald Reagan in 1980 that Americans elected their first, and so far only, divorced president.[73]

McAdoo's nervousness about the political consequences of his divorce grew as other members of his family passed through the divorce courts amidst considerable publicity. Harriet, Nona, Billy, and Ribbs all divorced during the 1930s, and soon after McAdoo's own divorce another scandal engulfed his second family.

Born in 1915, Ellen Wilson McAdoo had grown up in the public eye. She attended schools in California and Arizona, and then a finishing school in Paris with an eye to Vassar or Wellesley. When she was 19, however, her life changed course. In November 1934 the press announced that she wished to marry Rafael Lopez de Onate, a "Manila born motion picture actor," but that McAdoo's law partner William Neblett had initiated action to prevent the marriage because of de Onate's Filipino heritage. California law forbad mixed-race marriages, and McAdoo had apparently threatened to disinherit Ellen if she found a state that would marry her and Rafael. Nell was said to be "prostrated in bed" at the thought of what Ellen proposed to do. "Darling, don't feel so hopeless about Ellen!" her cousin Helen Bones wrote. "As I said to you before, she is a modern girl and if her marriage turns out unhappily you know she won't suffer the kind of agony your last years of married life were to you."[74]

De Onate maintained that his parents were Basque, not Filipino, and so the miscegenation laws did not apply. A month later the papers announced that the McAdoos had dropped their objection; Ellen and Rafael married three days later and left for Europe. "It all goes to show," McAdoo told reporters, "the truth of the old adage that 'love laughs at locksmiths.'"[75]

Ellen and Rafael stayed in Europe much longer than was usual for a honeymoon. "Oh darling Mac," Nell wrote in February 1935, "I know that she should be punished and she will be—she is bound to suffer—but please, please help her through this time." In April, five months after her wedding, Ellen gave birth to Ricardo. By then McAdoo had learned that his son-in-law had not come from a Spanish family at all, but had arrived in America "on a tramp ship from Manila as a deck hand" and had another wife and child in New York. McAdoo continued Ellen's monthly allowance but was mortified by her behavior. "In one letter she thinks I 'hate' her," he told Nell. "Of course I don't. Please tell her that—but I can't write about this matter. It always 'gets next to me' to think about it. I had such ambitions for her! But, alas, nothing can be done and nothing can be gained by grieving over the course she has taken."[76]

"Ricardito is enchanting and has my eyes," Ellen wrote from Austria in June 1935, "with huge pupils like Faith's. They are deep violet and too beautiful." She then warned that their stay in Europe would be lengthy:

Mummy dearest . . . we simply can't go back in October . . . We have to take four months off the baby's age (he's supposed to be born in July, making him an eight month baby). In October he will be seven months and we simply can't pass him off as three. He'll have teeth, will be sitting, and three month babies don't have teeth or sit . . . Also staying just a year is terribly obvious! Naturally everyone will know for certain that that's why we came here, and then everything would be ruined and all the money gone for nothing.[77]

Ellen, Rafael, and Ricardo stayed in Europe until the end of 1936. By then McAdoo had forgiven Ellen, but not her "scurvy husband." Two months after their return Ellen sued for divorce, alleging that Rafael was incapable of supporting her and had been mentally and physically abusive. He contested the divorce and the case received extensive newspaper coverage. Ellen testified that Rafael was often drunk and sometimes violent, and her father deposed that he had given them more than $8,000—their only income—during their marriage. Rafael countered that McAdoo had sought to prevent the marriage on racial grounds, had induced the couple to flee to Europe to avoid scandal, and now tried to prevent him from working as an actor.[78]

Ellen won her divorce, moved home with Nell, and lived from her father's allowance. She trained for a singing career and hoped to work in Hollywood, but her plans unraveled after she took to the stage drunk for her first performance. By the end of 1937 McAdoo was exasperated by Ellen's extravagance and her mother had lost patience with her. "She is really the most extraordinary child, such selfish egotism I have never seen in anyone so young. And such vanity." Ellen remarried in 1938, divorced in 1943, and died three years later from an overdose of sleeping pills.[79]

Mary Faith, Ellen's younger sister, was 14 when her parents divorced. She then lived with Eleanor and attended school in Los Angeles. Mac kept in close contact with Faith, supporting her financially and seeing her whenever he could. Faith was a sunny and agreeable child, but McAdoo was concerned that she might follow in Ellen's footsteps. "Do you not think," he wrote to Nell at the end of 1936, "that she may be getting too interested in the 'movies'? Heaven knows that one mistake of that sort is sufficient tragedy for a lifetime." Eleanor encouraged Faith to spend time with her father, but sometimes the strains of blending the fractured McAdoo clan made that difficult. Faith spent the summer of 1937 with her father and Harriet in Pasadena, but Eleanor stayed close at hand to "rescue Faith whenever I could. Harriet is a hard, disagreeable gold-digging horror and I knew that Faith would be pretty miserable, if she had to stay around the house with her all day." Nell's prickly relationship with McAdoo's first family did not improve; in 1938 she reminded him that "I am told by numerous people that some of your children feel very resentful toward me—that they speak of me with contempt and dislike."[80]

Faith stayed safely on the fringes of Hollywood society and showed promise as a writer. "I am so glad that you feel as I do about Faith's 'poems,'" Nell wrote to her sister Margaret at the end of 1937. "There is an exquisite purity in them that brings tears to my eyes." After her father's death, however, Faith reverted to her family's unsettled domestic patterns; she married Donald Thackwell, a Disney animator, in 1946 but married twice more before her death in 1988.[81]

United by their concern over Ellen and their pride in Faith, Eleanor and Mac soon re-established amicable relations. He sent money to pay for an operation in June 1935 and she replied warmly. "Ellen is such a heavy burden and I feel so deeply my responsibility for that tragedy that I hate to be an added burden. But I know your generosity and that you wouldn't want me to refuse your help."[82]

Eleanor never remarried but remained socially prominent. In 1937 there was press speculation that she would run for one of Los Angeles's congressional seats, but she concentrated instead on burnishing her father's legacy in magazine articles, as a consultant to Fox Studios for a movie on Wilson's life, and as the author of three books. McAdoo was supportive of Eleanor's literary efforts and put her in touch with publishers and agents. "You ought to write a novel next," he wrote in 1937. "You have a fine literary quality and with your imagination, I am sure you can do it."[83]

Nell took McAdoo's advice, but fortunately he did not live to see the result. In 1946 she published *Julia and the White House*, a thinly fictionalized account of her own life in which Eleanor was Julia, Ben King was Stephen Brady, and McAdoo was George Compton, solicitor general of the United States. Although engaged to Brady, Julia was swept off her feet by the much older and more urbane Compton and agreed to marry him instead. When she broke the news to Brady, he "kissed her roughly. 'Why, you little idiot,' he said. 'You stupid little idiot!' " Julia came to her senses, broke her engagement with Compton, and married Brady instead.[84]

⟳⊁⎜⊀⟲

"Your letters and postcards to [Faith] gave her great happiness," Nell told Mac in 1935. "I have done her a great wrong by getting a divorce—and you, too, of course. I am sure now that I was out of my mind when I did it . . . When I think of you and all we had together my heart breaks. Please forgive me for this—I know how disgusted you are with me and I'll try to take my medicine with more courage." Mac replied philosophically. "You must not blame yourself about the divorce. You did what you thought best . . . sometimes what I thought were mistakes turned out to be blessings."[85]

McAdoo had reason to be magnanimous, for he was soon to add another tangle to his family tree. In September 1935 the press announced that the 71-year-old senator would marry Doris Cross, a 26-year-old nurse. Reporters described Doris as "5 feet 2 inches in height, with eyes of blue, dark brown hair and of medium build," and her friends portrayed her as a "serious and quiet" Seventh Day Adventist. She was also very much in love with McAdoo; after lunch with him at a "little colonial inn," she noted in her diary, "I smothered him with kisses and told Mac how much I loved him. I call him P.M.—meaning Perfect Man."[86]

When Mac and Eleanor married in 1914, their twenty-six-year age difference attracted comment but not astonishment. In 1935, however, news of his marriage to a woman forty-five years his junior met amazement and ridicule. "He seems to have discovered the fountain of perpetual youth," one acquaintance declared. "All of the men and the attached women in your office send you hearty congratulations and best wishes for a long and happy future," William Neblett cabled from California. "The unattached and younger ladies of the force do not join enthusiastically in this message because of a tinge of jealousy." Another well-wisher thanked

McAdoo for his "remarkable courage in facing the common ridicule regarding May & October being united in marriage [that] gives me (in my seventieth year) a conviction that I should do likewise." Others were less charitable. "I was absolutely indignant when Mr. McAdoo married a young girl after his divorce from your sister," a friend told Margaret Wilson. "I still think he should have been ashamed of himself." Nell sent congratulations and Ben King, McAdoo's rival for her affections in 1914, sent his "genuine good wishes."[87]

Mac and Doris's time together was short but happy. Doris resigned from the Public Health Service and devoted herself to Mac's career. In 1936 she joined him on a flight to the Orient on Pan American Airways' China Clipper, and after he left the Senate in 1938 she took sea journeys with him to Hawaii and the Philippines. Younger than all of Mac's children except Ellen and Faith, Doris was able to bridge both sides of her husband's fragmented clan; at the end of 1940 she and Mac planned, but did not undertake, a trip to the Philippines with Harriet and Faith.[88]

McAdoo had one more surprise in store. In April 1937 the *Los Angeles Times* reported that he and Doris would soon become parents. The 73-year-old senator denied that "the stork" was expected, but in 1939 he did announce that he and Doris had adopted Ricardo de Onate, his 4-year-old grandson and Ellen's first child. Ellen had remarried in 1938 and moved to Kansas City, abandoning Ricardo to her father and Doris's care. "He is a fine little chap," McAdoo told Ellen, "and is getting to be very well behaved. Doris has certainly done wonders for him." Ricardo was renamed Richard Floyd McAdoo and became Mac's tenth child. He was forty-eight years younger than Harriet, McAdoo's oldest child, and only 5 when his grandfather and adopted father died. Richard attended the University of Southern California and became a management consultant in Washington. He died in 1993, having married three times, and was survived by two children. By then all of McAdoo's other children had died, but Doris survived them all. She died in July 2005, a few months before her ninety-sixth birthday and 141 years after William Gibbs McAdoo's birth. Mac's family circle had closed at last.[89]

Winter
1933–1941
❖

CHAPTER 14

The New Deal

McAdoo and Baker felt happier about politics at the end of 1932 than they had for nearly a decade. Although the Depression was three years old and more perplexing than ever, there was now hope of new ideas to address its causes and mitigate its effects. McAdoo, characteristically enough, was more optimistic than Baker, but even the skeptical Clevelander hoped that the New Deal might be a new beginning.

By the end of 1937, however, both men were disillusioned. Convinced that he was FDR's king maker in Chicago, McAdoo expected to play a major role in the new order. Although his political instincts, which valued decisiveness over deliberation and pragmatism over principle, coincided with those of the New Dealers, McAdoo soon chafed under the constraints of life in the Senate. As a legislator in a time of executive dominance he struggled to translate his self-proclaimed influence into substance. Far from being a central actor in the New Deal, he found himself in a supporting role that was too limited for his liking. He remained loyal to FDR and the New Deal throughout his term, but his loyalty became tinged with resentment at FDR's genial but firm refusal to allow him the prominence that McAdoo believed was his due. Unable to find significant fault with the ideas and policies of the New Deal, his disappointment with it was personal rather than ideological.[1]

Baker's disillusion was more profound. Although he had his doubts about FDR and the early New Deal, he suspended his disbelief for most of 1933 but then concluded that it represented so great a challenge to his values that he could no longer support it. By 1936 he had become a man without a party, too old-fashioned to remain a New Deal Democrat but too mindful of the past to become a Republican. Now out of political life, Baker instead became a spectator of a game that he no longer understood. Saved by his innate self-deprecation and fortified by his prominence at the bar, Baker did not descend into bitterness as the New Deal passed him by. Instead, he argued his case against it in terms that revealed his quiet refusal to adapt his values and convictions to the new conditions that swirled around him.

❧❦❧

"The independence of the Senatorship appeals to me," McAdoo told Daniel Roper, who was soon to become secretary of commerce. "I can do what I think is right, regardless of consequences . . . Old formulae have got to go into the discard and new and, if necessary, daring methods must be employed to save the country." Even before he took his seat in the Senate, he proposed an agricultural stimulus program, a federal bank deposit insurance scheme, and reorganization of railroads under federal control. "To hell with hoary formulas and outworn theories in times like these!"[2]

As a Senator McAdoo received a salary of $10,000 a year, less 15 percent docked by economy legislation, and a staff of four. He asked for seats on four of the Senate's most powerful committees, Agriculture, Foreign Relations, Banking, and Interstate and Foreign Commerce, although he conceded that it was too much to expect more than two of them. Unwilling to serve alongside Carter Glass, his old sparring partner over the Federal Reserve legislation, McAdoo left the Banking and Currency Committee off his wish list. In fact, he won none of his coveted committees but was assigned to Banking and Currency and the Patents Committee. During his term he received other committee assignments including Appropriations and Territories and Insular Affairs, and he became chairman of the Patents Committee. Even so, this was not the triumphant return he had hoped for and was a reminder that the Senate's seniority rules applied to all members, even those who had already distinguished themselves in the executive branch.[3]

When FDR and Congress set to work McAdoo was swept up in the urgency of the moment. "We are deluged by bills from the White House which we are expected to enact into law in short order," he told Eleanor. "It is somewhat bewildering." Although he had doubts about some of the bills pushed through during the Hundred Days, he did nothing to impede them. "I think I am doing some good work here," he told William Neblett, "although I have carefully avoided the limelight. I feel I can do much more as a new member by the course I am taking than if I were making speeches on the Floor of the Senate. That development will come later."[4]

McAdoo was sometimes critical of the New Deal but always kept his concerns private. He complained about the haste with which bills passed through Congress and worried that the Senate had become a mere cipher of the administration.

"Roosevelt continues to ask for unusual powers," he told Nell in March 1934. "I think we should pipe down a bit and try to assimilate some of the 'indigestibles' we have already prepared before we go further. There is wide discontent among business men and Conservatives and much uneasiness and confusion."[5]

Publicly, however, McAdoo was an enthusiastic New Dealer. In 1938 a conference of Californian Democrats hailed his "unbroken record as a militant New Deal Senator who has supported the administration on every issue" and as a pioneer of the whole reform program. McAdoo had been a friend to labor since his days at H&M and the US Railroad Administration (USRRA), and in the Senate he continued to support it. Except for his vote to condemn sit-down strikes in 1938 he voted for every major bill supported by organized labor, including a proposal in 1933 for a thirty-hour working week, the Labor Relations Board bill of 1935, and the provision of low-cost housing in 1936.[6]

McAdoo assumed that the promises made to him at the Chicago convention meant that he would be very influential in the new administration. FDR did consult him about cabinet appointments, but McAdoo sensed that the president-elect was already edging away from him. He was noncommittal about McAdoo's suggestions of Bernard Baruch for Treasury and George Creel for Navy, and about his view that a Californian should be in the cabinet. McAdoo objected to Carter Glass for Treasury and William H. Woodin for Commerce because of their conservatism, but soon after FDR nominated Woodin for Treasury and the equally conservative Claude Swanson for Navy, and his cabinet included no Californians. McAdoo agreed with FDR's choice of Cordell Hull for secretary of state and urged places for Thomas Walsh, who was nominated for attorney general, and Daniel Roper, who became secretary of commerce. Although FDR sent word that "he felt that the so-called McAdoo element of the party was well represented in the cabinet with Walsh, Hull and Roper," McAdoo was "astonished that the assurances given to me may be disregarded."[7]

Thenceforth McAdoo and FDR corresponded mainly over patronage and rarely over policy. Unusually among Roosevelt's correspondents, McAdoo addressed the president as "Dear Frank," but they had never been close friends. Although he consulted McAdoo over banking legislation in 1933, FDR otherwise kept McAdoo at arm's length. "I wish he would take some advice from older and experienced men instead of from the theorists only," McAdoo complained early in 1934. "Malignant people" claimed that he undermined the president "merely because I won't be a rubber stamp or stultify my intelligence. I have tried to help perfect measures which come before the committees of which I am a member but I have always supported the administration on the final votes." FDR appreciated McAdoo's support but rarely sought his advice. "I do hope that he will try to keep both feet on the ground during the next session," he told Claude Bowers in October 1934. "If he would only play with the team it would be best for him, as well as for the team."[8]

✪✪✪

Although McAdoo struggled to influence the administration's policies he was determined to control its patronage in California. He worked so hard toward that goal that he became known as one of the most enthusiastic and ruthless dispensers and withholders of patronage of any Democrat on Capitol Hill.[9]

McAdoo was inundated by requests for jobs from the moment he won election to the day that he left the Senate. "There are about six or seven million Democrats in the country who want jobs," he told the press in January 1933, "and from the way things are looking I don't blame them." Because he was the only Democratic senator from the nation's sixth most populous state McAdoo's mail was heavy with requests for federal jobs. "I think being a Senator in these strenuous times is worse than being at the head of a great department," he told George Fort Milton in 1934. "There, at least, one has an adequate organization to take care of the demands that are made upon him."[10]

McAdoo complained about the time he spent on patronage but reveled in the power it gave him. Reports that FDR was responsive to his requests helped salve his pride and conceal his failure to influence the president in other ways. "The man who was said to be 'out of it,' never to return," the *Kansas City Star* noted in April 1933, "is back in a big way and has procured enticing seats for a considerable group of his friends." W. H. Kiplinger claimed in his *Washington Newsletter* that "Mac" was "the one Senator who gets what he wants because Mr. Roosevelt fears him. McAdoo wants influence. He gets it through patronage. One year hence he will control more minor officials and more governmental policies than any other single Senator."[11]

"Kip" overstated his friend's influence but not his desire to acquire it. Hiram Johnson, California's other and senior senator, disdained patronage politics and left McAdoo free to use it to build up his own influence. George Creel in San Francisco and Hamilton Cotton in Los Angeles set up clearing houses to vet applicants for jobs, and they favored McAdoo's electoral base in the south of the state over Northern California. "Nothing is to be expected of [San Francisco]," Creel told McAdoo in January 1933. "The local Democratic party has been Republicanized so thoroughly that it will take another generation to work any change."[12]

Ideologically predisposed to an active state, McAdoo was also alive to its partisan possibilities. In June 1933 he criticized Secretary of the Interior Harold Ickes for consulting state governors and Chambers of Commerce before appointing public works administrators. Governors were too parochial and Chambers of Commerce were "usually highly reactionary. They do not represent the people. The Senators do." He asked that Hamilton Cotton be appointed administrator in California, but Ickes declined because he did not want his programs to become patronage machines. McAdoo had similar arguments with Secretary of Labor Frances Perkins, the Farm Credit Administration, and the Department of Agriculture. "Really, Frank," he complained to J. F. T. O'Connor, "I have never seen such a bunch of political simpletons as we have got at Washington . . . If they want to take the heart out of the Democratic party in California they are certainly pursuing the right course."[13]

McAdoo spent the rest of his term assiduously dispensing patronage while bemoaning his treatment by the administration. Cabinet secretaries did not understand politics, Washington bureaucrats made appointments without consulting him, and FDR seemed too partial to McAdoo's enemies within the party. "I really believe that I am capable of making suggestions about appointments in California," he told Attorney General Homer Cummings in August 1936, "even to infallible cabinet officers, which would be advantageous to the public service as well as to Party cohesion, but I despair." Two thousand men had already been discharged from public works projects in Los Angeles that summer, and another seven thousand would soon lose their jobs. "This is nuts for the Republicans," and FDR might lose California in the coming election unless saner heads like McAdoo's prevailed in Washington.[14]

Senator McAdoo also worked to direct federal largess to Californian industries. He insisted that the wine industry benefit equally with brewers in the unwinding of prohibition in 1933, and in 1936 used his position on the Appropriations Committee to tax offshore fish-processing to protect California's pilchard fishery. He worked with the movie industry to protect it from labor laws and with local quarries and bitumen makers to ensure that they supplied building and road projects in the state, and won compensation for lost logging revenues when Yosemite National Park was expanded in 1937. He was also a tireless advocate of agricultural irrigation. In 1933 he won funds to build a canal between the Colorado River and the Imperial Valley, and he supported a project to dam the San Joaquin and Sacramento Rivers to provide hydroelectric power and water storage for the Central Valley. In 1937 that project was enshrined in legislation, and FDR sent "Mac" one of the pens he used to sign it.[15]

Federal funding for infrastructure was plentiful in the early years of the New Deal, and despite their personal differences—Hiram Johnson privately referred to McAdoo as a "crook"—the two men cooperated to maximize their state's share of it. In Santa Barbara County alone they won a total of $22 million to build a National

Guard Armory, a reservoir at El Cielito, a water filtration plant at the Sheffield Reservoir, a county bowl amphitheater, and a sewerage system for La Mesa.[16]

Concentrating on Southern California while Johnson focused on the north, McAdoo won many federal projects, including expansion of the Port of Long Beach, flood control in Los Angeles County, deepening of the Stockton Shipping Channel, and construction of federal and municipal buildings. In 1936 the Agricultural Adjustment Administration (AAA) told him that it had paid Californian farmers more than $15 million in the previous year, and the Works Progress Administration (WPA) reported that it had allotted $79 million in grants and $17 million in loans to the state between 1933 and 1935. In 1937 McAdoo calculated that California had received nearly $1.5 billion in federal funds since 1933, including $507 million in Reconstruction Finance Corporation (RFC) loans, $265 million from the Farm Credit Administration, $105 million from the AAA, $137 million from the Home Owners' Loan Corporation, and $319 million from public works programs. The New Deal provided patronage and infrastructure on a grand scale, and McAdoo never let voters forget who brought the pork home.[17]

McAdoo also devoted time to his constituents' personal concerns. He helped radio stations negotiate with the Federal Communications Commission, followed up queries about veterans' pensions, pleaded with the Home Owners' Loan Corporation (HOLC) to save defaulters, and found room in Civilian Conservation Corps (CCC) camps and WPA rolls for his correspondents. In April 1934 he took up the case of Mearon Perkins, an African American janitor at the El Centro Post Office. Perkins had foiled a burglary and killed the intruder, but was now unemployed and destitute. McAdoo sponsored a bill to award Perkins $1,800 and successfully lobbied Postmaster General Farley to reinstate him. "There was a time when your El Centro friends didn't think you had a chance to benefit by your brave act," a friend told Perkins, "but when Senator McAdoo took an interest in your case we knew he would never stop trying, as he is a man who never forgets a promise."[18]

❖❖❖

In the Senate McAdoo voted for all the emergency measures proposed by the White House in 1933, breaking ranks only to support early payment of the veterans' bonus. His loyalty continued for the rest of his Senate term, which took in the 73rd, 74th, and 75th Congresses. Despite questioning some of their provisions, McAdoo voted for every significant New Deal measure between 1933 and 1938 and became one of FDR's most dependable supporters in the Senate.[19]

When McAdoo did vote against the White House, he usually erred on the side of liberalism; he voted for the soldiers' bonus in 1933 and 1934 and supported the Wagner-Costigan and Gavagan anti-lynching bills in 1935 and 1937 despite FDR's wishes. Yet his rebellions were only occasional and sometimes contradictory; in the same year that he supported the Gavagan bill he voted to confirm the administration's nomination of Senator Hugo Black to the Supreme Court despite Black's opposition to anti-lynching bills.[20]

Lacking strong support from the White House or the chair of a powerful committee, McAdoo introduced few major bills into the Senate. Even so he was a prolific legislator; during the 74th Congress he sponsored more than one hundred bills, the most important of which arose from his Patents Committee and concerned the implementation of the International Convention for the Protection of Industrial Property and the establishment of a court of patent appeals. He also introduced dozens of bills granting pensions to constituents and payments to individuals such as Mearon Perkins, to allow exhibits in the California Pacific International Exposition to enter the country free of tariffs, to exempt profits from the 1932 Los Angeles Olympic Games from taxation, to authorize the minting of commemorative coins to mark the opening of the Golden Gate Bridge, to authorize federal funding for adult education, to reduce the interest rate on late taxes, to construct a radio station to broadcast to Central America, and to pay Rosalie Rose $1,454.50 to settle her claim for injuries sustained in a collision with a Coast Guard truck.[21]

McAdoo's bills were referred to committees for further scrutiny, but only a dozen navigated the whole legislative process. He reintroduced some of the remainder during the first session of the next Congress and shoveled thirty more into the mill. His patent appeals court bill went back to the Patents Committee and his adult education bill received an adverse committee report. McAdoo's success rate was typical for that of senators of his day, but it was a far cry from the hopes that he had brought to the Capitol in 1933. Life in the Senate led him to conclude that he was a natural executive but an unhappy legislator.[22]

McAdoo focused on four main topics during his time in the Senate: banking reform, agricultural policy, court-packing, and foreign policy. As one of the self-proclaimed fathers of the Federal Reserve System, he was determined to protect and strengthen it. In 1913 he had tried to include a bank deposit guarantee in the Federal Reserve Act, and in 1932 he had sought to include the guarantee in the Democratic platform, but had lost those battles to Carter Glass. On the Senate Banking and Currency Committee in 1933 McAdoo again urged action on deposit insurance and for the expansion of the Federal Reserve System to cope with the banking crisis that threatened the whole economy.[23]

By then FDR had abandoned his opposition to deposit insurance, and even Glass had weakened. The Banking Subcommittee approved a bill covering deposits up to $10,000, and then on a sliding scale down to 50 percent of deposits over $50,000, to take effect in July 1934. Glass managed to water this plan down and in its final form the Glass-Steagall Banking Act of 1933 established the Federal Deposit Insurance Corporation (FDIC) but limited its coverage to $2,500 per deposit. McAdoo was disappointed that his more generous scheme and its immediate start had been thwarted, but he was delighted that the principle had been won.[24]

McAdoo remained on the Banking Committee but won few other victories. Early in 1934 he and Glass failed to block Treasury's appropriation of gold held by Federal Reserve Banks, but in other matters they were at loggerheads. McAdoo pushed for inclusion of all banks in the Federal Reserve System and increased powers for the FRB over the Reserve Districts, but Glass maintained his opposition to a more centralized structure. McAdoo also pushed for legislation to allow banks to open branches throughout their banking districts. He justified branch banking as a way to make banks more accessible to their customers, but his critics suspected that it was a gift to his political donor A. P. Giannini and the Bank of America, which wanted to open branches throughout the Twelfth Reserve District. Fearful of creating powerful banks remote from their depositors, Glass and other members of the Banking Committee blocked McAdoo's proposals throughout his Senate term.[25]

Agriculture, and especially measures to increase farm income, was another of McAdoo's interests and showed him willing to push government action beyond the limits imposed by the New Deal. In March 1933, as Congress began deliberations on what became the Agricultural Adjustment Act (AAA), McAdoo urged the creation of a United States Farm Mortgage Bank to refinance up to $5 billion in farm loans. Lenders could swap their mortgages for government bonds, and the Farm Mortgage Bank would renegotiate those mortgages on longer terms at lower interest rates. Current rates were about 6 percent, but McAdoo thought that mortgagees would accept 4 percent in return for certainty of repayment. Banks could use the new Farm Mortgages to offset their loans, and farmers and their communities would be spared further foreclosures. McAdoo's bill was sent to his Banking and Currency Committee, where it languished for want of approval from the White House.[26]

In the end McAdoo voted for the AAA, which embodied the administration's preferred strategy of crop reduction through payments funded by a tax on processors. When the Supreme Court found the AAA's processor tax unconstitutional, McAdoo proposed a constitutional amendment to empower federal regulation of agriculture. This was defeated 46–40 in the Senate, but at the end of 1937 he introduced an amendment to substitute a new agriculture bill with a proposal to impose federal control over the production of key agricultural commodities. Under McAdoo's Agricultural Equality Bill of 1937 the secretary of agriculture could determine the total annual production of cotton, wheat, corn, hogs, tobacco,

and rice and estimate the proportion of each crop that would be consumed do-
mestically. Producers could sell that proportion of their crop on the open market
at a price not less than a figure determined by the secretary of agriculture. The remainder of the crop, which was the exportable surplus, could be sold to a federal
agency that would export it at whatever price it could command. The president was
also authorized to impose tariffs on imported food to maintain domestic prices.[27]

McAdoo's ideas went far beyond the administration's plans. "My main objection to your bill," Secretary of Agriculture Henry Wallace wrote, "is that it would
take a . . . disastrous step into further economic isolation" by dumping farm sur-
pluses on Europe while inflating domestic prices through high tariffs. Secretary of
State Hull criticized the scheme as "an intolerable burden on American consumers of American products, and it would seriously disrupt all efforts to restore some
semblance of order and stability to international economic relations." "Let me
say," McAdoo replied, "that the American market for many years has been reserved to the American laboring man and the American manufacturer by tariff
rates which thoroughly protect them. The American farmer, on the other hand,
has never had any protection . . . In all fairness, how can we justify this economic
massacre of our farmers?" His bill died in committee and in 1938 he voted for a
new AAA based on crop reduction payments.[28]

McAdoo's reputation as a loyal but impatient New Dealer was cemented by his
support of court-packing in 1937. FDR's plan to nominate new judges to sit beside
those who refused to retire energized his opposition, but McAdoo remained on his
side. Court delays were caused by "technical tactics of clever lawyers, or by judges
who have become incompetent and dull-witted, who sit for life, and are not ac-
countable to any authority." The president's proposal did not usurp the Senate's
right to consent to judicial nominations, and no judge would be forced to retire.
"I am sure that Franklin Delano Roosevelt is not, by nature, character, or purpose,
susceptible to dictatorial rabies." Although he did not sit on the Judiciary Committee, McAdoo lobbied his fellow senators to support the president's plan. "I am
doing my best to help," he told a friend, "but I want to tell you . . . that the situation in the Senate is far from satisfactory. It is going to be a mighty close vote."[29]

As court-packing struggled in the Senate McAdoo suggested a compromise. If
the Supreme Court was expanded to fifteen judges it could hear appeals as of right
rather than at its discretion. An efficient court system with an open appeal structure
would allow more litigants their day in court and improve the current situation in
which the Court granted or denied certiorari without giving reasons. McAdoo
hoped his plan would remedy this "grave injustice" and win over wavering legislators. By then, however, court-packing had become so unpopular that compromise
was impossible. The Senate Judiciary Committee unanimously rejected McAdoo's

plan and reported adversely on the administration's bill. In the end McAdoo was one of only twenty Senators who remained loyal to FDR's doomed scheme.[30]

McAdoo also used his Senate pulpit to comment on foreign policy. He had moved away from internationalism during the 1920s, first by rejecting the League of Nations and then by demanding that Allied war debts be fully repaid. That had been important in securing William Randolph Hearst's support for his Senate campaign in 1932, and once elected McAdoo was less amenable to FDR's foreign policy than to his domestic program. Although he was abroad when the Senate considered joining the World Court in January 1935, McAdoo paired his vote against the bill. "You are certainly a great help in the oly [sic] favor I ever aed [sic] of you," Hearst cabled, "or evr [sic] will."[31]

McAdoo's insistence on payment of war debts also coincided with Hearst's views. He was appalled by the Allies' decision in 1932 to default on their war loans and was unsympathetic to linking repayment of the loans to renegotiation of reparations from Germany. The Allies had begged for American loans to save them during the war, and without them Germany would have won. While they now cried poor, Britain, France, and Italy spent lavishly on their military forces; between 1932 and 1936 Britain alone spent $618 million on its air force while it defaulted on $786 million in loan repayments. McAdoo would have no truck with the League of Nations or the World Court while Europeans treated their other obligations with contempt.[32]

McAdoo's support of the League of Nations was originally expedient and always contingent, and he became even less interested in internationalism during the 1930s. "I had a fine trip around the world," he told Josephus Daniels in 1935. "It added to my settled conviction . . . that we had better maintain the obstinate independence of the United States so far as European and Far Eastern affairs are concerned." Although McAdoo was hostile to Italian fascism and German Nazism—he supported a boycott of the 1936 Berlin Olympic Games to protest against Adolf Hitler's policies—he rejected collective action to contain them. Internationalism had been tried once and found wanting, and Wilson's "Crown Prince" declined to try it again.[33]

As McAdoo became more isolationist he became even less supportive of FDR's foreign policy. He voted for the Neutrality Act of 1937 against Roosevelt's wishes, and in 1938 called for the exemption of American shipping from Panama Canal tolls. This was contrary to Wilson's position in 1913 and embarrassed Roosevelt in 1938. Equal treatment of shipping through the canal had been guaranteed by treaty, but McAdoo argued that Britain and France, having defaulted on their war loans, were in no position to preach the sanctity of international agreements.[34]

For McAdoo isolationism did not mean disarmament and it did not lessen his appetite for territorial expansion. While Europe rearmed and Japan expanded, he argued in 1935, "we will be asinine to the one-thousandth degree if we are not ready for any situation which may face us in the future." The United States should be able to defend itself but remain neutral in other disputes that threatened world peace. "I believe in organizing and making our might the mightiest," he told Cordell Hull in 1939. "If we do that, we will be able at least to assure peace for ourselves."[35]

As a member of the Senate Committee on Territories and Insular Affairs Mc-Adoo joined the inaugural Pan American Clipper flight across the Pacific in October 1936. He and Doris flew eight thousand miles from San Francisco to Hong Kong and inspected facilities on Hawaii, Midway, Wake Island, Guam, and the Philippines on the way. He was proud to see the American flag flying over these islands, but saw that modern aviation had made them vulnerable. In the Atlantic and Caribbean, as well, foreign powers retained colonies that were close to American shores. Bermuda was only seven hundred miles from New York, and a bomber could cover that distance in two and a half hours. "If the American people are not an utter pack of damned idiots they will insist upon our acquisition of every West Indian possession of every foreign power so that these important islands . . . shall be under our flag. No debt settlement should even be considered without taking these islands as partial payment."[36]

Roosevelt had no intention of imposing McAdoo's dollar imperialism on Britain and France or even closer to home. In 1938 McAdoo suggested that Mexico sell its half of the Baja Peninsula and part of its state of Sonora to the United States and use the proceeds to compensate Americans who had lost their property to Mexican nationalization. "I know you will not misunderstand me when I say in all frankness that the Department would not be able to give favorable consideration to this proposal," Acting Secretary of State Sumner Welles replied. "I believe that the resentment in Mexico would probably be duplicated in other areas of the New World, and that much of the good will for the United States now existing in those countries might be impaired, if not altogether undermined, by such a suggestion on the part of this Government."[37]

❖❖❖

"I know that there is nothing in political life, except empty honors, and fierce antagonisms," McAdoo complained to William Neblett in May 1936. "I often wonder if the game is worth the candle." McAdoo had always protested too much about the burdens of public office but he was genuinely ambivalent over seeking another term in the Senate. He would be 75 by the time of the 1938 elections, and in 1937 he had supported the court-packing plan that portrayed 70-year-old judges as too old to be efficient. "I have never really liked this job," he told Tom Storke in January 1938, "and when I was elected in 1932, my mind was made up not to seek re-election." With a young wife to support, an ex-wife to maintain, and numerous children dependent on him, McAdoo once again dreamed of restoring his fortune. "It is not too late yet for me to redress my personal affairs if I devote my time to it for the next six years."[38]

Yet McAdoo enjoyed life in Washington and still seemed young for his years. In 1937 The Los Angeles Herald Express noted that he "cuts a gallant figure at Washington society dances and to the popular swing music, shakes a festive and non-rheumatic leg." Three Democrats had entered the race for his seat, so he would face a primary election if he sought another term. "It means the expenditure of money and energy," he told Storke. "I have plenty of the latter and damned little of the former, but maybe I can pull through if I finally decide that I want to come back here."[39]

McAdoo vacillated during the winter of 1937–1938. In a performance that would have been familiar to his supporters in 1920, 1924, 1928, and 1932, he agonized over his age, his poverty, and his alleged desire to live a private life. As he had done in 1924 McAdoo asked his friends to discuss his candidacy and how much they might contribute to his campaign. Storke reported that they all wanted him to run, but had little money to donate. Democrats in 1938 would win plenty of votes but few donations because of the current economic recession and dislike of FDR by the well-off, and McAdoo would suffer as "one of the administration's wheelhorses."[40]

McAdoo also asked local party leaders about his chances. They responded positively, complimenting him for winning federal projects and jobs, but they also relayed negative views. "I find some criticism of you, on the part of the women," Hensley Davis wrote from Napa, "because of your domestic experiences." Some voters there also objected to his support of Giannini's branch banking scheme. From Stanislaus Country came news that voters appreciated McAdoo's support of FDR and his ability to win projects, but that some criticized his divorce and re-marriage to a much younger woman. William Hill in San Joaquin County had heard no criticism of McAdoo's private life but plenty about the high-handed ways of his patronage boss William Neblett. Even so, Hill thought that McAdoo would win as long as he paid attention to the "cow counties" outside San Francisco and Los Angeles.[41]

By then McAdoo had decided to run. Jim Farley promised him support from Washington, but McAdoo sought a more personal endorsement. "The more I think of it," FDR replied, "the more convinced I have become that you ought to seek re-election. I do not need to tell you that I have always appreciated the fine support you have given to my Administration. Therefore, your retirement from the Senate would be a distinct loss to the public and all I can say is that I earnestly hope that you will run again." Convinced that FDR's support would win him the primary, McAdoo announced in March 1938 his candidacy for renomination.[42]

McAdoo faced four rivals. Peirson Hall was a US district attorney who had been prominent in the anti-McAdoo faction of the state party and had accused him of taking bribes from applicants for federal jobs. Hall's allegations were unsubstantiated, but they reinforced unease among some California Democrats that McAdoo had played the patronage game too enthusiastically and too greedily. Although McAdoo saw him as his most dangerous opponent, Hall withdrew from the race just before the filing date and after his charges against McAdoo began to unravel.[43]

Of his other opponents McAdoo worried most about John W. Preston, who had been a US district attorney and had sat on the California State Supreme Court. Preston ran as a conservative New Dealer who combined support of FDR with opposition to court-packing and reorganization. His campaign wilted in the face of McAdoo's huge patronage network, and he won only 9 percent of the vote in the primary.[44]

Sheridan Downey was a more dangerous rival. "He is looked upon as an unstable and smooth demagogue," McAdoo told Farley, "who is always only one or two jumps ahead of the sheriff." Downey had fallen in with Upton Sinclair's End Poverty In California movement and had been his running mate in the 1934 gubernatorial election. They lost badly, but Downey ran ahead of Sinclair and emerged as a popular orator. Although ostensibly loyal to FDR he advocated a more generous old age pension scheme than that instituted by the Social Security Act in 1935. He first supported Francis Townsend's plan for cash payments to all retired Americans over 60, but switched to the Ham and Eggs scheme that promised unemployed Californians over 50 a weekly payment of $30 in scrip. Recipients could use the scrip to buy goods and pay state taxes, and it would circulate at face value as long as it was endorsed each week by a 2 cent stamp sold by the state. After a year, and if the scrip had been stamped 52 times, California would redeem the scrip for $1 in currency to its holder at the time.[45]

Critics derided Ham and Eggs as a cruel fantasy. Merchants would not accept the scrip at face value, inflation would soar, and California would be flooded with $1.5 billion of scrip each year that it could not honor. Not surprisingly, however, Ham and Eggs was popular with California's burgeoning retiree population in and around Los Angeles. The movement boasted 270,000 members and collected 789,000 signatures on a petition to have the plan voted on as a state constitutional amendment in November. "The people have listened to you and your knockers," a

Ham and Eggs supporter told McAdoo in September. "They are tired of living in poverty and distress. Why not give it a try instead of going against the plan?"[46]

McAdoo was sure that the power of incumbency and FDR's support would see him home. He appointed George Creel to manage his campaign in the north and Tom Storke to oversee the south, and won endorsements from major newspapers, labor groups, and railroad organizations. "The President gets down on his knees and pleads with 'Dear Mac' to run again," the Los Angeles Times noted. "It would seem to assure Dear Mac of the nomination. The New Deal has slipped, but it hasn't slipped far enough to lick the White House favorite at the primary." Alert to criticism of his patronage machine, McAdoo forbad any pressure on federal employees to contribute to his campaign. Despite his earlier fears, little was made of his domestic life during the campaign, although his opponents certainly used his age against him.[47]

McAdoo may have been confident, but his advisors were worried. At the end of April Creel conceded that the primary would be difficult to win. Nearly half of California's Democrats lived in Los Angeles County, and they were entranced by Ham and Eggs. Newspapers there were overwhelmingly Republican and "viciously antagonistic" to McAdoo, but elsewhere in the state press opinion was friendlier and voters were receptive. McAdoo would have to win in his previously unfavored north and interior and aim to minimize his losses in Los Angeles. "The defeat of Mac is a matter that should concern you in Washington," Creel told Jim Farley. "I want to see an overwhelming victory, which I am sure we can have with proper financing."[48]

Every candidate found it hard to raise funds in 1938, and McAdoo was no exception. He told Bernard Baruch that "my enemies are . . . resorting to the most despicable methods, but I have no doubt that I can lick them. The problem, my dear fellow—and I hate to mention it—is the same old thing—money." Baruch had already sent $2,500 but declined to do more. McAdoo instead used $3,500 from his own funds, $1,000 from Huger, and $5,000 from the oil baron John Paul Getty, to augment his campaign chest. "Everyone tells me that I am away in the lead and that there is no doubt about the primary result," he told Creel, "unless some extraordinary thing should happen."[49]

Extraordinary things were happening in California, but McAdoo seemed only half aware of them. In his first campaign broadcast he stressed his commitment to the New Deal and his "devotion" to FDR, ignored Downey and Ham and Eggs, but promised to improve the Social Security Act so that "the disemployed will not starve, nor will our aged know poverty and sorrow."[50]

McAdoo campaigned throughout the summer but struggled to excite his electorate. Tom Storke thought that he was tired and unimaginative, resting on his laurels and refusing to engage with Downey and Ham and Eggs. "I was disappointed and distressed to see how Mac had slipped as a gladiator in the political arena where he had once reigned as a champion." He seemed old fashioned as he won endorsements from party leaders and editorial support from newspapers, stumped the state boasting of his experience and influence in Washington, and studiously ignored the tidal wave bearing down on him. One critic sniped that "it was characteristically kind of President Roosevelt to make a friendly gesture to an old man who is on his way out . . . For God's sake, why don't you get busy yourself, or quit!"[51]

McAdoo was more complacent than tired; he was sure that he would benefit from FDR's popularity in California and that the allure of Ham and Eggs would evaporate before the primary. In his campaign speeches he stressed his loyalty to FDR and the New Deal and his success in winning federal funds. "What is more," he told a radio audience at the end of the campaign, "I have not stooped to capitalize on poverty and unhappiness. No promise has been made that cannot be kept; no hope has been held out to human misery that cannot be fulfilled." Already more than $46 million had been paid to Californians under the Social Security Act, and much more would follow. Democrats should reject a "pink pill that will cure social evils over-night" and entrust their future to the experienced leadership of Roosevelt and McAdoo.[52]

Downey ran an effective campaign. Twenty years younger than McAdoo, he told voters that "the elderly junior senator is through; his record of non-accomplishment in office has proven his unfitness to represent the people." Even though the Ham and Eggs organization did not formally endorse Downey, he certainly championed it and that was enough to win its large constituency. He also publicized rumors that McAdoo's managers had indeed pressured federal employees to donate campaign funds. McAdoo angrily denied that charge as well as another that surfaced at the end of the campaign. Peirson Hall, who had once hoped to win the nomination before endorsing Downey, showed Catholic and Jewish audiences a photograph of what he said was McAdoo's Ku Klux Klan (KKK) "imperial passport" from 1924. McAdoo called the photo "utterly and wantonly false" and cited his endorsement by the *B'nai B'rith Messenger* and his criticism of Nazi Germany as proof of his hatred of bigotry.[53]

Allegations of shakedowns of federal employees and a fake KKK membership card were infuriating distractions, but the Ham and Eggs movement was McAdoo's major problem. "I am not scared," he told Marvin McIntyre in the White House ten days before the election, "but these fanatics who have grown hysterical over this '$30 every Thursday' may be able to ditch us." He asked FDR to "reexpress the hope that California will return me to the Senate to support the Administration." Roosevelt obliged by warning in a speech on Social Security against "short cuts to utopia," but otherwise McAdoo was left to face the Ham and Eggs movement on his own. Just before the election he reminded listeners that the scheme would be voted on as a state constitutional amendment in November, and so was irrelevant to the Senate contest.[54]

By then it was too late. On August 30, 1938, Downey won the primary by 136,000 votes, registering 46 percent of the vote to McAdoo's 34 percent. Downey ran up large majorities in Los Angeles and Southern California that outweighed McAdoo's majorities in the north. "I am still a bit stunned," Judge Emmet Seawell wrote from the California State Supreme Court, "but my calmer judgment persuades me that no human force could have stayed the surge of the multitude that was carried forward in the belief that Utopia's gates had been swung open to them and Mr. Downey had bidden them enter into the land of eternal plenty and happiness."[55]

McAdoo was mortified by his loss to a "cheap demagogue." He was sure that he would have won had he endorsed Ham and Eggs, but he would not support a scheme that would bankrupt the state. "I saved my honor and lost the job," he told Huger, "—and am satisfied." He did nothing to help Downey in the general election, which he won, and was pleased when the state party declared that pensions should be financed through the federal government. Once elected, Downey lost interest in Ham and Eggs and served as a conservative New Dealer.[56]

Commentators agreed that McAdoo had been swept away by Ham and Eggs, but their accounts of his political demise also shared a sense of wasted opportunity. He had entered the Senate as a lion of Wilsonian progressivism and as FDR's king maker, but left it as a much diminished figure who had traded the substance of office for its trappings. Frank Kent noted that Hiram Johnson was closer to FDR than the man who had helped him win the nomination, and that the widespread belief in 1932 that McAdoo would loom large in the Senate and with the White House had been dashed. "He has not counted for anything in either. It is true he succeeded in naming a good many of his constituents to office, but in no other direction was he heard of." Ray Tucker was even more damning. McAdoo had once conquered the Hudson River and been the dynamo of the Wilson administration, but in the Senate he had become a "patronage monger for California marshals, postmasters, fish inspectors, and district attorneys." He was now a "parochial patriot" who gave "too much heed to tracks and not sufficient thought to terminals; he has agitated himself over the mechanism and concerned himself only slightly with its meaning."[57]

Kent and Tucker ignored McAdoo's role in the creation of the FDIC, but they had a point: his reputation had significantly declined during his time in the Senate. Perhaps age had finally caught up with him, or perhaps he correctly saw himself as a better executive than legislator. He had languished in the Senate because he could not assert himself against its seniority system, or with an administration that humored the old lion but did not empower him, and because he was too vain to play the part of foot soldier to which FDR gently but firmly assigned him.[58]

Having lost the only elected office he had ever held, McAdoo was forced once again to consider his future. This time he was nearly 75 years old, but he refused to shuffle quietly into retirement. "You are too generous to suggest that I might be a leader to represent the cause of the people in 1940," he told two well-wishers after the primary, "but even if the plan were realizable I could not approve it because I shall never again seek an elective office. The remaining years of my life I want to devote to something else, chiefly to making adequate provision for those who are dependent upon me. Too long I have neglected my duty in this regard."[59]

⚔

Newton Baker did not hold public office during the New Deal, although there was speculation at the end of 1932 that FDR would appoint him secretary of state. "Of course it would be silly for a man at my time of life to decline to seek a chance at the presidency and then accept the secretaryship of state," he told Ralph Hayes. "As a matter of fact, I would far rather be president of the University of Virginia than either." Nevertheless he half expected Roosevelt's offer and would have accepted it from a sense of duty, but the idea was far-fetched. Through McAdoo, FDR owed much to William Randolph Hearst for his nomination, and choosing Baker to run his foreign policy would have alienated a powerful supporter. Nor was there a close personal bond between them; they were outwardly cordial but never close, and photographs of them together revealed a reserve that bordered on discomfort.[60]

In April 1933, after Cordell Hull's appointment as secretary of state, FDR did offer Baker the ambassadorship to Germany. This was an important post because Hitler had just assumed dictatorial powers after the Reichstag fire. "I have thought about it with real appreciation of your confidence and full realization of the importance of the service," Baker replied. "It is, however, quite clear to me that I am wholly unavailable."[61]

The two men corresponded cordially for the rest of 1933 and into 1934. In September 1933 Baker praised Roosevelt's call to the AEF to reprise its selfless patriotism to combat the Depression. "I can't tell you how particularly delighted I am by what you say," FDR replied. "I look forward to seeing you here some time real soon." In April 1934 he appointed Baker to lead an investigation into the Army Air Corps, then reeling from its attempt to deliver air mail, and to recommend its future disposition. Baker's board suggested an increase in the army's airpower and the creation of a general headquarters air force within the War Department, but it rejected calls to consolidate military aviation into a separate service.[62]

Roosevelt accepted all of Baker's recommendations on the Army Air Corps, but they met rarely and their correspondence grew fitful. In November 1934 FDR wrote about rumors that Baker had been retained to challenge the Tennessee Valley Authority (TVA). "One of my principle [sic] tasks is to prevent bankers and businessmen from committing suicide! . . . I am writing you thus frankly because it seems to me that in the public interest you and I should discourage suicide." The rumors were true, and Baker's role in the legal fight against the New Deal widened the distance between the two men. FDR did renominate him to the Permanent Court of Arbitration at the end of 1934, but by then Baker privately called him "der Fuhrer." "The President is to broadcast tonight," he told Bess in March 1937. "I am very reluctant to hear him because he always tries to make me envy or hate someone and I do not like either to hate or envy anybody." He did listen, but found FDR "all adrift and wrong from every possible point of view." For his part FDR thought that Baker had surrendered to conservatism. "Three years ago . . . I had a long talk with some of the University of Virginia Trustees and begged them to offer the Presidency to Newton," he told a friend in 1934. Had Baker taken that job he would have stayed liberal, but now he consorted with reactionaries. "I fear now . . . that he had [sic] definitely made his own bed!"[63]

By then Baker knew that he had fallen from presidential favor. He told his brother Frank in May 1935 that "I have heard that when people mention my name . . . they are told that 'Mr. Baker is a very estimable man, but his recommendation is of no importance in this administration.'" Apart from one uncharacteristically cruel jibe in 1936 that "I confess . . . that the fact that he could get infantile paralysis at fifty has seemed to me significant," Baker's differences with FDR were ideological rather than personal. "The President is moving too fast," he wrote in October 1937. "I do not doubt his intentions nor am I wholly out of sympathy with many of his purposes, but it is impossible to bundle up the fate of one hundred and twenty million people and commit it to one person to work out according to his own mind."[64]

At first, though, Baker tried hard to like the New Deal. Mindful of Republican failings during the 1920s and of the gravity of the Depression, he applauded the Hundred Days and paid tribute to FDR's "courage and good cheer." But the honeymoon was short-lived; in May 1933 Baker warned that Congress had ceded "dictatorial powers" that would be dangerous precedents, and in October he declined to speak in favor of the National Recovery Administration (NRA) because he disapproved of its collectivist ethos. "I do not believe that anything so vastly intricate and varying as the commerce and industry of a nation like the United States can be thus centrally administered," he told the head of the NRA's Speakers Division. "Of course, the whole progress of civilized society consists of limitations upon the liberties of savages in the interest of developing community responsibility and

advantages. My only anxiety . . . is that we do not take away too much liberty before we are . . . ready to replace it with community spirit."[65]

By the end of 1933 Baker found it increasingly difficult to reconcile his views
with the spirit of the New Deal. Reluctant to express his concerns publicly, and
torn between his disapproval of the old regime and his fear of the new order, Baker
used his correspondence to express growing disquiet about the recovery program.
In October 1933 he complained about its tendency to favor debtors over creditors;
he had no sympathy for the super-rich, but noted that most of the "creditor class"
were humble people who had worked hard, had saved diligently, and now faced
losses because of popular sympathy for their debtors. Speculative capitalism had
disgraced itself in the 1920s, but that was no excuse to impose a "collectivist revolution" that treated investors like Russian Kulaks and the improvident like heroes.
So far Roosevelt had resisted that temptation, but Baker feared that he would not
do so for much longer.[66]

His fears deepened during 1934. "I have asked myself a dozen times . . . why I
was instinctively cold to the so-called 'New Deal' experiments and I have thought
out the answer," he told a friend in May. It was too quick to trade individual liberty
for collective security, and the sight of bureaucrats in Washington running the
economy made him feel "as though the children in the kindergarten had ousted
the faculty and that the result of their activities was likely to do grave harm." Yet
"the job which President Roosevelt faced when he was inaugurated was both more
complex and more lonely than that of any statesman in our modern American history," and "he has certainly done far better than I would have known how to do."[67]

Baker aired his concerns more publicly from the beginning of 1935. News of his
retention to fight the TVA spurred inquiries as to why he had broken ranks. He
answered that the TVA "threatens an irreparable injury to all that I value most in
the Constitution." That document did not empower the federal government to
establish industries, to enrich one region at the expense of others, or to diminish
the value of private investment through publicly funded "yard-stick" competition.
The TVA was therefore unconstitutional, and Baker happily led the utilities' fight
against it.[68]

Baker's views on the TVA strengthened the belief that he had moved a long way
to the right since his time as mayor of Cleveland and in Wilson's cabinet. David
Lilienthal, the TVA's director, reminded a congressional hearing that Mayor Baker
had built a municipal electric plant to compete with private utilities, and that as
secretary of war he had approved federal generation and sale of power from Muscle Shoals. Others noted that he had endorsed the Water Power Act of 1920, which
granted leases for hydroelectric generation from navigable rivers, but now had
forgotten his principles to win briefs from wealthy clients.[69]

Baker denied any inconsistency. In Cleveland he had acted within his powers to stop rapacious monopolies, and at Muscle Shoals he had only supported the sale of power that was surplus to the government's proper function of producing munitions. This was very different from generating electricity solely as a commercial activity. After the war he thought that Muscle Shoals should be operated by a government-owned corporation devoted to the production of fertilizer and explosives. Surplus power could be sold to utilities for distribution to their customers, but Baker had never advocated direct federal distribution of electric power and he opposed it still.[70]

Baker did not live to see the unsuccessful outcome of his litigation against the TVA, but his faith in the rule of law remained strong. In 1935 he told the Ohio State Bar Association that lawyers should resist usurpation by the executive of powers reserved to the legislature and judiciary, but that he was hopeful that the checks and balances of constitutional federalism would endure. "I have never been very much disturbed about a revolution in the United States," he told Owen Young in January 1935, "as it seems to me that the necessary ingredients are not present, and I certainly am not disposed to assume that the President would try to pack the Supreme Court, or that the necessary majority of Congress would try to do so against his protest."[71]

Two years later he was not so sure. He was horrified by the court-packing plan, but hesitated to publicize this because of his prominence in the fight against the TVA. Privately, however, he made his objections clear. Although he was unsure about FDR's arguments that appeals on constitutional issues should proceed directly from the federal district courts to the Supreme Court and that worthwhile cases often failed to win certiorari, he was convinced that appointing younger judges to sit alongside those over 70 was an affront to judicial independence. Unlike McAdoo, Baker was convinced that court-packing would lead to executive tyranny. "If we were to elect a Ku Klux Congress and a Ku Klux President, as there have already been Ku Klux state legislatures and governors, the possibility of controlling the Supreme Court to effectuate their passionate legislation is an appalling thing to contemplate." FDR's claim that old judges were inevitably reactionary and inefficient was specious; in reviewing Supreme Court decisions Baker found that "the great landmarks of liberty vindicated by opinions which have become the very text books of freedom [were] written by hands almost trembling with age."[72]

As debate over court-packing intensified Baker grew more suspicious of FDR's motives in proposing it. It was tantamount to saying that "if the President tells the Congress that they must pass a certain piece of legislation and the Congress does it, then no court is allowed to hold it unconstitutional under pain of being superseded by one in sympathy with the President's wish." That would imperil every minority in the country, including Catholics, Jews, and white southerners. When Carter Glass attacked court-packing on those grounds, Baker thought that "his discussion of what the Supreme Court has meant and still means to the South in its effort to preserve white supremacy . . . may well rouse that whole section. For the first time I am beginning to feel that the proposal may be beaten and if it is the President's prestige will be shaken enough to make him behave for a while."[73]

Sometimes Baker criticized the New Deal for not enunciating its wider objectives, but in other moods he saw a clear plan at work. His case against the New Deal echoed that of the majority of former progressives who, in Otis Graham's phrase, evoked "a parade of imaginary horribles" of coercion, paternalism, collectivism, and class conflict. In November 1935 Baker condemned the National Youth Administration's assumption that public welfare was the best that young people could hope for. "I am troubled because most of our efforts nowadays seem to be to help youth," he told Daniel Willard, "rather than to make it possible for youth to help itself." He preferred nongovernmental means to help young people and served on the Youth Commission of the American Council on Education to assist groups such as the YMCA and the Boy Scouts.[74]

Baker also objected to the New Deal's propensity to ameliorate individual distress through legislation and taxation. "I have always believed, and still believe, that the duty of government is to let the citizens promote their own welfare." To think otherwise, he told an audience in 1937, was to espouse the "strange philosophies" of fascism and communism that placed the state above the individual. "When the idea is erected that the Government is a universal insurance society," he told a friend, "competition for the benefit of its protection ceases to be on the basis of deserts and comes to be a mere question of organized pressure for minority preference." In January 1936 he reacted to FDR's attack on "unscrupulous money-changers" by noting that the American economic system had produced many more wonders than injustices. "But now," he told Peggy, "the President summons the poor to hate the rich and practically tells every sloathful [sic] and improvident person in the country that instead of realizing his own shortcomings and redoubling his own efforts, he should look upon all successful people as enemies and join in a crusade to despoil them!"[75]

Taxation was the most obvious form of that despoliation. Although he was not as obsessed with taxes as some other critics of the New Deal, Baker's attitude to them changed as his skepticism about the New Deal deepened. He began with noblesse oblige, telling the retailing magnate E. A. Filene in February 1932 that "I am so made that I like to pay taxes and I am never sure that I can make as good use of any money I have as the Government will make for me." Three years later, after taxes had risen and the New Deal's redistributive agenda became clear, Baker liked paying taxes much less. The New Deal had created a huge debt that would take generations to repay, and the federal government had become an engine of economic redistribution that served partisan ends and special interests without regard to the common good.[76]

High income and gift taxes hit Baker hard because his wealth came from partnership dividends paid in cash and then diverted in gifts to his wife and children. Those gifts easily exceeded the tax threshold of $5,000 per year, and in 1935 Baker retained a lawyer to contest the taxation of gifts he had made to Bess. How, he wondered, could a transfer to his wife be classed as a taxable gift? Had he not taken a wedding vow to endow her with all his worldly goods? Like a latter-day champion of William Graham Sumner's 'Forgotten Man,' he told his brother Frank that "my concern is not for the prosperous or the well-to-do; they usually manage somehow to find bread and butter. But the people who live just above the economic margin . . . always have to pay." FDR had replaced the message of hope that had elected him in 1932 with a campaign of hate and envy to win re-election in 1936.[77]

Baker also objected to what he saw as a false dichotomy between property and personal rights. "When one says that he puts human relations above property and gives one man's property to another for some philanthropic or benevolent reasons," he told Frank in 1935, "he necessarily affects human relations in both directions." A widow who relied on income from a mortgage to support her children had every right to foreclose if her debtor could no longer pay. "Your illustration of the woman getting six % on a mortgage while the great mass of the people are out of work or on half time," Frank replied, "leaves me cold." Unabashed, Newton objected to a proposal to change the Fourteenth Amendment to deny its protection to corporate property. "I never represent a corporation without having a vivid feeling of all sorts and conditions of simple people who have entrusted their savings to its operations," he told the chairman of the Federal Power Commission in 1934. "A constitutional right or immunity today asserted by a great corporation may tomorrow be asserted by some poor devil as his only refuge from exploitation and oppression."[78]

Baker also saw signs of the New Deal's class war in its labor policies. Much attention had focused on employers' actions against employees, but intimidation by unions of nonmembers and employers had been ignored. Baker supported workers' rights to organize but worried that union leaders saw themselves in permanent conflict with employers. "I do not believe that there is any such inescapable opposition of interest," he declared in 1936, and "nor do I think it fair to charge all industrialists with a desire to oppress labor and all labor with a desire to rob capital and I am, therefore, deeply apprehensive of Federal legislation which recognizes any such conflict as either necessary or proper." Measures such as the National Labor Relations Act of 1935 were so intent on protecting workers' rights that they ignored the broader public interest. "My guess," Baker told Peggy in January 1937, "is that after a while we will all get tired of this incessant turmoil and decide that the consuming public has some rights which neither employer nor employee can be permitted to sacrifice."[79]

The New Deal forced Baker to reassert his own philosophy of the proper role of government. Liberalism under the New Deal had become more coercive than he could countenance. "Government at its best," he had written in 1918, "is the surrender by each individual of only so much of his individual right and liberty as must necessarily be surrendered for the common good." He had been adventurous in his use of municipal power in Cleveland, but that was within a single community; he had been enthusiastic in using federal power after 1916, but that had been in the context of a world war. Ordinarily, he wrote in 1936, "I am extremely jealous in the matter of making concessions from the reserved powers of the states to the general government." That was the assumption upon which the nation had been established, and to change it now was needless and sinister.[80]

Instead, Baker thought, the federal government needed to work within the framework established in 1789 and to modify it only by constitutional means. In June 1936 he told John H. Clarke, who had fought with him for the League of Nations but against him over the New Deal, that "I do not like to see our Government managing people or managing their business, though I concede that in certain respects and under proper safeguards, the latter may be increasingly necessary." Instead, he told another friend at the end of 1936, he preferred the principles by which he had governed Cleveland and served Woodrow Wilson in Washington:

> I started in life as a liberal. That term had very definite connotation to me. It meant a person who was in favor of liberty for others, and the others in question were considered as individuals and not as masses. I frankly think I am still just as much of a liberal and exactly the same kind of a liberal as I was forty years ago. In the meantime, a lot of people have adopted a new definition for the term and have excluded me from the ranks of liberalism because I reject their definition.[81]

⋙✦⋘

Baker's objections to the New Deal did not transform him into an uncaring reactionary. As he criticized the New Deal for its centralism and coercion he also helped local and voluntary associations to assist young people and the unemployed. He served on the Ohio Executive Committee of the Boy Scouts, continued to be generous to charities, and chaired the Cleveland Community Fund to raise funds for the Salvation Army, children's institutions, the YMCA, and local hospitals. He also stayed at the helm of the National Mobilization for Human Welfare to coordinate donations for distribution within the communities that raised them. In December 1934 Baker wrote to FDR that "we can feel that we did persuade the country that the Government has not taken over the whole relief and social service task, and that the need for local and personal assumption of responsibility was at least, in your phrase, no whit less necessary this year than last."[82]

Baker also supported the general cause of education and some individual educational institutions. He served on the boards of trustees of seven universities, including Johns Hopkins, Ohio State, and Tuskegee Institute during the 1930s, and in Cleveland supported the Western Reserve University and Cleveland College. The latter, an affiliate of Western Reserve and dedicated to adult education, held a special place in his affection. He taught courses there in international relations, donated generously to it, and bequeathed it his personal library. Western Reserve supported the college while it could, but during the Depression it needed more help. "I am unwilling to abandon what I think is the most valuable educational institution I have ever been connected with," Baker told potential donors in 1933. "The college really is necessary if we are to meet the possibility of discontent, if not rebellious sentiment, which the depression is creating on every hand." After slashing its budget by 50 percent, firing many of its staff, and cutting its courses, Cleveland College did survive and in 1937 had 4,800 students. By then Baker was chairman of its board of trustees.[83]

In 1928 Baker joined his fellow alumnus and friend John W. Davis on the board of trustees of Washington and Lee University. They watched as the Depression eroded the university's slender resources; in 1932 its endowment was $1.4 million and its enrollment stood at 862 students. Even so, he and Davis declined to accept New Deal funds to build dormitories and remodel its library because they believed that the federal government had no constitutional power to disburse funds for those purposes and because they feared for Washington and Lee's independence. "I did not see how our college could teach students to take a critical view of what is here proposed," Baker told Davis, "when the college was itself a beneficiary of the thing which to my mind ought to be criticized." They won the argument, but Baker was relieved when a bequest in 1936 allowed Washington and Lee to honor his scruples but also make its improvements.[84]

Social cohesion meant much to Baker during the 1930s. He worried that the values that held American society together had frayed, and saw religious tolerance as integral to that consensus. He therefore agreed to serve as Protestant cochairman of the National Conference of Jews and Christians (NCJC), an organization dedicated to dialogue between Christians and Jews, but felt uncomfortable in the role. Although nominally Episcopalian, he had long since ceased to be an active member of any congregation and preferred to keep his spiritual beliefs to himself. Religious intolerance, he thought, stemmed more from social behavior than the doctrinal differences that so concerned the NCJC; Jews and Christians clashed because of a shared misconception that their ways of life and worship were incompatible and because many Jews saw themselves as excluded from important areas of American society. Similarly, many Protestants disliked Catholicism because "the good Catholic acknowledges the temporal supremacy of an alien authority." Tolerance would therefore come from public education, social interaction, and intermarriage instead of doctrinal debate.[85]

Despite frequent offers to resign Baker remained as Protestant co-chairman and then honorary chairman of the NCJC until his death. As the NCJC came under pressure to mobilize American opinion against anti-Semitism in Germany, however, his unease returned. He had no sympathy for Hitler's anti-Semitism but insisted that the NCJC should concentrate on religious tolerance at home. "My sympathy and, to the extent I can be helpful, my aid will naturally go to those in other countries oppressed for religious and racial reasons," he told the head of the NCJC in June 1933, "but whenever activity in the foreign field might stir up religious or racial prejudice here, I am afraid that I shall have to stand aside." He told another correspondent that Americans would be affronted if a group of citizens in Berlin condemned their treatment of African Americans, and Germans deserved the same courtesy in return.[86]

There was indeed much work to be done at home to combat intolerance, but Baker had implied a moral equivalence between German reality and American possibility that eroded his ability to campaign effectively against either. When a correspondent accused him in March 1932 of pandering to "the shrewdness, smartness, and zeal of the kikes," and warned that "I have found . . . Jewish homes generally being private homes of prostitution, Christian girls hired as maids but forced to be slaves to Jewish passion," he reacted gently. "I propose that you pray for me and I will pray for you and the God in whom we both believe will probably then give the greater influence to that one of us whose spirit is most in accord with His divine will." His reaction was a model of moderation, but it smacked of moral complacency that belittled the evil unfolding in Europe.[87]

Even at home Baker's concern for social inclusion had limits. He watched the Great Migration of African Americans from the South to northern cities such as Cleveland with concern; his city's old black community, rooted in "the Oberlin tradition" of "self-respecting, industrious and educated colored people," was now swamped by newcomers who were "untrained, uneducated, and undisciplined . . . We now have in Cleveland sixty or seventy thousand negroes wholly unaccustomed to city life . . . so that our negro population comprises the greatest peril we have from the point of view of crime and vice." Housing projects, paid for by the New Deal, sprang up to accommodate Cleveland's new black immigrants, and Baker feared conflict between their inhabitants and the city's white population.[88]

Baker's composure soon returned. Racial prejudice, like religious intolerance, lay beyond the power of reason to eradicate because "as no one argues himself into a prejudice, of course it is impossible to argue one's self out of one." He thought that racism and bigotry were less evident in 1937 than they had been a generation earlier, and that they would continue to wither so long as they were not agitated. In that year, however, six African Americans were lynched in the United States and in Germany the Buchenwald concentration camp opened. Baker's serenity never veered so near to complacency and had never been so ill-timed.[89]

❧❦

Baker was less critical of Roosevelt's foreign policy than he was of the New Deal at home. The two men had been strong supporters of the League of Nations during Wilson's presidency, and they remained committed to it during the first half of the 1920s. Baker was much more so than Roosevelt, but by 1928 both had abandoned hope of immediate US entry into the League. Despite their differences over domestic politics Baker and FDR shared internationalist instincts and a conviction that the United States needed to engage with other nations to foster trade and encourage peace. Baker was thus prepared to give Roosevelt the benefit of the doubt on foreign policy after 1932 because he recognized the president's difficulties in dealing with isolationists in Congress and with movements that sought only domestic solutions to the Depression.

From the outset, however, Baker found good and bad in FDR's foreign policy. He was pleased by Cordell Hull's appointment as secretary of state, seeing him as a Wilsonian internationalist and champion of trade liberalization. Soon after, however, he was appalled by Roosevelt's scuttling of the London Economic Conference that convened in June 1933 to reduce tariffs and revalue currencies. Hull and James M. Cox led the American delegation to the conference, but at a crucial point in its deliberations FDR sent Raymond Moley to London to announce that he would not agree to stabilization of the dollar while the American economy was in crisis. Hull was left humiliated and the London Conference ended in disarray, but Baker refused to criticize the president. "Bad as the Economic Conference business is," he told Ralph Hayes in July 1933, "I frankly think there are a lot of worse things in the making and I prefer to play the part of Grisilda to that of Cassandra." FDR had been "unmannerly and rough" toward Hull and the conference, but he must have had good reason for his change of heart.[90]

Baker found much to worry about as he looked abroad in 1933. Italy, Germany, and the Soviet Union were in the hands of dictators, and in Asia things were no better. Japan was controlled by militarists determined to win hegemony over China and Southeast Asia and divided only over whether their main foe was Russia or the United States. Japan was already at war in China, and Baker urged the administration to work with the League of Nations to impose economic sanctions to force her to withdraw. The United States, with extensive Pacific possessions, had legitimate interests to protect against Japan, and Baker advised a combination of measures to appease and contain her. He suggested that Congress and states repeal their Japanese exclusion immigration and property laws and told his law partner Thomas Sidlo that "If I were Secretary of State, which thank the Lord I am not, I would have some conversations with Great Britain and France, looking to joint naval defense of the interests of the white races in the Orient."[91]

Japan posed the most obvious threat to American interests, but Baker also watched Europe closely. As he had shown within the NCJC, however, a combination of personal and intellectual factors made him slow to denounce Nazism as a mortal threat to world peace and democratic values. He had once spoken German fluently, read its classics, and had attended university at a time when German scholarship was the envy of the world. "I admired the social conscience of the Germans under the Empire and had more sympathy than I should have had with Bismarck's Kulturkampf." That had not prevented him from waging war against the Kaiser, but it had left him with respect for the German people and their capacity for intellectual greatness and social advancement. He had nothing but contempt for Nazism, but hoped in October 1933 that "time would be given to the real liberal elements among the Germans so to strengthen themselves so that when Hitlerism gives way or modifies, the choice will be in favor of intellectual liberalism rather than Communism on the one side or racial fanaticism on the other."[92]

Things, of course, only got worse. Baker told Peggy in 1935 that "the anti-Jewish riots in Germany seem to be growing more serious and I imagine mean that the Jews, Catholics and Protestants have been conspiring against Hitler . . . One might wish them success but for the fact that if they overthrow Hitler they are likely to go communist and take their turn at killing thousands of Nazis which will keep Central Europe boiling, like a volcano, with unpredictable results." Mussolini's invasion of Ethiopia that year was "abominable," but Baker told the director of the World Peace Foundation that it was futile merely to scold him. "I suppose it is very naughty of mankind to be so warlike, but I have no doubt that those of us who feel so must recognize that we cherish a minority opinion."[93]

What, then, was to be done? Unlike McAdoo, who reacted to the deteriorating global security situation by advocating armed isolation, Baker maintained a wan faith in multilateralism. Believing that public awareness of international affairs was vital, he remained active in groups such as the Foreign Affairs Council, the World Peace Foundation, and the Institute of Pacific Relations. Yet he saw more obstacles than opportunities as the 1930s wore on. "The tide of world affairs is running swiftly and strongly against every principle for the promotion of which the World Peace Foundation was organized," he told its director in March 1935. "And this tide is surging against the tenets of our belief not merely in Europe, Latin America and the Far East, but ever more heavily, if not yet irresistibly, in our own nation."[94]

Yet Baker refused to despair and restated his support of American entry into the League of Nations. His statement to the contrary in 1932 had not been a renunciation of the League, he claimed, but only a recognition that immediate entry was not then possible. In 1934, however, with FDR in the White House, Ralph Hayes no longer badgering him to improve his political prospects, and the world lurching toward Armageddon, Baker told the American Academy of Political and Social Science that the time had come to resume debate over what modifications to the League's Charter would be necessary for the United States to ratify it. "I would not be in favor of the United States joining the League of Nations with any commitment to send military or financial assistance abroad except as the wisdom and necessity of so doing should be voted by the American Congress," he wrote later, but it could still "bring very powerful aid to a single nation or a group of nations resisting aggression." He told another audience that the League had so far prevented Europe from plunging into another world war and that "it may yet save us from catastrophe."[95]

Baker continued to advocate American ratification of the World Court as another act of international engagement. He did not think that the court by itself could stop war, but, along with the League of Nations, he believed that it might strengthen the rule of law in international relations. Joining the World Court involved ratification by two-thirds of the Senate of the Statute of the Permanent Court of International Justice and of three reservations, which emphasized that the United States was not bound by World Court decisions and advisory judgments to which it did not consent, which were agreed to by the Senate before it rejected the court in 1926. These reservations were signed by Herbert Hoover in 1929, deferred by the Senate in 1931, and then revived in 1935.[96]

Baker urged ratification of the statute with the reservations and was grateful for FDR's support. In January 1935 he told a radio audience that "In our own country, as in every civilized country, the public peace is kept by a process of self-discipline, conciliation, arbitration and adjudication. If the peace of the world is to be kept, mankind has as yet developed no other agencies than these to accomplish that end." Now, thanks to FDR and because of the need for strong organizations dedicated to international peace, Americans had another chance to join fifty other states that were committed to justice rather than violence.[97]

Cowed by a furious campaign led by William Randolph Hearst and Father Coughlin, ratification of the World Court fell seven votes short of a two-thirds majority of the Senate in 1935. This was the same margin that had defeated the League of Nations in 1919, and Baker was disappointed that once again a minority of senators had blocked a great step forward in internationalism. He hoped, however, that this defeat would prompt a reduction in the Senate's powers over foreign policy. "That reform is far more important than mere membership in the World Court, gracious and reassuring as such membership would be both to ourselves and to the rest of the world."[98]

Repudiation of the World Court marked a strong isolationist turn on Capitol Hill, and Baker was dismayed to see Congress react to the deteriorating situation in Europe and Asia with a succession of neutrality acts. He saw this isolationist impulse as a throwback to a more ignorant era; in 1917 Woodrow Wilson had struggled to persuade his people of the need to intervene in the Great War, but now radio and newsreels had brought the world's problems directly into their homes. Many had reacted by reasserting old notions of isolationism, but the information Americans received was so distorted that their capacity to understand foreign affairs was limited.[99]

Baker saw neutrality legislation as an improper restraint on the president's power to conduct foreign policy. During his lifetime Congress passed three such laws, all of which FDR signed reluctantly and then tried to circumvent. The Neutrality Act of 1935 banned the sale of arms to belligerents and warned Americans not to sail on combatants' ships. The Neutrality Act of 1936 added a prohibition against American loans to nations at war, and in 1937 another Neutrality Act forbad shipment of passengers or cargo to belligerents on US vessels and banned American citizens from sailing on belligerents' ships. FDR won only one concession in 1937: a "cash and carry" clause to allow belligerents to buy American goods if they paid for them in cash and took responsibility for their transport. In 1935 isolationists also proposed the Ludlow Amendment to require a referendum before Congress declared war, but opposition from the White House buried it in the House Judiciary Committee.[100]

Baker supported FDR against the Neutrality Acts and the Ludlow Amendment. Isolationists had "sold the people on the idea that war can be prevented by some kind of abstention; that laws will keep us out of war. I wish I could believe it. What we really need is a concert of action among the well disposed nations." Americans had learned during the last world war that they could not stay on the sidelines while great issues of liberty were at stake, he told another group in 1937, and neutrality on questions of right and wrong was tantamount to moral blindness. The Ludlow Amendment was "incredibly wrongheaded" because it would create delay in the face of real crises and "a madhouse of popular discussion" over imaginary ones.[101]

Although he did not live to see the outbreak of World War II, Baker expected it to come. "With four aggressive nations loose and bent on world domination," he wrote in January 1937, "I should be in favor of any war necessary to restrain any one of [them]. As I understand the situation, freedom of speech, freedom of thought, religious and political, and other great principles upon which civilization as we know it rest, are denied by the philosophies of Russia, Germany, Italy and Japan. These civil and religious rights seem to me indispensable to human happiness and human growth and if war is necessary to preserve them, I should regret the necessity of making the choice, but would not hesitate for a moment in making it."[102]

Now deeply critical of the New Deal at home but supportive of it abroad, Baker hesitated to translate his attitude to it into tangible political form. When the American Liberty League was established by Pierre S. duPont, John J. Raskob, Al Smith, and John W. Davis in August 1934 to mobilize opposition to the New Deal, Baker was absent from its list of sponsors. In November he told a friend that he had not even seen any of the League's literature; like "the little old gentleman who sat in the corner in one of Dickens' novels, I have been quite overlooked."[103]

"From everything I know about the Liberty League," Baker told Davis when he was asked to join it, "my sympathies are warmly with it. I doubt, however, whether I want to join its ranks." He was a member of so many organizations that he did not have time for any more. Baker was certainly busy, but that was not the real reason for his hesitation. Although he was friendly with its leaders he saw the League as too closely connected to large corporate interests, too self-interested in its objection to high taxation, and too embittered in its opposition to FDR for him to join it. As much as he disliked the New Deal, he could not forgive those who had been cheerleaders for the values and policies during the 1920s that had made them rich but reduced the nation to poverty and despair. The Liberty League promised to reassert those ideas, and Baker would have nothing to do with it.[104]

As he rejected the Liberty League's version of pro-business Republicanism, Baker also refused to join the real thing. In a letter to Ogden Mills, a prominent New York Republican who had been Hoover's secretary of the treasury, Baker blamed the GOP for a litany of the nation's woes. It had entrenched the economic hegemony of the East over the South and West; after the Great War it had allowed

Henry Cabot Lodge to derail Wilson's new world order; and during the 1920s it had presided over "an entirely Babylonian prosperity" that had sown the seeds of the Great Depression. "The consequence of this seems to me to have been that President Roosevelt had to wade in a field in which it was impossible to step without sinking in the mud, but mud for the creation of which he was not in the slightest degree responsible."[105]

Baker was therefore torn as he contemplated the 1936 presidential election. Amid the welter of unwelcome initiatives emanating from the White House he found some that made him hesitate to jump ship. FDR's support of the World Court seemed entirely right and his struggle against isolationism was of great importance; Hull's campaign to liberalize trade was laudable, and in May 1935 Roosevelt's veto of the early payment of the veterans' bonus won Baker's wholehearted support. The result, he told Peggy in March 1936, was that "I find it difficult to be a Democrat and impossible to be a Republican."[106]

In this Baker was typical of many Democrats who had begun as progressives but who later opposed the New Deal. Of Wilson's cabinet only Albert Burleson, Josephus Daniels, and William McAdoo were publicly identified with the New Deal, and they felt self-conscious in their minority. McAdoo, who had long since lost his regard for Baker, resented his reputation as Wilson's true heir and as the exemplar of the Wilsonians' hostility to the New Deal. "That doesn't set well with me," McAdoo told Daniels in 1936. "You ought to have equal, if not greater, recognition. But for our Navy, we couldn't have handled the situation in Europe at all."[107]

In July 1935 John Owens, editor of the Baltimore Sun, noted that "it is hard to say which is the sadder spectacle—the plight of Mr. Roosevelt's administration without old fashioned liberal Democrats," or the plight of those Democrats who were ignored by the White House. Had FDR consulted men like Baker and Davis on the NRA he may have been spared its unanimous rejection by the Supreme Court; had he listened to Carter Glass on gold policy it might have been more successful. Instead, the administration was run by radicals and naïve experimenters, and Democrats like Baker and Glass were left with a choice between "recklessness and reaction."[108]

Baker was indeed torn between his dislike of the New Deal and his fear that a Republican victory in 1936 would return the nation to the old regime that he had so detested. "I think nobody could be more deeply sensible than I of the problems which the President and his Administration has had to face," he told Josephus Daniels in May 1936, ". . . but I find myself a very old-fashioned Democrat— perhaps too old-fashioned to be in touch with the necessities of this very modern situation. In any case, in all gentleness and with all respect I deeply disagree with many of the things the administration has done . . . so I have taken my sad thoughts off into a corner and withdrawn from political activities entirely."[109]

For the most part Baker see-sawed in private, but in June 1936 he and two other disaffected Democrats, FDR's first director of the Bureau of the Budget, Lewis W. Douglas, and Leo Wolman, a Columbia economist who had worked for Baker in the Council of National Defense (CND) during World War I and then for FDR in the NRA, wrote to *The New York Times* with suggestions for both parties' 1936 platforms. Equally critical of the Republican past and the Democratic present, Baker, Douglas, and Wolman railed against the subsidies and monopolies granted to special interests, including industry through Republican tariff policies, agriculture through the AAA, and labor groups through the NRA and the Wagner Act. "We believe that the New Era and the New Deal are two streams from the same source. The one fostered private monopoly in the name of national prosperity. The other has fostered state-controlled monopolies in the name of the national welfare. We believe that both are an aberration from the basic principles upon which this nation has grown great and has remained free." Baker and his companions then suggested that both parties promise to wind back subsidies, reduce government expenditure, and restore individual freedom and local autonomy.[110]

The Baker-Douglas-Wolman letter was widely noted but little heeded. It read like a throwback to nineteenth-century liberalism, and by 1936 the GOP and the Democrats were well accustomed to using the power of government to further their policies and assist their constituencies. Baker and his friends, Frank Kent wrote in *The New York Times*, "were writing against a long future and on the background of an almost forgotten past," and their even-handedness ensured that neither party would implement their suggestions.[111]

Baker's indecision lasted until Election Day. On November 3, the day before he went to the polls, he told a correspondent that "I have not separated myself from the Party this year, although my detachment from its present policies and theories is complete." A day later, however, he told Ralph Hayes that he had voted Republican. "As I sum it up my opposition to Landon was on economic grounds. My opposition to Roosevelt was on constitutional and ethical grounds. Economic mistakes seem to me more corrigible." Baker's vote against the party he had supported and served for so long was an intensely personal and conflicted protest; he later confessed to John H. Clarke that he had secretly hoped that FDR would be re-elected, but he could not bring himself to contribute to the landslide that he knew was coming.[112]

In the last year of his life Baker tempered disapproval of the New Deal with resignation. The "class war" that FDR had initiated still dismayed him, and he feared that society would be divided into "special and selfish interest groups clamoring for special privileges from Washington," but fair-mindedness prevented him from blaming the New Deal entirely for this decline. The United States, he told Josephus Daniels in December 1936, had never been a particularly law-abiding society; the nation's frontier past and its recent experience with prohibition be-spoke national characteristics and failings that long predated 1933:

> So far as the world is concerned I suppose it gets as good institutions and good government as it deserves, and when we look at what the world now is and what it faces, the only conclusion we can make is that it does not deserve any better. That is all very sad because there are a very large number of people who still have ideals and who exemplify . . . great faiths, but the major part of the world, I am afraid, is dancing the rhumba, going to picture shows, and turning its radio dials . . . These sentences do not mean that I am very pessimistic and disillusioned, but I have long believed that there is an undulatory theory of light and that from 1921 for a good many years we were in the trough rather than on the crest of the wave.[113]

Relegated to the sidelines, Baker now professed to have little interest in politics. When he traveled to Washington on business in April 1937, he told Bess that "I have singularly little impulse to look up any of our old friends here. They seem to me to have all gone mad! At least I feel like the only democrat left, with a little d, and these fascists, Nazis and totalitarians bore me. Carter Glass and Senator [Josiah] Bailey [of North Carolina] and a few others are sane, but no doubt they are busy and I avoid practicing the saying that 'A man who has an hour to waste usually does it with a man who hasn't.'"[114]

CHAPTER 15

"I have no quarrel with fate, no matter in what moods I have found her"

Newton Baker celebrated his sixty-fifth birthday on December 3, 1936. That put him well ahead of the average life expectancy of 45 for white American children born in 1871, but his chances of living until he was 78, the average age at death for men who turned 65 in 1940, were slim. Instead of looking forward to a long retirement, Baker was aware that his health was declining rapidly and that he did not have long to live.[1]

Self-conscious about his short stature and slight frame, Baker had never liked exercise. At home Bess attended to the garden, and although Newton occasionally played tennis with Jack when both of them were younger he preferred more sedentary recreation. In Washington he had worked six-day weeks and twelve-hour days, and in Cleveland he worked equally hard. After hours and on Sundays he gravitated to his armchair, his books, and his ever-present pipe. "My family . . . are all going to a night club tonight," he told his brother Frank in 1935. "When I declined to go one of them said, 'But you will be all alone, what will you do?' I replied quite truthfully, 'I shall spend the evening with Thucydides, do you not envy me?'"[2]

Baker had a fine mind but a weak heart, and in cultivating the former he neglected the latter. The heart murmur that his doctor had detected in 1889 haunted Baker all his life; he suffered his first heart attack in 1928, when he was 56, and then another in 1930. "All of a sudden I developed a devil of a fever which raged and stormed for a couple of days," he told Albert Burleson after his second attack. His heart then "gave a very flabby exhibition in appearance of its duty [and] served a notice which the doctors thought indicated an intention to quit on the job."[3]

Baker could afford the best treatment in a city already known for its medical facilities, but in the days before sophisticated medication, pacemakers, and open-heart surgery all his doctors could do was to prescribe rest. Even so, Baker was a

restless patient; he was happy at first to spend more time reading and to avoid activity, but he soon returned to his busy work schedule and to his many associations
and causes. When his doctors suggested that he stop smoking, Baker convinced
himself that this would cause more stress than benefit. He even saw his addiction
to nicotine as a sign of good health; in 1928 he told John W. Davis that he had lost
his desire to smoke for only a single day after his heart attack. "It, however, immediately returned with renewed force so I fancy my illness is more a thing of suspicion and guesses by doctors than of any very serious derangement of my internal
economics."[4]

In September 1933 Baker suffered another "mild heart disorder." He was confined to bed for ten days, still with his pipe, and returned to work promising to
behave. Three heart attacks in five years did little to change Baker's ways; his family and colleagues noticed little diminution in his workload and he seemed obliv-
ious to his doctors' concerns. "Life seems to me to grow more interesting all the
time," he told a friend soon after his third heart attack, "and I can only picture
myself at a hundred as breathlessly eager to learn more about it."[5]

In the summer of 1937 the Bakers went to Saratoga Springs, hoping that its
baths would alleviate Bess's arthritis and help Newton's heart. Bess's condition improved, but Newton's took a turn for the worse. In July he suffered what seemed at
first to be another heart attack, but his doctors later decided that it was a stroke: his
left arm and leg did not follow orders, his coordination was impaired, and he complained of mental confusion. He soon regained control over his limbs and mind,
but otherwise his recovery was slow. Later he was allowed to spend the mornings at
work if he scaled back his other commitments. He therefore resigned from the local
Democratic Party Committee, left the boards of the Mutual Life Insurance Company, Carnegie Corporation, and Ohio State University, and declined speaking
engagements. "My doctor has laid down a system of rules by which I can continue
to live a short time at the expense of most of the pleasures which life has for me."[6]

In October 1937 Baker collapsed during a trip to Chattanooga to discuss his
Tennessee Valley Authority (TVA) litigation, and he was again confined to bed. A
month later he described his recovery as steady but slow; he was back at work in
the mornings but he and Bess had dropped the idea of a Mediterranean cruise in
the winter. Another relapse in December 1937 sent him to bed for two weeks. "We
are having a very quiet Christmas at home this year," he told Peggy, "while I, staying at home most of the time, devote myself to books and other like matters and go
to bed at eight thirty each evening in the hope that a continuance of that discipline will have a curative effect upon me."[7]

To others Baker was more philosophical. His secretary Dorothy Cook thought
that he had lost his will to live as he realized that he would never recover his old

energy. He told Munson Havens that he now believed in the immortality of departed souls, and conceded to a relative that he had only a short time left. "This thing of being sixty-six years old turns out to have many disqualifications," he told Ralph Hayes, but he felt content with his life's work. He had seen extraordinary times in Washington and then sixteen years of fruitful work in Cleveland; his children were self-sufficient, and his only care was for Bess. "I hope the end will come suddenly when it does come and not leave me for any length of time a burden on Mrs. Baker's hands, to all of which she is entirely equal but the burden would be a sad one if she had to stand for any length of time the care of a sick old man."[8]

Baker's letter lay unsent while he was confined to bed. When Hayes did receive it on December 23, he sensed that Baker "was looking over Jordan when he wrote it and knew that the crossing was at hand." Hayes left for Cleveland that night and arranged to visit Baker on the afternoon of Christmas Day. That morning Baker was in his bedroom armchair, looking forward to lunch with his family and reading letters from well-wishers. "It is with regret that I read of the recurance [sic] of your mid-summer illness," one correspondent from Oregon wrote. He had been a private in the American Expeditionary Forces (AEF) and remembered meeting Baker in France in 1918. "You were a man of small stature, but when you spoke to me in apparent sincere solicitation, I forgot your size entirely and your humanity made you the biggest of 'big' men to me." Baker left the rest of his gifts and letters for the afternoon. Bess later told Josephus Daniels that "mine for him were never opened, for just as the children and the grandsons began to gather, his heart suddenly stopped beating. I try to be thankful that he was saved all pain and invalidation but nothing helps the terrible aching void."[9]

❖❖❖

News of Baker's death brought an avalanche of telegrams and letters from all over the United States and the Atlantic world; Dorothy Cook acknowledged a thousand of them in January 1938 alone. His body lay in state in Cleveland's Trinity Cathedral; a searchlight shone out over Lake Erie for two nights, flags at all army posts flew at half mast, hundreds of Clevelanders gathered for his funeral, a national radio broadcast eulogized him early in January 1938, and later hundreds of dignitaries assembled for a memorial service. In 1942 Western Reserve University bought a building to house Cleveland College and named it after Baker, and in 1943 the Council on World Affairs created the Newton D. Baker Lecture Fund to sponsor six lectures a year on American foreign policy. The first of these were given by Ralph Hayes and Walter Lippmann in December 1943 as the Allies began negotiations over what would become the United Nations Organization. "We must think of ourselves now as making a more and more perfect union of the nations which are already united throughout the world," Lippmann concluded. "That will be our tribute to Newton Baker, and his soul will rest in peace."[10]

Press coverage of Baker's death and career was generous; in a long obituary *The New York Times* noted that "aside from his historical service during the World War, Newton Diehl Baker had a prominent place in the modern American story." He had enhanced Cleveland's reputation as a beacon of reform; despite widespread derision he had raised, trained, and equipped four million men quickly and without massive corruption; after the war he had fought for the League of Nations and become one of the best lawyers of his generation. Baker's obituaries also made much of his more reluctant roles as FDR's rival for the 1932 presidential nomination and then critic of the New Deal, and all emphasized his high intellect, innate humanity, and genuine modesty. "We shall miss his genius for intimate friendship," the American Legion of Cleveland declared, "the sure, gentle voice of idealism speaking to our people; his sustained devotion to the best causes in our national life."[11]

Many of Baker's friends and associates sent more personal notes. "I loved him as a brother," Josephus Daniels wrote, "and [feel] sorrow that the world has lost so royal a spirit whose life ennobled our humanity." Baker's fellow Ohioan James Cox told Hayes that "if Newton had been a Republican he would certainly have been president." Henry Johnston, a Wall Street lawyer, asked Hayes "how different this country would be today had the Democratic Party been wise enough to have nominated Newton D. Baker for President in 1932 instead of Franklin D. Roosevelt. What a great leader your Secretary would have been!" An AEF veteran who had been wrongly included in a list of soldiers killed in action recalled Baker's kindness in personally assuring the soldier's mother that there had been a mistake; General Harbord described him as "one of the most distinguished Americans of all time," whose determination to fight for peace had done so much to win the war, and John J. Pershing recalled Baker's steadfast support of him and his determination that the AEF should fight as an independent army. "He stood the test of war, and will be remembered as the nation's ablest War Secretary."[12]

If McAdoo sent his condolences they were not preserved in either his own or Baker's files. Franklin Roosevelt did send Bess a cable, but it was perfunctory. "Mrs. Roosevelt and I offer sincere sympathy in the loss which has fallen so heavily upon you and yours in the untimely passing of a loved and loving husband and father," he wrote. "Newton D. Baker as Secretary of War directed the raising and equipment in the shortest time of the largest army ever made ready for action and he will be long remembered as a faithful and efficient public servant." The White House issued a more fulsome eulogy to the *Cincinnati Post*, which concluded that "No soldier gave more, fought harder or served more bravely than did this little man from Ohio who loved peace," but the damage had been done. "I try to think of what you wrote me when the ugly thought comes of the almost insulting message from the President," Bess told Daniels. "A mood of indignation swept this city over the way he damned Newton with faint praise."[13]

Bess repaid FDR's slight in spades; she endorsed Wendell Willkie for president in 1940 and condemned the New Deal for its reckless spending and dictatorial tendencies. "Mr. Roosevelt sowed the wind, when he coddled labor and promised them impossible things," she told Daniels in 1946, "and we are reaping the whirlwind." Her chauffeur had once been happy to earn $125 per month, but now he had gone on strike for that amount per week. "When one thinks of that stupid man, who was in school only through the fourth grade, making more money than college professors, it is a melancholy reflection upon our civilization."[14]

❧❋❧

Although McAdoo was eight years older than Baker he outlived him by three. In August 1938, when he lost his bid for renomination to the Senate, McAdoo was a month shy of his seventy-fifth birthday. Always frustrated as a legislator, he saw no reason to serve out his term as a lame duck. Before the primary he had urged the US Maritime Commission to save the Dollar Steamship Line, which was almost bankrupt and unable to maintain its fleet. McAdoo, as a member of the Senate Territories and Insular Affairs Committee and an advocate of the Merchant Marine, wanted to preserve the Dollar Line's routes between the United States and its Pacific possessions and to make it part of a naval reserve.[15]

Under a rescue plan negotiated in 1938 the Dollar Line received a $2.5 million loan from the Reconstruction Finance Corporation (RFC) as working capital, another $2 million from the Maritime Commission to repair its ships, and an annual subsidy of $3 million. In return the federal government took control of its stock and the right to replace its management. At the end of September 1938, with negotiations complete and the primary elections decided, news leaked out that McAdoo would serve as chairman of the Dollar Line's reconstituted board.[16]

McAdoo announced his resignation from the Senate on September 28, 1938. "It is going to keep me very busy until I get the thing on the water again with an adequate supply of first-class and efficiently managed ships," he told his ghost writer William Woodward. "I cannot make as much money out of this thing as I could if I resumed the practice of law, but . . . there is adventure in this game, and I find that, antique though I am, adventure still has an irresistible appeal for me." The Dollar Lines also closed the circle of his long career. Nearly fifty years before he had tried to save the Knoxville Street Railway Company; in 1902 he began a more successful project to complete the Hudson River tubes; and in 1918 he had nursed the nation's railroads through their wartime crisis. Now, twenty years later, he took charge of yet another struggling transportation concern.[17]

More than symmetry pushed McAdoo back to work. Out of office and feeling his age, he was again worried about money. Although his Senate salary and invest-ments had restored some of the losses he had suffered in 1929, his gains had been wiped out by the recession of 1937. Years of "unselfish service to the 'peeple,'" he told Huger in 1939, had left him poor. "When a man has passed 75, one must ex-pect some physical deterioration to set in. I have no serious impairment yet, but I realize that I can't run a foot race or vault a six foot pole, or dance all night or 'dissipate' repeatedly." He had perhaps five good years left, and needed to provide for Doris's and his children's futures. "If I can get a few big clients who can pay adequately for good service rendered, everything will be greatly simplified!"[18]

Patronage, not legal fees, came to McAdoo's rescue. Although FDR had kept him at arm's length in the Senate, he went out of his way to help him afterward. Whether from belated gratitude for McAdoo's role at the 1932 convention, or to recognize his steadfast support of the New Deal, or from guilt that he had not done enough to help him win renomination, Roosevelt gave McAdoo in 1938 one of the juiciest patronage plums in his gift. The Dollar Line job paid $25,000 a year, which was $10,000 more than McAdoo's Senate salary and $5,000 more than the chief justice of the Supreme Court earned. "Mac and Doris are living here in San Francisco now," George Creel told Margaret Wilson in June 1939. "Thank the Lord, he has a $25,000 a year job . . . for according to what he has let drop, his own affairs are in pretty bad shape."[19]

McAdoo was grateful for FDR's lifeline. He delayed his departure from the Senate until after the 1938 elections and then kept in frequent contact with the president about the Dollar Line. Aware of Roosevelt's love of the sea and eager to make the most of his friendly contact with him, McAdoo consulted him about the line's new name—FDR liked the "Seven Seas Steamship Company," but the board preferred "American President Lines" (APL)—and won it relief from Cus-toms fines and access to mothballed ships.[20]

Although he was no longer in the Senate, McAdoo remained active in politics. Still angry at Downey's support of the "asinine" Ham and Eggs scheme, he stayed aloof from the election over his old seat. Downey won, and expected to control federal patronage in California as McAdoo had done before him. McAdoo, how-ever, had other ideas; he argued that Downey had won the nomination and elec-tion under false pretenses and could not be trusted with the party's fate in Cali-fornia. He reminded FDR's patronage boss Jim Farley that he still sat on the Democratic National Committee (DNC), and "I think I should be consulted about major problems that arise in California. [By] playing with the radical elements now temporarily in the ascendancy, you are making the mistake of your life." FDR should treat Downey as an aberration and work with regular Democrats like McAdoo to prepare for the 1940 elections. To that end he collected patronage requests and forwarded them to Washington with his endorsement.[21]

Roosevelt was too respectful of Downey's senatorial prerogatives, and too willing to accept recommendations from Governor Culbert Olson, another of McAdoo's enemies, for McAdoo's liking. "We have a very unhappy situation in California," he told Attorney General Robert Jackson in January 1940. "It is unfortunate that [Downey] gets so much support from the Administration . . . I know how awkward it is to disregard a Senator, and I am not suggesting it. I only mean, to put it vulgarly, that he should not monopolize the trough."[22]

In November 1939 McAdoo confirmed his reputation as FDR's most loyal ally in California by endorsing him for a third term. He and George Creel organized a slate of delegates to contest the California primary for FDR, but in keeping with the clandestine nature of the third-term movement this was done without approval from the White House. Jim Farley eventually resigned over the issue, Vice President Garner made his opposition to it clear, and Roosevelt remained silent about his plans. "There is no doubt but that your ticket can win easily," one admirer wrote to McAdoo, "because the people know that President Roosevelt likes you better than any other man in this state . . . Today, you are more popular than you were at the last election. Voters realize the mistake they made on 'Ham and Eggs.'"[23]

Warned by his doctor against seeking election as a delegate, McAdoo still worked hard for FDR. "The world situation and our own as well are so uncertain and filled with such extraordinary potentialities for evil," he told Huger, "that it does seem to me that we are safer with Roosevelt at the helm than with some unknown and inexperienced person." Yet without encouragement from FDR McAdoo and his friends were hamstrung. "As things stand today—and I am referring only to California—everything is political chaos," he complained in February 1940. Garner had entered the primary, Downey had organized an uninstructed slate, and Governor Olson talked about leading a rival FDR ticket. McAdoo was happy to lead FDR's charge in California, but without word from the White House he could do nothing to stop Garner from winning the state as he had done in 1932. Robert Jackson was apologetic; Roosevelt had refused to either permit or forbid a third nomination, and "it seems to be a situation in which each of us has to act on his own."[24]

McAdoo and his friends did persist, and in May 1940 their slate won the California primary by more than 600,000 votes. In a radio address during the campaign McAdoo described the two-term tradition as nothing compared to the crisis facing the world. Hitler was on the march, Britain would soon face Germany alone, and America needed Roosevelt's leadership. FDR went on to win California in the general election, but apart from another radio speech McAdoo played little role in the president's victory. Out of office and replaced by Governor Olson on the DNC, his political career was over.[25]

Emboldened by the new warmth in Roosevelt's tone, McAdoo peppered him with personal notes and gifts. He sent avocado pears from his Santa Barbara estate, sought meetings when he went to Washington, invited FDR to tea when he visited California, and even joked about their wayward children. In lobbying for a diplomatic post for his former client and campaign donor John Paul Getty in 1940, McAdoo noted that Getty had been divorced three times. "I told the President jocularly that I didn't see how the Roosevelt or the McAdoo families could condemn any man because he has been divorced. He laughed heartily at this and seemed to concur in my view. It is a curious thing that his family and my family have been somewhat unlucky in this direction."[26]

McAdoo's role at APL grew significantly after its president Joseph Sheehan died in April 1940. McAdoo then combined the offices of chairman and president, and he ran APL until his own death less than a year later. By September 1939 APL had expanded its fleet from one to eleven, inaugurated a round-the-world service and augmented its Pacific routes, and nearly trebled its monthly revenues to $1.1 million. "Everybody considered this an impossible task," McAdoo boasted to Bernard Baruch in 1939, "but we are really conquering the problem." He was also aware that APL's growth sprang from federal subsidies that had ulterior motives. "We are entering upon the New Year—1939—invested by our Government with a great trust," he told his staff, "a trust which comprehends not only the successful transportation of our commerce on the high seas, but the creation and operation of a fleet of merchant vessels which can be swiftly converted into efficient auxiliaries for our Navy in time of national peril."[27]

The possibility of war weighed heavily on McAdoo after 1938. Although he had supported the Neutrality Acts of 1935 and 1937 his sympathy for isolationism had never extended to pacifism and had come under increasing strain. By the time he left the Senate his views on foreign policy had moved closer to FDR's and to a realization that war in Europe was almost certain and conflict in Asia highly likely. "I am more concerned with the hysteria in this country and the 'peace at any price' sentiment, than I am with what is happening in the rest of the world," he told Baruch in October 1939. "If we convince the world that we are unwilling to fight whenever our vital rights and our honor are jeopardized by the unlawful conduct of others, then we will sink to a low level in the scale of civilization."[28]

When war broke out in Europe in September 1939 McAdoo told the press that it would be "long and bitter," and that the United States would soon have to choose how to defend its honor, values, and commerce. He also wrote to "Dear Frank" to offer his services in whatever capacity the president saw fit. Two weeks later he wrote again, this time about oil storage facilities at Pearl Harbor. "These exposed tanks would be the first object of aerial attack if an enemy's planes should ever succeed in getting over the Island of Oahu."[29]

In August 1940, after France and the Low Countries had surrendered, McAdoo told his son-in-law that "I think that the European situation is so explosive that we may be compelled to get into the war sooner or later, even before the next election." By then he supported military and diplomatic preparations for war. He backed the destroyers-for-bases deal with Britain in August 1940 and urged that it be extended to Hong Kong and Singapore. He also praised the military training bill, tried to register for the draft, and congratulated FDR on his "Arsenal of Democracy" speech. FDR sent "many, many thanks," and invited Doris and Mac to lunch at the White House.[30]

Near the end of his life McAdoo reflected to his old friend Tom Storke about the war that was devastating Europe and that would soon engulf the United States:

> I hope that we may both live long enough to see a reordered and stabilized civilization with broader bases of economic and social justice for our own people as well as for the people of the world. This, alas, is perhaps an unrealizable dream. Christ had it and died for it almost two thousand years ago. I have long been convinced that civilization is on the wrong track in considering political aims the dominant factor in human life when the hard truth is that the economic and social order which most concern the welfare of humanity is the fundamental thing. Until men can be made to feel that there is security against want and war, especially the former, I doubt if we can ever produce a society which will banish both.[31]

McAdoo had long been famous for his vitality. Unlike Baker, he neither smoked nor drank and took regular exercise. Yet his health had never been robust; in addition to a breakdown in the 1890s, chronic sinusitis during the Great War, prostate surgery in 1924, four hernia operations, and carbuncles that laid him low in 1934, he suffered from many complaints that his doctors attributed to overwork and nervous tension. Despite his medical problems, which were magnified by his tendency to hypochondria, McAdoo was vain about his vigor and appearance. "It is the spirit and enthusiasm of the individual that means youth," he told Nona in 1930. "Take my case—sixty-six, and yet I am about thirty-three actually." In that year McAdoo ordered copies of a photograph of himself beside *Blue Streak*. "By the way, my hair is not quite so gray as it appears in this picture . . . I am not vain about this but if you could fix the picture so that it would look semi-gray, as it really is, I should like it."[32]

McAdoo published his autobiography in 1931, when he was 67. Ghost-written by William E. Woodward, *Crowded Years* covered his career only until 1918, but it encapsulated the restlessness that he maintained all his life: "What is life worth if one spends it like an oyster fastened securely to a rock? . . . My life has covered a wide range and it has been full of interesting and unexpected adventure. I have no quarrel with fate, no matter in what moods I have found her, and no matter what her decrees have been. I have had a glorious time!"[33]

By the late 1930s, however, McAdoo felt his age. In December 1938, soon after his seventy-fifth birthday, he complained of an "attack of indigestion." In fact, his former son-in-law and Manhattan physician Edward Cowles told him, he had suffered a mild stroke. He experienced no paralysis or confusion and needed only to rest. McAdoo obediently planned a holiday to Hawaii. "I have not allowed this thing to worry me at all," he told Cowles, "because I think I have a rational philosophy about life and death. I am not afraid to go, but I am not seeking an early exit."[34]

The McAdoos went to Hawaii for three weeks, but Mac's recovery was slow. His blood pressure remained high, and electrocardiograph tests in July 1939 revealed some arteriosclerosis and "a minor occlusion on the anterior cardiac surface." Cowles was now much more concerned and told McAdoo's doctor in San Francisco that his patient should reduce his working day to five hours and rest before any other activity. "I know that he is not afraid to die, but I am sure he would hate to be an invalid." McAdoo was headstrong and stubborn, but he was now an old and ill man.[35]

McAdoo continued on a restricted schedule for the rest of 1940. He tried to augment his salary through legal work from friends and companies associated with APL but resigned himself to the fact that his family would have to do without a large inheritance. McAdoo had always lived beyond his means, but before 1930 he had papered over his financial cracks through loans from wealthy friends, mortgages over his assets, and dividends from his speculations in oil and real estate. When the Great Depression and then the recession of 1937 blew down his financial house of cards, he went deeper into debt to maintain his large family in the style they were accustomed to and that the outside world assumed he could afford.[36]

McAdoo wrote his last will at the beginning of 1937. It named Doris, Eleanor, and six of his children as beneficiaries, each to receive 10 percent of his estate. Huger, by now financially secure and aware of his father's straitened circumstances, declined a share in the estate but asked to be appointed executor. McAdoo also made special provision for Mary Faith, who in 1940 was 20 and still single, and bequeathed his law library to William Neblett and a pair of gold cufflinks to George Creel. His gravesite, beside Robert's at Arlington National Cemetery, had already been chosen, and McAdoo reminded Huger about it in the last of his letters to him. "All of this is a painful subject to discuss, but I look upon these matters practically and think there is nothing like making provision in advance of the ultimate end of human existence."[37]

In January 1941 McAdoo and Doris went to Washington to attend FDR's inauguration and to take up his invitation to lunch at the White House. They stayed in Washington while McAdoo worked at APL headquarters, but in the early hours of February 1 he suffered a heart attack and died later that morning. "I cannot believe he has gone," Doris wrote to Josephus Daniels. "He was so vital and alive. I am so empty and lonely without him yet I know he died as he wanted to—with his boots on."[38]

As Huger had suspected, McAdoo left little behind. After his debts had been paid, his estate amounted to little more than $10,000. For a former senator who earned $25,000 a year at the time of his death and owned properties in Los Angeles and Santa Barbara, and who had once held extensive oil and real estate investments along with stocks and bonds, McAdoo's financial decline had been precipitate. The 1930 Census showed that his annual income exceeded $60,000 and that his household included six resident servants, but eleven years later there was almost nothing left. Newton Baker, on the other hand, had left behind a net estate of $155,000 in addition to the $500,000 he had given Bess and the children before his death. McAdoo had been generous to his children too, but never on the same scale. Despite or because of his financially adventurous and acquisitive ways, his hare had fallen far behind Baker's tortoise.[39]

❧✠❧

The Knoxville Journal's headline on February 2, 1941, "William G. McAdoo Dies; Entire Nation Mourns," was an exaggeration, but his passing was widely noted. Southern newspapers stressed his rise from Confederate ashes to the financial citadels of New York and the US Treasury; the New Orleans Times-Picayune remarked that he "must have been about the only Georgian that was ever grateful to William T. Sherman," because he had forced him to "start from scratch and learn to make his own way." As they had done for Newton Baker three years before, eulogists reviewed McAdoo's public career in some detail, but they dwelt longer on his personal life than they had for the quiet Clevelander. "Tall, erect William Gibbs McAdoo," the Sacramento Bee began, had been a "colorful figure in Washington political and social circles for more than a quarter of a century." He had risen from obscurity to conquer the Hudson River, help nominate and elect two presidents, create the Federal Reserve System, fund the war effort, control the nation's railroads, seek two Democratic presidential nominations, win election to the US Senate, and finally revive a shipping line. Along the way he had married three times, fathered nine children and adopted another, wooed and lost a president's daughter, and then married a woman forty-six years his junior. McAdoo, *The New York Times* observed, "was a man of singular persuasion and charm."[40]

McAdoo's obituaries also suggested that his career had been as notable for its failures as its achievements. "Although he could build tunnels and help run a country at war," *The New York Times* observed, "he could not get himself elected President." He had been a polarizing figure who had made powerful enemies without convincing his fellow citizens that his convictions were deep and his concern for them genuine. According to the *Tennessean* "there was something Jacksonian in his rise but he seemed to lack that common touch so necessary for highest honors." McAdoo was "more admired than loved," the *Times-Picayune* thought, and was "ever the man about whom the public could not quite make up its mind." The *Duluth News Tribune* conceded that he was brilliant but thought that his courting of publicity and controversy had divided the Democratic Party and the country "between men who admired him tremendously and men who disliked him intensely. History might have been different if McAdoo's had been a personality about which many could be neutral in their feelings."[41]

To many liberals McAdoo was a shallow egotist who had pandered to the Ku Klux Klan (KKK) in 1924 and then to William Randolph Hearst in 1932; to conservatives he was a radical who had attacked the banks too eagerly in 1914, run the railroads too firmly in 1918, and supported the New Deal too unquestioningly after 1932. Few of his eulogists saw much to praise in his time in the Senate, and this lent to their tributes a sense of disappointment; his brilliant achievements in New York and Washington had been derailed in 1924 and then lessened by a long journey along what the *Richmond Times-Dispatch* described as "the line of least resistance."[42]

Other obituaries reminded readers that even in his prime McAdoo had worked in a team, and not always as its leader. He had been a "servant and maker of presidents," the *Houston Post* noted, and had functioned best in that important but subordinate role. He, Wilson, and Baker had formed a triumvirate that led the United States in the last days of peace and through World War I, but McAdoo owed his position to Wilson and shared leadership of the cabinet with Baker. Even in Treasury, the Cleveland *Plain Dealer* noted, much of his success "was due to his ability to select capable subordinates. Some of those who were associated with him felt that he was not always generous in his appraisals of their service and was inclined too much to take credit and to shift blame." He had "wielded an influence in the World War cabinet second only to that of Newton D. Baker," but worked best in concert with Wilson or in cooperation with men such as Baruch.[43]

Although he was never close to the intellectuals and jurists who memorialized Baker through educational institutions and public lectures, McAdoo had his own parade of influential mourners. His funeral in Washington, conducted by the chaplain of the Senate, and his interment at Arlington were observed by prominent members of the political and business establishment. Secretary of Labor Francis Perkins described him as "an outstanding American [who] served his country with honor and distinction for many years," Cordell Hull called him "one of the outstanding leaders of the times," and Senate Majority Leader Alben Barkley mourned him as "one of the most colorful public figures in the history of the United States" who had made "great contributions to the history and welfare of our country." Even Hiram Johnson, who had never thought much of McAdoo in life, described him in death as "a man of very great ability and a Senator of renown."[44]

Franklin Roosevelt gave McAdoo a much warmer tribute than he had afforded Baker. Calling him "one of my oldest friends," the president told the press that "I join with the entire country in mourning him as one who has given many years of faithful service to the nation. My personal affection for him grew with the years." He and Eleanor wrote notes to Doris and sent a wreath to the funeral. "My heart is full of thanksgiving to you," Doris wrote back. "You took time to see Mac twice since we came Jan 19th [and] this meant more to him and to me than possibly you realize." FDR read Doris's note and did McAdoo one last favor. "See if she could come in to see me some time next week for about 10 or 15 minutes," he told his appointments secretary Pa Watson.[45]

❖❖❖

McAdoo's death coincided with the end of a formative era in American history. He had been born three months after the Battle of Gettysburg and died ten months before Pearl Harbor, and in those seventy-seven years the United States had fought a Civil War, reconstructed itself into a modern industrialized society, accumulated an empire, joined a world war that transformed it into the Western world's creditor, weathered the Great Depression, and reconfigured the scope and powers of its federal government. McAdoo, who had been born a Confederate and died an American, could and did claim a significant role in all these developments. When he began his tenure as secretary of the treasury in 1913, an office he would hold longer than any of his predecessors, his official transport was a horse-drawn carriage; when he left office in 1918 the horses had been pensioned off and he was director general of the nation's railroads. In between he had helped create the

Federal Reserve System, ushered in the federal income tax, and funded the American and Allied war effort. In retrospect those years saw him at the peak of his power and influence, but before them he had created a significant addition to New York City's transit system and afterward had twice sought the presidential nomination and won election to the US Senate.[46]

McAdoo's lifetime also encompassed Newton Baker's sixty-six-year span. Like McAdoo, Baker could claim an important role in the formation of the modern American state, but unlike his brasher colleague he felt uncomfortable doing so. Baker preferred smaller canvasses; he was happier being mayor of Cleveland than he was as secretary of war, and he was happiest of all arguing his law cases and advocating progressivism, Wilsonianism, and internationalism. His contributions to civic life were often harder won than McAdoo's; as Cleveland's city solicitor and mayor he played a pivotal role in expanding the authority and competence of its municipal government and, as perhaps the most unlikely secretary of war in American history, this avowed localist and erstwhile pacifist found himself at the helm of a massive mobilization that pushed him into uncharted and sometimes inhospitable territory. After the war Baker returned to his true vocation; happy in Cleveland and content as a lawyer, he remained prominent more out of duty than ambition, defending his versions of progressivism, internationalism, and American values against threats both real and apparent from Republican isolationism, Democratic New Dealism, and foreign tyranny.

McAdoo and Baker had very different personalities. Ray Stannard Baker thought McAdoo "dynamic rather than thoughtful," while Baker was the reverse. W. E. Woodward decided that "[McAdoo] has no metaphysics—and he does not care to dive down to the bottom of the ocean of life unless he can bring up a pailful of earth to show he has been there." In 1932, before Baker's half-hearted tilt at the presidential nomination, a graphologist saw "no urge for personal glorification in the hand, but the inherent strength and keenness of the mind would inevitably propel him to prominence . . . But there is a certain wearyness [sic] in the hand: something akin to a whimsical realization of futility." Baker was bookish and meditative; his favorite authors were Honoré de Balzac, William Shakespeare, Thucydides, and Ivan Turgenev, he hated jazz but loved Beethoven and Wagner. McAdoo, on the other hand, cared little for books and loved dancing to jazz. When Baker waxed philosophical he drew upon wide reading and deep reflection; when McAdoo did so he sounded like a self-improvement manual.[47]

McAdoo loved adventure and enjoyed controversy, while Baker admitted to dodging excitement but sometimes stumbling into it. "He is the most completely self-effacing man I have ever met," Raymond Fosdick observed, whereas no one ever accused McAdoo of modesty. He was driven by ego and ambition and rarely admitted to doubt or indecision; John Skelton Williams, who worked with him in Treasury, observed in 1914 that "his brain seems to be propelled by a great store of radium, lodged somewhere in his anatomy." George Creel knew both men well and attributed their differences to a clash of personalities that had deep roots:

> A talk with Mac developed that he also disliked Baker, because of differences while in Wilson's cabinet. No two men were ever more dissimilar, for the Secretary of War was scholarly, philosophical, and contemplative, while the Secretary of the Treasury shot ahead with the speed and directness of a bullet. Dynamic and intuitive, with supreme confidence in his abilities, Mac raged against Baker's cautious approach to problems, and the two were in continual dispute.[48]

These factors explain why Baker and McAdoo were never close friends, but they do not account for their complex interactions and relationship between 1912 and 1937. During their years in the cabinet they had been united in a common endeavor to serve Woodrow Wilson and shepherd the nation through peace and war. Baker thought McAdoo intrusive and self-serving and McAdoo saw Baker as indecisive and obstructive, but their battles also arose from their different views about the proper extent and nature of federal authority. McAdoo wholeheartedly embraced the need for expanded federal powers during his time in the cabinet and held that view for the rest of his career. This enabled him to advocate Washington-led reform during the 1920s and to become a cheerleader for the New Deal in the 1930s. Baker, on the other hand, began and ended his career as a localist, skeptical of the state when it was too far removed from its citizens, too convinced of its own wisdom, and too dismissive of individuals' autonomy. In between he grudgingly subordinated his views to the necessity of winning the war because he conceded that that task required significant but temporary expansion of federal activity and authority. Once the war was over, however, he returned to his old convictions and was not convinced that the Great Depression justified a return to the powerful wartime state.

McAdoo's and Baker's political careers were informed by each other's long after they left Wilson's cabinet. Their shared experience during that time left them as prominent figures widely seen as Wilson's most likely heirs and as future presidents, and the weight of those expectations weighed heavily on them both. Neither Baker nor McAdoo fulfilled that destiny, and Baker never quite decided whether he even wanted to. Even so, they remained important political actors who can tell us much about progressivism's diversity and fate, World War I and its legacies, the political ramifications of the Depression, and the debate over the New Deal. Examining McAdoo and Baker's work together and in opposition to each other sheds light not only on their contributions to the formation of the modern

American state but also on the whole process of modern state creation itself. So often in their careers Baker and McAdoo were two sides of the same coin, and our knowledge of both informs our understanding of the great changes that they observed, contributed to, and sometimes decried.

Baker's and McAdoo's professional and private experiences also have much to tell us, again as much by their differences as their similarities. Both were southerners, although being born outside Atlanta in 1863 marked McAdoo more deeply as a child of the Old South and its defeat than Baker, who was born six years after the war in the northern extremity of the Old Confederacy. McAdoo and Baker both became lawyers, although of different types and interests; Baker was much the more eminent and cerebral lawyer who was comfortable with complicated transactions and arcane courtroom argument, while McAdoo retained an instrumental view of the law that eschewed intellectualization and merged easily into entrepreneurship and lobbying.

Their families were also very different: Baker married once and his three children led conventional lives, while McAdoo married three times, suffered the suicide of his first wife and divorce from his second, fathered nine children and adopted a tenth, and for good reason worried about all but one of them. In its conventionality and stability Baker's home life was recognizable to his forebears and successors alike, but the volatility of McAdoo's reflected the uncertainties of modernity with its blended families, volatile marriages, and openly troubled children.

Despite their differences and conflicts, McAdoo and Baker have suffered similar fates at the hands of their eulogists and historians. Currents of wistfulness pervade both men's tributes and historical summations. Baker was Wilson's true heir but chose not to translate his prominence and reputation into elective office; he then became one of the country's best lawyers but did not ascend to the Supreme Court. "When he died in 1937," August Heckscher noted, "he left with large numbers of his countrymen a feeling that his career, useful and distinguished though it had certainly been, had fallen disconcertingly short of its promise." McAdoo suffered similar judgments but for different reasons. Baker's faults lay in his reticence and inability to adapt to new political and social imperatives arising from the Great Depression; McAdoo's weaknesses lay in his overweening ego and ambition. Wilson's Crown Prince wasted his talents by grasping too eagerly at personal wealth and political power, and in the process failed to win either. Unlike Baker, McAdoo's presidential ambitions were abundantly clear, and so his failure to achieve them in 1920 and 1924 lent a tone of failure to his entire career.[49]

Such judgments distort McAdoo's and Baker's significance. Describing Mc-Adoo as a man who wanted to be president but failed, and Baker as a man who might have been president but chose not to be, labels them as failures and disappointments rather than as exemplars and molders of powerful currents of American history. In Woodrow Wilson's cabinet Baker and McAdoo exercised enormous influence over state-making and statecraft during a critical time in the nation's development; as progressives they embodied the diversity and contradictions of an amorphous but powerful reform impulse; as lawyers they represented two different streams of professional activity; and as husbands and fathers they can tell us much about changes and continuities in domestic life during the first half of the twentieth century. They were therefore progressives at war: with their foes in Manhattan and Cleveland, the Kaiser's Germany, Republican normalcy, and Roosevelt's New Deal, with themselves, and with each other.

To return to the question that began this book: what is gained by looking at Baker and McAdoo together? Examined individually they were important actors in four decades of civic life, but studied together their differences become as important as their similarities, and their failures as telling as their achievements. They worked apart, together, and in opposition, and they lived very different private and business careers. Together they help show us the diversity and contradictions that lay within the modern American state that they did so much to build.

Abbreviations

Baker MSS	Papers of Newton Diehl Baker, Library of Congress, Washington, D.C.
Berkeley-WGM MSS	William Gibbs McAdoo, Letters to his Wife Eleanor (Wilson) McAdoo, University of California at Berkeley
Byrd MSS	Papers of Harry Flood Byrd Sr., Alderman Library, University of Virginia
Cummings MSS	Papers of Homer S. Cummings, Alderman Library, University of Virginia
Davis MSS	Papers of John W. Davis, Sterling Library, Yale University, New Haven, Connecticut
ELB	Elizabeth Leopold Baker
EWM	Eleanor Wilson McAdoo
FDR	Franklin Delano Roosevelt
FDR PPF	Franklin D. Roosevelt, President's Personal File, Franklin D. Roosevelt Library, Hyde Park, New York
FHB	Frank H. Baker
FHM	Francis Huger McAdoo
Huntington-WGM MSS	Papers of William Gibbs McAdoo, Huntington Library, San Marino, California
JCB	Julian C. Baker
LOC MSS	Library of Congress Manuscript Division
McAdoo MSS	Papers of William Gibbs McAdoo, Library of Congress, Washington, D.C.
n.d.	not dated
NDB	Newton Diehl Baker
n.f.	not filed
n.p.	not paginated
NYT	*The New York Times*
RHM	Robert Hazlehurst McAdoo
TR	Theodore Roosevelt

UCLA-WGM MSS	William Gibbs McAdoo Papers, University of California at Los Angeles
WGM	William Gibbs McAdoo
Wilson-McAdoo MSS	Papers of the Wilson-McAdoo Family, Library of Congress, Washington, D.C.
Wilson-McAdoo (SB) MSS	Wilson-McAdoo Collection, University of California at Santa Barbara
WRHA	Western Reserve Historical Association Library, Cleveland, Ohio
WRHA-Hayes MSS	Papers of Ralph A. Hayes, Western Reserve Historical Association Library, Cleveland, Ohio
WRHA-NDB MSS	Newton D. Baker Letters, Western Reserve Historical Association Library, Cleveland, Ohio

Notes

INTRODUCTION

1. Allan Bullock, *Hitler and Stalin: Parallel Lives* (London: HarperCollins, 1991); John Milton Cooper Jr., *Warrior and the Priest: Woodrow Wilson and Theodore Roosevelt* (Cambridge, Mass.: Belknap Press of Harvard University, 1983); Robert E. Sherwood, *Roosevelt and Hopkins: An Intimate History* (New York: Harper, 1948); Kristie Miller, *Ellen and Edith: Woodrow Wilson's First Ladies* (Lawrence: University Press of Kansas, 2010); and Daniel Mark Epstein, *Lincoln and Whitman: Parallel Lives in Civil War Washington* (New York: Random House, 2004).

2. Otis L. Graham, *Encore for Reform: The Old Progressives and the New Deal* (New York: Oxford University Press, 1967).

3. WGM, *Crowded Years: The Reminiscences of William Gibbs McAdoo* (Boston: Houghton Mifflin, 1931); Mary Synon, *McAdoo: The Man and His Times—A Panorama in Democracy* (Indianapolis: Bobbs-Merrill, 1924); Philip M. Chase, "William Gibbs McAdoo: The Last Progressive, 1863–1941" (PhD diss., University of Southern California, 2008); John J. Broesamle, *William Gibbs McAdoo: A Passion for Change, 1863–1917* (Port Washington, N.Y.: Kennikat Press, 1973); Jordan A. Schwarz, *The New Dealers: Power Politics in the Age of Roosevelt* (New York: Alfred A. Knopf, 1993); and Dale N. Shook, *William G. McAdoo and the Development of National Economic Policy, 1913–1918* (New York: Garland, 1987).

4. C. H. Cramer, *Newton D. Baker: A Biography* (Cleveland: World Publishing Company, 1961); Frederick Palmer, *Newton D. Baker: America at War*, 2 vols. (New York: Dodd, Mead & Company, 1931); and Daniel R. Beaver, *Newton D. Baker and the American War Effort, 1917–1918* (Lincoln: University of Nebraska Press, 1966).

5. Richard F. Fenno, *The President's Cabinet: An Analysis of Its Membership, and Its Strengths and Weaknesses in the Period from Wilson to Eisenhower* (Cambridge, Mass.: Harvard University Press, 1969), 119; Noble E. Cunningham, *Thomas Jefferson versus Alexander Hamilton: Confrontations That Shaped a Nation* (New York: Palgrave Macmillan, 2000); Doris Kearns Goodwin, *Team of Rivals: The Political Genius of Abraham Lincoln* (New York: Simon and Schuster, 2005); Arthur M. Schlesinger Jr., *Robert Kennedy and His Times* (Boston: Houghton Mifflin Company, 1978); and Philip A. Goduti Jr., *Kennedy's Kitchen Cabinet and the Pursuit of Peace* (New York: McFarland, 2009).

6. See Daniel T. Rogers, "In Search of Progressivism," in *The Promise of American History: Progress and Prospects*, ed. Stanley I. Kutler and Stanley N. Katz (Baltimore: Johns Hopkins University Press, 1982), 113–132; and Eldon J. Eisenach, *The Lost Promise of Progressivism* (Lawrence: University Press of Kansas, 1994). Robert L. Kelley, *The Transatlantic Persuasion: The Liberal-Democratic Mind in the Age of Gladstone* (New Brunswick, N.J.:

Transaction Publishers, 1990); Daniel T. Rodgers, *Atlantic Crossings: Social Politics in a Progressive Age* (Cambridge, Mass.: Harvard University Press, 1998); Nancy Cohen, *The Reconstruction of American Liberalism, 1865–1914* (Chapel Hill: University of North Carolina Press, 2002); and Cecelia Tichi, *Civic Passions: Seven Who Launched Progressive America* (Chapel Hill: University of North Carolina Press, 2011).

7. Ellis W. Hawley, *The Great War and the Search for a Modern Order: A History of the American People and their Institutions, 1917–1933* (New York: St. Martin's Press, 1979); David M. Kennedy, *Over Here: The First World War and American Society* (New York: Oxford University Press, 1980); William E. Leuchtenburg, "The New Deal and the Analogue of War," in *Change and Continuity in Twentieth Century America*, ed. John Braeman, Robert H. Bremner, and Everett Walters (Columbus: Ohio State University Press, 1968), 81–143; Lisa M. Budreau, *Bodies of War: World War I and the Politics of Commemoration in America, 1919–1933* (New York: New York University Press, 2010); Jennifer D. Keene, *Doughboys, the Great War, and the Remaking of America* (Baltimore: Johns Hopkins University Press, 2001); Stephen R. Ortiz, *Beyond the Bonus March and the GI Bill: How Veteran Politics Shaped the New Deal Era* (New York: New York University Press, 2010); and Richard Slotkin, *Lost Battalions: The Great War and the Crisis of American Masculinity* (New York: Henry Holt and Company, 2005).

CHAPTER 1: NEW SOUTH RISING, 1863–1901

1. William Gibbs McAdoo Sr., Diary Entry, October 31, 1863, McAdoo MSS, Container 353, File: "Oct. 31, 1930"; McAdoo MSS, Container 580, "Family Tree—1920"; and Tom L. Johnson, *My Story* (New York: B. W. Huebsch, 1911), 4.

2. McGuffey's report, more than one hundred pages long, can be found in Container 580 of McAdoo MSS. WGM to Mrs. Mary Hoss Headman, August 11, 1930, McAdoo MSS, Container 352, File: "August 11, 1930"; and WGM, *Crowded Years*, 3.

3. Charles McGuffey, "Information Concerning the McAdoo and Gibbs Families," 63, McAdoo MSS, Container 580. Six thousand dollars in 1840 was the equivalent, on the basis of changes to the Consumer Price Index, of $161,000 in 2011. www.measuringworth.com/uscompare/. WGM to Mrs. S. S. Cressnan, March 22, 1920, McAdoo MSS, Container 504; and Charles McGuffey, "Information Concerning the McAdoo and Gibbs Families," 56, McAdoo MSS, Container 580.

4. "Mrs. Mary M'Adoo Goes to Eternal Rest," *Knoxville Sentinel*, February 5, 1913, Harriman Papers, LOC MSS, Container 3, File: "McAdoo, William Gibbs, 1910–1918"; WGM to the Adjutant General of Georgia, August 12, 1930, McAdoo MSS, Container 352, File: "August 7, 1930"; and WGM to Colonel Thomas Darrah, December 7, 1925, McAdoo MSS, Container 321, File: "Dec. 7, 1925."

5. Charles McGuffey, "Scrapbook: Information Concerning the McAdoo and Gibbs Family," McAdoo MSS, Container 580; Broesamle, *William Gibbs McAdoo*, 3–4; and WGM to J. H. O'Neil, June 24, 1916, McAdoo MSS, Container 490-2. For more details, see WGM to Mrs. M. S. Ray, March 2, 1918, McAdoo MSS, Container 56, File: "Mar. 2, 1918." See "Mrs. Mary M'Adoo Goes to Eternal Rest," *Knoxville Sentinel*, February 5, 1913, Harriman Papers, LOC MSS, Container 3, File: "McAdoo, William Gibbs, 1910–1918"; and "Hon. William Gibbs McAdoo," *Sketches of Prominent Tennesseans*, in McGuffey, "Information Concerning the McAdoo and Gibbs Family," McAdoo MSS, Container 580.

6. For a photograph of McAdoo's birthplace, see Huntington-WGM MSS, Box 3, File 4.

7. WGM, Speech to Rotary Club luncheon, December 29, 1921, UCLA-WGM MSS, Box 5.

8. WGM to Mrs. I. K. Kenan, September 26, 1929, McAdoo MSS, Container 346, File: "Sept. 26, 1929"; WGM, *Crowded Years*, 11; WGM to Mark Sullivan, March 8, 1927, McAdoo MSS, Container 333, File: "Mar. 8, 1927"; and Chase, "William Gibbs McAdoo," 38ff.

9. WGM quoted in Synon, *McAdoo*, 11; "More about Mr. McAdoo's Boyhood, May 28, 1930," McAdoo MSS, Container 352, File: "May 28, 1930"; and WGM to Homer S. Cummings, December 20, 1939, McAdoo MSS, Container 470, File: "Dec. 20, 1939."

10. For Malcolm's reminiscence of his and Willie's boyhoods, see *NYT*, September 28, 1924, 4, 1:3; and WGM to Mark Sullivan, March 8, 1927, McAdoo MSS, Container 333, File: "Mar. 8, 1927."

11. For Knoxville's Civil War, see Robert Tracy McKenzie, *Lincolnites and Rebels: A Divided Town in the American Civil War* (New York: Oxford University Press, 2006).

12. Chase, "William Gibbs McAdoo," 42; and Gordon B. McKinney, "East Tennessee Politics: An Incident in the Life of William Gibbs McAdoo," *East Tennessee Historical Society's Publications* 48 (1976): 34–39.

13. See UCLA-McAdoo MSS, Box 14, File: "Unidentified Corresp"; WGM, *Crowded Years*, 24ff.; WGM Reminiscences, 2, McAdoo MSS, Container 349, File: "Mar. 5, 1930"; and Broesamle, *William Gibbs McAdoo*, 7–8.

14. "Home to the Hill: The second instalment of the life story of 19th century alumnus William G. McAdoo Sr.," *Tennessee Alumnus* 64, no. 4 (Fall 1984): 6–9, Huntington-WGM MSS, Box 3, File 1.

15. McAdoo to Florence Jaffray Harriman, February 3, 1913, Harriman Papers, LOC MSS, Container 3, File: "McAdoo, William Gibbs, 1910–1918." See also WGM, *Crowded Years*, 186.

16. WGM Reminiscences, 2, McAdoo MSS, Container 349, File: "Mar. 5, 1930"; and WGM, *Crowded Years*, 34.

17. WGM, *Crowded Years*, 34; and WGM to Hugh W. McDonald, August 30, 1939, McAdoo MSS, Container 469, File: "Aug. 30, 1939."

18. WGM Reminiscences, March 5, 1930, McAdoo MSS, Container 349, File: "Mar. 5, 1930"; and William Inglis, "Celebrities at Home: William Gibbs McAdoo," *Harper's Weekly* (n.d.), McAdoo MSS, Container 610.

19. Shook, *William G. McAdoo*, 146. See WGM to William G. McAdoo Sr., September 20, 1888, McAdoo MSS, Container 36, File: "Sept. 20, 1888"; Broesamle, *William Gibbs McAdoo*, 9; WGM, *Crowded Years*, 44; and Broesamle, *William Gibbs McAdoo*, 9.

20. WGM, *Crowded Years*, 47; and Broesamle, *William Gibbs McAdoo*, 10–11.

21. William Inglis, "Celebrities at Home: William Gibbs McAdoo," *Harper's Weekly* (n.d.), McAdoo MSS, Container 610.

22. WGM, *Crowded Years*, 47ff.; and Broesamle, *William Gibbs McAdoo*, 10ff. See also *Knoxville Sentinel*, March 3, 1897, McAdoo MSS, Container 630.

23. WGM, *Crowded Years*, 53.

24. WGM, *Crowded Years*, 50–54; and Broesamle, *William Gibbs McAdoo*, 15.

25. Broesamle, *William Gibbs McAdoo*, 16.

26. WGM to Elizabeth Klingberg, August 5, 1936, McAdoo MSS, Container 424, File: "Aug. 5, 1936"; Broesamle, *William Gibbs McAdoo*, 16–17; and WGM, *Crowded Years*, 53.

27. NDB to Ralph Hayes, May 18, 1926, Baker MSS, Container 114, File: "Ralph Hayes, 1926"; and NDB to Frederick V. Field, October 8, 1936, Baker MSS, Container 128, File: "Institute of Pacific Relations, 1936."

28. NDB to Mrs. R. Peterson, December 8, 1931, Baker MSS, Container 183, File: "Pa–Ph, 1931"; NDB to Franklin H. Baker, October 7, 1931, Baker MSS, Container 35, File: "Baa–Bar, 1931"; NDB to Willis F. Evans, February 11, 1927, Baker MSS, Container 91, File: "Eo–Ez, 1927"; and Palmer, *Newton D. Baker*, 1:79.

29. NDB to Elizabeth (Betty) Baker, December 14, 1923, WRHA-NDB MSS, Container 1, File 3.

30. NDB to Milton S. Billmire, December 1, 1931, Baker MSS, Container 42, File: "Bi–Bn, 1931"; NDB to George B. Cook, November 8, 1916, Baker MSS, Letterbooks, Reel 18; and NDB to Captain John W. Thomson, May 2, 1932, Baker MSS, Container 216, File: "Ta–Tn, 1932."

31. NDB to Willis F. Evans, February 11, 1927, Baker MSS, Container 91, File: "Eo–Ez, 1927"; and Cramer, *Newton D. Baker*, 18.

32. NDB to Greenhill Cemetery Association, Martinsburg, West Virginia, July 9, 1929, Baker MSS, Container 107, File: "Gr–Gz, 1929."

33. NDB to John H. Finley, December 10, 1928, Baker MSS, Container 93, File: "Fa–Fk, 1928"; and NDB to Charles M. Thomas, July 5, 1934, Baker MSS, Container 216, File: "Ta–Tn, 1934."

34. NDB to John H. Finley, December 10, 1928, Baker MSS, Container 93, File: "Fa–Fk, 1928"; and NDB to Munson Havens, June 19, 1922, Baker MSS, Container 111, File: "Hav–Hd, 1922."

35. NDB to Betty Baker, June 19, 1927, WRHA-NDB MSS, Acc. #4564, Folder 10; *NYT*, January 13, 1932, 2:1, and Palmer, *Newton D. Baker*, 1:158.

36. NDB to George B. Cook, November 8, 1916, Baker MSS, Letterbooks, Reel 18; and NDB to Thomas G. Frothingham, February 27, 1925, Baker MSS, Container 101, File: "Capt. Thomas G. Frothingham, 1925."

37. For some of NDB's fraternity correspondence, see Baker MSS, Container 266, Reel 1. NDB to Betty Baker, May 12, 1937, WRHA-NDB MSS, Acc. #4564, Folder 9; NDB to Tasker H. Bliss, November 6, 1928, Baker MSS, Container 42, File: "Bi–Bn, 1928"; NDB to Blanche Jacobi, June 13, 1911, Baker MSS, Container 130, File: "J, 1922"; Palmer, *Newton D. Baker*, 1:370; and NDB to Willis F. Evans, February 11, 1927, Baker MSS, Container 91, File: "Eo–Ez, 1927."

38. NDB to Max Stuart, November 10, 1933, Baker MSS, Container 213, File: "Sti–Stz, 1933"; Cramer, *Newton D. Baker*, 23; and NDB to Betty Baker, November 30, 1924, WRHA-NDB MSS, Acc. #4564, Container 1, Folder 5.

39. Cramer, *Newton D. Baker*, 23ff.; and NDB to Max Stuart, November 10, 1933, Baker MSS, Container 213, File: "Sti–Stz, 1933."

40. NDB to W. Calvin Chesnut, July 13, 1933, Baker MSS, Container 58, File: "W. Calvin Chesnut, 1933."

41. NDB to "Boyer," November 19, 1896, Baker MSS, Container 266, Reel 1; and NDB to "Kurt," November 10, 1896, Baker MSS, Container 266, Reel 1.

42. NDB to "Frank," January 27, 1897, Baker MSS, Container 266, Reel 1.

43. Cramer, *Newton D. Baker*, 23ff.; NDB to W. Calvin Chesnut, February 11, 1897, Baker MSS, Container 58, File: "W. Calvin Chesnut, 1932"; "Reminiscence of Louis Pauer to Philip W. Porter, April 10, 1962," Baker MSS, Container 262, File: "Pauer"; and Cramer, *Newton D. Baker*, 13.

44. Cramer, *Newton D. Baker*, 31; *NYT*, March 12, 1916, 6:11; and Johnson, *My Story*, 173.

45. See Broesamle, *William Gibbs McAdoo*, 35; and WGM to the Editor, *Atlanta Constitution*, May 26, 1923, McAdoo MSS, Container 278, File: "May 26, 1923."

46. See NDB to Peggy Baker, April 18, 1937, WRHA-NDB MSS, Acc. #4564, Container 3, Folder 20; and NDB to Walter H. Cook, March 4, 1914, Baker MSS, Letterbooks, Reel 13.

47. See NDB to M. R. Scott, September 23, 1916, Baker MSS, Cleveland Letterbooks, Reel 16.

48. For Wilson's attitudes to the Confederacy, see Sigmund Freud and William C. Bullitt, *Thomas Woodrow Wilson, Twenty-eighth President of the United States: A Psychological Study* (Boston: Houghton Mifflin Company, 1967), 11–12.

CHAPTER 2: GOTHAM'S CLASS A GENIUS AND CLEVELAND'S LITTLE DAVID, 1902–1911

1. Burton J. Hendrick, "William G. McAdoo and the Subway," *McClure's Magazine*, March 1911, 5, UCLA-WGM MSS, Collection 350, Box 11, File 1.

2. John K. Gomez, "The Hudson & Manhattan Railroad Company," www.jerseycityhistory.net/powerhousepagefourteen.html; *NYT*, March 13, 1904, 3:2; Broesamle, *William Gibbs McAdoo*, 17–18; and *NYT*, March 13, 1904, 3:2.

3. Burton J. Hendrick, "William G. McAdoo and the Subway," *McClure's Magazine*, March 1911, 5, UCLA-WGM MSS, Collection 350, Box 11, File 1; and WGM, *Crowded Years*, 66ff.

4. WGM, *Crowded Years*, 66ff.; and Broesamle, *William Gibbs McAdoo*, 19. Fifteen thousand dollars in 1902 was the equivalent, on the basis of changes to the Consumer Price Index, of $405,000 in 2011. www.measuringworth.com/calculators/uscompare/. Burton J. Hendrick, "William G. McAdoo and the Subway," *McClure's Magazine*, March 1911, 6, UCLA-WGM MSS, Collection 350, Box 11, File 1.

5. Anthony Fitzherbert, "The Public Be Pleased: William G. McAdoo and the Hudson Tubes," 3, www.nycsubway.org/us/path/hmhistory/.

6. Broesamle, *William Gibbs McAdoo*, 20; Anthony Fitzherbert, "The Public Be Pleased: William G. McAdoo and the Hudson Tubes," 3, www.nycsubway.org/us/path/hmhistory/; and John K. Gomez, "The Hudson & Manhattan Railroad Company," www.jerseycityhistory.net/powerhousepagefourteen.html.

7. *NYT*, March 13, 1904, 36.

8. McAdoo MSS, Container 588, "Scrapbooks"; Harvey Fisk and Sons, "Subways in New York," January 3, 1910, McAdoo MSS, Container 567; *Jersey City Journal*, November 26, 1906, UCLA-WGM MSS, Boxes 18–20; and *NYT*, February 26, 1908, 1:3.

9. WGM to Mayor Charles D. McGuffy, January 9, 1912, McAdoo MSS, Container 476-3; Harvey Fisk and Sons, "Subways in New York," January 3, 1910, McAdoo MSS, Container 567; Anthony Fitzherbert, "The Public Be Pleased: William G. McAdoo and the Hudson Tubes," 4, www.nycsubway.org/us/path/hmhistory/; and *New York Herald*, November 25, 1906, UCLA-WGM MSS, Box 20. For weekly reports on the tunnels' progress, see McAdoo MSS, Container 616.

10. *The Observer* (Jersey City, N.J.), February 22, 1909, UCLA-WGM MSS, Box 25, Vol. III.

11. Douglas Jasperson Church, "Thrilling Lives," *New York Herald*, May 2, 1909, UCLA-WGM MSS, Box 18, "Newspaper Clippings—Hudson and Manhattan RR."

12. *New York City*, April 22, 1909, UCLA-WGM MSS, Box 25, Vol. III; Broesamle, *William Gibbs McAdoo*, 24; John K. Gomez, "The Hudson & Manhattan Railroad Company," 5, www.jerseycityhistory.net/powerhousepagefourteen.html; and Chase, "William Gibbs McAdoo," 88.

13. Broesamle, *William Gibbs McAdoo*, 21–24; and Burton J. Hendrick, "William G. McAdoo and the Subway," *McClure's Magazine*, March 1911, 6–9, UCLA-WGM MSS, Collection 350, Box 11, File 1.

14. TR to WGM, February 17, 1908, Theodore Roosevelt Papers, LOC MSS, Series 2, Reel 348; Speech by WGM at Sherry's, February 25, 1908, McAdoo MSS, Container 563, File: "Speeches, 1908–1911"; and "Not Over It Yet," *Jersey City* (N.J.) *Journal*, July 20, 1909, UCLA-WGM MSS, Box 19, Vol. VI.

15. See UCLA-WGM MSS, Box 25, Vol. II, for five boxes of newspaper clippings celebrating the opening of the McAdoo Tunnels in February 1908. See also the two volumes of clippings collected by William Gibbs McAdoo Sr. and presented to his son: Huntington-WGM MSS, oversize volumes.

16. Burton J. Hendrick, "William G. McAdoo and the Subway," *McClure's Magazine*, March 1911, 13, UCLA-WGM MSS, Collection 350, Box 11, File 1.

17. See McAdoo MSS, Container 582, "Scrapbook"; UCLA-WGM MSS, Box 25, Vol. III; Hugh Hazleton to WGM, November 14, 1910, UCLA-WGM MSS, Box 11, Folder: "Hudson & Manhattan RR Coy, 1910"; WGM, "Decent Treatment of the Public by Corporations and Regulation of Monopolies," January 30, 1911, 7, UCLA-WGM MSS, Box 11, Folder 3; Burton J. Hendrick, "William G. McAdoo and the Subway," *McClure's Magazine*, March 1911, 14–15, UCLA-WGM MSS, Collection 350, Box 11, File 1; and Broesamle, *William Gibbs McAdoo*, 37–41.

18. Anthony Fitzherbert, "The Public Be Pleased: William G. McAdoo and the Hudson Tubes," 5, www.nycsubway.org/us/path/hmhistory/; and WGM, "Inpromtu [sic] address to the train employees of the Hudson and Manhattan Railroad," February 21, 1908, 2, 3, 4, McAdoo MSS, Container 563, File: "Speeches, 1908–1911."

19. Anthony Fitzherbert, "The Public Be Pleased: William G. McAdoo and the Hudson Tubes," 8, www.nycsubway.org/us/path/hmhistory/; and WGM, *Crowded Years*, 101.

20. Broesamle, *William Gibbs McAdoo*, 27. See also the complaint of Francis Dundon to the ICC claiming that the ladies-only cars were discriminatory against men, on April 24, 1909. The complaint was dismissed on the basis that men were merely discouraged, rather than prohibited, from sitting in the ladies-only cars. McAdoo MSS, Container 91, File: "Apr. 27, 1909." "Manhattan Losing Women Via Tunnel," *New York Herald*, April 8, 1909, UCLA-WGM MSS, Box 25, "Clippings Vol. III"; and Editorial, *New York Herald*, July 25, 1909, McAdoo MSS, Container 91, File: "July 25, 1909."

21. "The Public Be Pleased," *Boston Herald*, July 21, 1909, McAdoo MSS, Container 91, File: "July 22, 1909"; and *Boston Post*, December 11, 1910, McAdoo MSS, Container 583, "Scrapbook."

22. WGM, Speech to the Chamber of Commerce, Boston, Massachusetts, January 30, 1911, 3–5, UCLA-WGM MSS, Box 11, Folder 3. The underlining is WGM's.

23. WGM, Speech before the Chamber of Commerce, Boston, Massachusetts, January 30, 1911, 9, 10, UCLA-WGM MSS, Box 11, Folder 3.

24. WGM, "Inpromtu [sic] address to the train employees of the Hudson and Manhattan Railroad," February 21, 1908, 6, McAdoo MSS, Container 563, File: "Speeches, 1908–1911"; and Broesamle, *William Gibbs McAdoo*, 28–29.

25. Anthony Fitzherbert, "The Public Be Pleased: William G. McAdoo and the Hudson Tubes," 8, www.nycsubway.org/us/path/hmhistory/; WGM, *Crowded Years*, 106; Josephus Daniels, *The Wilson Era*, 2 vols. (Chapel Hill: University of North Carolina Press, 1946), 1:458; and WGM, "Susan B. Anthony," February 15, 1938, McAdoo MSS, Container 565, File: "Speeches 1938–1940."

26. WGM to Reverend Thomas R. Slicer, January 18, 1910, McAdoo MSS, Container 476, Part 1.

27. Hudson and Manhattan Railroad Company, Press Release, March 2, 1910, McAdoo MSS, Container 476, Part 1; Oliver T. Boyd to WGM, March 7, 1911, McAdoo MSS, Container 92, File: "Mar. 7–11, 1911"; and *Christian Science Monitor*, April 15, 1911, McAdoo MSS, Container 585, "Scrapbook."

28. WGM to Harvey Fisk & Sons, January 25, 1910, McAdoo MSS, Container 476, Part 1; and Hudson and Manhattan Railroad Company, Condensed Comparative Statement of Income, November 12, 1910, and January 17, 1911, McAdoo MSS, Container 616.

29. WGM to Pliny Fisk, August 10, 1911, McAdoo MSS, Container 93, File: "Aug. 5–10, 1911"; and John R. Stilgoe, *Train Time: Railroads and the Imminent Reshaping of the United States Landscape* (Charlottesville: University of Virginia Press, 2007), 12–13.

30. WGM, *Crowded Years*, 101. Twenty-five thousand dollars in 1908 was the equivalent of $630,000 in 2011. www.measuringworth.com/calculators/uscompare/. WGM to the Collector of Assessments and Arrears, New York City, January 25, 1910, McAdoo MSS, Container 476, Part 1; "Personal Check Account Ledgers, Nov. 29, 1911–Mar. 8, 1912," UCLA-WGM MSS, Box 2; and Broesamle, *William Gibbs McAdoo*, 34. For examples of WGM's driving record, see McAdoo MSS, Containers 410, 413, and 417, Files: "Sept 26, 1935," "Nov. 27, 1935," and "Feb. 10, 1936"; and *NYT*, September 27, 1935, 13:3.

31. Schwarz, *New Dealers*, 8. See McAdoo MSS, Container 91, for WGM's invitations, calling cards, and social calendars. Garnet Warren, "McAdoo, of Mighty Imagination," *New York Herald*, March 14, 1906, UCLA-WGM MSS, Box 21.

32. *New York Herald*, July 19, 1906, McAdoo MSS, Container 581, "Scrapbook (1)."

33. WGM to Sarah Fleming McAdoo, n.d., McAdoo MSS, Container 42, File: "May 16–19, 1910"; and WGM to Sarah, June 20, 1910, McAdoo MSS, Container 42, File: "June 20–21, 1910."

34. WGM to Dr. Samuel S. Drury, November 21, 1911, McAdoo MSS, Container 79; and Sarah McAdoo to WGM, January 8, 1909, McAdoo MSS, Container 41, File: "June 8, 1909."

35. Sarah McAdoo to WGM, July 2, 1909, McAdoo MSS, Container 41, File: "July 1–3, 1909"; and WGM to Sarah McAdoo, November 7, 1911, McAdoo MSS, Container 44, File: "Nov. 7–9, 1911."

36. WGM to Sarah McAdoo, January 25, 1912, McAdoo MSS, Container 45, File: "Jan. 25, 1912"; WGM to Clarence Graff, March 2, 1912, McAdoo MSS, Container 477-1; *NYT*, February 9, 1911, 9:2; and Wilson to WGM, February 26, 1912, in *The Papers of Woodrow Wilson*, ed. Arthur S. Link, 69 vols. (Princeton, N.J.: Princeton University Press, 1966–1994), 24:217.

37. W. E. Woodward to WGM, November 5, 1930, McAdoo MSS, Container 353, File: "Nov. 5, 1930"; Chase, "William Gibbs McAdoo," 149, n. 305; and WGM, *Crowded Years*, 128–129.

38. NDB to Ralph Hayes, May 18, 1937, Baker MSS, Container 37, File: "Newton D. Baker Personal, 1937"; Thomas F. Campbell and Thomas R. Bullard, "Baker, Newton Diehl," in *Biographical Dictionary of American Mayors, 1820–1920: Big City Mayors*, ed. Melvin G. Holli and Peter D'A. Jones (Westport, Conn.: Greenwood Press, 1981), 14; and NDB to "Miss Jennie," September 18, 1911, Baker MSS, Container 88, File: "Dr–Dz, 1922."

39. NDB to ELB, January 5, 1902, January 19, 1913, and June 28, 1904, WRHA-NDB MSS, Collection 3491, Container 1, File 1.

40. NDB to Mary H. Jamar, March 28, 1910, Baker MSS, Container 268; NDB to Mrs. Howard Leopold, March 14, 1910, Baker MSS, Container 268; NDB to Tom Johnson, September 12, 1910, Baker MSS, Container 268; and NDB to Mrs. Howard Leopold, July 18, 1910, Baker MSS, Container 268.

41. NDB to ELB, October 9, 1902, WRHA-NDB MSS, Collection 3491, Container 1, File 1; Cramer, *Newton D. Baker*, 42; NDB to P. J. Wagner, City Hall, May 9, 1904, Baker MSS, Cleveland Letterbooks, Reel 3; and NDB to Tom L. Johnson, March 25, 1908, Baker MSS, Cleveland Letterbooks, Reel 7. Five thousand dollars in 1902 was the equivalent, on the basis of changes to the Consumer Price Index, of $135,000 in 2011. www.measuring worth.com/uscompare/. NDB to ELB, January 7 and 11, 1903, and June 28, 1904, WRHA-NDB MSS, Collection 3491, Container 1, File 1.

42. NDB to Mrs. T. L. Johnson, September 17, 1921, Baker MSS, Personal Correspondence 1916–1922, Reel 11; and "New War Secretary As His Neighbors Know Him," *NYT*, March 12, 1916, 6:11.

43. Mark Sullivan, *Our Times: 1900–1925*, 6 vols. (New York: Charles Scribner's Sons, 1935), 3:471; Melvin G. Holli, *The American Mayor: The Best and Worst Big-City Leaders* (University Park: University of Pennsylvania Press, 1999), 52–54; NDB quoted in Cramer, *Newton D. Baker*, 13; and NDB, "Tom Loftin Johnson," entry for *The American Dictionary of Biography*, Baker MSS, Container 247, File: "1929."

44. George quoted in Holli, *American Mayor*, 52, and Sullivan, *Our Times*, 3:472. For Henry George's theories, see Steven L. Piott, *American Reformers, 1870–1920: Progressives in Word and Deed* (Lanham, Md.: Rowman & Littlefield Inc., 2006), 25–42.

45. Johnson quoted in Cramer, *Newton D. Baker*, 46; Thomas F. Campbell, "Johnson, Tom Loftin," in Holli and Jones, eds., *Biographical Dictionary of American Mayors*, 184; Shelton Stromquist, *Reinventing "the People": The Progressive Movement, the Class Problem, and the Origins of Modern Liberalism* (Urbana: University of Illinois Press, 2006), 157; Kenneth Finegold, *Experts and Politicians: Reform Challenges to Machine Politics in New York, Cleveland, and Chicago* (Princeton, N.J.: Princeton University Press, 1995), 82–100; and Steffens quoted in Holli, *American Mayor*, 58.

46. Campbell, "Johnson, Tom Loftin," in Holli and Jones, eds., *Biographical Dictionary of American Mayors*, 184; Holli, *American Mayor*, 56–57; NDB to V. V. McNitt, March 19, 1936, Baker MSS, Container 154, File: "McL–Md, 1936"; NDB to Walter Hurt, November 22, 1912, Baker MSS, Cleveland Letterbooks, Reel 14; and Cramer, *Newton D. Baker*, 36.

47. NDB to Mrs. T. L. Johnson, September 17, 1921, Baker MSS, Personal Correspondence 1919–1922, Reel 11. See also NDB, "The Boss from Whom I Learned the Most," *Red Barrel*, Coca-Cola Company, March 1927, Baker MSS, Container 247, Speeches and Writings, File: "1927"; NDB to Frank A. Scott, February 5, 1924, Baker MSS, Container 205, File: "Frank A. Scott, 1924"; and Cramer, *Newton D. Baker*, 41.

48. Finegold, *Experts and Politicians*, 99–100.

49. NDB to Edgar S. Morris, March 4, 1911, Baker MSS, Cleveland Letterbooks, Reel 12; NDB to Norman Weeks, February 17, 1908, Baker MSS, Cleveland Letterbooks, Reel 7; NDB to Richard H. Templeton, March 29, 1910, Baker MSS, Cleveland Letterbooks, Reel 10; and NDB to Horace Flack, April 5, 1908, Baker MSS, Cleveland Letterbooks, Reel 9.

50. NDB to John G. White, January 27, 1904, Baker MSS, Cleveland Letterbooks, Reel 2. The underlining is NDB's. Johnson, *My Story*, 173.

51. NDB to A. B. Lea, Director of Public Service, Cleveland, April 22, 1910, Baker MSS, Cleveland Letterbooks, Reel 10.

52. Holli and Jones, eds., *Biographical Dictionary of American Mayors*, 436.

53. NDB to W. J. Springborn, January 20, 1904, Baker MSS, Cleveland Letterbooks, Reel 2; NDB to W. H. Brett, City Librarian, October 30, 1905, Baker MSS, Cleveland Letterbooks, Reel 5; and NDB to M. A. Fanning, October 19, 1909, Baker MSS, Cleveland Letterbooks, Reel 9.

54. NDB to James L. Hughes, City Solicitor of Lorain, Ohio, October 21, 1904, Baker MSS, Cleveland Letterbooks, Reel 3.

55. NDB to Horace E. Adams, October 6, 1903, Baker MSS, Cleveland Letterbooks, Reel 1.

56. NDB to Reverend Casper W. Hiatt, May 19, 1903, Baker MSS, Cleveland Letterbooks, Reel 1.

57. NDB to Brand Whitlock, July 15, 1910, Baker MSS, Container 268; NDB to C. R. Green, December 31, 1908, Baker MSS, Cleveland Letterbooks, Reel 8; and NDB to Messrs. Drew and Campbell, December 7, 1908, Baker MSS, Cleveland Letterbooks, Reel 8.

58. NDB to Tom L. Johnson, October 19, 1904, Johnson Papers, Reel 3; and NDB to Joseph F. Cowern, November 7, 1908, Baker MSS, Cleveland Letterbooks, Reel 8.

59. NDB to Richard H. Templeton, March 29, 1901, Baker MSS, Cleveland Letterbooks, Reel 10; NDB, "Expression versus Suppression," *Social Hygiene* 4, no. 3 (July 1918): 309–310; and NDB to J. A. Leonard, Esq., March 30, 1905, Baker MSS, Cleveland Letterbooks, Reel 4.

60. NDB to Ohio Board of Pardons, July 13, 1906, Baker MSS, Cleveland Letterbooks, Reel 6; NDB to John Freeman, May 31, 1906, Baker MSS, Container 266, Reel 2; and NDB to O. B. Gould, September 18, 1908, Baker MSS, Cleveland Letterbooks, Reel 8. Baker was similarly forgiving toward a man who attempted to hold him up on a Cleveland street in 1912, and toward Walter Linton, who broke into the Bakers' house in 1914 and threatened Bess with a revolver. For the 1912 episode, see *NYT*, December 24, 1944. For Linton, see NDB to *New York Journal*, December 4, 1914, Baker MSS, Cleveland Letterbooks, Reel 14; and NDB to P. E. Thomas, Warden of the Ohio State Penitentiary, April 12, 1915, Baker MSS, Cleveland Letterbooks, Reel 15.

61. Price V. Fishback and Shawn Everett Kantor, "The Adoption of Workers' Compensation in the United States, 1900–1930," www.nber.org/papers/w5840.pdf; and NDB to E. W. Bemis, June 16, 1903, Baker MSS, Cleveland Letterbooks, Reel 1.

62. NDB to Board of Public Safety, August 7, 1905, Baker MSS, Cleveland Letterbooks, Reel 5; and NDB to E. W. Bemis, February 16, 1909, Baker MSS, Cleveland Letterbooks, Reel 8.

63. NDB to Brant [sic] Whitlock, January 20, 1906, Baker MSS, Cleveland Letterbooks, Reel 5; and NDB to Daniel E. Leslie, Board of Public Service, November 17, 1904, Baker MSS, Cleveland Letterbooks, Reel 3.

64. Cramer, *Newton D. Baker*, 42; and NDB to C. F. Harrison, October 19, 1912, Baker MSS, Cleveland Letterbooks, Reel 14.

65. Cramer, *Newton D. Baker*, 42.

66. *The City of Cleveland v. City Railway Company* (1904), 194 US 517; NDB to Cleveland City Council, April 24, 1903, Baker MSS, Cleveland Letterbooks, Reel 4; Holli, *American Mayor*, 57; NDB to Charles A. Thatcher, October 21, 1904, Baker MSS, Cleveland Letterbooks, Reel 3; NDB to J. M. Hackney, January 5, 1905, Baker MSS, Cleveland Letterbooks, Reel 4; *The City of Cleveland v. The Electric Railway Company* (1907), 201 US 529; *The Cleveland Electric Railway Company v. The City of Cleveland* (1907), 204 US 116; and see the Johnson Papers, LOC MSS, Reels 7 and 8.

67. *The North American*, December 7, 1907, Johnson Papers, LOC MSS, Reel 6; NDB to Charles A. Thatcher, October 21, 1904, Baker MSS, Cleveland Letterbooks, Reel 4; NDB to W. D. Thomas, January 30, 1905, Baker MSS, Cleveland Letterbooks, Reel 4; and Cramer, *Newton D. Baker*, 43.

68. NDB to the Editor, *Evening World* (Martinsburg, W.Va.), August 20, 1908, Baker MSS, Cleveland Letterbooks, Reel 8; and Cramer, *Newton D. Baker*, 44.

69. NDB to C. F. Harrison, October 17, 1912, Baker MSS, Cleveland Letterbooks, Reel 14; and NDB to Logan N. Coffinbury, January 22, 1910, Baker MSS, Cleveland Letterbooks, Reel 9.

70. NDB to George E. Lee, May 17, 1906, Baker MSS, Cleveland Letterbooks, Reel 6; NDB to Hon. Fred Bader, March 12, 1910, Baker MSS, Cleveland Letterbooks, Reel 10; and NDB to Hon. John Krause, Ohio Senate, March 4, 1911, Baker MSS, Cleveland Letterbooks, Reel 7.

71. NDB to Hon. Theodore E. Burton, February 24, 1904, and May 19, 1904, Baker MSS, Container 266, Reel 1, and Cleveland Letterbooks, Reel 3; and NDB to Hon. Richard Bartholdt, September 28, 1909, Baker MSS, Container 268.

72. NDB to W. B. Kilpatrick, June 23, 1910, Baker MSS, Container 268; NDB to John C. Long, December 20, 1927, Baker MSS, Container 147, File: "Li–Lz, 1927"; Willis Thornton, *Newton D. Baker and his Books* (Cleveland: The Press of the Western Reserve University, 1954), 43; and NDB to P. H. Callahan, June 10, 1933, Baker MSS, Container 52, File: "Colonel P. H. Callahan, 1933."

73. NDB to Frederick C. Howe, May 6, 1904, Baker MSS, Container 266; NDB to W. J. Bryan, July 12, 1904, Baker MSS, Container 266; and NDB to Robert Baker, August 4, 1908, Baker MSS, Container 267.

74. NDB to James E. Campbell, November 24, 1908, Baker MSS, Container 267.

75. NDB to George W. Norris, February 21, 1925, Baker MSS, Container 177, File: "No–Nz, 1925"; and NDB to "Miss Jennie," September 18, 1911, Baker MSS, Container 88, File: "Dr–Dz, 1922."

76. Finegold, *Experts and Politicians*, 102; and *NYT*, January 2, 1912, 15:3.

77. Chase, "William Gibbs McAdoo," 62–66 and 105.

CHAPTER 3: CHANGING ROLES

1. Robert R. Weiner, *Lake Effects: A History of Urban Policy Making in Cleveland, 1825–1929* (Columbus: Ohio State University Press, 2005), 94 and 203; Wellington G. Fordyce, "Immigrant Colonies in Cleveland," *Ohio History* 45 (1936): 320–340, 321; Michael Haverkamp, "Roosevelt and Taft: How the Republican Vote Split in Ohio in 1912,"

Ohio History 110 (Summer–Autumn 2001): 121–135, 128; Holli and Jones, eds., *Biographical Dictionary of American Mayors*, 436, 433, 438, and 440; and Maureen A. Flanagan, *America Reformed: Progressives and Progressivisms* (New York: Oxford University Press, 2007), 16.

2. Weiner, *Lake Effects*, 94.

3. Weiner, *Lake Effects*, 4–5.

4. *NYT*, March 12, 1916, 6:11; Finegold, *Experts and Politicians*, 103 and 105; Cramer, *Newton D. Baker*, 49; and Cleveland Chamber of Commerce, "Mayor Baker's Resignation from the Cleveland Chamber of Commerce, February 1914," WRHA-NDB MSS, PAM C1023.

5. Weiner, *Lake Effects*, 133–134 and 148–150.

6. Finegold, *Experts and Politicians*, 114 and 103; and Cleveland *Plain Dealer* quoted in Robert L. Briggs, "The Progressive Era in Cleveland, Ohio: Tom L. Johnson's Administration, 1901–1909" (PhD diss., University of Chicago, 1962), 207.

7. NDB to Chas L. Newton, February 25, 1914, Baker MSS, Cleveland Letterbooks, Reel 13. See also WRHA-NDB MSS, Container 2, for copies of annual reports by city government departments.

8. See WRHA-NDB MSS, Container 10, for patronage correspondence in 1913; and NDB to John D. Fackler, July 9, 1917, Baker MSS, Cleveland Letterbooks, Reel 11.

9. Cramer, *Newton D. Baker*, 53–54; NDB to E. C. Hopwood, Cleveland *Plain Dealer*, May 2, 1913, Baker MSS, Cleveland Letterbooks, Reel 11; and NDB to the Council of the City of Cleveland, January 6, 1913, Baker MSS, Cleveland Letterbooks, Reel 14.

10. Holli, *American Mayor*, 177; Finegold, *Experts and Politicians*, 5; and Cramer, *Newton D. Baker*, 55–59. For NDB's defense to this charge, see NDB to Professor C. C. Arbuthnot, April 14, 1916, Baker MSS, Cleveland Letterbooks, Reel 17.

11. See NDB to Harry L. Davis, December 8, 1915, Baker MSS, Cleveland Letterbooks, Reel 18; and WGM to NDB, n.d., McAdoo MSS, Container 480-1.

12. See NDB to Harry L. Davis, December 8, 1915, Baker MSS, Cleveland Letterbooks, Reel 18; and NDB to Edward C. Fischer, October 24, 1914, Baker MSS, Cleveland Letterbooks, Reel 14.

13. "Twenty-five Years of Home Rule," *Greater Cleveland: a Bulletin on Public Business by the Citizens League* 13 (December 30, 1937): 73–75, Baker MSS, Container 263, File: "1926–1934 Articles."

14. NDB, "Why Does Cleveland Need a New Charter?" n.d. [c. November 1912], Baker MSS, Cleveland Letterbooks, Reel 10; and NDB to John D. Fackler, July 9, 1917, Baker MSS, Cleveland Letterbooks, Reel 11.

15. NDB to George W. Norris, February 21, 1925, Baker MSS, Container 177, File: "No–Nz, 1925"; Finegold, *Experts and Politicians*, 103ff.; NDB to Cleveland Electric Illuminating Company, January 11, 1912, Baker MSS, Cleveland Letterbooks, Reel 13; NDB to Clement R. Wood, July 5, 1913, Baker MSS, Cleveland Letterbooks, Reel 14; and Cramer, *Newton D. Baker*, 51–54.

16. NDB to the Editor, *The Cleveland Press*, September 27, 1911, Baker MSS, Cleveland Letterbooks, Reel 8; NDB to James Weatherly, May 19, 1916, Baker MSS, Cleveland Letterbooks, Reel 16; and NDB to Henry L. Stimson, January 14, 1925, Baker MSS, Container 212, File: "Sti–Stz, 1925."

17. NDB to CEIC, January 12, 1912, Baker MSS, Cleveland Letterbooks, Reel 13.

18. NDB to the Council of the City of Cleveland, January 6, 1913, Baker MSS, Cleveland Letterbooks, Reel 14; NDB to L. H. Jenkins, November 12, 1914, Baker MSS, Cleveland

Letterbooks, Reel 16; and NDB to Henry L. Stimson, January 14, 1924, Baker MSS, Container 212, File: "Sti–Stz, 1925."

19. NDB to Haywood Scott, June 23, 1914, Baker MSS, Cleveland Letterbooks, Reel 14; NDB to Herbert R. Briggs, February 26, 1915, Baker MSS, Cleveland Letterbooks, Reel 14; and NDB to George W. Norris, February 27, 1925, Baker MSS, Container 177, File: "No–Nz, 1925."

20. NDB to George W. Norris, February 21, 1925, Baker MSS, Container 177, File: "No–Nz, 1925"; and NDB to Henry L. Stimson, January 14, 1925, Baker MSS, Container 212, File: "Sti–Stz, 1925."

21. *NYT*, November 30, 1913, 5, 9:1.

22. NDB to Clyde L. King, December 18, 1912, and NDB to Chas G. Merrell, October 9, 1914, Baker MSS, Cleveland Letterbooks, Reel 14.

23. NDB, "Expression versus Suppression," *Social Hygiene* 4, no. 3 (July 1918): 313–314; NDB to F. V. Faulhaber, December 16, 1912, Baker MSS, Cleveland Letterbooks, Reel 14; and NDB to the National Social Hygiene Society, January 31, 1918, in NDB, *Frontiers of Freedom* (New York: George H. Doran Company, 1918), 233ff.

24. NDB to D. C. Westenhaver, October 13, 1913, Baker MSS, Cleveland Letterbooks, Reel 12; NDB to H. Laughlin, September 5, 1913, Baker MSS, Cleveland Letterbooks, Reel 15; and NDB to Chas G. Merrell, October 9, 1914, Baker MSS, Cleveland Letterbooks, Reel 14.

25. NDB to Rolin H. White, September 23, 1915, Baker MSS, Cleveland Letterbooks, Reel 17; and NDB to Christian Trimmer, November 15, 1915, Baker MSS, Cleveland Letterbooks, Reel 18.

26. NDB to Reverend George H. Sandison, March 6, 1912, Baker MSS, Cleveland Letterbooks, Reel 13; and NDB to Edmund Vance Cooke, April 13, 1914, Baker MSS, Cleveland Letterbooks, Reel 15.

27. Finegold, *Experts and Politicians*, 106.

28. NDB to F. H. Goff, February 17, 1915, Baker MSS, Cleveland Letterbooks, Reel 14.

29. NDB to F. M. Creon, July 12, 1911, Baker MSS, Cleveland Letterbooks, Reel 7; and NDB to F. M. Barton, June 26, 1913, Baker MSS, Cleveland Letterbooks, Reel 11.

30. Weiner, *Lake Effects*, 110; NDB to Sabina Marshall, January 14, 1925, Baker MSS, Container 149, File: "Ma–Mb, 1925"; and NDB to E. C. Pearson, July 17, 1914, Baker MSS, Cleveland Letterbooks, Reel 16.

31. NDB to Sabina Marshall, January 14, 1925, Baker MSS, Container 149, File: "Ma–Mb, 1925"; and NDB to Cleveland Civil Service Commission, February 25, 1913, Baker MSS, Cleveland Letterbooks, Reel 14.

32. NDB to Harriet Taylor Upton, November 9, 1911, and NDB to Clarence E. Blume, February 12, 1912, Baker MSS, Cleveland Letterbooks, Reel 8; Steven H. Steinglass and Gino J. Scarselli, *The Ohio State Constitution: A Reference Guide* (Westport, Conn.: Praeger, 2004), 35 and 122–128; and NDB to C. E. Mason, February 15, 1912, Baker MSS, Cleveland Letterbooks, Reel 8.

33. For TR and judicial recall, see Gary Murphy, "'Mr. Roosevelt is Guilty': Theodore Roosevelt and the Crusade for Constitutionalism, 1910–1912," *Journal of American Studies* 36, no. 3 (2002): 441–457, 447–449, and 451–452; and Stephen Skowronek, *Building a New American State: The Expansion of National Administrative Capabilities* (New York: Cambridge University Press, 1982), 266–267. NDB to Frank H. Baker, March 1, 1912, and NDB to Louis F. Post, March 9, 1912, Baker MSS, Cleveland Letterbooks, Reel 8; and NDB to Frank H. Baker, June 3, 1912, Baker MSS, Cleveland Letterbooks, Reel 9.

34. NDB to Josephus Daniels, February 7, 1936, Baker MSS, Container 84, File: "Josephus Daniels, 1936"; NDB to FHB, June 3, 1912, Baker MSS, Cleveland Letterbooks, Reel 9; NDB to Daniel Kiefer, January 8, 1912, Baker MSS, Cleveland Letterbooks, Reel 8; and NDB to Professor Garrett Droppers, June 10, 1912, NDB to R. E. Byrd, April 4, 1912, and NDB to FHB, June 3, 1912, Baker MSS, Cleveland Letterbooks, Reel 9.

35. William F. McCombs to Woodrow Wilson, September 13, 1911, in Link, ed., *Papers of Woodrow Wilson*, 23:327; NDB to Professor E. W. Bemis, February 15, 1912, and NDB to Robert H. Grimes, January 10, 1912, Baker MSS, Cleveland Letterbooks, Reel 8.

36. NDB to Daniel Kiefer, January 8, 1912, and NDB to Professor E. W. Bemis, February 15, 1912, Baker MSS, Cleveland Letterbooks, Reel 8; NDB to C. W. Boyer, April 18, 1912, Baker MSS, Cleveland Letterbooks, Reel 9; and NDB to Daniel Kiefer, January 8, 1912, Baker MSS, Cleveland Letterbooks, Reel 8.

37. Cramer, *Newton D. Baker*, 65–66; NDB to Atlee Pomerone, May 23, 1912, and NDB to Professor Garrett Droppers, June 10, 1912, Baker MSS, Cleveland Letterbooks, Reel 9; and Francis W. Dickey, "The Presidential Preference Primary," *American Political Science Review* 9, no. 3 (August 1915): 467–487, 481.

38. Cramer, *Newton D. Baker*, 69; and NDB to Susan W. Fitzgerald, August 14, 1912, Baker MSS, Cleveland Letterbooks, Reel 13. The NDB-WGM correspondence is in Baker MSS, Cleveland Letterbooks, Reel 10.

39. US Bureau of the Census, *Historical Statistics of the United States* (Washington, D.C.: US Government Printing Office, 1975), 2:Y 79–83: 1073. For results in Cleveland, see Haverkamp, "Roosevelt and Taft," 127. NDB to Wilson, November 6 and 15, 1912, Baker MSS, Cleveland Letterbooks, Reel 18; Link, ed., *Papers of Woodrow Wilson*, 25:549; and "From the Diary of Edward M. House, February 18, 1913," in Link, ed. *Papers of Woodrow Wilson*, 27:118.

40. See NDB to Joseph Tumulty, August 13, 1913, Baker MSS, Cleveland Letterbooks, Reel 12; NDB to WGM, May 23, 1913, Baker MSS, Cleveland Letterbooks, Reel 11; NDB to Frederick C. Howe, March 17, 1913, Baker MSS, Cleveland Letterbooks, Reel 11; Woodrow Wilson to NDB and NDB reply, July 24 and October 4, 1913, in Link, ed., *Papers of Woodrow Wilson*, 28:69 and 359; NDB to WGM and WGM reply, May 23 and 28, 1913, Baker MSS, Cleveland Letterbooks, Reel 11; and McAdoo MSS, Container 100, File: "May 28, 1913."

41. NDB to WGM, January 1, 1914, and July 28, 1914, Baker MSS, Cleveland Letterbooks, Reel 13; NDB to WGM, August 21, 1914, Baker MSS, Cleveland Letterbooks, Reel 14; and NDB to Frederick C. Howe, March 17, 1913, Baker MSS, Cleveland Letterbooks, Reel 11.

42. NDB to D. C. Westenhaver, September 8, 1913, Baker MSS, Cleveland Letterbooks, Reel 12; NDB to Ernest Ludwig, March 6 and March 12, 1915, Baker MSS, Cleveland Letterbooks, Reel 14; and NDB to E. M. Baker, August 20, 1914, Baker MSS, Cleveland Letterbooks, Reel 13.

43. NDB to D. C. Matthews, July 6, 1914, Baker MSS, Cleveland Letterbooks, Reel 13; Cramer, *Newton D. Baker*, 80; and NDB to George Foster Peabody, September 23, 1915, Baker MSS, Cleveland Letterbooks, Reel 17.

44. NDB, *Why We Went to War* (New York: Harper & Brothers, 1936), 101–103; and NDB to Abraham Kolinsky, December 20, 1915, Baker MSS, Cleveland Letterbooks, Reel 18.

45. NDB to Joseph Tumulty, May 14, 1915, Baker MSS, Cleveland Letterbooks, Reel 15; and NDB to George Foster Peabody, October 21, 1915, Baker MSS, Cleveland Letterbooks, Reel 18.

46. NDB to Ernest Ludwig, March 6, 1915, Baker MSS, Cleveland Letterbooks, Reel 14; and NDB to FHB, January 2, 1916, WRHA-NDB MSS, Acc. #3491, Container 2, File 2.

47. NDB to Woodrow Wilson, December 15, 1915, Baker MSS, Cleveland Letterbooks, Reel 15.

48. Woodrow Wilson to NDB, November 12, 1915, in Link, ed., *Papers of Woodrow Wilson*, 35:193.

49. Daniels, *Wilson Era*, 2:444; WGM, *Crowded Years*, 340, Fenno, *President's Cabinet*, 209–211; NYT, February 12, 1916, 1:8; and Cooper, *Warrior and the Priest*, 299.

50. NYT, February 12 and March 7, 1916, 1:8 and 1:2; NDB to James M. Cox, May 11, 1914, Baker MSS, Cleveland Letterbooks, Reel 13; Daniels, *Wilson Era*, 1:449; and WGM, *Crowded Years*, 342.

51. NYT, March 7, 1916, 10:3 and 1:2. Riddell quoted in Meirion Harries and Susie Harries, *Last Days of Innocence: America at War, 1917–1918* (New York: Vintage Books, 1997), 50; Hermann Hagerdorn, *Leonard Wood: A Biography*, 2 vols. (New York: Harper & Brothers, 1931), 2:182; and NDB quoted in Beaver, *Newton D. Baker*, 1.

52. See WGM to Messrs. Delanoy and Delanoy, December 27, 1911, and WGM to R. B. Hay, January 4, 1912, McAdoo MSS, Container 476-3; WGM to Mr .and Thomas Vincent, January 30, 1912, McAdoo MSS, Container 477-1; WGM to B. C. Loder, May 27, 1912, McAdoo MSS, Container 477-3; NYT, November 29, 1922, 19:8, May 16, 1927, 23:8, and May 10, 1928, 48:1; and WGM to EWM, May 24, 1927, Wilson-McAdoo MSS, Container 1, File: "McAdoo, William G., 1926–27."

53. McAdoo MSS, Container 92, File: "Mar. 3–May 10, 1910"; and WGM to Jule Fleming, May 31, 1911, McAdoo MSS, Container 44, File: "May 18–21, 1913." See also WGM, "Memorandum: Automobile Accident," April 9, 1930, McAdoo MSS, Container 350, File: "Apr. 9, 1930"; NYT, May 19, 1911, 1:5, McAdoo MSS, Container 586, "Scrapbooks"; and WGM to Daniel C. Roper, February 23, 1925, McAdoo MSS, File: "Feb. 23, 1925."

54. See generally the Harriman Papers, LOC MSS, Container 31, "Biographical Details."

55. Mrs. J. Borden Harriman, *From Pinafores to Politics* (New York: Henry Holt and Company, 1923), 107; and WGM to Florence Jaffray Harriman, n.d., Harriman Papers, LOC MSS, Container 31, File: "McAdoo, William Gibbs, N.D." The emphasis is WGM's.

56. See WGM to Florence Jaffray Harriman, May 18 [1913], Harriman Papers, LOC MSS, Container 31, File: "McAdoo, William Gibbs, N.D."

57. WGM to Mr. Wentworth S. Micks, October 31, 1932, McAdoo MSS, Container 376, File: "Oct. 31, 1932"; and WGM to TR, November 16, 1903, Theodore Roosevelt Papers, LOC MSS, Reel 38.

58. WGM to TR, October 24 and November 26, 1904, McAdoo MSS, Container 581, File: "Scrapbook (1)"; TR to WGM, November 29, 1904, Theodore Roosevelt Papers, LOC MSS, Series 2, Reel 336; WGM to TR, January 16, 1911, Theodore Roosevelt Papers, LOC MSS, Reel 97; and WGM to TR, February 15, 1911, Theodore Roosevelt Papers, LOC MSS, Reel 99.

59. Broesamle, *William Gibbs McAdoo*, 43. WGM quoted in Shook, *William Gibbs McAdoo*, 69–70.

60. WGM to G. Grosvenor Dawe, February 28, 1911, McAdoo MSS, Container 92, File: "Feb. 27–28, 1911"; and Shook, *William Gibbs McAdoo*, 61. Newton quoted in Shook, *William Gibbs McAdoo*, 55.

61. WGM to TR, February 17, 1910, McAdoo MSS, Container 476, Part 1; WGM to Woodrow Wilson, October 11, 1910, in Link, ed., *Papers of Woodrow Wilson*, 21:265, 21:270, and 22:190; and *The Morning Sun* (New York City), December 13, 1910, McAdoo MSS, Container 584, "Scrapbook."

62. WGM to Arthur Brisbane, *New York Journal*, February 15, 1910, McAdoo MSS, Container 476-1.

63. Cooper, *Warrior and the Priest*, passim; James Chace, *1912: Wilson, Roosevelt, Taft & Debs—The Election That Changed the Country* (New York: Simon & Schuster, 2004), 128; and WGM to Major F. K. Huger, December 4, 1911, McAdoo MSS, Container 476-3. The emphasis is WGM's.

64. WGM to William Barton French, May 14, 1912, McAdoo MSS, Container 476-2.

65. William F. McCombs, *Making Woodrow Wilson President* (New York: Fairview Publishing Company, 1931), 109; Byron R. Newton, "Memorandum: The Wilson Campaign," 2–3, McAdoo MSS, Container 619; Godfrey Hodgson, *Woodrow Wilson's Right Hand: The Life of Edward M. House* (New Haven, Conn.: Yale University Press, 2006), 4; John Dos Passos, *Mr. Wilson's War* (Garden City, N.Y.: Doubleday & Company Inc., 1962), 54; WGM to George Foster Peabody, November 25, 1911, McAdoo MSS, Container 476-3; and WGM, *Crowded Years*, 118.

66. McCombs, *Making Woodrow Wilson President*, 41–42. WGM's letters can be found in McAdoo MSS, Container 477-2. WGM to J. E. Stern, January 8, 1912. McAdoo MSS, Container 476-3.

67. See WGM to F. L. Seely, December 21, 1911, McAdoo MSS, Container 476-3; WGM to George Foster Peabody, April 8, 1912, and WGM to Josephus Daniels, April 24, 1912, McAdoo MSS, Container 477-2; Pleasant A. Stovall, cable to WGM, April 22, 1912, McAdoo MSS, Container 477-2; Broesamle, *William Gibbs McAdoo*, 54–55 and 60; WGM to Earl Brewer, May 10, 1912, McAdoo MSS, Container 477-2; and WGM to W. H. Osborn, April 13, 1912, McAdoo MSS, Container 477-2.

68. Joseph P. Tumulty, *Woodrow Wilson As I Knew Him* (Garden City, N.J.: Doubleday, Page & Company, 1921), 135; and Ray Stannard Baker, "Memorandum of a Conversation with Mr. and Mrs. McAdoo and Miss Margaret Wilson at the Plaza Hotel, May 9, 1928," 4, Papers of Ray Stannard Baker, LOC MSS, Reel 79; Woodrow Wilson to WGM, November 10, 1911, and Wilson to Walter Hines Page, August 21, 1911, in Link, ed., *Papers of Woodrow Wilson*, 23:547 and 23:285; and Byron R. Newton, "Memorandum: The Wilson Campaign" 3, McAdoo MSS, Container 619.

69. Byron R. Newton, "Memorandum: The Wilson Campaign," 4, McAdoo MSS, Container 619.

70. Byron R. Newton, "Memorandum: The Wilson Campaign," 10, McAdoo MSS, Container 619; and Freud and Bullitt, *Thomas Woodrow Wilson*, 144.

71. WGM to George F. Peabody, June 3, 1912, McAdoo MSS, Container 477-3.

72. Cooper, *Warrior and the Priest*, 186.

73. Cooper, *Warrior and the Priest*, 120–121; WGM to George F. Peabody, May 29, 1912, McAdoo MSS, Container 477-3; and Ray Stannard Baker, "Interview with William Gibbs McAdoo, November 6, 1927," Papers of Ray Stannard Baker, LOC MSS, Reel 79.

74. WGM to Charles E. Hendrickson, April 16, 1929, McAdoo MSS, Container 343, File: "Apr. 16, 1929"; and WGM, *Crowded Years*, 145.

75. Ray Stannard Baker, "Memorandum of a Conversation with Mr. and Mrs. McAdoo and Miss Margaret Wilson at the Plaza Hotel, May 9, 1928," 4, Papers of Ray Stannard

Baker, LOC MSS, Reel 79. In his recent study of the 1912 election, Lewis L. Gould asserts that it was McCombs, and not McAdoo, who kept Wilson's message from the delegates. Gould does not, however, cite any source for his assertion, which is contrary to the accepted view: Lewis L. Gould, *Four Hats in the Ring: The 1912 Election and the Birth of Modern American Politics* (Lawrence: University Press of Kansas, 2008), 92. WGM to Joseph P. Tumulty, September 24, 1930, McAdoo MSS, Container 352, File: "Sept. 24, 1930"; Arthur S. Link, "The Baltimore Convention of 1912," *American Historical Review* 50, no. 4 (July 1945): 691–713, 708; and Broesamle, *William Gibbs McAdoo*, 62–63. For detailed accounts of the Baltimore convention, see Link, "Baltimore Convention of 1912"; Chace, *1912*, 143–166; Chase, "William Gibbs McAdoo," 110–116; and WGM, *Crowded Years*, 146.

76. Byron R. Newton, "Memorandum: The Wilson Campaign," 16, McAdoo MSS, Container 619; WGM to Woodrow Wilson, June 25, 1912, in *Woodrow Wilson: Life and Letters*, ed. Ray Stannard Baker, 8 vols. (Garden City, N.J.: Doubleday, Doran & Company, Inc., 1927–1939), 3:396; Broesamle, *William Gibbs McAdoo*, 64; and *New-York Tribune*, August 25, 1912, McAdoo MSS, Container 587, "Scrapbook."

77. Tumulty, *Woodrow Wilson As I Knew Him*, 135; *New-York Tribune*, August 17, 1912, McAdoo MSS, Container 587, "Scrapbook"; and Broesamle, *William Gibbs McAdoo*, 64–65.

78. Byron R. Newton, "Memo: Wall Street Funds, November 16, 1912," McAdoo MSS, Container 619; Newton, "Memorandum: The Wilson Campaign," 22, McAdoo MSS, Container 619; and WGM to William F. McCombs, October 24, 1912, McAdoo MSS, Container 619.

79. *The Globe* (N.Y.), October 3, 1912, McAdoo MSS, Container 588, "Scrapbooks"; "From the Diary of Edward M. House, October 20, 1912," and Woodrow Wilson to WGM, November 20, 1912, in Link, ed., *Papers of Woodrow Wilson*, 25:448 and 552; Paterson (N.J.) *Guardian*, March 13, 1913, McAdoo MSS, Container 589, "Scrapbooks"; *NYT*, February 6, 1913, 1:5; and *Journal of Commerce* (N.Y.), March 25, 1913, McAdoo MSS, Container 591, "Scrapbooks." Wilson quoted in Freud and Bullitt, *Thomas Woodrow Wilson*, 148.

80. Chicago *Post*, December 12, 1912, McAdoo MSS, Container 589, "Scrapbooks"; *NYT*, March 3, 1913, 2:3; Broesamle, *William Gibbs McAdoo*, 78; and Oswald Garrison Villard, *Fighting Years: Memoirs of a Liberal Editor* (New York: Harcourt, Brace and Company, 1939), 222–223.

81. WGM to Charles E. Hendrickson, April 16, 1929, McAdoo MSS, Container 343, File: "Apr. 16, 1929"; Villard, *Fighting Years*, 223; "From the Diary of Edward M. House, October 20, 1912," and William Jennings Bryan to Woodrow Wilson, December 25, 1912, in Link, ed., *Papers of Woodrow Wilson*, 25:448 and 622; and RHM to WGM, March 14, 1913, McAdoo MSS, Container 46, File: "Mar. 22 1912–Aug. 24 1913."

CHAPTER 4: NEWTON BAKER, WILLIAM MCADOO, AND PROGRESSIVISM

1. Robert Harrison, *Congress, Progressive Reform, and the New American State* (New York: Cambridge University Press, 2004), 4; Peter Filene, "An Obituary for 'The Progressive Movement,'" *American Quarterly* 22 (1970): 20–34; Dewey W. Grantham, *Southern Progressivism: The Reconciliation of Progress and Tradition* (Knoxville: University of Tennessee Press, 1983); Josephine Camhi, *Women Against Women: American Anti-Suffragism* (New York: Carlson Publishing, 1994), 214; and Keith W. Olson, *Biography of a Progressive: Franklin K. Lane, 1864–1921* (Westport, Conn.: Greenwood Press, 1979), 5.

2. Daniel Rodgers, "In Search of Progressivism," in *The Promise of American History: Progress and Prospects*, ed. Stanley Kutler and Stanley I. Katz (Baltimore: Johns Hopkins University Press, 1982), 113–132; James J. Connolly, "H-SHGAPE Bibliographical Essays: Progressivism," www.h-net.org/~shgape/bibessays/prog.html; and Robert D. Johnston, "Re-Democratizing the Progressive Era: The Politics of Progressive Era Political Historiography," *Journal of the Gilded Age and Progressive Era* 1, no. 1 (January 2002): 68–92, 77.

3. Alan Dawley, *Changing the World: American Progressives in War and Revolution* (Princeton, N.J.: Princeton University Press, 2003), 4–5; Cohen, *Reconstruction of American Liberalism*, 224; and Flanagan, *America Reformed*, 28.

4. Stromquist, *Reinventing "the People,"* viii; Flanagan, *America Reformed*, 32, Michael McGerr, *A Fierce Discontent: The Rise and Fall of the Progressive Movement in America, 1870–1920* (New York: The Free Press, 2003), 215–217; and David W. Southern, *The Progressive Era and Race: Reaction and Reform* (Wheeling, Ill.: Harlan Davidson Inc., 2005), 44–47.

5. McGerr, *Fierce Discontent*, xiv; and Pinchot quoted in John A. Thompson, *Reformers and War: American Progressive Publicists and the First World War* (Cambridge: Cambridge University Press, 1987), 43.

6. Robert Higgs, *Crisis and Leviathan: Critical Episodes in the Growth of American Government* (New York: Oxford University Press, 1987), 114; and Flanagan, *America Reformed*, 102 and 157.

7. James Weinstein, *The Corporate Ideal in the Liberal State: 1900–1918* (Boston: Beacon Press, 1968), xiv–xv.

8. Holli, *American Mayor*, 58–60; Cohen, *Reconstruction of American Liberalism*, 228; and Dawley, *Changing the World*, 15.

9. Flanagan, *Reforming America*, 102.

10. Higgs, *Crisis and Leviathan*, 115; and Olson, *Biography of a Progressive*, 5.

11. William B. Murphy, "The National Progressive Republican League and the Elusive Quest for Progressive Unity," *Journal of the Gilded Age and Progressive Era* 8, no. 4 (October 2009): 515–543, 516; Dawley, *Changing the World*, 4; and NDB quoted in Cramer, *Newton D. Baker*, 63.

12. Olson, *Biography of a Progressive*, 5.

13. NDB, "How Woodrow Wilson Met Domestic Questions," April 11, 1927, 15, Baker MSS, Container 247, File: "1927."

14. Rodgers, *Atlantic Crossings*, 52–75; and Johnston, "Re-Democratizing the Progressive Era," 88.

15. For examples of NDB-Johnson correspondence, see Baker MSS, Cleveland Letterbooks, Reels 3–7; Flanagan, *America Reformed*, 40; and Cramer, *Newton D. Baker*, 50.

16. Flanagan, *America Reformed*, 192–193.

17. Rodgers, *Atlantic Crossings*, 144, Martin J. Shiesl, *The Politics of Efficiency: Municipal Administration and Reform in America, 1880–1920* (Berkeley: University of California Press, 1977), 16; Rodgers, *Atlantic Crossings*, 112; and Flanagan, *America Reformed*, 28.

18. Cramer, *Newton D. Baker*, 187–190.

19. Thornton, *Newton D. Baker and his Books*; and Cramer, *Newton D. Baker*, 23.

20. Rodgers, "In Search of Progressivism," 123; Robert H. Wiebe, *Businessmen and Reform: A Study of the Progressive Movement* (Cambridge, Mass.: Harvard University Press, 1962); and Robert H. Wiebe, *The Search for Order, 1877–1920* (New York: Hill and Wang,

1968); 123–132. Broesamle, *William Gibbs McAdoo*, 30; and Chase, "William Gibbs McAdoo," 101–2.

21. Gabriel Kolko, *The Triumph of Conservatism: A Reinterpretation of American History, 1900–1916* (New York: The Free Press, 1963); and Higgs, *Crisis and Leviathan*, 114–116.

22. WGM, "Speech Delivered upon the Opening of the Hudson River Tunnels, July 19, 1909," 3, McAdoo MSS, Container 563, File: "Speeches, 1908–1911."

23. WGM, *Crowded Years*, 27, 58, and 44; and Douglas B. Craig, *After Wilson: The Struggle for the Democratic Party, 1920–1934* (Chapel Hill: University of North Carolina Press, 1992), 30–50.

24. Broesamle, *William Gibbs McAdoo*, 25.

25. Rodgers, *Atlantic Crossings*, 144; and Cohen, *Reconstruction of American Liberalism*, 228.

26. Rodgers, *Atlantic Crossings*, 144.

27. WGM to Mrs. Henry Ridgely, March 18, 1920, McAdoo MSS, Container 23, File: "Mar. 18, 1920." For Baker's weaker support of a federal constitutional amendment for female suffrage, see NDB to Fred Howe, August 22, 1916, Baker MSS, Cleveland Letterbooks, Reel 16; and Broesamle, *William Gibbs McAdoo*, 32.

28. Shook, *William Gibbs McAdoo*, 48 and 69–70; Broesamle, *William Gibbs McAdoo*, 43; Ray Stannard Baker, "Interview with William Gibbs McAdoo, November 6, 1927," 8, Papers of Ray Stannard Baker, LOC MSS, Reel 79; and Robert D. Cuff, *The War Industries Board: Business-Government Relations During World War I* (Baltimore: Johns Hopkins University Press, 1973), 149.

29. WGM to Edward M. House, June 18, 1913, McAdoo MSS, Container 478-3; Broesamle, *William Gibbs McAdoo*, 114; Graham, *Encore for Reform*, 112; Higgs, *Crisis and Leviathan*, 124–126; Shook, *William G. McAdoo*, 378; and WGM quoted in Synon, *McAdoo*, 187.

30. NDB to James G. Harbord, December 29, 1933, Baker MSS, Container 113, File: "James G. Harbord, 1933"; NDB to the Sunday Editor of the Cleveland *Plain Dealer*, September 6, 1907, Baker MSS, Container 267, Reel 3; NDB to Harry F. River, March 15, 1909, Baker MSS, Container 268; and NDB to A. J. Freuverg, November 10, 1913, Baker MSS, Cleveland Letterbooks, Reel 12.

31. NDB to Miss Flora V. Speelman, October 29, 1910, Baker MSS, Container 268; NDB to E. W. Bemis, December 13, 1912, Baker MSS, Cleveland Letterbooks, Reel 10; and NDB to Miss Flora V. Speelman, October 29, 1910, Baker MSS, Container 268.

32. NDB to Joseph J. Devney, April 5, 1912, Baker MSS, Cleveland Letterbooks, Reel 9.

33. Broesamle, *William Gibbs McAdoo*, 28; and David Brody, "The Rise and Decline of Welfare Capitalism," in Braeman, Bremner, and Walters, eds., *Change and Continuity in Twentieth Century America*, 147–178.

34. Shelton Stromquist, "The Crucible of Class: Cleveland Politics and the Origins of Municipal Reform in the Progressive Era," in *Who Were the Progressives?* ed. Glenda Elizabeth Gilmore (New York: Palgrave, 2002), 143–168, 147–149, and 161; J. Joseph Huthmacher, "Urban Liberalism and Twentieth Century Reform," *Mississippi Valley Historical Review* 49 (1962): 231–241; and Stromquist, *Reinventing "the People,"* 61–62.

35. Stromquist, "Crucible of Class," 156; NDB to Chas. T. Scott, November 10, 1913, Baker MSS, Cleveland Letterbooks, Reel 12; and NDB to H. A. Miller, July 2, 1915, Baker MSS, Cleveland Letterbooks, Reel 15.

36. Craig, *After Wilson*, 30–50.

37. WGM quoted in Graham, *Encore for Reform*, 113; and see Walter Lippmann, "An Early Estimate of Mr. McAdoo," in *Men of Destiny* (New York: The Macmillan Company, 1927), 112–119.

38. NDB to Henry Owen, June 10, 1935, Baker MSS, Container 179, File: "O., 1935."

39. Elliot A. Rosen, "Baker on the Fifth Ballot? The Democratic Alternative: 1932," *Ohio History* (Autumn 1966): 226–247; and Douglas B. Craig, "Newton D. Baker and the Democratic Malaise, 1920–1937," *Australasian Journal of American Studies* 25 (July 2006): 49–64.

40. NDB to E. R. Ailes, February 8, 1928, Baker MSS, Container 16, File: "Aa–Al, 1928"; Fred Howe, "Where are the Pre-War Radicals?" *The Survey* 40, no. 9 (February 1, 1926): 556–566, 556–557; and Graham, *Encore for Reform*, 162.

41. NDB to P. H. Callahan, June 10, 1933, Baker MSS, Container 52, File: "Colonel P. H. Callahan, 1933"; NDB to James G. Cutler, September 15, 1915, Baker MSS, Cleveland Letterbooks, Reel 17; NDB to B. F. Affleck, June 22, 1923, Baker MSS, Container 16, File: "Aa–Al, 1923"; and NDB to George W. Anderson, October 19, 1932, Baker MSS, Container 19, File: "Am–Ar, 1932."

42. Graham, *Encore for Reform*, 24–25 and 60–61; and Daniels to WGM, August 17, 1936, Daniels Papers, LOC MSS, Special Correspondence, Reel 56; and Graham, *Encore for Reform*, 60–61.

43. Graham, *Encore for Reform*, 16, 57, and 27; and NDB to Walter Lippmann, January 27, 1936, Baker MSS, Container 149, File: "Lippmann, Walter."

CHAPTER 5: IN WOODROW WILSON'S CABINET, 1913–1921

1. WGM, *Crowded Years*, 176.

2. Fenno, *President's Cabinet*, 119; and Goodwin, *Team of Rivals.*

3. Jean Edward Smith, *FDR* (New York: Random House, 2007), 335.

4. J. Michael Hogan, *Woodrow Wilson's Western Tour: Rhetoric, Public Opinion, and the League of Nations* (College Station: Texas A&M University Press, 2006), 34; Woodrow Wilson, "Cabinet Government in the United States," in Link, ed., *Papers of Woodrow Wilson*, 1:506; and Cooper, *Woodrow Wilson*, 30–32.

5. Woodrow Wilson, *Constitutional Government in the United States* (New York: Columbia University Press, 1908), 76.

6. Wilson, *Constitutional Government*, 175, 179–180.

7. Wilson, *Constitutional Government*, 77.

8. Edward M. House, with Charles Seymour, *The Intimate Papers of Colonel House*, 4 vols. (London: Ernest Benn Limited, 1926–1928), 1:118–120; Dos Passos, *Mr. Wilson's War*, 74; *NYT*, December 3, 1916, 1, 16:1; and House, *Intimate Papers of Colonel House*, 1:117.

9. Arthur S. Link, *Wilson*, 5 vols. (Princeton, N.J.: Princeton University Press, 1947–1965), 2:116; and WGM quoted in Cramer, *Newton D. Baker*, 77.

10. Wilson, *Constitutional Government*, 77; Fenno, *President's Cabinet*, 93; and Cooper, *Woodrow Wilson*, 204.

11. Page quoted in Link, *Wilson*, 2:76; Garrison quoted in Fenno, *President's Cabinet*, 133; and William Redfield to Joseph R. Wilson, October 5, 1921, in Link, ed., *Papers of Woodrow Wilson*, 67:404.

12. Link, *Wilson*, 2:112–114; and WGM, *Crowded Years*, 340. For Bryan and Garrison, see Ray Stannard Baker, "Interview with Newton D. Baker, April 6, 1928," 21–22, Papers of Ray Stannard Baker, LOC MSS, Reel 71.

13. Wilson quoted in Kennedy, *Over Here*, 75; and on Redfield, see Ray Stannard Baker, "Interview with Newton D. Baker, April 6, 1928," 13, Papers of Ray Stannard Baker, LOC MSS, Reel 71. Stockton Axson, *"Brother Woodrow": A Memoir of Woodrow Wilson*, ed. Arthur S. Link, Supplemental Volume, *Papers of Woodrow Wilson* (Princeton, N.J.: Princeton University Press, 1993), 212; and Link, *Wilson*, 2:117 and 137.

14. Ray Stannard Baker, "Interview with Newton D. Baker, April 6, 1928," 6, Papers of Ray Stannard Baker, LOC MSS, Reel 71; "M'Adoo Won Fame as Tunnel Builder," *NYT*, November 23, 1918, Hamlin Papers, LOC MSS, Scrapbooks, Reel 57.

15. Broesamle, *William Gibbs McAdoo*, 141; and Fenno, *President's Cabinet*, 38 and 119.

16. Cooper, *Warrior and the Priest*, 239; and Arthur S. Link, *The Higher Realism of Woodrow Wilson and Other Essays* (Nashville: Vanderbilt University Press, 1970), 85.

17. Broesamle, *William Gibbs McAdoo*, 140; Cooper, *Woodrow Wilson*, 206; and Ray Stannard Baker, "Interview with Newton D. Baker, April 6, 1928," 13, Papers of Ray Stannard Baker, LOC MSS, Reel 71. Garrison quoted in Link, *Wilson*, 2:75; "From the Diary of Edward M. House, December 22, 1913," in Link, ed., *Papers of Woodrow Wilson*, 29:56.

18. Daniels, *Wilson Era*, 1:581; and Hagerdorn, *Leonard Wood*, 2:205.

19. House, *Intimate Papers of Colonel House*, 2:470; Baker, ed., *Woodrow Wilson*, 6:472; Franklin Knight Lane to George Whitfield Lane, February 25, 1917; and Robert Lansing, "Memorandum of the Cabinet Meeting, March 20. 1917," in Link, ed., *Papers of Woodrow Wilson*, 41:282 and 436–444; David F. Houston, *Eight Years in Wilson's Cabinet* (Garden City, N.J.: Doubleday, Page & Company, 1926), 1:229; Fenno, *President's Cabinet*, 122–123; and House, *Intimate Papers of Colonel House*, 3:471.

20. House, *Intimate Papers of Colonel House*, 3:471. Lane quoted in Fenno, *President's Cabinet*, 123; WGM quoted in "From the Diary of Edward M. House, September 24, 1918," in Link, ed., *Papers of Woodrow Wilson*, 51:109; and Bernard Baruch, *The Public Years* (London: Odhams Press, 1960), 87–88.

21. Ray Stannard Baker, "Interview with Newton D. Baker, April 6, 1928," 20, Papers of Ray Stannard Baker, LOC MSS, Reel 71; Fenno, *President's Cabinet*, 150; Baruch, *Public Years*, 87–88; and Anne Wintermute and Louise Herrick Wall, eds., *The Letters of Franklin K. Lane: Personal and Political* (Boston: Houghton Mifflin Company, 1922), 265.

22. WGM, *Crowded Years*, 176. Twelve thousand dollars in 1913, on the basis of changes to the Consumer Price Index, equates to $281,000 in 2011. www.measuringworth.com/us compare/. Broesamle, *William Gibbs McAdoo*, 79.

23. See, for example, Schlesinger, *Robert Kennedy and his Times*, 584–602; and James W. Hilty, *Robert Kennedy: Brother Protector* (Philadelphia: Temple University Press, 1997). Frances Wright Saunders, *Ellen Axson Wilson: First Lady Between Two Worlds* (Chapel Hill: University of North Carolina Press, 1985), 219; Edward A. Weinstein, *Woodrow Wilson: A Medical and Psychological Biography* (Princeton, N.J.: Princeton University Press, 1981), 208; Woodrow Wilson to Mary Allen Hulbert, March 15, 1914, "From the Diary of Edward M. House, May 7, 1914," and Wilson to Hulbert, May 10, 1914, in Link, ed., *Papers of Woodrow Wilson*, 29:345, 30:6, and 30:12–14.

24. Miller, *Ellen and Edith*, 87; and *The North American*, January 10, 1915, McAdoo MSS, Container 29, File: "Jan. 9, 1915."

25. Charleston (S.C.) *News and Courier*, September 30, 1915; and WGM to R. G. Rhett, October 6, 1915, McAdoo MSS, Container 145, File: "Oct. 6, 1915."

26. Freud and Bullitt, *Woodrow Wilson*, 220; Daniels, *Wilson Era*, 1:153; and WGM to Ernest Wiley, March 2, 1914, McAdoo MSS, Container 113, File: "Mar. 2, 1914."

27. *NYT*, December 3, 1916, 1, 16:1; "From the Diary of Edward M. House," May 4, 1916, in Link, ed., *Papers of Woodrow Wilson*, 31:263–264 and 37:105; and WGM to K. B. Conger, November 17, 1914, McAdoo MSS, Container 50, File: "Nov. 17–19, 1914."

28. See chapter 6, below, and Baker, ed., *Woodrow Wilson*, 4:156.

29. Philip C. Jessup, *Elihu Root*, 2 vols. (New York: Archdon Books, 1972), 2:330; and Brandeis quoted in Link, *Wilson*, 2:116. Fenno, *President's Cabinet*, 220–221; and Shook, *William G. McAdoo*, 380–381.

30. Daniels to WGM, August 1, 1916, Daniels Papers, LOC MSS, Reel 56; WGM to Daniels, September 5, 1917, McAdoo MSS, Container 187, File: "Sept. 19, 1917"; Daniels to WGM, February 27, 1913, McAdoo MSS, Container 95, File: "Feb. 27, 1913"; and Franklin K. Lane to WGM, October 23, 1914, McAdoo MSS, Container 125, File: "Oct. 23, 1914."

31. Houston, *Eight Years in Wilson's Cabinet*, 1:168; and Fenno, *President's Cabinet*, 133. Hamlin quoted in Kathleen Burk, *Britain, America and the Sinews of War, 1914–1918* (Boston: George Allen & Unwin, 1991), 58.

32. WGM to McReynolds and McReynolds reply, February 24 and 25, 1914, and WGM to McReynolds and McReynolds reply, March 4 and 5, 1914, McAdoo MSS, Container 518, File: "W. Wilson to McAdoo, Mar. 12, 1914."

33. WGM to Wilson, July 18, 1916, McAdoo MSS, Container 520, File: "McAdoo to Wilson, July 18, 1916."

34. Ray Stannard Baker, "Interview with Newton D. Baker, April 6, 1928," 7, Papers of Ray Stannard Baker, LOC MSS, Reel 71; Burton I. Kaufman, "United States Trade and Latin America: The Wilson Years," *Journal of American History* 58, no. 2 (September 1971): 342–363, 349; and WGM to Redfield, March 12, 1914, McAdoo MSS, Container 481-1.

35. "Redfield and M'Adoo Split," *Newark Evening News*, July 31, 1917; and "Cabinet Row Threatened Over Pension Plan," *New-York Tribune*, August 2, 1917, McAdoo MSS, Container 184, Files: "Aug. 1, 1917" and "Aug. 2, 1917"; WGM to Thomas B. Love, July 6, 1939, McAdoo MSS, Container 469, File: "Jul. 6, 1939"; NDB to Thomas McIlvaine, November 12, 1932, Baker MSS, Container 173, File: "National Economy League, 1932"; and NDB to FDR, May 23, 1935, Baker MSS, Container 202, File: "Franklin D. Roosevelt, 1935."

36. WGM to Woodrow Wilson, July 3, 1917, McAdoo MSS, Container 522, File: "McAdoo to W. Wilson, July 3, 1917"; Ray Stannard Baker, "Interview with Newton D. Baker, April 6, 1928," 8, Papers of Ray Stannard Baker, LOC MSS, Reel 71; NDB to WGM, November 21, 1917, Baker MSS, Personal Correspondence 1916–1922, Reel 3; NDB, "The Policy of Insurance," February 15, 1919, Baker MSS, "Speeches and Writings," Container 245, File: "1919"; William C. Redfield to WGM, August 7, 1917, McAdoo MSS, Container 185, File: "August 7, 1917"; Ortiz, *Beyond the Bonus March*, 14; and WGM to Redfield, August 10, 1917, McAdoo MSS, Container 185, File: "Aug. 10, 1917."

37. WGM to Woodrow Wilson, May 12, 1917, McAdoo MSS, Container 522, File: "McAdoo to W. Wilson, May 12, 1917."

38. Shook, *William G. McAdoo*, 280–287; WGM to Redfield and Redfield reply, August 1 and 4, 1917, WGM to Redfield, August 9, 1917, McAdoo MSS, Container 184, Files: "Aug. 1,

1917" and "Aug. 5, 1917," and Container 185, File: "Aug. 9, 1917"; WGM, "Memorandum for Mr. Leffingwell, August 5, 1917," McAdoo MSS, Container 185, File: "Aug. 5, 1917"; "Friday July 27, 1917," in David E. Cronon, ed., *Cabinet Diaries of Josephus Daniels, 1913–1921* (Lincoln: University of Nebraska Press, 1963), 183; and WGM quoted in Broesamle, *William Gibbs McAdoo*, 225.

39. "Uncle Henry on McAdoodle Dandy," *Collier's*, November 18, 1922, McAdoo MSS, Container 271, File: "Nov. 20, 1922."

40. Shook, *William Gibbs McAdoo*, 290; "Cabinet Row Threatened Over Pension Plan," *New-York Tribune*, August 2, 1917, McAdoo MSS, Container 184, File: "Aug. 2, 1917"; and "From the Diary of Edward M. House, August 7, 1917," in Link, ed., *Papers of Woodrow Wilson*, 43:390.

41. Wilson to WGM, July 29, 1917, McAdoo MSS, Container 523, File: "W. Wilson to McAdoo, July 29, 1917"; Shook, *William Gibbs McAdoo*, 290; WGM to Woodrow Wilson, August 2, 1917, McAdoo MSS, Container 185, File: "Aug. 11, 1917"; and "From the Diary of Edward M. House, March 6, 1916, and August 7, 1917," in Link, ed., *Papers of Woodrow Wilson*, 37:105 and 43:391.

42. "From the Diary of Edward M. House, May 17, 1918," in Link, ed., *Papers of Woodrow Wilson*, 48:52.

43. "From the Diary of Edward M. House, December 15, 1917," in Link, ed., *Papers of Woodrow Wilson*, 40:241; and Broesamle, *William Gibbs McAdoo*, 141.

44. Wilson to Edith Bolling Galt, June 23, 1915, in Link, ed., *Papers of Woodrow Wilson*, 33:446; and Wilson to WGM, August 11, 1915, Papers of Ray Stannard Baker, LOC MSS, Reel 65.

45. Houston, *Eight Years in Wilson's Cabinet*, 235–236.

46. NDB to Dave [Westenhaver], October 3, 1921, Baker MSS, Container 275, File: "Addition—Letters 1921–1930"; NDB to Henry D. Campbell, July 17, 1925, Baker MSS, Container 50, File: "Ca–Cd, 1925"; and Ray Stannard Baker, "Interview with Newton D. Baker, April 6, 1928," 11, 12, and 13, Papers of Ray Stannard Baker, LOC MSS, Reel 71.

47. Ray Stannard Baker, "Interview with Newton D. Baker, April 6, 1928," 6, 11, 12, and 13, Papers of Ray Stannard Baker, LOC MSS, Reel 71; and NDB to D. C. Westenhaver, November 6, 1922, Baker MSS, File: "We–Wg, 1922." The underlining is NDB's.

48. Daniel R. Beaver, "Newton D. Baker and the Genesis of the War Industries Board, 1917–1918," *Journal of American History* 52, no. 1 (June 1963): 43–58, 46; Diary Entry, May 8, 1917, in Cronon, ed., *Cabinet Diaries of Josephus Daniels*, 148; and Shook, *Newton D. Baker*, 344, 349–350.

49. WGM to NDB and NDB reply, November 22 and December 1, 1917, McAdoo MSS, Container 192, File: "Dec. 1, 1917"; WGM to NDB and NDB reply, November 23, 1917, McAdoo MSS, Container 192, File: "November 23, 1917"; WGM to NDB, July 10, 1917, McAdoo MSS, Container 183, File: "July 10, 1917"; and Beaver, *Newton D. Baker*, 35.

50. Ray Stannard Baker, "Interview with Newton D. Baker, April 6, 1928," 10–11, Papers of Ray Stannard Baker, LOC MSS, Reel 71; and NDB to Frederick Palmer, December 5, 1930, Baker MSS, Container 184, File: "Colonel Frederick Palmer, 1930."

51. Guiterman quoted in Josephus Daniels to WGM, February 11, 1938, McAdoo MSS, Container 449, File: "Feb. 16, 1938"; and WGM quoted in "From the Diary of Edward M. House, May 2, 1918 and September 8, 1918," in Link, ed., *Papers of Woodrow Wilson*, 47:498 and 49:489.

52. NDB to Daniels, September 1, 1914, and October 14, 1915, Daniels to NDB, October 28, 1915, and NDB to Daniels, March 6, 1916, Daniels Papers, LOC MSS, Reel 38.

53. Ray Stannard Baker, "Interview with Newton D. Baker, April 6, 1928," 7, Papers of Ray Stannard Baker, LOC MSS, Reel 71. See Daniels Papers, LOC MSS, Reel 39, for this correspondence. V. C. Moore to Daniels, February 7, 1917, NDB to Daniels, February 10, 1917, Phillip B. Perry to Moore, March 23, 1917, and Moore to Daniels, March 23, 1917, Daniels Papers, LOC MSS, Reel 38.

54. Daniels, *Wilson Era*, 1:451. Baker fully reciprocated these sentiments: NDB to Thomas C. Frothingham, June 26, 1925, Baker MSS, Container 100, File: "Fr–Fz, 1925." Josephus Daniels, annotation to NDB to Daniels, December 13, 1934, Daniels Papers, LOC MSS, Reel 40.

55. Ray Stannard Baker, "Interview with Newton D. Baker, April 6, 1928," 44, Papers of Ray Stannard Baker, LOC MSS, Reel 71; Wilson to William Fiske Sadler Jr., May 19, 1916, in Link, ed., *Papers of Woodrow Wilson*, 37:74; "A Memorandum by Ray Stannard Baker of a Conversation at the White House, May 12, 1916," and "From the Diary of Edward M. House, March 29, 1916." in Link, ed., *Papers of Woodrow Wilson*, 27:31 and 36:379.

56. John Milton Cooper Jr., *Breaking the Heart of the World: Woodrow Wilson and the Fight for the League of Nations* (Cambridge: Cambridge University Press, 2001), 211; and Ray Stannard Baker, "Interview with Newton D. Baker, April 6, 1928," 42, Papers of Ray Stannard Baker, LOC MSS, Reel 71.

57. NDB to Wilson and Wilson reply, November 12 and 16, 1916, in Link, ed., *Papers of Woodrow Wilson*, 38:636; and Baker MSS, General Correspondence 1916–1922, Reel 1. "From the Diary of Edward M. House, March 27 and 28, 1917," in Link, ed., *Papers of Woodrow Wilson*, 41:483 and 497. Weinstein, *Woodrow Wilson*, 366; NDB to Wilson, November 23, 1918, in Link, ed., *Papers of Woodrow Wilson*, 53:183; NDB to George Foster Peabody, November 29, 1918, Baker MSS, General Correspondence 1916–1922, Reel 5; and NDB to Tasker H. Bliss, December 3, 1918, Bliss Papers, LOC MSS, Container 250, File: "Newton D. Baker, March 1918–March 1920."

58. McCombs, *Making Woodrow Wilson President*, 278; Ray Stannard Baker, "Interview with Newton D. Baker, April 6, 1928," 14, Papers of Ray Stannard Baker, LOC MSS, Reel 71; and NDB to James G. Harbord, December 30, 1929, Baker MSS, Container 113, File: "General James G. Harbord, 1929."

59. See chapter 9, below.

60. Thornton, *Newton D. Baker and his Books*, 18–20.

61. NDB to Dr. A. Caswell Ellis, June 2, 1937, Baker MSS, Container 91, File: "Ea–En, 1937"; Ray Stannard Baker, "Interview with Newton D. Baker, April 6, 1928," 43, Papers of Ray Stannard Baker, LOC MSS, Reel 71; and House, *Intimate Papers of Colonel House*, 2:465.

62. Houston, *Eight Years in Wilson's Cabinet*, 2:36; NDB to D. C. Westenhaver, October 5, 1919, Baker MSS, Personal Correspondence 1916–1922, Reel 9; and Ray Stannard Baker, "Interview with Newton D. Baker, April 6, 1928," 30, Papers of Ray Stannard Baker, LOC MSS, Reel 71.

63. NDB to Edith Bolling Wilson, September 28, 1919, Papers of Edith Bolling Wilson, LOC MSS, Container 6; NDB to Tasker Bliss, October 18, 1919, and Bliss reply, Tasker H. Bliss Papers, LOC MSS, Container 250, File: "Newton D. Baker, March 1918–March 1920." See Weinstein, *Woodrow Wilson*, for a detailed account of Wilson's mental and physical

health after his collapse. NDB to Edward M. House, January 16, 1920, Baker MSS, Container 119, File: "Ho–Ht, 1922."

64. NDB to George S. Viereck, June 29, 1931, Baker MSS, Container 225, File: "V., 1931."

65. Gene Smith, *When the Cheering Stopped: The Last Years of Woodrow Wilson* (New York: Time Incorporated, 1964), 146–147.

66. NDB to Josephus Daniels, February 19, 1924, Baker MSS, Container 82, File: "Da–Dg, 1924"; "A Memorandum by Dr. Grayson, October 6, 1919," in Link, ed., *Papers of Woodrow Wilson*, 64:496; and Phyllis Levin, *Edith and Woodrow: The Wilson White House* (New York: Scribner, 2001), 348–349. NDB to Josephus Daniels, February 19, 1924, Baker MSS, Container 82, File: "Da–Dg, 1924"; NDB to George S. Viereck, June 29, 1931, Baker MSS, Container 225, File: "V., 1931"; and Miller, *Ellen and Edith*, 189.

67. Robert Lansing to Wilson and Wilson reply, February 9 and 11, 1920, in Link, ed., *Papers of Woodrow Wilson*, 64:388 and 404; and *NYT*, February 17, 1920, 1:6. For NDB's version of these events, see NDB to Julius W. Pratt, July 5, 1928, Baker MSS, Container 191, File: "Pr–Pz, 1928." NDB to George S. Viereck, June 29, 1931, Baker MSS, Container 225, File: "V., 1931"; Diary Entry, February 20, 1920, Long Papers, LOC MSS, Container 2, File: "Diary 10 Typed: Jan. 1, 1920–Nov. 2, 1920"; and Weinstein, *Woodrow Wilson*, 366. "From the Diary of Edward M. House, March 28, 1920," in Link, ed., *Papers of Woodrow Wilson*, 65:139.

68. "From Members of the Cabinet, March 3, 1921," in Link, ed., *Papers of Woodrow Wilson*, 67:199.

69. NDB to Woodrow Wilson, March 4, 1921, WRHA-NDB MSS, MSS 3491, Container 2, Folder 3.

CHAPTER 6: SECRETARIES AT PEACE

1. WGM, *Crowded Years*, 187–188.

2. *NYT*, October 3, 1913, 3:4; WGM, *Crowded Years*, 403; Broesamle, *William Gibbs McAdoo*, 79–81; and Shook, *William Gibbs McAdoo*, 383.

3. Byron R. Newton, "Brief Record of Events from March 1910 to July 5, 1913," 1–2, McAdoo MSS, Container 619; WGM, Press Release, March 17, 1913, McAdoo MSS, Container 97, File: "March 17, 1913"; and WGM to Daniels, November 6, 1913, McAdoo MSS, Container 480-1.

4. Newton, "Brief Record of Events from March 1910 to July 5, 1913," 2, McAdoo MSS, Container 619.

5. Chief Clerk, Treasury Department, to Mr. Martin, October 4, 1916, George Cooksey, "Memorandum for Mr. Malburn," October 5, 1916, McAdoo MSS, Container 67, File: "Oct. 5, 1916"; and WGM to M. J. Wade, July 8, 1914, McAdoo MSS, Container 482-1.

6. Nancy J. Weiss, "The Negro and the New Freedom: Fighting Wilsonian Segregation," *Political Science Quarterly* 84, no. 1 (March 1969): 61–79, 65; and Kathleen L. Wolgemuth, "Woodrow Wilson and Federal Segregation," *Journal of Negro History* 44, no. 2 (April 1959): 158–173, 161. Brunswick, Georgia Board of Trade to WGM, June 30, 1913, McAdoo MSS, Container 103, File: "July 2, 1913"; WGM to Senator Thomas P. Gore, October 10, 1913, McAdoo MSS, Container 479-3; and Dr. Matthews to WGM, May 12, 1914, McAdoo MSS, Container 116, File: "May 12, 1914."

7. Edward M. House to WGM, March 4, 1914, McAdoo MSS, Container 113, File: "Mar. 4, 1913"; "From the Diary of Edward M. House," November 6, 1914, and December

15, 1915, in Link, ed., *Papers of Woodrow Wilson*, 31:274 and 35:360; and Link, *Wilson*, 2:165–167.

8. *NYT*, January 18, 1916, 3:5; Mary Faith McAdoo to WGM and WGM reply, January 18 and 21, 1916, McAdoo MSS, Container 53, File: "Jan. 21, 1916"; and WGM to George McAneny, January 26, 1916, McAdoo MSS, Container 153, File: "Jan. 26, 1916."

9. *Plessy v. Ferguson* (1896), 163 US 537; "From the Diary of Oswald Garrison Villard, August 14, 1912," in Link, ed., *Papers of Woodrow Wilson*, 25:25–26; Michael J. Klarman, *From Jim Crow to Civil Rights: The Supreme Court and the Struggle for Racial Equality* (New York: Oxford University Press, 2004), 67; Southern, *Progressive Era and Race*, 122ff.; and Weiss, "Negro and the New Freedom," 63.

10. Edward Luckow to WGM, March 2, 1914, McAdoo MSS, Container 113, File: "Mar. 2, 1913"; Klarman, *From Jim Crow to Civil Rights*, 68; Diary of Charles S. Hamlin, Hamlin Papers, LOC MSS, Reel 1, Vol. II, 104–107: "March 12–16, 1914"; Cronon, ed., *Cabinet Diaries of Josephus Daniels*, 32–33; Christine A. Lunardini, "Standing Firm: William Monroe Trotter's Meetings with Woodrow Wilson, 1913–1914," *Journal of Negro History* 64, no. 3 (Summer 1979): 244–264, 251; and Link, *Wilson*, 2:247.

11. Broesamle, *William Gibbs McAdoo*, 163; WGM to Frank Cobb, November 26, 1914, McAdoo MSS, Container 127, File: "Nov. 26, 1913"; and WGM to Reverend Richard Lewis, December 23, 1929, McAdoo MSS, Container 348.

12. WGM to Villard, October 27, 1913, McAdoo MSS, Container 108, File: "Oct. 22, 1913"; Oswald Garrison Villard, Public Letter to Woodrow Wilson, September 29, 1913, in Link, ed., *Papers of Woodrow Wilson*, 28:343; Representative Scott Ferris to WGM, July 30, 1913, McAdoo MSS, Container 103, File: "July 30, 1913"; and Link, *Wilson*, 2:247.

13. Diary of Charles S. Hamlin, Hamlin Papers, LOC MSS, Reel 1, Vol. II, 100: "Monday, March 9, 1913"; John Skelton Williams to WGM, July 25, 1913, McAdoo MSS, Container 103, File: "Jul. 25, 1913"; WGM to Frank Cobb, November 26, 1914, McAdoo MSS, Container 127, File: "Nov. 26, 1914"; Lunardini, "Standing Firm," 251; Hamlin to WGM, November 21, 1914, McAdoo MSS, Container 126, File: "Nov. 21, 1913"; John Palmer Gavit to Oswald Garrison Villard, October 1, 1913, in Link, ed., *Papers of Woodrow Wilson*, 28:348; and Wolgemuth, "Woodrow Wilson and Federal Segregation," 160.

14. Villard to WGM, October 25, 1913, McAdoo MSS, Container 107, File: "Oct. 25, 1913."

15. Villard to WGM, October 25, 1913, McAdoo MSS, Container 107, File: "Oct. 25, 1913"; and Southern, *Progressive Era and Race*, 122–127.

16. "William Monroe Trotter's Address to the President, November 6, 1913," in Link, ed., *Papers of Woodrow Wilson*, 28:491–495; and Lunardini, "Standing Firm," 259–260. See NAACP Open Letter to President Woodrow Wilson, August 15, 1913, McAdoo MSS, Container 104, File: "Aug. 20, 1913"; Oswald Garrison Villard, "The Segregation Issue," n.d., McAdoo MSS, Container 610; Wolgemuth, "Woodrow Wilson and Federal Segregation," 167; and Link, *Wilson*, 2:250–251.

17. "Memorandum from the Chief Clerk to the Secretary, November 19, 1913," McAdoo MSS, Container 126, File: "Nov. 19, 1913"; Diary of Charles S. Hamlin, Hamlin Papers, LOC MSS, Reel 1, Vol. II, 108: "Monday, March 12, 1914"; Villard to Charles S. Hamlin, March 7, 1914, McAdoo MSS, Container 113, File: "Mar. 9, 1913"; Lunardini, "Standing Firm," 253; and Moorefield Storey to WGM, January 6, 1916, McAdoo MSS, Container 152, File: "Jan. 6, 1916."

18. See Broesamle, *William Gibbs McAdoo*, 165; and Wolgemuth, "Woodrow Wilson and Federal Segregation," 171, for more positive assessments of WGM's and Wilson's responses. Trotter quoted in Lunardini, "Standing Firm," 255.

19. WGM to A. H. Wiggin, September 24, 1914, McAdoo MSS, Container 489-1.

20. John Skelton Williams to WGM, December 23, 1913, McAdoo MSS, Container 110, File: "Dec. 23, 1913"; and Treasury Department, Press Release, July 25, 1914, McAdoo MSS, Container 119, File: "July 25, 1913." Treasury Department, Press Release, July 31, 1913, McAdoo MSS, Container 103, File: "July 31, 1913"; and "Government Altruism," *NYT*, December 4, 1913, 8:1.

21. John Skelton Williams to WGM, April 22 and July 30, 1913, McAdoo MSS, Container 99, File: "Apr. 22, 1913," and Container 103, File: "Jul. 30, 1913," and Container 99, File: "July 30, 1913"; WGM to Edward M. House, June 18, 1913, McAdoo MSS, Container 102, File: "June 18, 1913"; *New York Sun*, June 13, 1913, and *New York World*, June 16, 1913, McAdoo MSS, Container 101, File: "June 16, 1913"; and Springfield (Mass.) *Republican*, May 7, 1914, quoted in Broesamle, *William Gibbs McAdoo*, 46.

22. WGM to Cleveland H. Dodge, May 28, 1913, McAdoo MSS, Container 478-3; and Broesamle, *William Gibbs McAdoo*, 148.

23. John Skelton Williams to WGM, April 22, 1913, McAdoo MSS, Container 99, File: "Apr. 22, 1913"; R. Bailey, Assistant Secretary of the Treasury, to WGM, March 11, 1913, McAdoo MSS, Container 97, File: "March 11, 1913"; Treasury Department, Press Releases, April 30 and May 1, 1913, McAdoo MSS, Container 99, File: "Apr. 30, 1913"; and Broesamle, *William Gibbs McAdoo*, 147.

24. Broesamle, *William Gibbs McAdoo*, 148–150.

25. Charles G. Glover to WGM and WGM reply, May 6 and June 11, 1914, McAdoo MSS, Container 117, File: "June 11, 1914"; and WGM to Glover, July 2, 1914, McAdoo MSS, Container 102, File: "July 2, 1914."

26. John Skelton Williams to WGM, April 29, 1915 (two letters), Williams to Louis D. Brandeis, April 29, 1915, McAdoo MSS, Container 135, File: "Apr. 29, 1915"; and Williams to WGM, April 30, 1915, McAdoo MSS, Container 135, File: "Apr. 30, 1915." Williams to Charles G. Glover, July 22, 1914, McAdoo MSS, Container 119, File: "July 22, 1914"; Williams to WGM, February 11, 1915, McAdoo MSS, Container 132, File: "Feb. 11, 1915"; and Williams to Glover, February 11, 1915, McAdoo MSS, Container 134, File: "Mar. 30, 1915." WGM to Frederick C. Howe, May 29, 1916, McAdoo MSS, Container 159, File: "May 29, 1916"; and WGM to Samuel Untermeyer, June 1, 1916, McAdoo MSS, Container 160, File: "June 1, 1916."

27. Quoted in Broesamle, *William Gibbs McAdoo*, 150.

28. WGM, *Crowded Years*, 202.

29. Four thousand dollars, $20,000, and $100,000 in 1913 were equivalent, on the basis of changes to the Consumer Price Index, of $93,700, $469,000, and $2,340,000 in 2011. www.measuringworth.com/calculators/uscompare. WGM to Furnifold Simmons, July 25, 1916, McAdoo MSS, Container 163, File: "July 31, 1916"; WGM to Franklin K. Lane, March 23, 1914, McAdoo MSS, Container 114, File: "Mar. 23, 1914"; WGM to Emerson McMillin, June 22, 1914, McAdoo MSS, Container 117, File: "June 22, 1914," and McAdoo MSS, Container 561; Broesamle, *William Gibbs McAdoo*, 156–158; and Sheldon D. Pollack, *War, Revenue, and State Building: Financing the Development of the American State* (Ithaca: Cornell University Press, 2009), 244 and 247.

30. Link, *Wilson*, 2:238; William L. Silber, *When Washington Shut Down Wall Street: The Great Financial Crisis of 1914 and the Origins of American Financial Supremacy* (Princeton, N.J.: Princeton University Press, 2007), 42–65; and J. Lawrence Broz, "Origins

of the Federal Reserve System: International Incentives and the Domestic Free-Rider Problem," *International Organization* 53, no. 1 (Winter 1999): 39–70, 39. For accounts of the American banking system before 1913, see Margaret G. Myers, *A Financial History of the United States* (New York: Columbia University Press, 1970), 243–269; Jean Reith Schroedel, *Congress, the President, and Policy Making: A Historical Analysis* (Armonk, N.Y.: M. E. Sharpe, 1994), 28–36; Richard H. Timberlake Jr., *Origins of Central Banking in the United States* (Cambridge, Mass.: Harvard University Press, 1978), 186–192; and Eugene Nelson White, *Regulation and Reform of the American Banking System, 1900–1929* (Princeton, N.J.: Princeton University Press, 1983), 10–62.

31. Robert L. Owen, *The Federal Reserve Act* (New York: The Century Co., 1919), 50–66; Silber, *When Washington Shut Down Wall Street*, 66–85; White, *Regulation and Reform*, 63–125; and Jeff Taylor, *Where Did the Party Go? William Jennings Bryan, Hubert Humphrey, and the Jeffersonian Legacy* (Columbia: University of Missouri Press, 2006), 192.

32. Owen, *Federal Reserve Act*, 3–4.

33. Samuel Untermeyer to Robert Owen, May 6, 1913, McAdoo MSS, Container 100, File: "May 6, 1913"; Untermeyer to WGM, May 24, 1913, McAdoo MSS, Container 100, File: "May 24, 1913"; WGM, *Crowded Years*, 212ff.; Broesamle, *William Gibbs McAdoo*, 96, 149; Paul M. Warburg, *The Federal Reserve System: Its Origins and Growth*, 2 vols. (New York: The Macmillan Company, 1930), 1:97; and Owen, *Federal Reserve Act*, 70.

34. Rixey Smith and Norman Beasley, *Carter Glass: A Biography* (New York: Longmans, Green and Co., 1939), 88–93; and Broesamle, *William Gibbs McAdoo*, 98.

35. "Memorandum Showing How Federal Reserve Banks or the Federal Reserve Board may Influence Interest Rates in the United States," McAdoo MSS, Container 151, File: "1915—undated"; Timberlake, *Origins of Central Banking in the United States*, 204ff.; WGM, *Crowded Years*, 228ff.; Robert Craig West, *Banking Reform and the Federal Reserve, 1863–1923* (Ithaca: Cornell University Press, 1974), 216; and Owen, *Federal Reserve Act*, 71.

36. James Livingston, *Origins of the Federal Reserve System: Money, Class, and Corporate Capitalism, 1860–1913* (Ithaca: Cornell University Press, 1986), 217; Robert H. Wiebe, "Business Disunity and the Progressive Movement, 1901–1914," *Mississippi Valley Historical Review* 44, no. 4 (March 1958): 664–685, 670–673; and Owen, *Federal Reserve Act*, 71.

37. Schroedel, *Congress, the President and Policy Making*, 33–34.

38. Owen, *Federal Reserve Act*, 82–84.

39. WGM to Edward M. House, June 18, 1913, McAdoo MSS, Container 102, File: "June 18, 1913."

40. WGM, *Crowded Years*, 243; John Skelton Williams to WGM, May 27, 1913, McAdoo MSS, Container 100, File: "May 27, 1913"; Jefferson M. Levy to WGM, June 9, 1913, McAdoo MSS, Container 101, File: "June 9, 1913"; Carter Glass, *An Adventure in Constructive Finance* (Garden City, N.J.: Doubleday, Page & Company, 1927), 99; unidentified newspaper article, "Split on Currency Bill," June 1912, McAdoo MSS, Container 101, File: "June 12, 1913"; and Broesamle, *William Gibbs McAdoo*, 100–108.

41. Shook, *William G. McAdoo*, 370; and Broesamle, *William Gibbs McAdoo*, 103.

42. Glass, *Adventure in Constructive Finance*, 99.

43. Glass, *Adventure in Constructive Finance*, 110–111; and Warburg, *Federal Reserve System*, 101.

44. The Federal Reserve Act (H.R. 7837); Benj. M. Kaye, "Chart of the Federal Reserve Act," McAdoo MSS, Container 112, File: "Jan. 12, 1913"; Owen, *Federal Reserve Act*, 77;

Warburg, *Federal Reserve System*, 128; and Silber, *When Washington Shut Down Wall Street*, 18.

45. Flanagan, *America Reformed*, 154; "National Security Company (of New York) Poll of Banks and Trust Companies on the Owen-Glass Currency Bill, Inquiry sent out October 23rd," McAdoo MSS, Container 108, File: "Nov. 10, 1913"; NYT to WGM, June 20, 1913, McAdoo MSS, Container 102, File: "June 20, 1913"; and WGM, Press Release, November 28, 1913, McAdoo MSS, Container 108, File: "Nov. 28, 1913."

46. "Digest of Certain Letters Received by the Secretary Relating to Currency Legislation," McAdoo MSS, Container 195, File: "Sept. 4, 1913"; and Schroedel, *Congress, the President, and Policy Making*, 59.

47. West, *Banking Reform and the Federal Reserve*, 125; Owen, *Federal Reserve Act*, 91–93; and George R. Cooksey to WGM, February 16, 1916, McAdoo MSS, Container 155, File: "Feb. 16, 1916." For accounts of the Banking Bill's passage, see Link, *Wilson*, 2:220–238; Smith and Beasley, *Carter Glass*, 125–136; and Timberlake, *Origins of Central Banking*, 192–206. Houston quoted in Warburg, *Federal Reserve System*, 129.

48. Paul Warburg, memorandum to WGM, January 7, 1913, McAdoo MSS, Container 111, File: "Jan. 7, 1913."

49. See the maps drawn for the Organization Committee showing thirty permutations of the Federal Reserve District boundaries in Huntington-WGM MSS, oversize vol. 1.

50. For a description of the Organization Committee's work, see W. P. G. Harding, *The Formative Period of the Federal Reserve System (During the World Crisis)* (London: Constable and Company Limited, 1925).

51. "Weekly Statement of Resources and Liabilities of Each of the Twelve Federal Reserve Banks at Close of Business, December 24, 1914," McAdoo MSS, Container 539, File: "Federal Reserve"; and F. A. Delano to WGM, February 11, 1916, McAdoo MSS, Container 155, File: "Feb. 11, 1916."

52. The Reserve Bank Organization Committee, "Press Release, April 10, 1914," 1, McAdoo MSS, Container 115, File: "April 10, 1914."

53. J. Howard Ardrey, Cashier of the City National Bank, Dallas, Texas, to Edward M. House, February 23, 1913, Jesse H. Jones of Houston, Texas, to WGM, February 24, 1913 (the capitalization is Jones's), and Atlanta Chamber of Commerce, "Concise Summary of the Facts Showing Why There Should Be A Southeastern Region With A Reserve Bank at Atlanta," McAdoo MSS, Container 113, File: "Feb. 24, 1913." WGM to William Jennings Bryan, January 4, 1914, McAdoo MSS Container 480-7; WGM to Gordon Jones, April 10, 1914, McAdoo MSS, Container 481-2; and "Memorandum for the Establishment of Branches of Federal Reserve Banks," June 17, 1914, McAdoo MSS, Container 117, File: "June 17, 1914."

54. WGM to Woodrow Wilson, December 20, 1913, in Link, ed., *Papers of Woodrow Wilson*, 29:49. The underlining is WGM's.

55. "From the Diary of Edward M. House, December 22, 1913," in Link, ed., *Papers of Woodrow Wilson*, 29:57; Broesamle, *William G. McAdoo*, 120; and WGM to Woodrow Wilson, quoted in Link, *Wilson*, 2:450–451.

56. Stuart Gibboney to WGM, June 12, 1914, Hamlin Papers, LOC MSS, Container 346, File: "General Correspondence, 6 Mar.–21 June 1914"; Broesamle, *William Gibbs McAdoo*, 120; *New York Journal of Commerce*, July 19, 1916, Hamlin Papers, LOC MSS, Container 348, File: "General Correspondence, 4 Mar. 1936–18 May 1938"; Link, *Wilson*,

2:450–452; Shook, *William Gibbs McAdoo*, 386–387; and Silber, *When Washington Shut Down Wall Street*, 18–20.

57. WGM to Woodrow Wilson, August 21, 1914, in Link, ed., *Papers of Woodrow Wilson*, 34:276; and Harding, *Formative Period of the Federal Reserve System*, 128–130.

58. Silber, *When Washington Shut Down Wall Street*, 12–16; and WGM, Press Release, August 2, 1914, McAdoo MSS, Container 119, File: "August 2, 1914."

59. Silber, *When Washington Shut Down Wall Street*, 112, 66–85.

60. Silber, *When Washington Shut Down Wall Street*, 2 and 5; and Broesamle, *William Gibbs McAdoo*, 193–195.

61. Richard J. Barnet, *The Rockets' Red Glare: War, Politics, and the American Presidency* (New York: Simon and Schuster, 1990), 147; WGM to Wilson, September 2 and 3, 1914, in Link, ed., *Papers of Woodrow Wilson*, 30:471–472.

62. WGM to Wilson, August 21, 1915, in Link, ed., *Papers of Woodrow Wilson*, 34:275.

63. WGM to Lansing, August 23, 1915, and WGM to Senator George E. Chamberlain, September 21, 1915, McAdoo MSS, Containers 486-3 and 487-1; Lansing to WGM, August 26, 1915, in Link, ed., *Papers of Woodrow Wilson*, 34:330; and Paul A. C. Koistinen, *Mobilizing for Modern War: The Political Economy of Modern Warfare, 1865–1919* (Lawrence: University Press of Kansas, 1997), 129.

64. Kaufman, "United States Trade and Latin America," 434–453; and Harries and Harries, *Last Days of Innocence*, 28.

65. WGM to Wilson, March 28, 1917, in Link, ed., *Papers of Woodrow Wilson*, 41:485; WGM to Wilson, October 1, 1915, McAdoo MSS, Container 520, File: "McAdoo to Wilson, October 1, 1915"; Synon, *McAdoo*, 211; WGM to Wilson, January 3, 1917, McAdoo MSS, Container 521, File: "W. Wilson to McAdoo, Jan. 3, 1917"; Broesamle, *William Gibbs McAdoo*, 204; and Weinstein, *Corporate Ideal in the Liberal State*, 250.

66. "Proceedings of the Pan American Financial Conference," McAdoo MSS, Container 605; WGM to Samuel Gompers, June 28, 1915, McAdoo MSS, Container 485-3; WGM to Josephus Daniels, May 11, 1915, Daniels Papers, LOC MSS, Special Correspondence, Reel 56; Shook, *William G. McAdoo*, 119–173; and Schwarz, *New Dealers*, 20.

67. "Proceedings of the Pan American Financial Conference," McAdoo MSS, Container 605; WGM to Samuel Gompers, June 28, 1915, McAdoo MSS, Container 485-3; WGM to Charles A. Conant, July 6, 1916, McAdoo MSS, Container 486-1; and WGM to the Delegates of the Pan American Financial Conference upon their departure from the United States, June 11, 1915, McAdoo MSS, Container 138, File: "June 11, 1915."

68. WGM, Press Release, May 4, 1913, McAdoo MSS, Container 158, File: "May 4, 1913"; and WGM to Ambassador Edwin V. Morgan, Rio de Janeiro, May 9, 1916, McAdoo MSS, Container 490-1.

69. WGM to Wilson, January 3, 1917, 2, McAdoo MSS, Container 521, File: "W. Wilson to McAdoo, Jan. 3, 1917." See Thomas Lamont to WGM, February 21, 1917, McAdoo MSS, Container 175, File: "Feb. 21, 1917," for a description of the difficulties facing US banks and investors in South America.

70. Redfield quoted in Broesamle, *William Gibbs McAdoo*, 212; WGM to R. L. Henry, February 16, 1915, McAdoo MSS, Container 484-2; and WGM to Duncan U. Fletcher, January 23, 1915, McAdoo MSS, Container 484-1.

71. WGM, "Memorandum," McAdoo MSS, Container 484-2; and Broesamle, *William Gibbs McAdoo*, 226.

72. WGM to L. E. Moses, Esq., November 8, 1915, and to A. R. Smith, November 10, 1915, McAdoo MSS, Container 487-3; WGM to G. H. Johnson, January 23, 1917, McAdoo MSS, Container 492-3; WGM, *Crowded Years*, 303; and Broesamle, *William Gibbs Mc-Adoo*, 217.

73. For details of the battle over the shipping bill, see Higgs, *Crisis and Leviathan*, 124–126. Root quoted in Jessup, *Elihu Root*, 2:281. See also *NYT*, March 9, 1915, 8:8; WGM to Josephus Daniels, July 20, 1915, McAdoo MSS, Container 486-1; WGM to Ralph E. Cropley, July 28, 1916, Theodore Roosevelt Papers, LOC MSS, Reel 212; and WGM to William Redfield, August 20, 1915, McAdoo MSS, Container 142, File: "Aug. 20, 1915."

74. Redfield to WGM, August 29, 1915, and September 13, 1915, McAdoo MSS, Containers 142 and 144, Files: "Aug. 20, 1915" and "September 13, 1915"; and WGM to Redfield, September 21 and 22, 1915, McAdoo MSS, Container 144, Files: "Sept. 21, 1915" and "Sept. 22, 1915."

75. Broesamle, *William Gibbs McAdoo*, 227–233; and WGM, *Crowded Years*, 303–316.

76. *NYT*, February 26, 1915, 8:2; and McGregor, "The Secretary of the Treasury," *Harper's Weekly*, October 24, 1914, 399–401, McAdoo MSS, Container 614.

77. Palmer, *Newton D. Baker*, 363; NDB to Thomas J. Howells, October 15, 1916, Baker MSS, Letterbooks, Reel 18; NDB to Robert Crosson, April 5, 1930, Baker MSS, Container 79, File: "Cr–Ct, 1930"; and NDB to ELB, March 12, 1916, and April 5, 1916, WRHA-NDB MSS, Container 1, Folder 2.

78. NDB to ELB, March 9, 1916, WRHA-NDB MSS, Container 1, Folder 2; NDB quoted in Dos Passos, *Mr. Wilson's War*, 162; and Beaver, *Newton D. Baker*, 1.

79. Elaine T. Wade, "Ralph A. Hayes: Private Secretary in the Newton D. Baker Administration of the War Department During World War I" (unpublished PhD diss., Georgia State University, 2001), 69–70; NDB to John McF. Howie, May 17, 1916, Baker MSS, Letterbooks, Reel 14; and NDB to Max Kolinsky, June 11, 1916, Baker MSS, Container 388, File: "Ki–Kq, 1922."

80. NDB to Dr. Howard White, May 8, 1925, Baker MSS, Container 256, File: "1925—May-Aug"; Paul A. C. Koistinen, *The Military-Industrial Complex: A Historical Perspective* (New York: Praeger, 1980), 30–31; Skowronek, *Building a New American State*, 96–97 and 235; Cramer, *Newton D. Baker*, 123; Thomas Fleming, *The Illusion of Victory: America in World War I* (New York: Basic Books, 2003), 104; and Wade, "Ralph A. Hayes," 3–9.

81. Skowronek, *Building a New American State*, 235; and Smith, *FDR*, 659.

82. For Villa's raid, see Friedrich Katz, "Pancho Villa and the Attack on Columbus, New Mexico," *American Historical Review* 83, no. 1 (February 1978): 101–130; Joseph Allen Stout, *Border Conflict: Villistas, Carrancistas, and the Punitive Expedition* (Fort Worth: Texas Christian University Press, 1999); and NDB to ELB, March 9 and 10, 1916, WRHA-NDB MSS, Container 1, Folder 2.

83. NDB to ELB, March 12, 1916, WRHA-NDB MSS, Container 1, Folder 2.

84. WGM to Carter Glass, March 11, 1916, McAdoo MSS, Container 156, File: "Mar. 11, 1916"; NDB to Frederick Funston, March 13, 1916, and NDB, "Memorandum for the Chief of Staff," March 16, 1916, in Link, ed., *Papers of Woodrow Wilson*, 36:298 and 323.

85. NDB, "Memorandum for the Adjutant General," June 22, 1916, in Link, ed., *Papers of Woodrow Wilson*, 37:283–286.

86. NDB to Charles R. Lingley, July 26, 1926, Baker MSS, Container 147, File: "Li–Lz, 1926"; and NDB to F. W. Kelsey, June 27, 1916, Baker MSS, Letterbooks, Reel 16.

87. NDB to Ellery Sedgwick, September 23, 1916, Baker MSS, Personal Correspondence 1916–1921, Reel 1; NDB to Thomas G. Frothingham, February 11, 1927, Baker MSS,

Container 101, File: "Captain Thomas G. Frothingham, 1925"; *NYT*, October 23, 1916, 9:5, and October 27, 1916, 2:2; NDB to Mrs. W. H. Conaway, October 31, 1916, NDB to Ben Cable, November 10, 1916, Baker MSS, Letterbooks, Reel 18; and NDB to Victor Blakeslee, March 21, 1936, Baker MSS, Container 43, File: "Bi–Bn, 1936." Letters criticizing Baker's speech are in Baker MSS, Container 244, "Speeches and Writings."

88. NDB to F. W. Kelsey, June 27, 1916, Baker MSS, Letterbooks, Reel 16.

89. NDB to Tasker H. Bliss, September 23 and October 15, 1916, Baker MSS, General Correspondence 1916–1922, Reel 1, and Letterbooks, Reel 18. Quotation is from the October 15 letter. NDB to Wilson, December 23, 1916, Baker MSS, General Correspondence 1916–1922, Reel 1.

90. NDB to John J. Pershing, February 6, 1917, Pershing Papers, LOC MSS, Container 19, File: "Baker, Newton D., 1916–1917"; NDB to Wilson, September 23, 1916, in Link, ed., *Papers of Woodrow Wilson*, 38:238; and NDB to Charles R. Lingley, July 26, 1926, Baker MSS, Container 147, File: "Li–Lz, 1926."

91. For a discussion of Wilson and preparedness, see Thomas J. Knock, *To End All Wars: Woodrow Wilson and the Quest for a New World Order* (Princeton, N.J.: Princeton University Press, 1992), 58–67. NDB to Wilson, "Memorandum on Preparedness as a Policy," April 7, 1916, WRHA-NDB MSS, MSS 4000, Container 4, Folder 73.

92. Cuff, *War Industries Board*, 11 and 35–38; and NDB to Thomas G. Frothingham, January 26, 1927, Baker MSS, Container 101, File: "Captain Thomas G. Frothingham, 1925." Robert D. Cuff, "The Cooperative Impulse and War," in *Building the Organizational Society: Essays on Associational Activities in Modern America*, ed. Jerry Israel (New York: The Free Press, 1972), 233–246, 233; and NDB to Josephus Daniels, November 14, 1916, Daniels Papers, LOC MSS, Reel 38.

93. NDB to Woodrow Wilson, "Memorandum on Preparedness as a Policy," April 7, 1916, WRHA-NDB MSS, MSS 4000, Container 4, Folder 73. See also NDB, "Industrial Preparedness," September 26, 1916, WRHA Pamphlet 697, 13; and *NYT*, May 24, 1916, 11:2.

94. Cuff, *War Industries Board*, 64, 246; and Koistinen, *Military-Industrial Complex*, 31.

95. Cuff, "Cooperative Impulse and War," 233–234; Koistinen, *Military-Industrial Complex*, 30–32; and NDB to Daniel Willard, December 5, 1931, Hayes Papers, LOC MSS, MSS 4000, Container 5, Folder 75.

96. Woodrow Wilson to WGM, August 11, 1915, Papers of Ray Stannard Baker, LOC MSS, Reel 65.

97. WGM to Dudley Field Malone, June 1, 1915, McAdoo MSS, Container 475-1; Link, ed., *Papers of Woodrow Wilson*, 34:74, n. 5; and Barnet, *Rockets' Red Glare*, 151.

98. WGM to J. H. O'Neil, June 18, 1915, McAdoo MSS, Container 485-2; WGM to Albert Krell, May 9, 1916, McAdoo MSS, Container 158, File: "May 9, 1916"; and WGM to Edward M. House, July 17, 1916, McAdoo MSS, Container 490-3.

99. WGM to Harriet McAdoo Martin, February 7, 1917, McAdoo MSS, Container 81.

100. NDB to Frank H. Baker, January 2, 1916, Baker MSS, Container 36, File: "Frank H. Baker, 1922." See also NDB to Dr. H. J. Gerstenberger, April 22, 1916, Baker MSS, Letterbooks, Reel 17.

101. NDB to Carl F. Schroder, April 20, 1916, Baker MSS, Letterbooks, Reel 17; and NDB to ELB, March 21 and May 17, 1916, WRHA-NDB MSS, Container 1, Folder 2. The underlining is NDB's.

102. NDB to ELB, April 21, 1916, WRHA-NDB MSS, Container 1, Folder 2.

103. NDB, *Why We Went to War*, 114; NDB to William A. Nitze, May 3, 1916, Baker MSS, Letterbooks, Reel 17; and Robert H. Zieger, *America's Great War: World War I and the American Experience* (Lanham, Md.: Rowman and Littlefield Publishers, 2000), 30.

104. NDB to Edward J. Cardozo, April 17, 1936, Baker MSS, Container 51, File: "Ca–Cd, 1936"; NDB, "Why We Went to War," *The American Legion Monthly*, August 1927, Baker MSS, "Speeches and Writing," Container 247, File: "1927"; and Franklin K. Lane and NDB, "War Measures and Purposes," in *The Nation in Arms* (Washington, D.C.: US Government Printing Office, 1917), 9.

105. NDB to Woodrow Wilson, February 7, 1917, in Link, ed., *Papers of Woodrow Wilson*, 41:151. Dooley quoted in Cramer, *Newton D. Baker*, 93.

CHAPTER 7: WARTIME SERVICE, 1917

1. NDB quoted in Edward M. Coffman, *Hilt of the Sword: The Career of Peyton C. March* (Madison: University of Wisconsin Press, 1966), 148; Houston, *Eight Years with Wilson's Cabinet*, 1:280; and John R. Rathom quoted in Beaver, *Newton D. Baker*, 98.

2. NDB to D. C. Westenhaver, April 30, 1917, Baker MSS, Container 228, File: "We–Wg, 1922."

3. Wade, "Ralph A. Hayes," 25–39, 210–243, 259. See Hayes Papers, LOC MSS, Container 4, Folder 73, Container 6, Folder 129; Baker MSS, Container 261, File: "1939–1949"; and Hayes to NDB, n.d. [1936], WRHA-Hayes MSS, Box 5, Folder 75; Hayes to NDB, "Dec. '35," Baker MSS, Container 261, File: "Dec. 1935"; and NDB to Hayes, December 23, 1933, Baker MSS, Container 260, File: "Dec. 1933."

4. Cuff, *War Industries Board*, 64; Josephine Goldmark, *Impatient Crusade: Florence Kelley's Life Story* (Urbana: University of Illinois Press, 1953), 128–129; Rodgers, *Atlantic Crossings*, 283–284; and Wade, "Ralph A. Hayes," 21.

5. Koistinen, *Military-Industrial Complex*, 30–32; and Skowronek, *Building a New American State*, 236–237.

6. Koistinen, *Mobilizing for Modern War*, 244–246; and NDB to Charles Warren, March 27, 1930, Baker MSS, Container 226, File: "Wa–Wd, 1930."

7. Wade, "Ralph A. Hayes," 125–132; Coffman, *Hilt of the Sword*, 51; and Koistinen, *Mobilizing for Modern War*, 245.

8. David F. Trask, *The AEF and Coalition Warmaking, 1917–1918* (Lawrence: University Press of Kansas, 1993), 25; Koistinen, *Military-Industrial Complex*, 39; and Koistinen, *Mobilizing for Modern War*, 244–246.

9. Cramer, *Newton D. Baker*, 125. NDB to Tasker H. Bliss, May 15, 1930, Baker MSS, Container 44, File: "General Tasker H. Bliss, 1930"; and NDB to Frederick Palmer, November 10, 1930, Baker MSS, Container 184, File: "Colonel Frederick Palmer, 1930."

10. NDB to Thomas G. Frothingham, February 21, 1927, Baker MSS, Container 101, File: "Capt. Thomas G. Frothingham, 1925."

11. Ray Stannard Baker, "Interview with Newton D. Baker, April 6, 1928," Papers of Ray Stannard Baker, LOC MSS, Reel 71; Wade, "Ralph A. Hayes," 139; NDB to ELB, January 7, 1922, WRHA-NDB MSS, Container 1, Folder 4; NDB to Thomas G. Frothingham, February 21, 1927, Baker MSS, Container 101, File: "Capt. Thomas G. Frothingham, 1925"; and James J. Cooke, *Pershing and his Generals: Command and Staff in the AEF* (Westport, Conn.: Praeger, 1997), 23. NDB quoted in Coffman, *Hilt of the Sword*, 151.

12. TR to NDB, July 6, 1916, in Elting E. Morison, ed., *Letters of Theodore Roosevelt*, 8 vols. (Cambridge, Mass.: Harvard University Press, 1954), 8:1087–1088; Seward W. Livermore, *Politics Is Adjourned: Woodrow Wilson and the War Congress, 1916–1918* (Middletown, Conn.: Wesleyan University Press, 1966), 25; TR to NDB, March 19, 1917, Baker MSS, Personal Correspondence, 1916–1922, Reel 2; and Cramer, *Newton D. Baker*, 110.

13. NDB to TR, March 20, 1917, TR to NDB, March 23, 1917, and NDB to TR, March 26, 1917, Baker MSS, General Correspondence 1916–1922, Reel 2.

14. TR to NDB, April 13, 1917, Baker MSS, General Correspondence 1916–1922, Reel 2.

15. TR quoted in Dos Passos, *Mr. Wilson's War*, 178; and Livermore, *Politics Is Adjourned*, 23–24.

16. TR to NDB, April 23, 1917, Baker MSS, General Correspondence 1916–1922, Reel 2.

17. NDB to Solomon B. Griffin, December 19, 1922, Baker MSS, Container 107, File: "Gr–Gz, 1922"; NDB to Woodrow Wilson, October 26, 1918, Baker MSS, General Correspondence 1916–1922, Reel 6; NDB to John H. Clarke, April 24, 1925, Baker MSS, Container 59, File: "Hon. John H. Clarke, 1925"; and Ray Stannard Baker, "Interview with Newton D. Baker, April 6, 1928," Papers of Ray Stannard Baker, LOC MSS, Reel 71.

18. NDB to Walter M. Moore, November 5, 1931, Baker MSS, Container 159, File: "Mo–Mx, 1934"; and NDB to Daniel Willard, December 5, 1931, WRHA-Hayes MSS, Container 5, Folder 75.

19. Gary Mead, *The Doughboys: America and the First World War* (London: Penguin Books, 2000), 120; Coffman, *War to End All Wars*, 49; Wilson to NDB, January 13, 1917, Baker MSS, General Correspondence 1916–1922, Reel 3; NDB to Daniel Willard, December 5, 1931, WRHA-Hayes MSS, Container 5, Folder 75; Cooke, *Pershing and his Generals*, 58; and Cramer, *Newton D. Baker*, 116.

20. NDB, "General John J. Pershing," *Army and Navy Journal*, August 22, 1934, Baker MSS, Container 179, File: "P., 1934."

21. Ray Stannard Baker, "Interview with Newton D. Baker, April 6, 1928," 2, Papers of Ray Stannard Baker, LOC MSS, Reel 71.

22. See NDB to General Thomas H. Barry, May 11, 1918, Baker MSS, Miscellaneous Correspondence, 1918, Reel 12; Palmer, *Newton D. Baker*, 2:229; and "Carbon Copy of General Leonard Wood's Interview with the Secretary of War, May 27, 1918," Wood Papers, LOC MSS, Container 352.

23. Wood to NDB, June 3, 1918, and NDB reply, June 5, 1918, Baker MSS, General Correspondence 1916–1922, Reel 6; Beaver, *Newton D. Baker*, 155–156; and Hagerdorn, *Leonard Wood*, 2:284.

24. NDB to Ralph Hayes, November 14, 1925, Baker MSS, Container 256, File: "1925 Nov-Dec"; Palmer, *Newton D. Baker*, 1:158–159; NDB to Daniel Willard, December 5, 1931, WRHA-Hayes MSS, Container 5, Folder 75; John J. Pershing, *My Experiences in the World War*, 2 vols. (New York: Frederick A. Stokes Company, 1931), 1:145 and 2:319; Ray Stannard Baker, "Interview with Newton D. Baker, April 6, 1928," 36, Papers of Ray Stannard Baker, LOC MSS, Reel 71; and NDB to Pershing, June 16, 1924, Pershing Papers, LOC MSS, Container 19, File: "Baker, Newton D., 1921-."

25. Beaver, *Newton D. Baker*, 186ff. and 210–211.

26. Coffman, *War to End All Wars*, 342; and Trask, *AEF and Coalition Warfare*, 156.

27. Kennedy, *Over Here*, 146.

28. John Whiteclay Chambers, *To Raise an Army: The Draft Comes to Modern America* (New York: The Free Press, 1987), 87, 175; Christopher Capozzola, *Uncle Sam Wants You: World War I and the Making of the Modern American Citizen* (New York: Oxford University Press, 2008), 21–23; and Beaver, *Newton D. Baker*, 103. NDB, "Newton D. Baker on Executive Influence in Military Legislation," *American Political Science Review* 50, no. 3 (September 1956): 700–701; and "Congress Again Shows a Leaning to Volunteers," *NYT*, April 10, 1917, 1:3.

29. See Beaver, *Newton D. Baker*, 28–30; and Chambers, *To Raise an Army*, 135. TR to William Allen White, August 3, 1917, in Morison, ed., *Letters of Theodore Roosevelt*, 8:1217; and Kennedy, *Over Here*, 149.

30. NDB to Ralph Hayes, June 12, 1922, Hayes Papers, LOC MSS, Container 4, Folder 66; and Capozzola, *Uncle Sam Wants You*, 25–26.

31. Chambers, *To Raise an Army*, 153ff.

32. Clark and Reed quoted in Higgs, *Crisis and Leviathan*, 131; and Nicholls and NDB quoted in John Dickinson, *The Building of an Army: A Detailed Account of Legislation, Administration, and Opinion in the United States, 1915–1920* (New York: The Century Company, 1922), 66–67.

33. Chambers, *To Raise an Army*, 163; Taft to NDB, April 8, 1917, Baker MSS, General Correspondence 1916–1922, Reel 2.

34. Ray Stannard Baker, "Interview with Newton D. Baker, April 6, 1928," 42, Papers of Ray Stannard Baker, LOC MSS, Reel 71. Crowder quoted in Kennedy, *Over Here*, 152; and NDB to Wilson, May 1, 1917, Baker MSS, General Correspondence 1916–1922, Reel 3.

35. Chambers, *To Raise an Army*, 180; and NDB to Ralph Hayes, June 12, 1922, Hayes Papers, LOC MSS, Container 4, Folder 66.

36. *NYT*, July 21, 1917, 10:5.

37. WGM to NDB, January 10, January 15, and May 22, 1918, McAdoo MSS, Container 497-3; NDB to Wilson, January 14 and May 25, 1918, in Link, ed., *Papers of Woodrow Wilson*, 45:583 and 48:151; WGM to Edward M. House, August 13, 1918, McAdoo MSS, Container 208, File: "Aug. 13, 1918"; Beaver, *Newton D. Baker*, 86; Kennedy, *Over Here*, 155; and Palmer, *Newton D. Baker*, 2:308.

38. WGM to NDB, July 10, 1917, McAdoo MSS, Container 495-1; Kennedy, *Over Here*, 155–156; and K. Walter Hickel, "'Justice and the Highest Kind of Equality Require Discrimination': Citizenship, Dependency, and Conscription in the South, 1917–1919," *Journal of Southern History* 66, no. 4 (November 2000): 749–780, 752.

39. Hickel, "'Justice and the Highest Kind of Equality Require Discrimination,'" 749; Gerald E. Shenk, *Work or Fight! Race, Gender, and the Draft in World War One* (New York: Palgrave Macmillan, 2005), 46–47; and Kennedy, *Over Here*, 155.

40. Chambers, *To Raise an Army*, 222; Coffman, *War to End All Wars*, 69; and Bernard C. Nalty, *Strength for the Fight: A History of Black Americans in the Military* (New York: The Free Press, 1986), 112.

41. Shenk, *Work or Fight!* 4–5, 155; Coffman *War to End All Wars*, 59–61; Chambers, *To Raise an Army*, 198, 230; Stephen Vaughn, *Holding Fast the Inner Lines: Democracy, Nationalism, and the Committee on Public Information* (Chapel Hill: University of North Carolina Press, 1980), 105; and Peyton C. March, *The Nation at War* (Garden City, N.J.: Doubleday, Doran & Company, 1932), 236.

42. NDB, "To the Rescue of a World in Flames," July 4, 1918, Baker MSS, Speeches and Writings, Container 244, File: "1918."

43. NDB to Wilson, July 18, 1919, in Link, ed., *Papers of Woodrow Wilson*, 61:530. The underlining is NDB's.

44. Zieger, *America's Great War*, 94; and March, *Nation at War*, 192.

45. James H. Hallas, *Doughboy War: The American Expeditionary Force in World War I* (Boulder, Colo.: Lynne Rienner Publishers, 2000), 52; Palmer, *Newton D. Baker*, 1:281; Cramer, *Newton D. Baker*, 98; and Wade, "Ralph A. Hayes," 104–105.

46. See Nancy K. Bristow, *Making Men Moral: Social Engineering During the Great War* (New York: New York University Press, 1996), 230–239, for a list of the locations and capacities of the thirty-two National Guard and National Army camps and cantonments; and Palmer, *Newton D. Baker*, 1:281, for a map of their locations. Livermore, *Politics Is Adjourned*, 46–47.

47. Kenneth McKellar to Woodrow Wilson, July 13, 1917, and Duncan U. Fletcher to NDB, July 11, 1917, Baker MSS, Personal Correspondence 1916–1922, Reel 3.

48. Livermore, *Politics Is Adjourned*, 46–47.

49. Ralph E. Cropley to WGM, December 13 and 20, 1917, McAdoo MSS, Container 193, Files: "Dec. 13, 1917" and "Dec. 20, 1917"; and Livermore, *Politics Is Adjourned*, 74–75.

50. Hearings Before the Committee on Military Affairs, US Senate, Sixty-Fifth Congress, Second Session, Part Four: Statement of Hon. Newton D. Baker, Secretary of War, January 28, 1918, 1943–1945 (Washington, D.C.: US Government Printing Office, 1918). Raymond B. Fosdick to NDB, January 14, 1925, Baker MSS, Container 94, File: "Fosdick, Raymond B., 1924."

51. Hayes to Carl Boyd, May 7, 1918, Pershing Papers, Container 19, File: "Baker, Newton D., 1918"; NDB to Woodrow Wilson, April 2, 1917, Baker MSS, General Correspondence 1916–1922, Reel 3; NDB to Surgeon General William Gorgas, December 3, 1917, Daniels Papers, LOC MSS, Special Correspondence, Reel 39; McGerr, *Fierce Discontent*, 297; and Coffman, *War to End All Wars*, 80.

52. Raymond B. Fosdick to NDB, December 15, 1917, Daniels Papers, LOC MSS, Special Correspondence, Reel 39; Bristow, *Making Men Moral*, 91–136. AEF soldier quoted in McGerr, *Fierce Discontent*, 300.

53. "Many Books Barred from Army Reading," NYT, September 1, 1918, 2, 2:5; and Bristow, *Making Men Moral*, 227–229.

54. Bristow, *Making Men Moral*, 11 and 89; Weldon B. Durham, "'Big Brother' and the 'Seven Sisters': Camp Life Reforms in World War I," *Military Affairs* 42, no. 2 (April 1978): 57–60, 60; NDB to Carl Boyd, May 4, 1918, Pershing Papers, LOC MSS, Container 19, File: "Baker, Newton D., 1918"; and NDB to Charles G. Frothingham, May 21, 1927, Baker MSS, Container 101, File: "Capt. Thomas G. Frothingham, 1925."

55. Edith Bolling Wilson, *My Memoir* (New York: The Bobbs-Merrill Company, 1938), 139. NDB entertained similar desires in 1918, but quickly renounced them: Ray Stannard Baker, "Interview with Newton D. Baker, April 6, 1928," Papers of Ray Stannard Baker, LOC MSS, Reel 71. WGM to Edward M. House, July 14, 1917 [but evidence suggests June 14, 1917], McAdoo MSS, Container 181, File: "June 14, 1917."

56. See chapter 6, above; and West, *Banking Reform and the Federal Reserve*, 216–217.

57. "Memorandum for the Secretary, July 27, 1916 and Further Revised Estimates of Receipts and Disbursements, Fiscal Year Ending June 30, 1917," W. H. Osborn to WGM, July 27, 1916, McAdoo MSS, Container 163, File: "July 27, 1916"; G. Calvin Mackenzie, "Old Wars, New Wars, and the American Presidency," in *New Challenges for the American*

Presidency, ed. George Edwards and Philip Davies (New York: Longman, 2004), 195–210, 199; Schwarz, *New Dealers*, 18; and Mead, *Doughboys*, 358.

58. See WGM to Claude Kitchin, April 30, 1917, McAdoo MSS, Container 178, File: "April 30, 1917."

59. WGM to Senator William J. Stone, June 6, 1917, McAdoo MSS, Container 180, File: "June 6, 1917." See Langbourne M. Williams to Woodrow Wilson, May 30, 1917, McAdoo MSS, Container 528, File: "May, 1917"; *NYT*, May 13, 1917, 6, 1:1; WGM to Senator Reed Smoot, June 21, 1917, McAdoo MSS, Container 182, File: "June 21, 1917"; and Kennedy, *Over Here*, 108.

60. WGM to Cleveland Dodge, April 14, 1917, McAdoo MSS, Container 493-3; George Cooksey, "Memorandum for WGM, July 5, 1917," McAdoo MSS, Container 183, File: "July 5, 1917"; WGM to Claude Kitchin, September 26, 1917, McAdoo MSS, Container 188, File: "Sept. 26, 1917"; "Income Tax Rates after the Revenue Law signed September 1917," McAdoo MSS, Container 561; and *NYT*, May 13, 1917, 6, 2:1.

61. Kennedy, *Over Here*, 109–110.

62. WGM to Claude Kitchin, June 5, 1918, McAdoo MSS, Container 295, File: "June 5, 1918."

63. Joseph P. Tumulty to Wilson, August 2, 1918, in Link, ed., *Papers of Woodrow Wilson*, 49:162–163; WGM to Kitchin, August 30, 1918, McAdoo MSS, Container 709, File: "Aug. 30, 1918"; and Synon, *McAdoo*, 238–239.

64. WGM to Edward M. House, August 13, 1918, McAdoo MSS, Container 499-3; WGM to Claude Kitchin, November 14, 1918, McAdoo MSS, Container 213, File: "Nov. 14, 1918"; Kennedy, *Over Here*, 111–113; and Pollack, *War, Revenue, and State Building*, 248–251.

65. WGM to Senator Robert L. Owen, April 25, 1917, McAdoo MSS, Container 178, File: "Apr. 25, 1917"; and Chase, "William Gibbs McAdoo," 137–138.

66. J. P. Morgan to WGM, April 10, 1917, McAdoo MSS, Container 177, File: "Apr. 10, 1917"; John Skelton Williams to WGM, April 20, 1917, McAdoo MSS, Container 177, File: "Apr. 20, 1917"; Paul Warburg to WGM, April 9, 1917, McAdoo MSS, Container 176, File: "Apr. 9, 1917"; Daniels, *Wilson Era*, 2:38; and Kennedy, *Over Here*, 101–102.

67. Cleveland H. Dodge to WGM, April 10, 1917, McAdoo MSS, Container 177, File: "Apr. 10, 1917." See also J. P. Morgan to WGM, April 27, 1917, McAdoo MSS, Container 178, File: "Apr. 27, 1917."

68. WGM to Cleveland H. Dodge, April 14, 1917, McAdoo MSS, Container 177, File: "Apr. 14, 1917"; and *NYT*, May 13, 1917, 6, 1:1.

69. John Skelton Williams to WGM, April 7, 1917, McAdoo MSS, Container 176, File: "Apr. 7, 1917"; White, *Regulation and Reform of the American Banking System*, 118–119; and Kennedy, *Over Here*, 103.

70. WGM to All Federal Reserve Banks, May 1, 1917, McAdoo MSS, Container 178, File: "May 1, 1917"; "The Liberty Loan," *The Bankers Magazine*, June 1917, McAdoo MSS, Container 180, File: "June 1, 1917"; and *NYT*, May 6, 1917, 1:2.

71. Kennedy, *Over Here*, 102–105; White, *Regulation and Reform of the American Banking System*, 118–11; and R. C. Leffingwell to WGM, June 21, 1918, McAdoo MSS, Container 260, File: "June 21, 1918."

72. Ervin Wardman to WGM, October 10, 1917, and Daniel C. Roper to George Cooksey, October 10, 1917, McAdoo MSS, Container 189, File: "Oct. 10, 1917"; and Kennedy, *Over Here*, 102.

73. WGM to NDB, October 31, 1917, Baker MSS, Personal Correspondence 1916–1922, Reel 2; R. C. Leffingwell to WGM, March 15, 1918, and Leffingwell, "Memorandum for the Secretary, March 15, 1918," McAdoo MSS, Container 198, File: "Mar. 15, 1918"; Paul M. Warburg to WGM, March 16, 1918, and George F. Norris to WGM, March 18, 1918, McAdoo MSS, Container 199, File: "Mar. 18, 1918"; and WGM, *Crowded Years*, 408.

74. William Jennings Bryan to WGM, March 5, 1918, and WGM to Bryan, March 11 and 22, 1918, McAdoo MSS, Container 198, File: "May 11, 1918"; WGM to A. B. Farquhar, July 15, 1917, McAdoo MSS, Container 495-1; Daniels, *Wilson Era*, 2:38; and Kennedy, *Over Here*, 101–106.

75. WGM, *Crowded Years*, 403; "Subscription to the Third Liberty Loan by States," McAdoo MSS, Container 552, File: "Liberty Loans"; J. O. Cole to WGM, October 29, 1917, McAdoo MSS, Container 190, File: "Oct. 29, 1917"; and Frank R. Wilson to WGM, "Summary of activities of the Bureau of Publicity during the Third Liberty Loan Campaign," May 25, 1918, 2, McAdoo MSS, Container 204, File: "May 25, 1918."

76. "Secretary McAdoo and the People of Buffalo," *Buffalo Times*, May 1, 1918, McAdoo MSS, Container 202, File: "May 4, 1918."

77. Chief Clerk, Treasury Department, to W. G. Martin, Secretary's Office, April 24, 1918, McAdoo MSS, Container 202, File: "Apr. 24, 1917"; and WGM, Cable to each Regional Director of the US Railroad Administration, September 1918, McAdoo MSS, Container 500-1, Part 1.

78. Kennedy, *Over Here*, 106; WGM to Senator Furnifold M. Simmons, June 9, 1917, McAdoo MSS, Container 181, File: "June 9, 1917"; WGM to Dr. Stockbridge, October 12, 1917, Stockbridge to WGM, and WGM reply, October 13 and 16, 1917, McAdoo MSS, Container 189, File: "Oct. 16, 1917"; and WGM to W. R. Compton, April 25, 1918, McAdoo MSS, Container 202, File: "April 25, 1918." H. J. Decker to WGM, October 27, 1917, McAdoo MSS, Container 190, File: "Oct. 27, 1917"; and "Farmer John, Krickrunn, Wisconsin," March 5, 1918, McAdoo MSS, Container 198, File: "Mar. 8, 1918."

79. Chase, "William Gibbs McAdoo," 133–136; and WGM to EWM, May 23, 1917, Wilson-McAdoo MSS, Eleanor Randolph Wilson McAdoo Papers, LOC MSS, Container 1, File: "McAdoo, William G., 1917."

80. WGM to EWM, May 23, 1917, Wilson-McAdoo MSS, Eleanor Randolph Wilson McAdoo Papers, LOC MSS, Container 1, File: "McAdoo, William G., 1917"; John B. Mills to Mr. Minor, June 5, 1917, and E. T. Meredith to R. R. Clagett, May 26, 1917, McAdoo MSS, Container 180, Files: "May 26, 1917" and "June 5, 1917"; and E. T. Meredith to WGM, June 13, 1917, McAdoo MSS, Container 181, File: "June 13, 1917." "Secretary M'Adoo," *The Milwaukee Journal*, May 19, 1917, 6:1, and *Wall Street Journal*, June 19, 1917, n.p., McAdoo MSS, Container 182, File: "June 28, 1917."

81. WGM, "Speech at Boston, June 5, 1917," McAdoo MSS, Container 191, File: "Nov. 5, 1917"; and "The Second Liberty Loan and the American Farmer," October 4, 1917, McAdoo MSS, Container 194, File: "Dec. 31, 1917."

82. WGM, "Speech at Boston, June 5, 1917," McAdoo MSS, Container 191, File: "Nov. 5, 1917."

83. WGM to Hon. William McAdoo, April 3, 1918, McAdoo MSS, Container 200, File: "Apr. 3, 1918"; WGM, "Address at Liberty Loan Dinner, New Orleans, April 13, 1918," McAdoo MSS, Container 564, File: "Speeches 1918"; and *NYT*, August 23, 1918, 8:6.

84. See Oscar T. Crosby to NDB, September 28, 1917, Baker MSS, General Correspondence 1916–1922, Reel 1; and Kathleen Burk, "The Diplomacy of Finance: British

Financial Missions to the United States, 1914–1918," *Historical Journal* 22, no. 2 (June 1979): 351–372.

85. PAGE to Secretary of State, March 5, 1917, McAdoo MSS, Container 175, File: "Mar. 5, 1917."

86. WGM to Frank I. Cobb, March 29, 1917, McAdoo MSS, Container 493-2; and "Mr. McAdoo's Great Task," *Washington Post*, April 11, 1917, McAdoo MSS, Container 178, File: "April 1917."

87. FRANCIS to Secretary of State, April 6, 1917, McAdoo MSS, Container 176, File: "Apr. 6, 1917"; and WGM to Secretary of State, April 12, 1917, McAdoo MSS, Container 177, File: "Apr. 12, 1917." WGM to Robert Lansing, July 9 and August 23, 1917, McAdoo MSS, Containers 495-1 and 495-3; WGM to NDB, July 6, 1917, McAdoo MSS, Container 495-1; WGM to Bernard Baruch, December 19, 1917, McAdoo MSS, Container 497-1; WGM to NDB, January 15, 1918, McAdoo MSS, Container 497-3; and WGM to Lansing, January 17, 1918, McAdoo MSS, Container 497-2.

88. Burk, *Britain, America and the Sinews of War*, 95.

89. WGM to Sir Arthur Cecil Spring-Rice, April 24, 1917, McAdoo MSS, Container 493-3; and WGM, *Crowded Years*, 414.

90. WGM to J. W. Alexander, January 22, 1917, McAdoo MSS, Container 173, File: "Jan. 22, 1917"; Richard Crawford to WGM, April 4, 1917, McAdoo MSS, Container 176, File: "April 4, 1917"; WGM to Wilson, April 30, 1917, McAdoo MSS, Container 522, File: "McAdoo to W. Wilson, May 1, 1917"; and WGM to NDB, July 7, 1917, McAdoo MSS, Container 183, File: "July 7, 1917."

91. Burk, *Britain, America and the Sinews of War*, 9 and 147; and Kennedy, *Over Here*, 323.

92. WGM to Wilson, July 10, 1917, McAdoo MSS, Container 522, Files: "July 10, 1917" and "July 16, 1917"; McAdoo MSS, Container 523, File: "July 16, 1917"; Sir Thomas White to WGM and WGM reply, September 5 and 19, 1917, McAdoo MSS, Container 187, File: "Sept. 10, 1917"; WGM to Wilson, November 15, 1917, McAdoo MSS, Container 523, File: "McAdoo to Wilson, Nov. 15, 1917"; and House, *Intimate Papers of Colonel House*, 3:113.

93. Kennedy, *Over Here*, 319–320.

94. Burk, "Diplomacy of Finance," 371; House to Wilson, August 10, 1917, in Link, ed., *Papers of Woodrow Wilson*, 43:425; and Wilson and House quoted in Kennedy, *Over Here*, 322.

95. Burk, *Britain, America and the Sinews of War*, 211. Lever quoted 132.

96. Burk, "Diplomacy of Finance," 368; and Kennedy, *Over Here*, 320–321.

97. WGM to Wilson, September 29, 1917, in Link, ed., *Papers of Woodrow Wilson*, 44:280–284; Kennedy, *Over Here*, 322–323; and Burk, *Britain, America and the Sinews of War*, passim.

98. See Chancellor of the Exchequer to WGM, July 30, 1917, in Link, ed., *Papers of Woodrow Wilson*, 43:326–333; Lord Balfour to the President and Secretary of the Treasury, July 20, 1917, in Link, ed., *Papers of Woodrow Wilson*, 43:223–230; and Sir William Wiseman to Sir Eric Drummond, September 20, 1917, in Link, ed., *Papers of Woodrow Wilson*, 44:230.

99. WGM to Wilson, January 2, 1918, and NDB to WGM, January 4, 1918, in Link, ed., *Papers of Woodrow Wilson*, 45:424–425 and 532–533; and Wilson to WGM, January 9, 1918, and WGM reply, January 14, 1917, in Link, ed., *Papers of Woodrow Wilson*, 45:546 and 588–592.

100. Mead, *Doughboys*, 134; WGM to Elihu Root, May 14, 1917, McAdoo MSS, Container 179, File: "May 14, 1917"; WGM to William Denman, April 28, 1917, McAdoo MSS, Container 493-3; Burk, *Britain, America and the Sinews of War*, 211; Kennedy, *Over Here*, 326; and WGM to Wilson, April 30, 1917, McAdoo MSS, Container 522, File: "McAdoo to W. Wilson, May 1, 1917."

101. WGM, Speech to Life Insurance Companies, July 2, 1917, McAdoo MSS, Container 183, File: "July 2, 1917."

102. Digest Made from Annual Reports to the Secretary of the Treasury on War Risk Insurance, McAdoo MSS, Container 562; WGM to Hon. William C. Adamson, August 24, 1917, McAdoo MSS, Container 495-3; and McAdoo, *Crowded Years*, 428.

103. "The Treasury Department during the First Year of the War: Some of the things it has done," McAdoo MSS, Container 207, File: "July 26, 1918"; and J. H. O'Neill to WGM, November 27, 1917, McAdoo MSS, Container 192, File: "Nov. 27, 1917."

CHAPTER 8: WARTIME SERVICE, 1918

1. Lane and NDB, "War Measures and Purposes," 12–13.

2. "Number of American Troops Disembarked in France, 1917 and 1918," Daniels Papers, LOC MSS, Special Correspondence, Reel 39.

3. Hallas, *Doughboy War*, 64; Mead, *Doughboys*, 175–176; and Trask, *AEF and Coalition Warmaking*, 42 and 53.

4. Mead, *Doughboys*, 175–176; Fleming, *Illusion of Victory*, 219, 226, and 265–274; and Trask, *AEF and Coalition Warmaking*, 78ff.

5. Trask, *AEF and Coalition Warmaking*, 125ff.; Cooke, *Pershing and his Generals*, 13, 33, 111, and 119; John Keegan, *The First World War* (New York: Vintage Books, 2000), 411; Fleming, *Illusion of Victory*, 185; Cooke, *Pershing and his Generals*, 123–133, 139, and 142; and Mead, *Doughboys*, 348. Dickman quoted in Fleming, *Illusion of Victory*, 228.

6. Niall Ferguson, *The Pity of War* (London: Penguin Books, 1988), 312; Keegan, *First World War*, 411; Ferguson, *Pity of War*, 312; Trask, *AEF and Coalition Warmaking*, 175–176; and Thornton, *Newton D. Baker and his Books*, 27.

7. NDB quoted in Palmer, *Newton D. Baker*, 1:178.

8. Skowronek, *Building a New American State*, 236; Grosvenor B. Clarkson, *Industrial America in the World War: The Strategy Behind the Line, 1917–1918* (Boston: Houghton Mifflin Company, 1923), 38–39; Beaver, *Newton D. Baker*, 46; Koistinen, *Mobilizing for Modern War*, 296; and Cuff, *War Industries Board*, 93–94.

9. See Baruch to WGM, May 27, 1919, UCLA-WGM MSS, Box 6, File: "Chairmanship for National Boy Scout Week I"; Beaver, *Newton D. Baker*, 71; Cuff, *War Industries Board*, 101–109; and Koistinen, *Mobilizing for Modern War*, 204.

10. Beaver, *Newton D. Baker*, 74; Weinstein, *Corporate Ideal and the Liberal State*, 219–220; Cuff, *War Industries Board*, 48 and 110; and Koistinen, *Mobilizing for Modern War*, 200.

11. Beaver, "Newton D. Baker," 55; Cuff, *War Industries Board*, 114; and Koistinen, *Mobilizing for Modern War*, 198.

12. Beaver, *Newton D. Baker*, 92ff.; and Cuff, *War Industries Board*, 140–141.

13. Beaver, "Newton D. Baker," 55; Baruch, *Public Years*, 46; and Cuff, *War Industries Board*, 143.

14. Clarkson, *Industrial America in the World War*, 55–58; and NDB to Woodrow Wilson, February 1, 1918, Baker MSS, Personal Correspondence 1916–1922, Reel 5.

15. Cuff, *War Industries Board*, 143; NDB to Grosvenor Clarkson, October 22, 1923, Baker MSS, Container 55, File: "Ce–Cn, 1923"; Baruch, *Public Years*, 51 and 55; Koistinen, *Mobilizing for Modern War*, 198; Skowronek, *Building a New American State*, 238–240; and Weinstein, *Corporate Ideal and the Liberal State*, 220.

16. Baruch, *Public Years*, 50–51; Margaret L. Coit, *Mr. Baruch* (London: Victor Gollancz, 1958), 170–171; NDB to Grosvenor Clarkson, October 22, 1923, Baker MSS, Container 55, File: "Ce–Cn, 1923"; Woodrow Wilson to Bernard Baruch, March 4, 1918, and Wilson to NDB, n.d., Baker MSS, Personal Correspondence 1916–1922, Reel 6.

17. Jordan A. Schwarz, *The Speculator: Bernard M. Baruch in Washington, 1917–1965* (Chapel Hill: University of North Carolina Press, 1981), 62; Beaver, *Newton D. Baker*, 104; Coffman, *War to End All Wars*, 164; and Samuel Untermeyer to WGM, May 30, 1917, McAdoo MSS, Container 180, File: "May 30, 1917."

18. Coit, *Mr. Baruch*, 170 and 198; Diary of Charles S. Hamlin, Vol. IX: 39, Hamlin Papers, LOC MSS, Reel 3: "Diaries"; NDB to Grosvenor Clarkson, October 22, 1923, Baker MSS, Container 55, File: "Ce–Cn, 1922"; NDB to Baruch, May 9, 1931, Baker MSS, Container 227, File: "War Policies Commission, 1931"; and NDB to Frank Scott, January 8, 1934, Baker MSS, Container 205, File: "Frank A. Scott, 1934."

19. Baruch, *Public Years*, 51 and 56; Clarkson, *Industrial America*, 71; Cuff, *War Industries Board*, 197; and WGM to Woodrow Wilson, March 6, 1918, McAdoo MSS, Container 524, File: "McAdoo to W. Wilson, Mar. 6, 1918."

20. Koistinen, *Mobilizing for Modern War*, 291–292; G. S. MacFarland to NDB, January 5, 1918, Baker MSS, General Correspondence 1916–1922, Reel 5; and Cuff, *War Industries Board*, 147.

21. Koistinen, *Military-Industrial Complex*, 40; Beaver, *Newton D. Baker*, 63; Weinstein, *Corporate Ideal in the Liberal State*, 225; and Cuff, *War Industries Board*, 149 and 190.

22. Beaver, *Newton D. Baker*, 108; and Coffman, *War to End All Wars*, 51.

23. Higgs, *Crisis and Leviathan*, 123; and Beaver, *Newton D. Baker*, 109.

24. James G. Grant, *Bernard Baruch: The Adventures of a Wall Street Legend* (New York: John Wiley and Sons, 1997), 149–153.

25. Clarkson, *Industrial America in the World War*, 407–409.

26. Pershing, *My Experiences in the World War*, 1:159ff.; NDB to Colonel C. C. Vestal, June 10, 1929, Baker MSS, Container 225, File: "V., 1929"; and NDB to David H. McClugage, September 2, 1924, Baker MSS, Container 152, File: "Mc, 1924."

27. NDB to David H. McClugage, September 2, 1924, Baker MSS, Container 152, File: "Mc, 1924"; Ray Stannard Baker, "Interview with Newton D. Baker, April 6, 1928," 39, Papers of Ray Stannard Baker, LOC MSS, Reel 71; and NDB to Tasker H. Bliss, April 29, May 7, and May 31, 1918, Bliss Papers, LOC MSS, Container 250, File: "Newton D. Baker, March 1918–March 1920."

28. NDB to Tasker H. Bliss, May 7, 1918, Bliss Papers, LOC MSS, Container 250, File: "Newton D. Baker, March 1918–March 1920"; NDB to David H. McClugage, September 2, 1924, Baker MSS, Container 152, File: "Mc, 1924"; NDB to Bliss, May 31, 1918, Bliss Papers, LOC MSS, Container 250, File: "Newton D. Baker, March 1918–March 1920"; Ray Stannard Baker, "Interview with Newton D. Baker, April 6, 1928," 39, Papers of Ray Stannard Baker, LOC MSS, Reel 71; and Cramer, *Newton D. Baker*, 152.

29. NDB, "Conclusion of the First Officers' Training Camp, Fort Myer, Virginia, August 13, 1917," *Frontiers of Freedom*, 64; "Army Rank Implies No Social Barrier," *NYT*, December 19, 1917, 4:4; Georges Clemenceau to General Chief of the French Mission, AEF, February 17, 1918, Baker MSS, Personal Correspondence 1916–1922, Reel 6; and NDB to Mr. H. Newcomb, May 13, 1933, Baker MSS, Container 162, File: "Na–Nn, 1933."

30. NDB to Woodrow Wilson, May 11, 1918, Baker MSS, Personal Correspondence 1916–1922, Reel 6; and Keene, *Doughboys*, 65.

31. NDB to Woodrow Wilson, May 1, 1918, Baker MSS, Container 234, File: "Wia–Wil, 1922"; NDB to Wilson, August 19, 1919, Baker MSS, Personal Correspondence 1916–1922, Reel 9; and NDB to Wilson, March 10 and August 14, 1920, in Link, ed., *Papers of Woodrow Wilson*, 65:78 and 66:34.

32. NDB, Independence Day Speech, July 4, 1917, and Speech to Trade Publication Editors, May 25, 1917, *Frontiers of Freedom*, 53 and 32; and NDB quoted in Beaver, *Newton D. Baker*, 237.

33. NDB to Russell H. Seibert, December 12, 1935, Baker MSS, Container 180, File: "Ohio State University, 1935"; Coffman, *War to End All Wars*, 76; Ray Stannard Baker, "Interview with Newton D. Baker, April 6, 1928," 41, Papers of Ray Stannard Baker, LOC MSS, Reel 71; and NDB to Wilson, July 1, 1919, in Link, ed., *Papers of Woodrow Wilson*, 61:366.

34. NDB to Wilson, October 1, 1917, Baker MSS, General Correspondence 1916–1922, Reel 3; and NDB to D. C. Westenhaver, October 11, 1917, Baker MSS, Container 228, File: "We–Wg, 1922."

35. Ray Stannard Baker, "Interview with Newton D. Baker, April 6, 1928," 41, Papers of Ray Stannard Baker, LOC MSS, Reel 71; Kennedy, *Over Here*, 165; NDB to Irita Van Doren, May 9, 1924, Baker MSS, Container 73, File: "Coa–Con, 1924"; Capozzola, *Uncle Sam Wants You*, 56–82; and Fleming, *Illusion of Victory*, 137.

36. Beaver, *Newton D. Baker*, 66ff.

37. NDB to Roger Baldwin, April 7, 1929, Baker MSS, Container 17, File: "Am–Ar, 1929."

38. Cooper, *Woodrow Wilson*, 408; and NDB quoted in Bristow, *Making Men Moral*, 144. See also Beaver, *Newton D. Baker*, 224 and 228; and Slotkin, *Lost Battalions*, 49. NDB to Charles H. Williams, August 4, 1923, Baker MSS, Container 234, File: "Wia–Wil, 1923"; NDB to Jesse B. Hearin, July 9, 1928, Baker MSS, Container 118, File: "He–Hh, 1928"; and NDB to George F. Peabody, July 10, 1930, Baker MSS, Container 258, File: "1930—July."

39. Nalty, *Strength for the Fight*, 112 and 109.

40. Hal S. Chase, "Struggle for Equality: Fort Des Moines Training Camp for Colored Officers, 1917," *Phylon* 39, no. 4 (1978): 297–310; John Milton Waldron and Thomas Montgomery Gregory to Wilson, May 11, 1917, in Link, ed., *Papers of Woodrow Wilson*, 42:321; and Jami Bryan, "Fighting for Respect: African-American Soldiers in World War I," 2, www.militaryhistoryonline.com/wwi/articles/fightingforrespect/.

41. NDB to ELB, August 31, 1918, WRHA-NDB MSS, 3491, Container 1, Folder 3; and NDB to Charles H. Williams, August 4, 1923, Baker MSS, Container 234, File: "Wia–Wil, 1923."

42. NDB to Wilson, August 22, 1918, Baker MSS, General Correspondence 1916–1922, Reel 6; and Nalty, *Strength for the Fight*, 103ff.

43. NDB to Wilson, August 23, 1918, Baker MSS, General Correspondence 1916–1922, Reel 6; and "A Petition to President Wilson," February 19, 1918, in Link, ed., *Papers of Woodrow Wilson*, 46:383.

44. Wilson to Pompey Long Hawkins, January 13, 1918, and Wilson to NDB, February 19, 1918, in Link, ed., *Papers of Woodrow Wilson*, 45:545 and 46:385; NDB to Wilson, August 23, 1918, Baker MSS, Personal Correspondence 1916–1922, Reel 6; and Nalty, *Strength for the Fight*, 105.

45. Nalty, *Strength for the Fight*, 111; and Slotkin, *Lost Battalions*, 552.

46. "Missy," Memorandum to "Bill," June 1, 1918, Papers of James Purroy Mitchel, LOC MSS, Box 24, Folder 2; and W. B. Engle to NDB, July 14, 1921, Baker MSS, Container 255, File: "1925." The capitalization is Engle's.

47. TR to William Allen White, August 3, 1917, in Morison, ed., *Letters of Theodore Roosevelt*, 8:1217; NDB to Matthew Page Andrews, October 19, 1927, Baker MSS, Container 18, File: "Am–Ar, 1927"; NDB to Cyril Clemens, December 17, 1936, Baker MSS, Container 57, File: "Ce–Cn, 1936"; and Livermore, *Politics Is Adjourned*, 100ff.

48. Ray Stannard Baker, "Interview with Newton D. Baker, April 6, 1928," 26, Papers of Ray Stannard Baker, LOC MSS, Reel 71; and Palmer, *Newton D. Baker*, 1:6. Chamberlain quoted in Trask, *AEF and Coalition Warmaking*, 29.

49. Ray Stannard Baker, "Interview with Newton D. Baker, April 6, 1928," 26, Papers of Ray Stannard Baker, LOC MSS, Reel 71; NDB to Tom Sidlo, December 25, 1917, Baker MSS, General Correspondence 1916–1922, Reel 2; and *NYT*, January 11, 1918, 1:5, 3:3, and 14:2, and January 12, 1918, 10: 1.

50. Ray Stannard Baker, "Interview with Newton D. Baker, April 6, 1928," 27, Papers of Ray Stannard Baker, LOC MSS, Reel 71; Grosvenor Clarkson to NDB, March 19, 1918, McAdoo MSS, Container 199, File: "March 19, 1918"; and Cronon, ed., *Cabinet Diaries of Josephus Daniels*, 271.

51. "Statement of Hon. Newton D. Baker, Secretary of War, January 28, 1918," Hearings before the Committee on Military Affairs, 1943–1985; and Tasker H. Bliss, "Notes of a Conference Held at the Trianon Palace, Versailles, on Tuesday January 29, 1918, at Noon," 7, Baker MSS, Container 253, File: "Report of General T. H. Bliss on the Supreme War Council."

52. WGM to NDB, January 22, 1918, Baker MSS, Personal Correspondence 1916–1922, Reel 5; David Lawrence to Wilson, January 28, 1918, Baker MSS, General Correspondence 1916–1922, Reel 5; *NYT*, February 24, 1918, 4:8; James quoted in Daniels, *Wilson Era*, 2:166. Ray Stannard Baker, "Interview with Newton D. Baker, April 6, 1928," 28, Papers of Ray Stannard Baker, LOC MSS, Reel 71; NDB to James A. Reed, May 1, 1918, Baker MSS, General Correspondence 1916–1922, Reel 5; March, *Nation at War*, 372, Wade, "Ralph A. Hayes," 248; and NDB to WGM, June 12, 1922, McAdoo MSS, Container 264, File: "Jun. 12, 1922."

53. Wilson to NDB, May 8, 1917, and NDB to Wilson, May 2 and 8, 1917, Baker MSS, Personal Correspondence 1916–1922, Reel 3; and Mead, *Doughboys*, 106.

54. NDB to Josephus Daniels, February 29, 1924, Baker MSS, Container 82, File: "Da–Dh, 1924"; and Kennedy, *Over Here*, 169.

55. NDB to Tasker H. Bliss, May 31, 1918 (No. 3), Bliss Papers, LOC MSS, Container 250, File: "Newton D. Baker, March 1918–March 1920"; Pershing, *My Experiences in the World War*, 1:93; Livermore, *Politics Is Adjourned*, 100ff.; and Wade, "Ralph A. Hayes," 207.

56. Bliss to NDB, December 23, 1917, Bliss Papers, LOC MSS, Container 250, File: "Dec. 1917–May 1918."

57. Bliss to NDB, January 22, 1918, Papers of Ray Stannard Baker, LOC MSS, Reel 62; and Fleming, *Illusion of Victory*, 187.

58. Bliss to NDB, February 2, 1918, Bliss Papers, LOC MSS, Container 250, File: "Dec. 1917–May 1918." The underlining is Bliss's. NDB to Wilson, March 28, 198, in Link, ed., *Papers of Woodrow Wilson*, 47:174; Wilson to NDB, February 4, 1918, Papers of Ray Stannard Baker, LOC MSS, Reel 62; Tasker H. Bliss, "Notes of a Conference Held at the Trianon Palace, Versailles, on Tuesday January 29, 1918, at Noon," 7, Baker MSS, Container 253, File: "Report of General T. H. Bliss on the Supreme War Council"; Bliss to NDB, February 2, 1918, Bliss Papers, LOC MSS, Container 250, File: "Dec. 1917–May 1918"; NDB to Bliss, April 29, May 7, and May 31, 1918, Bliss Papers, LOC MSS, Container 250, File: "Newton D. Baker, March 1918–March 1920"; and Cooke, *Pershing and his Generals*, 80.

59. NDB to Tasker H. Bliss, May 7, 1918 (No. 2), Bliss Papers, LOC MSS, Container 250, File: "Newton D. Baker: March 1918–March 1920"; NDB to Tasker H. Bliss, July 28, 1918 (No. 5), Bliss Papers, LOC MSS, Container 250, File: "Newton D. Baker, March 1918–March 1920"; NDB to Thos. G. Frothingham, August 6, 1925, Baker MSS, Container 101, File: "Capt. Thomas G. Frothingham, 1925"; and NDB to Wilson, March 28, 1918, in Link, ed., *Papers of Woodrow Wilson*, 47:175.

60. Beaver, *Newton D. Baker*, 149–150.

61. George to Lord Reading, April 14, 1918, in Link, ed., *Papers of Woodrow Wilson*, 47:338.

62. NDB to Wilson, January 3, 1918, in Link, ed., *Papers of Woodrow Wilson*, 45:438; Pershing to Bliss, January 9, 1918, Baker MSS, General Correspondence 1916–1922, Reel 5; Pershing to the Adjutant General, January 15, 1918, in Link, ed., *Papers of Woodrow Wilson*, 46:12; and Cooke, *Pershing and his Generals*, 40.

63. British War Cabinet report quoted in Kennedy, *Over Here*, 200; and Bliss to NDB, June 26, 1918, Bliss Papers, LOC MSS, Container 250, File: "May–July 1918."

64. Tasker H. Bliss, "Notes of a Conference Held at the Trianon Palace, Versailles, on Tuesday January 29 1918, at Noon," 4–8, Baker MSS, Container 253, File: "Report of General T. H. Bliss on the Supreme War Council"; and NDB to Bliss, December 23, 1918, Bliss Papers, LOC MSS, Container 250, File: "Newton D. Baker, March 1918–March 1920."

65. NDB to Wilson, December 5, 1918, Baker MSS, Personal Correspondence 1916–1922, Reel 6; NDB to Wilson, June 4, 1918, in Link, ed., *Papers of Woodrow Wilson*, 48:244; Palmer, *Newton D. Baker*, 1:175; Kennedy, *Over Here*, 199; and Slotkin, *Lost Battalions*, 5.

66. NDB to Colonel Lloyd C. Griscom, June 24, 1932, Baker MSS, Container 107, File: "Gr–Gz, 1932"; Mead, *Doughboys*, 298; and Pershing, *My Experiences in the World War*, 2:312–318.

67. NDB to "My dear little Miss Bunch" [Betty Baker], March 9, 1918, WRHA-NDB MSS, Acc. #4564, Container 1, Folder 1; NYT, March 22, 1918, 12:4; and NDB to Minnegerode Andrews, December 23, 1927, Baker MSS, Container 18, File: "Am–Ar, 1927." Harbord quoted in Frank Freidel, *Over There: The Story of America's First Overseas Great Crusade* (Philadelphia: Temple University Press, 1990), 195.

68. NDB to Minnegerode Andrews, September 25, 1927, Baker MSS, Container 18, File: "Am–Ar, 1927"; NYT, September 21, 1918, 19:4; Wade, "Ralph A. Hayes," 207–208; Cooke, *Pershing and his Generals*, 119; Mead, *Doughboys*, 284–297; NDB to ELB, September 15,

1918, WRHA-NDB MSS, Acc. #3491, Container 1, Folder 3; and NDB to Edward H. Smith, March 8, 1934, Baker MSS, Container 210, File: "Si–Sn, 1934."

69. NDB to James W. Kern, October 14, 1918, and Kern to NDB, October 19, 1918, Baker MSS, Personal Correspondence 1916–1922, Reel 4.

70. WGM, Address to the Third Annual Convention of the American Train Dispatchers Association, June 15, 1920, UCLA-Mac MSS, Box 12; George Creel, *Rebel at Large: Recollection of Fifty Crowded Years* (New York: G. P. Putnam's Sons, 1947), 269; and WGM, *Crowded Years*, 443.

71. Kennedy, *Over Here*, 253ff.; and J. Austin Kerr, "Decision for Federal Control: Wilson, McAdoo, and the Railroads, 1917," *Journal of American History* 54 (December 1967): 550–560, 551.

72. "The Railroads and the Government," *The West at Work* (July 1918): 24; Higgs, *Crisis and Leviathan*, 129; Koistinen, *Mobilizing for Modern War*, 174; and Palmer, *Newton D. Baker*, 1:133.

73. Kerr, "Decision for Federal Control," 557; and Skowronek, *Building a New American State*, 276.

74. WGM to Wilson, December 6, 1917, in Link, ed., *Papers of Woodrow Wilson*, 45:225–228; and J. Austin Kerr, *American Railroad Politics, 1914–1920: Rates, Wages and Efficiency* (Pittsburgh: University of Pittsburgh Press, 1968), 65.

75. Samuel Untermeyer to WGM, December 14, 1917, McAdoo MSS, Container 193, File: "Dec. 14, 1917"; and WGM to Wilson, December 15, 1917, in Link, ed., *Papers of Woodrow Wilson*, 45:304.

76. Theodore H. Price to Wilson, December 7, 1917, McAdoo MSS, Container 528, File: "Dec., 1917"; Tumulty to Wilson, December 7, 1917, in Link, ed., *Papers of Woodrow Wilson*, 45:232; Baruch, *Public Years*, 42; and WGM to Mary Synon, April 26, 1920, McAdoo MSS, Container 506.

77. Ray Stannard Baker, "Interview with Newton D. Baker, April 6, 1928," 10, Papers of Ray Stannard Baker, LOC MSS, Reel 71; Walker D. Hines, *War History of American Railroads* (New Haven, Conn.: Yale University Press, 1928), 245; Woodrow Wilson and NDB, "A Proclamation," December 26, 1917, and Wilson, "An Address to a Joint Session of Congress," January 4, 1918, in Link, ed., *Papers of Woodrow Wilson*, 45:358 and 421.

78. Higgs, *Crisis and Leviathan*, 145–147; Kennedy, *Over Here*, 254; Kerr, *American Railroad Politics*, 84–86 and 111–119; and Skowronek, *Building a New American State*, 277–278.

79. NYT, December 27, 1917, 1:5–8, 2:1–5; Kennedy, *Over Here*, 254; and Kerr, *American Railroad Politics*, 68.

80. New and Gillett quoted in NYT, December 28, 1917, 3:3. McCormick quoted in *Chicago Sunday Tribune*, August 25, 1918, 8, McAdoo MSS, Container 209, File: "Sept. 4, 1918."

81. Creel, *Rebel at Large*, 268; Synon, *McAdoo*, 9; *Life*, December 12, 1918, 897, McAdoo MSS, Container 215, File: "Dec. 14, 1918"; "William Gibbs McAdoo as War Finance Minister," *The West and the World* (July 1918), McAdoo MSS, Container 207, File: "July 29, 1918"; Thomas Randolph to WGM, December 31, 1917, and Bruce Barton to WGM, December 31, 1917, McAdoo MSS, Container 194, File: "Jan. 3, 1918." See also the Springfield (Mass.) *Republican*, December 31, 1917, and January 2, 1918, McAdoo MSS, Container 194, File: "Jan. 4, 1918," and "What Mr. McAdoes," *The Outlook*, n.d., McAdoo MSS, Container 199, File: "Mar. 21, 1918."

82. WGM, "To All Railroad Officers and Employees," January 8, 1918, McAdoo MSS, Container 194, File: "Jan. 8, 1918"; and WGM, *Crowded Years*, 460.

83. USRRA, "Order No. 1," December 29, 1917, McAdoo MSS, Container 556, File: "Gen. Orders Nos. 1–25"; WGM to Daniel Willard, February 4, 1918, and WGM to J. S. Peters, February 9, 1918, McAdoo MSS, Container 497-3; and Kerr, *American Railroad Politics*, 76 and 104.

84. WGM, "Report to the President," September 3, 1918, McAdoo MSS, Container 557, File: "Annual Reports"; WGM to Senator A. O. Stanley, September 5, 1921, McAdoo MSS, Container 255, File: "Sept. 5, 1921"; WGM, *Crowded Years*, 468ff.; and Kerr, *American Railroad Politics*, 81.

85. "Is Uncle Sam to Keep the Railroads?" *The Independent*, November 30, 1918, 286–287, McAdoo MSS, Container 611.

86. WGM, "How the Railroads Saved a Critical Situation in the Great War for the Allies," May 17, 1919, UCLA-WGM MSS, Box 12, Folder 1; and WGM to Herbert C. Hoover, March 15, 1918, McAdoo MSS, Container 198, File: "Mar. 15, 1918."

87. WGM to Senator Jos. E. Ransdell, September 4, 1918, and to Josephus Daniels, October 24, 1918, McAdoo MSS, Container 500-1, Part 1; and Synon, *McAdoo*, 325.

88. WGM, "Report to the President," September 3, 1918, McAdoo MSS, Container 557, File: "Annual Reports"; Carl R. Gray to WGM, January 20, 1918, McAdoo MSS, Container 195, File: "Jan. 20, 1918"; "Is Uncle Sam to Keep the Railroads?" *The Independent*, November 30, 1918, 286–288, McAdoo MSS, Container 611; Higgs, *Crisis and Leviathan*, 146; Hines, *War History of American Railroads*, 124; WGM, *Crowded Years*, 479–487; and NDB to WGM, June 13, 1918, McAdoo MSS, Container 206, File: "June 13, 1918."

89. Hines, *War History of American Railroads*, 154–155; and Kennedy, *Over Here*, 255.

90. Two hundred and fifty dollars in 1918 was equivalent, on the basis of changes to the Consumer Price Index, to $3,730 in 2011. www.measuringworth.com/uscompare. USRRA, "Railroad Wage Commission," January 18, 1918, McAdoo MSS, Container 195, File: "Jan. 18, 1918"; USRRA, "Report of the Railroad Wage Commission to the Director-General of Railroads," April 30, 1918, UCLA-WGM MSS, Box 14; USRRA, "General Order No. 27: Wages of Railroad Employees," May 25, 1918, McAdoo MSS, Container 556, File: "General Orders Nos. 24–27"; NYT, May 27, 1918, 1:1, 4:5–7; Hines, *War History of American Railroads*, 155 and 169–170; Kennedy, *Over Here*, 255, Kerr, *American Railroad Politics*, 93–100; WGM, *Crowded Years*, 488ff.; and Higgs, *Crisis and Leviathan*, 146.

91. NYT, May 27, 1918, 4:7.

92. Kennedy, *Over Here*, 255; NYT, June 1, 1918, 10:4; and WGM to Railroad Union Leaders, August 28, 1918, McAdoo MSS, Container 209, File: "Aug. 28, 1918."

93. WGM quoted in Higgs, *Crisis and Leviathan*, 146; NYT, February 4, 1923, 1, 8:1; and Clerks of the Northern Pacific Head of the Bay Freight Office to WGM, May 11, 1918, McAdoo MSS, Container 203, File: "May 11, 1918."

94. William T. McKinney to WGM, May 28, 1918, McAdoo MSS, Container 205, File: "May 31, 1918"; and Thomas R. Webb to WGM, October 18, 1937, Huntingdon-WGM MSS, Box 5, Folder 4.

95. NYT, May 27, 1918, 1:1; WGM to Ernest T. Atwell, November 21, 1918, McAdoo MSS, Container 213, File: "Nov. 21, 1918"; and WGM to George Foster Peabody, December 4, 1918, McAdoo MSS, Container 500-1, Part 2.

96. WGM to Arthur Brisbane, January 21, 1918, and WGM to B. L. Winchell of the USRRA, August 15, 1918, McAdoo MSS, Container 208, File: "Aug. 15, 1918"; WGM to

Walker D. Hines, October 25, 1918, McAdoo MSS, Container 212, File: "Oct. 25, 1918"; B. L. Winchell to WGM, October 15, 1918, McAdoo MSS, Container 211, File: "Oct. 15, 1918"; WGM to Ernest T. Attwell, November 21, 1918, McAdoo MSS, Container 500-1, Part 1; and B. F. Bush to WGM, November 27, 1918, McAdoo MSS, Container 214, File: "Nov. 27, 1918."

97. Richard H. Edmonds to WGM, August 13, 1918, McAdoo MSS, Container 208, File: "Aug. 13, 1918"; WGM to Theodore Price of the USRRA, July 29, 1918, McAdoo MSS, Container 207, File: "July 29, 1918"; "Is Uncle Sam to Keep the Railroads?" *The Independent*, November 30, 1918, 302, McAdoo MSS, Container 611; and *NYT*, August 20, 1918, 5:3.

98. WGM to Edward M. House, November 29, 1918, McAdoo MSS, Container 500-2; and WGM to Walker D. Hines, January 23, 1919, McAdoo MSS, Container 217, File: "Jan. 23, 1919."

99. WGM to Wilson, November 25, 1918, in Link, ed., *Papers of Woodrow Wilson*, 53:190; Walker D. Hines to WGM, November 26, 1918, McAdoo MSS, Container 214, File: "Nov. 26, 1918"; WGM to Representative T. W. Sims, December 11, 1918, McAdoo MSS, Container 500-2, Part 2; and WGM to William Sproule, December 14, 1918, McAdoo MSS, Container 215, File: "Dec. 14, 1918."

100. *NYT*, January 4, 1919, 1:3, and January 5, 1919, 8:3; WGM to Frank B. Miles, January 17, 1919, McAdoo MSS, Container 217, File: "Jan. 17, 1919"; and Kerr, *American Railroad Politics*, 135ff.

101. R. S. Lovett to WGM, "Outline of a Permanent Railroad Policy," November 27, 1918, McAdoo MSS, Container 214, File: "Nov. 27, 1918"; Dawley, *Changing the World*, 283–284; Kerr, *American Railroad Politics*, 161–174; and Thompson, *Reformers and War*, 256.

102. *NYT*, December 13, 1918, 14:1. See also *Journal of Commerce* (December 13, 1918), McAdoo MSS, Reel 57, "Scrapbooks."

103. WGM to Albert Shaw, December 31, 1918, McAdoo MSS, Container 216, File: "Dec. 31, 1918"; WGM and Walker D. Hines to Wilson, February 25 and 26, 1919, in Link, ed., *Papers of Woodrow Wilson*, 55:256–260; WGM to Hines, February 25, 1919, McAdoo MSS, Container 218, File: "Feb. 25, 1919"; Walker D. Hines to Wilson, April 4, 1919, in Link, ed., *Papers of Woodrow Wilson*, 56:620–623; WGM to Joseph P. Tumulty, November 24, 1919, McAdoo MSS, Container 226, File: "Nov. 24, 1919"; and Skowronek, *Building a New American State*, 279.

104. Skowronek, *Building a New American State*, 279–282; Dawley, *Changing the World*, 283; and Kerr, *American Railroad Politics*, 143–149 and 225–227.

105. WGM, Speech at Indianapolis, October 16, 1920, UCLA-WGM MSS, Box 12; and WGM to Professor Royal Meeker, April 28, 1920, McAdoo MSS, Container 506.

106. WGM to George Moore, November 19, 1920, McAdoo MSS, Container 244, File: "Nov. 19, 1920"; *NYT*, May 28, 1923, 28:2; WGM, *Crowded Years*, 495–504; WGM, "Address to 3rd Annual Convention of the American Train Dispatchers Association, June 15 1920," UCLA-WGM MSS, Box 12, Folder 3; WGM to Joseph H. O'Neil, July 30, 1921, McAdoo MSS, Container 253, File: "July 30, 1921"; and WGM to Joseph E. Eastman, December 6, 1923, McAdoo MSS, Container 287, File: "Dec. 6, 1923."

107. Hines, *War History of American Railroads*, 233, Kennedy, *Over Here*, 255–256; and McGerr, *Fierce Discontent*, 303.

108. E. Watkins to WGM, April 8, 1918, and E. Walter Giles to WGM, April 18, 1918, McAdoo MSS, Container 201, Files: "Apr. 12, 1918" and "Apr. 18, 1918"; "Goodbye

Mr. McAdoo," Macon (Ga.) *Daily Telegraph,* September 29, 1920, McAdoo MSS, Container 638; and WGM to John T. Ernhard, March 5, 1921, McAdoo MSS, Container 511.

109. *NYT,* February 5, 1922, 2, 6:1, and February 4, 1923, 1, 8:1; and "Mr. McAdoo's Blunder," *New-York Tribune,* September 12, 1923, 12:2, Papers of James Purroy Mitchel, LOC MSS, Box 24, Folder 2.

110. Kerr, *American Railroad Politics,* passim; Kennedy, *Over Here,* 253; Skowronek, *Building a New American State,* 279; Higgs, *Crisis and Leviathan,* 145–147; Shook, *William G. McAdoo,* 3 and 380; Leuchtenburg, "New Deal and the Analogue of War," 81–143; and Schwarz, *New Dealers,* 19.

111. WGM to Willard D. Straight, October 20, 1918, McAdoo MSS, Container 212, File: "Oct. 20, 1918"; WGM to EWM, October 30, 1918, Wilson-McAdoo MSS, Container 1, File: "McAdoo, William G., 1918–23"; WGM to K. B. Conger, November 8, 1918, McAdoo MSS, Container 213, File: "Nov. 8, 1918"; Beaver, *Newton D. Baker,* 200; Cronon, ed., *Cabinet Diaries of Josephus Daniels,* 343; and Fleming, *Illusion of Victory,* 299.

112. Diary of Henry Fountain Ashurst, November 11, 1918, in Link, ed., *Papers of Woodrow Wilson,* 53:35; NDB to Pershing, November 15, 1918, Pershing Papers, LOC MSS, Container 18, File: "Baker, Newton D., 1918"; and WGM to Callan O'Laughlin, November 16, 1918, McAdoo MSS, Container 500-1, Part 1.

113. WGM to Wilson, November 14, 1918, and Wilson reply, November 24, 1918, McAdoo MSS, Container 525, File: "McAdoo to W. Wilson, Nov. 14, 1918"; *NYT,* November 23, 1918, 1:8 and 2; WGM to Edward M. House, January 7, 1919, in Link, ed., *Papers of Woodrow Wilson,* 53:646; WGM to Walker D. Hines, January 13, 1918, McAdoo MSS, Container 217, File: "Jan. 13, 1918"; and Wilson to WGM, January 30, 1919, McAdoo MSS, Container 217, File: "Jan. 30, 1919."

114. *NYT,* November 23, 1918, 10:1, *Los Angeles Times,* November 29, 1918, n.p., and *Los Angeles Express,* November 25, 1918, n.p., McAdoo MSS, Container 214, File: "Nov. 29, 1918"; *New-York Tribune,* November 23, 1918, McAdoo MSS, Container 630; and WGM to J. H. Kirkland et al., November 30, 1918, McAdoo MSS, Container 500-1, Part 1.

115. WGM, Speech at Chattanooga, November 28, 1918, McAdoo MSS, Container 564, File: "Speeches, 1918"; WGM to Edward M. House, November 29, 1918, McAdoo MSS, Container 214, File: "Nov. 29, 1918"; WGM, Speech at KTMS, Santa Barbara, October 31, 1937, Huntington-WGM MSS, Box 5, Folder 3; McAdoo MSS, Container 204, File: "May 13, 1918," Container 206, File: "June 14, 1918"; WGM to Franklin K. Lane, November 7, 1918, McAdoo MSS, Container 213, File: "Nov. 7, 1918"; and Dr. Frank E. Miller to WGM, June 16, 1918, McAdoo MSS, Container 207, File: "June 11, 1918."

116. Cronon, ed., *Cabinet Diaries of Josephus Daniels,* 342; Franklin K. Lane to WGM, n.d., McAdoo MSS, Container 214, File: "Nov. 1918—undated"; WGM to K. B. Conger, December 19, 1914, McAdoo MSS, Container 483-3; WGM to Edward B. Alford, January 24, 1916, McAdoo MSS, Container 489-1; WGM to Cleveland H. Dodge, January 24, 1917, McAdoo MSS, Container 492-3; Dodge to WGM, February 7, 1917, McAdoo MSS, Container 493-1; WGM to Dodge, February 7, 1917, McAdoo MSS, Container 174, File: "Feb. 7, 1917"; and WGM to W. H. Osborn, November 15, 1918, McAdoo MSS, Container 500-2.

117. WGM to Wilson, November 22, 1918, in Link, ed., *Papers of Woodrow Wilson,* 53:74; WGM to Stuart A. Gibboney, November 29, 1918, McAdoo MSS, Container 500-1, Part 1; *NYT,* November 25, 1918, 2:3; and WGM to John B. Elliot, Los Angeles Collector of Customs, November 18, 1918, McAdoo MSS, Container 213, File: "Nov. 18, 1918."

118. Schwarz, *Speculator*, 176; (Providence) *Daily Journal*, November 25, 1918; "From the Diary of Edward M. House, December 15, 1918," in Link, ed., *Papers of Woodrow Wilson*, 53:401; *New-York Tribune*, November 23, 1918; *NYT*, November 25, 1918, McAdoo MSS, Container 630; and "From the Diary of Edith Benham, December 22, 1918," in Link, ed., *Papers of Woodrow Wilson*, 53:469.

119. "From the Diary of Edith Benham, December 22, 1918," in Link, ed., *Papers of Woodrow Wilson*, 53:468.

120. WGM to NDB, July 10, 1923, Baker MSS, Container 152, File: "Mc, 1923."

121. "From the Diary of Edward M. House, August 18, 1918," in Link, ed., *Papers of Woodrow Wilson*, 49:207.

122. NDB to WGM and WGM reply, November 23 and December 2, 1918, McAdoo MSS, Container 214, File: "Dec. 2, 1918."

123. NDB to Wilson, November 23, 1918, in Link, ed., *Papers of Woodrow Wilson* 53:182; Bliss to NDB, December 9, 1918, Bliss Papers, Container 250, File: "Nov. 1918–March 1919"; Pershing to NDB, December 19, 1918, Pershing Papers, LOC MSS, Container 18, File: "Baker, Newton D., 1918"; and Beaver, *Newton D. Baker*, 240.

124. NDB to WGM, July 3, 1923, Baker MSS, Container 152, File: "Mc, 1923"; and Diary of Charles S. Hamlin, February 5, 1924, Hamlin Papers, LOC MSS, Diaries, Vol. VIII, Reel 2, 16. See also "From the Diary of Edith Benham, December 22, 1918," in Link, ed., *Papers of Woodrow Wilson*, 53:468; and WGM to Edward M. House, December 12, 1918, McAdoo MSS, Container 500-2.

CHAPTER 9: THE HEIR APPARENT, THE CROWN PRINCE,
AND WOODROW WILSON, 1918–1924

1. Steve Neal, *Happy Days are Here Again: The 1932 Democratic Convention, the Emergence of FDR—And How America Changed Forever* (New York: HarperCollins Publishers, Inc., 2004), 66.

2. Chambers, *To Raise an Army*, 253; Coffman, *War to End All Wars*, 357; Cuff, *War Industries Board*, 259; NDB to Bliss, January 20, 1919, Bliss Papers, LOC MSS, Container 250, File: "Newton D. Baker, March 1918–March 1920"; and NDB to Edward R. Stettinius, November 11 and 16, 1918, Baker MSS, Personal Correspondence 1916–1922, Reel 5.

3. Bliss to NDB, November 22, 1918, Bliss Papers, LOC MSS, Container 250, File: "Nov. 1918–March 1919."

4. Pershing to NDB, November 28, 1918, and NDB to Pershing, December 2, 1918, Baker MSS, Container 255, File: "1918"; and Wade, "Ralph A. Hayes," 233.

5. Cooke, *Pershing and his Generals*, 140–141; Fleming, *Illusion of Victory*, 357; and *NYT*, May 8, 1919, 8:2–4.

6. Lippmann to NDB, January 15, 1919, Baker MSS, General Correspondence 1916–1922, Reel 7; NDB to Pershing, December 2, 1918, Container 255, File: "1918"; NDB to D. C. Westenhaver, December 30, 1918, Baker MSS, Container 228, File: "We–Wg, 1922"; *NYT*, May 8, 1919, 8:2; Pershing to NDB, Cable, n.d., Pershing Papers, LOC MSS, Container 19, File: "Baker, Newton D., 1919"; and March, *Nation at War*, 106.

7. Tasker H. Bliss to John J. Pershing, October 8, 1919, Pershing to NDB, November 29, 1919, and Ralph Hayes to Colonel Quekemeyer, December 2, 1919, Pershing Papers, LOC MSS, Container 19, File: "Baker, Newton D., 1919"; Wade, "Ralph A. Hayes," 280–282; and Budreau, *Bodies of War*, 15–48 and 248, n. 7.

8. US Army Signal Corps, Telegram, Brest to Paris, March 10, 1919, Pershing Papers, LOC MSS, Container 19, File: "Baker, Newton D., 1918"; and *NYT*, May 8, 1919, 8.

9. NDB to Mrs. Casserly, November 15, 1924, Baker MSS, Container 50, File: "Nov. 15, 1924 letter to Mrs John B. Casserly"; Zieger, *America's Great War*, 190–193; Ray Stannard Baker, "Interview with Newton D. Baker, April 6, 1928," 14–15, Papers of Ray Stannard Baker, LOC MSS, Reel 71; and Cramer, *Newton D. Baker*, 118–121.

10. NDB to Walter I. McKenzie, April 12, 1924, Baker MSS, Container 190, File: "Mc, 1924"; and NDB to Ralph Hayes, December 24, 1929, Baker MSS, Container 115, File: "Ralph Hayes, 1929."

11. "E.R." to Pershing, February 28, 1918, and March 6, 1918, and NDB to Wilson, November 27, 1918, Papers of Ray Stannard Baker, LOC MSS, Reel 62.

12. NDB to Wilson, November 27, 1918, Papers of Ray Stannard Baker, LOC MSS, Reel 62; NDB to Wilson, May 8, 1919, Bliss Papers, LOC MSS, Container 245, File: "Newton D. Baker, Nov. 1918–Oct. 1919"; NDB to H. C. Pahnke, January 2, 1926, Baker MSS, Container 82, File: "Pa–Ph, 1925"; NDB to C. W. Ackerman, January 18, 1932, Baker MSS, Container 16, File: "Aa–Al, 1932"; and Zieger, *America's Great War*, 190–193.

13. See Weinstein, *Woodrow Wilson*, for Wilson's physical and mental condition after October 1919.

14. NDB to Charles W. Dabney, November 18, 1919, Baker MSS, Personal Correspondence 1916–1922, Reel 7; and Smith, *When the Cheering Stopped*, 115–119.

15. NDB to Tasker H. Bliss, October 18, 1919, Bliss Papers, LOC MSS, Container 250, File: "Newton D. Baker, March 1918–March 1920."

16. Breckinridge Long, "Diary—10, Jan. 1 1920–Nov. 2, 1920," Long Papers, LOC MSS, Container 2; Ray Stannard Baker, "Interview with Newton D. Baker, April 6, 1928," 30, Papers of Ray Stannard Baker, LOC MSS, Reel 71; and NDB to ELB, January 4, 1924, WRHA-Baker MSS, Acc. #3491, Container 3, Volume 1.

17. Walter Lippmann to NDB, June 9, 1919, and NDB reply, June 13, 1919, Baker MSS, Personal Correspondence 1916–1922, Reel 7; NDB to Dave Westenhaver, December 26, 1919, Baker MSS, Container 228, File: "We–Wg, 1919"; and NDB to Charles Warren, December 24, 1928, Baker MSS, Container 226, File: "Wa–Wd, 1928."

18. See Cooper, *Breaking the Heart of the World*, 234–329.

19. "A Memorandum by Robert Lansing, December 16, 1919," in Link, ed., *Papers of Woodrow Wilson*, 64:193. The underlining is Lansing's.

20. NDB to Charles Dabney, November 18, 1919, Baker MSS, Personal Correspondence 1916–1922, Reel 7; "World Leadership Lost, Says Baker," *NYT*, February 9, 1920, 3:4; NDB to Charles S. Hamlin, September 8, 1926, Hamlin Papers, LOC MSS, Container 347, File: "General Correspondence, 29 Jan. 1926–26 March 1927"; NDB to Lippmann, January 20, 1920, Baker MSS, Personal Correspondence 1916–1922, Reel 10; and Cooper, *Breaking the Heart of the World*, 330–375.

21. Harvey Ingham to NDB and NDB reply, May 22 and 26, 1919, Baker MSS, Personal Correspondence 1916–1922, Reel 7; and Slotkin, *Lost Battalions*, 260–261.

22. Slotkin, *Lost Battalions*, passim; *NYT*, November 8, 1919, 8:1; and Bryan, "Fighting for Respect," 3.

23. L. L. Burkhead to WGM, September 29, 1919, WGM to Woodrow Wilson, October 8, 1919, and NDB to Wilson, October 14, 1919, WRHA-NDB MSS, 3491, Container 2, Folder 3.

24. WGM to Wilson, May 15, 1920, McAdoo MSS, Container 526, File: "McAdoo to W. Wilson, May 15 1920"; Palmer to Wilson, April 19, 1920, in Link, ed., *Papers of Woodrow*

Wilson, 65:203–211; and Ernest Freeberg, *Democracy's Prisoner: Eugene V. Debs, the Great War, and the Right to Dissent* (Cambridge, Mass.: Harvard University Press, 2008), 224–255.

25. NDB to Wilson, March 26, 1920, in Link, ed., *Papers of Woodrow Wilson*, 65:126; Dawley, *Changing the World*, 265; and NDB to a delegation from the Socialist Convention, n.d., Baker MSS, Container 251, File: "Misc., 1918–19."

26. NDB to Walter Lippmann, July 24, 1920, Baker MSS, Personal Correspondence 1916–1922, Reel 10; "From the Diary of Josephus Daniels, 1920 Tuesday 10 August," in Link, ed., *Papers of Woodrow Wilson*, 66:25; and Freeberg, *Democracy's Prisoner*, 224–225 and 292–300.

27. Dickinson, *Building of an Army*, 330–374; and Skowronek, *Building a New American State*, 244.

28. In 1913 the US Army had 92,756 officers and men, and in 1916 it had 108,399 personnel: *Historical Statistics of the United States*, 1:1141. NDB to Elizabeth Hauser, September 18, 1919, Baker MSS, Container 111, File: "Har–Hd, 1922."

29. WGM to Cleveland Dodge, December 7, 1918, McAdoo MSS, Container 214, File: "Dec. 7, 1918."

30. George Franklin to WGM, December 17, 1918, McAdoo MSS, Container 215, File: "Dec. 17, 1918"; WGM to FHM, January 28, 1919, and February 2, 1919, McAdoo MSS, Container 58, Files: "Jan. 29–30, 1919" and "Feb. 1–2, 1919"; WGM to Dodge, December 7, 1918, McAdoo MSS, Container 214, File: "Dec. 7, 1918"; and Schwarz, *New Dealers*, 26.

31. See, for example, Daniels, *Wilson Era*, 2:553; Dos Passos, *Mr. Wilson's War*, 105; Schwarz, *New Dealers*, 24; and Kennedy, *Over Here*, 99. WGM to Ray Stannard Baker, May 10, 1929, Papers of Ray Stannard Baker, LOC MSS, Reel 79; and "From the Diary of Edward M. House, April 28, 1914, and May 24, 1916," in Link, ed., *Papers of Woodrow Wilson*, 29:531 and 37:105.

32. Axson, "*Brother Woodrow*," 217–219.

33. "From the Diary of Thomas W. Brahany, March 26, 1917," in Link, ed., *Papers of Woodrow Wilson*, 41:474.

34. EWM to Edith Bolling Wilson, October 16, 1936, and August 19, 1942, Papers of Edith Bolling Wilson, LOC MSS, Container 26, File: "Eleanor Wilson McAdoo, 1915–1961"; Miller, *Ellen and Edith*, 121 and 258; Levin, *Edith and Woodrow*, 109; Link, *Wilson*, 4:4–5; Wilson, *My Memoir*, 78; Levin, *Edith and Woodrow*, 160; Charles S. Hamlin, Diary, October 9, 1925, Hamlin Papers, LOC MSS, "Diaries," Vol. IX: 47, Reel 3; WGM to Francis B. Sayre, October 5, 1926, McAdoo MSS, Container 328, File: "Oct. 5, 1926," and Container 329, File: "Nov. 22, 1926"; Edith Bolling Wilson to WGM, March 24, 1928, and December 4, 1930, and WGM reply, December 18, 1930, McAdoo MSS, Container 66, File: "March 25, 1926," and Container 68, File: "Dec. 4, 1930"; and WGM to Helen Bones, December 29, 1938, and January 18, 1939, and WGM to Tumulty, January 9, 1939, McAdoo MSS, Container 468, Files: "Dec. 9, 1938," "Jan. 18, 1939," and "Jan. 9, 1939."

35. WGM to Douglas Fairbanks, October 6, 1919, McAdoo MSS, Container 224, File: "Oct. 6, 1919"; WGM to C. S. Jackson, October 17, 1919, McAdoo MSS, Container 225, File: "Oct. 17, 1919"; and WGM to Frank I. Cobb, November 12, 1920, McAdoo MSS, Container 509.

36. WGM to John P. Dwyer, December 8, 1920, McAdoo MSS, Container 245, File: "Dec. 8, 1920"; and WGM to NDB, October 10, 1921, McAdoo MSS, Container 515, Vol. 23(1).

Only nine letters sent by McAdoo to Wilson between December 1918 and July 1919 are preserved in McAdoo MSS, Container 526: "Woodrow Wilson Correspondence." See "Politics: The Watchman," *Los Angeles Times*, September 26, 1919, 6, for gossip that McAdoo and Wilson were personally distant, if not estranged.

37. WGM to Mrs. J. Borden Harriman, November 9, 1919, Harriman Papers, LOC MSS, Container 31, File: "McAdoo, William Gibbs, 1919–1931."

38. WGM to Cary Grayson, February 13, 1920, McAdoo MSS, Container 503.

39. WGM to Wilson, May 14, 1920, McAdoo MSS, Container 234, File: "May 14, 1920."

40. WGM to Jouett Shouse, January 22, 1926, McAdoo MSS, Container 322, File: "Jan. 22, 1926."

41. Shouse to WGM, January 7, 1918, McAdoo MSS, Container 194, File: "Jan. 7, 1918." See also J. H. Fleming to WGM, March 18, 1918, McAdoo MSS, Container 199, File: "Mar. 18, 1918"; Isidore B. Dockweiler to WGM, February 3, 1919, McAdoo MSS, Container 217, File: "Feb. 3, 1919"; R. M. Barton to WGM, November 25, 1919, McAdoo MSS, Container 226, File: "Nov. 25, 1919"; Harriman, *From Pinafores to Politics*, 327; Baruch, *Public Years*, 173; and Charles C. Goetsch and Margaret L. Shivers, eds., *The Autobiography of Thomas L. Chadbourne* (New York: Oceana Publications Inc., 1985), 166.

42. See John B. Elliot to WGM, October 15, 1919, McAdoo MSS, Container 225, File: "Oct. 15, 1919"; Antoinette Funk to WGM, April 3, 1919, McAdoo MSS, Container 219, File: "Apr. 3, 1919"; Daniel C. Roper to WGM, October 28, 1919, McAdoo MSS, Container 225, File: "Oct. 28, 1919"; Jouett Shouse to WGM, August 12, 1919, McAdoo MSS, Container 223, File: "Aug. 12, 1919"; Robert W. Woolley to WGM, August 14, 1919, McAdoo MSS, Container 223, File: "Aug. 14, 1919"; Wesley M. Bagby, "William Gibbs McAdoo and the 1920 Presidential Nomination," *East Tennessee Historical Society's Publications* 31 (1959): 43–58, 47; Schwarz, *Speculator*, 178; and WGM to the Editor of *Labor*, March 30, 1920, McAdoo MSS, Container 232, File: "Mar. 30, 1920."

43. "If He Were President: William Gibbs McAdoo," *The Independent*, November 29, 1919, McAdoo MSS, Container 567, File: "Articles, 1910–32"; WGM to Homer S. Cummings, January 4, 1920, McAdoo MSS, Container 227, File: "Jan. 4, 1920"; WGM to G. W. Whitford, March 24, 1920, McAdoo MSS, Container 231, File: "Mar. 24, 1920"; WGM to C. A. Lyman, April 19, 1920, McAdoo MSS, Container 505; and WGM to Thomas B. Love, June 24, 1920, McAdoo MSS, Container 237, File: "June 24, 1920."

44. Bagby, "William Gibbs McAdoo," 57; Axson, *"Brother Woodrow,"* 198; "From the Diary of Edward M. House, January 27, 1918," in Link, ed., *Papers of Woodrow Wilson*, 46:116; Daniels, *Wilson Era*, 2:553; Levin, *Edith and Woodrow*, 447; Grayson quoted in Weinstein, *Woodrow Wilson*, 366; and Tumulty, *Woodrow Wilson*, 494.

45. Robert W. Woolley to WGM, August 14, 1919, McAdoo MSS, Container 223, File: "August 14, 1919"; "Politics is Hell," chapter 41, Papers of Robert W. Woolley, LOC MSS, Container 44; R. M. Barton to WGM, January 12, 1920, McAdoo MSS, Container 228, File: "Jan. 12, 1920"; Irwin Hood Hoover, *Forty-Two Years in the White House* (Boston: Houghton Mifflin Company, 1934), 106; Wilson to Joseph Tumulty, June 2, 1919, in Link, ed., *Papers of Woodrow Wilson*, 60:41; Bagby, "William Gibbs McAdoo" 43–45; Cary T. Grayson, *Woodrow Wilson: An Intimate Memoir* (Washington, D.C.: Potomac Books Inc., 1960), 116; "From the Diary of Homer S. Cummings, Monday May 31, 1920," in Link, ed., *Papers of Woodrow Wilson*, 65:344–350; NDB to A. S. Burleson, April 23, 1926, Baker MSS, Container 48, File:

"Bu–Bz, 1926"; and Wilson, "Random Notes, c. June 10, 1920," in Link, ed., *Papers of Woodrow Wilson*, 65:382.

46. Bagby, "William Gibbs McAdoo," 43; WGM to Miller S. Bell, February 17, 1920, McAdoo MSS, Container 605; WGM to Thomas B. Love, January 26, 1920, McAdoo MSS, Container 503; WGM to John B. Elliot, January 8, 1920, McAdoo MSS, Container 228, File: "Jan. 8, 1920"; "Statement of W. G. McAdoo at the Request of The United Press," March 24, 1920, McAdoo MSS, Container 231, File: "Mar. 24, 1920"; WGM to Janet A. Fairbanks, March 31, 1920, McAdoo MSS, Container 232, File: "Mar. 3, 1920"; WGM to Dixon C. Williams, February 7, 1920, McAdoo MSS, Container 229, File: "Feb. 7, 1920"; and WGM to Herbert Quick, January 29, 1920, McAdoo MSS, Container 503.

47. On Hoover, see WGM to John H. O'Neil, December 30, 1919, McAdoo MSS, Container 227, File: "Dec. 30, 1919"; WGM to Daniel C. Roper, January 15, 1920, McAdoo MSS, Container 501-1; and WGM to Labart St. Clair, March 7, 1920, McAdoo MSS, Container 504. On NDB, see Baruch to WGM and WGM reply, July 15 and August 20, 1919, McAdoo MSS, Container 223, File: "Aug. 20, 1919." On Palmer, see WGM to Thomas Ball, June 24, 1920, McAdoo MSS, Container 137, File: "June 24, 1920"; NYT, November 26, 1919, 3:1; Bagby, "William Gibbs McAdoo," 47; Josephus Daniels to George Foster Peabody, June 9, 1920, Daniels Papers, LOC MSS, Container 673, File: "Elections, 1920: May–Sept."; and on Cox, see WGM to Herbert Quick, January 23, 1920, McAdoo MSS, Container 228, File: "Jan. 23, 1920"; and WGM to W. D. Jamieson, July 7, 1920, McAdoo MSS, Container 507.

48. Albert S. Burleson to WGM, May 16 and 23, 1920, McAdoo MSS, Container 234, File: May 16, 1920," and Container 235, File: "May 23, 1920"; John Skelton Williams to WGM, April 1, 1920, McAdoo MSS, Container 232, File: "Apr. 1, 1920"; and Bagby, "William Gibbs McAdoo," 49.

49. NYT, June 13, 1920, 2, 6:1, and June 29, 1920, 1:4; WGM to Charlton G. Ogburn, March 7, 1920, McAdoo MSS, Container 230, File: "March 7, 1920"; Jouett Shouse to WGM, April 3, 1920, McAdoo MSS, Container 232, File: "Apr. 3, 1920"; Bruce Barton to WGM, January 12, 1920, McAdoo MSS, Container 228, File: "Jan. 12, 1920"; and Funk to WGM, April 3, 1920, McAdoo MSS, Container 232, File: "Apr. 3, 1920."

50. NDB to George F. Peabody, August 19, 1919, Baker MSS, Personal Correspondence 1916–1922, Reel 8; and NDB to D. C. Westenhaver, November 13, 1919, Baker MSS, Container 228, File: "We–Wg, 1922."

51. NDB to George F. Peabody, August 19, 1919, Baker MSS, Personal Correspondence 1916–1922, Reel 8; NDB to Lippmann, August 11, 1920, Baker MSS, Personal Correspondence 1916–1922, Reel 10; and Lippmann, *Men of Destiny*, 113–119.

52. NDB to Carter Glass, January 10, 1920, Baker MSS, Personal Correspondence 1916–1922, Reel 9; and NDB to D. C. Westenhaver, July 9, 1920, Baker MSS, Container 228, File: "We–Wg, 1922."

53. Julia Davis and Dolores E. Fleming, eds., *The Ambassadorial Diary of John W. Davis: The Court of St. James', 1918–1921* (Morgantown: West Virginia University Press, 1993), 107; NYT, May 19, 1920, 3:1, May 24, 1920, 3:4, and May 31, 1920, 2:3; *Independent Post* (N.Y.), November 28, 1919, 1, McAdoo MSS, Container 637; Robert Woolley to Daniel C. Roper, January 5, 1920, Woolley Papers, LOC MSS, Container 18, File: "Roper, Hon. Daniel C. 1917–1920"; *The Independent*, November 29, 1919, n.p., McAdoo MSS, File 567; WGM to W. H. Thomas, July 12, 1920, McAdoo MSS, Container 507; Jas F. Williamson to

WGM, June 1, 1920, McAdoo MSS, Container 235, File: "June 1, 1920"; McAdoo MSS, Container 508; and WGM to Mary Synon, July 2, 1920, Container 239, File: "Jul. 21, 1920."

54. "From the Shorthand Diary of Charles Lee Swem, 17 May 1920," in Link, ed., *Papers of Woodrow Wilson*, 65:291; WGM to EWM, January 5, 1920, Wilson-McAdoo MSS, Container 1, File: "McAdoo, William G., 1918–23"; and WGM to Cary T. Grayson, February 14, 1920, McAdoo MSS, Container 229, File: "Feb. 14, 1920."

55. WGM to EWM, May 5, 1920, Wilson-McAdoo MSS, Container 1, File: "McAdoo, William G., 1918–23." The underlining is WGM's.

56. WGM to Wilson, May 14, 1920, McAdoo MSS, Container 234, File: "May 14, 1920."

57. WGM to Jouett Shouse, June 18, 1920, McAdoo MSS, Container 236, File: "June 17, 1920"; Bagby, "William Gibbs McAdoo," 50; William McAdoo to WGM, June 23, 1920, McAdoo MSS, Container 237, File: "June 23, 1920"; WGM to Norman Hapgood, June 19, 1920, McAdoo MSS, Container 236, File: "June 19, 1920"; *NYT*, June 19, 1920, 1:8, and June 20, 1920, 2, 2:2; WGM to Charles A. Lyerly, August 3, 1920, McAdoo MSS, Container 239, File: "Aug. 3, 1920"; and WGM to Guy M. Bryan, August 7, 1920, McAdoo MSS, Container 240, File: "Aug. 7, 1920."

58. "A Memorandum by Carter Glass," in Link, ed., *Papers of Woodrow Wilson*, 65:435; Ralph Wammack to WGM, June 26, 1920, McAdoo MSS, Container 237, File: "June 26, 1920"; WGM to Harriet McAdoo, July 1, 1920, McAdoo MSS, Container 59, File: "Jul. 1–2, 1920"; and Bagby, "William Gibbs McAdoo," 53–54.

59. NDB to Walter Lippmann, July 15, 1920, Baker MSS, Personal Correspondence 1916–1922, Reel 10; Robert Woolley to Jouett Shouse, June 19, 1920, Woolley Papers, LOC MSS, Container 18, File: "Shouse, Hon. Jowett, 1914–1920"; and "Politics is Hell," chapter 41, Woolley Papers, LOC MSS, Container 44.

60. Antoinette Funk to WGM, June 21, 1920, McAdoo MSS, Container 237, File: "June 21, 1920"; Funk to WGM, July 6, 1920, McAdoo MSS, Container 238, File: "Jul. 6, 1920"; Bagby, "William Gibbs McAdoo," 56; David Burner, *The Politics of Provincialism: The Democratic Party in Transition, 1918–1932* (New York: Alfred A. Knopf, 1970), 59–63; and "From the Shorthand Diary of Charles Lee Swem, c. July 6 1920," in Link, ed., *Papers of Woodrow Wilson*, 65:499.

61. WGM to Funk, July 6, 1920, McAdoo MSS, Container 238, File: "Jul. 6, 1920"; WGM to S. R. Bertron, July 7, 1920, McAdoo MSS, Container 507; Bagby, "William Gibbs McAdoo," 43; Burner, *Politics of Provincialism*, 61; Cooper, *Breaking the Heart of the World*, 385; Craig, *After Wilson*, 16; *NYT*, July 7, 1920, 5:2; WGM to John B. Elliot, July 14, 1920, McAdoo MSS, Container 507; and Synon to WGM, July 6, 1920, McAdoo MSS, Container 238, File: "Jul. 6, 1920."

62. WGM to Mrs. Kellogg Fairbanks, July 15, 1920, McAdoo MSS, Container 238, File: "Jul. 15, 1920"; "Statement by W. G. McAdoo," July 29, 1920, McAdoo MSS, Container 239, File: "Jul. 29, 1920"; WGM to Richard S. Whaley, July 22, 1920, McAdoo MSS, Container 507; WGM to Wilson, October 2, 1920, McAdoo MSS, Container 526, File: "McAdoo to W. Wilson, Oct. 2, 1920"; WGM to Robert McAdoo, November 3, 1920, McAdoo MSS, Container 60, File: "Nov. 3–4, 1920"; WGM to Robert Woolley, November 3, 1920, McAdoo MSS, Container 509; and Carl E. Russell, Jas F. Moore, and Chas J. Long to WGM, November 2, 1920, McAdoo MSS, Container 243, File: "Nov. 2, 1920."

63. NDB to Ralph Hayes and NDB to Jesse W. Woodward, November 5, 1920, Baker MSS, Miscellaneous Personal Correspondence 1916–1921, Reel 13; and *NYT*, March 7, 1920, 10:7, and March 11, 1920, 5:4.

64. NDB to Ralph Hayes, July 28, 1934, Baker MSS, Container 117, File: "Ralph Hayes, 1934"; NDB to Solomon B. Griffin, November 29, 1922, Baker MSS, Personal Correspondence 1916–1922, Reel 12; and Daniels, *Wilson Era*, 2:172.

65. NDB to Calvin Coolidge, October 2, 1923, Coolidge to NDB, October 4, 1923, NDB et al. to Calvin Coolidge, November 28, 1923, Baker MSS, Container 191, File: "Pr–Pz, 1923"; Wilder H. Haines to NDB, December 1, 1923, and NDB to Haines, December 5, 1923, Baker MSS, Container 109, File: "Haa–Haq, 1923"; NDB to Irita Van Doren, May 9, 1924, Baker MSS, Container 224, File: "V, 1924"; and NDB to Roger Baldwin, March 30, 1929, Baldwin to NDB, April 3, 1924, and NDB to Baldwin, April 7, 1929, Baker MSS, Container 257, Files: "1929—March" and "1929—April."

66. For an affectionate account of Baker's style and achievements as secretary of war, see Frederick P. Keppel, "Newton D. Baker," in *Foreign Affairs* (April 1938), Pershing Papers, LOC MSS, Container 19, File: "Baker, Newton D., 1921-"; MacArthur to NDB, March 2, 1921, Baker MSS, Personal Correspondence 1916–1922, Reel 12; Cramer, *Newton D. Baker*, 163; Albert G. Ingalls to NDB, February 5, 1931, Baker MSS, Container 124, File: "I, 1931"; and *NYT*, March 15, 1929, 24:1.

67. Hagerdorn, *Leonard Wood*, 2:264; Palmer, *Newton D. Baker*, 2:161; and Villard, *Fighting Years*, 249.

68. Frank B. Davis to NDB and NDB reply, February 11 and 12, 1924, and NDB to Davis, Container 82, File: "Da–Dh, 1924."

69. Wilson to NDB, September 11, 1922, in Link, ed., *Papers of Woodrow Wilson*, 68:133; MacArthur to NDB, November 14, 1922, Baker MSS, Container 262, File: "Nov. 1922 Britannica"; and WGM to NDB, October 2, 1922, Baker MSS, Container 152, File: "Mc, 1922."

70. See Baker MSS, Containers 114 and 262, for copies of the letters sent on Baker's behalf. W. J. Cox to Leonard Ayers, March 30, 1928, Baker MSS, Container 262, File: "1927–1928: Britannica"; *NYT*, February 5, 1923, 32:3, July 3, 1924, 15:3, and November 19, 1926, 13:5; and NDB to J. L. Aasmed, December 22, 1923, Baker MSS, Container 16, File: "Aa–Al, 1923."

71. Beaver, "Newton D. Baker," 45.

72. NDB to Wilson, May 29, 1921, in Link, ed., *Papers of Woodrow Wilson*, 67:295. The underlining is NDB's. NDB to ELB, January 4, 1924, WRHA-NDB MSS, Acc. #3491, Container 3, Vol. 1.

73. *NYT*, March 2, 1922, 1:2; and WGM to NDB, April 29, 1922, Baker MSS, Container 152, File: "Mc, 1922."

74. George T. Webb to WGM, April 4, 1922, McAdoo MSS, Container 262, File: "Apr. 4, 1922"; Oscar W. Price to WGM, April 24, 1922, McAdoo MSS, Container 263, File: "Apr. 24, 1922"; and Robert E. Hennings, "California Democratic Politics in the Period of Republican Ascendancy," *Pacific Historical Review* 31, no. 3 (August 1962): 267–280, 269.

75. EWM to Wilson, March 2, 1922, in Link, ed., *Papers of Woodrow Wilson*, 57:562.

76. See Wilson to WGM, September 7, 1922, WGM to Wilson, December 19, 1922, and Wilson to WGM, December 26, 1922, in Link, ed., *Papers of Woodrow Wilson*, 68:129, 239, and 240, and McAdoo MSS, Container 526, for examples of their correspondence. WGM to Edith Bolling Wilson, March 26, 1928, Edith Bolling Wilson Papers, LOC MSS, Container 26, File: "Wm. G. McAdoo, 1926–1930."

77. "Statement of Honorable W. G. McAdoo," February 4, 1924, McAdoo MSS, Container 294, File: "Feb. 4, 1924"; and *NYT*, June 30, 1924, 14:3.

CHAPTER 10: LAWYERS AND BUSINESSMEN

1. WGM to NDB, March 9, 1921, Baker MSS, Personal Correspondence 1916–1922, Reel 12.

2. NDB to Hon. Willie Vickery, May 19, 1916, Baker MSS, Letterbooks, Reel 16. NDB quoted in Palmer, *Newton D. Baker*, 1:245.

3. NDB to M. P. Klingel, May 18, 1926, Baker MSS, Container 138, File: "Ki–Kq, 1926"; Thomas Sidlo to Stanley King, September 4, 1918, Baker MSS, Miscellaneous Correspondence 1916–1921, Reel 12; Cramer, *Newton D. Baker*, 171; NDB to Thomas Sidlo, July 27, 1916, Baker MSS, Letterbooks, Reel 16; NDB to George Henry Paine, April 11, 1935, Baker MSS, Container 184, File: "Pa–Ph, 1935"; and NDB to Joseph Musgrave, June 19, 1936, Baker MSS, Container 159, File: "Mo–Mx, 1936."

4. www.ech.case.edu/ech-cgi/article.pl?id=BH. For Baker and Hostetler's website, see www.bakerlaw.com/.

5. WGM, "list of retainers," McAdoo MSS, Container 216, File: "Jan. 1, 1919"; WGM to Stuart Gibboney, February 2, 1919, McAdoo MSS, Container 217, File: "Feb. 2, 1919"; *New York Telegram*, July 17, 1923, 1, McAdoo MSS, Container 642; "Ledger for Retainers 1919," UCLA-WGM MSS, Box 4; WGM to Bernard Baruch, March 22, 1919, McAdoo MSS, Container 218, File: "Mar. 22, 1919"; WGM to FHM, January 28, 1919, McAdoo MSS, Container 58, File: "Jan. 29–30, 1919"; McAdoo MSS, Container 218, File: "Mar. 13, 1919"; "Ledger, 1919," UCLA-WGM MSS, Box 4; "Various Statements of Firm, Jan. 1, 1920–May 29, 1920," UCLA-WGM MSS, Box 14; and WGM to Collector of Internal Revenue, New York, December 13, 1920, McAdoo MSS, Container 510.

6. McAdoo MSS, Container 265, File: "June 16, 1922"; Schwarz, *Speculator*, 170; WGM to GEC, December 30, 1918, McAdoo MSS, Container 216, File: "Dec. 30, 1918"; WGM to Owen D. Young, January 15, 1920, McAdoo MSS, Container 501-1; and WGM to Young, March 1, 1922, McAdoo MSS, Container 261, File: "March 1, 1922."

7. WGM to Douglas Fairbanks, April 2, 1920, McAdoo MSS, Container 501-2; L. R. Hoover to John Fairbanks, June 24, 1920, McAdoo MSS, Container 501-2; WGM to Dix W. Smith, October 13, 1921, McAdoo MSS, Container 515, Vol. 23(1); WGM to Urey Woodson, February 4, 1922, McAdoo MSS, Container 260, File: "Feb. 4, 1922"; *New York Telegram*, July 17, 1923, 1, McAdoo MSS, Container 642; *New York World*, April 30, 1923, McAdoo MSS, Container 277, File: "Apr. 30, 1923"; WGM to Leslie C. Garnett, June 28, 1923, WGM to Cary Grayson, June 28, 1923, and WGM to Joseph H. O'Neill, June 29, 1923, McAdoo MSS, Container 279, File: "June 28, 1923"; *NYT*, March 1, 1924, 1:7; *The World* (N.Y.) to WGM, February 26, 1924, McAdoo MSS, Container 296, File: "Feb. 26, 1924"; WGM to H. D. Jacobs, December 19, 1921, McAdoo MSS, Container 515; WGM to John Clifton Elder, November 26, 1920, McAdoo MSS, Container 510; and WGM to Wilson, June 2, 1922, in Link, ed., *Papers of Woodrow Wilson*, 68:72.

8. WGM to Edward L. Doheny, February 15 and 17, 1921, McAdoo MSS, Container 248, Files: "Feb. 15, 1921" and "Feb. 17, 1921"; WGM to President Obregon of Mexico, December 21, 1920, McAdoo MSS, Container 245, File: "Dec. 21, 1920"; and Joseph P. Tumulty to WGM, November 20, 1919, McAdoo MSS, Container 526, File: "McAdoo to W. Wilson, Nov. 20 & 21, 1919."

9. WGM, Press Release, February 22, 1924, McAdoo MSS, Container 297, File: "Feb. 27, 1924"; *NYT*, February 28, 1924, 1:7, 3:5; and David H. Stratton, "Splattered with Oil: William G. McAdoo and the 1924 Presidential Nomination," *Southwestern Social Science Quarterly* 44, no. 1 (June 1963): 62–75, 69. On McAdoo's work before the Departments of War and Navy and the USRRA, see McAdoo MSS, Containers 501-2 and 501-1; WGM to Carl R. Gray, Union Pacific Railroad, January 22, 1920, McAdoo MSS, Container 501-2; WGM to Ambassador from Chile, January 26, 1920, McAdoo MSS, Container 503; WGM to General Marlborough Churchill, War Department, January 8, 1920, McAdoo MSS, Container 501-2; WGM to Josephus Daniels, October 24, 1919, McAdoo MSS, Special Correspondence, Reel 56; and *NYT*, April 20, 1924, 1:5 and 2:4.

10. *The Nation* 118 (February 27 and March 5, 1924): 217 and 244.

11. Frankfurter to NDB, March 10, 1924, and NDB reply, March 12, 1924, Baker MSS, Container 100, File: "Fr–Fz, 1924"; NDB to George Foster Peabody, February 13, 1924, Baker MSS, Container 185, File: "George Foster Peabody, 1924"; and NDB to Orrin S. Good, May 21, 1929, Baker MSS, Container 103, File: "Gi–Gq, 1929."

12. McAdoo MSS, Containers 503, 508, and 514.

13. WGM to EWM, October 31, 1919, Wilson-McAdoo MSS, File: "McAdoo, William G."; and UCLA-WGM MSS, Box 11, File: "Federal Farm Loan System—Argument of WGM, October 30, 1919." Van Valkenburgh's decision was upheld by the Supreme Court: *Smith v. Kansas City Title and Trust Company* (1921), 255 US 180.

14. WGM to J. S. Wannamaker, January 19, 1922, McAdoo MSS, Container 259, File: "Jan. 17, 1922"; and WGM to Edward M. House, May 7, 1923, McAdoo MSS, Container 277, File: "May 7 1923."

15. NDB to ELB, December 7–8 and 14, 1929, WRHA-NDB MSS, Acc. #3491, Container 1, Folder 5.

16. NDB to ELB, February 27, 1906, WRHA-NDB MSS, Acc. #3491, Container 1, Folder 1; and Cramer, *Newton D. Baker*, 172.

17. Weiner, *Lake Effects*, 158; NDB to O. P. Van Sweringen, October 31, 1926, Baker MSS, Container 224, File: "V., 1926"; and Baker MSS, Container 225, Files: "V., 1928" and "Messrs O. P. and M. J. Van Sweringen, 1931."

18. "Memorandum, March 23, 1960, to "Bill" (William Bevis), WRHA-NDB MSS, Acc. #4564, Container 3, Folder 23.

19. R. T. Jackson, "Memorandum to Mr. Bemis," July 11 and 18, 1960, WRHA-NDB MSS, Acc. #4564, Container 3, Folder 23; *NYT*, January 25, 1933, 12:5; "Freedom of the Press: Argument of Newton D. Baker before the Court of Common Pleas, Cuyahoga County, Ohio, July 16, 1929," Baker MSS, Container 263, File: "1916–1934 Articles: Newton D. Baker"; *New-York Tribune*, July 29, 1929, and the *Pantograph* (Bloomington, Ill.), August 10, 1929, Baker MSS, Container 265, File: "Clippings—Cleveland Contempt Case, 1929"; and Cramer, *Newton D. Baker*, 171–186.

20. R. T. Jackson, "Memorandum to Mr. Bemis," July 11 and 18, 1960, WRHA-NDB MSS, Acc. #4564, Container 3, Folder 23; *NYT*, January 25, 1933, 12:5; NDB to Frank Baker, July 31, 1931, WRHA-NDB MSS, Acc. #3491, Container 2, Folder 2; NDB to George Peek, December 7, 1933, and Peek reply, December 9, 1933, and Ralph Hayes to NDB, February 9, 1934, Baker MSS, Container 262, File: "Sugar Processing Tax"; NDB to Urban A. Wernet, June 2, 1936, Baker MSS, Container 230, File: "We–Wg, 1936"; and R. T. Jackson, "Re: Doctor Kramer's attached letter and redraft of chapter X of his biography of Mr. Baker, July 18, 1960," WRHA-NDB MSS, Acc. #4564, Container 3, Folder 23.

21. Cramer, *Newton D. Baker*, 181–183; and *NYT*, April 27, 1930, 20:8.

22. NDB to Ralph Hayes, May 26, 1930, and Hayes reply, May 28, 1930, NDB to Hayes May 28, 1930, and Hayes reply, June 3, 1930, Baker MSS, Container 115, File: "Ralph Hayes, 1930."

23. NDB to Mrs. W. R. Atherton, November 23, 1935, Baker MSS, Container 33, File: "As–Az, 1935"; NDB to ELB, March 15, 1937, WRHA-NDB MSS, Acc. #3491, Container 2, Folder 1; and Cramer, *Newton D. Baker*, 173.

24. "Mirrors of Cleveland: Newton D. Baker," *The Cleveland Press*, January 17, 1922, Baker MSS, Personal Correspondence 1916–1922, Reel 12; and *NYT*, July 9, 1933, 2, 1:5.

25. W. H. Bemis to R. T. Jackson and Mr. Fiery, April 15, 1960, and "Memorandum to Bill (William Bemis)," March 23, 1960, WRHA-NDB MSS, Acc. #4564, Container 3, Folder 23. See Owen D. Young to NDB, May 27, 1925, for an example of NDB's submission of a "ridiculously low" bill: Baker MSS, Container 242, File: "X-Y-Z, 1925."

26. George Foster Peabody to NDB, December 20, 1934, and NDB reply, December 24, 1934, and NDB to Peabody, March 17, 1935, Baker MSS, Container 186, Files: "George Foster Peabody," 1934 and 1935.

27. Lynn Dumenil, "Women's Reform Organizations and Wartime Mobilization in World War I-Era Los Angeles," *Journal of the Gilded Age and Progressive Era* 10, no. 2 (April 2011): 213–245, 218.

28. Thomas M. Storke, *California Editor* (Los Angeles: Westernlore Press, 1958), 239ff.; WGM to E. F. Curry, November 24, 1922, McAdoo MSS, Container 271, File: "Nov. 24, 1922"; A. P. Giannini to WGM, December 31, 1921, McAdoo MSS, Container 258, File: "Dec. 31, 1919"; WGM to A. P. Giannini, January 6 and 28, 1922, and Giannini reply, January 30, 1922, McAdoo MSS, Container 259.

29. A. P. Giannini to WGM, December 31, 1921, McAdoo MSS, Container 258, File: "Dec. 31, 1922"; WGM to Baruch, April 10 and March 24, 1922, McAdoo MSS, Container 262; WGM to Doheny, October 12, 1922, McAdoo MSS, Container 269, File: "Oct. 12, 1922"; WGM to Daniel C. Roper, May 9, 1923, McAdoo MSS, Container 277, File: "May 9, 1922"; and William H. Neblett to WGM, July 21, 1924, McAdoo MSS, Container 307, File: "July 21, 1924."

30. WGM to E. J. Feuling, September 28, 1926, McAdoo MSS, Container 328, File: "Sept. 28, 1926"; Peter O. Knight to WGM and WGM reply, March 12 and 21, 1925, McAdoo MSS, Container 314, File: "Mar. 21, 1925"; WGM to Tom Chadbourne, November 17, 1924, McAdoo MSS, Container 309, File: "Nov. 16, 1924"; Neblett to WGM, April 24, 1926, McAdoo MSS, Container 325, File: "Apr. 24, 1926"; and WGM to David Blankenhorn, June 9, 1925, McAdoo MSS, Container 316, File: "Jun. 9, 1926."

31. McAdoo MSS, Container 325, File: "Apr. 24, 1926"; WGM to R. P. Williams, May 28, 1930, McAdoo MSS, Container 351, File: "May 28, 1930"; WGM to Mrs. Hancock Banning, April 1926, McAdoo MSS, Container 325, File: "April 1926—undated"; and the Los Angeles *Examiner*, March 15, 1925: 20, McAdoo MSS, Container 314, File: "Mar. 18, 1925."

32. WGM to Leo S. Rowe, October 31, 1924, McAdoo MSS, Container 308, File: "Oct. 31, 1924"; WGM to Dillon, Read, September 26, 1924, McAdoo MSS, Container 307, File: "Sept. 26, 1924"; Dillon, Read to WGM, April 2, 1925, Robert S. Freedman to WGM, April 9, 1925, WGM to Dillon, Read, April 16, 1925, Dillon, Read to WGM, April 23, 1924, Dillon, Read to WGM, April 26, 1925, McAdoo MSS, Container 314, File: "Apr. 2, 1925"; Dillon, Read to WGM, September 30, 1925, McAdoo MSS, Container 319, File: "Sept. 30, 1925";

and WGM to Dillon, Read, February 28 and July 11, 1928, McAdoo MSS, Containers 338 and 339.

33. WGM to H. P. Wilson, February 26, 1927, McAdoo MSS, Container 332, File: "Feb. 26, 1927"; and Wilson to WGM, March 23, 1927, McAdoo MSS, Container 333, File: "Mar. 23, 1927."

34. *NYT,* May 16, 1927, 23:2.

35. WGM to EWM, February 2, 1928 (the underlining is WGM's), Wilson-McAdoo-MSS, Container 2, File: "McAdoo, William G., Jan.–Feb. 1928"; Clagett to WGM, November 1, 1929, McAdoo MSS, Container 347, File: "November 1, 1929"; and WGM to Clagett, January 29, 1930, McAdoo MSS, Container 348, File: "Jan. 29, 1930."

36. McAdoo MSS, Container 86, File: "Personal Miscellany—Financial"; WGM to Brice Clagett, March 12, 1931, McAdoo MSS, Container 357, File: "Mar. 12, 1931"; and Clagett to WGM, March 16, 1929, McAdoo MSS, Container 342, File: "Mar. 16, 1929."

37. WGM to Clagett and H. P. Wilson, March 31, 1931, McAdoo MSS, Container 357, File: "Mar. 31, 1931"; WGM to Clagett, May 4, 1931, McAdoo MSS, Container 358, File: "May 4, 1931"; WGM to H. P. Wilson, February 1, 1933, McAdoo MSS, Container 382, File: "April 7, 1933"; Clagett to WGM, February 24, 1932, McAdoo MSS, Container 365, File: "Feb. 24, 1932"; Neblett to WGM, May 9, 1933, McAdoo MSS, Container 383, File: "May 9, 1933"; E. D. Flaherty to WGM, May 11, 1933, WGM, "Personal Ledger, 1926–1936," UCLA-WGM MSS, Box 14; and "McAdoo, Neblett, and Clagett: Final Accounts," McAdoo MSS, Container 383, File: "May 11, 1933."

38. WGM to Cummings and Cummings reply, July 23 and 29, 1933, McAdoo MSS, Container 386, Files: "July 23, 1933" and "July 29, 1933"; and WGM to Clagett, August 31, 1933, McAdoo MSS, Container 387, File: "Aug. 31, 1933."

39. McAdoo MSS, Container 86, File: "Personal Miscellany—Financial Summaries," Neblett to WGM, June 3, 1935, McAdoo MSS, Container 406, File: "June 5, 1936"; E. D. Flaherty to WGM, April 24, 1936, McAdoo MSS, Container 420, File: "Apr. 24, 1936"; WGM to Neblett, February 7, 1934, McAdoo MSS, Container 391, File: "Feb. 7, 1934"; and McAdoo, Neblett, and Warner, "Profit and Loss, Fees: Year 1936," McAdoo MSS, Container 433, File: "Apr. 7, 1937."

40. *Los Angeles Herald,* September 25, 1937, and WGM to Joseph B. Keenan, September 29, 1937, McAdoo MSS, Container 442, Files: "Sept. 25, 1937" and "Sept. 29, 1937"; Neblett to WGM, February 9, 1938, McAdoo MSS, Container 449, File: "Feb. 9, 1938"; Neblett to WGM, April 7, 1939, McAdoo MSS, Container 469, File: "Apr. 7, 1939"; WGM to Hon. Paul J. McCormick, February 21, 1938, McAdoo MSS, Container 448, File: "Feb. 21, 1938"; and WGM to Marie Harrison, July 13, 1938, Huntington-WGM MSS, Container 5, Folder 56.

41. WGM to John Dickinson, August 12, 1929, McAdoo MSS, Container 350, File: "Aug. 12, 1929."

42. NDB, "The Lawyer's Place in Society," April 12, 1932, Baker MSS, Container 263, File: "Speeches, 1931–1935."

43. Baker MSS, Containers 62 and 63, Files: "Cleveland Bar Association"; Baker MSS, Container 136, Files: "Judge Advocate General's Office, 1922–25"; Baker MSS, Container 20, File: "American Arbitration Assoc., 1927"; Baker MSS, Container 186, Files: "Permanent Court of Arbitration—Hague Tribunal 1928"; Manley O. Hudson, "American Members of the Permanent Court of Arbitration During Forty Years," *American Journal of International Law* 35, no. 1 (January 1941): 135–139; *NYT,* May 7, 1936, 3:5; Baker MSS, Container

22, Files: "American Bar Association, Jan. 1–April 1, 1937"; and NDB to Frank A. Quail, September 28, 1936, Baker MSS, Container 194, File: "Q., 1936."

44. NDB, "Labor Relations and the Law," *American Bar Association Journal* 8 (December 1922): 731–736; Baker MSS, Containers 171–173, Files: "National Crime Commission"; Baker MSS, Containers 61 and 62, Files: "Cleveland Association for Criminal Justice"; Baker MSS, Container 176, Files: "National Society of Penal Information, 1929"; and Baker MSS, Containers 167 and 168, Files: "NCLOE, 1931." For NDB and the Wickersham Committee, see chapter 12, below.

45. NDB, "Law, Police and Social Problems," *The Atlantic Monthly*, July 1915, 12–21, Baker MSS, Container 244, File: "Speeches, 1915, 1916."

46. NDB, "Crimes and the Criminal," *The Clevelander* 5 (July 1930): 3–5, Baker MSS, Container 247, File: "1930."

47. NDB to Bert M. Hardenbrook, September 4, 1921, Baker MSS, Container 111, File: "Har–Hd, 1925"; NDB to Wayne Moore, March 7, 1926, Baker MSS, Container 158, File: "Mo–Mx, 1928"; and NDB to Hon. Martin J. Wade, May 25, 1926, Baker MSS, Container 171, File: "National Crime Commission, Jan.–June 1926."

48. NDB to Hon. Dan B. Cull, May 9, 1930, Baker MSS, Container 81, File: "Cu–Cz, 1930"; NDB to Homer S. Cummings, December 23, 1933, Baker MSS, Container 81, File: "Cu–Cz, 1933"; NDB to Carl V. Weygandt, December 30, 1933, Baker MSS, Container 230, File: "We–Wg, 1933"; and NDB to Susanna M. Wood, December 1, 1937, Baker MSS, Container 239, File: "Wo–Wz, 1937."

49. NDB to Chief Justice Carrington T. Marshall, March 17, 1926, Baker MSS, Container 149, File: "Ma–Mb, 1926"; and NDB to George R. Farnum, September 24, 1936, Baker MSS, Container 94, File: "Fa–Fk, 1936."

50. Hon. Israel M. Foster, "McAdoo, the Lawyer," February 21, 1924, McAdoo MSS, Container 301, File: "May 2, 1924."

51. WRHA-NDB MSS, Acc. #4564, "Oversize Folder"; and Cramer, *Newton D. Baker*, 186.

52. Baker MSS, Container 182, File: "Pa–Ph, 1928"; and Baker MSS, Container 186, File: "Permanent Court of Arbitration—Hague Tribunal, 1928."

53. "Sample of Letter, (Irvington house)," n.d., McAdoo MSS, Container 78, File: "Undated"; WGM to Carl Priest, June 12, 1913, McAdoo MSS, Container 478-3; WGM to James H. Roper, January 24, 1937, McAdoo MSS, Container 430, File: "Jan. 25, 1937"; WGM to *Leslie's Weekly*, March 10 ,1921, McAdoo MSS, Container 511; WGM to Deputy Tax Commissioner, New York State, August 3, 1921, McAdoo MSS, Container 514, Vol. 22(2); and "Statement of All Expenses for 10 Years, 1924–1933," McAdoo MSS, Container 86, File: "Personal Miscellany—Financial Summaries." 2011 values are calculated on changes in the Consumer Price Index. www.measuringworth.com/uscompare. WGM to H. Ross McAdoo, June 29, 1925, McAdoo MSS, Container 322, File: "Jan. 29, 1925."

54. WGM to Chadbourne, June 24, 1922, McAdoo MSS, Container 265, File: "Jun. 24, 1922"; and WGM to Baruch, November 15, 1922, McAdoo MSS, Container 271, File: "Nov. 15, 1922."

55. "Ledger—Oct. 1923—June 1924," UCLA-WGM MSS, Box 4; Treasurer of Jameson Petroleum to WGM, September 1, 1925, McAdoo MSS, Container 318, File: "Sept. 1, 1925"; WGM to FHM, November 2, 1922, McAdoo MSS, Container 62, File: "Nov. 1–6, 1922"; WGM to Plymouth Petroleum, February 17, 1921, McAdoo MSS, Container 511; "Statement of Investments in Oil Leases and Royalties for Account W.G. McAdoo to May 1, 1926," McAdoo MSS, Container 325, File: "May 8, 1926"; E. D. Flaherty to WGM, February 2, 1929,

McAdoo MSS, Container 342, File: "Feb. 2, 1929"; and Flaherty to WGM, January 4, 1938, McAdoo MSS, Container 446, File: "Jan. 4, 1938."

56. WGM to W. F. Weeks, August 5, 1921, McAdoo MSS, Container 514, Vol. 22(2); Albert L. Cheney to WGM, May 12, 1924, McAdoo MSS, Container 303, File: "May 12, 1924"; and WGM to James Woodrow, October 12, 1927, McAdoo MSS, Container 336, File: "Oct. 12, 1927."

57. WGM to Baruch, October 24, 1924, McAdoo MSS, Container 308, File: "Oct. 24, 1924"; and WGM to Baruch, December 16, 1924, McAdoo MSS, Container 310, File: "Dec. 16, 1924."

58. WGM to O'Connor, April 2, 1925, and WGM to Lewis Humphrey, April 5, 1925, McAdoo MSS, Container 314, Files: "Apr. 2 and Apr. 5, 1925."

59. WGM to Baruch, April 20, 1925, and O'Connor to WGM, April 14, 1925, McAdoo MSS, Container 315, Files: "Apr. 20 and Apr. 14, 1925"; and WGM to Frederick I. Thompson, June 13, 1925, McAdoo MSS, Container 316, File: "Jun. 13, 1925."

60. *Time*, June 3, 1929, McAdoo MSS, Container 343, File: "May 31, 1929"; and WGM to EWM, February 18, 1929, Wilson-McAdoo (SB) MSS, Box 8, File: "William Gibbs McAdoo—Family Corres., Outgoing 1929, B-1." The underlining is WGM's.

61. Nona Cowles to WGM, January 16, 1928, Wilson-McAdoo (SB) MSS, Box 21, n.f.; WGM to Bellanca Aircraft Corp., January 7, 1929, McAdoo MSS, Container 341, File: "Jan. 7, 1929"; Buhl Aircraft Company to WGM, February 25, 1929, McAdoo MSS, Container 342, File: "March 16, 1929"; WGM to Lockheed Aircraft Co., June 22, 1929, McAdoo MSS, Container 344, File: "Jun. 22, 1929"; NYT, October 16, 1930, 25:4; and UCLA-WGM MSS, Box 14, "Personal Ledger 1916–1926."

62. WGM to James C. Edgerton, October 26, 1928, McAdoo MSS, Container 340, File: "Oct. 26, 1928"; WGM to Glen H. Curtiss, November 13, 1928, McAdoo MSS, Container 340, File: "Nov. 13, 1928"; and McAdoo MSS, Container 344, File: "July 12, 1929."

63. WGM, "The Southern Transcontinental Air Mail Route," McAdoo MSS, Container 341, File: "Jan. 28, 1929"; WGM, "Memorandum for Mr. Clagett," August 21, 1929, McAdoo MSS, Container 345, File: "Aug. 21, 1929"; WGM to Edwin P. Meissner, September 19, 1929, McAdoo MSS, Container 346, File: "September 19, 1929"; NYT, November 29, 1929, 3:3, and November 30, 1929, 5:1; and WGM to Thomas Gaunt, May 4, 1929, McAdoo MSS, Container 343, File: "May 4, 1929."

64. Baruch to WGM, June 19, 1929, McAdoo MSS, Container 344, File: "Jun. 19, 1929"; WGM to Brice Clagett, January 23, 1930, McAdoo MSS, Container 349, File: "Jan. 23, 1930"; and WGM to James C. Edgerton, April 3, 1930, McAdoo MSS, Container 350, File: "Apr. 3, 1930."

65. WGM to Douglas Fairbanks, April 8, 1919, McAdoo MSS, Container 219, File: "Apr. 8, 1919"; WGM to Fairbanks, October 1, 1920, WGM to Thomas M. Storke, October 1, 1920, and Storke to WGM, October 7, 1920, McAdoo MSS, Container 242, File: "Oct. 1, 1920"; and WGM to Fairbanks and WGM to Storke, November 16, 1920, McAdoo MSS, Container 244, File: "Nov. 16, 1920."

66. WGM to EWM, September 3, 1925, Wilson-McAdoo MSS, Container 1, File: "McAdoo, William G., 1925," and Container 2, File: "McAdoo, William G., 1929." The underlining is WGM's. WGM to Baruch, March 12, 1925, and April 20, 1925, McAdoo MSS, Containers 314 and 315, Files: "Mar. 12, 1925" and "Apr. 20, 1925"; and WGM to EWM, September 12, 1925, Wilson-McAdoo MSS, LOC MSS, Container 1, File: "McAdoo, William G., 1925."

67. WGM to John F. Sinclair, October 20, 1925, McAdoo MSS, Container 320, File: "Oct. 20, 1925."

68. "W. G. McAdoo: Balance Sheet, July 20, 1937," McAdoo MSS, Container 86, File: "Personal Miscellany—Financial Summaries."

69. WGM to FHM, August 9, 1926, McAdoo MSS, Container 648, File: "Aug. 1926 11"; and WGM, "Total Present Wealth," McAdoo MSS, Container 86, File: "Personal Miscellany—Financial Summaries." 2011 values have been calculated based on changes of the Consumer Price Index. www.measuringworth.com/uscompare.

70. NYT, May 25, 1933, 1:6–8, 13, and 15, and May 26, 1933, 14:1; McAdoo MSS, Container 605; J. P. Morgan & Co. to NDB, June 21, 1929, Baker MSS, Container 297, File: "Wim–Wn, 1929"; Arthur M. Schlesinger Jr., The Age of Roosevelt, 3 vols. (Boston: Houghton Mifflin Company, 1956–1960), 2:436.

71. WGM to Thomas J. Hamilton, February 6, 1929, McAdoo MSS, Container 34, File: "Feb. 6, 1929"; WGM to Jewel Perret, September 28, 1929, McAdoo MSS, Container 346, File: "Sept. 28, 1929"; WGM, "Personal Ledger, 1926–1936," UCLA-WGM MSS, Box 14; T. M. Storke to WGM, February 7, 1929, McAdoo MSS, Container 342, File: "Feb. 7, 1929"; WGM to FHM, October 30, 1929, McAdoo MSS, Container 68, File: "Oct. 30–31, 1929"; WGM to Bernard Baruch, April 21, 1930, McAdoo MSS, Container 350, File: "Apr. 21, 1930"; Standard Supervisory Service, "Mr. William Gibbs McAdoo, Schedule of Current Holdings, July 23, 1930," McAdoo MSS, Container 351, File: "July 9, 1930"; E. D. Flaherty to WGM, May 11, 1933, McAdoo MSS, Container 383, File: "May 11, 1933"; McAdoo MSS, Containers 366 and 405; McAdoo MSS, Container 357, Files: "Mar." and "Apr."; WGM to Oscar Howard, February 13, 1934, McAdoo MSS, Container 391, File: "Feb. 13, 1934"; and WGM to Howard, March 30, 1934, McAdoo MSS, Container 393, File: "Mar. 30, 1934."

72. WGM's patent for the flask was #1648992 of 1927: WGM to Ernest I. Mechlin, October 22, 1924, McAdoo MSS, Container 308, File: "Oct. 22, 1924"; WGM to RHM, August 8, 1935, McAdoo MSS, Container 408, File: "Aug. 8, 1935"; WGM to Mechlin and Mechlin reply, May 26 and 27, 1937, McAdoo MSS, Container 436, File: "May 27, 1937." WGM's razor patent was #1953248, issued in 1934: Thomas V. DiBacco, "William Gibbs McAdoo and his Patented Razor," History Teacher 4, no. 3 (March 1971): 48–56. NDB's book cleaner patent was #2036789, issued April 7, 1936: Baker MSS, Container 37, File: "NDB Personal, 1937." For drawings and details of all three of WGM's and NDB's patents, see www.freepatentsonline.com.html.

73. Cramer, Newton D. Baker, 173; and NDB to Ethel Vorce, n.d., Baker MSS, File: "V., 1934."

74. "Meeting of the FHBOMB syndicate, April 11, 1916," Baker MSS, Personal Correspondence 1916–1922, Reel 1; Carl Osborne to NDB, January 25, 1918, Baker MSS, Personal Correspondence 1916–1922, Reel 2; Osborne to NDB, July 2, 1918, Baker MSS, Miscellaneous Correspondence 1918, Reel 12; NDB to Osborne, December 20, 1916, Personal Correspondence 1916–1922, Reel 1; and Joseph Hostetler to NDB, May 9, 1918, Baker MSS, Personal Correspondence 1916–1922, Reel 4.

75. NDB to Daniel Willard, November 12, 1923, Baker MSS, Container 37, File: "Baltimore and Ohio Company, 1923"; NDB to Charles J. Faulkner, November 20, 1923, Baker MSS, Container 92, File: "Fa–Fk, 1923"; Baker MSS, Container 160, File: "The Mutual Life Insurance Company of New York, 1931"; NYT, May 20, 1933, 19:7; Baker MSS, Container 195, Files: "Radio Corporation of America," and Container 164, Files: "National

Broadcasting Company"; and Baker MSS, Container 106, Files: "Confidential: Goodyear Tire & Rubber Co. Board of Directors, 1934."

76. NDB to Betty Baker, December 14, 1923, WRHA-NDB MSS, Acc. #4564, Container 1, Folder 3.

CHAPTER 11:   LOST CAUSES, 1921–1929

1. Woolley to WGM, November 7, 1921, McAdoo MSS, Container 257, File: "Nov. 7, 1921"; WGM to John N. Garner, June 30, 1921, McAdoo MSS, Container 252, File: "June 30, 1921"; WGM to Edward L. Doheny, December 12, 1922, McAdoo MSS, Container 272, File: "Dec. 12, 1922"; WGM to Byron Newton, January 2, 1922, McAdoo MSS, Container 259, File: "Jan. 2, 1922"; Baruch to WGM, May 18, 1922, McAdoo MSS, Container 264, File: "May 18, 1922"; and WGM to F. W. Simmons, September 23, 1921, McAdoo MSS, Container 275, File: "Sept. 23, 1921."

2. WGM to J. W. Rixey Smith, January 3, 1922, McAdoo MSS, Container 259, File: "Jan. 3, 1922"; Keene, *Doughboys*, 171–175; and Ortiz, *Beyond the Bonus March and the GI Bill*, 23–27.

3. WGM to Byron Newton, January 2, 1922, McAdoo MSS, Container 259, File: "Jan. 2, 1922"; *NYT*, March 10, 1922, 17:2; and WGM to Dixon Williams, July 7, 1922, McAdoo MSS, Container 265, File: "Jul. 7, 1922."

4. *NYT*, November 13 and 14, 1922, 23:2 and 18:1; WGM, "The Living Wage," *Labor*, February 1923, McAdoo MSS, Container 657, File: "Articles, 1910–32"; and *NYT*, February 24, 1923, 7:4.

5. Baruch to WGM, April 10, 1922, McAdoo MSS, Container 262, File: "Apr. 10, 1923," and WGM reply, April 25, 1922, McAdoo MSS, Container 262, File: "Apr. 25, 1922"; Roper to WGM, Container 271, File: "Nov. 25, 1922"; Peabody to WGM, November 18, 1923, McAdoo MSS, Container 286, File: "Nov. 18, 1923"; NDB to Walter Lippmann, November 30, 1923, Baker MSS, Container 147, File: "Li–Lz, 1923"; NDB to E. M. Spelman, March 7, 1924, Baker MSS, Container 210, File: "So–Ss, 1924"; and Baker MSS, Container 173, File: "National Economy League, 1933."

6. WGM to Baruch, October 5, 1922, McAdoo MSS, Container 269, File: "Oct. 5, 1922"; WGM to Chadbourne, October 25, 1922, McAdoo MSS, Container 270, File: "Oct. 25, 1922"; WGM to Walsh, December 13, 1922, McAdoo MSS, Container 272, Files: "Dec. 6, 11, and 13, 1922"; and WGM to Claude Kitchin, McAdoo MSS, Container 272, File: "Dec. 11, 1922."

7. Baker MSS, Container 59, File: "Hon. John H. Clarke, 1923"; Baker MSS, Container 144, File: "League of Nations, 1923"; Baker MSS, Container 146, Files: "League of Nations Non-Partisan Association, 1922–26"; Baker MSS, Container 99, Files: "Foreign Policy Association"; Baker MSS, Containers 239–240, Files: "Woodrow Wilson Foundation"; Baker MSS, Container 78, Files: "Council on Foreign Relations"; and NDB to ELB, September 1923, WRHA-NDB MSS, Acc. #4564, Container 1, File 2.

8. NDB to ELB, January 18, 1922, WRHA-NDB MSS, Acc. #3491, Container 1, File 4; and NDB to Clarke, November 8, 1922, Baker MSS, Container 59, File: "Hon. John H. Clarke 1922." The underlining is NDB's.

9. WGM to NDB, April 29, 1922, Baker MSS, Container 152, File: "Mc, 1922"; and Cleveland Chamber of Commerce and "Correspondence between the Painters' Union and

Mr. Baker," May 10, 1922, Baker MSS, Container 64, File: "Cleveland Chamber of Commerce, 1922–23."

10. Gompers to NDB, August 19, 1922, Baker MSS, Container 102, File: "Gi–Gq, 1922."

11. NDB to Gompers, August 24, September 28, and November 23, 1922, Baker MSS, Container 102, File: "Gi–Gq, 1922."

12. Gompers to NDB, October 2, 1922, Baker MSS, Container 102, File: "Gi–Gq, 1922."

13. Frankfurter to NDB, January 19, January 22, and March 5, 1923, and NDB to Frankfurter, January 17, January 18, and March 8, 1923, Baker MSS, Container 100, File: "Fr–Fz, 1923"; NDB, "What Are We Aiming At In Industrial Relations?" *Current Affairs* 13 (January 15, 1923): 2–11, 9; and NDB to George N. Brown, March 13, 1923, Baker MSS, Container 47, File: "Bro–Bt, 1923."

14. Piott, *American Reformers*, 119; Tichi, *Civic Passions*, 123–163; NDB to Emily Marconnier, February 19, 1932, Baker MSS, Container 171, File: "National Consumers' League, 1932"; Goldmark, *Impatient Crusader*, 207; NDB to Kelley, May 31 and June 6, 1922, Constance Todd to NDB and NDB to Todd, August 14 and 24, 1922, NDB to Kelley, August 16, 1922, Kelley to NDB, August 29, 1923, and NDB to Kelley, September 24, 1923, Baker MSS, Containers 170 and 171, Files: "National Consumers' League, 1922–28 and 1937"; and Graham, *Encore for Reform*, 171, n. 8.

15. NDB to Kelley, June 9, 1922, Baker MSS, Container 170, File: "National Consumers' League, 1922–28"; *Hammer v. Dagenhart* (1918), 247 US 251; and NDB to Ralph Hayes, December 11, 1924, Baker MSS, Container 255, File: "1924—Nov.–Dec."

16. Preston J. Hubbard, *Origins of the TVA: The Muscle Shoals Controversy, 1920–1932* (Nashville: Vanderbilt University Press, 1962); and NDB to Ernest Greenwood, April 3, 1924, Baker MSS, Container 160, File: "Muscle Shoals 1924."

17. NDB to Charles A. Mooney, December 7, 1923, Baker MSS, Container 157, File: "Mo–Mx, 1923"; and NDB to Carter Glass, March 25, 1924, Baker MSS, Container 103, File: "Gi–Gq, 1924."

18. NDB to Grenville MacFarland, October 2, 1922, Baker MSS, Container 149, File: "Ma–Mb, 1926."

19. WGM to Baruch, February 1, 1923, McAdoo MSS, Container 274, File: "Feb. 1, 1923"; WGM to Chadbourne, March 10, 1923, McAdoo MSS, Container 275, File: "Mar. 10, 1923"; and Goetsch and Shivers, eds., *Autobiography of Thomas L. Chadbourne*, 199.

20. WGM to Byron Newton, April 29, 1922, McAdoo MSS, Container 263, File: "Apr. 29, 1922"; NDB to WGM, May 25, 1922, McAdoo MSS, Container 24, File: "Jun. 3, 1922"; NDB to WGM, October 7, 1922, McAdoo MSS, Container 269, File: "Oct. 7, 1922"; and Newton to WGM, April 18, 1922, McAdoo MSS, Container 263, File: "Apr. 18, 1922."

21. Roper to Chadbourne, January 11, 1924, McAdoo MSS, Container 292, File: "Jan. 19, 1924"; and Lee N. Allen, "The McAdoo Campaign for the Presidential Nomination in 1924," *Journal of Southern History* 29, no. 2 (May 1963): 211–228, 214. Fifty thousand dollars in 1924 was the equivalent, on the basis of the Consumer Price Index, of $658,000 in 2011. www.measuringworth.com/uscompare.

22. J. G. Doyle to WGM, December 2, 1923, McAdoo MSS, Container 287, File: "Dec. 2, 1923"; WGM to Rockwell, November 25, 1923, McAdoo MSS, Container 286, File: "Nov. 25, 1923"; WGM to Daniel Roper, September 8, 1923, McAdoo MSS, Container 282, File: "Sept. 8, 1923"; WGM to Tom Taggart, April 9 and May 2, 1924, McAdoo MSS, Container 304, File: "May 28, 1924"; Arthur F. Mullen to WGM, December 8, 1923, McAdoo MSS,

Container 288, File: "Dec. 12, 1923"; and Sam Abidon to WGM, January 22, 1924, McAdoo MSS, Container 293, File: "Jan. 22, 1924."

23. WGM to Kenneth McKellar, June 29, 1923, McAdoo MSS, Container 279, File: "June 29, 1923"; Long to Rockwell, March 31, 1924, Long Papers, LOC MSS, Container 172, File: "1924—XIII"; and Long, "Diary Entry 21 November 1923," Long Papers, LOC MSS, Container 3, File: "Diary—13: Handwritten 1923, scattered."

24. *NYT*, November 16, 1923, 1:7, and November 25, 1923, 9, 4:1.

25. WGM, "Jackson Day Address, January 8, 1924," "Fundamentals of Democracy, April 7, 1924," McAdoo MSS, Container 565, File; "Speeches, 1924–1926"; and WGM, "Open Letter to William L. O'Connell," March 21, 1924, McAdoo MSS, Container 565, File: "Speeches, 1924–1926."

26. *New York World*, March 27, 1924, McAdoo MSS, Container 299, File: "Mar. 28, 1924"; and Long to Edward M. House, January 19, 1924, Long Papers, LOC MSS, Subject File, Container 172, File: "1924 (V)."

27. WGM to Angus W. McLean, December 24, 1923, McAdoo MSS, Container 289, File: "Dec. 24, 1923"; WGM to Chadbourne, November 23, 1923, and December 10, 1923, McAdoo MSS, Containers 286 and 287, Files: "Nov. 23, 1923" and "Dec. 10, 1923"; WGM to Roper, January 2 and January 11, 1924, McAdoo MSS, Containers 290 and 291, Files: "Jan. 2, 1924" and "Jan. 11, 1924."

28. Charles H. V. Lewis to WGM, December 8, 1923, McAdoo MSS, Container 287, File: "Dec. 8, 1923." The capitalization is Lewis's. Burner, *Politics of Provincialism*, 130; and Angus Wilson McLean to WGM, December 13, 1923, McAdoo MSS, Container 288, File: "Dec. 13, 1923."

29. WGM to Edward Keating, March 16, 1931, McAdoo MSS, Container 357, File: "Mar. 16, 1931." The underlining is WGM's.

30. WGM to William B. Colver, April 1, 1924, McAdoo MSS, Container 299, File: "April 1, 1924—Folder #1"; and "The Case for Mr. McAdoo," *The Nation* 118 (June 25, 1924): 724.

31. WGM to Chadbourne, December 10, 1923, McAdoo MSS, Container 287, File: "Dec. 10, 1923"; and Randolph to WGM, December 13, 1923, McAdoo MSS, Container 288, File: "Dec. 13, 1923."

32. Clagett to J. C. Landreau, December 18, 1923, McAdoo MSS, Container 288, File: "Dec. 18, 1923"; and NDB to M. A. Daugherty, December 22, 1923, Baker MSS, Container 81, File: "Da–Dh, 1923."

33. WGM to Chadbourne, December 10, 1923, McAdoo MSS, Container 287, File: "Dec. 10, 1923"; Diary Entry, February 20, 1924, Long Papers, LOC MSS, Container 3, File: "Diary—14: Handwritten 1924"; Alfred Lucking to WGM, February 20, 1924, McAdoo MSS, Container 296, File: "Feb. 20, 1924"; and WGM to John H. Clarke, May 7, 1924, McAdoo MSS, Container 303, File: "May 7, 1924."

34. *Denver Post*, January 19, 1923, 10:1, McAdoo MSS, Container 634; *NYT*, November 3, 1923, 3:5; and WGM to Edith Galt Wilson, December 20, 1923, McAdoo MSS, Container 289, File: "Dec. 20, 1923."

35. Diary Entries, November 21, 1923, and May 31, 1924, Hamlin Papers, LOC MSS, Reel 2, Vol. VII:180 and Vol. VIII:174; EWM to Margaret Wilson, April 11, 1924, Wilson-McAdoo MSS, LOC MSS, Container 4, File: "McAdoo, Eleanor Randolph, 1922–33"; Link, ed., *Papers of Woodrow Wilson*, 68:476; Fosdick to NDB, July 14, 1924, Baker MSS, Container 99, File: "Fosdick, Raymond B., 1924"; and Cooper, *Woodrow Wilson*, 589.

36. Wilson, "Confidential Document," c. January 20, 1924, "Notes and Passages for an Acceptance Speech," and "Notes and Passages for a Third Inaugural Address," c. January 21, 1924, in Link, ed., *Papers of Woodrow Wilson*, 68:535–545; and Milton to WGM, January 13, 1924, McAdoo MSS, Container 291, File: "Jan. 13, 1924."

37. Shawn Lay, ed., *Invisible Empire in the West: Toward a New Historical Appraisal of the Ku Klux Klan of the 1920s* (Urbana: University of Illinois Press, 1992); Nancy McLean, *Behind the Mask of Chivalry: The Making of the Second Ku Klux Klan* (New York: Oxford University Press, 1994); and NDB to ELB, December 6, 1923, WRHA-Baker MSS, Acc. #4562, Container 1, File 3.

38. Walsh to WGM and WGM reply, November 28 and December 13, 1922, McAdoo MSS, Container 272, File: "Dec. 13, 1922."

39. Walsh to WGM, March 13, 1923, McAdoo MSS, Container 275, File: "Mar. 13, 1923"; WGM to Randolph Bolling, January 6, 1923, McAdoo MSS, Container 273, File: "Jan. 6, 1923"; and WGM to Daniel C. Roper, April 7, 1923, McAdoo MSS, Container 276, File: "Apr. 7, 1923."

40. Milton to WGM, January 13, 1924, McAdoo MSS, Container 291, File: "Jan. 13, 1924"; Murrell T. Bruckner to WGM, January 21, 1924, McAdoo MSS, Container 192, File: "Jan. 21, 1924"; and WGM to Joseph E. Davies, December 12, 1923, McAdoo MSS, Container 288, File: "Dec. 20, 1923."

41. Leon A. Dever to WGM, August 23, 1923, McAdoo MSS, Container 282, File: "Aug. 23, 1923." The capitalization is Dever's. James Bell to WGM, January 21, 1924, McAdoo MSS, Container 292, File: "Jan. 21, 1924"; Abidon to WGM, March 22, 1924, Huntington-WGM MSS, Folder 34; and Cato Sells to WGM, January 30, 1924, McAdoo MSS, Container 294, File: "Jan. 30, 1924."

42. Swope to WGM, October 25, 1923, McAdoo MSS, Container 285, File: "Oct. 25, 1923."

43. Shapforth to WGM, January 2, 1924, McAdoo MSS, Container 290, File: "Jan. 2, 1924"; Funk to WGM, April 9, 1924, McAdoo MSS, Container 300, File: "Apr. 9, 1924"; and Untermeyer to WGM, January 10, 1924, McAdoo MSS, Container 291, File: "Jan. 10, 1924."

44. WGM, "Masonry," October 8, 1923, McAdoo MSS, Container 567, File: "undated"; and WGM to Brother E. John H. Cowles, March 6, 1924, McAdoo MSS, Container 297, File: "Mar. 6, 1924."

45. Allen, "McAdoo Campaign," 218; WGM to Edward M. House, March 17, 1924, McAdoo MSS, Container 298, File: "Mar. 17, 1924"; P. H. Callaghan to WGM, May 16, 1924, McAdoo MSS, Container 303, File: "May 16, 1924"; and O'Neill to WGM, May 29, 1924, McAdoo MSS, Container 304, File: "May 29, 1924."

46. WGM to Claude Bowers, January 11, 1924, McAdoo MSS, Container 291, File: "Jan. 11, 1924."

47. Charles S. Hamlin, Diary Entry, February 28, 1924, Hamlin Papers, LOC MSS, Diaries, Reel 2, Vol. VIII; Cary Grayson to WGM, February 1, 1924, McAdoo MSS, Container 294, File: "Feb. 1, 1924"; WGM to Irving L. Lenroot, February 7, 1924, McAdoo MSS, Container 294, File: "Feb. 7, 1924"; Clarence N. Goodwin of Goodwin, Weitzel & Bresnahan, February 9, 1924, "Press Release, February 11, 1924"; and McAdoo MSS, Container 295, Files: "Feb. 7, 1924," "Feb. 9, 1924," and "February 12, 1924."

48. Hapgood to WGM, n.d., McAdoo MSS, Container 311, File: "1924"; Diary Entries, February 2, 6, and 8, 1924, Long Papers, LOC MSS, Container 3, File: "Diary—14: Handwritten 1924"; Baruch, *Public Years*, 173; House to WGM, February 23, 1924, McAdoo MSS,

Container 296, File: "Feb. 23, 1924"; Funk to WGM, February 13, 1924, McAdoo MSS, Container 295, File: "Feb. 13, 1924"; and Glass to WGM, February 22, 1924, McAdoo MSS, Container 297, File: "Feb. 22, 1924."

49. Goetsch and Shivers, eds., *Autobiography of Thomas L. Chadbourne*, 194–195; McAdoo MSS, Containers 294, 295, and 296; *New York World*, March 28 and July 1, 1924, McAdoo MSS, Container 299, File: "Mar. 29, 1924"; Frankfurter Papers, LOC MSS, Reel 47, File: "Lippmann, Walter 1924"; L. T. Russell to WGM, February 23, 1924, McAdoo MSS, Container 296, File: "Feb. 23, 1924"; and David C. Reay to Davis, February 13, 1924, Davis MSS, IV:25, Folder: "Feb. 13–15, 1924."

50. WGM to Rockwell, February 12, 1924, and Clagett to Milton, February 14, 1924, McAdoo MSS, Container 295, Files: "Feb. 12, 1924" and "Feb. 14, 1924"; Diary Entry, February 20, 1924, Long Papers, LOC MSS, Container 3, File: "Diary—14: Handwritten 1924"; and WGM to Baruch, March 4, 1924, McAdoo MSS, Container 297, File: "Mar. 4, 1924."

51. NDB to ELB, February 5, 1924, WRHA-NDB MSS, Acc. #4564, Container 1, File 3; Davis to Frank Polk, February 18, 1924, Davis Papers, IV:26; and Walsh to WGM, April 3, 1924, McAdoo MSS, Container 300, File: "April 3, 1924—Folder #1."

52. Baruch to WGM, March 5, 1924, McAdoo MSS, Container 297, File: "Mar. 5, 1924"; Baruch to Rockwell, April 16, 1924, McAdoo MSS, Container 301, File: "Apr. 16, 1924"; R. S. Jones, "Funds Raised by D. C. Roper," McAdoo MSS, Container 299, File: "Mar. 26, 1924"; Frazier to McAdoo for President Mailing List, March 9, 1924, McAdoo MSS, Container 298, File: "Mar. 9, 1924"; Roper to WGM, May 29, 1924, McAdoo MSS, Container 304, File: "May 29, 1924"; Angus McLean to WGM, April 5, 1924, McAdoo MSS, Container 300, File: "April 5, 1924"; Funk to WGM, June 6, 1924, McAdoo MSS, Container 305, File: "June 6, 1924"; WGM to Chadbourne, June 4, 1924, McAdoo MSS, Container 304, File: "June 4, 1924"; and Allen, "McAdoo Campaign," 219ff.

53. Louise Overacker, *The Presidential Primary* (New York: Macmillan Company, 1926), 248; and WGM to Thomas Chadbourne, March 22, 1924, McAdoo MSS, Container 299, File: "Mar. 22, 1924."

54. Leslie C. Garnett to Clagett, February 26, 1924, McAdoo MSS, Container 297, File: "Feb. 27, 1924"; Long to WGM, February 25, March 8, and April 5, 1924, Long Papers, LOC MSS, Container 172, Files: "1924: X," "1924: XI," and "1924: XIV"; WGM to C. C. Oliver, March 1, 1924, McAdoo MSS, Container 297, File: "Mar. 1, 1924"; and the *New York World*, n.d., McAdoo MSS, Container 299, File: "Mar. 28, 1924."

55. E. T. Meredith to Breckinridge Long, March 25, 1924, Long Papers, LOC MSS, Container 172, File: "1924: XIII"; Kelleher to WGM, March 12, 1924, McAdoo MSS, Container 298, File: "Mar. 12, 1924"; Key Pittman to Sarah George, June 3, 1924, Pittman Papers, LOC MSS, Container 12, File: "G"; *Los Angeles Herald*, March 13, 1924, McAdoo MSS, Container 627; and H. H. Worleleupht to WGM, March 28, 1924, McAdoo MSS, Container 299, File: "Mar. 28, 1924."

56. Nona McAdoo to WGM, January 29, 1924, McAdoo MSS, Container 63, File: "Jan. 27–31, 1924."

57. NDB to ELB, February 13 and June 1, 1927, WRHA-NDB MSS, Acc. #4564, Container 1, Folders 8 and 10; NDB to F. W. Kelsey, February 22, 1924, Baker MSS, Container 136, File: "Ke–Kh, 1924"; and NDB to William B. Wilson, December 24, 1923, Baker MSS, Container 234, File: "Wia–Wil, 1923."

58. NDB to Lippmann, October 25, 1923, Baker MSS, Container 147, File: "Li–Lz, 1923"; and NDB to ELB, December 2, 1923, WRHA-NDB MSS, Acc. #4564, Container 1, Folder 5.

59. NDB to Frankfurter, April 18, 1923, Frankfurter Papers, LOC MSS, Reel 13.

60. William H. Harbaugh, *Lawyer's Lawyer: The Life of John W. Davis* (Charlottesville: University Press of Virginia, 1990), 363; and NDB to ELB, October 24, 1923, WRHA-NDB MSS, Acc. #4564, Container 1, File 2.

61. NDB to Cox, January 16, 1924, Baker MSS, Container 76, File: "Coo–Cq, 1924."

62. Cummings to Rockwell, March 22 ,1924, McAdoo MSS, Container 299, File: "Mar. 22, 1924"; WGM to Alfred E. Smith, November 8, 1922, McAdoo MSS, Container 270, File: "Nov. 8, 1922"; Byron Newton to WGM, August 5, 1922, McAdoo MSS, Container 266, File: "Aug. 5, 1922"; and WGM to Chadbourne, September 19, 1923, McAdoo MSS, Container 283, File: "Sept. 19, 1923."

63. *New York Herald*, December 15, 1923, McAdoo MSS, Container 288, File: "Dec. 18, 1923"; and Chadbourne to WGM, June 4, 1924, McAdoo MSS, Container 304, File: "June 4, 1924."

64. WGM to Luke Lea, April 17, 1924, McAdoo MSS, Container 301, File: "Apr. 17, 1924"; and Lee N. Allen, "The Democratic Presidential Primary Election of 1924 in Texas," *Southwestern Historical Quarterly* 41 (April 1958): 474–493, 487.

65. Long to Robert J. Mitchell, May 23, 1924, Long Papers, LOC MSS, Container 173, File: "1924: XXI"; WGM to Lewis T. Humphrey, April 15, 1924, McAdoo MSS, Container 301, File: "Apr. 15, 1924"; and WGM to David Hunter Miller, May 5, 1924, McAdoo MSS, Container 302, File: "May 5, 1924."

66. Diary Entry, July 15, 1924, Long Papers, LOC MSS, Container 3, File: "Diary—14: Handwritten 1924"; NYT, June 24, 1924, 1:5, and June 24, 1924, 3:1; and NDB to ELB, June 26, 1924, WRHA-NDB MSS, Acc. #3491, Container 1, Folder 4.

67. Robert K. Murray, *103rd Ballot: Democrats and the Disaster in Madison Square Garden* (New York: Harper & Row Publishers, 1976), 129–133.

68. "Speech of Newton D. Baker Nominating James M. Cox," Baker MSS, Speeches and Writings, Container 246, File: "1924–25." The underlining is NDB's. NDB to ELB, June 27, 1924, WRHA-NDB MSS, Acc. #3491, Container 1, Folder 4.

69. NYT, June 28, 1924, 1:6; NDB to James Durbin, August 22, 1924, Baker MSS, Container 88, File: "Durbin, James M., 1922–36"; and *NYT*, June 28, 1924, 1:6.

70. "Speech of Newton D. Baker, June 28, 1924," Baker MSS, Speeches and Writings, Container 246, File: "1924–25."

71. NYT, June 29, 1924, 1:4; Pittman to L. L. Aitken, July 28, 1924, Pittman Papers, LOC MSS, Container 11, File: "A—General"; and Betty Glad, *Key Pittman: The Tragedy of a Senate Insider* (New York: Columbia University Press, 1986), 131.

72. NYT, June 30, 1924, 1:4 and 6:8; and NDB to Charles S. Hamlin, July 14, 1924, Baker MSS, Container 347, File: "General Correspondence, 4 Oct. 1923–20 Dec. 1924."

73. Diary Entry, July 15, 1924, Long Papers, LOC MSS, Container 3, File: "Diary—14: Handwritten 1924."

74. Murray, *103rd Ballot*, 153–159; and *NYT*, June 29, 1924, 1:6.

75. NYT, June 29, 1924, 1:6; and NDB to C. M. Gaylord, July 19, 1924, Baker MSS, Container 101, File: "Ga–Gh, 1924."

76. NDB to ELB, July 1, 1924, WRHA-NDB MSS, Acc. #3491, Container 1, Folder 4.

77. Josephus Daniels to WGM, n.d., Daniels Papers, LOC MSS, Special Correspondence, Reel 56.

78. James C. Prude, "William Gibbs McAdoo and the Democratic National Convention of 1924," *Journal of Southern History* 38, no. 4 (November 1972): 621–628, 623–627; Glad, *Key Pittman*, 132; Allen, "McAdoo Campaign," 226; and WGM to Tom Love, January 12, 1925, McAdoo MSS, Container 312, File: "Jan. 12, 1925."

79. NDB to ELB, July 5, 1924, WRHA-NDB MSS, Acc. #3491, Container 1, Folder 4.

80. Charles Cook to WGM, July 3, 1924, McAdoo MSS, Container 306, File: "July 3, 1924"; WGM to John Carter, July 4, 1924, McAdoo MSS, Container 306, File: "July 4, 1924"; Prude, "William Gibbs McAdoo," 627–628; Harbaugh, *Lawyer's Lawyer*, 213; and NDB to ELB, July 6, 1924, WRHA-NDB MSS, Acc. #3491, Container 1, Folder 4.

81. WGM to George Fort Milton, October 11, 1929, McAdoo MSS, Container 346, File: "Oct. 11, 1929"; and WGM to George Creel, March 12, 1927, McAdoo MSS, Container 333, File: "Mar. 2, 1927."

82. Murray, *103rd Ballot*, 199–205; and W. A. Palmer to WGM, July 8, 1924, McAdoo MSS, Container 306, File: "July 9, 1924."

83. WGM, "Public Statement," McAdoo MSS, Container 306, File: "July 12, 1924"; WGM to FHM, July 21, 1924, McAdoo MSS, Container 307, File: "July 21, 1924"; and Norman H. Davis to Charles S. Hamlin, September 24, 1924, Hamlin Papers, LOC MSS, Container 347, File: "General Correspondence, 4 Oct. 1923–20 Dec. 1923."

84. WGM to William Jennings Bryan, July 17, 1924, McAdoo MSS, Container 306, File: "July 17, 1924"; WGM to Homer Cummings, July 17, 1924, Cummings Papers, LOC MSS, Container 54, Folder: "1924 July 17–1925 April 30"; and WGM to Edith Wilson, August 9, 1924, Edith Bolling Wilson Papers, LOC MSS, Container 26, File: "Wm G. McAdoo, 1926–1930."

85. Davis to WGM, September 21, 1924, McAdoo MSS, Container 307, File: "Sept. 20, 1924"; WGM to George Fort Milton, October 1, 1924, McAdoo MSS, Container 308, File: "Oct. 1, 1924"; and Daniel Roper to WGM, November 11, 1924, McAdoo MSS, Container 309, File: "Nov. 11, 1924."

86. *NYT*, October 6, 1924, 1:2; Diary Entry, November 29, 1925, Hamlin Papers, LOC MSS, Reel 3, Diaries, Vol. IX:197; WGM to EWM, October 7 and 19, 1924, Wilson-McAdoo MSS, LOC MSS, Container 1, File: "McAdoo, William G., 1924"; WGM to Davis, October 4 and 24, 1924, McAdoo MSS, Container 306, File: "July 12, 1924"; *NYT*, October 29, 1924, 6:3; and WGM to Richard Lloyd Jones, November 3, 1924, McAdoo MSS, Container 308, File: "Nov. 3, 1924."

87. NDB to Leon Dessez, July 11, 1924, Baker MSS, Container 83, File: "Da–Dh, 1924"; NDB to S. W. Haynes, July 18, 1924, Baker MSS, Container 111, File: "Har–Hd, 1924"; NDB to Delos F. Wilcox, August 11, 1924, Baker MSS, Container 234, File: "Wia–Wil, 1924"; NDB to Wise, October 18 and November 10, 1924, Baker MSS, Container 237, File: "Wim–Wn, 1924"; NDB to Daniels, May 21, 1936, Baker MSS, Container 84, File: "Da–Dh, 1936"; and NDB to Davis, November 7, 1924, Davis MSS, IV:35, Folder: "Nov. 7, 1924."

88. WGM to Ed E. Leake, December 19, 1924, McAdoo MSS, Container 310, File: "Dec. 19, 1924."

89. WGM, "States' Rights and the Jeffersonian Idea," May 25, 1926, McAdoo MSS, Container 565, File: "Speeches, 1924–1926."

90. "Private Rights and Public Authority," in WGM, *The Challenge: Liquor and Lawlessness Versus Constitutional Government* (New York: Century Press, 1928), 106–145.

91. *NYT*, October 3, 1926, 9, 5:2, and October 4, 1926, 3:1; and *NYT*, October 24 1926, 9, 11:1.

92. WGM to John Sharp Williams, July 30, 1926, McAdoo MSS, Container 327, File: "July 30, 1926"; *Chattanooga News*, November 27, 1926, Cummings Papers, LOC MSS, Container 54, Folder: "1926 Jan. 1–Dec. 31"; Milton to WGM, January 13, 1927, McAdoo MSS, Container 331, File: "Jan. 13, 1927"; and Shouse to WGM, October 27, 1926, McAdoo MSS, Container 329, File: "Nov. 8, 1926."

93. *NYT*, January 27, 1927, 21:3, and January 29, 1927, 1:1 and 14:1.

94. *NYT*, January 31, 1927, 16:1.

95. *Los Angeles Examiner*, February 7, 1927, McAdoo MSS, Container 639; Mark Sullivan, "Will McAdoo Run?" *New York Herald Tribune*, March 13, 1927, and WGM to Sullivan, March 8, 1927, McAdoo MSS, Container 627; and WGM to Baruch, March 26, 1927, McAdoo MSS, Container 333, File: "Mar. 26, 1927."

96. Brisbane to WGM, March 2, 1927, McAdoo MSS, Container 333, File: "Mar. 2, 1927."

97. *NYT*, January 10, 1926, 1:7, and January 18, 1926, 3:1; WGM to Milton, January 7, 1927, McAdoo MSS, Container 331, File: "Jan. 7, 1927"; and Meredith to WGM, April 12, 1927, McAdoo MSS, Container 334, File: "Apr. 12, 1927."

98. *New York American* and New York *Evening Telegram*, April 16, 1927, McAdoo MSS, Container 627; Milton to WGM, May 19 and July 27, 1927, McAdoo MSS, Container 335, Files: "May 19, 1927" and "July 27, 1927"; and Milton to WGM, August 17, 1927, McAdoo MSS, Container 336, File: "Aug. 19, 1927."

99. WGM to Milton, August 27 and September 2, 1927, McAdoo MSS, Container 336, Files: "Aug. 27, 1927" and "Sept. 2, 1927"; and Milton to WGM and WGM reply, September 8 and 15, 1927, McAdoo MSS, Container 336, File: "September 15, 1927."

100. *The Nation* 123 (September 28 1927): 299; *NYT*, September 19, 1927, 24:1; and WGM to EWM, February 20, 1928, Wilson-McAdoo MSS, LOC MSS, Container 2, File: "McAdoo, William G., Jan.–Feb. 1928."

101. *NYT*, February 2, 1928, 1:4, and February 3, 1928, 1:6 and 22:1.

102. NDB to Ralph Hayes, September 22, 1927, Baker MSS, Container 114, File: "Ralph Hayes, 1927."

103. *NYT*, September 20, 1927, 1:3; WGM to Brian Mack, March 29, 1928, WGM to Jefferson Day Banquet, April 12, 1928, Walsh Papers, Container 181, File: "Mc"; Craig, *After Wilson*, 94–100; J. Leonard Bates, *Senator Thomas J. Walsh of Montana: Law and Public Affairs, from TR to FDR* (Urbana: University of Illinois Press, 1999), 265ff.; Mary Casey to Walsh, March 3, 1928, Walsh Papers, LOC MSS, Container 179, File: "Ce"; and Peter L. Peterson, "Stopping Al Smith: The 1928 Democratic Primary in South Dakota," *South Dakota History* 34 (February 1974): 439–454, 442.

104. Craig, *After Wilson*, 92–111; *NYT*, June 19, 1928, 9:2; WGM to Sally McAdoo, July 2, 1928, McAdoo MSS, Container 66, File: "July 2, 1928"; Newton to John J. Raskob, August 22, 1928, McAdoo MSS, Container 339, File: "Aug. 22, 1928"; and FDR to WGM, November 28, 1928, McAdoo MSS, Container 341, File: "Dec. 14, 1928."

105. *NYT*, November 4, 1928, 1:6; WGM to Furnifold M. Simmons, November 14, 1928, McAdoo MSS, Container 340, File: "Nov. 14, 1928"; and Cummings to WGM, November 26, 1928, Cummings Papers, LOC MSS, Container 55, Folder: "1928 Nov. 1–Dec. 18."

106. FDR to NDB and NDB reply, December 6 and 11, 1924, Baker MSS, Container 200, File: "Rog–Rz, 1924"; NDB to Walter Lippmann, November 14, 1927, Baker MSS,

Container 147, File: "Li–Lz, 1927"; and NDB to Samuel Dawson, May 17, 1927, Baker MSS, Container 82, File: "Da–Dh, 1927."

107. NDB to ELB, December 9, 1929, WRHA-NDB MSS, Acc. #3491, Container 1, Folder 5; NDB, "Inter-Allied Debts," *Trade Winds* (Cleveland, Ohio: Union Trust Company, October 30, 1926), NDB MSS, Container 256, File 246; and NDB to FHB, September 27, 1926, Baker MSS, Container 36, File: "Frank H. Baker, 1926."

108. *NYT*, August 31, 1926, 16:1; Fosdick to NDB, August 31, 1926, and "A True American" to NDB, September 1, 1926, Baker MSS, Container 252, Files: "War Debts Cancellation Article, F–L 1926" and "A–B 1926."

109. NDB to L. L. Wirt, February 7, 1927, Baker MSS, Container 237, File: "Wim–Wn, 1927"; and NDB to Hayes, June 26, 1929, Baker MSS, Container 257, File: "June 1929."

110. NDB to John G. Paxton, August 5, 1925, Baker MSS, Container 182, File: "Pa–Ph, 1925"; NDB to FHB, October 18, 1926, Baker MSS, Container 36, File: "Frank H. Baker, 1926"; and NDB to Ernest Harvier, November 26, 1926, Baker MSS, Container 109, File: "Haa–Haq, 1926."

111. NDB to Hayes, July 26, 1926, WRHA-NDB MSS, Acc. #4000, Container 4, Folder 73. The underlining is NDB's.

112. Hayes to NDB and NDB reply, June 28 and July 2, 1928, Baker MSS, Container 115, File: "Ralph Hayes, 1928"; and Lippmann to NDB, July 3, 1928, Baker MSS, Container 147, File: "Li–Lz, 1928."

113. Arthur M. Schlesinger Jr. and Fred L. Israel, eds., *History of American Presidential Elections 1789–1968*, 3 vols. (New York: Chelsea House, 1971), 3:2611–2624; NDB to Edith Bolling Wilson, July 7, 1928, Edith Bolling Papers, LOC MSS, Container 6, File: "Newton D. Baker, 1919–1932"; NDB to Ralph Hayes, July 2, 1928, Baker MSS, Container 115, File: "Ralph Hayes, 1928"; and NDB to FDR, July 6, 1928, Baker MSS, Container 200, File: "Rog–Rz, 1928."

114. NDB MSS, Container 85, File: "Democratic Committees 1928"; NDB to Hugh L. Scott, August 4, 1928, Baker MSS, Container 204, File: "Sch–Sd, 1928"; NDB to George Brown, October 6, 1928, Baker MSS, Container 47, File: "Bro–Bt, 1928"; NDB to FDR, November 6, 1928, Baker MSS, Container 200, File: "Rog–Rz, 1928"; *NYT*, November 1 and 4, 1928, 4:3 and 24:5; NDB to Ralph Hayes, November 7, 1928, Baker MSS, Container 115, File: "Ralph Hayes, 1928"; and NDB to William Dodd, November 12, 1928, Baker MSS, Container 86, File: "D–Dq, 1928."

CHAPTER 12: THE GREAT DEPRESSION

1. *NYT*, March 5, 1929, 6:3; and Fiona Ey, "Neither Wet nor Dry, Just Foggy: The Strange Case of the Wickersham Committee Report, 1923–1931" (unpublished history honors thesis, Australian National University, 1994), 25–27.

2. NDB to Peabody, April 5, 1923, Baker MSS, Container 185, File: "George Foster Peabody, 1923"; NDB to Moses Greenwood, July 5, 1927, Baker MSS, Container 107, File: "Gr–Gz, 1927"; NDB to Stanley H. Mullen, October 6, 1928, Baker MSS, Container 158, File: "Mo–Mx, 1928"; and NDB to Addison Hogue, August 2, 1928, Baker MSS, Container 120, File: "Ho–Ht, 1928."

3. WGM to Brice Clagett, March 22, 1929, McAdoo MSS, Container 342, File: "Mar. 22, 1929"; and WGM to George Fort Milton, July 30, 1929, McAdoo MSS, Container 342, File: "July 30, 1929."

4. Baker MSS, Containers 167 and 168, Files: "NCLOE"; and NDB to Reynolds Kinkade, May 23, 1929, Baker MSS, Container 167, File: "NCLOE." NDB to FHB, February 1, 1930, WRHA-NDB MSS, Acc. #3491, Container 2, Folder 2; NDB to Wickersham, October 17, 1930, Baker MSS, Container 167, File: "NCLOE, July–Dec. 1930"; NDB to James Fawcett, March 4, 1931, Baker MSS, Container 193, File: "Prohibition Report, 1931"; and NDB to R. W. Moore, March 5, 1931, Baker MSS, Container 158, File: "Mo–Mx, 1931."

5. Ey, "Neither Wet nor Dry," 42–55; and NDB, "Personal Statement to the Wickersham Report," Baker MSS, Container 167, File: "NCLOE, July–Dec. 1930."

6. Quoted in Ey, "Neither Wet nor Dry," iv.

7. WGM, Press Statement, January 21, 1931, McAdoo MSS, Container 355, File: "Jan. 21, 1931"; WGM to Daniel Roper, January 13, 1930, McAdoo MSS, Container 348, File: "Jan. 15, 1930"; NDB to Wickersham, December 16, 1931, Baker MSS, Container 236, File: "Honorable George W. Wickersham, 1931"; and NYT, January 21, 1931, 2:4.

8. NDB to James M. Beck, June 28, 1933, Baker MSS, Container 41, File: "Be–Bh, 1933"; and NDB to Byron Price, October 13, 1933, Baker MSS, Container 191, File: "Pr–Pz, 1933."

9. Gaunt to WGM, October 17, 1929, McAdoo MSS, Container 346, File: "Oct. 17, 1929"; WGM to Newton, November 2, 1929, McAdoo MSS, Container 347, File: "Nov. 2, 1929"; WGM to H. Hentz & Company, October 2, 1929, McAdoo MSS, Container 347, File: "October 30, 1929"; and WGM to EWM, November 12, 1929, Berkeley-WGM MSS, Box 8, Folder 8–1.

10. Baker MSS, Container 73, File: "Coa–Con, 1930"; and WRHA-NDB MSS, Acc. #4564, Folder 12. Three thousand three hundred dollars in 1931 was the equivalent, on the basis of changes to the Consumer Price Index, of $48,700 in 2011. www.measuringworth.com/uscompare/.

11. Anonymous to WGM, July 20, 1931, McAdoo MSS, Container 359, File: "July 20, 1931"; Eichler to WGM, July 5, 1931, McAdoo MSS, Container 359, File: "July 5, 1931"; and Edith Catterson to WGM, August 21, 1932, McAdoo MSS, Container 371, File: "Aug. 21, 1932." The underlining is Catterson's.

12. WGM to EWM, November 12, 1929, Berkeley-WGM MSS, Box 8, Folder: "Family Corresp., Outgoing 1929, 8–1"; and NYT, December 19, 1931, 6:4.

13. WGM to Richard E. Edmonds, June 12, 1929, McAdoo MSS, Container 344, File: "June 12, 1929"; and WGM to George W. Armstrong, June 8, 1931, McAdoo MSS, Container 359, File: "June 8, 1930."

14. WGM to W. E. Woodward, August 18, 1930, McAdoo MSS, Container 352, File: "Aug. 18, 1930"; NYT, June 5, 1931, 4:2; and WGM to F. W. Taussig, July 24, 1931, McAdoo MSS, Container 359, File: "July 9, 1931."

15. New York *Evening World*, October 20, 1930, McAdoo MSS, Container 353, File: "Oct. 20, 1930"; WGM to N. R. McCleskey, October 22, 1930, McAdoo MSS, Container 353, File: "Oct. 22, 1930"; and WGM to Senators Sam G. Britton and Joseph T. Robinson, December 22 and 29, 1930, McAdoo MSS, Container 355, Files: "Dec. 22, 1930" and "Dec. 29, 1930."

16. WGM to Orlando Weber, February 6, 1932, McAdoo MSS, Container 364, File: "Feb. 6, 1932."

17. NDB to Mary Fels, March 17, 1934, Baker MSS, Container 95, File: "Mrs. Joseph Fels, 1934"; and NDB to William G. Geier, January 5, 1933, Baker MSS, Container 102, File: "Ga–Gh, 1933."

18. NDB to Hayes, July 29, 1930, Baker MSS, Container 115, File: "Ralph Hayes, 1930"; NDB to FHB, August 23 and 31, 1930, Baker MSS, Container 136, File: "Frank H. Baker, 1930"; and WRHA-NDB MSS, Acc. #3491, Container 2, Folder 2.

19. NDB to Grosvenor Clarkson, August 7, 1934, Baker MSS, Container 56, File: "Ce–Cn, 1934"; NDB to Irving Fisher, July 20, 1931, Baker MSS, Container 93, File: "Fa–Fk, 1931"; NDB to Walter Lippmann, August 16, 1932, Baker MSS, Container 33, File: "Leonard P. Ayres, 1932"; NDB to Peabody, October 31, 1932, Baker MSS, Container 186, File: "George Foster Peabody, 1932"; NDB to Walter Gifford, August 24, 1931, Baker MSS, Container 192, File: "President's Organization on Unemployment Relief, 1931"; NDB to Daniel Roper, May 28, 1932, Baker MSS, Container 200, File: "Rog–Rz, 1932"; NDB, "To the *Press*," August 25, 1932, Baker MSS, Container 147, File: "Li–Lz, 1932"; and NDB to Robert J. Bender, March 31, 1932, Baker MSS, Container 41, File: "Be–Bh, 1932."

20. NDB, "To the Editor of the *Press*," August 25, 1932, Baker MSS, Container 147, File: "Liz–Lz, 1932"; NDB to Robert J. Bender, March 31, 1932, Baker MSS, Container 41, File: "Be–Bh, 1932"; and NDB to John H. Clarke, August 12, 1932, Baker MSS, Container 59, File: "John H. Clarke, 1932."

21. NDB, "Is Economic Planning Possible?" *The Cleveland Trust Monthly* 12, no. 10 (October 1931).

22. NDB, "To the Editor of the *Press*," August 25, 1932, Baker MSS, Container 147, File: "Li–Lz, 1932"; Baker MSS, Container 68, Files: "Cleveland Community Fund"; Baker MSS, Container 192-3, Files: "President's Organization on Unemployment Relief, 1931"; and *NYT*, August 1, 1932, 17:8.

23. NDB to Robert Leeper, September 1, 1932, Baker MSS, Container 143, File: "Le–Lh, 1932"; *NYT*, September 11, 1932, 8, 3:1; Baker MSS, Container 165, Files: "National Citizens Committee for the Welfare and Relief Mobilization of 1932"; *NYT*, November 11, 1932; Baker MSS, Container 166, File: "National Citizens Committee for Relief and Welfare Mobilization 1933"; and Baker MSS, Container 175, File: "National Relief Work (Alan Burns), 1935."

24. NDB to Peabody, September 27, 1932, Baker MSS, Container 186, File: "George Foster Peabody, 1932"; NDB, "Why Rebuild?" Baker MSS, Container 75, File: "National Relief Committee, 1934"; and NDB to W. A. Baldwin, October 10, 1932, Baker MSS, Container 35, File: "Baa–Bar, 1932."

25. *Saturday Evening Post* 207, no. 15 (October 13, 1934): 23.

26. NDB, "The Decay of Self-Reliance," *Atlantic Monthly* 154, no. 6 (December 1934): 726–733.

27. NDB in *NYT*, December 11, 1932, 8, 3:6; and Juliet Rose to NDB and NDB reply, March 12 and 13, 1934, Baker MSS, Container 201, File: "Rog–Rz, 1934." The underlining is Rose's. Mrs. F. F. Rutler to NDB and NDB reply, June 19 and 20, 1934, Baker MSS, Container 201, File: "Rog–Rz, 1934."

28. NDB to JCB, December 23, 1910, Baker MSS, Letterbooks, Reel 7; NDB to H. D. Baker, November 27, 1912, Baker MSS, Letterbooks, Reel 10; JCB to NDB, December 6, 1922, Baker MSS, Container 37, File: "Julian C. Baker, 1922"; G. V. Johnston to NDB,

December 28, 1923, Baker MSS, Container 34, File: "Baa–Bar, 1924"; NDB to FHB, February 1, 1930, WRHA-NDB MSS, Acc. #3491, Container 2, Folder 2; NDB to FHB, September 11, 1913, Baker MSS, Letterbooks, Reel 15; FHB to NDB, April 24, 1923, and FHB to NDB and NDB reply, August 7 and 8, 1925, Baker MSS, Container 36, Files: "Frank H. Baker, 1923 and 1925."

29. JCB to NDB, April 24, 1930, Baker MSS, Container 37, File: "Julian C. Baker, 1930"; Baker MSS, Container 37, Files: "Julian C. Baker, 1934–7"; and JCB to NDB, September 3, 1930, Baker MSS, Container 37, File: "Julian C. Baker, 1930."

30. JCB to NDB, n.d., Baker MSS, Container 37, File: "Julian C. Baker, 1933"; JCB to NDB, October 17, 1934, Baker MSS, Container 37, File: "Julian C. Baker, 1934"; and Baker MSS, Container 37, Files: "Julian C. Baker, 1936, 1937."

31. NDB to William E. Sweet, December 15, 1930, Baker MSS, Container 214, File: "Su–Sz, 1930"; and NDB to Ralph Hayes, September 7, 1931, Baker MSS, Container 115, File: "Ralph Hayes, 1931."

32. Baker MSS, Container 129, File: "Institute of Politics—Williamstown, Mass., 1931."

33. *Literary Digest*, August 15, 1931, 8; NDB to Peabody, April 9, 1931, Baker MSS, Container 186, File: "George Foster Peabody, 1931"; and NDB to Byron Newton, March 3, 1931, Baker MSS, Container 162, File: "Na–Nn, 1931."

34. Baker MSS, Container 262, Files: "Replies to Speech, 1931"; NDB to Hayes, August 6, 1931, WRHA-Hayes MSS, Container 4, Folder 74; and NDB to Ethel Vorce, September 12, 1931, Baker MSS, Container 225, File: "V., 1931."

35. Lippmann quoted in Ronald Steel, *Walter Lippmann and the American Century* (New York: Vintage Books, 1980), 291 and 292; Baker MSS, Container 115, File: "Ralph Hayes, 1931"; and Lippmann, "Baker for President," *New York Herald Tribune*, June 29, 1932, Baker MSS, Container 149, File: "Walter Lippmann, 1932."

36. Craig, *After Wilson*, 225–247; *NYT*, April 3, 1932, 7, 5:8; Hayes to NDB, September 3 and 10, 1931, and Hayes to John H. Clarke, September 17, 1931, Baker MSS, Container 115, File: "Ralph Hayes, 1931"; and FDR to Daniels, May 14, 1932, Papers of Franklin D. Roosevelt: Papers as Governor, Series 1, Box 19, Folder: "Josephus Daniels 1932."

37. NDB to Martin L. Davey, December 31, 1931, Baker MSS, Container 82, File: "Da–Dh, 1931"; and NDB to Hayes, September 7, 1931, Baker MSS, Container 115, File: "Ralph Hayes, 1931."

38. Havens, "Copy of Pencilled Memo, November 3, 1931," Baker MSS, Container 112, File: "Har–Hd, 1931"; NDB to Redmond C. Stewart, December 21, 1931, WRHA-Hayes MSS, Container 5, Folder 75; and William T. Reed to Harry Flood Byrd, December 28, 1931, Byrd MSS, Container 108, Folder: "William T. Reed, July–Dec. 1931."

39. Breckinridge to Robert Woolley, April 16, 1931, Woolley Papers, LOC MSS, Container 2; Bowers to FDR, June 7, 1931, Papers of Franklin D. Roosevelt: Papers as Governor, Series 1, Box 7, Folder: "Claude G. Bowers"; and Bowers to Josephus Daniels, December 19, 1931, Daniels Papers, LOC MSS, Reel 42, "Bowers, Claude G."

40. Hayes to NDB, November 29, 1931, Baker MSS, Container 115, File: "Ralph Hayes 1931 (2)."

41. R. W. Scott to Hayes, January 29, 1932, and Hayes to Jesse Strauss, April 28, 1932, Baker MSS, Container 116, Files: "Hayes, Ralph, Jan.–Feb. 1932," and "April 1932."

42. Hayes to NDB, January 20, 1932, Baker MSS, Container 116, File: "Hayes, Ralph, Jan.–Feb. 1932." The underlining is Hayes's.

43. *NYT*, January 16, 1932, 14:2; NDB to John H. Clarke, January 16, 1932, WRHA-Hayes MSS, Container 5, Folder 75; NDB to Norman C. Smith, March 17, 1932, Baker MSS, Container 209, File: "Si–Sm, 1932"; and NDB to Hayes, January 22, 1932, Baker MSS, Container 116, File: "Hayes, Ralph, Jan.–Feb. 1932."

44. Baker MSS, Containers 116 and 264, Files: "Hayes, Ralph, May–June 1932," and "Hayes, Ralph, Feb.–Mar. 1932"; WRHA-Hayes MSS, Container 6; and NDB to George Stewart Brown, February 18, 1932, Baker MSS, Container 47, File "Bro–Bt, 1932."

45. NDB to R. R. Thompson, January 19, 1932, Baker MSS, Container 216, File: "Ta–Tn, 1932"; NDB to Hayes, February 16, 1932, Baker MSS, Container 116, File: "Hayes, Ralph, Jan.–Feb. 1932"; and NDB to Norman Hapgood, February 18, 1932, Baker MSS, Container 111, File: "Norman Hapgood, 1932."

46. Daniel C. Roper to James Farley and Louis Howe, May 6, 1932, Democratic National Committee Papers, Box 99, Folder: "District of Columbia, R–Z"; NDB to Clarke, February 22 and March 3, 1932, Baker MSS, Container 59, File: "Hon. John H. Clarke, 1932"; NDB to Joseph H. Clarke, Baker MSS, Container 56, File: "Ce–Cn, 1932"; and NDB to Hapgood, February 18, 1932, Baker MSS, Container 111, File: "Norman Hapgood, 1932."

47. George Creel, "Newton D. Baker's Measure," *Collier's: The National Weekly* 89 (March 19 ,1932): 7ff.; Frankfurter to Charles C. Burlingham, February 10, 1932, Frankfurter Papers, LOC MSS, Reel 19; and Oswald Garrison Villard, "Newton D. Baker—Just Another Politician," *The Nation*, April 13, 1932, 414–418.

48. Walter Lippmann, "Baker for President," *New York Herald Tribune*, June 29, 1932, Baker MSS, Container 149, File: "Walter Lippmann, 1932"; *NYT*, May 1, 1932, 1:4; and Hayes to NDB, April 1 and February 18, 1932, Baker MSS, Container 116, File: "Hayes, Ralph, April 1932."

49. WGM to Nona McAdoo, April 16, 1929, McAdoo MSS, Container 67, File: "Apr. 16–17, 1929."

50. WGM to Daniels, April 5, 1930, McAdoo MSS, Container 350, File: "Apr. 5, 1930."

51. Craig, *After Wilson*, 184–193.

52. WGM to Brice Clagett, February 20, 1931, and Clagett reply, February 25, 1931, McAdoo MSS, Container 356, Files: "Feb. 20, 1931" and "Feb. 25, 1931"; WGM to Raskob, March 2, 1931, McAdoo MSS, Container 356, File: "Mar. 2, 1931"; and *NYT*, April 9, 1931, 3:1.

53. Craig, *After Wilson*, 192.

54. WGM to J. F. T. O'Connor, September 17, 1930, McAdoo MSS, Container 352, File: "Sept. 17, 1931"; WGM quoted in *NYT*, April 9, 1931, 3:1; WGM to George Creel, January 27, 1931, McAdoo MSS, Container 356, File: "Jan. 27, 1931"; and WGM to Frank C. Davis, March 10, 1931, McAdoo MSS, Container 357, File: "Mar. 10, 1931."

55. WGM to Edward M. House, January 10, 1931, McAdoo MSS, Container 355, File: "Jan. 10, 1931."

56. WGM to Baruch, May 7, 1931, McAdoo MSS, Container 358, File: "Apr. 27, 1931."

57. WGM to Frank Gannett, January 27, 1931, and Milton to WGM, February 2, 1931, McAdoo MSS, Container 356, Files: "Jan. 27, 1931" and "Feb. 2, 1931"; WGM to Newton, September 17, 1931, McAdoo MSS, Container 361, File: "Sept. 17, 1931"; and NDB to Newton, January 7, 1931, McAdoo MSS, Container 356, File: "Jan. 27, 1931."

58. WGM to W. M. Kiplinger, June 16, 1930, McAdoo MSS, Container 351, File: "June 16, 1930"; and WGM to Charles F. Horner, April 6 and May 7, 1931, McAdoo MSS, Containers 357 and 358, Files: "April 6, 1931" and "May 7, 1931."

59. Rosen, "Baker on the Fifth Ballot?" 234; WGM to Thomas Hamilton and Hamilton reply, September 24 and October 14, 1931, McAdoo MSS, Container 361, Files: "September 24 and October 14, 1931"; and Hampton to WGM, July 21, 1931, McAdoo MSS, Container 360, File: "July 29, 1931."

60. NYT, October 3, 1931, 9:3; WGM to Wayne C. Williams, October 21, 1931, McAdoo MSS, Container 361, File: "Oct. 21, 1931"; and Outlook and Independent, October 14, 1931, in George Fort Milton to WGM, November 2, 1931, McAdoo MSS, Container 362, File: "Nov. 2, 1931."

61. Byron Newton to WGM, August 17, 1931, McAdoo MSS, Container 360, File: "Aug. 17, 1931"; WGM to Claude Bowers, October 28, 1931, McAdoo MSS, Container 361, File: "Oct. 28, 1931"; and Moyle to WGM, November 18, 1931, McAdoo MSS, Container 362, File: "Nov. 18, 1931."

62. Baruch to WGM, April 27, 1931, McAdoo MSS, Container 358, File: "Apr. 27, 1931"; Baruch, Public Years, 223; Milton to WGM, February 18, 1931, McAdoo MSS, Container 356, File: "Sept. 24, 1931"; Clagett to WGM, September 24, 1931, McAdoo MSS, Container 361, File: "Sept. 24 1931"; and FDR to Cummings, January 25, 1932, Democratic National Committee Papers, Box 86.

63. WGM to Simmons, September 30, 1931, McAdoo MSS, Container 361, File: "Sept. 30, 1931."

64. NYT, February 19, 1932, 1:3; Rosen, "Baker on the Fifth Ballot?" 245; WGM to W. E. Woodward, February 18, 1932, McAdoo MSS, Container 365, File: "Feb. 17, 1932"; and Hayes to NDB, May 13, 1932, Baker MSS, Container 116, File: "Hayes, Ralph, May–June 1932."

65. Matthew Josephson and Hannah Josephson, Al Smith, Hero of the Cities: A Political Portrait Drawing on the Papers of Frances Perkins (London: Thames and Hudson, 1969), 242–250; Hearst quoted in Cramer, Newton D. Baker, 253; Russell M. Posner, "California's Role in the Nomination of Franklin D. Roosevelt," California Historical Society Quarterly 39, no. 2 (June 1960): 121–139, 124; Craig, After Wilson, 200–204; and Neal, Happy Days are Here Again, 58–64.

66. Storke, California Editor, 299.

67. Roper to FDR, February 19, 1932, Cummings MSS, Container 62.

68. NYT, February 20, 1932, 3:1; and March to NDB, April 5, 1932, Baker MSS, Container 259, File: "April, 1932: 1–5."

69. WGM, "Radio Address for John N. Garner," April 11, 1932, McAdoo MSS, Container 565, File: "Speeches, 1932." The capitalization is WGM's. Ed. J. Dunn to WGM, April 12, 1932, McAdoo MSS, Container 366, File: "April 12, 1932."

70. W. E. Woodward to WGM, May 4, 1932, McAdoo MSS, Container 367, File: "May 4, 1932"; NYT, May 8, 1932, 3, 6:4; Daniels in the Chicago Herald and Examiner, June 24, 1932, McAdoo MSS, Container 637; and Posner, "California's Role in the Nomination of Franklin D. Roosevelt," 130.

71. Schlesinger, Age of Roosevelt; Neal, Happy Days are Here Again; and Rosen, "Baker on the Fifth Ballot?" 227.

72. Hayes to John H. Clarke, July 6, 1932, Baker MSS, Container 116, File: "July–Dec. 1932."

73. NDB, "Statement," June 25, 1932, Baker MSS, Container 192, File: "Presidential Campaign 1932."

74. Storke, California Editor, 304; Rosen, "Baker on the Fifth Ballot?" 245; NYT, June 24, 1932, 1:7; and Rosen, "Baker on the Fifth Ballot?" 242.

75. *NYT*, June 9, 1932, 2:4; NDB to R. J. Clinchy, July 11, 1932, Baker MSS, Container 192, File: "Presidential Campaign, 1932"; WGM to John T. Gaffey, June 13, 1932, McAdoo MSS, Container 368, File: "June 13, 1932"; WGM to Thomas J. Walsh, November 15, 1932, McAdoo MSS, Container 377, File: "Nov. 15, 1932"; and WGM to John B. Elliot, August 15, 1932, McAdoo MSS, Container 371, File: "Aug. 15, 1932."

76. Donald A. Ritchie, *Electing FDR: The New Deal Campaign of 1932* (Lawrence: University Press of Kansas, 2007), 104.

77. Hayes to John H. Clarke, July 6, 1932, Baker MSS, Container 116, File: "Hayes, Ralph, July–Dec. 1932"; Hayes to William E. Dodd, July 25, 1932, Baker MSS, Container 116, File: "Hayes, Ralph, July–Dec. 1932"; Rosen, "Baker on the Fifth Ballot?" 237; and Ritchie, *Electing FDR*, 196.

78. Hayes to John H. Clarke, July 6, 1932, Baker MSS, Container 116, File: "Hayes, Ralph, July–Dec. 1932"; NDB to John Stewart Bryan, August 6, 1932, Baker MSS, Container 47, File: "Bro–Bt, 1932"; and FDR quoted in Rosen, "Baker on the Fifth Ballot?" 245.

79. Kennedy quoted in Neal, *Happy Days are Here Again*, 274–275; Roy W. Howard to NDB, July 12, 1932, Baker MSS, Container 122, File: "Roy W. Howard, 1932"; and Brice Clagett, "Personal and Confidential" Memo, February 22, 1933, McAdoo MSS, Container 380, File: "Feb. 22, 1933."

80. Garner quoted in "The Daily Washington Merry Go Round," October 9, 1933, Baker MSS, Container 260, File: "Oct. 1933"; and WGM to Rayburn, September 20, 1938, McAdoo MSS, Container 464, File: "Sept. 20, 1938," and April 28, 1939, McAdoo MSS, Container 469, File: "Apr. 28, 1939."

81. Farley quoted in Neal, *Happy Days are Here Again*, 124.

82. Storke to WGM, May 12, 1934, McAdoo MSS, Container 384, File: "May 12, 1934"; Cotton to WGM and Storke, September 26, 1938, McAdoo MSS, Container 465, File: "Sept. 26, 1938"; Brice Clagett, "Personal and Confidential," February 22, 1933, McAdoo MSS, Container 380, File: "Feb. 22, 1933"; Roper to WGM, January 7, 1939, McAdoo MSS, Container 468, File: "Jan. 13, 1939"; and Smith, *FDR*, 273.

83. Storke, *California Editor*, 314ff.; Neal, *Happy Days are Here Again*, 284–290; WGM to Sam Rayburn, April 28, 1939, McAdoo MSS, Container 469, File: "Apr. 28, 1939"; "Proceedings of the Democratic National Convention—1932," McAdoo MSS, Container 469, File: "Apr. 28, 1939"; and Smith quoted in Neal, *Happy Days are Here Again*, 285.

84. H. L. Mencken, *On Politics: A Carnival of Buncombe* (Baltimore: Johns Hopkins University Press, 1996), 263; and *Collier's*, November 12, 1932, McAdoo MSS, Container 630.

85. Rosen, "Baker on the Fifth Ballot?" 245; and Neal, *Happy Days are Here Again*, 283.

86. Howard to NDB, July 12, 1932, Baker MSS, Container 122, File: "Roy W. Howard, 1932"; and Wade to NDB, July 9, 1932, Baker MSS, Container 192, File: "Presidential Campaign 1932."

87. NDB to Hayes, July 1, 1932, Hayes MSS, LOC MSS, Container 5, Folder 77; NDB to John Stewart Bryan, July 4, 1932, Baker MSS, Container 47, File: "Bro–Bt, 1932"; NDB to Nathan Strauss, July 7, 1932, Baker MSS, Container 192, File: "Presidential Campaign 1932"; and NDB to P. H. Callahan, September 8, 1936, Baker MSS, Container 52, File: "Colonel P. H. Callahan, 1936."

88. NDB to John Stewart Bryan, July 4, July 7, and August 6, 1932, Baker MSS, Container 47, File: "Bro–Bt, 1932"; and NDB to George Foster Peabody, July 4, 1932, Baker MSS, Container 186, File: "George Foster Peabody, 1932."

89. NDB to William E. Dodd, July 23, 1932, Baker MSS, Container 87, File: "Di–Dq, 1932"; NDB to John Stewart Bryan, July 4 and 7, 1932, Baker MSS, Container 47, File: "Bro–Bt, 1932"; NDB to P. H. Callahan, July 9, 1932, Baker MSS, Container 52, File: "Colonel P. H. Callahan, 1932"; FDR to NDB, August 30, 1932, Baker MSS, Container 200, File: "Rog–Rz, 1932"; and NDB to Moley, September 10, 1932, Baker MSS, Container 159, File: "Mo–Mx, 1932."

90. NDB to Byron R. Newton, October 17, 1932, Baker MSS, Container 162, File: "Na–Nn, 1932"; Cleveland *Plain Dealer*, October 21, 1932, and *The Cleveland Press*, November 2, 1932, Baker MSS, Container 248, File: "1932"; and the *Boston Evening Transcript*, November 2, 1932, Baker MSS, Container 45, File: "Boston Address, November 2, 1932."

91. WGM to Thomas Love, December 29, 1925, McAdoo MSS, Container 321, File: "Dec. 29, 1932."

92. WGM to Clagett, January 23, 1932, McAdoo MSS, Container 364, File: "Jan. 23, 1932"; WGM to Baruch, February 27, 1932, McAdoo MSS, Container 365, File: "Feb. 27, 1932"; WGM to Woodward, February 18, 1932, McAdoo MSS, Container 365, File: "Feb. 17, 1932"; and *NYT*, January 13, 1932, 2:2.

93. Roy B. Maxey to WGM, September 1, 1932, McAdoo MSS, Container 373, File: "Sept. 8, 1932"; and Posner, "California's Role in the Nomination of Franklin D. Roosevelt," 133.

94. Dockweiler to Farley, August 20, 1932, FDR PPF 4649.

95. John B. Elliot to WGM, July 28, 1932, McAdoo MSS, Container 370, File: "July 28, 1932"; George Creel to WGM, August 31, 1932, McAdoo MSS, Container 372, File: "Aug. 31, 1932"; WGM, Radio Speech, August 29, 1932, McAdoo MSS, Container 565, File: "Speeches 1932"; WGM to Creel, August 7, 1932, McAdoo MSS, Container 371, File: "Aug. 17, 1932"; and Arthur J. Lovell to WGM, August 4, 1932, McAdoo MSS, Container 371, File: "August 4, 1932."

96. M. B. O'Connor to J. F. T. O'Connor, September 6, 1932, McAdoo MSS, Container 373, File: "Sept. 9, 1932."

97. William Hubbard to George Lynn, October 18, 1932, McAdoo MSS, Container 375, File: "Oct. 18, 1932"; Statement by WGM to the AAPA, September 28, 1932, McAdoo MSS, Container 374, File: "Sept. 28, 1932"; WGM to Long, October 20, 1932, Long Papers, Container 174, File: "Pol. Camp. 1932 IX"; and WGM to FDR, October 5, 1932, McAdoo MSS, Container 374, File: "Oct. 5, 1932."

98. "McAdoo for US Senate Memorandum," September 8, 1932, McAdoo MSS, Container 373, File: "Sept. 8, 1932."

99. George W. Lynn to WGM, September 24, 1932, McAdoo MSS, Container 373, File: "Sept. 24, 1932"; Josephus Daniels to Bernard Baruch, September 27, 1932, Daniels Papers, LOC MSS, Reel 41, "Baruch, Bernard M. 1930–1933"; WGM to Mrs. J. F. Harty, October 27, 1932, McAdoo MSS, Container 375, File: "Oct. 27, 1932"; WGM to Kemper Campbell, October 18, 1932, McAdoo MSS, Container 375, File: "Oct. 18, 1932"; WGM, Campaign Speech, October 7, 1932, McAdoo MSS, Container 565, File: "Speeches 1932"; WGM to G. B. Hjelm, October 31, 1932, McAdoo MSS, Container 376, File: "Oct. 31, 1932: Folder #2"; and "Wm. G. McAdoo for United States Senator," Campaign Pamphlet, McAdoo MSS, Container 378, File: "1932."

100. WGM, "Campaign Speech, October 1932," McAdoo MSS, Container 565, File: "Speeches 1932"; and "Campaign Speech, October 1932," McAdoo MSS, Container 606, File: "Miscellaneous."

101. WGM, "Campaign Speech, October 1932," McAdoo MSS, Container 606, File: "Miscellaneous"; and "Wm. G. McAdoo for United States Senator," McAdoo MSS, Container 378, File: "1932."

102. William Hubbard to George Lynn, October 18, 1932, McAdoo MSS, Container 375, File: "Oct. 18, 1932"; Maurice Harrison to WGM, October 31, 1932, McAdoo MSS, Container 376, File: "Nov. 2, 1932"; WGM to FDR, November 3, 1932, McAdoo MSS, Container 376, File: "Nov. 3, 1932"; and Garner to WGM, November 5, 1932, McAdoo MSS, Container 377, File: "November 5, 1932."

103. "Official Vote, November 8, 1932," McAdoo MSS, Container 378, File: "Dec. 13, 1932"; Nellie Donohue to WGM, November 8, 1932, and WGM to Charles E. Russell, November 15, 1932, McAdoo MSS, Container 377, Files: "Nov. 8 and 15, 1932"; and WGM to Creel, November 28, 1932, McAdoo MSS, Container 377, File: "Nov. 27, 1932."

CHAPTER 13: HUSBANDS AND FATHERS

1. NDB to Munson Havens, December 13, 1915, Baker MSS, Cleveland Letterbooks, Reel 18.

2. NDB to ELB, January 15, 1903, WRHA-NDB MSS, Acc. #3491, Container 1, Folder 1.

3. NDB to F. J. Andrew, March 27, 1933, Baker MSS, Container 33, File: "Am–Ar 1933"; and NDB to ELB, December 3, 1929, WRHA-NDB MSS, Acc. #3491, Container 1, Folder 5.

4. NDB to Ralph H. Leopold, March 28, 1914, Baker MSS, Letterbooks, Reel 13; and NDB to H. A. Garfield, April 30, 1931, Baker MSS, Container 102, File: "Ga–Gh, 1931."

5. NDB to Mary E. Raymond, December 5, 1931, Baker MSS, Container 194, File: "Ra–Rh, 1931"; and NDB to Mrs. Stanley McCormick, March 13, 1934, Baker MSS, Container 153, File: "McA–McD, 1934."

6. ELB to Addie Daniels, n.d. [1916], Daniels Papers, LOC MSS, Reel 38; and NDB to ELB, April 18 and April 7, 1916, WRHA-NDB MSS, Acc. #3491, Container 1, Folder 2.

7. ELB to Addie Daniels, n.d. [1916], Daniels Papers, LOC MSS, Reel 38; and NDB to ELB, April 7, 1916, WRHA-NDB MSS, Acc. #3491, Container 1, Folder 2.

8. NDB to Dr. J. W. Kern, December 31, 1928, Baker MSS, Container 137, File: "Ka–Kh, 1928."

9. NDB to Margaret Baker, November 8, 1930, WRHA-NDB MSS, Acc. #4564, Container 1, Folder 11.

10. NDB to Nell Whitlock, October 16, 1936, Baker MSS, Container 234, File: "Wh, 1936"; NDB to ELB, March 18, 1937, WRHA-NDB MSS, Acc. #3491, Container 2, Folder 1; NDB to Margaret Baker, May 2, 1937, WRHA-NDB MSS, Acc. #4564, Container 3, Folder 20; and NDB to John J. Pershing, June 25, 1937, Baker MSS, Container 184, File: "Pa–Ph, 1937."

11. NDB to ELB, April 7, 1919, WRHA-NDB MSS, Acc. #3491, Container 1, Folder 4; NDB Memo to Ralph Hayes, "ca July 1918," Baker MSS, Container 255, File: "1918"; and NDB to Betty Baker, September 16, 1923, WRHA-NDB MSS, Acc. #4564, Container 1, Folder 2.

12. NDB to Mrs Edith Stevenson Wright, May 27, 1930, Baker MSS, Container 238, File: "Wo–Wz, 1930"; NDB to Mlle Schenker, September 29, 1923, WRHA-NDB MSS, Acc. #4564, Container 1, Folder 2; NDB to Betty Baker, October 17, 1923, WRHA-NDB

MSS, Acc. #3491, Container 3, Vol. 1, and March 1, 1924, WRHA-NDB MSS, Acc. #4564, Container 1, Folder 4.

13. Betty Baker to NDB, n.d., and NDB reply, September 22, 1924, Baker MSS, Container 154, File: "Mr. and Mrs. John P. McGean (Betty Baker)"; NDB to Betty Baker, September 28, 1924, WRHA-NDB MSS, Acc. #4564, Container 1, Folder 4; and NDB to Betty Baker, November 30, 1924, and January 22, 1925, WRHA-NDB MSS, Acc. #4564, Container 1, Folder 5.

14. NDB to Betty Baker, January 8 and February 17, 1925, WRHA-NDB MSS, Acc. #4564, Container 1, Folder 6; Lee Phillips to NDB, January 28 and June 18, 1926, Baker MSS, Container 182, File: "Pa–Ph, 1926"; and Wedding Invitation, Pershing Papers, LOC MSS, Container 19, File: "Baker, Newton D. 1921-."

15. NDB to Betty Baker, June 12, 1927, WRHA-NDB MSS, Acc. #4564, Container 1, Folder 10; Lee Phillips to Walton McGean, September 9, 1927, W. H. McGean to J. P. McGean, September 12, 1927, and NDB to Betty Baker, September 14, 1927, Baker MSS, Container 154, File: "Mr. and Mrs. John P. McGean (Betty Baker)."

16. NDB to Peggy Baker, April 17, 1932, WRHA-NDB MSS, Acc. #4564, Container 2, Folder 3; and NDB to Betty Baker, January 22, 1925, WRHA-NDB MSS, Acc. #4564, Container 1, Folder 5.

17. NDB to Bess Baker, WRHA-NDB MSS, Acc. #3491, Container 2, Folder 1.

18. NDB to Jackie Baker, April 3, 1916, WRHA-NDB MSS, Acc. #3491, Container 1, Folder 2.

19. G. B. Gould to NDB, March 6 and April 26, 1923, Baker MSS, Container 103, File: "Gi–Gq, 1923."

20. NDB to Betty Baker, September 22, 1924, Baker MSS, Container 154, File: "Mr. and Mrs. John P. McGean (Betty Baker)"; and NDB to A. R. Hoxton, October 22, 1924, Baker MSS, Container 120, File: "Ho–Ht, 1924."

21. NDB to Frank A. Scott, May 13, 1926, Baker MSS, Container 205, File: "Frank A. Scott, 1926"; NDB to Alfred B. Percy, March 27, 1927, Baker MSS, Container 182, File: "Pa–Ph, 1927"; NDB to A. N. Sheriff, January 25, March 4, August 21, and October 25, 1926, Roxbury School Reports, Baker MSS, Container 207, File: "She–Shz, 1926"; and Jack Baker to NDB correspondence, Baker MSS, Container 34, File: "Baa–Bar, 1926."

22. NDB to Clarence N. Goodwin, May 25, 1934, Baker MSS, Container 105, File: "W. B. Gongwer, 1935"; and NDB to Hayes, August 28, 1928, Baker MSS, Container 257, File: "Aug. 1928."

23. NDB to Peggy Baker, May 31, 1931, WRHA-NDB MSS, Acc. #4564, Folder 12; NYT, July 25, 1932, 17:6; NDB to John H. Clarke, January 16, 1932, WRHA-NDB MSS, Acc. #4000, Container 5, Folder 75; NDB to Peggy Baker, January 17, 1932, WRHA-NDB MSS, Acc. #4564, Folder 13; NDB to Dr. Allen Krause, February 17 and March 15, 1932, Baker MSS, Container 37, File: "Newton D. Baker III, 1932"; NDB to Dr. Marcusson, May 14, 1932, Baker MSS, Container 151, File: "Ma–Mb, 1932"; and NDB to ELB, November 12, 1937, Baker MSS, Container 36, File: "Baa–Bar, 1937."

24. NDB to Miss H. J. Patterson, February 22, 1924, Baker MSS, Container 182, File: "Pa–Ph, 1924."

25. Harriet Farnsworth Gulick to NDB and NDB reply, July 21 and 24, 1925, Baker MSS, Container 107, File: "Gr–Gz, 1925"; and NDB to Peggy Baker, October 1, 1930, WRHA-NDB MSS, Acc. #4564, Folder 11.

26. NDB to Mabel Wiley Kelly, September 18, 1931, Baker MSS, Container 203, File: "Sarah Lawrence College, 1931"; and NDB to Peggy, November 30, 1930, WRHA-NDB MSS, Acc. #4564, Folder 11.

27. NDB to Peggy, March 1, 1931, WRHA-NDB MSS, Acc. #4564, Folder 12; NDB to Peggy, January 12, 1933, Baker MSS, Container 242, File: "Sarah Lawrence College, 1933"; NDB to Constance Warren, June 9, 1933, Baker MSS, Container 203, File: "Sarah Lawrence College 1933"; and NDB to Peggy Baker, June 3, 1934, WRHA-NDB MSS, Acc. #4564, Container 2, Folder 13. NDB to J. Lionberger Davis, June 14, 1934, Baker MSS, Container 83, File: "Da–Dh, 1934"; NDB to Fulton Wright, October 11, 1934, Baker MSS, Container 239, File: "Wo–Wz, 1934"; NDB to Wright, April 25, 1935, Baker MSS, Container 242, File: "Mr. & Mrs. Fulton Wright, 1935"; NDB to Peggy Baker, November 2, 1936, Baker MSS, Container 242, File: "Mr. & Mrs. Fulton Wright, 1936"; and NDB to Peggy Baker, December 27, 1936, WRHA-NDB MSS, Acc. #4564, Container 3, Folder 19. Twenty-one thousand five hundred dollars in 1934 was the equivalent, on the basis of changes to the Consumer Price Index, of $361,000 in 2011. www.measuringworth.com/uscompare/.

28. See the newspaper cuttings in "Wilson Family Clippings, Eleanor McAdoo Wilson: Wedding Scrapbooks 16–1," Wilson-McAdoo (SB) MSS, Box 16; and EWM, *The Woodrow Wilsons* (New York: The Macmillan Company, 1937), 258.

29. EWM Reminiscences, n.d., Wilson-McAdoo (SB) MSS, Box 7, Folder 8; *NYT*, March 13, 1914, 1:6; and Saunders, *Ellen Axson Wilson*, 170–171, 194, and 218–219.

30. EWM, *Woodrow Wilsons*, 273.

31. WGM to EWM, December 25, 1913, Wilson-McAdoo MSS, LOC MSS, Container 1, File: "McAdoo, William G., 1913–14"; EWM to WGM, January 22, 1914, McAdoo MSS, Container 47, File: "Jan. 2–26, 1914"; and Saunders, *Ellen Axson Wilson*, 270.

32. WGM to EWM, January 25, 1914, Wilson-McAdoo MSS, LOC MSS, Container 1, File: "McAdoo, William G., 1913–14." The underlining is WGM's. Grayson to WGM, February 6, 1914, McAdoo MSS, Family Correspondence and Related Material, Container 47, File: "Feb. 6–7, 1914"; WGM to EWM, February 20, 1914, Wilson McAdoo MSS, LOC MSS, Container 1, File: "McAdoo, William G., 1913–14"; Saunders, *Ellen Axson Wilson*, 330; and McAdoo MSS, Container 90, Diary for 1937.

33. *NYT*, March 14, 1914, 1:6; WGM to Major F. K. Huger, March 23, 1914, McAdoo MSS, Container 48, File: "Mar. 23, 1914"; and "Disparity of Age in Marriage," Quincy *Journal*, 1914, McAdoo MSS, Container 48, File: "April 3, 1914."

34. Saunders, *Ellen Axson Wilson*, 80; *NYT*, May 8, 1914, 1:4; and "Wilson Family Clippings, Eleanor McAdoo Wilson: Wedding Scrapbooks," Wilson-McAdoo (SB) MSS, Boxes 7 and 16.

35. WGM, *Crowded Years*, 347; WGM to Ruth Hamilton Walsh, January 9, 1912, McAdoo MSS, Container 476–3; and WGM to Seth Barton French, March 8, 1912, McAdoo MSS, Container 476–2.

36. WGM to Irving W. Bonbright, March 19, 1913, McAdoo MSS, Container 478–1; WGM to K. B. Conger, November 12, 1915, McAdoo MSS, Container 478–3; WGM to Harriet Martin, July 18, 1915, McAdoo MSS, Container 53, File: "July 17–18, 1916"; *NYT*, June 9, 1918, 16:1; and Harriet Martin-Platt to WGM, July 8, 1935, McAdoo MSS, Container 72, File: "July 7–8, 1935."

37. WGM to Ross McAdoo, March 30, 1917, McAdoo MSS, Container 54, File: "Mar. 30, 1917"; and WGM to FHM, December 18, 1917, McAdoo MSS, Container 55, File: "Dec. 17–20, 1917."

38. WGM to F. K. Huger, June 11, 1920, McAdoo MSS, Container 236, File: "June 19, 1920," WGM to FHM, March 5, 1929, McAdoo MSS, Container 67, File: "Mar. 5, 1929"; and Ethel McAdoo to WGM, n.d., McAdoo MSS, Container 343, File: "Apr. 18, 1929."

39. WGM to Sally, April 21, 1922, McAdoo MSS, Container 61, File: "Apr. 18–29, 1922"; WGM to FHM, August 16, 1926, McAdoo MSS, Container 648, File: "Aug., 1926: 11."

40. WGM to EWM, January 8, 1928, Berkeley-WGM MSS; Link, ed., *Papers of Woodrow Wilson*, 55:412; and Chase, "William Gibbs McAdoo," 170.

41. *Houston Chronicle*, March 11, 1913, McAdoo MSS, Container 590, "Scrapbooks"; "On the Inside at Washington," *The Sunday Herald* (Washington, D.C.), April 2, 1914, McAdoo MSS, Container 51, File: "Mar. 6–9, 1914."

42. WGM to Cleveland (Ohio) *Leader*, February 27, 1914, McAdoo MSS, Container 484-3; WGM to NDB and NDB reply, February 27 and March 1, 1915, McAdoo MSS, Container 51, File: "Mar. 6–9, 1915"; WGM to Samuel Untermeyer, March 11, 1915, McAdoo MSS, Container 484-3; and WGM, Press Release, June 2, 1915, McAdoo MSS, Container 51, File: "Jun. 1–3, 1915."

43. Wilson to Edith Galt, August 31, 1915, in Link, ed., *Papers of Woodrow Wilson* 34:394. The underlining is Wilson's. EWM to Nona, November 15, 1918, McAdoo MSS, Container 78, File: "undated."

44. WGM to Baruch, March 22, 1919, McAdoo MSS, Container 218, File: "Mar. 22, 1918."

45. Nona to WGM, November 15, 1922, McAdoo MSS, Container 62, File: "Nov. 13–16, 1922."

46. WGM, *Crowded Years*, 348; and WGM to Nona McAdoo, December 17, 1926, McAdoo MSS, Container 65, File: "Dec. 17–18, 1926."

47. *New York American*, May 12, 1935, and Edward S. Cowles to WGM, December 9, 1935, McAdoo MSS, Container 73, File: "Dec. 8–9, 1935." Nona McAdoo to WGM, November 24, 1935, McAdoo MSS, Container 73, File: "Nov. 23–25, 1935."

48. WGM to Billy McAdoo, July 26, 1914, and June 6, 1916, McAdoo MSS, Containers 80 and 81.

49. WGM, "Family War Service," McAdoo MSS, Container 77, File: "undated"; William G. McAdoo III to Nona de Mohrenschildt, September 9, 1918, Wilson-McAdoo (SB) MSS, Box 15, Folder: "Wilson Family Ephemera—Robert H. McAdoo"; WGM to Billy, September 24, 1918, Wilson-McAdoo MSS, Container 7, File: "General Correspondence, William Gibbs McAdoo, 1923–37"; and WGM to Billy, May 6, 1921, McAdoo MSS, Container 60, File: "May 4–6, 1921."

50. WGM to Charles Page, October 28, 1921, McAdoo MSS, Container 256, File: "Oct. 28, 1921"; WGM to Billy and WGM to Charles Page, November 12, 1921, McAdoo MSS, Container 61, File, "Nov. 12, 1921"; WGM to Edwin Hobby, February 28, 1921, McAdoo MSS, Container 511; and WGM to J. R. Burnett, November 18, 1921, McAdoo MSS, Container 515, Vol. 23(2).

51. WGM to Billy McAdoo, November 18, 1921, McAdoo MSS, Container 61, File: "Nov. 18, 1921"; EWM to WGM, March 16, 1928, McAdoo MSS, Container 66, File: "Mar. 16, 1928"; Helen W. Bones to Margaret W. Wilson, n.d., Wilson-McAdoo MSS, LOC MSS, Container 4, File: "Bones, Helen W., undated"; Molly McAdoo to EWM, March 6, 1933, Wilson-McAdoo (SB) MSS, Box 15, Folder 7; and Molly McAdoo to WGM, February 10, 1935, McAdoo MSS, Container 72, File: "Feb. 10, 1935."

52. *NYT*, May 2, 1936, 10:2; WGM to Billy McAdoo, November 18, 1921, McAdoo MSS, Container 61, File: "Nov. 18, 1921"; EWM to WGM, March 16, 1928, McAdoo MSS, Container 66, File: "Mar. 16, 1928"; WGM to Edward Cowles, May 19, 1930, McAdoo MSS, Container 350, File: "May 19, 1930"; Edward Cowles to WGM, November 8, 1932, and WGM reply, November 15, 1932, McAdoo MSS, Container 70, File: "Nov. 14–17, 1932."

53. *NYT*, March 20, 1934, 25:4; WGM to Hearst, January 11, 1934, McAdoo MSS, Container 71, File: "Jan. 8–11, 1934"; and WGM to EWM, March 21, 1934, Wilson-McAdoo MSS, Container 2, File: "McAdoo, William G., 1934." The underlining is WGM's.

54. *NYT*, October 14, 1934, 2, 2:2, and June 9, 1937, 12:3; Billy McAdoo to WGM, June 15, 1937, McAdoo MSS, Container 75, File: "June 12–15, 1937"; Charles F. Horner of the NAA to WGM, June 5, 1932, McAdoo MSS, Container 72, File: "June 13, 1935"; and Billy McAdoo to WGM, January 18, 1937, McAdoo MSS, Container 74, File: "Jan. 17–19, 1937."

55. WGM to Billy, November 1, 1937, McAdoo MSS, Container 75, File: "Nov. 1, 1937"; WGM to Marguerite de Heczey, April 29, 1938, McAdoo MSS, Container 454, File: "Apr. 29, 1938"; and Chase, "William Gibbs McAdoo," 160.

56. WGM to William Scudder, September 30, 1915, McAdoo MSS, Container 487-2; Norman Hamilton to WGM, January 3, 1918, McAdoo MSS, Container 50, File: "Jan. 1–3, 1918"; McAdoo MSS, Container 77, File: "undated"; WGM to RHM, October 31, 1917, McAdoo MSS, Container 55, File: "Oct. 31, 1917"; and Chase, "William Gibbs McAdoo," 165.

57. W. F. Magie to WGM and reply, July 20 and 21, 1921, McAdoo MSS, Container 239, File: "Jul. 21, 1920"; and WGM to RHM, December 6, 1920, McAdoo MSS, Container 60, File: "Dec. 6–8, 1920."

58. WGM to RHM, July 28, 1922, McAdoo MSS, Container 266, File: "Jul. 28, 1922." The underlining is WGM's.

59. RHM to WGM, November 25, 1922, McAdoo MSS, Container 271, File: "Nov. 25, 1922"; and WGM to William B. Joyce, September 17, 1923, McAdoo MSS, Container 283, File: "Sept. 17, 1923."

60. *NYT*, January 11, 1937, 10:1; WGM to Senator William H. King, October 16, 1929, McAdoo MSS, Container 346, File: "Oct. 16, 1929"; WGM to W. W. Mattson, January 22, 1937, and WGM to E. D. Flaherty, January 29, 1937, McAdoo MSS, Container 430, File: "Jan. 22, 1937." The McAdoo graves at Arlington are Numbers 4977, 4968, and 4969. www.arlingtoncemetery.net/rhmcadoo.htm.

61. EWM to Margaret Wilson, November 8, 1937, Wilson-McAdoo MSS, LOC MSS, Container 4, File: "Margaret Woodrow Wilson"; WGM to EWM, September 14, 1915, Berkeley-WGM MSS; and EWM to WGM and EWM to WGM, October 30, 1919, McAdoo MSS, Container 58, File: "Oct. 30–31, 1919."

62. WGM to Frank A. Munsey, July 1, 1914, McAdoo MSS, Container 118, File: "July 1, 1914"; and the *Boston Sunday Globe*, December 4, 1932, 2:1, Wilson-McAdoo (SB) MSS, Box 16, Folder 2: "Wilson Family Clippings."

63. WGM to EWM, December 31, 1927, Wilson-McAdoo MSS, Container 1, File: "McAdoo, William G., 1926–27"; WGM to EWM, January 17 and 20, 1928, Wilson-McAdoo MSS, LOC MSS, Container 2, File: "McAdoo, William G., Jan.–Feb. 1928"; and EWM to WGM, February 7, 1928, McAdoo MSS, Container 66, File: "Feb. 7, 1928."

64. EWM to WGM, March 2, 1928, McAdoo MSS, Container 66, File: "Mar. 2, 1928," and WGM reply, March 8, 1928, Wilson-McAdoo MSS, LOC MSS, Container 2, File: "McAdoo, William G., Mar.–Apr. 1928."

65. WGM to EWM, March 18, 1928, Berkeley-WGM MSS; and EWM to WGM, April 7, 1928, McAdoo MSS, Container 66, File: "Apr. 8–10, 1928."

66. EWM to WGM, McAdoo MSS, Container 78, File: "undated"; and WGM to EWM, December 1, 1928, Wilson-McAdoo MSS, LOC MSS, Container 2, File: "McAdoo, William Gibbs, May–Dec. 1928." The underlining is WGM's. EWM to WGM, June 28, 1929, McAdoo MSS, Container 78, File: "undated"; and WGM to EWM, June 28, 1929, Wilson-McAdoo MSS, LOC MSS, Container 2, File: "McAdoo, William Gibbs, June–July 1929."

67. Newton to WGM, October 10, 1929, McAdoo MSS, Container 346, File: "Oct. 10, 1929." The capitalization is Newton's. Thomas Gaunt to WGM, June 4, 1931, McAdoo MSS, Container 359, File: "June 4, 1931"; Jessie Wilson Sayre to Margaret Wilson, August 7, 1931, Wilson-McAdoo MSS, LOC MSS, Container 5, File: "Sayre, Jessie Wilson, 1926–32"; and WGM to Thomas Gaunt, April 25, 1930, McAdoo MSS, Container 350, File: "Apr. 25, 1930."

68. See McAdoo MSS, Containers 71–72 and 648. WGM to EWM, May 10, 1934, Wilson-McAdoo MSS, LOC MSS, Container 2, File: "McAdoo, William G., 1934"; and Francis B. Sayre to EWM, May 6, 1934, Wilson-McAdoo MSS, LOC MSS, Container 2, File: "Sayre, Francis B., 1932, 1934." The underlining is Sayre's.

69. WGM to EWM, May 23, 1934, Wilson-McAdoo MSS, LOC MSS, Container 2, File: "McAdoo, William G., 1934."

70. "Property Settlement," McAdoo MSS, Container 86, File: "Personal—Financial Material"; Eugene Overton to EWM, July 16, 1934, Wilson-McAdoo MSS, LOC MSS, Container 3, File: "O–P, 1934"; McAdoo MSS, Container 87, File: "Personal Miscellany—Financial Material"; and NYT, July 20, 1934, 15:2. Six thousand dollars in 1934 was the equivalent, on the basis of changes to the Consumer Price Index, of $101,000 in 2011. www.measuringworth.com/uscompare/.

71. For press reports of the McAdoo divorce, see McAdoo MSS, Container 632; and NYT, July 18 and 19, 1934, 1:3 and 1:2, July 25 and August 9, 1934, 19:2 and 37:3. W. H. Neblett to WGM and WGM reply, July 27 and 30, 1934, McAdoo MSS, Container 396, File: "July 30, 1934."

72. Sally to WGM, July 18 [1934], McAdoo MSS, Container 78, File: "undated"; McGerr, *Fierce Discontent*, 11 and 45; *Historical Statistics of the United States*, 1:64, and Elaine Tyler May, *Great Expectations: Marriage and Divorce in Post-Victorian America* (Chicago: University of Chicago Press, 1980), 167.

73. May, *Great Expectations,* passim; Garry Wills, *Under God: Religion and American Politics* (New York: Touchstone Books, 1990), 35; NDB to Peggy Baker, December 13, 1936, WRHA-Baker MSS, Acc. #4564, Container 3, File 19; NDB to Hayes, November 27, 1937, Baker MSS, Container 117, File: "Ralph Hayes, 1937"; and NDB to Vernon Richardson, December 15, 1936, Baker MSS, Container 199, File: "Ri–Rof, 1936."

74. NYT, November 8, 1934, 25:2; Travis Hoke, "Tragedy of Ellen McAdoo," *American Weekly*, March 23, 1947, 3; and Helen Bones to EWM, March 9, 1935, Wilson-McAdoo MSS, LOC MSS, Container 1, File: "Bones, Helen W., 1931–1937."

75. NYT, November 11, 1937, 20:2; McAdoo MSS, Container 637; Wilson-McAdoo (SB) MSS, Box 7, Folder 14: "Ellen Wilson McAdoo—Personal Ephemera"; and Box 4, Folder 3: "Ellen Wilson McAdoo, Professional Correspondence, Unidentified."

76. EWM to WGM, February 3, 1935, McAdoo MSS, Container 72, File: "Feb. 3, 1935"; Eva Scott to WGM, December 5, 1934, McAdoo MSS, Container 72, File: "Dec. 5–6, 1934"; and WGM to EWM, March 10, 1935, Berkeley-WGM MSS.

77. Ellen Wilson McAdoo to EWM, June 25, 1935, Wilson-McAdoo MSS, LOC MSS, Box 7. The underlining is Ellen's.

78. WGM to EWM, February 7, 1937, Wilson-McAdoo MSS, LOC MSS, Container 2, File: "McAdoo, William G., 1935–37, n.d."; Wilson-McAdoo MSS, LOC MSS, Box 16; *NYT*, April 3, 1937; *Los Angeles Examiner*, February 27, 1937, and *Los Angeles Evening Herald and Express*, April 2, 1937, McAdoo MSS, Container 74, File: "Feb. 27–28, 1937"; and Hoke, "Tragedy of Ellen McAdoo," 3. For the transcript of Ellen's divorce trial, see McAdoo MSS, Container 77, File: "undated."

79. Ellen to WGM, June 7, 1937, McAdoo MSS, Container 74, File: "May 5–8, 1937"; William H. Neblett to WGM, August 6, 1937, McAdoo MSS, Container 440, File: "Aug. 6, 1937"; WGM to Ellen, August 6, 1937, McAdoo MSS, Container 74, File: "May 5–8, 1937"; EWM to Margaret Wilson, November 8, 1937, Wilson-McAdoo MSS, LOC MSS, Container 4, File: "Margaret Woodrow Wilson"; Los Angeles *Herald and Express*, September 24, 1943, Wilson-McAdoo (SB) MSS, Box 16, Folder 2; Hoke, "Tragedy of Ellen McAdoo," 3; and Chase, "William Gibbs McAdoo," 405.

80. WGM to Faith McAdoo, September 25, 1935, McAdoo MSS, Container 73, File: "Sept. 25–26, 1935"; WGM to EWM, December 21, 1936, Berkeley-WGM MSS; EWM to Margaret Wilson, September 3, 1937, Wilson-McAdoo MSS, LOC MSS, Container 4, File: "Margaret Woodrow Wilson"; and EWM to WGM, May 10, 1938, McAdoo MSS, Container 75, File: "May 10, 1938."

81. EWM to Margaret Wilson, November 8, 1937, Wilson-McAdoo MSS, LOC MSS, Container 4, File: "Margaret Woodrow Wilson"; and "Genealogy of President Woodrow Wilson," www.wc.rootsweb.ancestry.com.

82. EWM to WGM, June 4, 1935, McAdoo MSS, Container 72, File: "June 4, 1935."

83. EWM to Margaret Wilson, September 3, 1937, Wilson-McAdoo MSS, LOC MSS, Container 4, File: "Margaret Woodrow Wilson"; Margaret Wilson to EWM, May 11, 1938, Wilson-McAdoo MSS, LOC MSS, Container 3, File: "Wilson, Margaret Woodrow, 1934–39"; Wilson-McAdoo (SB) MSS, Box 16, File 2: "Wilson Family Clippings"; *NYT*, April 7, 1967, 37:4; WGM to EWM, March 14, 1934, and n.d., Wilson-McAdoo MSS, Container 2, Files: "McAdoo, William G., 1934" and "1935–37 and undated"; and EWM to Margaret Wilson, September 6, 1943, Wilson-McAdoo MSS, LOC MSS, Container 4, File: "Margaret Woodrow Wilson."

84. EWM, *Julia and the White House* (New York: Dodd, Mead & Company, 1946), 164.

85. EWM to WGM, March 4, 1935, McAdoo MSS, Container 72, File: "Mar. 4 1935"; and WGM reply, March 10, 1935, Berkeley-WGM MSS.

86. *NYT*, September 14, 1935, 17:6; and Doris McAdoo, Diary, McAdoo MSS, Container 89, n.f.

87. *NYT*, September 14, 1935, 17:6; Neblett to WGM, September 13, 1935, McAdoo MSS, Container 410, File: "Sept. 13, 1935"; F. P. Clark to WGM, September 15, 1935, McAdoo MSS, Container 72, File: "Sept. 15, 1935"; Etna C. Roberts to Margaret Wilson, March 27, 1941, Wilson-McAdoo MSS, LOC MSS, Container 6, File: "Etna C. Roberts, 1941–43"; EWM to WGM, September 12, 1935, McAdoo MSS, Container 72, File: "Sept. 11–12, 1935"; and King to WGM, September 15, 1935, McAdoo MSS, Container 72, File: "Sept. 15, 1935."

88. Associated Press, December 15, 1936, McAdoo Huntington MSS, Box 4, Folder 27; WGM to Tom Connally, November 4, 1936, McAdoo MSS, Container 427, File: "Nov. 4, 1936"; and WGM to Francis B. Sayre, October 29, 1940, McAdoo MSS, Container 473, File: "Oct. 29, 1940."

89. *Los Angeles Times*, April 12, 1937, McAdoo MSS, Container 632; WGM to Ellen, October 24, 1938, Wilson-McAdoo (SB) MSS, Box 8, Folder 3: "William Gibbs McAdoo, Family Corres., Incoming 1938"; *NYT*, October 13, 1939, 26:3; "McAdoos Adopt Grandson," unidentified newspaper clipping, McAdoo Huntington MSS, Box 10, Folder 49; and "Genealogy of President Woodrow Wilson: Richard Floyd McAdoo," www.wc.rootsweb.ancestry.com.

CHAPTER 14: THE NEW DEAL

1. Schwarz, *New Dealers*, 30–31.

2. WGM to Roper, November 17, 1932, McAdoo MSS, Container 377, File: "Nov. 17, 1932"; and WGM to Edward M. House, December 12, 1932, McAdoo MSS, Container 378, File: "Dec. 12, 1932."

3. Charles F. Pace to WGM, February 3, 1933, McAdoo MSS, Container 379, File: "Feb. 3, 1933." Ten thousand dollars in 1933 was the equivalent, on the basis of changes to the Consumer Price Index, of $174,000 in 2011. www.measuringworth.com/uscompare/. WGM to Brice Clagett, November 30, 1932, McAdoo MSS, Container 377, File: "Nov. 30, 1932."

4. WGM to EWM, April 21, 1933, Wilson-McAdoo MSS, LOC MSS, Container 2, File: "McAdoo, William G., 1930–33"; and WGM to Neblett, April 7, 1933, McAdoo MSS, Container 382, File: "Apr. 7, 1933."

5. Storke, *California Editor*, 395; and James T. Patterson, *Congressional Conservatism and the New Deal: The Growth of the Conservative Coalition in Congress, 1933–1939* (Lexington: University of Kentucky Press, 1967), 1, 40; WGM to Storke, January 10, 1934, McAdoo MSS, Container 390, File: "Jan. 10, 1934"; WGM to EWM, January 28 and March 6, 1934, Berkeley-WGM MSS; and Wilson-McAdoo MSS, LOC MSS, Container 2, File: "McAdoo, William G., 1934."

6. "Legislative Record of Measures of Interest to Labor," McAdoo MSS, Container 450, File: "Feb. 22, 1938"; "Speech of Senator McAdoo Representative at the Young Democratic Regional Conference, May 28, 1938," Huntington-WGM MSS, Box 5, Folder 38; and Patterson, *Congressional Conservatism and the New Deal*.

7. FDR to WGM, January 6, 1933, McAdoo MSS, Container 379, File: "Jan. 6, 1933"; *NYT*, January 16, 1933, 2:8; Brice Clagett, "Personal and Confidential," February 22, 1933, McAdoo MSS, Container 380, File: "Feb. 22, 1933"; and WGM to Daniel C. Roper, February 13, 1933, McAdoo MSS, Container 380, File: "Feb. 13, 1933."

8. WGM to FDR, March 8, 1933, McAdoo MSS, Container 388, File: "Mar. 8, 1933"; WGM to EWM, January 6 and February 7, 1934, Wilson-McAdoo MSS, LOC MSS, Container 2, File: "McAdoo, William G., 1934"; and FDR to Bowers, October 6, 1934, FDR PPF 730.

9. Kevin Starr, *Endangered Dreams: The Great Depression in California* (New York: Oxford University Press, 1996), 199.

10. *NYT*, January 16, 1933, 2:8; and WGM to Milton, January 22, 1934, McAdoo MSS, Container 391, File: "Jan. 22, 1934."

11. *Kansas City Star*, April 15, 1932, McAdoo MSS, Container 383, File: "Apr. 26, 1933"; and *Kiplinger Washington Newsletter*, June 24, 1933, McAdoo MSS, Container 386, File: "July 19, 1933."

12. Johnson to WGM, October 15, 1935, McAdoo MSS, Container 411, File: "Oct. 14, 1935"; and Creel to WGM, January 30, 1933, McAdoo MSS, Container 379, File: "Jan. 30, 1933."

13. WGM to Ickes and Ickes reply, June 29 and 30, 1935, McAdoo MSS, Container 385, Files: "June 29, 1933" and "June 30, 1933"; WGM to Daniel C. Roper, December 13, 1933, McAdoo MSS, Container 389, File: "Dec. 13, 1933"; and WGM to O'Connor, July 20, 1933, McAdoo MSS, Container 386, File: "July 20, 1933."

14. WGM to Cummings, August 15, 1936, McAdoo MSS, Container 424, File: "Aug. 15, 1936."

15. On wine, see WGM to James B. McSheehy, April 11, 1933, McAdoo MSS, Container 382, File: "Apr. 11, 1933," and NYT, March 16, 1933, 1:3; on pilchards, see McAdoo MSS, Container 418, File: "Mar. 12, 1936," and WGM to Robert M. LaFollette, June 9, 1936, McAdoo MSS, Container 422, File: "Jun. 9, 1936." For the movie industry, see WGM to William Randolph Hearst, April 5, 1933, McAdoo MSS, Container 382, File: "Apr. 5, 1933." For granite and bitumen, see McAdoo MSS, Container 397; and for Yosemite, see McAdoo MSS, Container 440, File: "Aug. 14, 1937." For the Central Valley Water Project, see McAdoo MSS, Container 408, File: "July 24, 1935," Container 410, File: "Sept. 12, 1935," and Container 442, File: "Sept. 27, 1937."

16. Johnson quoted in Chase, "William Gibbs McAdoo," 347, n. 800; Storke, *California Editor*, 342; and McAdoo MSS, Container 386, files for July and August 1933.

17. For the USDA, see McAdoo MSS, Container 425, File: "Sept. 16, 1936"; and for the WPA, see D. Wilder to WGM, September 25, 1936, McAdoo MSS, Container 426, File: "Sept. 25, 1936." California expenditures are from "Federal Expenditures (Partial) in California," McAdoo MSS, Container 617. See also WGM to William H. Neville, May 4, 1938, McAdoo MSS, Container 454, File: "May 4, 1938."

18. See McAdoo MSS, Containers 394, 397, 406, and 407, and William Rowe to WGM, June 9, 1937, McAdoo MSS, Container 437, File: "June 9, 1937." For Mearon Perkins, see WGM to Farley and Cummings, McAdoo MSS, Container 393, File: "Apr. 11, 1934"; and WGM to Ernest R. Utley, September 10, 1935, and WGM to Perkins, September 24, 1935, McAdoo MSS, Files: "Sept. 10, 1935" and "Sept. 24, 1935."

19. For WGM's voting record, see *Congressional Record*, 73rd Congress, Second Session, 78741ff., 74th Congress, Second Session, 88359ff.; WGM, handwritten lists of major votes, 73rd to 75th Congresses, McAdoo MSS, Containers 606, 615, and 618; Patterson, *Congressional Conservatism and the New Deal* and "A Conservative Coalition Forms in Congress, 1933–1939," *Journal of American History* 52, no. 4 (March 1966): 757–772, 757; Lewis L. Gould, *The Most Exclusive Club: A History of the United States Senate* (New York: Basic Books, 2005), 129; Ortiz, *Beyond the Bonus March and the GI Bill*, 127–148; and WGM, Speech, April 7, 1937, *Congressional Record*, 137373, UCLA-WGM MSS, Box 11, "Loose Material."

20. Patterson, "A Conservative Coalition Forms in Congress," 766. See the anti-lynching materials in McAdoo MSS, Container 608; and WGM to J. L. Caston, November 15, 1937, McAdoo MSS, Container 443, File: "Nov. 15, 1937." For the Black nomination, see McAdoo MSS, Container 440, File: "Aug. 18, 1937"; and Gould, *Most Exclusive Club*, 147.

21. "History of Bills and Resolutions Introduced in the United States Senate Seventy-Fourth Congress, Senator McAdoo," McAdoo MSS, Container 615, and McAdoo MSS Container 618; WGM to Eugene Flaherty, September 9, 1935, McAdoo MSS, Container 410, File: "Sept. 9, 1935"; and David Dillingham, "Some Pertinent Reasons why the McAdoo Bill [for Adult Education] Should receive Favorable Consideration," n.d., McAdoo MSS, Container 620.

22. "Bills & Resolutions by WGM, January 6–August 18, 1937," McAdoo MSS, Container 89, n.f.; and O. R. Altman, "First Session of the Seventy-Fifth Congress, January 5, 1937, to August 21 1937," *American Political Science Review* 31, no. 6 (December 1937): 1071–1093, 1084.

23. W. H. Woodin to WGM, April 9, 1933, McAdoo MSS, Container 382, File: "Apr. 9, 1933." See also WGM, *Crowded Years*, 254; chapter 6, above; and *Santa Barbara Daily News*, March 16, 1933, McAdoo MSS, Container 381, File: "Mar. 17, 1933."

24. Federal Deposit Insurance Corporation, "The First Fifty Years: A History of the FDIC, 1933–1983," www.fdic.gov/bank/analytical/firstfifty/; and WGM to FDR, May 10, 1933, McAdoo MSS, Container 383, File: "May 10, 1933."

25. *NYT*, January 17, 1934, 1:8; McAdoo MSS, Container 405, File: "May 21, 1935"; McAdoo MSS Container 346, File: "June 7, 1937"; WGM, Press Release, November 29, 1937, McAdoo MSS, Container 444, File: "Nov. 29, 1937"; and WGM to J. C. O'Neill, February 2, 1938, McAdoo MSS, Container 448, File: "Feb. 2, 1938."

26. "Memorandum by Senator McAdoo Re United States Farm Mortgage Bank," March 30, 1933, McAdoo MSS, Container 382, File: "Mar. 30, 1933"; and *NYT*, March 30, 1933, 1:6.

27. WGM to M. W. Thatcher, March 9, 1936, McAdoo MSS, Container 418, File: "Mar. 9, 1936"; McAdoo MSS, Container 447, File: "Jan. 11, 1938;" and "Amendments to S. 2787," November 16, 1937, UCLA-WGM MSS, Box 11, Folder: "Cotton."

28. Wallace to WGM, September 4, 1937, and WGM reply, October 6, 1937, McAdoo MSS, Container 441, File: "Sept. 4, 1937"; Hull to WGM, October 28, 1937, McAdoo MSS, Container 443, File: "Oct. 28, 1937"; and WGM to all Senators, December 13, 1937, McAdoo MSS, Container 445, File: "Dec. 13, 1937."

29. Patterson, *Congressional Conservatism and the New Deal*, 85–88 and 110; Gould, *Most Exclusive Club*, 143; and Altman, "First Session of the Seventy-Fifth Congress," 1086–1088. WGM to EWM, March 19, 1937, McAdoo MSS, Container 74, File: "Mar. 18–20, 1937"; WGM to Rodney Yoell, February 9, 1937, McAdoo MSS, Container 430, File: "Feb. 9, 1937"; WGM, "Reform of the Federal Judiciary," Radio Address, February 16, 1937, McAdoo MSS, Container 565, File: "Speeches 1937"; *NYT*, March 6, 1937, 2:2; and WGM to William E. Woodward, March 12, 1937, McAdoo MSS, Container 432, File: "Mar. 12, 1937."

30. WGM to William H. Neblett, May 18, 1937, McAdoo MSS, Container 435, File: "May 18, 1937"; WGM to Eugene Stockwell, April 15, 1937, McAdoo MSS, Container 436, File: "June 3, 1937"; W. H. Neblett to WGM and WGM reply, June 1 and 3, 1937, McAdoo MSS, Container 436, File: "June 3, 1937;" and *NYT*, May 13, 1937, 8:2.

31. *NYT*, October 27, 1933, 12:6; WGM to Mary Workman, February 26, 1935, McAdoo MSS, Container 402, File: "Feb. 26, 1935"; and Hearst to WGM, McAdoo MSS, Container 401, File: "Jan. 28, 1935."

32. WGM, Radio Speech, December 30, 1936, McAdoo MSS, Container 428, File: "Dec. 30, 1936."

33. WGM to Daniels, February 25, 1935, Daniels Papers, LOC MSS, Reel 56; and WGM to Committee on Fair Play in Sports, November 26, 1935, McAdoo MSS, Container 410, File: "Sept. 16, 1935."

34. *NYT*, January 13, 1938, 8:2; and WGM to Albert Lee Stephens, January 24, 1938, McAdoo MSS, Container 448, File: "Jan. 24, 1938." See McAdoo MSS, Container 621, for the inventory bill.

35. WGM to Eleanor McFarland, March 29, 1935, McAdoo MSS, Container 403, File: "Mar. 29, 1935"; WGM, Radio Speech, December 30, 1936, McAdoo MSS, Container 428, File: "Dec. 30, 1936"; and WGM to Hull, February 13, 1939, McAdoo MSS, Container 468, File: "Feb. 13, 1939."

36. WGM, Radio Speech, December 30, 1936, McAdoo MSS, Container 428, File: "Dec. 30, 1936"; WGM to Reynolds, July 27, 1934, McAdoo MSS, Container 396, File: "July 27, 1934"; and WGM to Admiral William Leahy, August 4, 1939, McAdoo MSS, Container 463, File: "Aug. 4, 1939."

37. WGM to Cordell Hull, April 4, 1938, and Welles to WGM, April 21, 1938, McAdoo MSS, Container 452, File: "Apr. 4, 1938"; and Thaddeus G. Armstrong to WGM, March 3, 1940, McAdoo MSS, Container 470, File: "Mar. 5, 1940."

38. WGM to Neblett, May 8, 1936, McAdoo MSS, Container 420, File: "May 7, 1936"; Elliot DeWitt to WGM, July 22, 1938, Huntington-WGM MSS, Container 8, Folder 5; and WGM to Storke, January 24, 1938, McAdoo MSS, Container 448, File: "Jan. 24, 1938."

39. *Los Angeles Herald Express*, June 12, 1937, 2, in McAdoo MSS, Container 437, File: "June 16, 1937"; and WGM to Storke, December 18, 1937, McAdoo MSS, Container 445, File: "Dec. 18, 1937."

40. Storke to WGM and WGM reply, January 31 and February 1, 1938, and WGM to Storke, February 4, 1938, McAdoo MSS, Container 448, Files: "Jan. 31, 1938," "Feb. 1, 1938," and "Feb. 4, 1938"; Storke to WGM and WGM reply, February 10 and 19, 1938, McAdoo MSS, Container 449, File: "Feb. 19, 1938."

41. WGM to Wallace Shepard, March 16, 1938, McAdoo MSS, Container 451, File: "Mar. 16, 1938"; Henley S. Davis to WGM, April 7, 1938, Harold L. Rogers to WGM, April 18, 1938, and W. H. Hill to WGM, March 30, 1938, McAdoo MSS, Container 453, Files: "Apr. 13, 1938," "Apr. 18, 1938," and "Apr. 18, 1938."

42. WGM to FDR, March 8, 1938, and FDR reply, March 16, 1938, FDR PPF 308.

43. Chase, "William Gibbs McAdoo," 372–374.

44. WGM to FDR, July 2, 1938, McAdoo MSS, Container 458, File: "July 2, 1938."

45. WGM to Farley, October 25, 1938, Huntington-WGM MSS, Box 10, Folder 2. For the Ham and Eggs plan, see Jackson K. Putnam, *Old-Age Politics in California: From Richardson to Reagan* (Palo Alto, Calif.: Stanford University Press, 1970), 89–113; Starr, *Endangered Dreams*, 197–222; and Chase, "William Gibbs McAdoo," 278–371.

46. "Memorandum on the California Retirement Life Payments Plan," n.d., McAdoo MSS, Container 621; WGM to Harold Ickes, September 14, 1938, McAdoo MSS, Container 464, File: "Sept. 14, 1938"; R. Michael Alvarez, William Deverell, and Elizabeth Penn, "The 'Ham and Eggs' Movement in Southern California: Public Opinion on Economic Redistribution in the 1938 Campaign," USC Law School and California Institute of Technology, Center for the Study of Law and Politics Working Paper No. 12, February 21, 2003, www.lawweb.usc.edu/centers/cslp/assets/docs/cslp-wp-012.pdf. Putnam, *Old-Age Politics in California*, 96; Starr, *Endangered Dreams*, 206; and A. R. Jagunich to WGM, September 17, 1938, McAdoo MSS, Container 464, File: "Sept. 17, 1938."

47. WGM to Creel, July 19, 1938, McAdoo MSS, Container 459, File: "July 19, 1938"; WGM to James Hollister, April 27, 1938, McAdoo MSS, Container 454, File: "Apr. 27, 1938"; Huntington-WGM MSS, Container 55, Folder 66, "Fletcher, Ed, 14 June 1938"; WGM to J. C. Tutt of *The Labor Advocate*, May 23, 1938, McAdoo MSS, Container 456, File: "May 23, 1938"; WGM to George White, June 4, 1938, McAdoo MSS, Container 457, File: "June

4, 1938." On WGM's age, see *San Francisco Chronicle*, July 22, 1938, Huntington-WGM MSS, Box 8, Folder 6.

48. Creel to Farley, April 29, 1938, McAdoo MSS, Container 454, File: "Apr. 9, 1938."

49. WGM to Baruch, July 18, 1938, McAdoo MSS, Container 459, File: "July 18, 1938." A partial account of WGM's 1938 campaign finances is in McAdoo MSS, Container 76, File: "Aug. 30, 1938"; "Questionnaire on Campaign Expenditures," McAdoo MSS, Container 464, File: "Sept. 21, 1938"; and WGM to Creel, June 17, 1938, McAdoo MSS, Container 457, File: "June 17, 1938."

50. "Opening Speech by Senator Wm. G. McAdoo," July 6, 1938, McAdoo MSS, Container 606.

51. Chase, "William Gibbs McAdoo," 379; Storke; *California Editor*, 308–309 and 395; and Joseph P. Doakes to WGM, May 21, 1938, McAdoo MSS, Container 456, File: "May 26, 1938."

52. WGM, Radio Speech, August 10, 1938, McAdoo MSS, Container 565, File: "Speeches 1938–1940"; and Patterson, *Congressional Conservatism and the New Deal*, 277.

53. "California's next U.S. Senator," McAdoo MSS, Container 638; and Putnam, *Old-Age Politics in California*, 99. For allegations of shakedowns of federal employees, see George Creel to WGM, July 27, 1938, and WGM to Morris Sheppard, July 28, 1937, McAdoo MSS, Container 459, Files: "July 27, 1938" and "July 29, 1938"; and *Los Angeles Times*, August 12, 1938, McAdoo MSS, Container 639. For The KKK "passport," see *Los Angeles Examiner*, August 23, 1938, McAdoo MSS, Container 462, File: "Aug. 23, 1938"; WGM, Radio Speech, August 29, 1938, McAdoo MSS, Container 565, File: "Speeches, 1938–1940"; WGM to Creel, September 24, 1938, McAdoo MSS, Container 465, File: "Sept. 24, 1938"; P. J. Domingues to WGM, n.d., McAdoo MSS, Container 468, File: "1938 [2]"; WGM to Trippe, August 1, 1938, Huntington-WGM MSS, Box 4, Folder 22; and *B'nai B'rith Messenger*, August 26, 1938, 1, Huntington-WGM MSS, Box 8, Folder 64.

54. WGM to McIntyre, August 18, 1938, FDR PPF 308; Putnam, *Old-Age Politics in California*, 9; and WGM Radio Address, August 29, 1938, McAdoo MSS, Container 565, File: "Speeches, 1938–1940."

55. www.ourcampaigns.com/RaceDetail.html?RaceID=379496; WGM to H. H. Whiting, November 3, 1938, McAdoo MSS, Container 466, Files: "Oct. 27, 1938" and "Nov. 3, 1938"; and Seawell to WGM, September 2, 1938, FDR PPF 308.

56. WGM to FHM, September 8, 1938, McAdoo MSS, Container 648, File: "July–Dec., 1938: 36"; WGM to James A. Farley, September 10, 1938, Huntington-WGM MSS, Box 10, Folder 1; WGM to FDR, September 2, 1938, FDR PPF 308; WGM to Josephus Daniels, September 12, 1938, McAdoo MSS, Container 464, File: "September 12 ,1938"; and J. R. Files to WGM, September 17, 1938, McAdoo MSS, Container 464, File: "Sept. 17, 1938."

57. Kent, "He Did Not Shine: William McAdoo in Eclipse," *Baltimore Sun*, n.d., McAdoo MSS, Container 632; and Tucker, "The McAdoo Myth," *The Commentator*, June 1937, 33–38, McAdoo MSS, Container 606.

58. Chase, "William Gibbs McAdoo," 345.

59. WGM to Mr. and Mrs. Benton Fremont, September 13, 1938, McAdoo MSS, Container 464, File: "Sept. 13, 1938."

60. NDB to Hayes, October 12, 1932, Baker MSS, Container 116, File: "Hayes, Ralph, July–Dec. 1932"; and Hayes to John H. Clarke, November 18, 1932, Baker MSS, Container 116, File: "Hayes, Ralph, July–Dec. 1932."

61. NDB to FDR, April 21, 1933, FDR PPF 669.

62. NDB to FDR, September 19, 1933, and October 3, 1933, and FDR to NDB, October 6, 1933, FDR PPF 669. See *NYT*, July 23, 1934, 1:1, for the Army Air Corps review.

63. John C. O'Laughlin to NDB, September 1, 1934, Baker MSS, Container 179, File: "O., 1934"; FDR to NDB and NDB reply, November 8 and 9, 1934, Baker MSS, Container 201, File: "Rog–Rz, 1934"; FDR to NDB, January 9, 1935, FDR PPF 669; NDB to ELB, December 30, 1934, WRHA-NDB MSS, Acc. #4564, Box 2, Folder 14; NDB to ELB, March 9 and 10, 1934, WRHA-NDB MSS, Acc. #3491, Box 2, Folder 1; and FDR to George Foster Peabody, November 28, 1934, FDR PPF 660.

64. NDB to FHB, May 28, 1935, Baker MSS, Container 36, File: "Frank H. Baker, 1935"; and NDB to Henry James, October 24, 1936, Baker MSS, Container 132, File: "J., 1932." The underlining is NDB's. NDB to William L. Ransom, October 27, 1937, Baker MSS, Container 195, File: "Ra–Rh, 1937."

65. *NYT*, March 17, 1933, 3:1, and May 20, 1933, 7:1; NDB to Raymond Hudson, July 8, 1936, Baker MSS, Container 124, File: "Hn–Hz, 1936"; NDB, Radio Address, March 17, 1933, NDB MSS, Container 263, File: "1926–1934 Articles"; NDB to Louis J. Alber, October 5 and 11, 1933, NDB MSS, Container 16, File: "Aa–Al, 1933"; and Graham, *Encore for Reform*, 29.

66. NDB to Arthur E. Seagrave, October 5, 1933, Baker MSS, Container 206, File: "Se–Shd, 1933"; and NDB to E. M. Gilkeson, October 10, 1933, Baker MSS, Container 104, File: "G–Gq, 1933."

67. NDB to E. A. Filene, May 22, 1934, Baker MSS, Container 95, File: "E. A. Filene, 1935."

68. NDB to Fred Schulder, January 19, 1935, Baker MSS, Container 204, File: "Sch–Sd, 1935"; NDB to Stephen Early, April 1, 1935, Baker MSS, Container 202, File: "Franklin D. Roosevelt, 1935"; *NYT*, November 26, 1934, 1:6, and September 13, 1935, 8:3; Joseph C. Swidler and Robert H. Marquis, "TVA in Court: A Study of TVA's Constitutional Litigation," *Iowa Law Review* 32 (1946–1947): 296–326, 313; and Edwin C. Goddard et al., "Notes: The Constitutionality of the TVA as a Power Development Program," *Harvard Law Review* 48 (1934–1935): 806–815, 807, n. 5.

69. "From Testimony of D. E. Lilienthal Before the House Committee on Military Affairs, March 28, 1935," Baker MSS, Container 157, File: "Me–Mn, 1935"; Link, *Wilson*, 2:132, n. 137; and Olson, *Biography of a Progressive*, 105.

70. NDB to John J. McSwain, April 3 and 8, 1935, and April 4 1932, Baker MSS, Container 154, Files: "McL–Md, 1935" and "McL–Md, 1932."

71. *Tennessee Electric Power Company v. Tennessee Valley Authority* (1939), 306 US 118; Swidler and Marquis, "TVA in Court," 317"; Ohio Bar Hears Baker Challenge New Deal," *Cleveland News*, January 26, 1935, Baker MSS, Speeches and Writing, Container 50, File: "1935"; NDB to Young, January 24, 1935, Baker MSS, Container 243, File: "X–Y, 1935"; and NDB to Samuel D. Pettengill, February 2, 1937, Baker MSS, Container 184, File: "Pa–Ph, 1937."

72. NDB to Walter Lippmann, February 4, 1937, Baker MSS, Container 149, File: "Walter Lippmann, 1937"; NDB to Rabbi Morris S. Lazaron, April 1, 1937, Baker MSS, Container 142, File: "La–Ld, 1937"; NDB to Bulkley, February 9 and 12, 1937, Baker MSS, Container 50, File: "Bu–Bz, 1937"; and NDB to Samuel B. Pettengill, April 23, 1937, Baker MSS, Container 184, File: "Pa–Ph, 1937."

73. NDB to A. C. Denison, February 17, 1937, Baker MSS, Container 84, File: "Da–Dh, 1937"; NDB to Walter Lippmann, March 10, 1937, Baker MSS, Container 149, File: "Walter Lippmann, 1937"; NDB to FHB, March 9, 1937, Baker MSS, Container 37, File: "Frank H. Baker, 1937"; and NDB to ELB, March 30, 1937, WRHA-NDB MSS, Acc. #3491, Box 2, Folder 1.

74. Graham, *Encore for Reform*, 25 and 66–69; NDB to Willard, July 1, 1935, Baker MSS, Container 237, File: "Daniel Willard, 1935"; Baker MSS, Container 75, File: "Commission on Care and Education of American Youth"; and NDB to Paul Kellogg, November 26, 1935, Baker MSS, Container 215, File: "Survey Associates, 1935."

75. NDB to Peggy Baker, January 5, 1936, WRHA-NDB MSS, Acc. #4564, Box 3, Folder 17; NDB, "Address to the American Iron and Steel Institute," May 27, 1937, Baker MSS, Container 27, File: "American Iron and Steel Institute Address, 1937"; and NDB to John H. Clarke, May 15, 1936, Baker MSS, Container 60, File: "John H. Clarke, 1936."

76. NDB to Filene, February 16, 1932, Baker MSS, Container 95, File: "E. A. Filene, 1932"; NDB to Arthur A. Craven, June 1, 1936, Baker MSS, Container 80, File: "Cr–Ct, 1936"; and NDB to Jonathan Daniels, May 21, 1936, Container 84, File: "Da–Dh, 1936."

77. NDB to Walter Wyatt, April 30, 1935, Baker MSS, Container 239, File: "Wo–Wz, 1935"; NDB to Peggy Baker, n.d., WRHA-NDB MSS, Acc. #4564, Box 2; NDB to FHB, July 7, 1936, WRHA-NDB MSS, Acc. #3491, Box 2, Folder 2; NDB to Maurice William, September 10, 1936, Baker MSS, Container 236, File: "Wia–Wl, 1936"; and NDB to William Allen White, November 2, 1936, Baker MSS, Container 234, File: "Wh, 1936."

78. NDB to FHB and FHB reply, May 8 and 14, 1935, Baker MSS, Container 36, File: "Frank H. Baker, 1935"; NDB to Edward Lee, December 30, 1936, Baker MSS, Container 144, File: "Le–Lh, 1936"; and NDB to Frank R. McNinch, December 12, 1934, Baker MSS, Container 154, File: "McL–Md, 1934."

79. NDB to E. A. Filene, May 25, 1935, Baker MSS, Container 95, File: "E. A. Filene, 1935"; NDB to Harris Creech, June 1, 1936, Baker MSS, Container 72, File: "The Cleveland Trust Company, 1936"; NDB to Milton Esberg, July 17, 1936, Baker MSS, Container 93, File: "Eo–Ez, 1936"; and NDB to Peggy Baker, January 3, 1937, WRHA-Baker MSS, Acc. #4562, Box 3, Folder 20.

80. NDB, *Frontiers of Freedom*, 208; NDB to A. Duncan Yocum, February 15, 1936, Baker MSS, Container 243, File: "X–Y, 1936"; NDB to Harry M. Ayers, June 8, 1935, Baker MSS, Container 33, File: "As–Az, 1935"; and NDB to Francis Pickens Miller, October 19, 1936, Baker MSS, Container 157, File: "Me–Mn, 1936."

81. NDB to Clarke, June 18, 1936, Baker MSS, Container 60, File: "Hon. John H. Clarke, 1936"; Carl Wittke, "Mr. Justice Clarke—A Supreme Court Judge in Retirement," *Mississippi Valley Historical Review* 36, no. 1 (June 1949): 27–50, 43; and NDB to Frank F. Gentsch, December 15, 1936, Baker MSS, Container 102, File: "Ga–Gh, 1936."

82. Baker MSS, Container 45, Files: "Boy Scouts of America"; Baker MSS, Container 67, Files: "Cleveland Community Fund, 1936"; NDB to FDR and FDR reply, September 6 and 11, 1933, FDR PPF 669; and NDB to FDR, December 7, 1934, FDR PPF 669.

83. Baker MSS, Container 218, Files: "Tuskegee Institute"; NDB to Raymond Fosdick, June 6, 1934, Baker MSS, Container 100, File: "Fosdick, Raymond B., 1934"; NDB to Fosdick, April 28, 1933, Baker MSS, Container 66, File: "Cleveland College, 1933"; and see generally, Container 68, File: "Cleveland College, 1937." Thornton, *Newton D. Baker and his Books*, 63–85; and Cramer, *Newton D. Baker*, 197.

84. Baker MSS, Containers 227 and 228, Files: "Washington & Lee University, 1928" et seq.; and Davis to Francis P. Gaines, April 17, 1935, and NDB to Davis, June 7, 1935, Baker MSS, Container 84, File: "John W. Davis, 1935."

85. NDB to Reverend J. E. Carhart, February 12, 1923, Baker MSS, Container 50, File: "Ca–Cd, 1923"; NDB to Addie Daniels, February 19, 1917, Daniels MSS, Reel 38; NDB to Hayes, July 9, 1929, Baker MSS, Container 115, File: "Ralph Hayes, 1929"; Baker MSS, Containers 169 and 170, Files: "NCJC"; and NDB to Everett R. Clinchy, January 30, 1935, March 30, 1932, and March 29, 1933, Baker MSS, Container 169, Files: "NCJC, 1935, 1932, and 1933."

86. NDB to James Wise, March 11, 1932, Baker MSS, Container 169, File: "NCJC, 1932"; NDB to Clinchy, June 5, 1933, Baker MSS, Container 169, File: "NCJC, 1933"; NDB to Robert A. Ashworth, June 5, 1933, Baker MSS, Container 169, File: "NCJC, 1933"; NDB, Address to NCJC, August 1935, Baker MSS, Container 169, File: "NCJC, 1935"; NDB to Clinchy, February 5, 1937, Baker MSS, Container 169, File: "NCJC, 1937"; and NDB to Salmon O. Levinson, November 1, 1933, Baker MSS, Container 144, File: "Le–Lh, 1933."

87. Richard Nelson to NDB and reply, March 10, 1932, Baker MSS, Container 169, File: "NCJC, 1932."

88. NDB to Robert Lester, December 26, 1934, Baker MSS, Container 53, File: "Carnegie Corporation, 1934."

89. NDB to Ida L. Jackson, January 30, 1937, Baker MSS, Container 132, File: "J., 1937"; and NDB to Mark Womack, April 17, 1937, Baker MSS, Container 239, File: "Wo–Wz, 1937."

90. NDB to Hayes, July 6, 1933, Baker MSS, Container 260, File: "July, 1933."

91. *New York Herald Tribune*, February 20, 1932, Baker MSS, Container 131, File: "J., 1932"; NDB to Frances Perkins, September 30, 1933, Baker MSS, Container 183, File: "Pa–Ph, 1933"; and NDB to Sidlo, July 12, 1932, Baker MSS, Container 209, File: "Si–Sn, 1933."

92. NDB to Brainard Avery, October 24, 1933, Baker MSS, Container 32, File: "As–Az, 1933."

93. NDB to Peggy Baker, July 28, 1935, WRHA-NDB MSS, Acc. #4564, Box 2, Folder 16; NDB to Fosdick, July 1, 1935, Baker MSS, Container 100, File: "Fosdick, Raymond B., 1935"; and NDB to Raymond Rich, July 20, 1935, Baker MSS, Container 241, File: "World Peace Foundation, 1935."

94. Baker MSS, Container 97, Files: "Foreign Affairs Council," Containers 240–243, Files: "World Peace Foundation," and Containers 125–127, Files: "Institute of Pacific Relations"; NDB to Raymond T. Rich, March 1935 and March 1936, Baker MSS, Containers 242 and 243, Files: "World Peace Foundation, 1935 and 1936."

95. NDB to S. M. Babson, November 13, 1934, Baker MSS, Container 17, File: "Academy of Political Science Speech, November 7, 1934"; NDB to Ellen Gowen Hood, April 6, 1935, Baker MSS, Container 121, File: "Ho–Ht, 1935"; NDB to Louis J. Keller, March 23, 1937, Baker MSS, Container 138, File: "Ka–Kh, 1937"; and NDB, "The World Crisis and What We Can Do About It," NBC, Radio Address, March 28, 1936, Baker MSS, Container 250, File: "1936."

96. NDB to Louis Keller, March 23, 1937, Baker MSS, Container 138, File: "Ka–Kh, 1937"; Baker MSS, Container 176, Files: "National World Court Committee"; NDB to Pittman, March 10, 1934, Baker MSS, Container 190, File: "Pi–Pq, 1934"; *NYT*, January 29, 1934, 16:1; and Michael Dunne, *The United States and the World Court, 1920–1935* (London: Pinter Publishers, 1988), chapters 5 and 8.

97. NDB, "Radio Address on behalf of the World Court Resolution in the Senate of the United States," January 29, 1935, Baker MSS, Container 249, File: "1935."

98. NYT, January 30, 1935, 2:1; NDB to S. G. Knebel, February 2, 1935, Baker MSS, Container 139, File: "Ki–Kq, 1935"; and Robert D. Accinelli, "The Roosevelt Administration and the World Court Defeat, 1935," Historian 40, no. 3 (May 1978): 463–478.

99. NYT, May 16, 1937, 2, 1:5.

100. Robert Dallek, Franklin D. Roosevelt and American Foreign Policy, 1932–1945 (New York: Oxford University Press, 1979), 102–108, 117–120, and 139–140; and David M. Kennedy, Freedom From Fear: The American People in Depression and War, 1929–1945 (New York: Oxford University Press, 1999), 393–395 and 400–401.

101. Kansas City Times, February 27, 1937, Baker MSS, Container 250, File: "1937"; and NYT, May 16, 1937, 2, 1:5.

102. NDB to E. M. Baker, January 22, 1937, Baker MSS, Container 36, File: "Baa–Br, 1937"; and NYT, April 18, 1937, 36:6.

103. NDB to Andrew Kelly, November 15, 1934, Raskob Papers, File 61: "American Liberty League: Correspondence, 1934."

104. NDB to Davis, January 18, 1935, Baker MSS, Container 84, File: "John W. Davis, 1935"; Ralph Hayes to Douglas Allen, September 13, 1934, Baker MSS, Container 117, File: "Ralph Hayes, 1934"; Craig, After Wilson, 274–297 and 283–284; and George Wolfskill, Revolt of the Conservatives: A History of the American Liberty League (Boston: Houghton Mifflin, 1962).

105. NDB to Mills, January 21, 1935, FDR PPF 669.

106. NDB to Raymond Hudson, July 8, 1936, Baker MSS, Container 124, File: "Hn–Hz, 1936"; and NDB to Peggy Baker, March 6, 1936, WRHA-NDB MSS, Acc. #4564, Box 3, Folder 7.

107. Graham, Encore for Reform, passim; and WGM to Daniels and reply, September 1 and 8, 1936, Daniels Papers, LOC MSS, Special Correspondence, Reel 56.

108. Jouett Shouse to NDB, July 10, 1935, Baker MSS, Container 207, File: "She–Shy, 1935."

109. NDB to Daniels, May 2, 1936, Baker MSS, Container 84, File: "Josephus Daniels, 1936."

110. NYT, June 3 and 4, 1936, 20:7 and 22:1.

111. NYT, June 4, 1936, 20:7.

112. NDB to Joseph K. Hull, November 2, 1936, Baker MSS, Container 124, File: "Hu–Hz, 1936"; NDB to Hayes, November 3, 1936, WRHA-NDB MSS, Acc. #4000, Box 5, Folder 77; and NDB to Clarke, November 20, 1936, Baker MSS, Container 60, File: "Hon. John H. Clarke, 1936."

113. NDB to Daniels, December 9, 1936, Daniels Papers, LOC MSS, Reel 40.

114. NDB to ELB, April 2, 1937, WRHA-NDB MSS, Acc. #3491, Box 2, Folder 1. The underlining is NDB's.

CHAPTER 15: "I HAVE NO QUARREL WITH FATE, NO MATTER IN WHAT MOODS I HAVE FOUND HER"

1. Michael Haines, "Fertility and Mortality in the United States," EH.Net Encyclopedia, www.eh.net/encyclopedia/article/haines.demography; and Social Security Administration "Life Expectancy for Social Security," www.ssa.gov/history/lifeexpect.html.

2. NDB to J. Kellog, October 8, 1934, Baker MSS, Container 138, File: "Ka–Kh, 1934;" NDB to Peggy Baker, n.d., WRHA-NDB MSS, Acc. #4564, Box 2, Folder 16; and NDB to FHB, December 22, 1935, WRHA-NDB MSS, Acc. #3491, Box 2, Folder 2.

3. NDB to Walter Lippmann, October 31, 1928, Baker MSS, Container 147, File: "Li–Lz, 1928"; NYT, April 30, 1930, 5:2; and NDB to Burleson, May 8, 1930, Baker MSS, Container 49, File: "Bn–Bz, 1930."

4. Drs. Hill and Thomas, "Results of NDB's Chest Examination," Baker MSS, Container 119, File" Hi–Hn, 1930"; and NDB to Davis, November 6, 1928, Baker MSS, Container 82, File: "Da–Dh, 1928."

5. NDB to Ralph Hayes, September 13, 1933, Baker MSS, Container 230, File: "Sept. 1933"; NYT, September 9, 1933, 11:5; and NDB to W. D. Connor, December 15, 1935, Baker MSS, Container 74, File: "Coa–Con, 1935."

6. NDB to Peggy Baker, July 7, 1937, WRHA-NDB MSS, Acc. #4564, Box 3, Folder 20; NYT, July 16, 19, and 20, 1937, 21:4, 2:8, and 9:1; NDB to Clarke, August 26, 1937, Baker MSS, Container 60, File: "Hon. John H. Clarke, 1937"; NDB to Daniel Willard, n.d., WRHA-NDB MSS, Acc. #3491, Box 2, Folder 3; NDB to David F. Houston, September 9, 1937, WRHA-NDB MSS, Box 2, Folder 3; and Dorothy Cook to Mrs. Harry Fulks, December 13, 1937, Baker MSS, Container 101, File: "Fa–Fz, 1937."

7. NDB to John H. Clarke, November 26, 1937, Baker MSS, Container 60, File: "Hon. John H. Clarke, 1937"; NDB to Havens, December 17, 1937, WRHA-NDB MSS, Acc. #3491, Box 2, Folder 3; and NDB to Peggy Baker, December 16, 1937, Baker MSS, Container 242, File: "Mr. and Mrs. Fulton Wright, 1937."

8. Cook to Ralph Hayes, January 18, 1938, Baker MSS, Container 261, File: "Jan. 1938"; NDB to Havens, December 17, 1937, and NDB to Mary Mobley, December 17, 1937, WRHA-NDB MSS, Acc. #3491, Box 2, Folder 3; and NDB to Hayes, December 17, 1937, WRHA-Hayes MSS, Acc. #4000, Box 5, Folder 77.

9. Hayes to John H. Clarke, January 3, 1938, WRHA-Hayes MSS, Acc. #4000, Box 5, Folder 83; V. M. Sackett to NDB, December 19, 1937, Baker MSS, Container 203, File: "Sa–Scg, 1937"; ELB to Daniels, January 22, 1938, Daniels Papers, LOC MSS, Special Correspondence, Reel 40; and ELB to John J. Pershing, January 9, 1938, Pershing Papers, LOC MSS, Container 19, File: "Baker, Newton D., 1921-."

10. Cook to Hayes, January 18, 1938, Baker MSS, Container 261, File: "Jan. 1938"; War Department, General Order No. 10, December 27, 1937, Pershing Papers, LOC MSS, Container 19, File: "Baker, Newton D., 1921-"; NYT, December 26, 1937, 1:3 and 16, December 27, 1937, 2:5 and 14:2, December 28, 1937, 21:4, December 29, 1937, 21:3, and January 3, 1938, 2:7; "In Memoriam: Newton Diehl Baker, January 30 1938," and assorted newspaper clippings, Baker MSS, Container 261, File: "1938"; Ralph Hayes, Eulogy for NDB, January 30, 1938, Baker MSS, Container 261, File: "Jan. 1938"; NYT, February 26, 1938, 13:7, and April 19, 1942, 2, 6:6; Council on World Affairs, "Newton D. Baker Lecture Fund," Baker MSS, Container 263, File: "Speeches—Memorial, 1938–1943"; and "Newton D. Baker Memorial Lectures, December 3, 1943," Baker MSS, Container 261, File: "Baker, Newton D.: Memorial Meeting, 1943."

11. NYT, December 26, 1937, 1:3 and 16, December 27, 1937, 2:5 and 14:2; and American Legion of Cleveland, December 25, 1937, Baker MSS, Container 261, File: "Baker, Newton D.: Funeral."

12. Daniels, "Appreciation of Hon. Newton D. Baker," Pershing Papers, Container 19, File: "Baker, Newton D., 1921-"; Ralph Hayes to Daniels, January 10, 1938, Baker MSS,

Container 261, File: "Baker, Newton D.: Funeral"; Cox to Hayes, December 7, 1943, Baker MSS, Container 261, File: "Baker, Newton D.: Memorial Meeting"; Johnston to Hayes, December 27, 1937, Baker MSS, Container 261, File: "Baker, Newton D.: Funeral"; Benjamin H. Namm, "A Tribute to Newton D. Baker," Baker MSS, Container 261, File: "Baker, Newton D.: Funeral"; Harbord, Radio Address, January 2, 1938, Baker MSS, Container 261, File: "Feb. 1938"; Pershing to ELB, December 25, 1937, and Radio Address, January 2, 1938, Pershing Papers, LOC MSS, Container 19, File: "Baker, Newton D., 1921-."

13. FDR to ELB, and Stephen Early to the *Cincinnati Post*, December 27, 1937, FDR PPF 669; and ELB to Daniels, January 22, 1938, Daniels Papers, LOC MSS, Special Correspondence, Reel 40.

14. *NYT*, September 25 and November 5, 1940, 18:3 and 21:4; and ELB to Josephus Daniels, January 9, 1946, Daniels Papers, LOC MSS, Special Correspondence, Reel 40.

15. Thomas Woodward to WGM, August 13, 1938, McAdoo MSS, Container 460, File: "Aug. 13, 1938."

16. E. D. Flaherty to WGM, September 21, 1938, McAdoo MSS, Container 464, File: "Sept. 21, 1938"; and *NYT*, September 28, 1938, 51:1.

17. WGM to Woodward, September 27, 1928, McAdoo MSS, Container 465, File: "Sept. 27, 1938."

18. WGM to FHM, August 19 and May 31, 1939, McAdoo MSS, Container 648, File: "1939: 37"; and WGM to Bernard Baruch, August 4, 1939, McAdoo MSS, Container 469, File: "Aug. 4, 1939."

19. Frank R. Kent, "The Great Game of Politics," November 18, 1939, McAdoo MSS, Container 642; and Creel to Margaret Wilson, June 27, 1939, Wilson-McAdoo MSS, LOC MSS, Container 5, File: "C—1925–40." Twenty-five thousand dollars in 1938 was the equivalent, on the basis of changes to the Consumer Price Index, of $399,000 in 2011. www. measuringworth.com/uscompare/.

20. FDR to WGM, October 11, 1938, McAdoo MSS, Container 466, File: "Oct. 11, 1938"; WGM to FDR, October 17, 1938, McAdoo MSS, Container 466, File: "Oct. 17, 1938"; and WGM to FDR, McAdoo MSS, Container 467, File: "Dec. 9, 1938."

21. WGM to Carter Glass, December 29, 1938, McAdoo MSS, Container 468, File: "Dec. 29, 1938"; WGM to FDR, November 4, 1938, McAdoo MSS, Container 466, File: "Nov. 4, 1938"; WGM to Farley, July 19, 1939, McAdoo MSS, Container 469, File: "Jul. 19, 1939"; WGM to FDR, May 17, 1939, McAdoo MSS, Container 469, File: "May 29, 1939"; and see McAdoo MSS, Container 467, for WGM's patronage correspondence.

22. WGM to Jackson, January 23, 1940, McAdoo MSS, Container 471, File: "Jan. 23, 1940."

23. *NYT*, November 14, 1939, 6:5; WGM to Creel, January 12, 1940, McAdoo MSS, Container 470, File: "Jan. 12, 1940"; and Al Neish to WGM, March 5, 1940, McAdoo MSS, Container 470, File: "Mar. 7, 1940."

24. WGM to FHM, March 30, 1940, McAdoo MSS, Container 648, File: "1940: 38"; and WGM to Robert Jackson and Jackson reply, February 6 and 14, 1940, McAdoo MSS, Container 471, Files: "February 6 and 14, 1940."

25. McAdoo MSS, Container 471, File: "May 9, 1940"; McAdoo MSS, Container 565, File: "Speeches, 1938–1940"; *NYT*, July 21, 1940, 4, 10:7; Dr. Hilmar Koefod to WGM, March 23, 1940, McAdoo MSS, Container 471, File: "Mar. 23, 1940"; *Los Angeles Examiner*, July 17, 1940, Huntington-WGM MSS, Box 10, Folder 47; WGM to Hamilton Cotton, July 23, 1940, McAdoo MSS, Container 472, File: "July 23, 1940"; and McAdoo MSS, Container 473, File: "Nov. 12, 1940."

26. WGM to FDR, May 13, 1939, FDR PPF 308; FDR to WGM, May 24, 1939, Huntington-WGM MSS, Box 10, Folder 21; WGM to E. M. Watson, August 25, 1939, McAdoo MSS, Container 469, File: "Aug. 25, 1939"; WGM to Watson, October 15, 1940, McAdoo MSS, Container 473, File: "Oct. 15, 1940"; Chase, "William Gibbs McAdoo," 386; and WGM to Thomas Corcoran, August 10, 1940, McAdoo MSS, Container 472, File: "Aug. 10, 1940."

27. Chase, "William Gibbs McAdoo," 384 and 390; WGM to Baruch, August 4, 1939, McAdoo MSS, Container 469, File: "Aug. 4, 1939"; and WGM to Employees of APL, January 1, 1939, McAdoo MSS, Container 468, File: "Jan. 1, 1939."

28. WGM to Baruch, October 3, 1939, McAdoo MSS, Container 470, File: "Oct. 3, 1939."

29. *NYT*, September 3 1939, 14:7; WGM to FDR and FDR reply, September 5 and 13, 1939, McAdoo MSS, Container 470, Files: "Sept. 5 and 14, 1939"; and WGM to FDR, September 19 and October 3, 1939, and FDR reply, September 26, 1939, FDR PPF 308.

30. WGM to Brice Clagett, August 9, 1940, McAdoo MSS, Container 473, File: "Aug. 19, 1940"; WGM to FDR, August 22, 1940, FDR PPF 308; WGM to Hull, August 29, 1940, McAdoo MSS, Container 473, File: "Aug. 29, 1940"; "Statement of Honorable Wm G. McAdoo, October 16, 1940," McAdoo MSS, Container 473, File: "Oct. 16, 1940"; and WGM to FDR and FDR reply, December 30 and 31, 1940, McAdoo MSS, Container 474, File: "Dec. 30, 1940."

31. WGM to Storke, November 13, 1940, McAdoo MS, Container 473, File: "Nov. 13, 1940."

32. WGM to Thomas Storke, January 26, 1921, McAdoo MSS, Container 512; WGM to William E. Woodward, August 3, 1931, McAdoo MSS, Container 360, File: "Aug. 3, 1931"; WGM to Nona McAdoo, June 27, 1930, McAdoo MSS, Container 68, File: "June 26–27, 1930"; Newton to WGM, May 28, 1922, McAdoo MSS, Container 263, File: "May 28, 1922"; and WGM to William Phillips, July 19, 1930, McAdoo MSS, Container 359, File: "July 19, 1930."

33. WGM, *Crowded Years*, 528.

34. *NYT*, December 7, 1938, 2:7; and Cowles to WGM and WGM reply, January 2 and 7, 1939, McAdoo MSS, Container 468, File: "Jan. 7, 1939."

35. Cowles to Rodney A. Yoell, July 1, 1939, McAdoo MSS, Container 469, File: "July 1, 1939."

36. WGM to Baruch, October 3, 1939, McAdoo MSS, Container 470, File: "Oct. 3, 1939."

37. WGM, "Memorandum for Mr. Neblett," October 10, 1935, McAdoo MSS, Container 405, File: "May 28, 1935"; WGM to FHM, August 29, 1935, McAdoo MSS, Container 648, File: "1935: 29"; "Last Will of William Gibbs McAdoo," February 2, 1937, McAdoo MSS, Container 75, File: "September 27, 1937"; and WGM to FHM, January 28, 1941, McAdoo MSS, Container 648, File: "1941: 39."

38. *Santa Barbara News-Press*, February 1 and 2, 1941, Wilson-McAdoo MSS, LOC MSS, Boxes 8 and 16, Files 14 and 5; Chase, "William Gibbs McAdoo," 393; *NYT*, February 2, 1941, 1:5; *Sacramento Bee*, February 2, 1941, Huntington-WGM MSS, Box 10, Folder 55; and Doris McAdoo to Daniels, n.d., Daniels Papers, LOC MSS, Special Correspondence, Reel 56.

39. Roots Web's WorldConnect Project: "Genealogy of President Woodrow Wilson," 2: www.we.rootsweb.ancestry.com/cgi-bin/igm.cgi?op=GET&db=woodrow_wilson&id=I0021;

and Cramer, *Newton D. Baker*, 173. Ten thousand dollars in 1941 was the equivalent, on the basis of changes to the Consumer Price Index, of $153,000 in 2011, and $155,000 and $500,000 in 1938 were the equivalents of $2,470,000 and $7,980,000 in 2011. www.measuring worth.com/uscompare/.

40. New Orleans *Times-Picayune*, February 3, 1941, and *Knoxville Journal*, February 2, 1941, Huntington-WGM MSS, Box 10, Folder 57; *Sacramento Bee*, February 2, 1941, Huntington-WGM MSS, Box 10, Folder 55; and *NYT*, February 2, 1941, 1:5.

41. *NYT*, February 2, 1941, 1:5; Nashville *Tennessean*, February 2, 1941, Huntington-WGM MSS, Box 10, Folder 58; *Times-Picayune*, February 3, 1941, Huntington-WGM MSS, Box 10, Folder 57; and *Duluth News-Tribune*, February 3, 1941, Huntington-WGM MSS, Box 10, Folder 56.

42. *Louisville Times*, February 3, 1941, *Philadelphia Inquirer*, February 2, 1941, and *Richmond Times-Dispatch*, February 2 1941, Huntington-WGM MSS, Box 10, Folder 57.

43. *Houston Post*, February 3, 1941, Cleveland *Plain Dealer* and *Cincinnati Enquirer*, February 2, 1941, Huntington-WGM MSS, Box 10, Folder 56.

44. *Sacramento Bee*, February 2, 1941, Huntington-WGM MSS, Box 10, Folder 55; and *NYT*, February 2, 1941, 1:5.

45. *NYT*, February 2, 1941, 1:5; Doris McAdoo to FDR, February 6, 1941, and FDR annotation, FDR PPF 308.

46. McAdoo MSS, Container 96; and Chase, "William Gibbs McAdoo," 107.

47. Baker, *Woodrow Wilson*, 2:235; Woodward, "Note About W.G. McAdoo," McAdoo MSS, Container 349, File: "Mar. 12, 1930," H. D. Mehling, "analysis of NDB's handwriting, May 5, 1932," Baker MSS, Container 37, File: NDB Personal, 1937"; NDB to Henry E. Stone, May 11, 1928, Baker MSS, Container 213, File: "Sti–Stz, 1928"; *The Clevelander*, August 1935, Baker MSS, Container 65, File: "Cleveland Chamber of Commerce, 1935"; Baker MSS, Container 196, File: "Radio Corporation of America, 1936"; and WGM to Sally McAdoo, January 11, 1924, McAdoo MSS, Container 63, File: "Jan. 9–12, 1924."

48. Cramer, *Newton D. Baker*, 275; Daniels, *Wilson Era*, 2:183; Williams to Wayne McVeagh, November 25, 1914, McAdoo MSS, Container 127, File: "Nov. 25, 1914"; and Creel, *Rebel at Large*, 270.

49. August Heckscher, "A Career That Fell Short of its Promise," *New York Herald Tribune*, Paris, April 8–9, 1961, WRHA-NDB MSS, Acc. #4564, Box 3, Folder 23; and Schwarz, *New Dealers*, 11.

Essay on Sources

William McAdoo and Newton Baker lived well-documented lives that spanned the seventy-eight years between the Battle of Gettysburg and the bombing of Pearl Harbor. Baker was too modest to pay much attention to his place in history, but McAdoo was not. He paid a genealogist to research his family's history, commissioned a biography, and published an autobiography. Aspects of his and Baker's lives after 1900 were also covered in local and national newspapers and in the memoirs and biographies of many of their friends, rivals, and colleagues.

And then there are the McAdoo and Baker Papers. Most of them are held in the Library of Congress Manuscript Division, but there are smaller collections in Cleveland for Baker and in California for McAdoo. In both cases, however, historians should begin their work in the Library of Congress. Separately the McAdoo and Baker collections there are exhaustive and exhausting; McAdoo's includes 35,000 files in hundreds of archive boxes stuffed with correspondence and reports, and Baker's is no less intimidating.

These huge collections, with a combined total of 600,000 items, are seldom explored and sometimes dismissed as arid. Neither is easy to browse: Baker's and McAdoo's incoming and outgoing correspondence is organized by date rather than by correspondent, and both collections are too large to be usefully navigated from their finding guides. The entire Baker and McAdoo collections took me more than two years to read, and those who seek material on only a portion of their careers face a daunting task. Yet these two collections will reward historians of the United States' first forty years of the twentieth century as much as any other currently available to them. The Baker and McAdoo Papers provided this book not only with its archival backbone but also its rationale: separately they made possible biographies of both men; together they provided an irresistible case for a double biography.

The Library of Congress holds many other collections that were very important to this book. Foremost of these for McAdoo are the Papers of the Wilson-McAdoo Family, which focus on the parents, siblings, and children of Eleanor Wilson McAdoo, and those of Charles S. Hamlin, Florence Jaffray Harriman, Breckinridge Long, Edith Bolling Wilson, and Robert W. Woolley. For Baker the Library of Congress holds collections from Tasker H. Bliss, Felix Frankfurter, Tom L. Johnson, John J. Pershing, and Leonard Wood. Valuable material on Baker and McAdoo can also be found in the Papers of Ray Stannard Baker, Josephus Daniels, and Woodrow Wilson.

The Baker and McAdoo collections contain many photographs and cartoons, and the Library of Congress's Prints and Photographs Division also holds images of both men. These pertain chiefly to their time in Woodrow Wilson's cabinet, although there are several photographs of McAdoo taken during his time in the US Senate.

Other collections of Baker and McAdoo's papers are held in a variety of institutions. As regards Baker, the Western Reserve Historical Association Library in Cleveland holds an important collection of his letters that cover his whole career and include many letters between Baker, his wife, and his children. The Papers of Ralph A. Hayes provide another perspective on Baker, this time from his protégé and close friend. Although there is some overlap between these collections and the Baker Papers in the Library of Congress, they are important additions, not least for the insights they afford into the Bakers' home life.

McAdoo's papers outside Washington, D.C., are scattered in four small collections in California. The most useful of these are in the Huntington Library and the Davidson Library at the University of California at Santa Barbara. Both collections include important family and business correspondence. Two still smaller collections, one at the University of Southern California and the other at the University of California at Berkeley, contain materials on McAdoo's business and political activities and some of his family correspondence.

A full list of this book's manuscript sources, which total thirty collections in ten institutions, forms part of the bibliography available at http://www.press.jhu.edu/.

Baker and McAdoo were both published authors in their own right. Although he never published an autobiography, Baker was a frequent contributor to public debate after 1916. In a number of articles in periodicals, including the *Saturday Evening Post*, the *Atlantic Monthly* and *Foreign Affairs*, he wrote about the war effort of 1917–1918, the need for the United States to engage fully with the League of Nations and to improve its industrial relations, and on the shortcomings of the New Deal. These works are listed in the notes and bibliography, but the most useful of them are his *Why We Went to War* (New York: Harper & Brothers, 1936) and *Frontiers of Freedom* (New York: George H. Duran, 1918). Unlike McAdoo, Baker did not use ghost writers, and so his works bear his personal stamp not only in their arguments but also in their expression.

McAdoo produced a collection of speeches defending national prohibition and proposing its stricter enforcement entitled *The Challenge: Liquor and Lawlessness Versus Constitutional Government* (New York: The Century Press, 1928), and three years later released his autobiography *Crowded Years: The Reminiscences of William G. McAdoo* (Boston: Houghton Mifflin, 1931). The latter was written by a ghost writer, William E. Woodward, and so is less useful to a biographer than it might otherwise have been. *Crowded Years* also ends in 1930 and was never updated. Like Mary Synon's *McAdoo: The Man and His Times—A Panorama in Democracy* (Indianapolis: The Bobbs-Merrill Company, 1924), *Crowded Years* reads more as an advertisement for himself than as a window into McAdoo's thought and deeds.

A number of other primary sources proved more useful. Foremost of these is the sixty-nine-volume *Papers of Woodrow Wilson*, edited by Arthur S. Link and published by Princeton University Press between 1966 and 1994. This collection provided vital insights into Baker's and McAdoo's relationship with Wilson and their work in his cabinet. Superbly indexed and broad in its sweep, the *Papers of Woodrow Wilson* include material from a wide range of Wilson's friends, enemies, and observers, many of whom had important things to say about Baker and McAdoo. Ray Stannard Baker, Wilson's official biographer, devoted some attention to McAdoo and Baker in his eight-volume *Woodrow Wilson: Life and Letters* (Garden City, N.J.: Doubleday, Doran & Company, 1927–1939), while Cary Grayson's *Woodrow Wilson: An Intimate Memoir* (Washington, D.C.: Potomac Books, Inc., 1960), Edward M. House and Charles Seymour's *Intimate Papers of Colonel House* (London: Ernest Benn Limited, 1926–1928), and Joseph P. Tumulty's *Woodrow Wilson As I Knew Him*

(Garden City, New Jersey: Doubleday, Page & Company, 1921) have more to say about McAdoo than Baker.

Other sources from Wilson's family were valuable. Stockton Axson, Wilson's brother-in-law, contributed insights into the president's relationship with McAdoo in *"Brother Woodrow": A Memoir of Woodrow Wilson*, published as part of Link's *Papers of Woodrow Wilson* in 1993. Eleanor Wilson published a biography of her parents in 1937, a collection of their letters in 1946, and a thinly fictionalized account of her courtship by McAdoo in *Julia and the White House* (New York: Dodd, Mead & Company, 1962). Each is useful for its portrayal of the family into which McAdoo married and the marriage that he contracted. Another, more jaundiced, account of McAdoo's relationship with the Wilsons can be found in Edith Bolling Wilson's *My Memoir* (New York: The Bobbs-Merrill Company, 1938).

A number of McAdoo's and Baker's associates within the Wilson administration have left a rich trove of memoirs. Of Baker and McAdoo's cabinet colleagues, Josephus Daniels's diaries (Lincoln: University of Nebraska Press, 1963) and his two-volume *Wilson Era* (Chapel Hill: University of North Carolina Press, 1946), Secretary of Agriculture David F. Houston's *Eight Years with Wilson's Cabinet* (Garden City, N.J.: Doubleday, Page & Company, 1926), and Anne Wintermute and Louise Herrick Wall's edited collection of *The Letters of Franklin K. Lane: Personal and Political* (Boston: Houghton Mifflin Company, 1922) have been very useful.

For Baker, Tom Johnson's *My Life* (New York: B.W. Huebsch, 1911) and Peyton C. March's *The Nation at War* (Garden City, N.Y.: Doubleday, Doran & Company, 1932) are valuable for his career in Cleveland municipal politics and then as secretary of war. For McAdoo, Bernard Baruch's *Public Years* (London: Odhams Press Limited, 1960), George Creel's *Rebel at Large: Recollections of Fifty Crowded Years* (New York: George Putnam's Sons, 1947), and Thomas M. Storke's *California Editor* (Los Angeles: Westernlore Press, 1958) include affectionate reminiscences from his friends, while Charles C. Goetsch and Margaret L. Shivers's edition of *The Autobiography of Thomas L. Chadbourne* (New York: Oceana Publications, Inc., 1985) and William F. McCombs's *Making Woodrow Wilson President* (New York: Fairview Publishing Company, 1931) contain less flattering observations.

Prominent in national political life for thirty years, Baker and McAdoo were well covered by the press. I have mainly used *The New York Times*, but both men's papers contain hundreds of clippings from newspapers across the country. Articles and commentary from *Collier's*, *The Literary Digest*, *The Nation*, and the *Atlantic Monthly* have also been useful, as has the *Congressional Record* for McAdoo's term in the US Senate and the published hearings before the Senate Committee on Military Affairs for Baker's difficulties as secretary of war.

As McAdoo, Baker, and their associates have left us a wealth of primary sources, historians have amassed a huge volume of work that explores aspects of their social and political milieu. The notes in this book refer to books and articles in print and digital form that have provided context and significance to Baker's and McAdoo's public and private lives. Those sources are too numerous to be individually discussed here, but a brief discussion of my chapters' sources reveals their many strengths and surprising silences.

As noted in the introduction, neither McAdoo nor Baker has received his full biographical due. Baker has only one published biography, C. H. Cramer's *Newton D. Baker: A Biography* (Cleveland: World Publishing Company, 1961). Cramer's biography is painstaking, but provides little contextualized or critical analysis of Baker's attitudes, achievements, and failures. Cramer did devote a long chapter to Baker's legal career, but almost no space to his family. Other studies, such as Frederick Palmer's *Newton D. Baker: America at War* (New York: Dodd, Mead & Company, 1931) and Daniel Beaver's *Newton D. Baker and the American War Effort, 1917–1918* (Lincoln: University of Nebraska Press, 1966), have focused only on his work as secretary of war. Palmer worked with Baker during the war and was determined to rescue him from his Republican critics, while Beaver provided a more balanced account of Baker's strengths and shortcomings as the organizer of the United States' first foray into modern total war.

Apart from Elliot A. Rosen, who published an important study of Baker's candidacy for the 1932 Democratic presidential nomination ("Baker on the Fifth Ballot? The Democratic Alternative: 1932," *Ohio History* 30 [1966]: 226–247) more than forty years ago, historians have contented themselves with seeing Baker not so much as an actor in his own right but as a loyal understudy—first to Tom Johnson in Cleveland and then to Woodrow Wilson in Washington—and later as an archetype of a progressive turned conservative, eager to sell his legal talents to the highest bidder in support of corporate interests and in opposition to the New Deal. This view underpins Otis L. Graham's treatment of Baker in *Encore for Reform: the Old Progressives and the New Deal* (New York: Oxford University Press, 1967), and few historians have bothered to question it since.

McAdoo has also suffered from historians' neglect. He has only one full biography, Philip M. Chase's thorough but unpublished dissertation ("William Gibbs McAdoo: The Last Progressive, 1863–1941" [University of Southern California, 2008]), available at www.digitallibrary.usc.edu/assetserver/controller/item/etd-Chase-2497.pdf). Chase's dissertation provides an excellent account of McAdoo as a politician who professed to be a "progressive" but who too often favored the politics of influence over those of conviction. McAdoo also has two published but partial biographies. The oldest of these, John J. Broesamle's *William Gibbs McAdoo: A Passion for Change, 1863–1917* (Port Washington, N.Y.: Kennikat Press, 1973), ends with US entry into World War I, while Dale N. Shook's *William G. McAdoo and the Development of National Economic Policy, 1913–1918* (New York: Garland Publications Inc., 1987) deals only with McAdoo's tenure as secretary of the treasury.

Without a deep reservoir of secondary sources on McAdoo and Baker's early years to draw on, I have relied on their papers to piece together their genealogies and childhoods. It was only in 1902, when Baker joined Tom Johnson's administration in Cleveland and McAdoo began work on the Hudson River tunnels, that their lives become accessible from other sources. Robert R. Weiner's *Lake Effects: A History of Urban Policy Making in Cleveland, 1825–1929* (Columbus: Ohio State University Press, 2005) was especially valuable, as was Kenneth Finegold's *Experts and Politicians: Reform Challenges to Machine Politics in New York, Cleveland, and Chicago* (Princeton, N.J.: Princeton University Press, 1995) and Melvin Holli's *The American Mayor: The Best and the Worst Big-City Leaders* (University Park: University of Pennsylvania Press, 1999). McAdoo's work with the Hudson River tunnels is well covered by Anthony Fitzherbert, "'The Public Be Pleased': William G. McAdoo and the Hudson Tubes" at www.nysubway.org/us/path/hmhistory. McAdoo's and Baker's gravitation to Woodrow Wilson in 1911 and 1912 is also explored in the many biographies of him and accounts of the 1912 presidential campaign that are referred to in the notes and bibliography.

Chapter 4 of this book, which deals with Baker's and McAdoo's attitudes to and places within progressivism, owes much to the recent surge of interest in this movement. Alan Dawley's *Changing the World: American Progressives in War and Revolution* (Princeton,

N.J.: Princeton University Press, 2003), Maureen Flanagan's *America Reformed: Progres-sives and Progressivisms, 1890s–1920s* (New York: Oxford University Press, 2007), Michael McGerr's *A Furious Discontent: The Rise and Fall of the Progressive Movement in America, 1870–1920* (New York: The Free Press, 2003), Daniel T. Rodgers's *Atlantic Crossings: Social Politics in a Progressive Age* (Cambridge, Mass.: Harvard University Press, 1998), and Shel-ton Stromquist's *Reinventing "the People": The Progressive Movement, the Class Problem, and the Origins of Modern Liberalism* (Urbana: University of Illinois Press, 2006) have breathed new life into the idea of a progressive movement and reawakened our apprecia-tion of its significance to modern state competence and civic reform.

This book builds on that literature to argue that Baker and McAdoo were self-conscious "progressives" who felt part of a movement they were better at describing than defining. McAdoo emphasised enlightened labor practices and corporate ethics that saw no conflict between profitability and civic responsibility; Baker saw progressivism more as a state of mind than a specific platform. He was connected to a myriad of good-government organi-zations, foreign policy institutes, consumer activist groups, and charitable foundations all dedicated to improving not only the substance but also the spirit of municipal, state, fed-eral, and even international government. Yet, different as they were, Baker and McAdoo saw themselves as part of a broad—a very broad—progressive movement. Later in their lives they diverged as McAdoo backed the New Deal as a logical extension of the statism that had marked his activities within the Wilson administration, while Baker opposed it as an ugly stepchild of World War I-era regimentation and centralization that he had come to see as a necessary evil to win the war but from which he resiled as soon as it was over. Baker and McAdoo recognized each other as fellow, but different, progressives until the late 1920s, and their similarities and differences underline the diversity—once dismissed as the utter incoherence—of progressives and their movement.

Part II of this book covers McAdoo and Baker's experiences in Woodrow Wilson's cabi-net between 1913 and 1921. Between them their cabinet tenures encompassed the whole of Wilson's presidency, with McAdoo dominating the cabinet in Wilson's first term and Baker increasingly influential during his second. There is very little published work on the cabi-net in general, or on Wilson's in particular, other than Richard F. Fenno's venerable *The President's Cabinet: An Analysis of its Membership, and its Strengths and Weaknesses in the Period from Wilson to Eisenhower* (Cambridge, Mass.: Harvard University Press, 1959); this important institution of the federal government has been neglected by historians and po-litical scientists alike. Nowhere is this more surprising than for Wilson's presidency; key cabinet members, led by McAdoo and Baker, have left significant archival resources that illuminate the ways in which cabinet members interacted with each other, the president, and the federal bureaucracy, and Wilson himself theorized (but did not practice) its proper role in *Constitutional Government in the United States* (New York: Columbia University Press, 1908) and "Cabinet Government in the United States" (*Papers of Woodrow Wilson,* 1:506).

Wilson's cabinet may be neglected, but some of McAdoo's and Baker's major initiatives within it are not. In McAdoo's case, Broesamle and Shook's books, and Chase's disserta-tion, as well as McAdoo's *Crowded Years* and Mary Synon's *McAdoo,* cover his work as sec-retary of the treasury in some detail.

For the creation of Federal Reserve System the papers of Carter Glass at the University of Virginia and those of Robert L. Owen in the Library of Congress have useful, if self-interested, insights into McAdoo's role, as do their published accounts of the creation of the new banking system: Carter Glass, *An Adventure in Constructive Finance* (Garden City, N.J.: Doubleday, Page & Company, 1927) and Robert L. Owen, *The Federal Reserve Act* (New York: The Century Co., 1919). W. P. G. Harding's *The Formative Period of the Federal Reserve System (During the World Crisis)* (London: Constable and Company Limited, 1925), and Paul M. Warburg's *The Federal Reserve System: Its Origins and Growth* (New York: The Macmillan Company, 1930) are also useful accounts by those present at the Fed's creation. My account of McAdoo's work with the Federal Reserve is also indebted to James Livingstone, *Origins of the Federal Reserve System: Money, Class, and Corporate Capitalism, 1890–1913* (Ithaca: Cornell University Press, 1986), Allan H. Meltzer, *A History of the Federal Reserve, Vol. 1: 1913–1951* (University of Chicago Press, 2003), Richard H. Timberlake, *The Origins of Central Banking in the United States* (Cambridge, Mass.: Harvard University Press, 1978), Robert Craig West, *Banking Reform and the Federal Reserve, 1863–1923* (Ithaca: Cornell University Press, 1974), and Eugene Nelson White, *The Regulation and Reform of the American Banking System, 1900–1929* (Princeton, N.J.: Princeton University Press, 1983).

Other accounts of McAdoo's work in Treasury can be found in Kathleen Burk, *Britain, America and the Sinews of War, 1914–1918* (Boston: George Allen & Unwin, 1991), Burton I. Kaufman, "United States Trade and Latin America: The Wilson Years," *Journal of American History* 58 (1971): 342–363, and Sheldon D. Pollack, *War, Revenue and State Building: Financing the Development of the American State* (Ithaca: Cornell University Press, 2009). The USRRA, which preoccupied McAdoo in 1918, has received little attention since Walker D. Hines, *War History of American Railroads* (New Haven: Yale University Press, 1928) and K. Austin Kerr, *American Railroad Politics, 1914–1920* (Pittsburgh: University of Pittsburgh Press, 1968), and is overdue for attention from political and economic historians.

Baker's work as secretary of war is better covered, but by a literature that is showing its age. John Dickinson's *The Building of an Army: A Detailed Account of Legislation, Administration and Opinion in the United States, 1915–1920* (New York: Century Company, 1922), Frederick Palmer's 1931 account, Cramer's 1961 biography, and Daniel Beaver's *Newton D. Baker and the American War Effort*, published in 1966, all focus on Baker's performance as secretary of war, but without the benefit of the recent upsurge of historical research into America's Great War. Some aspects of the Department's work, however, have received attention from historians determined to reawaken interest in and debate over the Great War and its impact on American society.

Two areas of this new scholarship warrant mention here. The first concerns the devising and implementation of conscription in 1917 and 1918, sometimes subsumed into a rubric of a new conception of citizenship that emerged from progressive reform. A number of historians have contributed to this historiography, and their works have significantly influenced my own account. These include Nancy Bristow's *Making Men Moral: Social Engineering during the Great War* (New York University Press, 1996), Christopher Capozzola's *Uncle Sam Wants You: World War I and the Making of the Modern American Citizen* (New York: Oxford University Press, 2008), John Whiteclay Chambers's *To Raise an Army: The Draft Comes to Modern America* (New York: The Free Press, 1987), Jennifer D. Keene's *Doughboys, the Great War, and the Remaking of America* (Baltimore: Johns Hopkins University Press, 2001), and Gerald E. Shenk's, *Work or Fight!: Race, Gender, and the Draft in World War I* (New York: Palgrave Macmillan, 2005).

Another area of interest has been in the formation and functions of federal wartime coordination bodies operated, at least for a time, by the Department of War. Grover B.

Clarkson, in *Industrial America in the World War: The Strategy Behind the Line, 1917–1918* (Boston: Houghton Mifflin Company, 1923), produced an insider's account of these bodies and a generally favorable view of Baker and his department's roles within them, as did Daniel Beaver in "Newton D. Baker and the Genesis of the War Industries Board," *Journal of American History* 52 (1963): 43–58. Bernard Baruch, in *The Public Years*, was much less complimentary. Robert D. Cuff, in *The War Industries Board: Business-Government Relations During World War I* (Baltimore: Johns Hopkins University Press, 1973), Paul A. C. Koistinen in *Mobilizing for Modern War: The Political Economy of Modern Warfare, 1865–1919* (Lawrence: University Press of Kansas, 1997), and Baruch's biographer Jordan A. Schwarz, in *The Speculator: Bernard M. Baruch in Washington, 1917–1965* (Chapel Hill: University of North Carolina Press, 1981) have followed suit. My account of Baker's relationship with the WIB is similarly critical.

McAdoo's and Baker's roles in the state-building project of the first half of the twentieth century is central to my analysis of their historical significance. In this I have been influenced by the large body of work on the development of American public and private bureaucratic competence led by Robert Wiebe in *The Search for Order, 1877–1920* (New York: Hill and Wang, 1968) and Ellis Hawley in *The Great War and the Search for a Modern Order: A History of the American People and their Institutions, 1917–1933* (New York: St. Martin's Press, 1979), and which now includes Robert Higgs, *Crisis and Leviathan: Critical Episodes in the Growth of American Government* (New York: Oxford University Press, 1987) and Stephen Skowronek, *Building a New American State: The Expansion of National Administrative Capabilities* (Cambridge: Cambridge University Press, 1982).

The triangular relationship between Baker, McAdoo, and Wilson, explored in chapter 9, draws upon the papers of all three men and from the work of Wilson and his family's biographers. Apart from Arthur S. Link's monumental *Wilson* (Princeton University Press, 1947–1965), my thinking has been influenced by John Milton Cooper Jr.'s recent *Woodrow Wilson: A Biography* (New York: Alfred A. Knopf, 2009), and by two double biographies: Phyllis Levin, *Edith and Woodrow: The Wilson White House* (New York: Scribner, 2001) and Kristie Miller, *Ellen and Edith: Woodrow Wilson's First Ladies* (Lawrence: University Press of Kansas, 2010). These works recognize McAdoo and Baker as important figures in Wilson's presidency, and all note McAdoo's dual role as his son-in-law and secretary of the treasury, but none have explored its development and denouement and so have underplayed the bitterness with which they regarded each other after 1918.

Other silences haunt chapters 10 and 13 of this book, which deal with McAdoo's and Baker's careers as lawyers and their lives as husbands and fathers. Normally voluminous, both men's papers are rightfully thin in their coverage of their legal work; because of lawyer-client confidentiality the two men's papers have been purged of material about individual clients and particular cases. For less obvious reasons, other than William H. Harbaugh's superb *Lawyer's Lawyer: The Life of John W. Davis* (Charlottesville: University Press of Virginia, 1990), there are few published works that shed light on the legal profession during Baker and McAdoo's time or on the ways in which lawyers plied their trades, either within large firms specializing in corporate law, as was Baker's lot, or in small legal-lobbying firms of the kind that kept McAdoo in varying degrees of comfort after 1918.

In the case of Baker's and McAdoo's family lives, this problem is less acute because both men's papers provide voluminous and frank material about their marriages and families. Even so, the McAdoo Papers contain almost no correspondence on his divorce from Eleanor Wilson. That silence aside, both collections provide much raw material for analysis of

McAdoo's and Baker's private lives, but there was little in the secondary literature available to me to give it context. Other than Elaine Tyler May's *Great Expectations: Marriage and Divorce in Post-Victorian America* (Chicago: University of Chicago Press, 1983), which focuses on the period 1870–1920, I could not find much on the social and political consequences of divorce, or of suicide, or of the impact of depressive alcoholism, or of "shotgun marriages" among Baker's and McAdoo's peers. Yet these issues were integral to McAdoo's family, and peripheral to Baker's, and to many other American families of their time, and we need to understand much more about them.

No such problems beset our understanding of McAdoo's and Baker's political activities during the 1920s and after the onset of the Great Depression, which are covered in chapters 11 and 12 of this book. In both cases the published record is fulsome, and I have used parts of it to put McAdoo's and Baker's ideas and activities in context. McAdoo's tilts at the Democratic presidential nomination in 1920 and 1924, and Baker's championing of the League of Nations throughout the decade, are well documented by press reports, contemporary commentary, and works such as David Burner, *The Politics of Provincialism: the Democratic Party in Transition, 1918–1932* (New York: Alfred A. Knopf, 1970), John Milton Cooper Jr., *Breaking the Heart of the World: Woodrow Wilson and the Fight for the League of Nations* (Cambridge: Cambridge University Press, 2001), Michael Dunne, *The United States and the World Court, 1920–1935* (London: Pinter Publishers, 1988), Nancy MacLean, *Behind the Mask of Chivalry: The Making of the Second Ku Klux Klan* (New York: Oxford University Press, 1994), Robert K. Murray, *The 103rd Ballot: Democrats and the Disaster in Madison Square Garden* (New York: Harper and Row, 1976), and my *After Wilson: The Struggle for the Democratic Party, 1920–1934* (Chapel Hill: University of North Carolina Press, 1992) and "Newton D. Baker and the Democratic Malaise, 1920–1937," *Australasian Journal of American Studies* 25 (2006): 49–64.

McAdoo's and Baker's roles in the nomination and election of Franklin D. Roosevelt in 1932 are well known, thanks to Rosen's early work on Baker (noted above) and a number of recent studies including Steve Neal, *Happy Days Are Here Again: The 1932 Democratic Convention, the Emergence of FDR—and How America Changed Forever* (New York: HarperCollins, 2004), Donald A. Ritchie, *Electing FDR: The New Deal Campaign of 1932* (Lawrence: University Press of Kansas, 2007), and Jean Edward Smith, *FDR* (New York: Random House, 2007).

The final section of this book—the winter of Baker's and McAdoo's lives—canvasses their different reactions to the New Deal. There is no shortage of secondary literature on the New Deal and its political and social context, but Baker and McAdoo do not figure prominently in it. David M. Kennedy's *Freedom From Fear: the American People in Depression and War, 1929–1945* (New York: Oxford University Press, 1999) is a recent addition to this canon, but it and its forebears, such as Arthur M. Schlesinger Jr.'s *The Age of Roosevelt* (Boston: Houghton Mifflin, 1956–1960), deal with the New Deal's champions more fully and more sympathetically than they do its critics. Even so, they have little to say about McAdoo, whose work in the Senate between 1933 and 1938 has received no detailed attention other than in Chase's dissertation (noted above), and brief references in Stephen R. Ortiz's *Beyond the Bonus March and GI Bill: How Veteran Politics Shaped the New Deal Era* (New York: New York University Press, 2010), Jackson K. Putnam's *Old Age Politics in California: From Richardson to Reagan* (Stanford University Press, 1970), Kevin Starr's *Endangered Dreams: The Great Depression in California* (New York: Oxford University Press, 1996), and R. Michael Alvarez et al.'s "The 'Ham and Eggs' Movement in Southern Cali-

fornia," (USC Center for the Study of Law and Politics Working Paper no. 12, 2003: www
.nber.org/papers/w5480.pdf).

If McAdoo's support of the New Deal has gone unnoticed, Baker's opposition to it has
fared little better. James T. Patterson's *Congressional Conservatism and the New Deal: The
Growth of the Conservative Coalition in Congress, 1933–1939* (Lexington: University of Kentucky Press, 1967) and George Wolfskill's *Revolt of the Conservatives: A History of the American Liberty League* (Boston: Houghton Mifflin, 1962), despite their age, still influence our
understanding of the conservatives' complaints against the New Deal, but they have little
to say about Baker, who was a member of neither Congress nor the Liberty League. Even
Otis Graham's *An Encore for Reform* (noted above), treated him as one disaffected progressive among many rather than as an eminent New Deal critic worthy of detailed study.
Baker's "The Decay of Self-Reliance" (*Atlantic Monthly* 154 [1934]: 726–733), Cramer's biography, and my "Newton D. Baker and the Democratic Malaise," (noted above) provide
some detail about Baker's journey through New Deal politics and ideology, as does Robert
F. Burk in *The Corporate State and the Broker State: The Du Ponts and American National
Politics, 1925–1940* (Cambridge, Mass.: Harvard University Press, 1990).

This essay is by no means comprehensive in its treatment of this book's sources. Readers
are encouraged to check the notes to each chapter and to refer to the bibliography at www
.press.jhu.edu.

Index